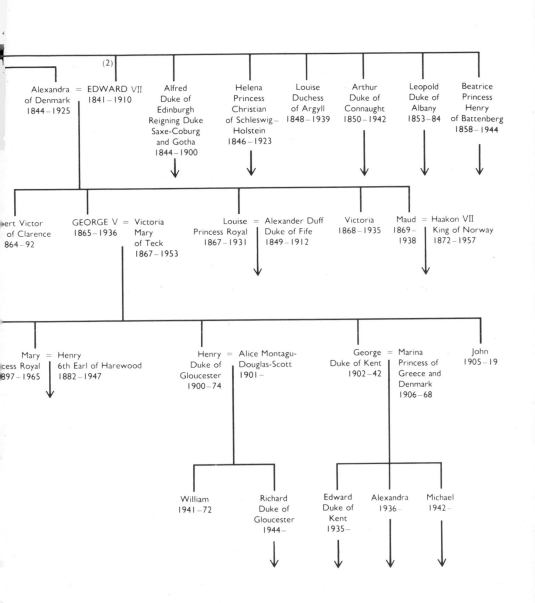

The Reluctant King

THE RELUCTANT KING

The Life & Reign of George VI
1895–1952

Sarah Bradford

St. Martin's Press / New York

In memory of my father
Hilary Anthony Hayes
1901–84

THE RELUCTANT KING: THE LIFE AND REIGN OF GEORGE VI
1895–1952. Copyright © 1989 by Sarah Bradford. All rights
reserved. Printed in the United States of America. No part of this
book may be used or reproduced in any manner whatsoever without
written permission except in the case of brief quotations embodied
in critical articles or reviews. For information, address St. Martin's
Press, 175 Fifth Avenue, New York, N.Y. 10010.

Library of Congress Cataloging-in-Publication Data

Bradford, Sarah.
        The reluctant king: the life and reign of George VI,
1895–1952
    Sarah Bradford.
            p.   cm.
        ISBN 0-312-04337-6
        1. George VI, King of Great Britain, 1895–1952.
    2. Great Britain—Kings and rulers—Biography.
    3. Great Britain—History—George VI, 1936–52.   I. Title.
    DA584.B69   1990
    941.084′092—dc20
    [B]   89-78016
                                                       CIP

First Published in Great Britain by George Weidenfeld & Nicolson
Ltd.

First U.S. Edition

10   9   8   7   6   5   4   3   2   1

CONTENTS

ILLUSTRATIONS

Edward VII as Prince of Wales (*Bassano & Vandyke*)

Queen Victoria with her great-grandchildren, 1899 (*reproduced by gracious permission of HM The Queen*)

Queen Alexandra outside Sandringham Kennels with her three eldest grandchildren. Painting by Fred Morgan and Thomas Blinks (*reproduced by gracious permission of HM The Queen*)

Prince Albert aged two (*Mansell Collection*)

The Prince and Princess of Wales with their children, 1906 (*reproduced by gracious permission of HM The Queen*)

The Duchess of York's boudoir at York Cottage, 1897 (*reproduced by gracious permission of HM The Queen*)

York Cottage (*reproduced by gracious permission of HM The Queen*)

Prince Edward and Prince Albert with their tutor, Mr H. P. Hansell, at Sandringham, 1911 (*Popperfoto*)

Prince Albert as a midshipman in 1914 (*reproduced by gracious permission of HM The Queen*)

Jutland. Unpublished letter from Prince Albert to Mrs Godfrey-Faussett, 11 June 1916 (*author's collection*)

'Coaling': Prince Albert and shipmates dressed for the job, HMS *Cumberland* 1913 (*reproduced by gracious permission of HM The Queen*)

Louis Greig, November 1914 (*courtesy of Mr Carron Greig*)

The Prince of Wales and Prince Albert in France, 1918 (*Imperial War Museum*)

Prince Albert in the Officers' Mess at Cranwell (*RAF College, Cranwell*)

Phyllis Monkman (*courtesy of Mr John Blythe*)

Lady Maureen Stanley (*Hulton–Deutsch Collection*)

Mrs Ronald Greville in 1891, by Carolus-Duran (*courtesy of the National Trust, Polesden Lacey*)

Mabell, Countess of Airlie (*National Galleries of Scotland*)

The Duke of York and Lady Elizabeth Bowes-Lyon on their engagement, January 1923 (*Weidenfeld Archives*)

The Duke and Duchess of York leaving Buckingham Palace after their wedding on 26 April 1926 (*Popperfoto*)

The Duke and Duchess of York on their honeymoon at Polesden Lacey, 1923 (*Weidenfeld Archives*)

The wedding of Prince Paul of Serbia and Princess Olga of Greece in Belgrade, 22 October 1923 (*Press Association*)

The christening of Princess Elizabeth at Buckingham Palace, 29 May 1926 (*Syndication International*)

The Duke of York at the Wimbledon Lawn Tennis Championships, June 1926 (*Popperfoto*)

The Duke of York with Princess Elizabeth (*reproduced by gracious permission of HM The Queen*)

The Duke of York speaking outside Parliament House, Canberra, 1927 (*courtesy of Australia House*)

By the swimming-pool at Fort Belvedere (*Weidenfeld Archives*)

The Yorks with daughters and dogs in 1936 (*Hulton–Deutsch Collection*)

Edward VIII with Mrs Simpson, 1936 (*Weidenfeld Archives*)

Stanley Baldwin (*Syndication International*)

Alexander Hardinge (*reproduced by gracious permission of HM The Queen*)

Walter Monckton (*Weidenfeld Archives*)

Halifax and Hitler at Berchtesgaden, November 1937 (*Topham*)

Neville Chamberlain (*Weidenfeld Archives*)

Alan Lascelles (*Hulton–Deutsch Collection*)

Coronation of King George VI and Queen Elizabeth, 12 May 1937 (*Syndication International*)

The King about to be crowned (*Syndication International*)

The Duke and Duchess of Windsor after their wedding at the Château de Candé, 3 June 1937 (*Popperfoto*)

The King and President Roosevelt, June 1939 (*Popperfoto*)

The Blitz: The King and Queen inspecting bomb damage at Buckingham Palace, September 1940 (*Popperfoto*)

The Blitz: The King and Queen with people bombed out of their homes in Sheffield (*Syndication International*)

The royal family with Mrs Eleanor Roosevelt at Buckingham Palace, October 1942 (*Popperfoto*)

The King entering the Grand Harbour of Valletta, Malta (*Imperial War Museum*)

The King meets Field-Marshal Montgomery's terrier in Holland, 15 October 1944 (*Imperial War Museum*)

ACKNOWLEDGMENTS

I am most grateful to Her Majesty Queen Elizabeth II for her gracious permission to quote from previously unpublished letters by King George VI and from material in the Royal Archives.

I am most grateful to Her Majesty Queen Elizabeth The Queen Mother for gracious assistance provided by Clarence House and for permission to quote from previously unpublished letters as well as other copyright material.

Many people have helped me in my research for this book, some of whom would prefer not to be named. I respect their wishes and thank them for their kindness. Among those who have been particularly generous with their help and advice I should like to thank first of all Hugo Vickers, whose expert knowledge on aspects of this subject has been invaluable and freely given. The Countess of Longford gave me much-needed encouragement at the start of the project and provided me with introductions; General Sir John Hackett gave me guidance in the military field; Professor John Charmley's knowledge of British archives and Professor Douglas Johnson's of French sources were of great assistance as was the help which Professor Arthur Schlesinger, Jr, gave with introductions to archives in the United States. Dr Hugh L'Etang kindly provided guidance in the medical field; Kenneth M. Duke gave me the benefit of his knowledge of the captured German documents; Leonard Miall his advice on broadcasting while David Williamson provided expert advice on European royalty and on the Family Tree featured on the endpapers of this book.

I am extremely grateful to the following people for help generously given in interviews, permission to quote from copyright material in their possession, information and advice: The Lady Priscilla Aird; Michael Bloch; John Blythe; Lord Bonham-Carter; Professor D. Cameron Watt; the Earl of Carnarvon; Professor Sir Raymond Carr; Barbara Cartland; The Hon. Sir Edward Cazalet; the late Mrs Thelma Cazalet-Keir; M.L.R. Chambers; Lord Charteris of Amisfield; Peter Coats; Baron Geoffroi de Courcel; Nicholas Courtney; Lord Crathorne; The late Helen, Lady Dashwood; The Hon. Malcolm Davidson; Lord Deedes; Dorothy Dickson; Professor David Dilks; Lady Donaldson; The Marchioness of Douro; Grace, Countess of Dudley; Nick Duval; Baroness Elliot of Harwood; The Hon. Mrs David Erskine; Margaret Fawcus; Robert Fawcus; The Dowager Lady Fermoy; Lady Fielden; Kyril Fitzlyon; The Rt Hon. Michael Foot MP; M.R.D. Foot; Alastair Forbes; Sir Edward Ford; General Sir David Fraser; Alastair Goodlad MP; Cecilia Goodlad; Professor Doris Kearns Goodwin; The Hon. Lady Goulding; Dr Malcolm Graeme; Lord Graves; Henry Carron Greig; John Grigg; The

Viscount Hambleden; The Dowager Viscountess Hambleden; the late Professor Sir Keith Hancock; Lord Hardinge of Penshurst; Duff Hart-Davis; Sir Rupert Hart-Davis; The Hon. John Harvey; Charles Higham; The Rt Hon. the Lord Home of the Hirsel; Anthony Howard; Lady Lorna Howard; Philip Howard; Derek Hudson; Lieutenant-General Sir Ian Jacob; Professor Denis Judd; Peter Kemp; Lord Keyes RN (retd); Sir Hector Laing; Mrs Derek Lawson; Evelyn Laye; The Hon. Lady Lindsay of Dowhill; Sir David Llewellyn; The Rt Hon. the Earl of Longford; Eileen Macleod; Mrs Susan Lowndes Marques; Brian Masters; Professor John P. Matthews; Vice-Admiral Sir Ian McGeoch; David Metcalfe; Dr R.K. Middlemas; Captain George Mitchison; Major-General the Viscount Monckton of Brenchley; The Viscount Montgomery of Alamein; Dr H. Montgomery Hyde; The Hon. Lady Mosley; Nigel Nicolson; Sir Gordon Pirie; The Hon. Shaun Plunket; Count Poklewski-Koziell; Stuart Preston; Dr David Reynolds; Robert Rhodes James MP; Neil Roger; Kenneth Rose; Anthony Rota; The Dowager Duchess of Rutland; Lady George Scott; Lady William Scott; The Rt Hon. the Earl of Selkirk; Francis Sitwell; David Smith-Dorrien; Baroness Soames; John Stefanidis; Captain J.S. Stevens RN (retd); Dr Gerald Swyer; Michael Thornton; J.C. Trewin; M.T. Turnbull; Peter Vansittart; Christopher Warwick; the late Francis Watson; Dr Jack Weir; Lady Wheeler-Bennett; Professor Frank Whitford; The Rt Hon. the Lord Wilson of Rievaulx; Captain A.V. Yates RN (retd); Philip Ziegler.

Lastly, I would like to express my great gratitude to my publishers, to George Weidenfeld, Bud Maclennan and Christopher Falkus; to my editor, Linda Osband; to my agent, Pat Kavanagh; to my researchers, Saul Kelly and Padraic Sweeney; to Douglas Matthews who compiled the index; and most of all for the support and encouragement which he has given me over more than four years on this book, to my husband, William Ward.

For their invaluable help in the relevant archives and libraries, I am grateful to the following:
Oliver Everett, Librarian and Assistant Keeper of the Royal Archives, Windsor; the Keeper and staff of the Public Record Office, Kew; Dr B.S. Benediksz, Sub-Librarian Special Collections, University of Birmingham; Dr Alan Borg, Director, Mr Roderick Suddaby, Keeper of the Department of Documents, and Mrs Margaret Brooks, Keeper of the Department of Sound Records, the Imperial War Museum; Mrs Jean M. Buckberry, College Librarian and Archivist, Royal Air Force College, Cranwell; J.D. Brown, Head of Naval Historical Research, Ministry of Defence; John Hamill, Grand Librarian and Curator to the Library and Museum of the United Grand Lodge of England; Michael Hyde, Secretary, and Gilles Desmons, the Industrial Society; the staff of the Photographic Administration, British Library Newspaper Library, Colindale; the Hans Tasiemka Archive, London; Dr A.P.W. Malcolmson and the staff of the Public Record Office of Northern Ireland; Dr David M. Smith, Director, Borthwick Institute of Historical Research, University of York; Dr Penelope Bulloch, Librarian, Balliol College, Oxford; Dr John Tanner, former Director of the Royal Air Force Museum; Air Commodore H. Probert, Head of the Air Historical Branch (RAF); Melanie Aspey, Archivist, News International plc Record Office; R.C. Yorke, Archivist of the College of Arms; Correlli Barnett, Keeper, and Elizabeth Bennett, Archivist, Churchill Archives Centre, Churchill College, Cambridge; D.J. Butler, County Archivist, Durham County Record Office. R.C. Trebilcock, Librarian, and Mrs P.A. Judd, Assistant Librarian, Pembroke College, Cambridge; Mrs Sarah Tyacke, Keeper, Dr R.C. Snelling and Dr Christopher Wright, Department of Manuscripts, British Library; Mrs Mary Clapinson, Keeper of Western Manuscripts, and Helen Langley, Assistant Librarian, Bodleian Library, Oxford; Patricia Methven, Archivist, Liddell Hart Centre for Military Archives, King's College, London; Alison Cowden, Institute of United States Studies; A.J. Farrington, Deputy Director, and David Blake, European Manuscripts Section, India Office Records; Christopher Rowell, Historical Buildings Adviser, National Trust; Eric Freeman, Librarian, Wellcome Institute

for the History of Medicine; the Clerk of the Records, House of Lords, and the Trustees of the Beaverbrook Foundation; Brenda Mee, Higher Library Executive, House of Commons Library; Douglas Matthews and the staff of the London Library; Dr E.G.W. Bill, Librarian, and Melanie Barber, Deputy Librarian, Lambeth Palace Library; Mark Jones, Manager, and the staff of the BBC Sound Archives.

Monsieur Jean Batdebat, Ministre Plenipotentiaire Directeur des Archives & de la Documentation, Archives des Affaires Etrangères, Quai d'Orsay; Monsieur Georges Dethan, Conservateur en Chef, Chef de la Division Historique, Ministère des Affaires Etrangères.

John Wickman, Director, Dr Martin M. Teasley, Assistant Director, and James W. Leyerzapf, Supervisory Archivist, the Dwight D. Eisenhower Library; Dr Elizabeth Valkenier, literary executor of the papers of TRH Prince Paul and Princess Olga of Yugoslavia, and Ellen Scaruffi, Curator, Bakhmeteff Archive, Columbia University; Louise T. Jones, Manuscripts and Archives Librarian, Historical Society of Pennsylvania; John N. Jacob, Archivist Librarian, George C. Marshall Foundation; Sally M. Marks, Reference Services Branch, National Archives and Records Administration, Washington, DC; Emil P. Moschella, Chief, FOIPA Section, Records, Federal Bureau of Investigation; John F. Stewart, John F. Kennedy Library; Dr William Emerson, Director, and Raymond Teichman, Supervisory Archivist, Franklin D. Roosevelt Library; Benedict K. Zobrist, Director, Harry S. Truman Library.

Bruce Whiteman, Research Collections Librarian, Mills Memorial Library, McMaster University; George F. Henderson, Assistant Archivist (Public Service), Queen's University Archives, Kingston.

FOREWORD

Two weeks after the death of King George VI on 6 February 1952, René Massigli, Ambassador of France to the Court of St James, wrote a considered report on the life and reign of the late King for the information of his Foreign Minister, Maurice Schumann. 'If the "greatness" of a King', he wrote, 'can be measured by the extent to which his qualities correspond to the needs of a nation at a given moment in its history, then George VI was a great King, and perhaps a very great King.' George VI reigned through the most critical times for his House of Windsor, for his country and, indeed, for the world. Acceding to the throne in the unprecedented circumstances of his brother's abdication, he was immediately faced by the turmoil in European politics in the years leading up to the Second World War, six years of war itself, followed by a period of austerity, social transformation and loss of Empire. Nor were public problems the only or, even for him, the most difficult with which he had to contend. He suffered from that most debilitating handicap for a man in public life, a stammer, and, arising from that, a shyness which could make public occasions painful. As if that were not enough, he succeeded a brother who had been idolized as no royal prince has been either before or since and in whose shadow he had lived almost since the day he was born. With courage, determination, dedication and a fine understanding of the nature and meaning of constitutional kingship, he succeeded in leaving to his daughter, Queen Elizabeth II, in Massigli's judgement, 'a throne more stable than England has known throughout almost her entire history'. At his funeral the wreath from his old companion-in-arms and Prime Minister, Winston Churchill, bore the simple inscription 'For Valour'.

It is now more than thirty years since Sir John Wheeler-Bennett's weighty but unrevealing official biography was published and in the intervening years no major study of the King has appeared, although under the thirty-year rule much new evidence has been recently released in public records illuminating some of the principal events of his reign including the Abdication. From archives in the United Kingdom, France and the United States, from private diaries, correspondence and memoirs a wealth of new evidence has emerged throwing light on the King in his private as well as his public relations, including his long and bitter quarrel with his brother. Many people have been able to recall the King as they knew him in their lifetime, enabling a picture of George VI to be built up infinitely more revealing than has been hitherto known. The King's reputation has dimmed over the three decades since his death; the aim of this book is to provide a reappraisal in the light of our vastly increased knowledge of the period of his life and reign.

The Reluctant King

1

HERITAGE

'The British Crown is the greatest inheritance a man can have.'
W.E. Gladstone

PRINCE Albert Frederick Arthur George of York came almost apologetically into a world largely ruled by his relations. The latest member of the British royal family had chosen to be born at 3.10 a.m. on 14 December 1895, a date traditionally held sacred in the family as 'Mausoleum Day', the anniversary of the death from typhoid of his German great-grandfather, Prince Albert of Saxe-Coburg and Gotha, thirty-four years before, and the death from diphtheria seventeen years later of Prince Albert's and Queen Victoria's third child, Princess Alice of Hesse.

The first thought of the baby's father, Prince George, Duke of York, was not so much joy at the birth of his second son as apprehension at the reaction of the child's great-grandmother, Victoria, Queen of Great Britain and Ireland, Empress of India, then at Windsor Castle preparing to spend the dreaded anniversary in the deepest mourning. The tiny, plump, seventy-six-year-old widow exercised an influence over her family quite disproportionate to her physical stature. Her children and her grandchildren lived in awe of her; her eldest son, Albert Edward, Prince of Wales, the new-born Prince's grandfather, still sweated with nerves when hauled over the coals by his formidable mother. From Windsor he wrote to his son, Prince George:

Grandmama was rather distressed that this happy event should have taken place on a darkly sad anniversary for us, but I think – as well as most of us in the family here – that it will 'break the spell' of this most unlucky date.

The Queen's other children hastened to follow the Prince's line, hoping to make their mother look on the bright side of the little Prince's unfortunate birthday. Victoria's eldest daughter, the Dowager German Empress, wrote to her mother from Berlin on 17 December:

On the one hand I thought it rather to be regretted that the dear little Baby was born on a day of such inexpressibly sad memories to us, – but on the other – it is a gift from Heaven and a very precious one ... on this *darkest* day of your Life a ray of sunshine is sent in after years! and I like to look at it in this light!

Fortunately the Queen herself had come to the same conclusion. Entering the baby's birth in her diary, she noted with approval: 'Georgie's [the Duke of York's] first feeling was one of regret that this child should be born on such a sad day. I have a feeling it may be a blessing for the dear little boy and may be looked upon as a gift from God!' She was further mollified by 'Georgie's' tactful decision (suggested by his father as a sop to the Queen) to name the child Albert and to ask Victoria to be his godmother. She wrote to 'Darling Georgie':

It is a great satisfaction to us all that it should be a second boy & I need not say how *delighted* I am that my great wish—viz. that the little one born on that sad anniversary shd. have the dear name of *Albert*—is to be realised.

As a mark of her extreme approval, she ordered a bust of Albert to be sent to Sandringham as a christening present for the baby Prince who was to bear his name. Most of the family did not care for the name Albert (Albert's son, Albert Edward, always known in the family as 'Bertie', positively refused to be called Albert I when he succeeded his mother, dropping Albert for Edward). '*George* will be his *last* name,' his maternal grandmother, Princess Mary Adelaide, wrote of the baby who was to become King George VI to his uncle, Prince Alge, '& we hope may some day *supplant* the *less favoured* one!' [1] The baby Albert was to be unfortunate over his christening date as well as his birthday. Set for 3 February at Sandringham, it had to be postponed for the funeral of his great-uncle, Prince Henry of Battenberg, husband of Victoria's youngest daughter Beatrice, who, having succumbed to malaria in Sierra Leone while a volunteer with the Ashanti Expeditionary Force, died on the voyage home. Once again the Queen was plunged in grief and, although everyone sympathized, one of Prince Albert's godmothers, his great-aunt, the Grand Duchess Augusta of Mecklenburg-Strelitz, thought it was hard on the baby. 'Rather odd', she commented, 'that a Babe can't be made a *Christian* of, because poor Henry is dead!' Prince Albert was finally christened in the church at Sandringham appropriately dressed in the Honiton lace christening robe used by the royal family since the birth of Victoria and Albert's first child. His godparents represented a roll-call of royal and princely relations, including the Queen; her eldest daughter, the Empress Frederick, widow of the German Emperor and mother of Kaiser Wilhelm II; her third son, Arthur, Duke of Connaught; the Crown Prince of Denmark, the baby's great-uncle on his grandmother's side; Prince Adolphus 'Dolly' of Teck, his mother's brother; and the Grand Duke and Duchess of Mecklenburg-Strelitz. During the ceremony Prince Albert yelled with all his might, provoking his elder brother, Prince Edward, to bawl in sympathy.

The baby's father had wanted a girl, and said so, but the rest of the world saw the birth of his second son as a double insurance to the royal succession. 'I am delighted that they have got their king guarded,' the baby's black-sheep uncle, Prince Frank of Teck, wrote to his mother, using the gaming terminology to which he was unfortunately accustomed (he was at the time on his way out to India in disgrace as a result of a huge gambling debt, which he had been unable to pay).[2] The *Morning Advertiser* put the same point on 16 December, although in more sedate language, adding, 'He may never be called upon, as his father was, to step into the place on the steps of the throne, vacated under such sorrowful circumstances by an elder brother. . . .' Curiously, and in view of events forty years later, the birth of the baby Prince's elder brother, Edward Albert Christian George Andrew Patrick David, the future Edward VIII, had been the occasion of a prophecy by the Labour leader, Keir Hardie, in the House of Commons, which was to prove uncannily accurate:

From his childhood onward this boy will be surrounded by sycophants and flatterers by the score and will be taught to believe himself as of a superior creation. A line will be drawn between him and the people he is to be called upon some day to reign over. In due course, following the precedent which has already been set, he will be sent on a tour round the world, and probably rumours of a morganatic alliance will follow and the end of it all will be the country will be called upon to pay the bill.

Keir Hardie's remarks were greeted by a storm of scandalized abuse, which was primly printed as usual on such occasions in the parliamentary report as 'loud cries of "Oh! Oh!" and "Order"'. Forty-two years later Edward VIII would abdicate in order to marry Wallis Simpson, but it was his younger brother, Prince Albert, rather than the country, who would pay the bill.

Keir Hardie was right, and not only in his prediction of Prince Edward's destiny. The little Princes could not but be aware that, in one sense at least, they were 'of a superior creation'. They were members of a caste with privileges and rules as rigid as the Brahmins of India, the royal families of Europe. At the time of Prince Albert's birth there were twenty reigning monarchs in continental Europe, and he was related to all of them by ties of blood or marriage. Through his great-grandmother, Queen Victoria, and her nine children, four sons and five daughters, he was linked with the German Emperor, the Tsar of Russia and the Kings of Spain, Portugal, Belgium, Bulgaria and Romania. Through his grandmother, Alexandra, he was related to the royal families of Greece and Denmark, and his aunt, Princess Maud, would become Queen of Norway. And then there were the German relations: the princes and princesses, margraves and margravines, grand dukes and ex-Kings of Württemberg, Hanover, Saxe-Coburg and Gotha, Hesse-Darmstadt, Mecklenburg-Strelitz and Battenberg, an inextricably entangled collection to which Victoria referred as 'the royal mob'.

Prince Albert's grandfather, King Edward VII, was once asked whether he thought an English duke should take precedence over a minor Indian rajah. 'Certainly not,' he replied indignantly. While still Prince of Wales he went further and aroused the fury of the German Embassy by insisting that Kalakua, King of the Cannibal Islands (Hawaii), take precedence over his sister's husband, the Crown Prince of Germany. The Prince's friend, Liberal politician Sir Charles Dilke, noted in his diary:

At a party given by Lady Spencer at the South Kensington Museum, Kalakua marched along with the Prince of Wales, the Crown Prince of Germany following humbly behind; and at the Marlborough House Ball Kalakua opened the first quadrille with the Princess of Wales. When the Germans remonstrated with the Prince, he replied, 'Either the brute is a King, or else he is an ordinary black nigger, and if he is not a King, why is he here?'[3]

In 1903, after his accession as King Edward VII two years earlier, Britain broke off diplomatic relations with Serbia in protest at the brutal assassination of King Alexander and Queen Draga. When pressure was put on him by Germany and Italy to restore friendly relations, King Edward told them roundly that British public opinion was too outraged for him to consider it, adding:

I have another, and, so to say, a personal reason. *Mon métier à moi est d'être Roi.* King Alexander was also by his *métier 'un Roi'.* I cannot be indifferent to the assassination of a member of my profession.... We should be obliged to shut up our businesses if we, the kings, were to consider assassination of kings as of no consequence at all....[4]

It was this same feeling of royalty as an exclusive profession, but a profession none the less, which would lead his grandson, King George VI, to refer to the British monarchy as 'the family firm'.

Like most castes, royalty laid an excessive emphasis on outward forms, which, in the case of the British royal family, expressed itself in an obsessive concern with clothes, uniforms, medals and decorations. The royal eye would unfailingly detect any false note and sharp reprimands would be issued to prime ministers, duchesses, even a woodwind player at Covent Garden Opera House who had the temerity to appear in the orchestra pit wearing a black tie instead of a white one. Edward VII was a particular stickler in this respect, a characteristic which his grandson George VI would inherit to a marked degree. Once, when his Prime Minister, the absent-minded Marquess of Salisbury, appeared at a Buckingham Palace drawing-room in a curious mixture of uniforms having dressed in a hurry without the help of his valet. Edward, then Prince of Wales, fell into a literal passion. 'Here is ... Europe in a turmoil,' he shouted, ' – twenty ambassadors and ministers looking on – what will they think – what *can* they think of a premier who can't put on his clothes?' Lord Salisbury coolly responded to the royal tantrum by remarking that it was a dark morning and 'I am afraid that at the moment my mind must have been occupied by some subject of less importance.'[5]

Propriety in the inferior orders demanded in return a rigid code of behaviour in royalty. The royal family was not to be seen laughing in public. 'Did you see that ridiculous Photo of them all, *laughing*,' Prince Albert's great-aunt Augusta, herself very conscious of being a descendant of George III, wrote indignantly to his mother, Princess May; 'Lily grinning, no, too funny & not Royal!'[6] Royal humour tended towards *schadenfreude*. As Lord Granville once quipped, wit was wasted on the royal family since nothing made them laugh like hearing one had shut one's finger in the door. Queen Victoria, according to her biographer, Elizabeth Longford, 'laughed immoderately' when Napoleon III spilt coffee over his cocked hat and when Lord Kinnoull tumbled head over heels down a slope, but when her own cap was accidentally twitched off in front of Court ladies at a drawing-room, she described it as a 'dreadful misadventure'.[7] Royalty were only really free to relax with each other. 'In our position which is so totally different from other people's', she advised her daughter, the Crown Princess of Germany, 'one ought not to be left alone, without a Child or a near Relation.' As Sir Charles Cust, King George V's greatest friend, pointed out, royalty were a race apart: 'there are three kinds of people in the world: blacks, whites and Royalties'.[8] It might have been more accurate to say that as far as royalty was concerned, there were only two, royalties and the rest. Another royal intimate, George Gage, told Harold Nicolson that he believed royalties never saw any difference or gradations between non-royalties, and that to them the Duke of Devonshire was much the same as any other commoner.[9]

Within that royal caste there was a clearly defined pecking order based on criteria not only of ancient lineage but also of present power. Prime Minister Gladstone called the British throne the greatest of all inheritances; the family into which Prince Albert had been born was the most prestigious of the world's ruling families. His great-grandmother, Victoria, was the world's longest-serving sovereign; having ascended the throne as an eighteen-year-old girl in 1837, she was now within two years of her Diamond Jubilee in 1897, an occasion when a display of imperial pomp and power would be staged unseen since the days of the Roman Empire. As Queen of Great Britain and Ireland and Empress of India, Victoria was the titular head of an empire which included a quarter of the world's population and nearly a quarter of its land surface, an empire whose proud boast was that the sun never set upon it. Within five years the first cracks in the unwieldy imperial edifice would appear, but in the year of Prince Albert's birth the British Empire was at its apogee and it would last, an imperial royal heritage, into his future reign.

The British royal family was not only powerful and well connected, but it was also extremely rich: its collection of jewels was perhaps only equalled by the Russian royal family and some of the more opulent Indian princes, and its paintings, drawings and works of art were worth literally billions at Buckingham Palace in London and at Windsor Castle. While a considerable proportion of these magnificent objects, such as the Crown Jewels, the Queen's pictures including Mantegnas, Rubens and drawings by Raphael, da Vinci, Michelangelo and Rembrandt, and buildings such as Buckingham Palace, St James's Palace, Windsor Castle and Hampton Court, were inalienable Crown property, many of the jewels were the Queen's personal property, as were the estates of Balmoral and Osborne and the Prince of Wales's large country property and 300-room house at Sandringham in Norfolk. The Queen and the Prince of Wales both had very large private incomes derived from the Duchies of Lancaster and Cornwall, which with skilful investment increased in value over the years, untouched by the taxation paid by their subjects. Their comfort and luxury were ministered to by a select band of utterly loyal and devoted courtiers, drawn from the aristocracy or from well-connected, upper-class families, who looked upon Court service as an hereditary profession, and an army of servants – the royal yacht alone had thirty-one servants and 300 crew.

Queen Victoria represented the apex of the pyramid of this world-wide edifice of power and magnificence. After nearly sixty years on the throne she was an object of veneration and awe, not only to her family, but to her millions of subjects all over the globe. Widowed at forty-two, the Queen spent the rest of her life in mourning for the husband she had so passionately loved, preserving the rooms where he lived and died as shrines exactly as he left them; his favourite chair in his study at Windsor bore a commemorative plaque and rumour had it that she always took a pair of his flannel drawers to bed with her. All the family houses and gardens were filled with mementoes of the dead: locks of hair, fading photographs, figurines, portrait busts and statues. Victoria's great-grandson remembered Osborne, the summer palace which Victoria and Albert had built on the Isle of Wight, as 'the family necropolis', so crammed was it with family relics. Victoria herself always wore mourning black; when she wanted to be specially smart, a few diamond stars would be added to the white widow's cap with streamers which was always part of her daily attire. Her bracelets were gold chains from which hung various lockets containing the hair of her children and grandchildren, and by day she always wore round her neck a two-sided locket with portraits of her dead daughter, Princess Alice of Hesse, and of her haemophiliac son, Leopold, Duke of Albany.

All this mourning and the isolation in which she lived, added to the almost total silence with which she liked to be surrounded, must have made visiting 'Gangan' a depressing ordeal for her great-grandchildren. At Balmoral, the Scottish baronial castle which she and Albert had built on Deeside and which she dearly loved, she lived a life of almost mythical isolation, sometimes not seen by her Household or her few guests for days at a time, when she would retreat to the Glassalt Shiel, a small house on the estate. Her Household communicated with each other by writing notes, often of suppressed venom, and one of her principal ladies-in-waiting – Jane, Marchioness of Ely – was known as 'Whispering Jane', so inaudible was her voice. Balmoral was a shrine to Prince Albert (who had chosen the site because it reminded him of his native Germany), made gloomy by the dark ginger paint which covered all the panelling and woodwork, and the tartan curtains, carpets and even sofas. The Prime Minister, Lord Rosebery, once said that he had thought the drawing-room at Osborne was the ugliest room in the world until he saw the drawing-room at Balmoral. It was not only gloomy but freezing cold as the Queen loathed heated rooms. Windows were open on the coldest days and the fireplaces were left empty. The Queen's passion for open air was such that she would go for drives in open carriages in the coldest weather (but with a bottle of whisky in a box under the driver's seat to help keep out the cold) and, unless there was snow on the ground, she would always breakfast outside, in 'summerhouses' in winter, or under a tented awning in summer. At breakfast she would be attended by two Indian Khitmagars in scarlet and gold uniforms, and everything on the table would be of gold, even the egg-cup and spoon with which she ate her boiled egg.

Demanding and repressive with her Household, Victoria was astonishingly indulgent to her servants, particularly to her favourite Indians and Scotsmen. Drunkenness was rife at Balmoral — 'the amount of whisky consumed by the servants at Balmoral was truly stupendous,' the Queen's Assistant Private Secretary, Sir Frederick 'Fritz' Ponsonby, remembered. The annual commemoration of Prince Albert, held at the cairn built in his memory on Craig Lurigan, was treated by the ghillies as an excuse to get thoroughly drunk, as was the annual ghillies' ball presided over by the Queen, a nimble and enthusiastic dancer. In contrast rules for the Household and the royal family when visiting were extremely stiff. The Queen could not bear smoking, which, as Ponsonby pointed out, was curious since 'all her family smoked like chimneys'. No one was allowed to smoke in any part of Osborne where a whiff might reach the royal nostrils. At first a smoking-room was built in the garden there, unconnected with any part of the house; then it was allowed in the billiards-room only. Statues of the Queen's much-indulged Scottish servant, John Brown (wrongly rumoured to have married her secretly), who had been thoroughly and deservedly hated by the royal family and Household, stood in the grounds as a memorial to her devotion to him.

'Gangan's' world of silent gloom was in dark contrast to the 'perpetual sunlight' with which the lives of Prince Albert's paternal grandparents seemed to their grandchildren to be bathed. The Prince of Wales, the Queen's eldest son and heir to the throne, was fifty-four when Prince Albert was born. He was almost bald, his fair beard turning grey, and he had become exceedingly stout, a fact concealed as far as possible by his excellent tailor. Despite his weight, which was due entirely to over-indulgence in food, he walked swiftly on his sturdy legs, invariably followed by his scruffy and aggressive brown and white terrier, Caesar, which was given to attacks upon the trousers of even the most exalted members of his master's Household. Restless and easily bored, the Prince of Wales remained full of a zest for life and a relentless capacity for enjoyment, at which, since his formidable mother had allowed him to do nothing else for the past thirty or so years of his life, he had become something of an expert. He was an enthusiastic and hearty eater, his appetite for food, rich and in quantity, unaffected by the huge cigars and large numbers of Egyptian cigarettes which he smoked. By the time he sat down to breakfast he had already smoked two cigarettes and one cigar, while by dinner he would often have got through twenty more cigarettes, which he smoked exhaling reflectively through his nose, and twelve more large cigars. Despite this, on shooting days at Sandringham he would devour platefuls of bacon and eggs, haddock and chicken, and buttered toast, in a matter of minutes. An hour or so later out shooting he would fortify himself with hot turtle soup, and at half-past two a large luncheon. At tea in the saloon, he would tackle poached eggs, *petits fours*, preserved ginger, rolls, scones, hot tea-cakes, sweet cakes and his favourite Scottish shortbread. Some three hours later at dinner at half-past eight, he would confront at least twelve courses, taking a considerable portion of each. He was relatively abstemious, however, where alcohol was concerned, drinking only a few glasses of champagne with dinner, rarely anything else, and sometimes a glass of brandy afterwards, port almost never.

Women were only allowed one glass of wine each as he hated to see their faces flushed with alcohol. Women were his passion and his weakness, and in his earlier years as Prince of Wales his succession of mistresses had outraged the British public who adored the Princess of Wales. Even in his later years, when the Hon. Mrs George Keppel had become his established favourite, he continued to enjoy casual encounters with willing women in Paris, Marienbad, Homburg and Baden-Baden. For the Prince of Wales, as for his eldest grandson, Prince Edward, women helped to assuage his restlessness and exorcise the ever-present spectre of boredom. Although far from a fool, he was no intellectual; he never read a book and abominated intellectual conversation, particularly at dinner, where he preferred to be entertained with jokes, funny stories or gossip, preferably whispered in his ear by a beautiful woman. He liked the company of millionaire financiers such as Sir Ernest Cassel, smart racing aristocrats and court jesters and, at this stage in his life, his public image was of a pleasure-loving prince with a taste for buffoonery. His mother's favourite Prime Minister, Disraeli, habitually referred to him with a tinge of light contempt, as 'Prince Hal'.

Within the family and Household, however, the Prince was held in some awe. He could be formidable and possessed in full measure the famous 'Hanoverian spleen', an explosive temper which his grandson, Prince Albert, would inherit. When angry he would 'roar like a bull' and indulge in extravagant gestures. His fits of temper were often prompted by the most minor accidents, as on one occasion at dinner when he accidentally splashed his starched shirt front with spinach. When rubbing with his napkin failed to remove the spot and only made it worse, he dunked the napkin furiously in the spinach and rubbed it all over his shirt. On another occasion, when one of his grandchildren irritated him by fidgeting and accidentally knocking something off the table, he roared 'Damn you, boy!' and hurled a huge melon to the floor.

Prince Albert's grandmother, Alexandra, had captivated the British public since the day in 1863 when, hailed by Tennyson as 'the Sea King's daughter from across the sea', she had arrived from Denmark to marry the heir to the British throne. One of three beautiful daughters of Prince Christian of Schleswig-Holstein-Sonderburg-Glücksburg, who succeeded to the Danish throne later that same year as King Christian ix, Alexandra had natural chic and style and a slim, athletic figure, which she was to bequeath to her grandson, Prince Albert. The children of her family had all been athletic and brought up on gymnastics –

Alexandra sometimes demonstrated her athleticism by performing *le grand jeté*. She loved riding and was a very proficient horsewoman and an excellent, though reckless, whip, who liked to drive her phaeton and pair as fast as they would go. She had been brought up in comparative poverty in a happy family background, where she had received education in French, English and religion but little else. The Danish royal family were exceptionally close and remained so throughout their lives, as Queen Victoria, commenting on the quarrelsomeness of royalty in general, noted rather enviously: '. . . one remarkable exception is the Danish Royal Family; they are wonderfully united—and never breathe one word against each other, and the daughters remain as unspoilt and as completely Children of the Home as when they were unmarried. I do admire this. . . .'

Alexandra's beauty was matched by her high spirits and a tomboyishness encouraged by her family's passion for practical jokes. Like her husband, she was restless, gregarious and completely unintellectual; the tragedy of her life was to be her deafness from otosclerosis, which she inherited from her mother, Princess Louise of Hesse-Cassel. With her third pregnancy in 1867, when she caught rheumatic fever which left her with a pronounced limp, Alexandra became increasingly deaf. Her deafness cut her off from the social life which was her husband's chief interest and, although she put up a brave pretence of hearing everything that was said to her and was an excellent and lively hostess, her disability, combined with her natural inclinations, tended to make her home, her children, her horses, dogs and other animals the centre of her life. She had beauty, goodness, sympathy, charm and intuition, but she had very little brain, and her husband, who liked the company of clever women, turned to them for amusement. Alexandra tolerated this, perhaps because she had no alternative. She was none the less surprised by it, as her artless remark on the subject to Margot Asquith showed: 'But I thought I was *so-o-o* beautiful. . . .'[10] Childlike by nature, she remained exceptionally youthful-looking into old age, a physical trait which her two eldest grandsons were to inherit.

Edward and Alexandra had six children: three boys, Albert Victor, George and Alexander, who lived only a few hours, and three girls, Louise, Victoria and Maud, known collectively as 'the Hags'. That Prince George should have been in direct line of succession to the throne was due to a tragedy which turned out to be a very fortunate accident for the British monarchy. Born in June 1865, he was not the first but the second son of Edward and Alexandra. His elder brother, Prince Albert Victor, Duke of Clarence and Avondale, always called Eddy, who was born prematurely in January 1864, appeared destined to be the heir to the throne. But as Prince Eddy grew up, it became apparent even to his doting parents that he was poor material for kingship. He was a seven-month child, always delicate; unkind courtiers described him as 'practically wanting'. Taller and thinner than his brother George, he had brown wavy hair, large slightly protuberant eyes and an excessively long neck, which, as he grew up, he tried to conceal by wearing a very high starched collar (matched by starched cuffs so that he was nicknamed 'Collar and Cuffs'). Always in delicate health,

Prince Eddy grew up backward, lazy and uninterested in anything except polo, which he was too indolent to practice, and sex. He and Prince George shared a girl whom they kept in St John's Wood, but, where Prince George showed a reasonable restraint, Prince Eddy's pursuit of physical pleasure landed him in hot water and alarmed his parents. He was despatched to India in the autumn of 1889 to keep him out of trouble, but not before he had managed to catch a mild form of venereal disease. In view of his ardently heterosexual nature it was, therefore, somewhat unfair that his name should have been publicly mentioned in the autumn and winter of 1889 in connection with the unsavoury Cleveland Street case, involving Society figures – one of whom, Lord Arthur Somerset, was a friend of the Prince of Wales's and superintendent of the Prince's stables – and a male brothel. If Prince Eddy had, indeed, visited Cleveland Street with one of the accused aristocrats, Lord Euston, it was under the mistaken impression that it was offering *poses plastiques*, the female striptease of the day.[11] When not in pursuit of more plebeian pleasure, Prince Eddy managed to fall in love with an unsuitable princess, Hélène, daughter of the Comte de Paris, pretender to the French throne. Hélène offered to give up her Catholic religion in order to marry Prince Eddy, but her father, backed by the Pope, refused to allow it. Prince Eddy's escapades and the public scandal of the Cleveland Street case were to have a very marked effect on Prince George's attitude to his sons when they were young men, when he was to show an almost obsessive fear of their falling into unsuitable entanglements.

The question of a suitable marriage for Prince Eddy was clearly becoming urgent when the royal family's thoughts turned to the twenty-four-year-old Princess May of Teck. She was poor, but none the less descended on her mother's side from George III; her only disadvantage as the wife to the heir to the throne lay in her morganatic blood on her father's side. Prince Franz, Duke of Teck, was looked upon as tainted by the morganatic marriage of his father, Duke Alexander of Württemberg, who would otherwise have been heir apparent to the reigning King of Württemberg, to the Hungarian Countess Claudine Rhedey of Kis-Rédé. Duke Alexander's marriage had ended in tragedy when his wife was thrown from her horse while watching a military review near Vienna and trampled to death by a charging cavalry squadron. She was buried in the mountains of Transylvania whence her family came, in the little church of Erdó Szent-György. To the caste-conscious royalties of Europe, however, romance was no substitute for legitimate royal blood, and when it was suggested to the Empress Augusta of Germany that her brother, the Duke of Schleswig-Holstein, a worthless individual whom Queen Victoria called 'that odious Gunther', might marry Princess May, she was much offended and declared that 'her Brother would not dream of making such a *messalliance*!!!' Princess May's membership of the exclusive royal club was honorary, due to her mother's father's royal blood and, as her biographer James Pope-Hennessy put it, 'though the life-members of this exclusive club were kind and courteous to her, they were well aware of the difference between a Serene Highness [like her father, Franz of

Teck] and a Royal one'. Then she was relatively poor and only a very rich member of the English peerage could afford to marry her. She was, as Pope-Hennessy said, 'Too Royal to marry an English gentleman and not Royal enough for Royalty.'[12] More important, perhaps, than her imperfect royalty, was that the percipient Queen Victoria liked her, pronouncing her after a ten-day inspection at Balmoral in November 1891 'a superior girl, – quiet and reserved *till* you know her well – . . . & so sensible and unfrivolous. . . .'[13] A month later during a house-party at Luton Hoo, home of the Danish Minister, Baron von Falbe, Prince Eddy proposed to Princess May and was accepted.

For a woman like Princess May, high-principled and inhibited, marriage to a weak, indolent but passionate man like Prince Eddy could only have led to the deepest unhappiness. There were signs that she was beginning to have doubts herself, asking her mother anxiously, 'Do you think I can *really* take this on, Mama?' Fate, however, intervened. While Princess May and her parents were staying with the Prince and Princess of Wales at Sandringham in January 1892, Prince Eddy felt unwell while out shooting on the 7th, the day before his twenty-eighth birthday. Two days later his illness was diagnosed as influenza with incipient pneumonia and by the 13th he was delirious. While the dying young man raved, his parents, brother, sisters and fiancée sat in the small sitting-room next to his own claustrophobic little bedroom. For Princess May the ordeal was made worse by the fact that in his delirium Prince Eddy frequently referred to his love for Hélène, and his shouts of 'Hélène, Hélène,' echoed through the rooms and down the passages. At 9.35 on the morning of 14 January, only a week after he had been taken ill, it was all over. The heir to the throne of England was dead.

'The dear girl looks like a crushed flower,' Queen Victoria noted of the bereaved Princess May, although, the shrewd old Queen wrote, the Princess had 'never been in love with poor Eddy'.[14] Whatever Princess May's doubts about Prince Eddy, she would not have been human had she not been bitterly disappointed that the glittering dream of being Queen of England had abruptly vanished. The abiding passion of her life was and would always be the British monarchy and the royal family to which, as a great-grand-daughter of George III, she belonged. There were practical problems too as her aunt and confidante, the Grand Duchess of Mecklenburg-Strelitz, was not slow to point out. Princess May's parents were wildly extravagant and permanently broke and had even, at one point in Princess May's girlhood, had to take the time-honoured expedient of going abroad to avoid creditors and reduce expenditure. 'What will happen about the Trousseau!' the Grand Duchess wrote, 'who will pay for it and for all the expenses incurred? this is a very serious consideration . . . it is hard enough to lose poor Eddy but to be still more ruined, cannot be expected!'[15]

The sudden death of Prince Eddy sent a shock wave through not only his immediate family but also his grandmother's dominions. The male succession to the throne no longer seemed secure, since his only brother, Prince George, was also unwell, suffering the after-effects of an attack of typhoid. The royal family quickly made up its mind: 'Georgie' must marry immediately and the best candidate to hand was Princess May. Only Princess May seemed shocked at the idea. After a miserable stay with her dead fiancé's grief-stricken parents at Compton Place, Eastbourne, over the period which should have included her wedding day (27 February), when they generously presented her with the magnificent diamond rivière which was to have been their wedding present to her, she went abroad with her parents, refusing to return to England because of rumours of her engagement to Prince George. The Prince of Wales and Prince George, however, later visited the Tecks at Cannes; a few weeks later a fire at Strelitz, where Princess May and her mother were staying, symbolically destroyed all the photographs she possessed of Prince Eddy. At the end of November she and Prince George were together at Sandringham for the morbid anniversary of her engagement to Prince Eddy, 3 December. In the meantime, the only other serious candidate for Prince George's hand, the pretty, flirtatious 'Missy' (Princess Marie of Edinburgh), had been pushed by her pro-German mother into a far less glittering match with the Hohenzollern heir to the throne of Romania. At Christmas Prince George and Princess May exchanged presents and heartfelt letters about Eddy; on 3 May 1893 they were engaged and two months later they were married. They spent their honeymoon at York Cottage, Sandringham, the Prince of Wales's wedding gift to his son, an odd place for the young couple to choose under the circumstances. 'The young people go to Sandringham to the Cottage after the Wedding wh. I regret & think rather *unlucky* & sad,' Queen Victoria commented.[16]

The marriage aroused unkind comment as Prince George and Princess May were aware. '... people only said I married you out of pity and sympathy,' Prince George wrote to his wife years later; 'that shows how little the world really knows what it is talking about.' The world saw only a shy, inhibited couple who showed little affection for each other in public, but in private they were writing each other touching love letters. Shortly before their marriage on 6 July 1893, Princess May wrote to her future husband:

I am very sorry that I am still so shy with you, I tried not to be so the other day, but alas failed, I was angry with myself! It is so stupid to be so stiff together & really there is nothing I would not tell you, except that I *love* you more than anybody in the world, & this I cannot tell you myself so I write it to relieve my feelings. . . .

Prince George replied the same day:

Thank God we both understand each other, & I think it really unnecessary for me to tell you how deep my love for you my darling is & I feel it growing stronger & stronger every time I see you; although I may appear shy & cold. . . .[17]

This inability to show the love they truly felt was to have serious consequences in their relationship with their children.

At the time of his marriage and, indeed, during the years in which his elder children were born, Prince George was a naval officer. A naval career was the only one he had ever contemplated and been trained for until his brother's death placed him in direct line of succession to the throne. Since birth, he had been brought up in close tandem with Prince Eddy, acting as a stiffener for his brother's indolent nature. His father, the Prince of Wales, remembering with bitterness the ferociously strict educational regime to which he had been subjected by his parents, had determined that his sons should not be made to suffer in the same way. The result was that the two boys had only the most rudimentary education under their tutor, Mr (later Canon) Dalton, described by Prince George's biographer as 'a muscular Christian' who 'would ask after their dogs, while he slipped in a useful historical fact or a moral saw'.[18] One of Prince George's fondest memories of his tutor was of him teaching his brother and himself archery and allowing them to shoot at him as if he were a running deer. It is hardly surprising, therefore, that when Prince George was eleven years old, Mr Dalton was forced to admit that the boys' educational standard was below that of their contemporaries at private school. Instead of sending them to public school which might have widened their knowledge, the two Princes were sent for two years as naval cadets on the training ship *Britannia* (forerunner of the Royal Naval College at Dartmouth) and then for a two-year cruise round the world in HMS *Bacchante*. By the year of Prince Albert's birth, the thirty-year-old Prince had been in the Navy since adolescence and that disciplined, blinkered, masculine world had formed his whole experience. Even after he left the Service in 1898, the habits, routine and outlook he had learned in it continued to regulate his daily life. His oldest and best friends continued to be the friends he had made while in the Navy and, in his son's words, 'he retained a gruff, blue-water approach to all human situations, a loud voice, and also that affliction common to Navy men, a damaged ear-drum'.[19] Through the Navy he had acquired a salty sense of humour, a fondness for such unroyal expressions and expletives as 'damn fool!', and a lifelong habit of consulting the barometer first thing in the morning and last thing at night.

Facially he resembled his father with bright blue, slightly prominent eyes and fair hair; he also inherited his father's physical agility, although he never acquired his father's bulk, his weight remaining more or less at ten stone throughout his adult life. He shared his father's short-fuse temper whenever orders he had given were misunderstood or arrangements he had sanctioned went awry. Where his father would 'roar like a bull', Prince George would explode. Sir Derek Keppel, the Master of his Household, would recall: 'He would call me every name under the sun, but always, as I was leaving the room after an "explosion", he would call me back and make his peace with, "Derek, did you ever hear this story?"'[20] He did not inherit his father's supreme self-confidence, which had survived all Victoria's attempts to dent it, or the tactful charm and instinct for doing the right thing, which was to make Edward VII a force in European diplomacy. His father was the dominant influence on his life as he himself was to be, directly or indirectly, upon the life of his son, Prince Albert, until the latter's marriage. As his biographer put it:

Prince George's devotion to his father was from first to last tinged with something more than reverence, something more approaching to awe. Kindly, tolerant, sympathetic and sunny as was the Prince's nature, his power to inspire fear increased as his political influence and reputation grew; and no one can read through the letters which Prince George wrote to him from childhood to middle age without observing how dominant was this condition, how constantly he subordinated not only his inclinations but his whole nature to his father's.[21]

Prince George's cousin, 'Drino' Carisbrooke, said somewhat unkindly that King Edward's affection for George was due to the fact that the latter was prepared to be his complete slave. Edward was, said Carisbrooke, 'horrible' to his daughters, and Princess Louise was so frightened of him that she would faint in the carriage on her way to Buckingham Palace.[22]

Prince George regarded his father with reverential awe, but he adored his beautiful mother and their relationship was exceptionally close. Even when he was grown up he would read aloud to his mother during her evening ritual of hair-brushing and would say his prayers with her as if he were still a child. The whimsically affectionate terms of their letters to each other read embarrassingly today; it was, as Alexandra's biographer points out, the eternal nursery world of Peter Pan, except that in their case it was not the boy who refused to grow up but the mother who would not allow him to do so, expressed in Alexandra's hope that 'I shall always find my little Georgie quite the same and unchanged in every respect'. This was written when 'little Georgie' was nineteen; six years later, when he was twenty-five and commanding a gunboat, she ended a letter to him 'with a great big kiss for your lovely little face'. Her son responded in kind: 'I wonder who will have that sweet little room of mine, you must go and see it sometimes and imagine that your Georgie dear is living in it', appealing to her to 'think sometimes of your poor boy so far away but always your devoted and loving little Georgie'.[23] This sickly terminology was not uncommon at the time; it was, moreover, a feature of the Danish royal family's correspondence, which was always liberally sprinkled with 'dear little' or 'poor little' followed by a diminutive. Alexandra was not only extremely maternal, but she was also demanding and possessive towards her children in a way that she never was towards her husband. Six months after Prince Eddy's death Alexandra, always known to her children as 'Mother dear', wrote to her son: 'You know my Georgie that you are everything to us now – & must give us *double* affection for the one that has gone before us!'; again, shortly before his engagement, the thought of which filled her with unconscious jealousy, she wrote of 'the bond of love between us – that of Mother & child – which *nothing* can ever diminish or render less binding – & *nothing* & *nobody* can or shall ever come between me & my darling Georgie boy'.[24]

It was hardly an encouraging prospect for a future wife. It was not difficult for Alexandra to retain her hold over 'darling Georgie'. To him everything about his mother was perfect, as was everything about his family and childhood. The Wales children, George, Eddy and his three sisters, Victoria, Maud and

Louise, had been and continued to be in adulthood a mutual admiration society; after her marriage, therefore, Princess May had not only to contend with a constant and concealed tug-of-love over her husband with her mother-in-law, but with her sisters-in-law as well, particularly Victoria and Louise, who constantly denigrated her. 'Poor May, with her Württemberg hands,' Princess Louise, Duchess of Fife, would sigh theatrically,[25] while Prince George's unmarried and favourite sister, Princess Victoria, whom he described as 'my sweet angel of a sister', used her daily telephone conversations with her brother as a channel for disparaging remarks about his wife and, later, for trouble-making gossip about his children.

It says a great deal for Princess May's fortitude of spirit that she endured the veiled hostility and sometimes downright unkindness of her in-laws without complaining. Fortitude had been bred into her in her upbringing with the Teck family. Her parents, otherwise devoted to each other, were always squabbling, as were her three younger brothers; Princess May, as the eldest child and only daughter, had to keep the peace. Her shyness, which had been a torture to her since childhood, was exacerbated by the exuberant behaviour of her mother, Princess Mary Adelaide, who attacked life with the same delighted avidity with which she revelled in a cream bun, 'r-r-rich c-r-ream' the Princess would say, rolling her rs lusciously. The Princess adored food, as she loved all the good things in life, and by the age of twenty-four the American Ambassador to the Court of St James's had estimated that she must have weighed some 250 pounds. Her bulk caused her self-conscious daughter agonies of embarrassment; at Madame Taglioni's dancing classes in Connaught Square the other children would giggle when they saw that Princess Mary Adelaide needed two gilt chairs instead of one to sit upon. Princess Mary Adelaide made things worse by talking about May's shyness in public, emphasizing it and pressing her daughter to match her own excessive volubility. The more she did this, the more Princess May would retreat into her shell. Her father's behaviour was equally embarrassing to her. Prince Franz of Teck was extremely touchy about his honour and position and would fly into violent public rages, which his family termed 'breezes', if he thought himself slighted. Both he and his wife were childishly extravagant about money. Princess May found her father's insistence on having far more servants than he could afford, his lack of a sense of proportion about trifling matters and his consequent public tantrums extremely distressing. 'Poor man,' she wrote of him, 'if only he was less proud and foolish about that sort of thing, what can it matter how many servants one has as long as one can live comfortably?'[26] Poor Princess May was born to be a 'grown-up'. Intelligent, warm-hearted, longing to be loved and appreciated but vulnerable to criticism and inhibited in her capacity for self-expression, she was not to blossom as a personality until the days of her widowhood.

Nor could she feel at home at Edward and Alexandra's Court, where 'romps' and 'rags' were the order of the day, apple-pie beds were made and soda-siphons squirted. When the Wales children were young they had taken part in all this boisterous horse-play, egged on by their mother who encouraged them to crawl about under the table at luncheon pinching the guests' legs, once mistaking those of the Prime Minister, Disraeli, for their usual victim, Christopher Sykes. Even when she became Queen, Alexandra did not give up her family's passion for practical jokes and on one occasion made her nephew, Prince Christopher of Greece, dress up in the outfit Queen Victoria had worn in the days of her youth to open the Great Exhibition in Paris under Napoleon III. Arrayed in this with a feathered bonnet on his head, and equipped with a lace parasol, 'Christo' was trooped by the Queen through the corridors of Buckingham Palace, past scandalized servants, to entertain his sick aunt, the Dowager Empress of Russia. Among the Danish royal family and their offshoots, the Greeks, the special joke was to make funny noises and yell if they saw anyone trying to write a letter. There were no 'in' jokes to play on anyone bold enough to read a book since none of them did. Princess May's sense of restraint and dignity, said her lifelong friend and lady-in-waiting, Mabell, the Countess of Airlie, recoiled from what she herself described as the 'surfeit of gold plate and orchids' of the life at her father-in-law's Court. As a result people criticized her and said she was dull and boring, of which she was well aware, writing sadly of herself to her old governess and friend, Mademoiselle Bricka, as 'old me who am always criticised and generally condemned'. The result of this treatment was to make her withdraw even further into her shell, as Lady Airlie, who had known her as a child, discovered when she joined her Household in 1902:

Even as a girl she had been shy and reserved, but now her shyness had so crystallised that only in such moments of intimacy [on greeting the recently widowed Lady Airlie with tears in her eyes] could she be herself. The hard crust of inhibition which gradually closed over her, hiding the warmth and tenderness of her personality, was already starting to form.[27]

For Prince Albert and his brothers and sister, like many upper-class children of their day, their parents were 'Olympian figures', part of a dimly perceived, grown-up universe. For them the real world was their nursery and the servants and nurses who looked after them at York Cottage, Sandringham.

2

A CLOISTERED WORLD

'[Prince George and Princess May] were more conscientious and more truly devoted to their children than the majority of parents in that era. The tragedy was that neither had any understanding of a child's mind ... they did not succeed in making their children happy.'

Mabell, Countess of Airlie

S ANDRINGHAM, where Prince Albert was born and where one day he would die, was the place which, above all the other royal houses, he and his family regarded as home.

Situated in the remote, peaceful county of Norfolk on the southern shore of the great grey indentation of the eastern coast of England known as the Wash, the estate had been purchased in 1866 by Prince Albert's grandfather when Prince of Wales. The move had been applauded by the Prince's parents, since they hoped it would remove their son from the rackety life which he led in London. Their hopes were in vain, for the Prince of Wales simply moved his social circle of buffoons, beauties and millionaires down to Sandringham for the two months, November and December, which he spent there for the shooting. The original house being neither large enough nor comfortable enough to accommodate the Prince's taste, he had it pulled down and, with the help of a London architect named Humbert and a local builder, Mr Goggs, he began a new house in 1870, enlarging it with another London architect, R.W. Edis, in 1883 and again in 1891, after a fire destroyed thirteen bedrooms. By the time Prince Albert was born, the 'Big House' at Sandringham looked more like an hotel than a country house, built in red brick edged with stone in what a local historian politely called 'a modified Elizabethan' style. One royal biographer thought it resembled a Scottish golf hotel; it could equally well have been the home of some Edwardian sauce or mustard magnate, a house built by an extremely rich man who wanted comfort but not extravagance. It is neither ugly nor ill-proportioned, but it is not beautiful either, the only touches of fantasy on its rather monotonous exterior being the tall, decorated Elizabethan chimneys and tower with a weather-vane and a stone *porte-cochère* in the style of a Loire château. Inside, the hall, dominated when Prince Albert was a child by a ferocious stuffed baboon holding a tray for visitors' cards, opened into the saloon, the chief meeting-place, with cream-coloured, stone-faced walls, Eliz-abethan-style fireplace, gallery, ornate piano made out of oak from the estate and sofas upholstered in the royal racing colours of red, blue and gold. The drawing-room faced down over lawns to the lake, its elaborate plasterwork and pretty painted ceiling panels looking like a very expensive suite in the Ritz. There were no antiques or ancestral portraits; perhaps the family felt they had quite enough in their other houses and palaces. A celebrity photograph screen, which belonged to Edward and Alexandra, is a microcosm of their age and includes a range of personalities from Gladstone and Ruskin to Nellie Melba and Camille Clifford, the original Gibson Girl. Although eighty years have passed since Edward vii died and it is over sixty years since the death of Queen Alexandra, the Big House at Sandringham, although cleared by Queen Mary of the incredible clutter with which Alexandra loved to surround herself, remains in spirit theirs.

If the presiding spirit of the Big House is Edward vii, then that of York Cottage, the house where Prince Albert was born, is George v. 'Until you have seen York Cottage,' the Duke of Windsor told his father's biographer, Harold Nicolson, 'you will never understand my father.' York Cottage stands a few hundred yards from the Big House on a grassy mound backed by a grove of oak trees and overlooking a pond presided over by a melancholy-looking lead pelican designed (but never used) as a fountain. The first thing that strikes a visitor about the house itself is its smallness and ugliness. Architecturally it is a higgledy-piggledy building with no merit whatsoever, of small rooms, bow windows, turrets and balconies, built of mixed carstone, a dark reddish-brown stone found on the estate, and pebble-dash, with black-painted half-timbering. It looks rather less imposing than a villa built in a south coast resort of the 1890s, perhaps at Bournemouth, where Edward vii, then Prince of Wales, carried on his amour with Lillie Langtry. Yet this is the house where George v and Queen Mary lived, first as Duke and Duchess of York, then as Prince and Princess of Wales, and finally as King and Queen, with six children, equerries and ladies-in-waiting, private secretaries, four adult pages, a chef, valet, dressers, ten footmen, three wine butlers, nurses, nursemaids, housemaids and handymen for thirty-three years.

George v was essentially a simple man. The smallness, lack of pretension and, it must be said, of taste, about York Cottage suited him. He found it cosy and homelike, its limited dimensions better suited to his personality than palaces, and gave him a good excuse not to entertain. He was not mean, but he was shy and did not like Society with a capital S, preferring even when at Buckingham Palace to dine alone with his wife. Princess May, whose ideas of a suitable setting for royalty certainly did not fit York Cottage, was less enthusiastic. Moreover, she enjoyed interior decoration and cannot have been pleased to find, on her arrival at York Cottage for her honeymoon, that her husband had ordered 'the Maples' man' to decorate the house throughout in standard upholsterer's taste. Prince George liked living as the vast majority of his subjects lived. Like his grandmother, Queen Victoria, one of his greatest strengths as a sovereign was his instinctive knowledge of, and sympathy with, their reactions. Lord Salisbury said of the Queen: 'I have always felt that when I knew what the Queen thought, I knew pretty certainly what view her subjects would take, and especially the middle class of her subjects.'[1] This sense of identity with the feelings and aspirations of the mass of their subjects was one of the most important qualities which George v bequeathed to his second son.

Prince Albert, always known in the family as his grandfather had been before him as 'Bertie', was born in his mother's bow-fronted bedroom on the first floor overlooking the pond. Its measurements – 20'6" by 18'6" – were far from palatial, but it was none the less one of the largest rooms in the house and only slightly smaller than the drawing-room in which the whole family and the Household gathered. He was a sturdy child, weighing nearly eight pounds at birth, almost the same as his elder brother Prince Edward, known as 'David' to his family, born eighteen months previously in the far grander surroundings of White Lodge in Richmond Park. It seemed somehow fitting that the glamorous heir to the throne should have been born at the high point of the English royal social season, Ascot week, and that his birth should have been announced by his proud grandfather during the course of a ball; it was also fitting that Prince Albert, who was to live for much of his life in his brother's shadow, should have been born out of the limelight in the country whose life suited him so well.

Prince Albert's birth was followed by that of Princess Mary, his only sister, in 1897, Prince Henry in 1900, Prince George in 1902 and lastly Prince John in 1905. In keeping with the generally accepted principle that children should never be heard and only seen on appropriate and carefully regulated occasions, a swing door was put across the passage on the first floor beyond the bedrooms of their parents and certain members of the Household, and beyond it two small, simply furnished rooms were designated for the children. One was the 'Day Nursery', where the children ate, played and had their first lessons. It was so cramped that there was hardly any room for toys, only one small-sized rocking-horse; fortunately Princess Mary did not care for dolls. The other, slightly larger room was the 'Night Nursery', where the three elder children slept with a nurse and had their baths in round tin tubs filled with hot water brought by a servant from the bowels of the house. Through the windows they could look out over the pond, with its little, wild, bramble-covered island reached by a bridge, to the park where tiny, web-antlered Japanese deer grazed, or lie in bed listening to the quacking of the wild duck on the pond at dawn and at dusk, the cooing of the wood-pigeons in the trees of the park and the occasional call of their grandfather's cock-pheasants in the woods.

But life in the nursery in the early years was far from idyllic. Like all upper-class children of the period their lives were ruled by nurses and their happiness depended not upon their parents but upon the temperament of their nannies. Parents were generally unaware of what went on behind the baize doors where their children were confined, usually to be brought down washed, brushed and dressed in their best once a day at tea-time for perhaps one hour of the twenty-four. That left at least eight hours during which the children were at their nurses' – or governesses' – mercy, and some of them were undoubtedly sadists as memoirs of upper-class Edwardian childhoods reveal. Lady Diana Manners (later Cooper), grand-daughter of the Duke of Rutland, and Loelia Ponsonby, daughter of Sir Frederick Ponsonby, both suffered at the hands of cruel nurses and governesses. Sir Frederick, who was brave enough to tackle George v over his bullying of his sons, was quite unaware of the unhappiness of his own daughter. The little Princes were no exception; their first nurse was dismissed for being impudent to their grandmother, the Duchess of Teck, but the second, a secret sadist, remained undetected for some time, torturing the heir to the throne and neglecting his brother. Every evening the nanny would carry the young Prince Edward down to spend tea-time with his parents, and just outside the door of the drawing-room she would pinch and twist his arm to make him cry. 'The sobbing and bawling this treatment invariably invoked', the Duke of Windsor recalled in his memoirs, 'understandably puzzled, worried and finally annoyed' his parents and would result in his being peremptorily removed from the room before further embarrassment was inflicted upon them. The same nurse, whose cruelty to Prince Edward was probably prompted by jealousy of his parents, a common tendency in nannies, was also given to favouritism and neglected Prince Albert in favour of his elder brother, an early taste of the treatment he was to receive throughout the first part of his life. She often gave him his afternoon bottle while driving in a vehicle known as a C-spring victoria, which gave a notoriously bumpy ride, with the result, according to his official biographer, that the baby Prince developed chronic stomach trouble which led to the gastric problems he was to suffer as a young man. Eventually the nurse had a nervous breakdown, and Princess May was astounded to discover that she had not had one day off in three years and dismayed to find that she had been the cause of her elder son's disappointing behaviour in the drawing-room. It had taken her three years to find this out.

Prince George and Princess May were anxious, loving but unsuccessful parents. That this was so was mainly due to the martinet attitudes of Prince George as a father, but Princess May, too, must bear some of the blame. She was not by nature a maternal woman, finding the whole process of pregnancy and childbearing distasteful and embarrassing, nor did she take great pleasure in cuddling the children and giving them their baths as both their grandmothers did. She was uninterested in babies and did not understand children, expecting them to behave like tiny adults. 'What a curious child he is,' she wrote of her eldest son when he was two, perhaps the most fidgety age of all for any child. 'David was "jumpy" yesterday morning, however, he got quieter after being out.' On another rare occasion all went well: 'Baby was delicious at tea this evening, he is in a charming frame of mind ... I really believe he begins to like me at last, he is most civil to me,' she wrote to her husband in terms distinctly odd for a mother to use about her own child.[2] She never succeeded in establishing a close relationship with her sons, apart, perhaps, from Prince George, her favourite; Prince Albert and Prince Edward were both to seek, and to find, mother-figures in their wives.

Lady Airlie, who knew them intimately, denied that Prince George and Princess May were 'stern and unloving parents'. 'Remembering them in my early days at Sandringham,' she wrote, 'before their family was even complete, I believe that they were more conscientious and more truly devoted to their children than the majority of parents in that era. The tragedy was that neither had any understanding of a child's mind.' Lady Airlie was a courtier, a breed that normally would rather die than say or write a word that might be construed as reflecting badly on the royals they serve, but she was also an honest woman and a friend of the family, who wrote the truth as she saw it. It was, she thought, curious that both of them had been brought up in particularly loving homes with adoring mothers and yet 'they did not succeed in making their children happy'.[3]

Part of the trouble undoubtedly was that the children saw so little of their parents and when they did they were rarely alone. On almost all occasions, certainly at tea-time in the drawing-room, Prince George and Princess May would be accompanied by a lady or a gentleman, whoever happened to be in waiting. While the children spent most of their time at Sandringham in the early years, first with their nurse and then with their tutor, their parents were frequently away, either on official tours or following an unvarying routine social calendar.

The children saw considerably more of their mother than of their father. Prince George never lingered over his tea in the drawing-room but would stride off alone to his study, inaccurately known as 'the Library', to read *The Times*, deal with correspondence, write up his game book or pore over his extraordinary stamp collection, remaining there until dinner. Princess May, however, would be in the drawing-room entertaining the children. Sometimes they would gather round the card-table to play an educational card game using cards with the counties of England on them, for example. Sometimes, with a lady-in-waiting at the piano, she, 'Bertie' and 'David' sang together, songs like 'Swannee River', 'The Camptown Races', 'Oh, My Darling Clementine' and 'Funiculi, Funicula'. But the time they liked most to spend with their mother was the hour before dinner, when she rested in her boudoir with its sprigged and striped wallpaper, chintz-covered chairs, painted, mirrored overmantel like thousands of other suburban villas throughout the land, and photographs everywhere, even stacked in a shelf-tidy because space was so limited. Hanging on the walls were prints, copies of paintings which in the case of the boudoir tended to the sentimental (elsewhere they would be copies of Old Masters of the type known as Alinari and sold in the better class of tourist shop in Florence); there was not one good original picture in York Cottage. At 6.30 they would come in to find their mother, dressed in a négligée, lying on the *chaise longue*, with her workbox on the lower shelf of a two-tiered table beside her, the top of which was covered with delightful miniature trinkets. The children would sit beside her on little chairs while she read to them, often royal history, her favourite subject. She taught them how to make woollen 'comforters', tubular scarves five foot long, by looping wool over brass pegs fitted on to a wooden ring, which were sent to one of her charities. Her son remembered how 'her soft voice, her cultivated mind, the cosy room overflowing with personal treasures were all inseparable ingredients of the happiness associated with this last hour of a child's day'.[4]

Prince George had a repressive effect on his wife as well as on his children. Her natural high spirits, which she only showed with those who knew her well, went underground after her marriage. It is a sad comment on the Princes' relationship with their father that his eldest son's happiest memories of his childhood always involved his mother's presence and his father's absence. He told his mother's biographer, James Pope-Hennessy:

My father was a very repressive influence. When he used to go banging away for a week or two at some shoot in the Midlands, and my mother never would go to those things; we used to have the most lovely time with her alone – always laughing and joking down at Frogmore or wherever we might be – she was a different human being away from him.

When the boys teased their French master, Monsieur Hua, by serving him tadpoles on toast as a savoury, the Duke recalled that their mother thought it 'highly amusing'; 'my father would have been furious. She liked anything of that sort when she was on her own with us.'[5]

When Prince Albert was five his father wrote him a characteristic letter on his birthday:

Now that you are five years old I hope you will always try & be obedient & do at once what you are told, as you will find it will come much easier to you the sooner you begin. I always tried to do this when I was your age & found it made me much happier.

At five, Prince Albert was still in the nursery, but his father was already determined that he should be brought up under strict discipline. It may be that his naval experience had taught him to regard obedience to orders as the highest of virtues and insubordination as the cardinal sin. Seemingly he had forgotten his own early childhood when he and his brother and sisters had been described by their grandmother as 'wild as hawks', remembering only the quarterdeck discipline to which he and Prince Eddy had been subject on *Britannia*. His own children were not expected to behave as children. They were expected to keep to their own quarters and, when they left them, to behave as primly as any adult member of the Household. Lady Airlie never saw them run along the corridors, 'they walked sedately, generally shepherded by nurses or tutors'. Prince George once wrote of his family as 'a regiment', and his children certainly felt that they were always on parade. Any irregularity in the children's behaviour or dress would be greeted with an outburst worthy of the quarterdeck. When one of the boys dared to appear before his father with his hands in the pockets of his sailor suit, Lalla Bill, the children's nurse, was immediately summoned and ordered to sew up the pockets of all their suits to prevent a recurrence of the offence.

Transgressions such as having dirty hands or wriggling in church would be followed by the dreaded summons to their father's presence. The Duke of Windsor wrote years later:

No words that I was ever to hear could be so disconcerting to the spirit as the summons, usually delivered by the footman, that 'His Royal Highness wishes to see you in the Library'.... Just as my mother's room came to represent a kind of sanctuary at the end of the day, so the Library became for us the seat of parental authority, the place of admonition and reproof.[6]

Sometimes the 'admonition' would be physical: Prince George would put his boy over his knee and spank him.

The way to the Library led through a dark-panelled hall with a huge carved oak fireplace, and the door would open on a small cheerless room with a dark oak dado and wall coverings the colour of dried blood made from the regulation red cloth then used by the French army for soldiers' trousers. The room was crowded with photographs on every available surface, all of the Prince's numerous relations. Reproduction lithographs of dull paintings hung on long wires on the walls and the general effect was one of cluttered gloom. Somehow two leather chairs, a sofa and a large desk with two Empire lamps were fitted into the room, not to mention a glass-fronted case containing the Prince's cherished collection of shot-guns. Books, in fact, were conspicuously absent from the Library: the shelves beside the Prince's desk housed his fabulous stamp collection, which, apart from shooting and sailing, was his principal hobby. The Prince would sit at the desk with his back to the north-facing window (he had a mirror panel set in the wall to his left so that he could see anyone coming up the drive at a glance). Prominent on the desk was a placard which summed up the sense of duty which ruled his life; upon it he had copied in his sloping, childish hand a precept from the nineteenth-century American Quaker, Stephen Grellet: 'I shall pass through this world but once. Any good thing, therefore, that I can do or any kindness that I can show any human being, let me do it now. Let me not defer nor neglect it, for I shall not pass this way again.'

Why was Prince George, a good, kind and not insensitive man, such an ogre to his children when they were growing up? It may well be that the true cause of his behaviour as a parent lay in his own relationship with his father. The story that he once told Lord Derby, 'My father was frightened of his mother, I was frightened of my father, and I am damned well going to see to it that my children are frightened of me', may or may not be apocryphal, but is certainly revealing of his point of view. Lacking both the self-confidence and natural authority of his father, he assumed an attitude which he believed to be correct towards his children, and, since temperamentally he could not show the love he truly felt, could not temper his fierceness with affection. This was all the more strange because he was by nature an emotional man, easily moved to tears. Harold Nicolson records in an unpublished diary that one of Prince George's favourite books which he read frequently in 1887, seven years before he became a father himself, and which always made him cry, was a Fauntleroy-style sentimental novel called *Wrong on Both Sides*. Its theme was of a harsh old earl who snubs and bullies the beautiful young viscount, his son, but loves him deeply underneath. 'Interesting psychologically,' Nicolson commented.[7]

There is reason, too, to think that Prince George, kind and sensitive as he was in his treatment of women, notably his daughters-in-law, Princess Marina, Duchess of Kent, and Prince Albert's wife, Elizabeth, was irritated by boys and young males in general. His daughter, Princess Mary, was his favourite child, and he doted on his grand-daughter, Princess Elizabeth. His harsh treatment of his sons has already been noted and it became worse rather than better as they grew up. His grandson, Lord Harewood, Princess Mary's eldest son, remembered him as an awesome, impatient figure who was always finding fault:

The possibility of getting something wrong was, where my grandfather was concerned, raised to heights of extreme probability, and our visits to Windsor for Easter usually provided their quota of uneasy moments. In 1931 [Harewood, or the Hon. George Lascelles as he then was, was aged just eight] he had been dangerously ill and was terrified of getting a cold. I had started to get hay fever and at the end of April, as we went to say goodbye to him in his sitting-room after breakfast, I started to sneeze, either from the pollinating grass or sheer nerves, and no amount of assurance that I had hay fever could stop the shouts of 'Get that damn child away from me', which made a rather strong impression on an awakening imagination.[8]

Understandably, after several such incidents as this, Harewood gained the impression that his grandfather did not really care much for children.

Moreover, Prince George suffered from dyspepsia, which affected his far from even temper. The Duke of Windsor told James Pope-Hennessy:

Off the record, my father had a most horrible temper. He was foully rude to my mother. Why, I've seen her leave the table because he was so rude to her, and we children would all follow her out; not when the staff were present of course, but when we were alone.[9]

It is not difficult to see how this essentially kind and open-hearted man could appear intimidating to his family. 'They were all frightened of him,' said a courtier. If this was true of his wife, whom he sincerely loved and admired while treating her with an almost Oriental imperiousness, so much the more so his children, whom he believed it was his duty to dominate.

Prince Albert's fifth birthday was to be the last of his nursery childhood. Just under a month later, in January 1901, Queen Victoria died at Osborne, sinking slowly 'like a great three-decker ship' in the words of her son-in-law, the Marquess of Lorne, as the nineteenth century closed and the twentieth began. Her passing was seen by contemporaries as the end of an era which had become identified with stability, opening the way for an age which many viewed with dread. The tiny figure lying in state at Osborne dressed in white, with her lace wedding veil covering her face (she had forbidden black because her death reunited her with her adored Albert), represented an image of the prestige and responsibilities of the British monarchy which would be a heavy burden for her great-grandsons to carry in the troubled century to come.

Just under eighteen months later, on 9 August 1902, the three eldest children watched the Coronation of their grandparents as King Edward VII and Queen Alexandra. The Coronation was less splendid than it should have been, since it had originally been scheduled for June but had had to be put off when the King developed appendicitis. The galaxy of crowned heads who had gathered in London for the occasion had already gone home, with the exception of the Abyssinian representative, who simply did not dare to return with the news that he had not attended the Coronation after all. The ceremony which took place in Westminster Abbey, where the Kings and Queens of England, his ancestors, had been crowned over the past 800 years, was Prince Albert's first experience of the historic splendours surrounding the British Crown. With Prince Edward, both of them dressed in identical Balmoral kilts and jackets, with the inevitable Eton collars, he watched as the grandparents he knew so well were transformed by the age-old rites into fairy-tale figures. Queen Alexandra, looking as young and slender as ever, shimmered in a dress of gold tissue. King Edward was an impressive figure dressed in uniform cloaked in purple velvet and a cape of ermine, and, blazing with jewels on his head, the same Crown of State which his grandson had recently seen among the Crown Jewels in the Tower of London. The two boys, unused to such a long ceremony, fidgeted and whispered throughout except for the moving moment when their father knelt in homage to the King. But when one of their great-aunts dropped her heavily embossed Order of Service over the edge of the royal box in which they sat, and it fell with a clatter into a large gold vessel below, the Princes were seized with irrepressible fits of giggles. Both these giggling little boys would be Kings, but only one of them was destined to be crowned.

The death of their legendary great-grandmother and the accession as King of their grandfather marked a significant change in the lives of the two eldest male grandchildren. It also marked the end of their father's private life as Duke of York, those seventeen years in which, to the despair of his biographer, he had 'done nothing except kill animals and stick in stamps'. On 9 November 1901, the King's birthday, Edward created his eldest son Prince of Wales, in recognition of the fact that Prince George was now heir to the throne. From now on Prince George, as Prince of Wales, would have to lead a more conspicuously public life as the scope of his duties, and indeed the scale of his style of living, were officially expanded. In March 1901, now Duke of Cornwall as well as of York, he had embarked with Princess May on a six-month tour of Australia and New Zealand (during which the delighted children followed their magnificent grandparents round their various residences being thoroughly spoiled and indulged by them). As the King took over Buckingham Palace, Windsor Castle and Balmoral, those 'Scottish funeral parlours' as he had been wont to refer to them in his mother's time, so he handed over to his son the imposing Marlborough House as his London residence, Frogmore House in the Home Park of Windsor Castle, and Abergeldie, a dour little castle on the River Dee near Balmoral.

For the Princes Albert and Edward, this change in status was manifested by their abrupt removal from the warm feminine atmosphere of the nursery shared with Princess Mary and ruled over by the beloved Lalla, their surrogate mother. One morning, without any warning, the boys were told that from then on the nursery footman, Frederick Finch, would wake them in the morning and that they would be under his care. The boys already knew Finch, a tall, handsome, thirty year old, who had been their nursery footman for the past three years. In the absence of Lalla, Finch would act as male nanny-cum-valet to them, shining their shoes, seeing that they washed their face and hands, kneeling beside them when they said their evening prayers, nursing them when they were sick and occasionally disciplining them. He would remain with them, an understanding friend and reassuring male presence, until Prince Edward went to Oxford, acting as valet and then butler to him when he became Prince of Wales.

The parting from Lalla and the transfer to Finch was followed by an event which even more clearly marked the end of nursery childhood. The Duke of Windsor recalled the scene one morning at their London home, York House, in the spring of 1902:

. . . Bertie and I heard my father stamping up the stairs. He had a particularly heavy footfall, but on that particular morning it sounded more ominous than ever. Besides, it was not his habit to come often to our room. In some apprehension we watched the door. When it opened, it revealed next to my father a tall, gaunt, solemn stranger with a large moustache.

'This is Mr Hansell,' my father said coldly, 'your new tutor,' and with that he walked out of the room, leaving us alone with Mr Hansell, who was no doubt as embarrassed as we were. . . .[10]

The man to whom the boys had been so abruptly introduced, and who was to become an enforced and inseparable part of their lives until they were grown up, was a typical product of his age and class. Henry Peter Hansell, then aged thirty-nine, was the son of a local Norfolk country gentleman. Educated at a good minor public school, Malvern College, where he was a member of the school cricket and football teams and apparently gained distinctions in English and History, he had then gone on to Magdalen College, Oxford, where he played football and emerged with a respectable second-class honours degree in History. In the tradition of impecunious sons of the middle classes who were otherwise unfitted to earn their living, Hansell had taken the line of least resistance and become a preparatory schoolmaster. Then, probably through his local Norfolk connections, he had got a job as Prince Arthur of Connaught's tutor. Prince Arthur having passed into Eton, Hansell was temporarily unemployed. Tall, good-looking and taciturn, a crack rifle shot and six-handicap golfer, he was also, thanks to his background on the Norfolk broads, a keen sailor, a quality particularly calculated to appeal to the Prince of Wales, who was a passionate and expert yachtsman. Always dressed in tweeds, an ever-present pipe in his mouth, and given to staring silently into the middle distance, Hansell was earnest, conscientious, uninspired and uninspiring. 'Melancholy and incompetent', as his eldest charge was to characterize him, the task of inspiring two little boys to the pursuit of knowledge in utter isolation from their contemporaries and the outside world was a far from enviable one. It is hardly surprising that he did not succeed. It is to his credit that he never believed he would. He thought that the boys should be sent to a preparatory school like any other children of their age, but their father's obstinate clinging to the ways of the past meant that his sons should be educated, or rather non-educated, alone with a tutor just as he and Prince Eddy had been with Canon Dalton. The new Princess of Wales was too intelligent not to have doubts about Hansell's capabilities, however much she tried to deceive herself, but her husband, characteristically, would attribute his sons' lamentable educational standards not to any defect in their tutor but to their stupidity.

Hansell emerges as a rather sad, solitary figure from the memoirs of his eldest pupil. A bachelor, he had to devote twelve years of his life to the royal children, a life lived mainly within the strict confines of York Cottage, his only relaxations outside this royal 'prison' being expeditions to examine churches and cathedrals in the company of equally serious and like-minded companions. Looking back, the Duke of Windsor suspected that his tutor 'developed a form of mental claustrophobia' from this position in the closely knit household:

Close to York Cottage on the way to the kennels there was a slight rise of ground. Every morning after breakfast Mr Hansell would disappear in that direction, to be gone fifteen minutes. From the top of the rise one had a view over the open plough-land. There Mr Hansell used to stand, smoking his pipe, meditating, and looking abstractedly into space. This habit puzzled Bertie and me. We finally decided that Mr Hansell liked to be alone, but in later years I was to think that these brief withdrawals had a deeper meaning. Once when he took us there I asked him what he found to look at in so dull a view. He looked at me in surprise. 'I don't think you will understand,' he said, 'but for me it is freedom.' Thereafter that spot became known to us as 'Freedom', and in my own time I was to realise fully what Mr Hansell meant.[11]

The arrival of 'Mider', as the boys called Hansell in a childish corruption of the word 'Mister', was a disquieting portent of unwelcome things to come. In other ways for the children that spring and summer of 1902 represented their first real emancipation from the confines of York Cottage. They spent Easter at Frogmore, an attractive Georgian house just down the hill from Windsor Castle where their grandparents held Court and where King Edward now patrolled the corridors with his terrier Caesar and his artistic advisers at his heels, rootling out the rubbish which had accumulated over the long years of his mother's reign. Frogmore was completely unmodernized, having neither electric light, central heating, nor even a bathroom, and the children's rooms up under the roof leads could be stifling on a hot day, but there they enjoyed a freedom that they never had in the cramped spaces of York Cottage within earshot of their father. On fine days they would bicycle round the well-kept paths of the romantic garden with its huge cedars and winding lake with water lilies and weeping willows.

Shrieking with delight the elder boys and their sister would race their bicycles round the Rotunda, the imposing classical memorial built by Queen Victoria after the death of her mother. The house itself was, like all Queen Victoria's homes, a 'family necropolis', the grounds of which resembled a cemetery of marble monuments to departed relations, servants and pets, while the interior of the house was cluttered with enough marble busts and life-size statues to fill a small museum. The delighted children noted that one of them, a statue of Queen Victoria's father, Edward, Duke of Kent, bore a striking likeness to one of their parents' footmen, a stout, jolly man named Smithson, the resemblance being heightened when they borrowed one of Smithson's caps which he wore off duty and placed it on the Duke's head. Their mother was amused but felt compelled to admonish them not only for making fun of their great-great-grandfather but also of a servant, but Smithson, when shown the children's handiwork, was not offended but highly flattered to be thought to resemble the royal Duke and the children spotted him afterwards standing admiringly in front of the bust. Windsor Castle itself, under the happy reign of their grandparents, was no longer a place of gloom and silence. In the great corridor built by George IV to accommodate some of the most splendid paintings of the royal collection, the children ran races and played hide-and-seek among the marble busts on their tall pedestals. In the magnificent Library built by William IV to house his father's fabulous collection of books and Old Master drawings, they would seize the tall library ladder and give each other rides upon it, wheeling it up and down the Gothic corridors among the bookshelves. Or they would have tea with their grandfather, who perhaps allowed them to play the great game of sliding buttered fingers of bread down the stripes of his trousers, as little Sonia Keppel did when the man she knew as Kingy visited her mother, Alice.

In that same summer of 1902 they went for the first time to Abergeldie Castle, which had a tall stone tower haunted not only by bats but also, they were told, by the ghost of one unfortunate Kittie Rankie, who had been burned as a witch on the hill overlooking the Castle. From their rooms in the ancient house they could hear the delicious sound of the River Dee splashing and gurgling round the granite boulders in the stream-bed below. While their father disappeared for days on end with his gun to shoot grouse or stalk stags on the moors, the children and their mother would drive out in a carriage with a picnic basket. When no one was looking they raced across the swinging suspension foot-bridge across the Dee, especially on windy days when the bridge swung violently in the gale.

It was to be their last truly carefree, childish summer; that autumn Prince Albert and his elder brother were sent back to York Cottage to settle down to school lessons with Mr Hansell. Mary, too, was given a female Finch in the form of a buxom, kindly German nursemaid whom they all loved, named Else Korsukawitz, and a Hansell represented by a sharp-tongued Frenchwoman, Mademoiselle José Dussau, whom the two elder Princes came to loathe. For Prince Albert, a shy, sensitive, highly strung child, removal from the sheltering world of the nursery to the unfamiliar terrors of the schoolroom was far worse than for his less inhibited brother and sister. The three elder children had always formed a trio and Prince Albert suffered in comparison with his siblings in the unenviable position of middle child. Prince Edward, as the eventual heir to the throne, was the star, the boy whom everybody noticed. Mary, as the only girl and her father's favourite, was indulged by him even to the point of forgiving her her unpunctuality, a cardinal sin in Prince George's eyes. Lady Airlie recorded that 'although his jokes at her expense often made her cheeks crimson, she was rarely scolded by him'. People tended not to notice the shy, second son. When he did bring attention on himself by being naughty, and he was generally blamed for any misdemeanour by the trio, he received the dreaded summons to his father's room. The effect of his father's intimidating sternness, his unintentionally cruel manner of 'chaffing' his children, and his high expectations of them upon a child like Prince Albert can only be conjectured. It was, however, at this period that he developed the stammer which was to haunt him throughout life.

Sir John Wheeler-Bennett, the future King George vi's official biographer, who himself suffered the same disability, has written movingly of a stammerer's predicament:

Only those who have themselves suffered the tragedies of the stammerer can appreciate to the full their depth and poignancy – the infuriating inhibitions and frustrations, the bitter humiliation and anguish of the spirit; the orgies of self-pity; and the utter exhaustion, mental and physical; perhaps, above all, the sense of being *different* from others and the shrinking from help prompted by pity. Only [he adds] by the exercise of the greatest tact and sympathy and understanding can the lot of the sufferer be mitigated, and these factors were not predominant in the climate of ideas at York Cottage.

As far as Prince Albert's father, a naturally impatient man, was concerned, sympathetic understanding was the last thing the boy could expect. 'Get it out', he would command him sharply as the hapless boy struggled with a word.

Prince Albert, like many of the best natural athletes, was born left-handed and, like all left-handed children of his era, was forced to write with his right hand, something which can, apparently, produce a psychological condition known as a 'misplaced sinister'. It has, moreover, been proved statistically that the incidence of stammering is much higher among people who are born left-handed and with a more developed right-hand side of the brain. Stammering is also a nervous condition, which produces a muscular spasm so that the stammerer is literally 'stuck for words'. Anything which contributes to the nervousness, such as the treatment which Prince Albert received at the hands of his father, can only serve to make the condition worse. Almost certainly, too, the other children teased him about his impediment, increasing his sense of helpless isolation.

Lady Airlie has, however, left an attractive picture of the six-year-old Prince, whom she liked the best of the royal children. Hardly knowing him when she first arrived, it was he who made the first approach. He made her an Easter card and waylaid her one morning as he came out of his mother's boudoir, but at the last moment his courage failed him and, thrusting the card into her hand without a word, he darted away. He was not a boy who made friends easily, she said: 'intensely sensitive over his stammer he was apt to take refuge either in silence – which caused him to be thought moody – or in naughtiness. He was more in conflict with authority than the rest of his brothers.'[12] Once she succeeded in gaining his confidence, however, she found that, far from being backward, he was an intelligent child with more force of character than anyone suspected. Years later his father would acknowledge this when he told a friend, 'Bertie has more guts than the rest of them put together.'

Prince Albert's self-confidence and peace of mind can hardly have been helped by the drastic treatment devised by his father's doctor, Sir Francis Laking, to combat knock-knees, from which his father and all his brothers except Prince Edward suffered. From the age of about eight Prince Albert was forced to wear a set of splints on his legs for several hours during the day and to sleep in them at night. A letter of his to his mother, dated 26 February 1904, makes pathetic reading. 'This is an experiment!' he wrote to her from Marlborough House, into which his parents had moved in the spring of 1903. 'I am sitting in an armchair with my legs in the new splints and on a chair. I have got an invalid table, which is splendid for reading but rather awkward for writing at present. I expect I shall get used to it.' On one occasion Finch, whose duty it was to put the splints on Prince Albert's legs at night, was so moved by his tearful pleas that he allowed him to sleep without them. Somehow Laking heard of this and reported him to the Prince of Wales, who summoned Finch to the Library. 'Look at me,' he expostulated to Finch, holding his trousers tight against his legs.' If that boy grows up to look like this, it will be your fault.' Possibly because of this inhuman treatment, Prince Albert grew up with perfectly straight legs, but the psychological effect of having been forced to wear such humiliating and inhibiting objects can hardly have helped a boy who already had a disabling stammer to cope with.

It is not, therefore, surprising that Prince Albert did not respond well to the new regime. Hansell had done his best to impart a serious atmosphere to the proceedings by setting up a schoolroom on the second floor with standard wooden school desks with hinged lids and attached chairs with hard seats and straight backs, a blackboard, wall maps and school books. He drew up a daily time-table based on the schedule of an ordinary preparatory schoolboy. Finch woke the Princes at seven and oversaw their progress to the schoolroom half an hour later for three-quarters of an hour 'prep' – homework – before breakfast. In winter it would still be dark outside as the two small boys sat glumly in the cold room grappling with unfamiliar problems, their stomachs rumbling with hunger. At 8.15 precisely, Hansell would appear to take them down to breakfast, and at nine they would be back at their desks, to work, with an hour's play-break, until lunch. Lunch was followed by a walk, or perhaps kicking a football around on the lawn, then another hour's work until tea-time – jam, muffins and milk – their last meal of the day. Then, hands, faces and knees scrubbed and hair smoothly brushed, they would be summoned down to the drawing-room where their parents and the Household were having tea.

Both boys, and Prince Albert in particular, found lessons unfamiliar and baffling. Their nursery lessons with Mademoiselle Bricka, the plump, elderly Alsatian lady who had been their mother's much-loved governess and confidante, had not prepared them for the educational curriculum faced by schoolboys their age. Hansell's written reports to the Prince of Wales on his sons' progress make dismal reading, their note being one of plaintive complaint: 'Both boys must give a *readier* obedience. I often describe them to myself as obedient boys at the second time of asking' (20 September 1902). Prince Albert in particular seems to have disappointed his tutor; he was hopeless at mathematics and frequently caused trouble with fits of temper. 'The work in simple division sums is most disheartening,' the wretched Hansell wrote on 25 July 1903. 'I really thought we had mastered division by 3 but division by 2 seems to be quite beyond him now.' And on 16 January 1904, 'I am very sorry to say that Prince Albert has caused two painful scenes in his bedroom this week. On the second occasion I understand that he narrowly escaped giving his brother a very severe kick, it being absolutely unprovoked & Finch being engaged in helping Prince Edward at the time.' Hansell's concern would seem quite out of proportion to the offence, but no doubt it evoked the dreaded summons to the Library. The splints and Prince Albert's resentment of them did not help his concentration when he was forced to wear them day and night, as is clear from Hansell's repeated complaints during 1904. '*Prince Albert's* early morning work is rendered almost useless by the *splints*, which I must say, appear to suit him much better and to be doing good already,' he wrote on 21 May. 'Under the conditions however small results can only be obtained by very great and sustained efforts on the part of the teacher.' Six weeks later he wrote: 'Practically all *Prince Albert's* work with me has been combined with the splints. It is now quite certain that *such a combination is impossible.*'

In his efforts to make the little schoolroom at York Cottage as much like a real school as possible, Hansell assembled a small team of teachers to help him educate the Princes, a team of which he clearly regarded himself as headmaster. Hansell took himself and his position seriously without the faintest glimmer of humour. By the early summer of 1905 he had reached the end of the second volume of his Report Book, writing on 20 May 1905:

On this, the last page of the second volume of the Report Book, it will not be out of place if I put down a few observations on the important subject of how the Princes are to be kept up to the mark in their work and in their conduct. A careful survey of the Report Book for each day will show that the reports of bad work have been noted and dealt with by me. The strong lever of a report book, to be handed into His Royal Highness after each lesson, will be used by Dr Oswald, Mr David and Monsieur Hua. With regard to my own work & the responsibility of surveillance, I propose only to make a direct report for special misbehaviour or idleness, such report only to be made after due consideration and with full conviction.

In keeping with the Prince of Wales's clinging to his own childhood experience, three of Mr Hansell's four colleagues had taught Prince George in his youth, which to anyone less conservative might not have appeared a necessary qualification for the task of imparting knowledge to his young children. Monsieur Gabriel Hua, a heavily bearded Frenchman with a deep voice, had taught French to Prince George in *Britannia* with a singular lack of success, mainly due to his pupil's detestation of things foreign. The Prince of Wales, regarding French as an effeminate language, would deliberately mispronounce French words when presented with a menu. Hua, however, had since gone on to become a celebrated and popular master at Eton and was now distinguished enough for the Prince to appoint him his Librarian, a post that entitled him to a position in the Prince of Wales's Household and to wear at dinner the special blue Household evening coat with black velvet collar and gilt buttons bearing the Prince of Wales's feathers. Hua had been called in as a direct result of the cold war which raged between the two elder boys and Princess Mary's French governess, Mademoiselle Dussau, whom Prince Edward described as 'that dreadful woman whom Bertie and I find it hard to refrain from poisoning when we are at home'.[13] Mademoiselle Dussau disliked small boys and frequently engineered their summons to the Library; she also, to their dismay, influenced their beloved sister to support her in her efforts to suppress their high spirits with threats of 'I'll tell Mama'. Worst of all, in their view, she made it compulsory to speak French at meals when she was present, supported by Hansell and an obedient Princess Mary. The Duke of Windsor recalled:

For my brother and me these meals were humiliating ordeals. Far from firing us with enthusiasm for Mlle Dussau's native language, they produced a completely opposite effect on us. And rather than lend ourselves to an experiment that, if successful, would only enhance Mlle Dussau's position, we resolved to try to defeat it by limiting our conversation to simple monosyllabic responses.[14]

Reports of this filtered back to the Prince of Wales and Hua was summoned out of retirement, but, despite his great experience of boys, he made little progress with Prince Albert, whose stammer made it more difficult for him to pronounce unfamiliar words and who already had a built-in hostility to the language.

'Prince Albert's excitable temperament, his hasty disposition and the readiness with which he reacts to the slightest reproof are obstacles which have to be fought against and overcome,' Hua was to write of the twelve-year-old Prince on 14 July 1908. In later life, however, when he was King, George VI's French was good enough for him to be able to make speeches in the language without hesitating and to converse without difficulty with French generals. His elder brother's accent and grasp of French, however, remained lamentable and in this, as in many other things, he was to show a marked preference for German.

Prince Albert, however, resisted the attempts of Professor Eugen Oswald, a wizened old man with a tobacco-stained beard and a guttural accent, a former teacher of the Prince of Wales during his brief sojourn at Heidelberg in 1892, to teach him German. All the children knew some German, since they had had a German nursemaid who made them repeat grace in German before and after every meal in the nursery. It was, after all, the mother tongue of most of their European relations, but only Prince Edward showed any aptitude for it. Prince Albert, Dr Oswald wrote in his weekly report to the Prince of Wales, was 'inattentive and playful' during the lessons at Marlborough House. When the Prince of Wales sent for him to ask for more details, the wretched Dr Oswald was embarrassed: 'Your Royal Highness, it isn't only that Prince Albert is inattentive; but, when I scold him, he just pulls my beard.'[15]

Parental insistence on foreign languages almost spoilt the family birthday rituals, turning them into a public ordeal for Prince Albert. The children's own birthdays, at which proceedings focused on a table covered with presents and a white tablecloth with a garland of wired flowers in the shape of the birthday child's initial, were pure pleasure, but those of their parents and grandparents involved a trying and embarrassing tradition. Each child was supposed to memorize a poem, copy it out on sheets of white paper which were then tied together with coloured ribbons, recite the verses in public, bow and then present the person whose birthday it was with the scroll on which they were written. At first it was always Shakespeare or Tennyson, which was bad enough, the children thought, but when they began their French and German lessons, their respective tutors considered it would be a good idea to show their progress in those languages by reciting French and German poems, La Fontaine's fables or ballads by Goethe. At Sandringham, where both their grandparents' birthdays were held, on 9 November and 1 December, these occasions, to which their grandparents liked to invite their guests, became a nightmare for Prince Albert. The experience of standing in front of the glittering company of grown-ups known and unknown, and struggling with the complexities of Goethe's *Der Erl König*, painfully conscious of the contrast between his halting delivery and that of his 'normal' brother and sister, was a humiliating one which may well have laid the foundations for his horror of public reviews when he was King.

The children had other tutors, their religious teacher being Canon Dalton. Stooped, bony, and possessed of a deep sepulchral voice, the Canon was an oily courtier but an abominable tyrant to his fellow canons at Windsor whom he would terrorize by flaunting his royal connections. Unlike their loyal father, who cherished an affection for the old Canon, the young Princes seemed to have felt no warmth for Dalton and they certainly disliked his son Hugh, later Chancellor of the Exchequer in King George vi's post-war Government. In the spring of 1906 a maths master was foisted on them, the consequence of an embarrassing day at Abergeldie when, their father having asked them to compute the average weight of the stags he had shot the previous season at Balmoral, they utterly failed to come up with an answer remotely tallying with the correct one. Mr Martin S. David, a master at Tonbridge school, appeared to coach them during holidays at York Cottage. Prince Albert loathed mathematics, a subject which he found difficult to grasp and which easily reduced him to nervous rage. 'You must really give up losing your temper when you make a mistake in a sum,' his father admonished. 'We all make mistakes sometimes, remember now you are nearly 12 years old and ought no longer to behave like a little child of 6. . . .'

The teacher whom Prince Albert liked was the local village schoolmaster, Walter Jones, a Yorkshireman with a rich accent and a deep laugh, who taught the children of the estate workers at the village of West Newton and replaced Hansell in the York Cottage schoolroom when he went on holiday. Jones was a considerable figure on the Sandringham estate and had become an intimate of the Prince of Wales, who even took him with him on his Empire tour of 1901. A self-taught naturalist with an encyclopaedic knowledge of the botany and animal life of Norfolk, he would take the Princes on fascinating expeditions through the woods and marshes of Sandringham, his lean frame striding tirelessly through the bracken in search of the nesting places of birds. The estate abounded in game, woodcock and pheasant in the woods of tall Scots and Corsican pines and slender birch-trees, rabbits in the fields, wild duck and migratory birds on the ponds and in the rough grass of the flat lands stretching down to the Wash, covered by the sea at high tide, laced with tiny creeks like veins when the water was out. Prince Albert, like his father, was a countryman at heart; in later life he was to be an expert wildfowler and a crack shot. Much of his understanding and knowledge of the Norfolk countryside and its ways he learned walking with Mr Jones through the bracken brakes of Sandringham under the open sky.

Prince Albert was a natural athlete inheriting the physical grace and slender figure of his grandmother, Queen Alexandra. He learned to ride at an early age, went hunting with the West Norfolk hounds and became an excellent horseman, although Princess Mary was braver on a horse than either of her brothers. He learned skating with the boys on the estate when the lakes froze over in mid-winter; later he and Prince Edward would organize ice-hockey teams there. The two boys were given some old golf clubs to practise on the nine-hole golf course which their grandfather had laid down, and sometimes they tagged along after Hansell, Jones, Finch and Mr Sayward, the stationmaster at Wolferton. Prince Albert had a natural swing and, although in later life Prince Edward developed a passion for the game, the younger brother who cared about it less was always the better golfer. Sometimes Mr Jones organized football games with the boys from the West Newton school. A photograph exists of the Sandringham team which played a local team from Glebe House at Hunstanton; dated 1906, it shows the team, which included Prince Albert, posing with its captain, Prince Edward; the result is not recorded. No less than three of those sturdy Norfolk boys in their long shorts and thick stockings were to be killed in the First World War.

Prince Albert was to witness two world wars in his comparatively short life and his earliest childhood memories were connected with war and soldiers. The

Boer War broke out in the autumn of 1899 and lasted until 1901; little else was talked about in the family or the nursery. Princess May's three brothers were all on active service and their letters from the front were read out to the children; in the nursery they pored over the nurses' newspapers, where artists' illustrations gorily depicted Highlanders dying on the barbed wire before Magersfontein or Royal Artillery guns captured at Colenso. For the first time it was clear that the British Army was not invincible; it was the first fissure in the monolithic but ill-assorted structure of the British Empire, whose accelerating dissolution was to be a major issue of Prince Albert's future reign. For the children, however, on their comparatively rare visits to London, the excitement of the war was seeing troops drilling in Hyde Park, or swinging in columns through the streets marching to brass bands playing 'Soldiers of the Queen'. At Marlborough House, the children were impressed by the huge, highly coloured murals by La Guerre on the walls of the great saloon and the two main staircases depicting in dramatic fashion the Duke of Marlborough's victories, the heroic figures of the generals, the twisted bodies of the dead and dying soldiers and horses, the shattered cannon. The children themselves played at soldiers, drilled by two of their favourites among their father's servants, veterans of the Boer War, Henry Forsyth and Findlay Cameron.

Forsyth had been a pipe major in the Scots Guards and, in 1901, became personal piper to the Prince of Wales. Every morning just before eight, wearing the kilt and carrying his bagpipes, he would appear beneath the Prince's window and, on the stroke of the hour, the air would be rent by the skirl of the pipes. Cameron was a Highlander and the children's hero. Dressed in livery with a kilt, with a row of medals on his robust chest, and a huge handlebar moustache, he was an imposing figure. He had fought in the Sudan and South Africa and would thrill the children with self-glorifying tales of his heroic hand-to-hand combats with the 'Fuzzie-Wuzzies' and desperate shoot-outs with the Boers. It was later discovered that Cameron had a weakness for whisky and on one occasion he tripped as he entered the dining-room catapulting a huge ham among the guests. To the children, however, he was a larger-than-life figure, representing the exciting world outside the quiet enclosed purlieus of San-dringham and Marlborough House. Their biggest thrill was to watch the Changing of the Guard at close quarters in Friary Court, St James's Palace, just over the wall from Marlborough House, when Hansell would understandingly allow them time off, supervised by Cameron and Forsyth. The two old soldiers organized the three elder children into a squad; armed with wooden rifles, they paraded every morning with Cameron as drill sergeant and Forsyth marching ahead playing his pipes. Sometimes, when the King was at Sandringham, he would walk down from the Big House to inspect them.

York Cottage, Sandringham, remained 'home' to the children, even after their father became Prince of Wales and occupied Marlborough House, Frogmore House and Abergeldie, between which the family moved in an annual unchanging routine. The Prince and Princess of Wales would spend January at

York Cottage for the last weeks of the pheasant shooting, where the children remained while they went to London in February to fulfil their public duties – levees, banquets, State visits, charitable functions – until the end of March, when they rejoined the children, either at Sandringham or at Frogmore. May and June were spent in London for the balls, garden-parties and presentation-parties of the social Season, interrupted by a ten-day sojourn at Frogmore in June for Ascot week races. In July the children, with their mother, who disliked yachting and had had enough of shooting-parties at Sandringham, would retire to Frogmore while their father embarked on his regular summer sporting programme: first Goodwood, staying with the Duke of Richmond for the racing; then Cowes, yachting with the King on the *Victoria & Albert*; then from the 'Glorious Twelfth' of August, when the grouse-shooting started, visiting the grouse moors of his friends – at Abbeystead in Lancashire with the Earl of Sefton, at Bolton Abbey with the Duke of Devonshire, or at Studley Royal with the Marquess of Ripon; then at Moy Hall in Inverness-shire, home of the Mackintosh of Mackintosh; and finally to Abergeldie, where the children and their mother would join him. Although they loved Scotland, they always felt sorry when they boarded the train at the end of August to join their father, for it meant a renewal of the strict regime he enforced when at home. By early September, the best of the grouse-shooting being over, the Prince of Wales would spend his days 'on the hill' deer-stalking; by the end of the month the weather would have turned colder and the first snow whitened the hill-tops before the family returned south in the second week of October, the children with their tutors and nurses to York Cottage, their parents to Marlborough House. The Prince and Princess of Wales would come down on occasions for the partridge and then the pheasant shoots, and there was always a great shooting-party at Sandringham for King Edward's birthday on 9 November. At Christmas the whole family would be reunited there, the Prince and Princess of Wales with their children at York Cottage, the King and Queen at the Big House.

For the children, the annual arrival of their grandparents at Sandringham early in November was a magical interruption of their daily routine, an explosion of light, music, laughter and excitement. A few days before, the shuttered Big House stirred as an army of servants arrived from London to bring it to life, fires were lit and exotic plants carried in from the greenhouses. Then, without a word of warning, all the clocks in the estate would be put half an hour ahead; this was Sandringham Time, introduced by the King in imitation of his neighbour, the Earl of Leicester at Holkham, in order to squeeze the maximum daylight out of the dying year for the shooting-parties. This, for the children, was a signal for festival. That same evening, the great house on the hill would blaze with lights, and the crunch of gravel and the clatter of horses' hoofs on the drive would herald the arrival of the King and Queen, with twenty or thirty guests and their attendant valets and maids. If the two Princes had their homework well in hand, they would be allowed to run up to the Big House after tea to say goodnight to their grandparents. After the sedate, enclosed atmosphere of overcrowded York Cottage, the boys felt a charge of excitement as they approached the Big House, looming out of the dusk like a great ocean-liner, and entered the saloon, filled with beautifully dressed people, the ladies in ravishing tea-gowns, glowing with ropes of pearls, sparkling with diamonds, the men in velvet suits, chatting to each other or playing bridge in the adjoining drawing-room while Gottlieb's orchestra played music from Strauss operettas in the gallery. The air would be filled with the scent of perfume, flowers and expensive cigars, the air tingling with an underlying sense of sex and power, what Lord Esher called the 'electric excitement' of Edward vii's Court. All too soon, for their father had laid down a rule that they had to be home by seven, the two Princes would have to leave this enchanted world, and all too often, since their grandparents 'seemed to delight in conspiring to defeat that particular point of parental discipline', these delightful excursions would end in the Library, with their father upbraiding them for being late.[16]

King Edward's Sandringham was a happy place where he relaxed and enjoyed playing the part of country squire instead of monarch. It was a big, well-run, lavishly kept-up, sporting and agricultural estate, the property of a benevolent landlord with a bottomless purse and a keen interest in its success. The King bred prize-winning cattle and shire horses, the powerful animals then used for ploughing. His racing stud at Wolferton was one of the most successful in the country with two Derby winners, Persimmon and Diamond Jubilee, and the King himself, when he was Prince of Wales, had been one of the country's top owners with an income from racing of £30,000 a year. The estate was run on paternalistic lines and employed some 300 workers housed in purpose-built cottages in the villages of West Newton, Dersingham and Wolferton, with schools and village social clubs founded and funded by the King. There was also a Technical School started by Queen Alexandra, where the children of the estate workers were taught woodcarving and other crafts.

A romantic painting by Frederick Morgan and T. Blinks shows Queen Alexandra, slim, auburn-haired, beautifully dressed and as youthful-looking as ever, standing on the summer grass at Sandringham surrounded by children and dogs – Prince Albert, Prince Edward and Princess Mary, and an assortment of borzois, wolfhounds, collies, bassets and pomeranians. Sandringham was a paradise for children and animals, of which there were a great many. The Queen adored animals (she even fed pheasants on the terrace as if they were chickens and woe betide her son George if any of them disappeared during the shooting season) and had her favourites modelled in miniature by Fabergé. In the stables there were her favourite ponies, Lady Love and Ruby Mine; two splendid chestnuts, Faithful Boy and Margate Buoy, which she would drive harnessed to her park phaeton; her riding pony, Violet, which she took with her wherever she went; and the King's big, bay horse, Tooting, which he liked to drive himself in a buggy. There were numbers of old retired ponies, and a small and frisky Italian donkey which the Queen's grandchildren would harness to a special miniature trap. In the saddle-room the children would stare wide-eyed at a Mexican saddle presented to their grandfather by the hero of the Wild West, 'Buffalo Bill' Cody. The children's and their grandmother's favourite place, however, was the kennels, where seventy-five dogs were kept—basset-hounds, borzois, deer-hounds, Great Danes, spaniels, bull-dogs, pugs, dachs-hunds and every kind of terrier—especially at the four o'clock feeding time when the dogs were fed on Scottish oatmeal and bullocks' paunches all cooked by the kennel staff in big coppers. Near the kennels were the pigeon houses where the King's racing pigeons and the Queen's doves were kept, overseen by Mr Jones.

For the children there was also the excitement of a ride in one of their grandparents' motor cars, a Daimler or a Mercedes. Queen Alexandra, who liked to drive her horses at a rattling pace, was nervous of motoring and annoyed her husband by tapping the chauffeur on the shoulder with her parasol when she thought he was going too fast. The King liked speed and preferred motoring alone with his chauffeur and his motor engineer, Mr C.W. Stamper, who sat in front with his tool-bag, ready to jump down and deal with any fault as it occurred. Although the speed limit on public roads was raised to twenty miles per hour in 1903, the King, not being subject to the laws of his realm, was very proud of himself for having driven along the Brighton road at sixty miles per hour in 1906. After a day such as this he would always say as he got out of the car, rolling his guttural rs, 'a very good run, Stamper; a very good run indeed.'

The two Princes were sometimes allowed to watch an afternoon's shooting with their grandfather. Between 10,000 and 12,000 pheasants a year were reared on the estate to be slaughtered by the King and his guests during the shooting season, which traditionally opened on his birthday, 9 November. Those were the days of the *grandes battues,* when the gamekeepers wore bowler hats trimmed with gold cords, coats of green velveteen, introduced by the Prince Consort from Germany, with brass buttons, and tight cord breeches and gaiters, while the head-keeper, Mr Jackson, to show his superior status, wore a half top-hat called a 'cheerer' and a green brass-buttoned coat of melton cloth, and carried a silver horn on a cord of red braid with tassels. The beaters, not less than sixty of them, wore smocks and black felt hats with red and blue ribbons known as 'chummies'. The King himself wore baggy knickerbockers of bold checked tweeds with spats stretching almost to the knee, and a voluminous Inverness tweed cape of an equally bold pattern. Shooting at Sandringham under Edward VII was not a very sporting affair, since the King regarded it primarily as a way of entertaining his guests; the bigger the bag the better he was pleased, and the whole day's shooting was stage-managed to provide His Majesty and his guests with the greatest number of the easiest targets in the intervals before and after a gargantuan luncheon.

The focal point of the Sandringham year was Christmas, aptly described by King Edward's grandson as 'Dickens in a Cartier setting'. Just before Christmas seven of the fattest bullocks were slaughtered to provide joints of meat for every family on the estate, widows included, and the distribution took place in the coach house. Great tables covered with white tablecloths were ranged with bloody joints of meat, each tagged with the name of the recipient. All the workers on the estate gathered – gamekeepers, gardeners, foresters, stable and kennel hands, farm workers and their wives, some 300 in all – in the stable yard, before filing in in turn to receive their joint of meat and to be wished a Happy Christmas by the King, seated with all his family at the door. In the evening after tea, the royal children piled into their father's omnibus, which was usually used for transporting the servants, and drove up to the Big House. In the saloon their grandparents waited with some of the older members of the Household who usually spent Christmas with them. After minutes of excited anticipation, a gong sounded the signal for the appearance of one of the upper servants disguised as Santa Claus who led the way to the ballroom. The double doors were flung open to reveal a Christmas tree from the Sandringham woods, twenty-seven feet high, blazing with candles in the centre of the room, its top almost touching the barrel ceiling, its branches decorated with tinsel, glass balls and patches of white cotton wool imitating snow. Round it were trestle tables running the length of the room, covered with white cloths and loaded with presents, each section marked off for each member of the party, which always included the local doctors and clergy as well as the family and Household. While Gottlieb's band played in the gallery, the King and Queen led each person in turn up to their presents, 'a rather trying experience', Fritz Ponsonby remembered, with the 'the King on one side and the Queen on the other explaining who gave what present and giving particulars about the various articles'. Each person received an amazing number of presents – prints, water-colours, silver cigarette-cases, inkstands, pins, studs and books. The King's and Queen's presents from all their royal relations in Europe were magnificent, particularly the Fabergé objects sent by the Tsar. Through all this ceremony the children were dying with excited anticipation, for they were made to wait until everyone else had received their presents before they were allowed to fall upon the tables set aside for them and to open their presents on the ballroom floor covered with a sea of wrapping paper. The presents were left out on the tables so that every evening after dinner the King and Queen and their party could examine each other's gifts until New Year's Eve, when they were cleared away to make room for the present-giving for the servants and estate-workers. Each person was given two tickets as they came in and the Queen's daughters and members of the Household distributed the numbered presents, some 800 in all. Then finally, the tree was stripped and all the toys and sweets which had hung on it were given to the children.

Although Prince Albert and Prince Edward were always coupled together in their early childhood, it was clearly understood that Prince Edward was the heir to the throne. That his superior destiny was already recognized by his younger brother was illustrated by a curious incident which Lord Esher witnessed at

Windsor on 25 May 1904, when, as he was looking through a weekly paper with the children, they came upon a picture of Prince Edward with the caption 'our future King'. 'Prince Albert at once drew attention to it,' Lord Esher noted, ' – but the elder hastily brushed his brother's finger away and turned the page. . . .'[18] On that occasion, when Prince Edward was just under ten years old and Prince Albert nine, Esher noticed that the elder brother acted as 'a sort of head nurse' to the other children. 'I could always manage Bertie,' the Duke of Windsor was to write years later when he was in exile and his brother King of England. It was not long, however, before Prince Albert began to resent his elder brother's assumption of authority, and as the brothers approached puberty there were signs that he was no longer easy to 'manage'. By January 1907, when Prince Edward was approaching thirteen years old and Prince Albert was in his twelfth year, Hansell was finding it difficult to keep the peace in the schoolroom. 'It is extraordinary how the presence of one acts as a sort of "red rag" to the other,' he reported. Conflict in the schoolroom, however, ended that month when a tearful Prince Edward, smartly dressed in naval cadet's uniform, left to begin his first term at the Royal Naval College, Osborne. Exactly two years later Prince Albert followed him there. His experience of life outside the cloistered world of York Cottage was about to begin.

UGLY DUCKLING AND COCK PHEASANT

'I had a miserable time in the Navy. . . .'
HRH Prince Albert in conversation with the Marchioness of Granby

ON 16 January 1909 Prince Albert, aged just thirteen, arrived at Osborne accompanied by Hansell. His tutor's report at the end of his York Cottage schoolroom days was one in which any note of optimism was heavily tempered by doubts about the future:

... I can state as a fact that he has reached a good standard all round but we must remember that he is at present a 'scatter-brain' and it is perfectly impossible to say how he will fare ... at Osborne under the influence of all the excitement attendant on the new life.... Like his brother he cannot get on without 'a bit of a shove' and, after our experience of Prince Edward's first two terms, I do hope that he will not be left too much to himself. At present they *must* have a certain amount of individual help and encouragement, especially encouragement, a too literal interpretation of the direction that they are to be treated exactly the same as other boys, who have had three or four years at private school, must lead to disaster [Hansell warned] ... he requires a firm hand, but in that respect the excellent discipline of Osborne will be just what he requires. I have always found him a very straight and honourable boy, very kind-hearted and generous; he is sure to be popular with the other boys.

Prince Albert had been equipped like the other cadets by Gieves, the naval outfitters in Savile Row, in tailor-made blue trousers and jacket with brass buttons and white collar tabs, topped with a naval cap. According to regulations, trousers were to be made without pockets, to prevent either the cut from being spoilt by overstuffing, or possibly the boys' fingers from straying in an indecent manner; monkey jackets were tailored without side pockets, only one outside pocket on the left breast and one inside on the right being permitted. Mr Gieve could not, however, bring himself to comply with the Prince of Wales's instructions that his son should be outfitted exactly the same as any other naval cadet entering Osborne and had substituted fine quality cashmere for the rough blue wool of Prince Albert's 'rug of uniform pattern', which, emblazoned with the cadet's initials in scarlet, was to lie neatly folded at the end of each bed.

Hansell had reason to be pessimistic; the culture-shock of being thrown in at the deep end of the English public-school system for a boy who, like Prince Albert, had been brought up in an enclosed and sheltered atmosphere, would have been considerable. His contemporaries would already have had five years' experience of being separated from their parents and families for most of the year and plunged into the tribal world of the British preparatory school with its severe discipline, physical discomfort, hierarchical organization and esoteric customs. They would have been brought up to expect the even more demanding second stage of that system which they entered at the age of thirteen: the utter subjugation of the younger 'new' boys to their older schoolfellows, the fagging, bullying, covert and overt homosexuality, appalling food, Spartan comforts and daily regimentation of life at a British public school. Prince George had done his best to prepare his sons in some ways for the school experience with his insistence on discipline, even over petty matters, and his absolute determination that they should not be brought up to think themselves superior to other people. He could not, however, prevent them from feeling themselves to be different, and had even fostered this feeling by discouraging them from contact with children of their own age. Almost the only occasions on which Prince Albert and his brothers and sister had met other children had been twice-weekly private dancing classes with carefully selected upper-class children in London and the somewhat unreal football matches with the sons of estate workers at Sandringham. Even courtiers' children rarely mixed with the Princes, Loelia Ponsonby remembered only very occasional children's parties at the palaces, or nursery expeditions in the holiday atmosphere at Balmoral. Royalty cannot approach too closely to a subject, however much they might ask 'to be treated as other people'.

It was, therefore, with very little conception of what other children in the herd were really like, that an apprehensive Prince Albert faced life as a naval cadet. His sense of strangeness was no doubt increased by the fact that the college was housed in the stable block of Osborne House, the huge Italianate villa on the Isle of Wight in which 'Gangan' Victoria had died just under eight years ago. King Edward had absolutely refused to take on the house, which he regarded as a white elephant, and, to the indignation of his sisters and in defiance of his mother's will, had given it to the nation to be used as a convalescent home for officers, while the stable block was to be turned into a preparatory training college for naval cadets. Queen Victoria's rooms remained as she had left them, closed up behind shutters in the great house, while her great-great-grandson was to sleep on a hard iron bed in a dormitory housed in temporary buildings made of a substance called Luralite – asbestos sprinkled with sand – which had already deteriorated so much in the five or so years since the college opened that the boys could stick their feet through the walls.

Osborne's motto, a quotation from Nelson, was emblazoned in large brass letters on the central oak crossbeam in the main hall which bore his name, 'There Is Nothing The Navy Cannot Do'. The British Navy was regarded as not only omnipotent but also invincible and infallible; the all-embracing justification for anything done in its name was 'for the good of the Service'. From the moment that Prince Albert crossed the threshold of his great-grandmother's former stable block he was absorbed in an organization with a triumphant pride in its historic tradition, a sense of superiority to any other Service and a clear consciousness that it was vital to the defence of the British Empire. Osborne and Dartmouth, to which Prince Albert was, with considerable difficulty, to graduate two years later, were designed by his grandfather's great friend, the First Sea Lord, Admiral of the Fleet Sir John 'Jackie' Fisher, to replace the old wooden training ship, *Britannia*, in which Prince George and Prince Eddy had served, as training colleges to produce officers technically prepared for the great war against Germany which Fisher was convinced would soon come. Only two months after Prince Albert entered Osborne there was a nationwide war scare; the Germans, it was predicted, would be ahead of the British in naval armaments by 1912, there was a rash of war novels and spy stories predicting a German invasion of Britain, like Erskine Childers's *Riddle of the Sands*, and rumours of 6,500 German spies already operating in Britain in advance of the invader. It cannot have been long before Prince Albert became aware of the possibility that he might have to fight a war against the Navy of the Kaiser, his father's first cousin, whom he knew as 'Uncle Willy'.

The college was run on predominantly naval lines, headed by a captain, Arthur Christian, who had been on *Britannia* with Prince Albert's father, and staffed by twenty-seven officers who ran the administration and the discipline with the teaching staff, from the headmaster down, occupying a subordinate position. On arrival, the new boys were divided into six terms named after famous admirals, Prince Albert's being Grenville; the boys of each term were allotted two dormitories labelled under two 'watches', starboard for the clever boys, port for the others – both the royal Princes landed up in the port watch. Discipline was strict, but not, according to former cadets, unkindly, although the life was Spartan, beginning at 6 a.m. in summer and 6.30 in winter, when the boys, woken by a bugler playing reveille, were expected to leap out of bed at the first stroke of the cadet captain's gong, kneel down and say their prayers, then at two strokes of the gong start brushing their teeth and, at three, jump all at once in the green-tiled, cold-water plunge pool at the end of the dormitory. Everything at Osborne was done at the double: cadets were expected to run everywhere and at the end of the day they were given only three minutes to undress, fold up their clothes and brush their teeth, although extra time was allowed for prayers. Food was unappetizing; the boys supplemented their unap-pealing diet by spending their one shilling a week pocket money in the canteen, a hut on the playing-fields where a naval pensioner sold fruit, ice-cream, stuffed dates and sweets.

Life at Osborne is remembered by Prince Albert's contemporaries as tedious rather than brutal. There was not a great deal of bullying, but what there was seems to have been concentrated on the unfortunate Princes, whose royal birth and secluded upbringing marked them out as 'different', a cardinal sin in the eyes of the other boys. Prince Edward was in his final year when Prince Albert arrived but, due to the rigid seniority system which divided the years or 'terms', there was little practical help he could give his brother beyond snatching a prearranged walk round the playing-fields together. What he had to report of the 'hazing' he had had to undergo was hardly a comfort to his younger brother, including as it did a crude re-enactment of the decapitation of their ancestor, Charles I, which involved pushing the unfortunate Prince Edward's head through a classroom window and banging the sash down on his neck. One cadet contemporary at Osborne during Prince Albert's time remembered him as 'having rather a rough time, he was rather bullied'. On one occasion Cadet Denham, as he then was, was coming out of the mess-hall after breakfast when he found a figure tied up in a hammock in the gangway calling for help. It was Prince Albert, trussed up by the cadets of his own term.[1] The Prince was small and fragile in physique, which led to his being nicknamed 'Sardine'. Games were compulsory; Prince Albert, being almost totally unused to playing football or cricket as team games on a regular basis, was at a disadvantage here as he was with the school curriculum which, as Osborne was basically a technical school, concentrated on mathematics, navigation, science and engineering. Although he enjoyed the practical side of the engineering course in the workshops on the River Medina and the turns taken crewing a small steamer called the *Beta*, mathematics classes involved public humiliation. Years later he told a friend how sometimes he would have to remain silent when asked a question in maths class because his stammer would not allow him to pronounce the 'f' of the word fraction. This earned him the reputation of being stupid and recalcitrant, although his father, always more understanding at a distance than he was face to face, wrote to Hansell: 'Watt [Prince Albert's Osborne tutor] thinks Bertie shy in class. I expect it is his dislike of showing his hesitating speech that prevents him from answering. . . .' In the circumstances, Prince Albert's first letter home to his mother on 19 January 1909 was obviously a brave lie, as was his brother's reassuring letter, 'Bertie is getting on well.' His father was not deceived. 'No doubt it will take a term or two for Bertie to settle down,' he wrote to Hansell.

Prince Albert must have surmounted most of his difficulties at least as far as his fellow cadets were concerned since Denham remembered him as 'likeable' and 'generally popular'. His academic record remained, however, disastrous. It was noted by those who scanned the examination lists that 'Bertie' was always either bottom or very near it, at any rate in a position which would probably have earned a boy of less illustrious parentage the sack. Prince Albert's progress from Osborne to Dartmouth was accompanied by the inevitable exhortations from his disappointed parent and nervously despairing comment by his tutors. His father wrote:

My dearest Bertie, I am sorry to say that the last reports from Mr Watt with regard to your work, are not at all satisfactory, he says you don't seem to take your work seriously, nor do you appear to be very keen about it. My dear boy this will not do, if you go on like this you will be at the bottom of your Term, you are now 71st & you won't pass your examination ... if you don't take care.

The warnings were of no avail; in the final examinations in December 1910, Bertie's place was 68th out of 68. Watt wrote to Hansell:

I am afraid there is no disguising to you the fact that P.A. [Prince Albert] has gone a mucker. He has been quite off his head, with the excitement of getting home, for the last few days, and unfortunately as these were the days of the examinations he has quite come to grief.... I am afraid Their Majesties will be very disappointed, and I can well understand it. But after all the boy must be at the least stable part of his mental development, and I expect another year will produce a great change in him....

None the less, despite going 'a mucker' and coming bottom of his term, Prince Albert went on in January 1911 to the second stage of his naval education, joining his elder brother, then in his final term, at Dartmouth Royal Naval College. Within a month of his arrival both Princes suffered one of the last hazards of childhood, an illness which was to have considerable bearing on Prince Edward's future and may have had some slight effect on Prince Albert. In February 1911 there was an epidemic of measles and mumps at Dartmouth during which two cadets died. Prince Albert and Prince Edward caught both diseases severely enough for bulletins to be issued to the press and for the prestigious medical journal, *The Lancet*, to print a reassuring, but misleading, statement: 'The Princes are at the age of least danger, and the important measure of confinement to bed, to the lack of which so many complications and *sequelae* are frequently due, is being enforced....'[2] Among the complications following upon mumps is orchitis, which affects the testicles and can impair procreative capacity, something which, in the case of the heir to the throne, would be of overriding importance. On the outbreak of the epidemic the Princes were isolated in the commandant's house in the hope that they would escape; in fact, far from being, as the *The Lancet* claimed, 'at the age of least danger', as adolescents they were very vulnerable indeed to complications. While orchitis as a result of mumps is rare in childhood, it is a definite risk in adolescent and adult males, and where it occurs some degree of infertility can be expected in one in ten patients. In a few cases where both testicles are affected, sterility can result. In Prince Albert's case whatever complication there may have been was clearly minor, but in that of Prince Edward, it seems to have been serious. Although extremely active sexually as a young man, he never had any children, while from hints dropped by those close to him it appears that it was known to them that he had something 'wrong with his gland', as the euphemism went, and specifically that it 'went wrong' 'on reaching puberty'.[3] It was noticed that his body hair was sparse and that he rarely needed to shave. Knowledge of, or fear of, being sterile can prompt the obsessive sexual life to which the Prince was prone; the knowledge that he was unlikely ever to father a child could even have been a factor in his willingness to abdicate the throne.

In the interval a transformation had taken place in Prince Albert's family's position; since the death of Edward VII on 6 May 1910, he was not just the grandson but the son of the King. Prince Albert had been in London on holiday and had seen his grandfather several times in the week preceding the King's death. On 27 April, the night of the King's return from Biarritz, where he had been on holiday with Mrs Keppel, the Prince and Princess of Wales and their two elder sons had accompanied the King to the opera to hear *Rigoletto*, starring the enormously fat Tetrazzini. The following day, after entertaining Lord Kitchener to lunch, the same family party went to a Private View at the Royal Academy; the next day they all lunched together at Buckingham Palace. It was the last time he was to see his grandfather alive; King Edward caught a chill at Sandringham that weekend and returned to Buckingham Palace very unwell on the Monday. On Thursday 5 May, Prince Albert and Prince Edward accompanied their father to Victoria Station to meet Queen Alexandra, who had hurried back from the Continent on hearing the news. On Friday morning, 6 May, the King saw his old friend, the millionaire Sir Ernest Cassel, tried to smoke a cigar but could not enjoy it. That afternoon, standing by the cage of his favourite canaries, he collapsed and fell to the floor. Refusing to be put to bed, he sat in a chair saying feebly, 'No, I shall not give in; I shall go on; I shall work to the end.' But it was clear that he was dying, suffering a series of heart attacks. The doctors could do nothing for him but give him morphia to ease his pain; they had already given him oxygen and injections of strychnine, tyramine and ether. Later that afternoon the Prince of Wales walked over from Marlborough House to tell him that his horse, Witch of the Air, had won the 4.15 race at Kempton Park. The King replied, 'Yes, I have heard of it. I am very glad.' They were his last coherent words; he later lapsed into a coma and died without a struggle at a quarter to midnight. His grief-stricken son entered into his heritage as King George V, writing sorrowfully in his diary, '. . . I have lost my best friend and the best of fathers. . . .'

Prince Albert had been the first of King Edward's grandchildren to realize that he was dead. Looking out of the window of Marlborough House early the following morning, his horrified cry wakened Prince Edward, 'Look, the Royal Standard is at half-mast!' No one needed to tell the two royal princes what that meant. While they were dressing, Finch came in to tell them that their father wished to see them downstairs. His face grey with fatigue, the new King informed his sons that their grandfather was dead. Prince Edward replied that they already knew as they had seen the Royal Standard at half-mast. At first the King seemed not to hear as he described to them the scene at their grandfather's death-bed; then the significance of Prince Edward's words touched an atavistic royal nerve.

'What did you say about the Standard?' he asked sharply.

'It is flying at half-mast over the Palace,' they told him. The King frowned and muttered, 'But that's all wrong,' and repeating to himself the ancient saying, 'The King is dead. Long live the King!', he sent for his equerry and ordered that a mast be rigged at once on the roof of Marlborough House.[4] Two days later the two boys stood at the salute at the wall of Marlborough House as their father was proclaimed King in Friary Court, St James's Palace, opposite. For both of them it was one step nearer the throne.

As Prince Albert, wearing his naval cadet's uniform, walked at his father's side behind the gun-carriage bearing his grandfather's coffin out of Buckingham Palace along the route lined with silent crowds to Westminster Hall, he must have been aware, perhaps for the first time now that he was old enough to realize it, the importance of the public face of kingship and the deep emotions which centred on the person of the King. The private image of his grieving grandmother refusing to allow his grandfather's body to be put in the coffin was subsumed in the magnificently stage-managed ceremonial obsequies of the King. Kingship had transformed Edward VII from a playboy prince into the 'Uncle of Europe', an internationally respected statesman. It would transform his father and, in time, it would transform him too.

The fact that his father was now King–Emperor had a considerable impact on Prince Albert's life. Not only had his parents inherited the invisible but powerful aura of reigning sovereigns, but physically also they had moved into the palaces of the royal inheritance. In London they now occupied Buckingham Palace, which more than any of the King's other houses symbolizes the British monarchy in the public mind. Newspapers talk of stories emanating from the 'Palace' when they mean the Court. Huge, grey and as soulless as a bank headquarters, with magnificent reception-rooms and endless corridors, to the British monarchy it was simply the headquarters of the family firm. Then there was Windsor Castle, the huge fortress-palace outside London, and Balmoral, where the new Queen endeavoured to lighten the Victorian gloom by stripping the panelling of its dark, marmalade-coloured paint. She dared not tackle what King George's biographer called the 'tartan-drenched interior' for fear of offending her husband's almost pathological attachment to the past. Indeed, 'We are back in Victorian times,' Lord Esher wrote describing King George's 'peaceful and domestic' life at Windsor, where the new King, despite his reverence for his glamorous father, preferred to revive the simplicity of his grandmother's way of life and the customs he remembered as a child – dinner in the Oak Room, sitting in the corridor before tea, driving out in the park with the children in a carriage drawn by the Windsor Greys. At Sandringham, however, life for Prince Albert went on much as it had before. King Edward had bequeathed the Big House to Queen Alexandra, who continued to live there while the new King–Emperor, his growing family, courtiers and servants squeezed into York Cottage as if nothing had changed.

The change in his father's status also perceptibly altered the relationship, already sufficiently weighted in the elder Prince's favour, in which Prince Albert stood to his elder brother. Prince Edward was now the Prince of Wales, heir to the throne, and would inevitably in the course of time become King–Emperor. The dominant feature of Prince Albert's life was undoubtedly the invidious comparison between his elder brother and himself drawn by all but the very few people who knew him intimately. Although he came to accept it as a fact of life, he minded it deeply; it had an enormous effect upon him, giving him an inferiority complex vis-à-vis his brother which even the love of his wife and family and the admiration of a nation would never quite succeed in eradicating. Years later, only a few weeks after he had become King, George VI confessed to Mrs Baldwin, the homely wife of his Prime Minister, how all his life he had been outshone by his brilliant brother and 'there had been times when as a boy he had felt envious that eighteen months should make so much difference'.[5]

At home in his childhood, the women of his family circle appreciated him, being sensitive enough to see the qualities beneath the shyness. He was his grandmother's favourite (apart from Prince John, who, remaining virtually a baby, appealed to her strongly developed maternal sense); in 1905, when he was ten, his grandmother was to write of him to his parents who were then in India as 'sweet Bertie, my particular friend', while Lady Airlie, as has been noted, liked him best of the children. The male courtiers, however, were charmed by Prince Edward, notably Lord Esher, his grandfather's *éminence grise*, a man of towering intellect and romantic, if voyeuristic, homosexual proclivities. Esher used to invite the elder three children to tea in his room at Windsor Castle during their grandfather's reign and afterwards confide to his journal the most enthusiastic praise of Prince Edward, 'as clever and composed as ever', 'a most charming boy; very direct, dignified and clever'. By the time the Prince of Wales was sixteen, the age at which Esher found boys most attractive, he was a little in love with him. 'The boy is a darling. Backward but sweet,' was his verdict. The infatuated courtier barely mentioned Prince Albert, dismissing him as 'a commonplace character'. Even Captain Bryan Godfrey-Faussett, his father's old friend and equerry, a straightforward, unimaginative naval officer, while recording in his diary Prince Albert's sporting prowess without comment could not refrain from remarking on the elder brother's charm. At Osborne and Dartmouth the first public comparisons with the Prince of Wales began to be made by his tutors and his fellow cadets. His tutors found Prince Edward, although no scholar, quicker and more enthusiastic than his younger brother. 'One could wish', Mr Watt wrote of Prince Albert, 'that he had more of Prince Edward's keenness and application.' As the Princes grew older, the differences between them became more noticeable, between the quick charm and 'pretty' blond looks of the elder brother, the shyness and more ordinary appearance of his self-effacing younger brother. It was, a contemporary wrote of the Osborne and Dartmouth days, 'like comparing an ugly duckling with a cock pheasant'.

There was only one area in which Prince Albert outshone his elder brother. He had a natural athleticism and co-ordination of hand and eye, which enabled him to excel at any individual sport he undertook, and it was in this area that he received the only plaudits he could expect in his father's circle. It must have given him considerable private satisfaction simply to be better than 'David' at every game they tried. 'Played racquets with PA [Prince Albert] who is quite good & much better than his elder brother,' Godfrey-Faussett noted in his diary for 21 April 1910.[6] At Windsor at Easter 1914, the royal Household played golf with the Princes: 'Prince Albert is very good and will be very good indeed, right shape and form etc....'[7] Hansell's reports on Prince Albert's prowess with a gun were in marked contrast to his comments on the Prince's dismal performance in the schoolroom. Writing to Fritz Ponsonby and Godfrey-Faussett from Balmoral in August 1911, he retailed Prince Albert's progress stalking and shooting grouse. 'He really does shoot *well* for a boy,' he wrote after a day 'on the hill' after stags, and, grouse-shooting, 'Prince Albert shot really well and killed all his birds clean ... he has an eye like a hawk and is thoroughly keen.'[8]

A shared passion for shooting was a bond between Prince Albert and his father. King George was one of the best shots in the country as Prince Albert would be in his time. The King kept a shotgun beside his bed so that he could practise putting it to his shoulder and aiming it when he got up in the morning. At Sandringham, while maintaining his father's tradition of lavish shooting-parties, heavy lunches and mass slaughter of pheasants, he preferred the 'small days' rough shooting without beaters, accompanied by Mr Jones, some of the tenant farmers and, as soon as they were old enough, his sons. Prince Albert learned a good deal about wild game and its habits following his father through his favourite coverts, heathland and marshes, all of which the King knew well and each of which to him had its history of game shot and – rarely – missed, places with names like Whin Hill, Grimston Car, Captain's Close, Cat's Bottom, Folly Hang and Ugly Dale. The party would set out from York Cottage on foot with dogs to retrieve and keepers to carry the game, and walk all day with only a brief stop for a light lunch, the aim being to 'fill the card', i.e. to get at least one of the species of game listed on the printed card. On these occasions the King would be in his element, relaxed, the cares of State forgotten, laughing and joking with the keepers and his sons.

Prince Albert had his first day's shooting at Sandringham just before Christmas 1907, nine days after his twelfth birthday. That evening he sat down to fill in his game book as he was to do meticulously for the rest of his life in that sloping, schoolboyish hand which was so like both his father's and his elder brother's. 'December 23rd, 1907 Sandringham, Wolferton Warren. Papa, David and myself. My first day's shooting. I used a single barrel muzzle loader with which Grand-papa, Uncle Eddy and Papa all started shooting. I shot 3 rabbits.' Just over a year later he graduated to his first pheasant on 5 January 1909, but it was not until the same day the following year when he was fourteen that he was allowed to join a grown-up party. A year later in August 1911 at Balmoral he brought down his first grouse, and on 1 September, the opening day of the partridge season, his first partridge. It was the beginning of a lifelong passion.

By the end of the year of the Coronation relationships in the royal family circle had already begun to develop in the direction they were to take over the following years. In December 1911 Prince Albert returned from Dartmouth to find his place as his elder brother's companion taken by Prince George, who was almost exactly seven years younger than he was. Prince Edward had spent the winter at York Cottage cramming for Oxford with Hansell. That winter, according to his memoirs, he found in his much younger brother 'qualities that were akin to my own; we laughed at the same things ... we became more than brothers – we became close friends'. Prince George was the most talented of the brothers and the only one not to have incurred the family curse of shyness from which even the Prince of Wales suffered to a certain degree. Queen Mary used to say of him that he was the only one of her sons who communicated with her, who was not, as she put it, *'boutonné'*. He shared her passion for collecting *objets d'art* and paintings and grew up with all the social talents, handsome, charming, with a good sense of humour, a talent for playing the piano and a taste for clever, amusing people. He could at times, however, be moody and difficult and, like his brothers, was to be to a certain extent a victim of his father's repressive parenting. Forced into the Navy against his will and subsequently into the unsuitable role of factory inspector, the Prince's reaction was to break loose into a wild social life which was to fulfil all his father's gloomier predictions. His relationship with his eldest brother remained his closest bond until the advent of Wallis Simpson in his brother's life.

There is no sign that Prince Albert minded this change very much, if at all, although it must have contributed to the isolation caused by his stammer. He remained on the best of terms with his elder brother, although he was now, for convenience sake, bracketed with his younger brother, Prince Henry, always known as 'Harry'. Prince Henry was five years younger than Bertie and generally regarded as the dunce of the family, outshone in looks, charm, athletic ability and even brains by his three brothers. Although he later became robust in appearance, Prince Henry as a boy was considered delicate, suffering frequently from severe colds; like Prince Albert he was knock-kneed and subjected to the same severe regime of splints. 'Perhaps not surprisingly', his biographer commented on the unfortunate princes, 'these high-spirited and vigorous young boys showed serious signs of nervous tension.' It seems, however, more likely that this was a result of their repressive upbringing in general rather than of the splints in particular, since all three elder brothers displayed symptoms of inner tension: 'David' had a habit of looking down rather than at the person he was speaking to and fidgeted nervously with his tie and collar, 'Bertie' stammered, 'Harry' was given to outbursts of nervous laughter and all three tended to drink a little too much, while George had no nervous habits but went wild as a young man and even experimented with drugs.

Prince Albert's only sister, Princess Mary, was perhaps the shyest of the family, resembling her mother in her reluctance to show emotion. Her elder son recalled that his demonstrations of affection as a child were regarded as 'slightly embarrassing and something I would grow out of.... We did not talk of love and affection and what we meant to each other, but rather – and even that not easily – of duty and behaviour and what we ought to do....'[9] Princess Mary was a tomboy as a girl; she was the best and bravest rider of the family, a quality which she bequeathed to her great-niece, Princess Anne. 'My sister', George VI later said of her, 'was a horse until she came out.' She grew up as her mother had, with the role of peacemaker to her brothers thrust upon her. She was gentle, kind and obedient. Like Prince Albert, she dreaded public appearances, so much so that even opening a fête would be an ordeal for her. She was not beautiful, nor even pretty, although she had a lovely complexion and a charming habit of wrinkling up her nose when she smiled. She kept her brothers in order, but was totally subservient to her parents in an almost Victorian manner. Her father treated her with far less sternness than he did her brothers, but he was strict with her as she grew up, allowing her few friends or parties and no fashionable clothes of which he disapproved. In 1912, when Princess Mary was fifteen, her mother planned a princely future for her with Ernst August von Hanover, heir to the Duke of Brunswick and the only descendant in the male line of King George III, what Queen Mary, being, through her mother, a member of it, proudly called the 'old' royal family, to distinguish it from the new and lesser dynasty of Saxe-Coburg and Gotha introduced to the throne of Great Britain with Prince Albert, Victoria's Prince Consort. Ernst August, however, married the German Emperor's only daughter the following year, and Queen Mary's hopes of finding a suitably bred, inevitably German, princeling for her daughter were dashed by the First World War.

The youngest child of the family, Prince John, was rarely mentioned. Born in 1905, he suffered from epileptic fits which developed when he was four. He seems also to have been born with some form of mental retardation. In his childhood, however, he was still normal enough for any abnormality not to be noticed – at least by other children. Loelia Ponsonby remembered him as 'a nice little boy' at Balmoral when she was a child, noticing nothing unusual about him apart from the fact that when they climbed the hills he was roped to his nurse, which the other children thought 'sissy'. His aunt-by-marriage (and cousin), Princess Alice, Countess of Athlone, recalled 'Johnny' as 'very quaint ... one evening when Uncle George [George V] returned from stalking he bent over Aunt May and kissed her, and they heard Johnny soliloquize, "She kissed Papa, *ugly* old man." '[10] His abnormality, or perhaps his liability to fits, must have increased as he grew older for he was permanently separated from his family in 1917, living at secluded Wolferton Farm at Sandringham in the care of Lalla Bill and dying there in 1919.

From the winter of 1911/12 the two elder boys' paths diverged. While Prince Edward went to Magdalen College, Oxford, to lead the relatively free life of an undergraduate, even one anxiously supervised by his father from not very far, Prince Albert returned to Dartmouth to begin his second term. Here in a less restricted ambience, and free from the debilitating presence of his elder brother, he did better than at Osborne. His term officer, Lieutenant Henry Spencer-

Cooper, encouraged him to take up the sports he was good at, riding, tennis and cross-country running. He went beagling and pheasant shooting with Spencer-Cooper, and sailed in the College 'Blue Boats', which the cadets could take up river to Totnes and have tea on the lawn of a hotel. The Dartmouth curriculum placed less emphasis on the classroom subjects and more on the professional aspects of a naval officer's career: Morse code, semaphore, flag signals, seamanship, the organization and discipline of a ship's company and, considered all-important in the Royal Navy which was still, despite Fisher's efforts, the most snobbish of the Services, naval etiquette. His name appeared in the College Punishment Book for minor crimes: one day's No. 1A punishment for 'skylarking outside the Quarter Deck [Assembly Hall] with eight other cadets', one day's No. 3 punishment for 'Talking before Grace' and another for 'Talking outside Study', while he and sixteen other cadets were beaten – six strokes of the cane each – for letting off illegal fireworks on Guy Fawkes's night. His final examination position, although far from brilliant, was the best he had yet attained, 61st out of 67.

Shortly after his return to Dartmouth in January 1912, Prince Albert was made aware of the disruptive forces at work beneath the apparently smooth surface of British life and of the exposed position occupied by the monarchy in any clash between the classes. In February 1912 King George and Queen Mary returned triumphant from the great Coronation Durbar held in Delhi to be confronted with the threat of civil war in Ireland and industrial troubles at home. The King had planned to visit the Naval College in March, a visit which he later cancelled because of the prolonged coal strike, which had begun on 26 February; within a few days of his arrival from India an innocent letter from Prince Albert touched him on the raw. It was rumoured that some of the Dartmouth cadets planned to celebrate the royal visit by painting the King's statue red. The horrified captain ordered a twenty-four-hour watch on the statue which involved recruiting civilian staff, some of whom threatened to go on strike and were dismissed. This was reported in the newspapers and Prince Albert, thinking his parents might be amused by it, wrote to his mother on 28 February:

Papa's statue has been placed at the end of the quarterdeck today with Grandpapa's picture on the right of it. It looks very well indeed. Have you seen that small paragraph in todays [sic] Daily Graphic on page 9. It is headed 'The Statue and the Strike'. It is supposed that some cadets were going to paint it, so the cadets' servants were told to watch it at night, to prevent anybody from doing so.

The idea of the use of red paint on his statue, combined with the fact that the country was in the grip of the coal strike, moved the King deeply and he at once demanded an explanation from the captain.

It was also made clear to Prince Albert in March that monarchs, in Europe at least, faced dangers more fatal than red paint on their images. An attempt was made on the life of King Victor Emmanuel III of Italy, prompting the

Prince to write from Dartmouth to his father: 'I saw in the papers the other day that one of those beastly anarchists tried to kill the King of Italy'; he added with a bloodthirsty expression of royal solidarity, 'What a good thing he was killed by the crowd.' Only a year later, in March 1913, an assassination attempt succeeded, this time the victim being a royal relation, his great-uncle, King George I of Greece, Queen Alexandra's favourite brother. 'We were all terribly shocked & grieved last Tuesday, the 18th inst, to receive the sad news that dear Uncle Willy the King of Greece had been assassinated at Salonica, by a Greek,' the King wrote. 'It is too horrible he was out for a walk as usual in the street, when this brute came up behind him & shot him through the heart.' Fifteen months later, the shooting in Sarajevo of another royal prince, the Archduke Franz Ferdinand, set off a train of events which was to give Prince Albert his first experience of total war.

War was very much in the air when Prince Albert, still a Dartmouth cadet, accompanied his father on the royal yacht, the *Victoria & Albert*, for the great review of the Fleet off Weymouth from 7 to 11 May 1912. Destined as he was for a career as a naval officer, Prince Albert could not have failed to have been impressed by the appearance of what was then the largest and most modern war fleet in the world, equipped with the latest huge dreadnoughts and battle-cruisers and even a submarine in which, with his father, he experienced his first underwater dive. The shadowy presence in the back of everyone's minds was that of the German High Seas Fleet far away in the Baltic ports. Cousin Willy, the Kaiser, had visited the country the previous year for the unveiling of the great white marble monument to Queen Victoria. As usual he had been most agreeable and attracted favourable attention from the London crowds, but at the last minute, on the eve of his departure from Portsmouth, he had spoilt things by uttering 'threats and curses against England' to Prince Louis of Battenberg, a high-ranking admiral and cousin of the King. In the spring of 1912 the promulgation of the German Navy Law had raised the prospect of an immediate escalation of the naval armaments race. 'The maintenance', Winston Churchill, now First Lord of the Admiralty, wrote to a colleague, 'of twenty-five [German] battleships (which, after the next four or five years, will all be Dreadnoughts) exposes us to constant danger, only to be warded off by vigilance, approximating to war conditions.'[11] Churchill accompanied the King at the naval review of 1912 and was present when the King and Prince Albert went for their submarine dive; it was Prince Albert's first meeting with the man who, twenty-eight years later, would be his Prime Minister in the Second World War.

At Easter that year, Prince Albert was confirmed in the church at Sandringham by the Rt Rev. William Boyd-Carpenter, Bishop of Ripon, in the presence only of his father and mother, elder brother and sister. He had learned a simple, deep faith in God from his grandmother, Queen Alexandra, which was always to be of great importance to him. Although no great reader, one book on the historical truth of the Resurrection, *The Empty Tomb*, made a great impression on him and he frequently referred to it. His confirmation, signifying that he had entered into full membership of the Church of England and could now take Holy Communion, meant a good deal to him as appears from a letter he wrote to Boyd-Carpenter on the second anniversary of his confirmation, when he was a midshipman on HMS *Collingwood*: 'It is just two years ago tomorrow that you confirmed me in the small church at Sandringham. I have always remembered that day as one on which I took a great step in life.' A sustaining faith in God was something which he would need to support him through the coming years, which were to be perhaps the most miserable of his life, and again, many years later, when he would be at the head of a nation at war.

In January the following year, 1913, Prince Albert embarked in the cruiser *Cumberland* on the final six-month training cruise which would qualify him as a midshipman and a regular member of the Royal Navy. His father had seen to it that he had two friends and protectors on board *Cumberland*, Lieutenant Spencer-Cooper and, as ship's surgeon, Louis Greig, the doctor who had looked after him during a bout of whooping cough at Osborne. Neither of them, however, could protect him from the interest which he aroused in the public as the son of the King of England. *Cumberland*'s cruise took him on a round trip of the Empire in the Western Atlantic – the West Indies and Canada. Even at their first port of call, Spanish Tenerife, he was driven round the town with the ship's captain, Aubrey Smith, to allow the local population to demonstrate their enthusiasm, which they did greatly to his embarrassment. 'In the afternoon I drove round the town with Captain Smith and Major Golding [the British Consul], as the people wanted to see me,' he wrote to his mother. 'They followed the carriage all the time and made a great noise.' In the British West Indies it was even worse. While Prince Albert stuttered his way through the prepared text of a speech opening the Kingston Yacht Club in Jamaica, the local girls vied with each other to see who could touch his trousers the most times. Unlike his elder brother, who took such episodes quite in his stride, Prince Albert found public appearances and crowds an ordeal and on minor occasions he got a friend who was a 'double' to stand in for him. Sporting occasions were less painful, giving him an opportunity to shine. At a gymkhana in Barbados he won the distance Handicap for polo ponies and was placed in an event called the Polo Scurry. He also won the Farmyard Race crossing the line first braying like a donkey. From the West Indies *Cumberland* sailed up the Canadian coast; Prince Albert visited Niagara Falls, 'hunted all the time by photographers and also by the Americans who had no manners at all and tried to take photographs', as he noted in his diary. The social occasions in Quebec where all the girls competed to dance with the Prince were no more of a pleasure. At seventeen he was immature, shy and unused to girls; he flatly refused to dance until Spencer-Cooper drew him out and made him laugh by pretending that his back braces buttons had come off and his trousers were in danger of falling down.

The unrestrained public adulation and extraordinary interest which he excited merely by being the King's son was a new and unwelcome experience. It was on board *Cumberland*, too, that he first experienced the way in which innocent, gullible royalty can be made use of for personal and social advancement. Once the *Cumberland* tour was over, the burning question for the cadets was to be transferred as a midshipman to a good ship. Several, for the right or the wrong reasons, saw HRH Prince Albert as the best means of achieving this. Good-naturedly the Prince wrote to Godfrey-Faussett enlisting his help:

HMS *Cumberland*, The Nore, July 21 1913

Dear Captain Faussett,

I am writing to you on behalf of the cadets of my term, who are very keen on getting on the same ship as myself. But I do not want you to mention anything to Papa, as I have already asked him to try and get three others with me. Their names are C— and de Berniere Smith. The former is a son of a friend of yours, and the latter has been told by Admiral Tripper that he can get him whatever ship he likes. Well C— has written to his father to ask you if you can get him into the 'Collingwood' as I said that I was very likely going to her, as she had a Lieutenant Tait on board who so Papa told me was in the 'Hindustan' when David was in her, and that he wanted him to be head of my division. I received a letter today from Papa who told me that he had not yet decided which ship I was going to. So do you think you could try and get them into the same ship as I get, and directly I hear from Papa what the ship is, I will let you know. I hope I am not troubling you very much about this, but we have always been together ever since we knew each other. . . .[12]

Within the following twenty-four hours, however, the Prince learned something about C— which caused him to write hastily the next day to Godfrey-Faussett:

I am very sorry for troubling you again about this same ship business, but I have been told a piece of information that I am afraid must alter the arrangements in the previous letter. It is absolutely confidential and I ask you not to mention it to a soul, even if the person concerned asks you the reason, or his father. It is about C—. I have discovered that he is trying to gain his own ends, and that if he is with me in my first ship, he will want to remain with me afterwards, and then I shall not be able to do anything to get rid of him. He is one of those people that one must be very careful about. So do you think you could counteract that to get him out of the same squadron as I am in, otherwise there will be complications. Please do all you can in your power and you will be doing the greatest favour for me that anybody has ever done. . . .[13]

To the Prince's relief, Godfrey-Faussett replied firmly that he could not do anything in any case without asking the King first and that it was far better to leave these things to chance. Prince Albert, who signed himself to Godfrey-Faussett as 'Albert', carefully underlining his name with a curlicue and a flourish, had learned the first lesson of royalty vis-à-vis the outside world: be wary.

On 15 September 1913, Prince Albert, aged seventeen, received his first commission as midshipman on the 19,250-ton battleship, HMS *Collingwood*. It was his official entry into the career which, like his father, he thought he was destined to follow. Whether he was as absolutely committed to the Navy as his father had been at the same age is perhaps open to question. He was liable to sea-sickness and, therefore, did not share his father's passion for the sea and sailing;

indeed after visiting his elder brother at Magdalen College, Oxford, he had confided to his mother that he wished he had been there rather than at sea.

None the less, willingly or with reservations, into the Navy he went, as his father had planned, joining the flagship of an old friend and former shipmate of King George, Vice-Admiral Sir Stanley 'Cecil' Colville, commander of the First Battle Squadron. This did not mean he would now be treated as an officer; a junior midshipman (known as a 'snotty' because his uniform jacket had three buttons on the cuffs, allegedly to prevent him wiping his nose on it) was considered by the officers to be the lowest form of life and was completely at the mercy of the sub-lieutenant in charge of the 'Gunroom' (the midshipmen's mess). Charles Morgan's novel, *The Gunroom*, published in 1919, gave a vivid picture of the worst that 'snotties', or 'warts' as they were known, could expect at the hands of a sadistic sub-lieutenant. Aristocratic, even princely, birth was no protection, as Prince Albert's cousin 'Dickie', son of Prince Louis of Battenberg, discovered in July 1916 when he joined the Fleet as a junior midshipman on *Lion*, where 'snotties' were regularly beaten for failing to complete nonsensical and humiliating tasks. Fortunately for Prince Albert, however, the senior sub-lieutenant in charge of the Gunroom for most of his time on *Collingwood*, Harry Hamilton, was no sadist; a cheerful, sporting young man, he had a healthy respect for the Court connection, even harbouring an ambition for a post aboard the royal yacht.

Prince Albert was given no preferential treatment as far as quarters were concerned, sleeping like the other midshipmen in a hammock slung in the 'flat' outside the Gunroom at night and stowed away during the day. His only private piece of furniture was his solid ironbound sea-chest containing three drawers below for shoes, underclothes and suits, three trays above, one being tin-lined for washing things, and a lid to the inside of which the 'snotties' pinned photographs of their families or pin-ups of music-hall actresses of the day.[14] There was no privacy but at least there was no squalor; for the ratings conditions, despite all Jackie Fisher's attempts to ameliorate them, remained not much better than in Nelson's day. One near-contemporary of Prince Albert, F. J. Chambers, who joined the Grand Fleet as a midshipman in 1915, recalled that the contrast between the living conditions of the ratings forward and the officers aft was something which in those days was taken for granted. But he was shocked to discover that the men's 'heads' (i.e. WCs) had only half-doors to prevent them from being used as homosexual rendezvous. 'It struck me, even at the age of sixteen, as being an insult to decent men,' Chambers wrote.[15]

Between a privileged young man brought up like Prince Albert and the ratings of the lower deck there was a gulf bridged only by the petty officers, the naval equivalent of sergeants. It was the petty officers rather than their superior officers who taught the midshipmen the basic skills of their profession – signals, Morse and semaphore, rifle drill and handling the ship's heavy armament. It was through them that the trainee officers learned how the lower deck thought and reacted and that midshipmen came to have a knowledge of the men they would eventually have to lead. A petty officer taught Prince Albert how to handle the ship's picket boat, a privilege which Chambers described as 'the height of [a snotty's] ambition'. Within months of his arrival on *Collingwood* Prince Albert had achieved this coveted privilege, running the ship's picket boat, 52 feet long with sleek lines, gleaming brass funnels, 250 horse-power engines driven by water tube coal-fired boilers, and a speed of around 16–18 knots. Early in June 1914 he had the task of bringing his picket boat alongside his old training ship, the *Cumberland*, as the navigating officer, Lieutenant F. J. Lambert, reported to his brother, Guy, describing the Prince as 'a small, red-faced youth with a stutter ... when he reported his boat to me he gave a sort of stutter and an explosion. I had no idea who he was and very nearly cursed him for spluttering at me!'[16]

Confronting senior officers brought out Prince Albert's shyness. Sub-Lieutenant Hamilton wrote of his charge, officially known as 'Johnson', presumably for security reasons:

Johnson is very well full of young life and gladness, but I can't get a word out of him, he treats me with great respect and seems to be in an awful funk of me! Thank goodness he is treated exactly the same as all the other minor snotties. It was quite a pretty sight seeing him polishing the brightwork this morning before divisions![17]

Hamilton seems to have succeeded in winning 'Johnson's' confidence none the less, reporting in a letter of 13 June 1914 that he had been playing golf with him. He seems to have been disappointed as far as the royal yacht was concerned, but he seems to have had hopes of deriving some benefit from his position vis-à-vis the Prince:

It is a bad bussiness [*sic*] about the Yacht isn't it but as the King has made a new billet in the Royal Household for me (Controller of the Royal Morals) I think in the end it may be a better show. If Johnson doesn't write home and say I bully him. . . .[18]

Essentially, of course, it was a farce to pretend that HRH Prince Albert, son of the King of England and Emperor of India, was the same as any ordinary midshipman. While it undoubtedly helped him to gain insight into the way in which ordinary men lived and acted, his was also a false and somewhat uncomfortable position, always in the public eye, always experiencing the ambivalence with which people react to royalty. As far as routine duties went, he may have been treated 'exactly the same as all the other minor snotties', but on other occasions the spotlight was on him as the son of the King. When, shortly after he joined his ship, *Collingwood* had gone on manœuvres in the Mediterranean from the end of October to the end of December 1913, the Commander-in-Chief, Admiral Sir Berkeley Milne, and Sir Stanley Colville took him with them to stay with his father's friend, Lord Kitchener, at the Agency in Cairo, where he was presented to the Khedive and taken to see the Pyramids. At the top of the Great Pyramid, his grandfather's vandalistic scrawled initials 'AE' remained to be seen from his visit there aged twenty. On 24 November 1913 the Field Marshal gave a ball for the Fleet attended by over a thousand guests. 'I went to bed at 3.0 a.m. having danced nearly every dance,' Prince Albert recorded in his diary. When the Fleet reached Salamis Bay early in December the pretence of the Prince's being an ordinary 'snotty' had again to be dropped when the King and Queen of Greece paid him a visit on board ship; he had a bad cold and received them in the Admiral's cabin. On 1 December he was well enough to go ashore and see 'Uncle Tino' (his father's first cousin, King Constantine), 'Aunt Sophie' (the former Princess Sophie Dorothea of Prussia, sister of Kaiser William 11) and 'the cousins', Prince George and Prince Alexander.

'My eighteenth birthday and I am allowed to smoke,' he wrote in his diary for 14 December 1913. His mother had thoughtfully sent him a cigarette case as a birthday present, and from Toulon he wrote to thank her and to report on the social round with the French Navy:

The French fleet are giving us a very good time here, and have arranged all kinds of dances and theatres for us. Last night I went to a ball given by the Municipality, which was a very funny affair. There were 6000 guests, and it was in a theatre. There was no room to dance and you could not move at all. All the guests were ordinary people in the town and most of them got drunk at supper.... I am so glad that you enjoyed your visit to Chatsworth... and that you found the house interesting with some old things [he added dutifully].

Christmas 1913, his first away from home, he spent on board ship at Gibraltar, but by New Year's Eve he was with his family again at Sandringham. 'Last night', Queen Mary wrote to her Aunt Augusta of Mecklenburg-Strelitz on 2 January 1914, 'we all dined with Mama [Queen Alexandra] & even danced afterwards much to the enjoyment of the young people. God grant that this year may be a peaceful one & that the clouds over these dear Islands may disperse!!!'[19] It was a vain hope. On 28 June Prince Albert was on board *Collingwood* at Portland when the assassination of the Archduke Franz Ferdinand and his wife at Sarajevo lit the fuse which was to lead to war. Neither Prince Albert, his parents, the Government nor the nation realized the potential significance of the Archduke's murder. Whereas to the Austrians it was, as H.A.L. Fisher pointed out, 'as if at a moment of acute political tension, the Prince of Wales had been murdered in Ireland', King George and Queen Mary regarded it in a family light as yet one more episode in the anarchistic assault on dynasties. 'Terrible shock for the dear old Emperor,' the King wrote in his diary, while Prince Albert did not even mention it in his; the arrival on board of fifty Roedean schoolgirls when the ship lay off Brighton on 1 July seemed a much more interesting event: 'After lunch at 2.30 50 girls arrived from the Rodine [*sic*] School,' he wrote. 'We showed them over the ship and danced before tea.'

There was to be little time left for dancing. On 10 July, with war only three weeks away, the order went out for a test mobilization of the Third Fleet, soon to be called the Grand Fleet. Almost incredibly, the timing of the mobilization was purely fortuitous, Churchill, as First Lord of the Admiralty, having suggested to Prince Louis of Battenberg, the First Sea Lord, on 22 October the previous year that, as an economy measure, a test mobilization be substituted for the usual summer manœuvres in 1914. Mobilization began on 15 July, and on 17–18 July a grand review of the whole fleet was held at Spithead. 'It constituted', Churchill later wrote, 'incomparably the greatest assemblage of naval power witnessed in the history of the world.' On 18 July Prince Albert boarded the *Victoria & Albert* to meet his father, attended by Godfrey-Faussett and the Prince of Wales, and sat down to dinner with seventeen admirals; the following day he stood proudly to attention aboard *Collingwood* as the huge fleet steamed past the royal yacht. The King came on board to inspect the ship and, according to Hamilton, 'spent a long time in the Gunroom asking questions about everything and talking about all the pictures'.[20] The King left while his son was still on duty in the gun turret, but the Prince of Wales and Godfrey-Faussett stayed behind chatting with him in the Gunroom for an hour afterwards.

It was the last time Prince Albert was to see either his father or his brother for a considerable time. The King wrote to him on 28 July:

I have just heard from yr. Captain that for the moment all leave is stopped on account of the European situation & he has asked for my instructions concerning your coming on leave on Friday as arranged. I have answered that of course you could not leave until the situation became normal again. I am sure you would be the last to wish to be treated differently to anybody else. But I do hope that things are going to come right & that there will be no war & that you may be able to come on Friday or very soon.

Harry, with his usual cold, and George would be coming home before the end of the week, but the King's immutable summer sporting routine had been seriously disrupted by the political situation. He told his son:

I have had to give up my visit to Goodwood where I was to have gone yesterday & up till now, on account of the political situation I have made no arrangements yet for going to Cowes on Saturday. I shall indeed be disappointed if we are unable to go. I hoped to have raced in the 'Britannia' at least 4 times next week. . . .

On that day, the 28th, Austria declared war on Serbia and Churchill ordered the Fleet to War Station. The King was not the only one to have his sporting programme disrupted. '. . . the silly Austrians have messed up everything,' Hamilton wrote home, foreseeing nothing but a temporary inconvenience in the cancellation of his leave. 'As a matter of fact it is rather a good thing as the leave will come along with the partridges [partridge shooting season begins on 1 October]. . . .'[21]

On 29 July the Battle Squadrons left Portland for Scapa Flow in the Orkney Islands off the extreme northern tip of Scotland. Churchill wrote:

We may picture this great Fleet, with its flotillas and cruisers, steaming slowly out of Portland Harbour, squadron by squadron, scores of gigantic castles of steel wending their way across the misty, shining sea, like giants bowed in anxious thought. We may picture them again as darkness fell, eighteen miles of warships running at high speed and in absolute darkness through the Narrow Straits, bearing with them into the broad waters of the North the safeguard of considerable affairs.[22]

Two days later, *Collingwood*, with the other battleships of the Fleet, lay in the desolate waters of Scapa Flow, guarding the northern entrance to the North Sea. Five hundred miles to the south on the Baltic and North Sea coasts of Germany, the German High Seas Fleet waited in their heavily defended bases. At 11 p.m. (midnight German time) on the night of 4 August the British ultimatum to Germany expired and the Admiralty flashed the signal to all HM ships and naval establishments, 'Commence hostilities against Germany.' Prince Albert, as midshipman of the middle watch, midnight to 4 a.m., was asleep at the actual moment the signal was received and for some reason put down the time of the declaration of war as 2 a.m. in the diary which he carefully kept each day, noting also the text of his father's telegram to the Fleet. In Buckingham Palace, the sound of cheering crowds outside ringing in his ears, the King, like any other father, was thinking of his eighteen-year-old son, the only one of his children to be in the front line. 'Please God that it will soon be over', he wrote in his diary, '& that he will protect dear Bertie's life.'

It soon became apparent, however, that the threat to Prince Albert's well-being was not external but internal, the beginning of a pattern of serious ill-health which was eventually to force him out of the Navy. At Dartmouth he had had attacks of gastric trouble which he apparently concealed in keeping with the stiff-upper-lip ethos of the Service. Three weeks after the war started, on 23 August, he went down with a violent pain in his stomach and had difficulty breathing. Morphia was administered and hot fomentations on the stomach, but beyond easing the pain they could not cure it; two days later appendicitis was diagnosed. 'Johnson poor fellow has got appendicitis and has gone home very fed up with life. Rotten bad luck, isn't it?' Hamilton reported.[23] Prince Albert was transferred to the hospital ship *Rohilla* at Wick and examined there by Sir James Reid, Queen Victoria's favourite physician, who had been called in by the King. At that point *Rohilla* was recalled to the Fleet, but Reid and Fleet Surgeon Lomas, having examined the Prince, decided it was not safe to move him and, escorted through the mined waters by two destroyers, the ship left for Scapa Flow. There the Prince's health improved enough for him to be landed, with forty-five other invalids, in cots by crane to tugs and hence to the quay at Aberdeen on 29 August. On 9 September he had his appendix removed by Professor Marnoch, Professor of Surgery at Aberdeen University, with Reid in attendance, reporting to the King by telephone.

Prince Albert wrote in his simple, still quite childish style to his father from the Northern Nursing Home, Aberdeen, showing more concern for his father than for himself:

I am afraid you must have been rather frightened when you heard I was ill. I am much better now and feel quite happy.... The pain has practically gone away now although it hurt a good deal last Sunday. [Everyone] has been very kind to me in every way and everything is most comfortable here. You must be very sorry at not being able to go up to Scotland this year as usual. You must be very tired after all this very trying time with so much work to do, and so many people to see, and never getting a rest....

The King was too busy to travel to Aberdeen, but on 19 September the Prince of Wales, now an officer in the Grenadier Guards, and Hansell visited him and later Princess Mary, accompanied by the hated Mademoiselle Dussau.

The inevitable comparison with his elder brother became even more invidious during these miserable years which Prince Albert, a semi-invalid at nineteen, was to spend in and out of hospitals or convalescing at Sandringham or in London in the company of his parents and his sister, while his contemporaries fought and died in Flanders and the North Sea. On 16 November the Prince of Wales left for France, where he was attached to the staff of Field Marshal Sir John French, Commander-in-Chief of the British Expeditionary Force, but the monotony of Prince Albert's life was broken only by such episodes as shooting a rutting stag at Sandringham which had become dangerous and had attacked Bland, the keeper, Princess Mary and himself when they were riding. At the end of November his father arranged for him to join the War Staff at the Admiralty, where at least he could wear uniform. He was pathetically grateful for the opportunity, writing optimistically to his father on 26 November: 'it will be very interesting, and now people cannot say that I am not doing anything'. For someone of his age it was very hard to be at home and in civilian clothes while other young men were at the front. Men who were not in the Services were talked of as cowards and sent white feathers through the post, and Prince Albert felt conspicuously out of it and vulnerable to criticism. That he was criticized in the war years for staying at home is apparent from a letter which the Prince of Wales was to write to the Queen on 6 December 1918, urging that Prince Albert should stay on in France after the Armistice:

Bertie can be of far more use in this way than sitting in England where he has spent most of the war not that this was his fault!! But by remaining with the armies till peace is signed he will entirely erase any of the very unfair questions some nasty people asked last year as to what he was doing you will remember.

Sadly, routine at the Admiralty turned out to be very far from interesting. 'Nothing to do as usual' and 'It seems such a waste of time to go there every day and do nothing' became typical entries in his diary. 'Life here is very dull', he wrote to Commander Spencer-Cooper, who had taken part in the Battle of the Falkland Islands, 'and I am longing to get back to the "Collingwood".'

In February 1915 he did get back to *Collingwood* but not for long. 'I have been very fit on the whole since I returned here but just lately the infernal indigestion has come on again,' he told Hansell on 15 May. 'I thought I had got rid of it but it has returned in various forms.' By 20 June it had become serious. 'Johnson is very far from well,' Hamilton reported, '& my Godfather, Swish [Sir William Watson Cheyne, Professor of Clinical Surgery at King's College, London, and President of the Royal College of Surgeons], has been up here to report progress. Apparently he is sick every time he swallows any food and is very mouldy. In fact wasting away....'[24] 'Swish' recommended that Prince Albert be sent to a hospital ship for observation again and on 12 July, three days after a visit by the King to the Fleet – the first time Prince Albert had seen his father for six months – he was transferred from *Collingwood* to the *Drina*. He was, in fact, suffering from a stomach ulcer, but the diagnosis of Dr Willan on board the *Drina* was 'weakening of the muscular wall of the stomach and a consequent catarrhal condition', for which rest, careful diet and a nightly enema were prescribed, treatments which Prince Albert, always fascinated by medicine, described at some length and in considerable detail in a letter to his mother. He did not, however, make a sustained recovery, which, considering that the diagnosis was wrong from the outset, is hardly surprising. At the beginning of August the doctors told Prince Albert's captain, Captain Ley, 'that it would be most unadvisable [*sic*], even dangerous' to the Prince's health for him to rejoin his ship. The captain was in a quandary; he had given Prince Albert his word before he left *Collingwood* that if the Fleet put to sea for action he would be on board. Ley wrote to the King conveying the doctors' opinion and asking for advice, receiving in reply, via the King's secretary, Lord Stamfordham, a letter expressing Roman sentiments:

... [HM] attaches the utmost importance to keeping faith with Prince Albert with regard to the promise given HRH that in the event of the Fleet putting to sea, he should return to 'Collingwood' ... no doubt the idea of the Prince's not being allowed to proceed into action with his ship would prey upon his mind and undo all the good effects of his treatment. Therefore HM cannot agree to Dr Sutton's suggestion.

There is in the King's opinion only one alternative and that is to declare that the Prince is medically unfit for service; to send him on sick leave and place him in a nursing home under special treatment.

This course His Majesty would however strongly deprecate.

From what you report, HRH has evidently improved considerably; there is no reason to expect any early naval engagement, but even were the unexpected to happen and the Fleet were ordered to sea the day after you receive this letter, the King would prefer to run the risk of Prince Albert's health suffering than that he should endure the bitter and lasting disappointment of not being in his ship in the battle line.

In these circumstances please say nothing to Prince Albert and let us hope that he will continue to progress every day & be able to return to duty before 'the day' comes.

... HM also remembers that you think the Prince's illness gets somewhat on his nerves which seems to be another reason for refraining from any action likely to upset HRH.

As it turned out, there was no need for dramatic decisions. 'The day' when the British Grand Fleet should sally forth to deal the knock-out blow to the German High Seas Fleet had still not materialized when, two months later, it became apparent that a prolonged diet of enemas and cramming for his sub-lieutenant's examinations on a hospital ship was doing no good for Prince Albert's health or morale. The King consulted Admiral Colville, who sensibly suggested that a spell ashore might do the trick and the Prince was, therefore, despatched to Abergeldie in the uninspiring company of Dr Willan and Hansell. Given that the Prince was suffering from an undiagnosed ulcer, this prescription of isolation and boredom did not effect a complete cure. When he returned from

Scotland to Sandringham at the end of October he was still unfit for duty.

Anxiety over his father's state of health after a serious accident in France made Prince Albert's condition worse. On 28 October 1915, while inspecting a unit of the Royal Flying Corps at Hesdigneul, the King's horse, a chestnut mare provided by General Haig, despite careful preliminary training with gunfire and regimental drums, alarmed by 'the extraordinary noise of 20 flying men trying to cheer', reared up and fell over backwards on top of the King. He was severely injured, fracturing his pelvis and experiencing a great deal of pain and shock; he continued to suffer the after-effects of the accident to the end of his life. In November, when he returned from France, the King's recovery was slow and painful; concern for his father aggravated Prince Albert's ulcer. He loved his father deeply; they had grown close in the few years since he had left Dartmouth, a closeness enhanced by his long periods of convalescence when he and Princess Mary were the only children left at home. King George's letters to his son have a touching note of tenderness and understanding; in character and outlook on life they had a good deal in common. 'May God bless and protect you my dear boy is the earnest prayer of your devoted Papa,' the King had written shortly after the outbreak of the war. 'You can be sure that you are constantly in my thoughts.' 'I was really very sorry to leave last Friday', the nineteen-year-old Prince told his father in February 1915 on rejoining his ship, 'and I felt quite homesick the first night....' 'I miss you still very much especially at breakfast,' the King replied.

In those days at home alone with his father, Prince Albert absorbed a good deal of the business of kingship which was to stand him in good stead later on. His father talked or wrote to him of his preoccupations including political questions. They corresponded regularly, discussing the news of the war, the casualties such as the death of Lord Stamfordham's only son on the Western Front – 'Poor John Bigge's death came as a great shock to me,' Prince Albert wrote. 'He was such a very nice man. Lord Stamfordham must be heart broken ...' – and the activities of the German U-boats: 'we heard to-day that the "Lusitania" had been sunk off the south-west coast of Ireland. A terrible catastrophe with so much loss of life. It makes one so angry to think that after a thing like the "Lusitania" going down we cannot do anything in revenge. Here we are absolutely ready the whole time and still we have to wait,' he wrote angrily to his father in May 1915.

The King agreed that the sinking of the *Lusitania* was 'a dastardly outrage & a great crime against civilisation', but he refused to take part in the rabid tide of anti-German feeling which swept over England. He replied sternly to a request from Prince Henry at Eton asking whether he could go and look at a camp of German prisoners of war: 'I think it is in very bad taste, I don't wish you to go there at all.... How would you like it if you were a prisoner for people to come and stare at you as if you were a wild beast?'[25] The royal family had, after all, the closest blood ties with Germany and the King and Queen had never shared Edward VII's dislike of the Kaiser, despite his faults. Queen Mary and the children had wept when Princess Mary's beloved German maid, Else, had to return to Germany at the beginning of the war or face internment in England. The King had been embarrassed when his first cousin by marriage, Prince Louis of Battenberg, was hounded from office as the First Sea Lord in October 1914 because his father had been a German. Pre-war ties with the German relations had been close; not only had Queen Mary hoped for a Hanoverian prince as a husband for Princess Mary, but in 1913 the Prince of Wales had twice been sent to Germany to stay with relations, visiting the King and Queen of Württemberg in April and 'Uncle Henry of Prussia' in August, visits which may have inspired his lifelong admiration for things German.

None the less the King, despite centuries of German blood, considered himself British to the backbone and, when H.G. Wells sneered at 'an alien and uninspiring Court', King George's riposte was, 'I may be uninspiring, but I'll be damned if I'm an alien.' In 1917, in what his biographer, Kenneth Rose, called a momentary loss of nerve and an uncharacteristically theatrical gesture, the King decided to rid the royal family of its Germanic taint by changing the family name to Windsor. Nobody, however, seemed to be quite sure exactly what their previous family name was. Harold Nicolson, the King's official biographer, was fascinated by this predicament:

What indeed was their existing name? . . . it wasn't Guelph as had at first been supposed. It wasn't Wettin [the Prince Consort's family name] which they had been told it ought to have been. It was Wipper, which distressed them very much. Wipper would not do at all, even though it had to be changed. Then it was suggested to the King that in adopting Windsor [Lord Stamfordham's proposal], the Earl of Plymouth, one of whose surnames [the family name was Windsor-Clive] it was, ought, perhaps, as a matter of courtesy, to be consulted. The King said that double names did not count, and anyway, Lord Plymouth's family ought to feel honoured. Lord Plymouth was not consulted, and presumably did feel honoured.[26]

The Kaiser ridiculed his cousin's change of name, declaring that he was looking forward to seeing 'The Merry Wives of Saxe-Coburg-Gotha', but the King's decision was extremely popular in Britain as was the wholesale rechristening of the King's relations at his orders. His Serene Highness Prince Louis of Battenberg Anglicized his name to Mountbatten and became Marquess of Milford Haven; his elder son, Prince George, became Earl of Medina and his younger son, Prince Louis, was styled Lord Louis Mountbatten, while another Battenberg, Prince Alexander, was created Marquess of Carisbrooke. Queen Mary's two surviving Teck brothers dropped Teck in favour of their maternal grandmother's family name of Cambridge, Dolly, the eldest, becoming Marquess of Cambridge, and Alge, the younger, Earl of Athlone. It was an imaginative, well-executed stroke and a brilliant exercise in public relations, much as the King would have detested to have it thought of as such.

Buckingham Palace and, indeed, Sandringham, where Prince Albert spent much of his time, were dreary places in wartime. There was no alcohol and comparatively little food at the King's table from April 1915, when 'the King's

Pledge' was announced to the nation, as an example specifically aimed at drunken munitions workers; as King George told Prince Albert in the spring of 1915, 'We must have more ammunition before we can try another advance. We can't turn it out fast enough, drink I am afraid has something to do with it, so I have set the example by giving it up during the war.' Lady Desborough reported

a sad account of Windsor Castle on the wagon. Tempers were but little improved by temperance and a crêpe wreath was fastened to the cellar door and Charlie Cust [the King's greatest friend and equerry] fainted the first night after dinner; the only cheerful person being Margot [Asquith, wife of the Prime Minister], who took copious swigs out of a medicine bottle and talked a great deal, but no one else spoke except to contradict her.[27]

The lack of alcohol made the austerity regime imposed at the royal table harder to bear because both the quality and the quantity of the food had already been severely reduced. At York Cottage for instance, Fritz Ponsonby recalled, if you were late for breakfast you got nothing and, due to

the wonderful punctuality of the King and Queen, one was late if the clock sounded when one was on the stairs.... In order to be sure of getting enough to eat you had to be before time. Lord Marcus Beresford dogged the Queen's footsteps. There was just enough and no more for everyone so that if people helped themselves too generously there was nothing left for the person who came last. Godfrey-Faussett came late one day after having been kept on the telephone and, finding nothing to eat, rang and asked for a boiled egg. If he had ordered a dozen turkeys he could not have made a bigger stir. The King accused him of being a slave to his inside, of unpatriotic behaviour and even went so far as to hint that we should lose the war on account of his gluttony.[28]

Austerity such as that practised at Court was certainly not the order of the day at the headquarters in France of His Majesty's Brigade of Guards, where Prince Albert went in January 1916 to visit his brother. The King would have been shocked at the delicacies which his officers consumed, even in the trenches: plovers' eggs, foie gras, roast woodcock, cold partridge and Port-Salut cheese. For Prince Albert it was his first real experience, however diluted, of war; hitherto he had only read about it in the newspapers or in letters from his brother. He watched a British bombardment of a German position and the enemy retaliation. 'I saw several houses shelled by the Boches and the women and children running out by the back door,' he wrote. 'That makes one think of the horrors of war and those people are shelled every day.' He could not help contrasting his own sheltered existence with his brother's experiences; the Prince of Wales had narrowly escaped being killed a few months earlier in September 1915, when his driver had been hit by a burst of shrapnel near Vermelles, and had visited the front line near Loos after a gas attack.

Reluctantly Prince Albert returned to the tedium of his existence in London, which can be glimpsed from his letters to Godfrey-Faussett, who, with his wife, seems to have done what he could to lighten it. Apart from brief shooting expeditions to Sandringham with his father, a treat to which he greatly looked forward was an expedition arranged by the Godfrey-Faussetts to a matinée at the Hippodrome on 26 January 1916, to which the Prince specifically asked them to invite 'Portia' Cadogan (Lady Sybil Cadogan, eldest daughter of Viscount Chelsea, later 6th Earl of Cadogan). That this was a special event in his life is evident from the fact that he wrote no less than three letters to Godfrey-Faussett about it between 23 January and 27: 'I should love to go. . . . Will you ask Portia Cadogan to come that day as well?' and, two days later, 'I am so looking forward to tomorrow . . . I hope Portia will be able to come. . . .' If it was a budding romance, it was not a successful one; 'Portia' became engaged on 26 May 1917 to Edward, Lord Stanley, eldest son of the 17th Earl of Derby, when Prince Albert, perhaps somewhat wistfully, wrote to Godfrey-Faussett, 'old Edward is a very lucky fellow'.[29] After the Hippodrome expedition, 'Dear Captain Faussett' became 'Dear Godfrey'. Prince Albert undertook his first public engagement, opening the House of Commons rifle range, when he had to make a speech. 'I hope that all the people on your list won't be there,' he wrote to Godfrey-Faussett on 13 March 1916, 'as I shall be very nervous in any case. I shall certainly take my paper there in case of accident. It ought not to be very difficult to learn by heart.'[30] His other official duty was to entertain the Crown Prince of Serbia (later King Alexander of Yugoslavia): 'I am still leading the quiet life with a Serbian Prince thrown in last week,' he wrote to Louis Greig. 'Pretty stiff time with him, as he can't talk English.' Otherwise, his letters early that year report frequent consultations with doctors: 'They don't think I shall be able to go to sea again till April,' he wrote on 27 January 1916. 'What an awful thought, another 3 months to come before that. I am longing and have been longing for centuries to get back to my ship. . . .'[31]

He was, however, back on *Collingwood* at Scapa Flow by mid-May in time to take part in the great Battle of Jutland at the end of the month. While the focus of the war had been centred on the land offensives on the Western Front, the principal function of the Navy had been the somewhat inglorious one of keeping the German High Seas Fleet bottled up in their harbours, and it was not until May 1916 that the stalemate at Verdun, and the deteriorating position of Germany in terms of manpower and supplies, forced the German Navy to take the initiative against the British in a controversial heavyweight bout which was to be the last naval battle between massed fleets.

Prince Albert was, once again, in the sick-bay, this time as a result of eating soused mackerel in the Gunroom of *Invincible* on Sunday night, when *Collingwood* put to sea with the main fleet under the Commander-in-Chief, Admiral Sir John Jellicoe, on the evening of Tuesday 30 May. At noon that day the Admiralty had warned Jellicoe and Admiral Beatty that the High Seas Fleet would probably put to sea early next morning; then at 5.40 p.m., after intelligence reports of a highly important operational signal having been sent to the German Navy, the Admiralty ordered Jellicoe to concentrate the Grand Fleet eastward of the 'Long Forties' (about 100 miles east of Aberdeen), 'ready for eventualities'. By 10.30 p.m., Jellicoe and the main fleet were at sea, heading for the rendezvous with

Beatty and the Battle Cruiser Fleet off the Skagerrak. By the time the call to action came for *Collingwood* at 4.30 p.m. the following day, Beatty had already fought a duel with the German battle-cruiser fleet under Admiral Hipper and suffered severe losses. At 5.37 p.m., according to the meticulous account which Prince Albert kept of his ship's part in the battle, *Collingwood* opened fire on some light German cruisers. *Collingwood*'s second salvo hit one of them, setting her on fire; after two more salvoes, she sank and *Collingwood* turned to another light cruiser, which also sank. A big battle-cruiser – either the *Derfflinger* or Hipper's flagship the *Lutzow* – loomed up through the banks of mist and smoke; a salvo from *Collingwood* hit her behind the aft turret, which burst into flames, and she turned away and disappeared into the mist. By then it was too dark to fire and the crew went to Night Defence Stations. They never saw the enemy again and on Friday 2 June returned to Scapa Flow, their ship unscathed despite torpedoes passing ahead and astern and various salvoes straddling it. Prince Albert recounted his personal experience of being shelled:

I was in A turret and watched most of the action through one of the trainer's telescopes as we were firing by Director, when the turret is trained in the working chamber and not in the gun house. At the commencement I was sitting on top of A turret and had a very good view of the proceedings. I was up there during a lull, when a German ship started firing at us, and one salvo 'straddled' us. We at once returned the fire. I was distinctly startled and jumped down the hole in the top of the turret like a shot rabbit!! I didn't try the experience again. The ship was in a fine state on the main deck. Inches of water sluicing about to prevent fires from getting a hold on the deck. Most of the cabins were also flooded.

The hands behaved splendidly and all of them in the best spirits as their heart's desire had at last been granted, which was to be in action with the Germans. Some of the turret's crew actually took on bets with one another that we should not fire a shot. A good deal of money must have changed hands I should think by now.

My impressions were very different to what I expected. I saw visions of the masts going over the side and funnels hurtling through the air etc. In reality none of these things happened and we are still quite as sound as before. No one would know to look at the ship that we had been in action. It was certainly a great experience to have been through and it shows that we are at war and that the Germans can fight if they like.

He was disappointed that *Collingwood*'s part in the action had not been more dramatic. 'Bertie is very proud of being in action but is sorry that his ship was not hit (although she was straddled by several salvoes) as she has nothing to show she has been in the fight,' the King wrote to his uncle, the Duke of Connaught. 'Oh, if only they would come out again and we could meet them, but this time in the early morning, we should have better light and more daylight to deal with them,' Prince Albert wrote to the Prince of Wales. He had seen ships sunk in flames and had passed the shattered wreck of the *Invincible* in which he had dined only a few days before, her bows and stern sticking up out of the shallow water, where 1,026 of her crew, including Admiral Hood, had died, but visibility had been too bad for the full horror of death like this to come home to him (when *Invincible* blew up some of the men in the other British ships had cheered, thinking she was German), and *Collingwood* herself had suffered no casualties. War seemed heroic and exciting, and the Battle of Jutland itself fought in mist and smoke lit by the flare of bursting shells like the most dramatic of battle pictures. As he wrote to his brother:

In a war on such a scale as this of course we must have casualties and lose ships & men, but there is no need for everyone at home to bemoan their loss when they are proud to die for their country. They don't know what war is, several generations have come and gone since the last great battles....

Above all, he was surprised and pleased that he had not felt afraid. 'When I was on top of the turret I never felt any fear of shells or anything else,' he added. 'It seems curious but all sense of danger and everything else goes except the one longing of dealing death in every possible way to the enemy.'

Jutland, however, was a disputed victory, a reaction based on a mismanaged official communiqué by the Admiralty issued on Friday 2 June which, in giving the relative losses in men and ships between the British and German Fleets, not only failed to claim a victory but succeeded in conveying the impression that there had been a disaster. News that the Kaiser was celebrating the Battle of the Skagerrak as a German victory with such slogans as 'The spell of Trafalgar has been broken' did not help matters. The facts were that, statistically, in losses of ships and men the German High Seas Fleet had had the best of it. The Germans lost 11 ships of 62,000 tons as against British losses of 14 ships of 111,000 tons, total casualties of 3,058 or 6.79 per cent of their ships' companies as compared with British casualties of 6,097 men representing 8.84 per cent of the Grand Fleet's strength. The British Navy, it was claimed, had lost not only ships and men at Jutland but the reputation for invincibility which had overawed the navies of the world since Trafalgar. It was, none the less, a victory in the sense that the Germans had been forced to retreat and, in the words of the historian of the battle, Arthur J. Marder:

From the strategical point of view, which is what really matters – that is, the effect of the battle on the outcome of the war – the Grand Fleet was, beyond the shadow of a doubt, the winner. Scheer [the German Commander-in-Chief], who had set out to cut off and overwhelm part of Jellicoe's advance forces, had been compelled to retreat to his harbours. Albeit a successful retreat, it had not changed the naval position. *The British control of the sea communications was unimpaired.*[32]

The real casualty was the Navy's own self-esteem. Both the Admirals commanding at Jutland felt a sense of bitter frustration that they had not been able to inflict an out-and-out defeat on the German fleet. Jellicoe told Beatty, 'I missed one of the greatest opportunities a man ever had,' while Beatty confided to his wife that it was 'one of the saddest days of my life, on which I lost many old and valued friends and trusted comrades, and the Navy missed one of the greatest opportunities of achieving the greatest and most glorious victory'.[33]

Britain's great fleet, the most powerful ever assembled, had failed to live up to the exploits of the past.

For Prince Albert the experience of battle action had been therapeutic, as he wrote on 11 June to Mrs Godfrey-Faussett:

I am quite all right and feel very different now that I have seen a German ship filled with Germans and have seen it fired at with our guns. It was a great experience to have gone through and one not easily forgotten. How and why we were not hit beats me, as we were fired at a good part of the time ... it was a great nuisance getting ill again but the action put me all right at once....[34]

'I'm so glad old Bertie was in the fight, as it will buck him up a lot,' the Prince of Wales wrote to Godfrey-Faussett, thanking him for sending him a copy of Prince Albert's Jutland letter, '& it seems to have cured him of the slight return of his old complaint which was a d—d bore as I really hoped he was cured once & for all!!' The Prince of Wales had been awarded the recently instituted Military Cross, much to his chagrin, for, as he said, he had never been in the trenches; for once, he envied his brother's more active role. 'What wouldn't I give to get up to the Forth & Scapa & see them all!!' he wrote. 'Life out here is pretty dull & monotonous for us all up in the Ypres area....'[35]

It was not long, however, before Prince Albert was writing with the same refrain. The result of Jutland was to convince Scheer and even the Kaiser that this sea battle between the two fleets must, and would, be the last. From then on the German Naval Command placed their reliance on unrestricted U-boat warfare. For Prince Albert and the rest of the Grand Fleet, this meant a return to the tedious job of maintaining the blockade of Germany from their northern base at Scapa Flow, a dreary place with dreadful weather and a treeless landscape of wild moorland and rocks. '... life is going on as usual, very dull and monotonous,' the Prince wrote to Mrs Godfrey-Faussett on 9 July. 'The action seems years ago and we are longing for another one.'[36] The tedium seems to have aggravated his complaint, for, although he wrote optimistically to his father that month, 'I really think now that I have got over all my inside troubles. I have not had any recurrence of pains or sickness', within six weeks, on 26 August, he was in acute pain. Relays of doctors examined him and he was transferred to Windsor, where further doctors – Sir Frederick Treves, Sir Bertrand Dawson and Dr Hewett – finally agreed that he had a duodenal ulcer. A fortnight's rest at the Imperial Hotel, Torquay, accompanied by Lieutenant Campbell Tait, his turret officer in *Collingwood* (during which time he visited Dartmouth and left a pound to buy bananas and cream for the cadets), was followed by a spell of shore duty with Admiral Colville, then Commander-in-Chief at Portsmouth. On 14 December 1916, he celebrated his twenty-first birthday at Buckingham Palace, where his father invested him with the Order of the Garter, the order for which he conceived a lifelong passion. 'I cannot thank you enough for having made me a Knight of the Garter,' he wrote to his father. 'I feel very proud to have it, and will always try to live up to it.'

'One sometimes doubts whether he will be able to continue in the navy,' Lord Stamfordham had written to Sir James Reid with a gloomy résumé of Prince Albert's state of health, but on 8 May 1917 the Prince returned to Scapa Flow, this time as acting lieutenant on the 27,500-ton battleship, *Malaya*. With him was his friend Campbell Tait, later appointed by the King as his 'Hon. and Extra' equerry; shortly afterwards Louis Greig joined as the ship's second surgeon. The Prince was delighted, writing of Greig to his mother, 'It is so nice having a real friend as a messmate and he is very cheery.' *Malaya* was one of the Queen Elizabeth class of new battleships, capable of doing twenty-five knots as opposed to the twenty-one knots of the older battleships in the Grand Fleet. Presented by the Federated Malay States, she had suffered over 100 casualties to her company at Jutland. Her captain was Captain the Hon. Algernon Boyle, whom a recently joined midshipman, Andrew Yates, recalled as an excellent seaman and a popular and just officer, but 'not very cordial and seldom speaks to midshipmen except to strafe them'. Prince Albert, however, had graduated from the Gunroom to the wardroom and was now an officer, whom the midshipmen called 'Sir'. He was second in command in his gun turret to Campbell Tait, now a commander, and had dropped the sobriquet 'Johnson', being known as 'PA'. He had grown considerably in confidence since his days as a midshipman in *Collingwood*, when Lambert had described him as 'a red-faced, stuttering youth'. Yates, who was midshipman in his turret, remembers that 'PA never had a sign of a stammer then. . . . No stammer at all.' PA, he said, did not worry about King's Regulations when it came to smoking. Officially, one was not allowed to smoke until one was eighteen, but Yates smoked a pipe two years before his eighteenth birthday and Lieutenant Prince Albert turned a blind eye to his breach of regulations. The Prince was very keen on deck hockey, which was one thing they could play in harbour: 'We only did it with walking sticks and a piece of wood that wouldn't go very far. It got quite rough and we knocked each other around. . . . I remember one midshipman got knocked down, and the scrum going on round him to get the ball and PA saying "Hit him again, he's still breathing." '[37]

Prince Albert's service on *Malaya* was destined to be extremely brief. 'I have quite settled down here and am as happy as possible,' he had reported to Godfrey-Faussett on 7 July 1917, just a month after his arrival on board. By the end of the month he was ill again and, on 4 August, was transferred ashore to South Queensferry Hospital. The ship's chaplain, who visited him there, found him looking thin and ill. He was deeply depressed and, although his father exhorted him to have patience and courage , he felt he could not go on. He had already come to the conclusion that his naval career was over. 'Personally I feel that I am not fit for service at sea, even when I recover from this little attack,' he told his father. He had spent nearly eight years of his life either training for or serving in the Navy; in his four years as a serving officer, he had spent just twenty-two months at sea. It was a defeat, a disappointment to himself and, he well knew, to his father.

Still, he was not prepared to retire into civilian life while the war was still on. He decided to transfer to the Royal Naval Air Service and was amazed to find that his father agreed without any argument. 'My own suggestion for once came off and Papa jumped at the idea,' he told Hansell. 'Greig is going there as well ... he is a perfect topper.' Louis Leisler Greig, a big, bluff, ebullient, kind-hearted Scot, had become an increasingly important figure in the Prince's life and a rock of support and companionship. From this time on until the Prince's marriage, he dedicated himself to the Prince's service, occupying a position somewhere between father-figure and friend, acting as a buffer between the shy young man and the outside world, smoothing the Prince's path, at sport, at work and even, on occasion, in love. Fifteen years older than the Prince, Greig had been born in Glasgow of middle-class parents and educated at Merchiston Castle School, Edinburgh, and the University of Glasgow, from which he graduated in Medicine and Surgery in 1905. His chief claim to fame had been as an outstanding rugby player, first for Scotland against the All Blacks in 1905 and then, after joining the Navy as a surgeon in 1906, captaining the Navy side against the Army in 1907, 1909 and 1910. When Prince Albert first met him at Osborne in 1909 Greig was, therefore, at twenty-eight, a sporting hero in the eyes of the cadets. Greig first came into contact with the Prince as his medical adviser when the Prince caught whooping cough at the end of the summer term of 1909; the Prince being in quarantine at Barton Manor on the Isle of Wight, where he had been staying with his parents for the Tsar's visit, Greig must have then met the royal family. He was subsequently medical officer on board the training ship *Cumberland* when Prince Albert was a cadet on the ship, and it must have been at this time that the two became friends since by early 1916, after Greig returned from a spell as a prisoner of war at Halle in Germany, the Prince was already corresponding with him. It was, therefore, no coincidence that, shortly after the Prince joined *Malaya* in 1917, Greig was appointed the ship's second surgeon. From that time over the next six years they were to be virtually inseparable and when the Prince transferred to the Naval Air Service the King asked Greig if he would do so too.

It was Greig, apparently, who backed Prince Albert in his desire to have an operation. 'I don't think I can get any better without an operation and I should like to get it over and done with,' the Prince pleaded with his father in September. The royal doctors, however, as they were to do in the case of his serious illnesses as King, havered for a period of two months until a crisis in his condition forced their hands. 'It is decided that poor Bertie is to have an operation to-morrow as he does not seem at all well & has constant pain,' his mother noted in her diary for 28 November 1917. 'He is most cheerful about it....' The operation took place the following day and was successful. '... they found the cause of all the trouble he has been having since 1915,' the Queen wrote. Failure to diagnose 'the cause of all the trouble' had cost the Prince nearly three years of wretchedness, physical pain and mental depression.

At the beginning of February in the last year of the war, 1918, Prince Albert and Greig reported for duty at HMS *Daedalus*, alias the training station at Cranwell in Lincolnshire. Although still officially attached to the Navy, with effect from 1 April the Prince was to be given the rank of captain in the newly constituted Royal Air Force, which was to consist of the Royal Naval Air Service amalgamated with the Royal Flying Corps. The new Service was a hybrid with schizophrenic tendencies with the former Naval Service employing naval terminology while the Flying Corps ran on Army lines. The station itself had started life as 'HMS' and continued to be run as though it were afloat. Grass was cut on the 'quarterdeck', the men were divided into port and starboard watches and talked of 'going ashore' when they left the station on leave. 'Men were not allowed to go ashore except when the "liberty boat" [actually the small camp steam train to Sleaford] was alongside', Wing-Commander A.E.F. McCreary recalled of the old Cranwell, '... and they were inspected at the Master at Arms' Office by a petty officer and the Officer of the Watch to see that they were clean and of credit to the Force before they were allowed to go ashore.'[38]

The makeshift nature of the whole enterprise in its beginnings was symbolized by the fact that the RAF had no distinctive uniform of its own. Naval officers had arrived in, and retained, their naval uniforms, although adopting Army rank, while the Army officers kept their rank but wore uniforms and insignia of the various corps and regiments to which they had belonged. Therefore, the announcement of the first royal visit by the King and Queen, which was to take place on Thursday, 11 April 1918, occasioned a panic rush on London naval and military outfitters. The moment the date of the royal review was known, everyone was ordered into new khaki uniform, the later Air Force blue not yet having been adopted. The King, who had chosen the title of 'General-in-Chief of the RAF', was greatly interested in the subject, even down to the uniform of the RAF band. Three NCO 'models' were paraded before him only to receive the cutting royal comment, 'Porters at a cinema!'; orders were given to cut down on the gold braid.

Prince Albert must have been well aware that his father, a Senior Service man to the backbone, was, as one of his Secretaries of State for Air, Samuel Hoare, testified, 'strongly prejudiced against flying, the Air Ministry and the Air Force',[39] and consequently regarded his second son's new career very much as a *pis-aller*. This cannot have helped the Prince's confidence, and indeed he was in a state of some confusion not only about the direction his future would take but even about the viability of the present. A letter which he wrote to Godfrey-Faussett on 1 March 1918 expresses this confusion: 'I have already given up all idea of flying. I think it is an overrated job altogether. What is going to happen to me at the Amalgamation [of the two Services] I don't know yet, but I expect to be seconded from the R[oyal] N[avy] for a time.'[40] By 'all idea of flying', the Prince meant becoming a flying officer, for three days later, on 4 March, he made his first flight, piloted by Lieutenant Richard Peirse (later Air Chief Marshal Sir Richard Peirse). The weather on the day proved stormy and rainy and the officer in charge of training wanted to postpone the flight, but the Prince insisted; he was not at all looking forward to the experience, but felt that putting it off would only make it worse. His reactions to his first flight were mixed. 'It was a curious sensation', he wrote to his mother the next day, 'and one which takes a lot of getting used to. I did enjoy it on the whole, but I don't think I should like flying as a pastime. I would much sooner be on the ground!! It feels safer!!' It was, indeed, safer on the ground, flying at that time being very much of a hit-and-miss affair; it may have given Prince Albert wry amusement to know that his elder brother was not allowed to risk his precious life in the air at this stage but that he, as second son, was expendable.

Prince Albert was doing his best, but finding that the Cranwell establishment did not run on the oiled wheels that he had learned to expect from his service in the Navy. The essential cogs on which the naval machinery depended, the petty officers, were, according to the Prince, 'all hopeless & understand nothing about discipline and organisation. The difference between this place and a ship is quite extraordinary.'[41] The Prince found himself 'Officer Commanding Boys' in charge of No. 4 Boys' Squadron made up of 500 former Navy Boys, with an ex-civilian, McCreary, as his second in command. It was hardly an elevated position and, given the lack of experienced petty officers or even a trained second in command to help him, Prince Albert found it very hard work, as he told his father. He was entirely responsible for the boys, down to punishments and permission for leave, even to seeing that they kept their huts clean. Anxiety to do well at an unfamiliar job made him heavy-handed and over strict. Wing-Commander S.E. Townson, who arrived on 6 April 1918 with a contingent of RFC boy-entrants to join their RNAS counterparts to train as aero-engine fitters, recalled: 'The O.C. Boys' Wing was a lean dark young man with an embarrassing stutter who signed our passes "Albert, Prince" in very boyish handwriting but was extremely strict for all that.'[42] Wilfred A. Goss, who had joined the RNAS as a Boy mechanic the previous December, aged seventeen, wrote in an unpublished memoir that 'the then Duke of York', as he incorrectly described him, 'was not over popular in the wardroom and at best his presence could only be described as unfortunate'.[43] McCreary was more sympathetic. 'He had great ability to apply himself to any job he undertook,' he wrote. 'He worked long hours and there was nothing which was too much trouble for him. . . . I remember on occasions querying his punishments or perhaps his authorisation of requests, but never did I find him without a very sound answer for what action he had taken.' McCreary quoted the case of a boy who asked for weekend leave as his consumptive mother was due to go away that Sunday to a convalescent home. The Prince refused the request, afterwards giving as his reason, when McCreary asked if he had not been a little hard, that it would be better for the boy to go later when his mother was properly settled in and not now when the likelihood was that she would be extremely upset. 'I think the boy should be spared this emotional upheaval.'

McCreary seems to have been an amiable perhaps somewhat plodding personality who regarded Prince Albert as a being from outer space whose meaning and motivations he found difficult to fathom. The Prince's view of McCreary is perhaps best illustrated by a story which McCreary himself retails. At the end of the Second World War replacements became necessary for some of the Windsor Greys at Buckingham Palace Mews whose duty it is to draw the State coaches. When the new horses arrived, the Master of the Horse asked King George VI if he would go down to the Mews and suggest names. 'The first horse was led in,' McCreary wrote, 'big, broad – the usual type of Windsor Grey. Immediately the King said: "Oh, I know the name here. Call it McCreary of the Royal Air Force!"' At first McCreary was hurt when he heard the story, but was mollified when he heard that the King had named a second horse 'Eisenhower'.[44]

Cranwell was something of a new social experience for a prince brought up in a narrow Court circle and whose only experience hitherto outside that circle had been of the strictly hierarchical and aristocratic Royal Navy, so exclusive that the historian Marder wrote that even Nelson under existing circumstances would have been unable to enter it. The establishment itself was makeshift and lacking in any kind of atmosphere or tradition of the kind to which the Prince had been accustomed. Situated on the flat windswept Lincolnshire fields, the majority of its buildings were corrugated iron, painted black, the only concession to comfort being their lining of panelled wood to keep out the draughts. When he was on watch during the night, the Prince, however, managed to wangle a bunk in the only brick building, later known as York House, and the services of a marine batman in the morning. As for his fellow officers, the Prince found them, as he wrote to his mother within a month of his arrival there, 'very nice, though a curious mixture of people in every walk of life'. Where the Prince of Wales in the Grenadiers was surrounded by 'all my friends & the friends of my friends at home', Prince Albert did not make friends at Cranwell as he had in the Navy, nor did he feel part of the establishment in the way in which he had felt part of the small world of *Collingwood* or *Malaya*. Partly this was because he was in an unfamiliar milieu and, at the end of a long period of illness and depression, suffering from a repressed sense of failure; it was also because he did not commit himself socially to Cranwell. He was living in a house at South Rauceby with Louis Greig and his wife, Phyllis Scrimgeour, whom Greig had married in 1916.

For the Prince, the only real advantage of Cranwell over his previous Service life was that it was on land and offered the sporting amenities denied him at sea. He hunted with the Cranwell beagles, the Blankney and the Belvoir hunts and played tennis at the Physical Training School where Greig was an officer. Cranwell turned out a fine tennis team and Greig coached the Prince to a standard good enough to win the RAF doubles title and, in 1926, to play at Wimbledon. Greig also taught him to drive while at Cranwell, motor cars being considered socially correct by the King whereas motor cycles, which all the officers at Cranwell used for getting round the base, were quite beyond the pale. 'Only bounders ride motor bicycles,' the King pronounced. When McCreary asked the Prince whether he would like a 'gharry', as motor cycles were called, he replied with a smile, 'Oh, you don't know my father. He doesn't even allow me a push-bike!'

The Prince's royal expertise in matters of protocol and Service etiquette came in useful in the inter-Service confusion at Cranwell caused by that establishment's dual naval/military character. The station had a 'Lighter than Air' section composed of two rigid airships and a number of Blimps. When these machines were on the ground they came under the commanding officer, Lieutenant-Colonel Calvert, but the moment they were airborne, the Navy took over command, which naturally tended to create problems. 'One day', McCreary remembers, 'the office door burst open and Lt-Col. Talbot came in and said: "PA these ruddy leathernecks [marines] they're getting at me and wanting to know why I still fly the white ensign [flown only by the Royal Navy and the Royal Yacht Squadron]. I refuse not to fly it. What's the correct answer?" PA looked up and within a moment said: "Oh, the answer, Sir, is HMS Daedalus is still List of Navy." '[45]

The squabbling and confusion among the Cranwell command reflected bitter disagreements at the top. Even before the official formation of the RAF on 1 April 1918, the dashing leader of the Royal Flying Corps, Major-General Trenchard, designated as the new Chief of the Air Staff, had a monumental disagreement with the Secretary of State, Lord Rothermere, and resigned, a resignation which was made public on 13 April and came as a disheartening surprise to the officers of the new Air Force. His departure was followed by further quarrels and resignations, which had unhappy echoes at Cranwell. 'Everything here as you may imagine is in a very unsettled state, owing to the changes in the Air Board, and nothing is settled yet as to what routine we are working under,' Prince Albert wrote to his father. 'We are now having a mixture of naval and military routine, which is not a great success.' His own by now carefully established routine of training the Boys' Squadron was being disrupted. 'I am rather depressed about the whole affair as you may imagine, as I was very keen on this job, and was doing my best to make it a success,' he complained in mid-May, objecting to the removal of his old instructor. 'Now I am afraid I have rather lost interest until I know exactly what is going to happen. I am telling you all this as I am certain you would want to know what sort of things do go on, and this is quite a serious question and I am involved in it personally.' The King clearly could not intervene in such low-level squabbles and it is clear from a letter of the Prince's a month later that things had not improved: 'The whole of my show is upside down and no one knows what is likely to happen. I am pretty fed up and don't feel like staying here for good.'

He must have renewed his complaints in person in July when he spent a brief leave in London with his parents to celebrate their silver wedding with a Thanksgiving Service in St Paul's and, for the Prince and King, both keen sports fans, a rather more enjoyable day out at Stamford Bridge football ground in Chelsea where the US Army were playing the US Navy at baseball. The King, quite carried away, pronounced this unfamiliar game 'very exciting' and autographed a ball to be sent to President Woodrow Wilson. In any event, the Prince soon obtained his release from Cranwell; on 2 August he assumed duty with the 5 Cadet Wing at RAF Headquarters at St Leonard's, commanded by Brigadier-General Critchley. At St Leonard's at least, the Air Force Headquarters was not bedevilled by divided loyalties and the King, for once, was enthusiastic about the establishment and its commander, writing to congratulate his son after an inspection there at the end of the month: 'I thought your squadron did wonderfully well considering they had only been at drill for a week.... I certainly think you are in a better place than at Cranwell, the whole spirit is different.'

Prince Albert did not stay at St Leonard's for long; he was anxious to see action in France where the war in the West was at last coming to an end. The great German initiative of March 1918 had failed and its army was being pushed stubbornly back, fighting all the way. The Prince longed to see the front before the final collapse and on 23 October he was flown to France in a Handley Page bomber by Greig (who with remarkable determination had succeeded in gaining his wings at the age of forty) to join Trenchard's Independent Air Force Headquarters at Autigny as Staff Officer 3/Air. It was his first experience of warfare in the air and he was full of admiration for the cool courage of the pilots, writing to his mother on 6 November: 'The officers all seem in very good spirits and never look upon a raid as more than an ordinary flight, which of course is only right.' He was also extremely impressed by Trenchard's pugnacity and energy, writing to his father in November: 'General Trenchard won't allow anybody to talk about peace here. I have never seen a man more engrossed in his command. He knows a great deal more about what a Squadron should have than the Squadron Commander. He fairly keeps everybody up to their work.' Yet, despite Trenchard's refusal to admit it, the war was virtually over. At eleven o'clock on 11 November 1918 the guns on the Western Front fell silent. 'The great day has come & we have won the war,' the King wrote to Prince Albert. 'It has been along time coming, but I was sure if we stuck to it, we should win & it is a great victory over one of the most perfect military machines ever created.'

Prince Albert's part in the 'great victory' had not – apart from the brief glorious day at Jutland – been a particularly happy or active one. The years between 1913 and 1918 were perhaps the unhappiest and loneliest of his life, but the experience he had gained of the working and organization of the Services at war was to be invaluable to him twenty-one years later as Commander-in-Chief in the Second World War.

4

LOVE AND DUTY

'... he is a man who will be made or marred by his wife.'
Cecilia Countess of Strathmore to Mabell, Countess of Airlie, March 1921

IN THE months following the armistice of November 1918, Prince Albert learned the crucial lesson that the first duty of a King, as trustee of his Crown and his dynasty, is to survive. He learned, too, that in order to survive, the monarchy required not merely the passive consent of its subjects but their active support and an enthusiasm which had to be seen to be both earned and deserved.

The situation facing his father in 1918 was analogous in many respects to the one with which he was to be confronted in 1945. The social, ideological and political pressures generated by the Great War, a war affecting masses on the military and home fronts, had raised social expectations, toppled dynasties and changed the face of Europe. At the end of the war in 1918, the three great imperial thrones of continental Europe – those of Austria, Germany and Russia – had fallen, the throne of Greece seemed insecure, in Holland a strong republican movement threatened the future of the House of Orange, and in Germany all the royal relations of King George v and Queen Mary had lost their rights and positions: 'Uncle Willie' Württemberg had abdicated, the young Grand Duke of Mecklenburg-Strelitz had done likewise and also shot himself, the Duke of Saxe-Coburg and Gotha ruled in Coburg no longer, and both branches of the Hesse family were deprived of even nominal power. Prince Albert had had first-hand experience of this when he visited Germany for the first time at the end of the year, meeting at Bonn his father's first cousin, Princess Viktoria of Schaumburg-Lippe, sister of the recently deposed Kaiser. The events, however, which had eclipsed all others, sending a shock wave through Europe, were the Bolshevik Revolution and the murder of the Tsar and the Russian royal family.

King George's decision to deny asylum to his much-loved first cousin, Nicholas II, in order to avoid dangerous repercussions against his own throne, was the prime example of how far a monarch, even a kindly and loyal man like George v, would go to protect his dynasty. Whether Prince Albert actually knew of the decision his father had taken between the end of March and mid-April 1917 is uncertain. Although he was stationed at Cranwell at the time, he was at home for Easter at Windsor on 14 and 15 April and would, at the very least, have been aware of his father's distress over the question. Given the fact that George v was, in private conversation, notoriously garrulous and indiscreet, it is unlikely that he hid the nature of his preoccupations from his son. The lesson of the spring of 1917 that his first duty was to the interests of 'the family firm' was not lost upon Prince Albert; in his time, he, too, would have to suppress his private opinions and loyalties in favour of public policy. He had learned the lesson which his brother's abdication was to reinforce: that a King is a public figure first and a private man only second.

He was well aware of the preoccupation of the Court with the dangers to the Crown on both the home and imperial fronts. Ominous events during the war had pointed to the growing unpopularity of British rule and the imperial connection: a rebellion of Afrikaner generals in South Africa in 1914 and an uprising in Ireland in 1916 were followed after the war by an almost general crisis of empire in India, Ireland and Egypt, beginning with 379 Indians shot dead at Amritsar in 1919. At home the situation also had potential for danger. The King in public put on a confident face, although it was plain that the future of the monarchy was in the forefront of his mind. The Earl of Crawford, Lord Privy Seal, described an interview with him just before the Armistice:

... his voice rather more shrill, his gestures more syncopated than when I last saw him. ... He is clearly asking himself what the future has in store for the royal family: and on the whole he is fairly confident. 'Why should our people have a revolution? We are the victors, we are the Top Dog. ...'[1]

The King's confidence was, however, shaken by reports of the Labour Party meeting at the Albert Hall to launch their election campaign on 14 November, less than one week later, when Mr Bob Williams, Secretary of the Transport Workers' Union, declared that he hoped to see the Red Flag flying over Buckingham Palace; Willie Gallacher, describing himself as 'a Bolshevik from Glasgow', admitted he was out for revolution; the 'Red Flag' was sung and cheers given for 'The Bolsheviks' and 'Lenin and Trotsky'. The King obtained a first-hand impression of the discontent under the surface when, accompanied by the Prince of Wales, he rode to Hyde Park to review a parade of some 15,000 discharged, disabled soldiers; the men, at first sullen and unresponsive, burst into shouts of 'Where is this land fit for heroes?' (a reference to Lloyd George's wartime promise), broke ranks and surrounded the King. Prince Albert, wearing the uniform of the RFC to present the prizes at the Services' boxing championships in the National Sporting Club, was equally taken aback when one of the winners, also wearing the RFC uniform, on being routinely congratulated and asked if there were anything the Prince could do for him, replied bluntly, 'Yes. You can get me out of this bloody uniform as quick as you like!'[2]

The spectre of Bolshevism and the class war was an anxiety shared and, indeed, fanned by the courtiers. 'The Monarchy and its cost will have to be justified in the future in the eyes of a war-worn and hungry proletariat, endowed with a huge preponderance of voting-power,' Esher had written to Stamfordham on 4 November 1918. The 'selling' of the image of the family firm to the people who would have to pay for it was to be a major royal preoccupation in the post-war years. In this campaign the two elder Princes both had a part to play: while his elder brother represented the Crown as the link of Empire in a series of spectacularly successful overseas tours, on the home front Prince Albert carved himself a niche in industrial relations.

The Prince's involvement stemmed from the initiative of the Reverend Robert Hyde, a churchman with a considerable background in social welfare who had worked with the Ministry of Munitions during the war promoting better conditions in the factories. In April 1918 he had set up the Boys' Welfare Association, specifically devoted to boys in industry. His approach to Buckingham Palace through the Archbishop of Canterbury, Dr Davidson, had been received with extreme caution by Stamfordham and the new Assistant Private Secretary, Clive Wigram. The involvement of the Palace in industrial welfare in an official capacity could be taken to imply criticism of the Government's omissions in that area. 'Are you going to set the King's son against the King's Government?' they asked Hyde in response to his suggestion that Prince Albert should become the first President of his Association. Satisfied that the round-faced, ill-dressed and enthusiastic clergyman had no ulterior motive, Prince Albert was allowed to accept on his own terms, 'no fuss, no publicity, no red carpet', becoming President of the Boys' Welfare Association on 21 March 1919. Later that year, the Association's scope was widened to include all industrial workers under the title of the Industrial Welfare Society. Its principal aim was to ameliorate relations between the workforce and the employers by improving physical conditions of work, providing canteens, medical care and other benefits. The Society, initially viewed with suspicion by trade unionists, government departments and some industrialists, was entirely dependent on voluntary subscription for its financing; royal patronage was, therefore, extremely helpful in persuading both industry to join the welfare schemes and businessmen to provide the funds.

Prince Albert took his duties as President seriously, earning the plaudits of the *Daily Sketch*:

Prince Albert looks like being in future the Royalty who will be most in touch with social welfare and work and kindred philanthropic enterprise. As President of the Industrial Welfare Society, he is taking his duties very seriously and pays visits to factories and works, but so unostentatiously does he set about things that nothing is heard about his work.

His assiduity in visiting factories, mines and shipyards earned him the nickname 'the Foreman' from his brothers. In fact, he took a real interest in technical processes of which he had some knowledge from his days in the engineering workshops at Osborne and Dartmouth and was later to have his own workshop at Windsor during the war. One plant manager told Hyde that of all the visitors he had shown over the works Prince Albert had been the one to ask the most sensible questions and show the greatest understanding of the problems. He undertook fund-raising tours for the Society, putting pressure on industrialists to contribute for the Society was on a precarious financial footing until 1933, when he was able to report that he had obtained a donation of £33,000, enough then to secure its future. Over the years between the wars he gained invaluable first-hand knowledge of the workings of industry such as few people in the country had acquired. A trade unionist wrote to Hyde in the spring of 1923:

At no time in the history of this or any other country has anyone, occupying a similar position to the Duke of York [Prince Albert had been created Duke of York by his father on 5 June 1920], done so much to establish and maintain harmonious relationships between employers and workmen ... [he] has placed the community under an obligation to him for the kindliness and the effectiveness with which he has performed the tasks allotted to him.[3]

Easily the most publicized of the Prince's initiatives in the field of social relations was the annual institution known as the Duke of York's Camp, the first of which was held in August 1921. In March that year the welfare officer of one of the member firms of the iws, Briton Ferry Steelworks, wrote to the Society saying that a number of boys in the works, keen footballers, had saved up their money to give themselves a trip to London and requesting that the Society arrange a match against a London team for them. Prince Albert, a keen football spectator himself, passed the idea on to the Palace with the suggestion that he, as President, should attend. Once again the Palace showed extreme caution about royal dealings with the working classes. The Scottish Biscuit King, Alexander Grant, whom the Prince had met on his first factory visit to the McVitie & Price works at Harlesden and who had become his firm ally and mentor in the industrial field, was summoned to Buckingham Palace to give his opinion, as the Grant family record puts it, 'on Prince Albert going amongst the younger generation of the working classes. ... Mr Grant expressed the opinion that Royalty's interest in Industry was long overdue.'[4] Presumably Grant was able to reassure the King and Queen that working-class boys were not dangerous, for the Prince, accompanied by Grant, did attend the match between the Briton Ferry boys and a team from Westminster School at the Vincent Square ground. It was after this match that Grant told Hyde that he thought the idea of bringing together boys from different backgrounds could be significant and that he would put up the money to finance any scheme which the Duke of York might approve. Hyde went 'hotfoot to the Duke and told him of the offer. After various ideas had been mulled over, the Duke said, "Let's have a camp!"'

The idea was that the Duke of York should personally invite 400 selected boys, 200 from public schools (two from each) and 200 from member firms of the iws, to be his guests for a week in August at an annual summer camp, the site to be at a disused airfield on Romney Marshes near the sea. Financed by Grant to the tune of £1,100, and organized by Hyde and a team of ex-naval and military men, the first camp took place in August that year in somewhat chaotic conditions, which, if the idea had not been thoroughly thought out, could have proved disastrous. The boys assembled for lunch in the Royal Mews at Buckingham Palace where, intimidated by their surroundings and shy of each other, they met in embarrassed silence. Social differences were underlined by the fact that to the working-class boys this meal was 'dinner' while to their public-school equivalents it was 'lunch'. When they arrived down at New Romney things did not go smoothly, the caterer having hired such unskilled local assistants as an ancient shepherd whose life had been spent on Romney Marshes, the ex-coxswain of the local lifeboat and the captain of the village fire brigade. Hyde recalled:

Catering in any of its branches was an entirely novel experience with all of them. Food ran short, utensils remained unwashed, and owing to lack of organisation, these old men were so tired out by the second afternoon that we sent them off to take a rest. As soon as they had cleared off the kitchen revealed the presence of nearly 3,000 dirty dishes as well as knives and forks.

The 'catering matron' who doled out the food could only count up to thirteen and, as there were twenty boys at each section table, she guessed 'with very uneven results'. The concert hall where the evening entertainments were held was a swelteringly hot, low-roofed concrete building; one day there was a near-riot by Scottish boys who felt that one of them had been victimized when his bagpipes were confiscated.

Apart from such early inconveniences, the experiment was a success. It had been carefully designed to ensure that class differences should not be brought out. The atmosphere was informal: everyone wore shirts and shorts, even the rolypoly Hyde, whom Prince Albert teased as 'the worst-dressed man in England', and the Prince himself when he visited on what became known as 'the Duke's Day'. The boys were divided into sections under a leader and inter-section games were devised to eliminate the advantage that playing organized team games would have given the public-school boys. There was bathing on the nearby beach, free biscuits donated by Grant and entertainments got up by the boys themselves. On his 'Day' Prince Albert took part in all the camp activities and liked to lead the singing and miming of 'Under the Spreading Chestnut Tree'. The grand finale was the chairing of the camp commander and the singing of 'Auld Lang Syne' round a huge bonfire on the beach.

It was simple innocent fun in a Baden-Powellesque age and it worked, as the boys' own accounts in school and works magazines showed. The boys were quite aware of the purpose behind the camp: 'It would take too long to describe all we saw and experienced,' wrote two boys from the Bournville iron works, 'but you can take it from us that the chumming-up was a very real thing and there are at least two chaps who are ready to go again.' A Scottish boy, James Anderson, from the North British Diesel Engine Works, wrote touchingly in *The Shipyard* about the 1923 camp: 'There was genuine regret at parting from our English friends.... In my opinion the English Public School boy is the perfect type of gentleman.' The *Eton College Chronicle*, looking down from the top of the social pyramid, drew the moral lesson:

Quite apart from merely giving pleasure, the camp is of very great service both socially and nationally, for it does show us to each other under the best conditions. It has helped us to see that those with whom we seldom come in touch, whether they come from another public school, or from an office, from a factory or from a mine, can be really good fellows. We believe that it points the way to the solution of many of the problems of the day, for it is the very best way of curing the disease of class-hatred, which is at the bottom of nearly all our troubles at the present time.[5]

The camps received enormous publicity in the years between the wars – camp entertainments even being broadcast live on the BBC – so much so that the surroundings of New Romney became crowded with sightseers. In 1935, therefore, the camp site was moved to Southwold in Suffolk, where, with success, arrangements became more lavish. Chefs from Harrods, the Savoy Hotel and the Kit-Kat Club, assisted by their *sous-chefs*, planned the menus for the week, while Mr Stapley, the stage carpenter from the Hippodrome Theatre in London, acted as stage manager for the entertainments. The uncomfortable straw pail-lasses on which the boys used to sleep were banished; there was even a camp tie, dark blue with red, yellow, red, white and green stripes, chosen by the Prince and made up by a London maufacturer. Etonian Sir David Llewellyn, who attended the 1935 camp, recalled that 'the whole thing was marvellously organised and the food was very good.... There wasn't any regimentation – it was all very much on trust.' Like the works boys, he remembered it with 'enormous pleasure ... there wasn't a semblance of class war in any shape or form'.[6] Denis Thatcher, a veteran of the 1932 camp, wrote regretfully: 'Its ideas and ethos 40 years on, are totally outdated....' The last camp was held at Balmoral in 1939; with the outbreak of war they were to be discontinued, although revived during the war by Hyde in a somewhat different form. The Duke of York's Camps were an idealistic experiment whose value was more symbolic than real, but within their limited scope and in the context of their time they were a success and, by the publicity engendered by the Prince's connection with them, presented a positive image of responsible and concerned royalty.

The Prince's work for the Society and the camps gave him a personal satisfaction, a sense that he was doing something of value which had been lacking in his unprofitable years of sickness during the war. Meeting people and sensing their appreciation of him contributed to his confidence, while he was playing a role in industry which no member of his family had done before. He was still trying to prove himself in various ways, even flying, which, as he suffered from a fear of heights and a certain related claustrophobia, took considerable courage on his part. He was not afraid to admit it, as the memoirs of an American First World War pilot recalled. James Warner Bellah met the Prince

at 'an aerodrome in England during the last months of the First World War' –
it is more likely to have been the early summer of 1919 since Prince Albert was
appointed captain in May 1919 having commenced flying instruction on 1 March
1919 at Croydon, although it could possibly be April 1918, a month after his
first flight on 4 March – describing him as 'a slender young man with a nice
smile and pleasant grace . . . infinite courtesy and a diffident manner'. The Prince's
popularity in the mess rose when he admitted, on being asked how he enjoyed
flying, 'Not too much,' showing, Bellah said, 'that he was more honest than the
rest of us'. During a visit by the Prince of Wales, his brother asked him if he
knew anything about the De Haviland aeroplane. 'Practically nothing,'
responded Prince Albert. 'That pleased us greatly', Bellah wrote, 'for neither
did we, although that was the plane we were flying.' He continued:

What established him as a regular guy was an incident that happened one night in the
senior officers' mess. . . . Another guest was a famous air fighter who wore the ribbons
of the Distinguished Service Order, the Distinguished Flying Cross, the Air Force Cross
and a few assorted French numbers. He had imbibed freely, and his good taste had
become dulled.

After staring for a long moment at the then wingless ribbons on the diffident captain's
left breast he said, 'Captain, what are all those ribbons?'

For an equally long moment the captain looked down at his ribbons as if he had never
seen them before. Then he looked up and smiled and said, 'I'm not quite sure. The tailor
puts them there whenever I have a uniform made.'

No one present failed to feel the quiet lash of the remark. . . .[7]

On 1 March 1919, Prince Albert began a course of flying instruction at
Waddon Aerodrome near Croydon with, as his instructor in the little Avro
504K, Lieutenant Alec Coryton (later Air Chief Marshal Sir Alec Coryton). He
had already taken some instruction while in France, with an old Etonian pilot
named Dudley Hobbs, but Hobbs had gone down with scarlet fever and the
second instructor designated for the Prince, this time at Croydon, Major Bird,
had crashed on a test flight, breaking both legs, preliminary to taking the Prince
up for the first time. Despite this unpromising start, Prince Albert, according
to Coryton, proved a

very apt pupil . . . his eye and hand were what I'd call accustomed to working together.
No trouble teaching him to land or anything like that, but I don't think he enjoyed it,
didn't really like it. But I think it was his father's idea that one son should be in the
Army and one in the Navy and one in the Air Force.

The Palace would not allow him to go solo, ostensibly on medical grounds, but
it seems more likely to have been over-protectiveness which was not entirely
unjustified. Engines were unreliable, there was no communication between
ground and air, and the crash rate for pilots under instruction going solo was
appallingly high. The prohibition, however, did little for the Prince's morale
since he naturally and undoubtedly correctly interpreted it as meaning that his

parents would not trust him to fly solo, and therefore it was to him yet another sap to his confidence. One rather sad little incident, narrated by Coryton, illustrated this:

One day I must have corrected him through the voice pipe and during that trip he got depressed and I said to him, 'If this was the training of war pilots, you'd be solo tomorrow!' That cheered him up and when he got back he must have told the Queen this, because when I was on weekend leave I suddenly got a telephone message that I had to report to Colonel Newall of Inland Area [later Air Chief Marshal Sir Cyril Newall, Chief of the Air Staff] and I went there and Louis Greig who was the Prince's ADC, he'd heard about this and told me what was happening, and he said, 'I'll get on to Newall so that you aren't torn to pieces in the morning!'[8]

The Prince took his Category A test in two parts on 28 and 31 July 1919, an experience made more nerve-racking by the presence of the Air Officer Commanding South Eastern Area, Brigadier-General T.I. Webb-Bowen, who had come down to Croydon specially for the occasion. He passed the test, obtaining his official certificate on which it stated he had 'completed 23 hours and 10 minutes in the air'. During the flying test, Coryton had to sit in the front seat of the plane, but put his hands on the struts to show that he had nothing to do with flying the aircraft. 'I think he enjoyed it,' Coryton said of the Prince; 'he gave me a cigarette case afterwards with *In Memoriam* on it. . . .' Asked if the Prince would have been good enough to fly solo, Coryton said that he would. Coryton kept another memento of the future King's flying training, salvaging the Avro's joystick, which he subsequently presented to the King, a graceful gesture prompted by Louis Greig to whom the King wrote on 20 December 1949: 'What a good idea of yours and I propose putting it at Windsor along with armour, battleaxes, swords and pistols etc., used by my ancestors. It will give a real modern touch.'[9]

On obtaining his certificate, Prince Albert was appointed to the rank of captain (aeroplane) flying, then attached in October 1919 to Headquarters Midland Area and promoted again the following month to squadron leader, promotions which were purely formal since the King had already decided that the Prince would be of more use to the dynasty on the civilian front, for which he was to be prepared by a brief spell of higher education. He was to go to Trinity College, Cambridge, thus tactfully spreading the royal patronage between the two senior universities, the Prince of Wales having been to Oxford. 'I am giving up a Service career now and go to Cambridge for a year, to learn everything that will be useful for the time to come,' he had written to Campbell Tait in July, displaying a somewhat naive view of the practical value of a university education, particularly one as curtailed as his was to be. It is far from clear precisely what the King intended his two younger sons (Prince Henry was to accompany Prince Albert to Cambridge) to learn at university in the space of just one year. Indeed, Prince Henry, who had attended Eton and then the Royal Military College at Sandhurst and been commissioned as a lieutenant in the

Army in July 1919, was possessed, as even his official biographer admitted, of 'a somewhat less than natural intellectual talent'. He went to sleep in lectures and, when directed by his brother to answer his mother's query as to what he did all day, replied: 'Bertie told me that you had asked him what I did all day here and that you were surprised when he answered that I killed mice,' proudly confessing that he had killed fifty mice in traps which he set in the conservatory of Southacre, the house on the outskirts of Cambridge which his father had rented for the brothers to share with Louis and Phyllis Greig.

At Oxford the Prince of Wales at least had been allowed to live in college, where, although trammelled by the presence of Hansell and an equerry of impeccably aristocratic descent specially selected by his father, he had thoroughly enjoyed himself. The two younger Princes, however, were to be allowed no such freedom, a restriction due to their father's increasing obsession that they might find themselves in bad company. The result was that they enjoyed practically no company at all, Prince Albert being the worse off of the two since Prince Henry at least knew a few men there from Eton. Living out of college they did not get many opportunities to meet other undergraduates except at weekly Sunday night gatherings after dining with the Chancellor, Dr Shipley. Moreover, at most formal academic gatherings they did not get the chance to talk to any undergradutes at all, but found themselves surrounded by sycophantic dons eager to meet the King's sons. Almost the only friend they had of their own age at Cambridge who was acceptable to their father was their cousin, Lord Louis Mountbatten, five years younger than Prince Albert, who had also come up to Cambridge in October 1919 as an undergraduate at Christ's. Mountbatten, tall, exceptionally good-looking and eager to make friends with his royal cousins, lightened the Princes' lives by inviting them to drop in for tea whenever they liked and dining frequently with them at Southacre. With Mountbatten they attended the Cambridge Union to hear him argue against a decrease of armaments and on another occasion when Winston Churchill spoke against a motion advocating a Labour government. Prince Albert acted as very much the elder brother towards the unsophisticated Prince Henry, who still tended to behave like a schoolboy, 'shrieking with laughter at everything' as a courtier's wife noted at the time. He treated his cousin, however, as a contemporary. On one occasion Mountbatten planned to take a girl he was in love with to the Oxford and Cambridge rugby match in December in a party including Prince Henry, but at the last moment the King decided to attend and, to Mountbatten's annoyance, the scared young Prince called it off. 'Harry is so young, he can't stand up to his father like I can,' wrote the twenty-four-year-old Prince Albert, excusing his brother. 'Of course, he ought to have told him he had a party of his own. He doesn't understand, like you and me, the trouble it is to get these girls to do anything, otherwise he wouldn't have let the King spoil it all.'[10] He used his influence with his father to allow Mountbatten to go as aide-de camp to the Prince of Wales on the first of his world tours in March 1920, but, although Mountbatten continued to correspond with him on this and subsequent voyages, he was to transfer his affection and loyalty to the heir to the throne for the next sixteen years.

Probably the only lasting benefit which Prince Albert derived from his time at Cambridge was his knowledge of the British Constitution learned from the solid pages of Dicey's *Law of the Constitution*, and the more brilliant exposition of the subject by Walter Bagehot, whose analysis of the nature of monarchy remains unsurpassed. These authorities laid down the ground rules for the constitutional monarchy of Great Britain, the wider relations between Crown and people and the more trammelled one between the monarch and his government. Prince Albert became an expert on the subject and on occasion showed a greater perception of constitutional implications than either his official legal adviser or even Winston Churchill. The Prince, like his mother, was fascinated by history, tradition and ritual. Just as he had cherished the King's bestowing upon him the Order of the Garter, so he deeply appreciated his father granting him the title of Duke of York (he was also to be Earl of Inverness and Baron Killarney) on 5 June 1920. 'I am very proud to bear the name that you did for many years, and I hope I shall live up to it in every way,' he wrote to his father from Cambridge. The King replied with one of his characteristically kindly letters expressing an affection which he seemed incapable of expressing in his children's presence:

Dearest Bertie,

I was delighted to get your letter this morning, & to know that you appreciate that I have given you that fine old title of Duke of York which I bore for more than 9 years & is the oldest Dukedom in the country. I know that you behaved very well in a difficult situation for a young man & that you have done what I asked you to do. I feel that this splendid old title will be safe in your hands & that you will never do anything which could in any way tarnish it. I hope you will always look upon me as yr. best friend & always tell me everything [he added somewhat pathetically] & you will find me ever ready to help you & give you good advice.

Looking forward to seeing you to-morrow.

Ever my dear boy,

Yr. very devoted Papa.

Prince Albert's interest in ritual and his feeling for family tradition found expression in freemasonry. Both he and the Prince of Wales were initiated as members of the Brotherhood in 1919, the Prince of Wales entering the socially exclusive Household Brigade Lodge, whose membership was confined to the officers of the Brigade of Guards, in May and Prince Albert the Navy Lodge, No. 2612, reserved for senior naval officers, in December. Freemasonry had been closely linked with the Prince's family since their arrival in Britain in 1714; indeed, it has been surmised that freemasonry was involved in the overthrow of the Stuart dynasty. Whether or not there is any truth in this, the principal body in English freemasonry, Grand Lodge, was founded in 1717, just three years after George I succeeded to the throne. Since then every British monarch except Queen Victoria (who as a woman would have been ineligible) and

George v had been members of the Craft as it is called, as had many other male members of the royal family. Edward vii had been an enthusiastic mason until his accession and at the time of Prince Albert's initiation his great-uncle, Prince Arthur, Duke of Connaught, was Grand Master.

It was, perhaps, his grandfather, Edward vii, who first aroused in Prince Albert an enthusiasm for masonry which was to remain a serious interest all his life. He told his brother masons at his initiation (with, naturally, Louis Greig) at Princes' Galleries, Piccadilly, on the evening of 2 December 1919:

I have always wished to become a Freemason, but owing to the war I have had no opportunity before this of joining the Craft. All my life I have heard of Freemasonry, and though there has always been a certain mystery attached to it, I have learned that Freemasons in this country have been a great help to the poor and friendless, and have been notable for their efforts on behalf of children. One can see, by the great Masonic Institutions and Schools, how successful their work has been in this cause, and I like to think that in the future I shall be associated in their great work.[11]

The ideals of the Craft – brotherly love, service and truth – appealed to him; it was a logical extension in some ways of the industrial charity work he had already begun.

The social aspect of masonry, the sense of belonging to a circle of initiates bound together by a secret bond, was also attractive to someone like Prince Albert, who, being both royal and shy, had been somewhat isolated, providing him with an instant network of contacts. Freemasonry had a firm grip on the Court and the higher echelons of the Services. Rear Admiral Sir Lionel Halsey, Comptroller of the Prince of Wales's Household, was a mason, the son of a high-ranking mason, Comp.[anion] Sir Frederick Halsey, Bart, Second Grand Principal of the United Royal Arch Chapter, No. 1629. It appears to have been Lionel Halsey who arranged for the initiation of both Princes into the higher ranks of masonry. On 7 February 1921 Halsey wrote to Brother Colonel Hope Willis, a mason of the 30th Degree and a member of the exclusive United Royal Arch Chapter, making arrangements for Willis to instruct the two royal brothers in the masonic rite, known as 'the word', to enable them to take the first step on the rung of the thirty-three degrees leading to the most exalted ranks of masonry. They had already progressed through the three preliminary degrees, Entered Apprentice, Fellow Craft and Master Mason, attained by the vast majority of ordinary masons. The two Princes, accompanied by their Comptrollers, Greig and Halsey, were also to be admitted on 11 February into the United Rose Croix Chapter, No. 169, of the Ancient and Accepted Rite, in the ceremony of Perfection, part of which was conducted by Willis himself. Four days later, on 15 February, again with Halsey and Greig (who caused some mirth by referring wryly to his meteoric rise through the masonic ranks), they took part as 'Exaltees' in the ceremony of Exaltation making them members of the United Royal Arch Chapter, No. 1629.

Membership of the United Royal Arch and hence the higher degrees of masonry is by invitation of the Supreme Council only, a guarantee of exclusivity, and, according to *The Freemason* (19 February 1921), was at that time largely drawn from the Household Brigade and Navy Lodges into which Prince Albert and the Prince of Wales had been first initiated. The First Grand Principal or head of the United Royal Arch was the Duke of Connaught, the Pro First Grand Principal, Lord Ampthill, the Second Grand Principal, Sir Frederick Halsey, Bart, and the Third Grand Principal was the Very Rev. Dean Brownrigg, who, as representatives of the royal family, the military, political and clerical aristocracy respectively, could fairly be said to represent the Establishment of England. The Princes' initiation ceremonies of Exaltation and Perfection took place at No. 10 Duke Street, St James's, suitably situated in the heart of that aristocratic, male-dominated quarter, within easy reach of White's Club, Locks the hatters, Lobb the boot and shoemakers, the shirt-makers, hosiers, gentlemen's outfitters, antique and art dealers and auction houses, which provided the niceties of the Establishment world. No. 10 Duke Street was, in its way, even more exclusive than White's, then as now largely the preserve of the landed aristocracy. Known to higher masonic initiates as the Grand East, it was the headquarters of the Supreme Council, the governing body of the thirty higher degrees of masonry, as opposed to Grand Lodge, based in the monumental Freemasons' Hall (the present building was not completed until 1933) in the more plebeian surroundings of Great Queen Street, Holborn, which controlled the three lower degrees of masonry.

Prince Albert was to become First Grand Principal of the United Royal Arch Chapter in 1928, having made a rapid ascent of the masonic ladder (Master of his Lodge in 1920, Senior Grand Warden of his brother's Household Brigade Lodge in 1923, and Provincial Grand Master of the Middlesex Lodge in 1924). He became Grand Master of the Grand Lodge of Scotland in 1936 (having been initiated into Scottish masonry by the village postmaster at Glamis) and would have succeeded his great-uncle, the Duke of Connaught, on the latter's retirement in 1938, as Grand Master of the Grand Lodge, had he not become King. When the former King Edward VIII left the country for exile in December 1936, the new king, George VI, noted in his diary, 'we said goodbye as Masons'. In accordance with precedent established by his ancestor, George IV, George VI gave up his masonic offices on his accession, but he went so far as to break with precedent when, as Past Grand Master, he installed three successive Grand Masters, including his brother, Prince George, Duke of Kent. He continued to take a fervent interest in masonry; on 11 June 1946 he issued two stamps in celebration of victory in the Second World War, during which masonry had been suppressed by the Nazis, one of which depicted a dove bearing an olive branch, with the masonic symbols, bricks, a trowel, and a square and compass, the message being that peace (the dove and olive branch) could only be built on the sure foundations of brotherly love (the masonic square and compasses). In the last year of his life, when illness prevented him from personally installing the Earl of Scarbrough as Grand Master, he was to write of the important part which freemasonry had to play in the 'spiritual and moral regeneration of the world'.

While the Prince of Wales was constantly overseas on imperial tours, Prince Albert carried on his duties on the home front and in Europe, which was considered infinitely less important than either England or the Empire, as his father's representative to the European royalties, particularly in the Balkans where there was a high concentration of royal family connections. It was to give him a certain experience of personalities and countries in what was to be one of the most disputed areas in the Second World War.

The outstanding personality in the Balkans was Queen Marie of Romania, George v's first cousin, always known as 'Missy', with whom he had once been a little in love. 'Missy', daughter of Queen Victoria's son, Prince Alfred, Duke of Edinburgh, and his wife, the Grand Duchess Marie, daughter of Tsar Alexander II, had, however, married an unimpressive Hohenzollern prince, Ferdinand, who had succeeded his uncle as King of Romania. Queen Marie in her youth had been a beauty, blonde, voluptuous and irresistible to men. Now bosomy, double-chinned and distinctly middle-aged, she was still possessed of an extravagant temperament and a marked tendency to fantasy, given to leaving notes in her own hand about her palaces, declaring 'Marie of Romania—one of the most wonderful women in the world. A woman like that is born once in a century.'[12] Prince Albert already knew 'Cousin Missy' when, with her daughters Marie and Ileana, she had stayed at Buckingham Palace in March 1919. In April 1922, Queen Marie invited George v to act as Chief Sponsor at the marriage of her daughter Marie to King Alexander of Serbia, and to send one of his sons as his representative. Wary of inflaming revolutionary passions, Stamfordham on behalf of the King consulted the Foreign Office, who replied on 11 April 1922 that there was no political objection in this case but rather, as Sir Eyre Crowe minuted to the Foreign Secretary, Lord Curzon, 'some advantage to Great Britain standing forth as the foremost supporter of a monarchical regime where this is not running counter to nationalist sentiment.'[13]

There was, however, a threat to Prince Albert's security which the Foreign Office took remarkably lightly. Early in April, the Foreign Office had received from the Secret Intelligence Service's representative in Austria a report of a plot by Croatian revolutionaries aided and abetted by Bulgarian Macedonian revolutionaries, to assassinate King Alexander during the wedding festivities, the whole thing masterminded by shadowy Hungarian intriguers. King Alexander, a Serb, was later assassinated, a victim of the divided racial make-up of the recently formed kingdom of Yugoslavia, when he was shot in Marseilles in 1933 by a Croat. His throne, which had come into being as a result of the First World War, was not destined to survive the Second. On this occasion, however, or perhaps because neither King George nor the Prince of Wales was involved, the Foreign Office seem to have taken a relaxed view of the threat until the very eve of the wedding (which took place on 8 June and not, as Wheeler-Bennett incorrectly states, on the 9th), when Miles Lampson sent a report dated 6 June to Sir Eyre Crowe with the minute dated 7 June: 'The wedding is for tomorrow. As the Duke of York is Chief Sponsor and will therefore be in close proximity to the King during the festivities, perhaps we *ought* to telegraph? I am always inclined to doubt these reports but we can hardly take risks. . . .'[14] In fact, a most urgent Code R telegram had already been sent to Belgrade in the early hours (2.5 a.m.) of 5 June, following information from Sir Wyndham Childs, the Assistant Commissioner of the Metropolitan Police:

Following from Scotland Yard. Confidential information has been received from a trustworthy source that the Bulgarian–Macedonian Committee have recommended a man called Marian Kilifanski to seditious groups in Serbia as a suitable man to assassinate King Alexander of Serbia at the wedding. Kilifanski also said to be in touch with the Serbian Communists.[15]

Prince Albert was no doubt quite unaware of the threat of Kilifanski as he rode in the perilous place of honour following the bridegroom's carriage on a particularly skittish Irish horse from the Serbian royal stables. He cannot, however, have been unaware of the difference between being a member of a Balkan royal family and his own. Although his biographer wrote of 'enthusiastic cheers of the crowd who thronged the route', in fact, as Sir William Strang of the Foreign Office reported, the crowds could not be described as 'very great. . . . Nor was there the lusty cheering to which one is accustomed in England, perhaps because the Serbian "Zivpo" [meaning 'long live'. Sir William's Serbian orthography was shaky, the correct spelling being 'Zivo'] does not lend itself to lustiness.' The smallness of the crowd, he said, was probably due to a heavy police presence and massive security precautions.[16]

At this royal wedding in 1922, Prince Albert met a crowd of royal relations. He had already met King Alexander as the non-Anglophone Crown Prince of Serbia in London in 1916; he was on friendly terms with King Alexander's cousin, the cultivated, Anglophile Prince Paul of Serbia, who had recently been an undergraduate at Oxford. The Greek royal family was there in force, including Prince George of Greece, Queen Alexandra's great-nephew, the future King George II of Greece, whom he had first met at Athens in 1913 when he was on *Cumberland*. Prince George had married the previous year Queen Marie's eldest daughter, Elisabetha, a haughty, difficult girl, a dynastic, loveless match which was not destined to last. His younger sister, Princess Helen of Greece, had married two years previously the Romanian Crown Prince, Queen Marie's son, Carol. But, by the time Prince Albert joined the Romanian royal family for the wedding in June 1922, his cousin Helen's marriage was already falling apart. The susceptible Carol had become infatuated with Elena Lupescu, wife of an officer in the Romanian army; three years later, after attending Queen Alexandra's funeral in England, he suddenly eloped with her to Italy, abdicating his throne.

Four months later the Prince was back in the Balkans, again at 'Cousin

Missy's' instigation, in an attempt to shore up her husband's recently implanted dynasty with the help of her royal relations. The occasion was essentially an artificial one, the 'Coronation' of Marie and her husband, Ferdinand, as King and Queen of 'Greater Romania', an area which had fallen to Romania as the spoils of the First World War at Hungary's expense, despite the Romanian army's Hunnish behaviour in sacking Budapest. Greater Romania now included Transylvania, the homeland of Prince Albert's maternal great-grandmother, Countess Rhedey. George v, recognizing a tinsel occasion when he saw one and feeling, in any case, the need for economy as a result of a drastic cut in his income due to war taxation, had attempted to evade the invitation on the grounds of expense. The Foreign Office had, however, pressed it, offering to pay 'if the Duke of York could go out'. And so, on 12 October 1922, Prince Albert arrived at the Romanian royal castle at Sinaia, where Queen Marie had succeeded in assembling a respectable official party including her sister, the Infanta Beatrice of Spain, known as 'Baby Bee', and her husband, the Infante Alfonso, Prince Paul of Serbia, Queen Marie's royal daughters, Elisabetha and Marie, the Duke of Genoa, brother of the Queen of Italy, and Marshal Foch. After a weary overnight train journey to remote Alba Julia in Transylvania, where the Coronation was to take place in a huge, purpose-built church, Prince Albert endured an even wearier day with ritual in the cathedral followed by a mock-medieval ceremony on a dais outside, stage-managed by the Queen. There was an *ersatz* quality about the whole affair; the crown was a Paris-made copy of a sixteenth-century original and the Queen's jewels were by Cartier. 'So very picturesque,' was the Prince's comment as he took his leave of his cousin at the end of two further days of wearisome celebration in Bucharest.

Allowing for the hyperbole frequently indulged in by diplomats making official reports on the performance of members of the royal family, Sir Herbert Dering's despatches from Bucharest to Lord Curzon made it clear that Prince Albert had played his role in the tedious Ruritanian charade extremely well. The reports of HM Minister in Bucharest were passed on to the King, who, apparently, remained unimpressed, so much so that Stamfordham ventured to take him to task for it through the easier medium of Queen Mary:

I venture to trouble Your Majesty with this letter in case you may not realise what an unqualified success the Duke of York was in Rumania. I happened to be in the King's room when His Majesty was talking on this subject to Your Majesty. *I* had been talking to Colonel Waterhouse [Prince Albert's Private Secretary] . . . and I felt that His Majesty's praise was quite inadequate.

For Colonel Waterhouse said he could not exaggerate how admirably in every way His Royal Highness had done – and that when he got away 'on his own' he was a different being and never failing to 'rise to the occasion', and proved himself to be far away the most important of the foreign visitors at the Coronation.

The King was once again as negative and critical in his attitudes towards his male children in their young manhood as he had been when they were in the schoolroom. The 'inadequate' response which he accorded to Prince Albert's successful visit to Romania contrasted strangely with his 'warm praise' widely reported in the press when, in September 1919, the Prince shot a 'Royal' stag weighing twenty-three stone, the largest killed at Balmoral for thirteen years. The King seemed to take a positive pleasure in thwarting the Princes' social plans about which he always seemed to be uncannily well informed. Intelligence reports about their movements would reach him from various sources, of which the most malicious were Princess Victoria, his favourite sister, and Sister Agnes Keyser, his father's confidante, founder of the King Edward VII Hospital for Officers, whose house King Edward used to use for assignations with Mrs Keppel. These ladies, both spinsters, would feed the King's anxieties with disquieting gossip, no difficult task for, as Prince Albert later told his father's biographer, King George was extraordinarily anxious about the possibility of his sons getting mixed up with 'bad women' and harried them unmercifully until they were married. Another reason for the King's repressive attitude towards his sons' social lives was his absolute detestation of the twentieth century and his fanatical devotion to the past. He hated everything about the post-war world, a long list which included Soviet Russia, cocktails, jazz, and the habit of going away for weekends, but which would have been headed by the new young woman with her short skirts, bobbed hair and painted nails.

Buckingham Palace, where Prince Albert lived when he was in London, which he was most of the time after leaving Cambridge in the summer of 1920, was like a time capsule in which the ageing King and Queen lived an unvarying dignified routine surrounded by courtiers, who, even if not actually elderly themselves, were mentally adjusted to the rhythm of another age. It was a dull place for a young man, as Queen Mary's biographer put it:

The comparative seclusion in which King George V and Queen Mary were living in the nineteen-twenties contrasted strangely with the contemporaneous revival of social life in London and with the wild jazzy tone of that post-war decade. An absolute quiet reigned within Buckingham Palace, which to young members of the family seemed not at all unlike that royal court of the Perrault fairy-tale under the spell of Carabosse. They became restive, and seized upon or manufactured opportunities to avoid family evenings which ended at ten or ten-thirty, and during which the King would interrogate one or other of them as to what he had been doing latterly and why he had been doing it....[17]

The unvarying routine of Court life, and the dead weight of tradition for tradition's sake which accompanied it, began to pall on Prince Albert. He felt that his parents should go out more into public life and accustom themselves to the modern world, writing to the Prince of Wales in February 1922, on the occasion of their sister's marriage, that he hoped it might jolt them into Society. 'I feel that they can't possibly stay in & dine together every night of their lives', he wrote, '& I don't see what they are going to do otherwise, except ask people here or go out themselves....'[18] Blinkered, opinionated and, it must be said, selfish as he had become, King George had, however, no intention of changing his ways. He was, none the less, surprised that his sons spent as little time at

Balmoral as they could, and when he asked J.H. Thomas, a former railwayman and his favourite Labour minister, why this should be so, he received a straight answer: 'It's a dull 'ouse, Sir, a bloody dull 'ouse.' Considering that among the regular house guests every year there were Sister Agnes Keyser and the Archbishop of Canterbury, Dr Cosmo Lang, that no card games were ever played or cocktails drunk, and that house traditions were those laid down by Queen Victoria, it was hardly surprising that the Princes should have found it dull. The Sergeant Footman, as the head butler was called, always served lunch and dinner dressed in shepherd's plaid, for no better reason than that his predecessors in the Prince Consort's day had often been required to stand in for the Prince while Landseer had been painting the royal portrait.

Even at Windsor during Ascot week, when the King and Queen traditionally held a house-party to attend the races, the entertainment was as measured and formal as a courtly minuet. The annual banquet in the Waterloo Room followed ground rules laid down at least a century before, the forks on the table laid face downwards, a custom dating from the days when the lace ruffles on the male guests' cuffs might otherwise have caught in the prongs. The surroundings were sumptuous, the tables loaded with magnificent gold or silver plate, but as entertainment the evenings lacked any spark of gaiety, as Prince Albert complained to Lady Airlie, during one such evening:

No new blood is ever introduced, and as the members of the party grow older every year there's no spring in it, and no originality in the talk – nothing but a dreary acquiescence in the order of the day. No one has the exciting feeling that if they shine they will be asked again next summer – they know they will be automatically, as long as they are alive. Traditionalism is all very well, but too much of it leads to dry rot.[19]

After he returned from Cambridge in the summer of 1920, Prince Albert was the son who spent most time at home. From August 1919, when the Prince of Wales left for the first of his world tours, this time to Canada and the United States, until the end of the decade, he was almost constantly overseas, and had, in any case, from July 1919 set up his own independent Household in York House, St James's Palace. Prince Henry had joined a cavalry regiment at Aldershot, while Prince George, after leaving Dartmouth, went on a training cruise and then, reluctantly, into the Navy. Prince John, who had been living in seclusion at Wolferton, had died suddenly after an epileptic fit on 18 January 1919, while Prince Albert was still in France. Prince Albert did not return to England for the funeral at Sandringham later that month; it is unlikely that his brother's death meant a great deal to him and it was generally regarded as a merciful release by his family since the wretched Prince John had suffered increasingly from epilepsy since the age of four.

Fortunately for Prince Albert, Princess Mary played the part of principal companion to her parents, the classic role of the only daughter of the house, just as her aunt, Princess Victoria, was the sole companion of her mother, Queen Alexandra. It was an invisible bondage from which the only escape was marriage, and Princess Mary's brothers, who doted on her, became increasingly worried that such an outcome was growing unlikely. Princess Mary lived in complete subjection to her parents, her life one dreary round of public duties with her mother or on her own, inspecting Girl Guides and attending charity bazaars, or of family rituals, such as luncheon at Marlborough House to mark Queen Alexandra's birthday or wedding anniversary. The Prince of Wales had confided to Lady Airlie in 1919:

I don't feel that she is happy but she never complains. The trouble is that she is far too unselfish and conscientious. That's why she was so overworked at her lessons. When my brothers and I wanted her to play tennis she used to refuse because she had her French translation to do, or she hadn't read *The Times* for the day. Is that normal for a girl?

On one occasion when Prince Albert wanted her to make up a four at tennis with Louis Greig and his equerry, James Stuart, Princess Mary refused because she would not have time to change her tennis shoes before having tea with her parents, explaining that her father would never excuse her. On another occasion when she came down in a fashionable sleeveless evening dress, the King roared at her and forced her to go upstairs and change into an old-fashioned one with sleeves. During the war she had trained and worked as a VAD but afterwards, when her contemporaries were having fun, the Princess was allowed very little. At a *thé dansant* when asked to dance she had replied with repressive royalty, "We don't reverse. . . .'

Prince Albert was, therefore, delighted when she became engaged in November 1921 to Viscount Lascelles; he spontaneously stood up at dinner in the great dining-room at Belvoir Castle, where he was staying, to propose his sister's health, but, as so often, his stutter let him down and there was an embarrassing pause as the large house-party waited for him to get the words out.[20] Princess Mary was twenty-four, her prospective bridegroom nearly forty, but, although unkind gossips said that Lascelles had proposed to the Princess to win a bet in his club, they were genuinely attached to each other and well suited, both of them being emotionally undemonstrative, deeply traditional and fond of horses. Lascelles, a Grenadier Guards officer during the war, an impeccable dandy in manner and a collector of considerable taste, was not the Hanoverian royal prince Queen Mary had dreamed of, but in many ways he was a suitable husband for the Princess. He was extremely rich, having inherited a fortune from his great-uncle, Lord Clanricarde, and in 1929 was to inherit an earldom and a stately home, Harewood House, in Yorkshire. He was, like his brother-in-law, Prince Albert, a leading freemason and a devotee of *petit point*.

Princess Mary's marriage in February 1922 left Prince Albert as the only occupant of the upper-floor rooms overlooking the Mall which had been designated for the 'children'. He was by now anxious to escape from the Palace embrace and had already decided on the road he wanted to take. He needed, as his Private Secretary, Colonel Waterhouse, had told Stamfordham, to be 'on his own', away from the dominating presence of his father, and still more to establish his own personality in counterpoint to his publicly idolized elder brother, now regularly referred to in the press as 'Prince Charming'. He had been working away, quietly and conscientiously at his public duties and trying, with the help of an Italian speech therapist, to conquer his stammer. Lord Crawford drew a sympathetic portrait of the Prince at twenty-four fulfilling a public engagement at the Civil Service Athletic Club:

... the Duke of York ... attended to distribute the prizes. I thought the whole thing very fatiguing. The Duke thought so too but showed admirable endurance and was delightful to everybody and got an excellent reception when making a little speech at the end of the proceedings. He is an amusing youth – more so I think than his brother, though much less of a personality. He has a really bad stammer but by dint of careful training he has almost mastered this infirmity – and apart from halting pauses between his words, he gets along much better than the average of his contemporaries.[21]

Instinctively Prince Albert was drawn towards women to provide the reassurance and appreciation so notably lacking at home. According to James Stuart, who became his equerry in 1920, the Prince had no close male friends of his own age, his closest friend being Louis Greig, who was fifteen years older than he was, while the friends he corresponded with included Bryan Godfrey-Faussett, who was almost the same age as his father, and Campbell Tait, his senior by several years. This was partly due to his isolated upbringing and to the inevitably distancing factor of being royal; it was noted of the Prince of Wales, too, that he had no real male friend except, perhaps, for Major Edward 'Fruity' Metcalfe, a dashing Indian cavalry officer who joined his staff in 1921. At this stage of their lives, in fact, the two brothers were close friends and often together when the elder Prince was in England. It may, indeed, have been the Prince of Wales who put the idea behind Prince Albert's first relationship into his brother's mind.

Phyllis Monkman was a star of the London theatrical world of the 1920s. Like so many troupers of the time, she was born, on 8 January 1892, into a family connected with the stage: her father, Jack Harrison, was a well-known theatrical costumier who founded the Eccentric Club. She studied dancing under Madame Sismondi and made her first appearance as a dancer at the age of twelve at the Prince of Wales's Theatre in *Lady Madcap*, with, among others, Lord Esher's future daughter-in-law, Zena Dare. Before she was twenty she had appeared in a series of shows with stars like Gladys Cooper and Gertie Millar. During most of the war years she had been principal dancer at the Alhambra and when that contract ended she went as leading lady to the Comedy Theatre, working for the impresario André Charlot, with, among her leading men, Jack Hulbert and Jack Buchanan. Phyllis Monkman had personality and physical grace rather than beauty, apart from her much-admired legs. 'Looks have never been my strong suit,' she was to scrawl with characteristic honesty across a typescript biography of her stage career. Petite, with a pocket-Venus figure, a bubbling sense of humour and a character which made and kept her life-long friends, such as Noël Coward and Ivor Novello, as well as a succession of admirers, she was exactly the type of woman to appeal to the Prince. In 1919 she was starring with Jack Buchanan in *Tails Up* at the Comedy when, according to one version of her story, Greig came to her dressing-room to tell her that Prince Albert wanted to meet her and would like her to dine with him, which she apparently later did, meeting the Prince in rooms at Half Moon Street. More than that she would not say and no more is known of this romance, beyond rumours in the social–theatrical world of annual presents of jewellery on her birthday and the fact that among her effects when she died, aged eighty-four, on 2 December 1976, was a small scuffed leather wallet with a flap purpose-made to hold one photograph and stiff enough to stand on its own like a miniature frame. Inside it was a portrait of Prince Albert in a dark blue peaked cap with wings, soft shirt collar pinned behind a dark blue tie, the lapels of his Service greatcoat just visible.

Prince Albert was also, briefly, attracted to another bright, confident woman, Lady Maureen Vane-Tempest-Stewart, daughter of the 7th Marquess of Londonderry and his wife, the formidable hostess, Edith, always known as 'Circe'. Lady Maureen's father, 'Charlie' Londonderry, was a millionaire Anglo–Irish aristocrat, a descendant of Britain's great Foreign Secretary, Lord Castlereagh. Londonderry was an exceptionally proud and handsome man with great estates in England and Northern Ireland and valuable mining interests in County Durham. He also had political ambitions and an interest in flying, being Air Minister in several Conservative governments. His wife was the greatest political hostess in London, a patroness of writers and friend of Shaw and Yeats; the first Labour Prime Minister, Ramsay MacDonald, fell in love with her and some people attributed his political isolation from his own party to the taste for royal and aristocratic society to which Circe Londonderry had introduced him. The Londonderrys were on friendly terms with the royal family, Princess Helena Victoria, the King's cousin, being a founder member of Circe's Ark Club at Londonderry House, to which most notable political figures belonged. Apart from the Ark Club and the grand soirées, Lady Londonderry gave Wednesday dances for her children and it may well have been at one of these that Prince Albert fell for Lady Maureen. His interest was serious enough for Lady Londonderry later to tell Harold Nicolson that her daughter might have been Queen of England. Lady Maureen was beautiful and assertive, with an organizing talent which she inherited from her mother. She was not, for some reason, generally loved, but Prince Albert always showed a penchant for her, bringing the Queen to dine at her house when he was King and even forgiving her for inviting their arch *bête noire*, Lord Beaverbrook, at the same time. In 1920, however, Lady Maureen preferred Oliver Stanley, younger son of the 17th Earl of Derby (and younger brother of the Edward Stanley who married Portia Cadogan), becoming engaged to him in July 1920 and marrying him in November that year. By that time Prince Albert, too, was no longer interested: he had met the girl who was to change his life.

On 10 June 1920, Prince Albert accompanied his mother, sister and Prince Henry to a large dinner-party given by Lady Farquhar, whose husband was a great friend of the King's and reputedly a very rich man (although to everyone's astonishment, when he died three years later, he was discovered to be deeply in debt, and of lavish legacies he had bequeathed to the royal family they received not a penny). It was Derby Night, traditionally a date for celebration in London Society and, while the King gave his annual dinner at Buckingham Palace to the members of the Jockey Club, the Queen and the Princes dined at Lady Farquhar's house, 7 Grosvenor Square, before the ball which was to take place later in the evening. About sixty people sat down to dinner at three tables set with antique porcelain and decorated with sweet peas; afterwards several hundred people arrived for the ball. Among them, although unmentioned by the social columnists, was the nineteen-year-old Lady Elizabeth Bowes-Lyon.

It was not, apparently, the first time they had met; at a children's party given by Lady Leicester the five-year-old Lady Elizabeth, dressed in long blue-and-white dress and with a floppy bow in her hair, is said to have presented the ten-year-old Prince with a cherry off her cake. If this story is true then it was an early instance of the future Queen's famous ability to make friends with a charming gesture and a childish act of considerable self-sacrifice as well for she always had a sweet tooth. According to one account, Prince Albert first saw Elizabeth at the Farquhars' ball talking to James Stuart, went up to him and said, 'Who was that lovely girl you were talking to? Introduce me to her.'[22] Whatever the exact sequence of events, Lady Elizabeth's effect on her future husband was instant; he confessed to Lady Airlie three years later that he had fallen in love with her, although unconsciously, that evening.

Lady Elizabeth was small, about 5 foot 4 inches, with a dazzling complexion, vivid blue eyes in a heart-shaped face, a radiant smile and dark hair cut in an unfashionable fringe. Her clothes, too, were old-fashioned and could be described as picturesque rather than chic. Lady Airlie, a neighbour in Scotland who knew her well, wrote of her that 'she was very unlike the cocktail-drinking, chain-smoking girls who came to be regarded as typical of the nineteen-twenties', and what was more, she added, 'her radiant vitality and a blending of kindness and sincerity make her irresistible to men'.[23] Lord David Cecil, a childhood friend and Hertfordshire neighbour, recalled, many years later, Lady Elizabeth as a child: 'she had sweetness and a sense of fun; and a certain roguish quality. The personality which I see now was there already.'[24]

Lady Elizabeth was not only attractive, but she was also an aristocrat, with a family tree stretching back into the Middle Ages and royal descent, sharing with Prince Albert a common ancestor in King Robert the Bruce of Scotland. Born on 4 August 1900, Lady Elizabeth Angela Marguerite Bowes-Lyon was the ninth child and fourth daughter of the 14th Earl of Strathmore and Kinghorne,

Viscount Lyon and Baron Glamis, Tannadyce, Sidlaw and Strathdictie in Scotland; Baron Bowes of Streatlam Castle in the county of Durham, and Lundale in the county of York in the United Kingdom. Her family owned one of the largest and most beautiful castles in Scotland, Glamis, which was also the oldest inhabited building in the country, with the usual bloodstained Scottish history and uncommonly grisly array of ghosts, including the famous Monster, probably a misshapen child of the house kept locked away from public view.[25] They also possessed another more modest castle, Streatlam, in the north-east of England, an early eighteenth-century mansion, St Paul's, Walden Bury, in Hertfordshire, and an imposing town house in what was then the most aristocratic of all London squares, St James's. Her family had owned Glamis since the fourteenth century when, in 1370, Joan, daughter of King Robert II of Scotland, took as her second husband, Sir Robert Lyon, known as 'the White Lyone' on account of his blond hair, and brought with her the lands of Glamis with the quasi-royal title of Thane of Glamis, the right to maintain a private army and a private hangman. The Strathmores were also rich, though not excessively so, their wealth based, like the Londonderrys', on mining interests in County Durham brought to the family by an eighteenth-century heiress, Mary Eleanor Bowes, who married John Lyon, 9th Earl of Strathmore, in 1767, bringing with her 43,000 acres of land, £21,000 in rents, £600,000 in trust, coal mines and ironworks, a castle, Streatlam, and Gibside, an impressive part-Gothic, part-classical house by James Paine, and finally St Paul's, Walden Bury.

The Strathmores, although an undeniably 'grand' Scottish noble family, were neither courtiers nor socialites. Nor did they share the mystical awe with which many of their peers regarded the royal family. 'As far as I can see, some people have to be fed royalty like sea-lions fish,' Lady Strathmore was heard to remark. Lady Elizabeth's father, Claude George Bowes-Lyon, a handsome, heavily moustachioed figure, was a popular and conscientious landlord, an expert on forestry, with a high sense of duty and social responsibility – he was Lord Lieutenant of Angus for many years. He was also a keen and skilful shot and an above-average cricketer. Described as a 'quiet, courteous, religious man', he was of somewhat melancholy temperament. The males of the Bowes-Lyon family tended to follow the classic pattern: military service in a Scottish regiment, the Black Watch, their recreations shooting, fishing and cricket. Lady Elizabeth's mother, Lady Strathmore, herself came of an equally 'grand' though, compared with the Lyons' 600 years, perhaps slightly more 'nouveau' family, the Cavendish-Bentincks, the family of the Dukes of Portland, descended from the Dutch favourite of William of Orange. Born Nina-Cecilia Cavendish-Bentinck, she was the daughter of a clergyman who had been the heir to the fabulously rich 5th Duke of Portland, but who had unfortunately died before the Duke, thus leaving his daughters in a far less glittering position than they might otherwise have enjoyed.

Lady Strathmore provided an injection of sturdy Anglo-Saxon blood to the Bowes-Lyon's Celtic temperament. She was the key figure in the family and the strongest influence on her youngest daughter. As a clergyman's daughter she had strong religious principles; she was also artistic, a passionate gardener and a gifted pianist. Despite her castles, houses and possessions, she had very little regard for material considerations. Once, when a concerned visitor to St Paul's, Walden Bury, anxiously pointed out that water was pouring down a wall, she simply sighed, 'Oh dear, we'll have to move the sofa again.' Unlike her husband, she had a natural gaiety and sense of fun which Lady Elizabeth inherited in full measure. Another child remembered her as

always finding something fresh to interest her. Something new—not necessarily something prudent . . . buying a house . . . going to a sale . . . entering a fresh field. Mother retained this immense zest for living, this intense interest in everything going on—particularly to the people she loved—just as she kept her sense of gaiety, right to the end.[26]

Largely due to the atmosphere her mother created, Lady Elizabeth, unlike Prince Albert, had had an idyllic childhood. 'I have nothing but wonderfully happy memories of childhood days at home,' she wrote to her friend, Osbert Sitwell, when her father died six years later, 'fun, kindness, & a marvellous sense of security.'[27] She was the second youngest of a large family, the eldest of whom was already grown up by the time she was born; Patrick, Master of Glamis, was twenty, John, fourteen, Alexander, thirteen, Fergus, eleven, and Michael, seven. She had three elder sisters, Violet, who died before she was born, Mary and Rose. Elizabeth was born after a seven-year gap on 4 August 1900[28] and followed two years later by David, the last of the Strathmores' children. By the time she was four years old, her father had inherited the earldom and with it Glamis and the other family houses, so that Lady Elizabeth and her younger brother were brought up among ancestral splendours, moving between St Paul's, Walden Bury, their large London house in St James's Square and Glamis. Surrounded by ponies and pets of every description, spoiled by indulgent servants and, in Lady Elizabeth's case, cooks and still-room maids in particular, and with the comforting maternal presence of Cecilia Strathmore, Lady Elizabeth's childhood had been as different as could possibly be imagined from Prince Albert's regimented and restricted upbringing.

Lady Elizabeth was, therefore, exactly the type of woman to attract Prince Albert, both physically and in her sparkling, warm, confident personality, which was ideally suited to draw him out of his shyness. She was also mature for her age, with the maturity of those girls who were projected from the schoolroom into the adult world by their experience of the Great War. When the First World War broke out on 4 August 1914, her fourteenth birthday, four of her brothers had joined the army; Fergus was killed in the Battle of Loos the following year, while Michael, reported as 'believed dead' in 1917, was wounded and taken prisoner. Glamis itself was turned into a convalescent hospital for wounded soldiers; Elizabeth entertained the soldiers, playing the piano and singing to them, and was responsible for running the whole establishment in the summer of 1918 when her mother was seriously ill. The war had delayed her debut in Society so that this season of 1920 was her first as a debutante: she was officially to be presented to the King and Queen at the Palace of Holyrood in Edinburgh on 15 July. Prince Albert, stimulated by his interest in her, threw himself wholeheartedly for the first time into the social round, so much so that the Society columnists remarked on his presence at 'dinners and dances galore'. Among the parties he attended was the coming-out ball given by the Duchess of Buccleuch in July for her daughter, Lady Alice Scott, Prince Henry's future bride; Prince Henry and Prince Paul of Serbia were also there.

His pursuit of Lady Elizabeth, however, was not to be an easy one. She was soon one of the most popular debutantes of her year and surrounded by admirers. Her attractions were increased by the magical atmosphere of Glamis when the traditionally minded half of Society headed north from London for the shooting season beginning with the 'Glorious Twelfth'. Describing Glamis as 'a place where time stood still', Lord Gorell, one of Lady Elizabeth's admirers, confessed to her biographer, Lady Longford:

I was madly in love with her. Everything at Glamis was beautiful, perfect. Being there was like living in a van Dyck picture. Time, and the gossiping, junketing world, stood still. Nothing happened ... but the magic gripped us all. I fell *madly* in love. They all did.[29]

Prince Albert arrived at Glamis at the end of September for his first visit there, no doubt glad to escape from Balmoral, where the Archbishop of Canterbury and Sister Agnes Keyser were as usual among the guests. In fact, after a duty week at Cowes and Ryde with his parents early in August, the Prince had spent comparatively little time at Balmoral, preferring to stay in neighbouring Scottish castles shooting and attending parties which might include Lady Elizabeth. At the end of August he was at Drummond Castle with the Earl and Countess of Ancaster; he then went to Balmoral to see his brother, Prince George, who was briefly at home after a cruise in Scandinavian waters on the training ship *Téméraire* and was soon to continue to the Mediterranean. He was at the Braemar Gathering in mid-September with his parents and Princess Mary and then stayed with the Mackintosh of Mackintosh at Moy Hall for the Northern Meeting at Inverness, where he was to be guest of honour at two balls. Before the end of the month he was at Glamis, where Lady Elizabeth had asked a young party, including Princess Mary, who came over from Cortachy where she had been staying with Lady Airlie for one of her Girl Guide inspections at Dundee, accompanied by Ladies Airlie and Strathmore, and Helen Cecil, future wife of the King's Assistant Private Secretary, Alec Hardinge. 'Elizabeth is a perfect angel as usual,' Helen wrote to her mother on 15 September 1920. 'They have got the Duke of York coming here and Elizabeth specially asked me to stay and help with him though I think it is just politeness on her part and she can't want me really. . . .'[30]

History does not relate what happened on this first visit to Glamis, but there is no doubt Elizabeth and her romantic castle had their effect on the already susceptible Prince. By the winter even Queen Mary was well aware of her son's feelings. One afternoon, while out driving with Lady Airlie, she told her that Lloyd George had advised the King that the country would not tolerate a foreigner for the Prince of Wales and that the Duke of York should also look for a bride among the British aristocracy. 'I don't think Bertie will be sorry to hear that,' the Queen added. 'I have discovered that he is very much attracted to Lady Elizabeth Bowes-Lyon. He's always talking about her. She seems a charming girl but I don't know her very well. . . .' Lady Airlie replied that she had known her all her life 'and could say nothing but good of her'. It seems that the attraction had been mutual. Mabell Airlie went on:

Very soon after that the Duke and Lady Elizabeth started dropping in at my flat, on various pretexts, always separately but each talked of the other. She was frankly doubtful, uncertain of her feelings, and afraid of the public life which would lie ahead of her as the King's daughter-in-law. The Duke's humility was touching. He was deeply in love. . . .'[31]

It was, however, one thing to be in love with Elizabeth, quite another to get her to marry him. She was surrounded by men who were in love with her, including Prince Albert's equerry, the handsome James Stuart, two other Scots—the millionaire Christopher Glenconner and Archie Clark-Kerr, the same age as the Prince and already a promising diplomat—and George Gage, the heir to an aristocratic Sussex family, among others. The favoured candidate seems to have been James Stuart, at least so the tradition in his family goes. Stuart was a dashing young man two years younger than the Prince, with a background of Eton and the Royal Scots, with whom he had fought on the Somme and won an MC. Elizabeth's friends hold differing views. 'No, he was in love with her but she was not the least bit in love with him. If she had been she would have married him,' said one. 'Well he was certainly in love with her and perhaps she was just a little with him. He was awfully attractive. Everybody was in love with James Stuart,' said another. It is now impossible to know the truth; all that is certain is that whether or not he was his employer's rival in love, Stuart remained his equerry for another year—the visitors' book at Polesden Lacey shows him accompanying the Prince there for the weekend of 2–4 July the following summer. In 1922, perhaps to distance himself from an awkward situation, he went to Oklahoma to work in the oilfields, returning the following year to marry Lady Rachel Cavendish in the summer of 1923, just after the Prince's marriage to Lady Elizabeth. 'Stuart's romantic attachments were not very profound,' was the general opinion. 'If he did "behave well" by removing himself then that would have been the first time. . . .'[32] The tone of Stuart's memoirs is noticeably lukewarm when referring to his time as equerry with

Prince Albert: 'He was not an easy man to know or to handle, and I cannot pretend that I ever became a close friend.' This may have been due to a rankling male jealousy, but the two men were not at all the same type and did not get on.

Perhaps Mabell Airlie was right, Lady Elizabeth simply was not ready to give up her independence for the restricted life of the Court. In any case when Prince Albert proposed to her in the spring of 1921, she refused him. Lady Airlie and her friend, Lady Strathmore, were equally distressed by the Prince's discomfiture. 'The Duke looked so disconsolate,' Mabell wrote. 'I do hope he will find a nice wife who will make him happy.' Cecilia Strathmore wrote to her: 'I like him so much and he is a man who will be made or marred by his wife.' But Prince Albert was not interested in finding another 'nice wife', he wanted Elizabeth and, with the determination that had carried him through the difficulties of his life so far, he did not give up hope.

Prince Albert desperately wanted to marry, for his own reasons: he had met the right woman, it might well be said the only woman, he was in love with her and she was not indifferent to him; he wanted very much to get away from his family and to make his own life; and lastly, he was under a certain amount of pressure from his family to get married for the sake of the dynasty. Queen Mary had 'mentioned' the subject to him in the spring of 1920; the Prince of Wales was passionately in love with a married woman, Freda Dudley Ward, and, having been forbidden two years earlier by his father to marry the only suitable girl upon whom his fancy ever lighted, Lady Rosemary Leveson-Gower, was now showing no signs whatever of intending marriage. Indeed, the Prince and Freda Dudley Ward, like the rest of Prince Albert's family, were encouraging him to pursue his suit of Lady Elizabeth Bowes-Lyon. Moreover, weddings were in the air that spring. In February Helen Cecil married Alec Hardinge; among her bridesmaids dressed in blue tulle over silver tissue – the Cecil colours – was Lady Elizabeth. In April another friend, Mollie Lascelles, married the Earl of Dalkeith, Lady Alice Scott's elder brother and heir to the Duke of Buccleuch. After his proposal had been rejected that spring, Prince Albert and Lady Elizabeth remained on good terms and in September, accompanied by an inquisitive Queen Mary, he went over to Glamis, where Lady Elizabeth was acting as hostess during the illness of her mother. He spent a few days there, reporting to the Queen, 'It is delightful here & Elizabeth is very kind to me. . . .' Queen Mary, after her visit of inspection to Glamis, was, she told Mabell Airlie, 'more than ever convinced that this was "the one girl who could make Bertie happy". But', the Queen added, 'I shall say nothing to either of them. Mothers should never meddle in their children's love affairs.' Mabell Airlie, however, felt that she was in a better position to meddle and was to prove a useful go-between. 'Although the romance seemed at an end I continued to plead his cause from time to time,' she wrote, adding significantly, 'and Lady Elizabeth continued to visit me.'[33]

There were more weddings in 1922. Princess Mary married Viscount Lascelles in February; Lady Elizabeth was among her eight bridesmaids. In April the

engagement was announced between Lord Louis Mountbatten and Edwina Ashley, heiress grand-daughter of Edward VII's friend Sir Ernest Cassel. In June
there was the Serbian wedding which Prince Albert attended. Whether the
oppressive atmosphere of Buckingham Palace was beginning to weigh upon
him after his sister left, or whether the emotions aroused by the two weddings
had unsettled him, by midsummer of 1922, after his return from the Serbian
wedding, the Prince seems to have reached a crisis in his life.

On 25 July 1922 he was due to lay the cornerstone of a memorial to the
Dover Patrol at Dunkirk in the presence of French and British dignitaries. A
few days before, John Colin Campbell Davidson, a thirty-three-year-old Scot,
MP for Hemel Hempstead and Parliamentary Private Secretary to the Prime
Minister, Andrew Bonar Law, received a telephone call from Louis Greig,
mysteriously urging him to make a point of attending the ceremony on 25 July.
Davidson, therefore, took a place on the chartered ship carrying Members of
both Houses of Parliament from Harwich to Dunkirk for the ceremony, which
passed off without incident. Davidson was just about to board the ship to return
when he saw Greig running along the quayside, beckoning to him. Greig then
took him aboard the destroyer *Versatile,* which had brought the Prince to
Dunkirk, led him down to the wardroom and left the two men alone together.

Thirty years later, at the time of King George VI's death, Davidson set down
what he remembered of this curious interview, sending a copy to the Queen
Mother.

I had not been in the Duke's presence more than a few minutes before I realized that he
was not only worried but genuinely unhappy. He seemed to have reached a crisis in his
life, and wanted someone to whom he could unburden himself without reserve. He
dwelt upon the difficulties which surrounded a King's son in contrast with men like
myself who had always had greater freedom at school and university to make their own
friends and a wider circle to choose from. We discussed friendship, and the relative
value of brains and character, and all the sort of things that young men do talk about in
the abstract when in reality they are very much concerned in the concrete.

He told me that sometimes the discipline of the formality of the court proved
irksome, and I sensed that he was working up to something important. I felt moved
with a great desire to help him if I could, he was so simple, frank and forthcoming.

Then out it came. He declared that he was desperately in love, but that he was in
despair for it seemed quite certain that he had lost the only woman he would ever
marry. I told him that however black it looked he must not give up hope; that my
wife had refused me consistently before she finally said yes, and that like him, if she
persisted in her refusal, I would never have married anyone else.[34]

No one seems to know why the Prince should have chosen to unburden
himself to Davidson, although the Queen Mother confirmed that he had done
so. Davidson was on friendly terms with the Princes and he was certainly *persona
grata* with the royal family. The following year he was appointed Chancellor of
the Duchy of Lancaster, largely a political sinecure with responsibility for one
source of the king's income. He was a political insider and a confidant of

the Prime Minister although relatively young. It may be simply that the Prince
was seeking reassurance and disinterested advice from a man with a reputation
for sagacity and dexterity in confidential matters. Encouraged, perhaps, by his
conversation with Davidson at the end of July, Prince Albert doggedly pursued
his courtship. In September 1922 he was at Glamis again, in a party which
included the American diarist, politician and socialite, Henry 'Chips' Channon.
Over twenty years later when Elizabeth's father died, aged eighty-nine, Channon remembered that late summer at Glamis:

The then Duke of York, afterwards King, used to come into my bedroom in the
evening, and we would talk of the Glamis monster and the admittedly sinister atmosphere in the castle and of the other ghosts. . . . One rainy afternoon, we were sitting
about and I pretended that I could read cards, and I told Elizabeth Lyon's fortune and
predicted a great and glamorous royal future. She laughed, for it was obvious that the
Duke of York was much in love with her. As Queen she has several times reminded
me of it. I remember the pipers playing in the candlelit dining-room, and the whole
castle heavy with atmosphere, sinister, lugubrious, in spite of the gay young
party. . . .[35]

The Prince's obvious devotion and continuing passion was beginning to put
pressure on the normally carefree Lady Elizabeth. Her mother now noticed for
the first time that her daughter was 'really worried', saying 'I think she was torn
between her longing to make Bertie happy and her reluctance to take on the
responsibilities which this marriage must bring.'[36]

On Friday, 5 January 1923, the *Daily News* announced, 'Scottish Bride for
Prince of Wales Heir to the throne to wed Peer's daughter an Official Announcement imminent. . . . One of the closest friends of Princess Mary. . . .'
The strong hint was that this 'young Scottish lady of noble birth . . . daughter
of a well-known Scottish peer, who is owner of castles both north and south of
the Tweed,' could hardly have been anyone else than Elizabeth Bowes-Lyon. At
Firle in Sussex, where Lady Elizabeth was spending the weekend in a house-
party at the home of her admirer, George Gage, Channon noted that she was
not her usual happy self:

The evening papers have announced her engagement to the Prince of Wales. So we all
bowed and bobbed and teased her, calling her 'Ma'am': I am not sure that she enjoyed
it. It couldn't be true, but how delighted everyone would be! she certainly has something on her mind. . . . She is more gentle, lovely and exquisite than any woman
alive, but this evening I thought her unhappy and distraite. I longed to tell her I
would die for her, although I am not in love with her. Poor Gage is desperately fond
of her – in vain, but he is far too heavy, too Tudor and squirearchal for so rare and
patrician a creature as Elizabeth.[37]

Why should teasing on the subject of her supposed engagement to the Prince
of Wales have disturbed Elizabeth's normally sunny composure? Some people
have deduced that it was because she herself had hoped to marry the heir to the
throne and that this secret disappointment was one of the reasons for her

subsequent hostility to Wallis Simpson. It is still a rumour in some aristocratic circles, but notably among people at least a generation younger than her. If it really had been a probability at the time, Channon would certainly have had something more definite to say on the subject, than 'It couldn't be true. . . .' Channon, an extremely well-informed gossip, knowing that Prince Albert was in love with her and the Prince of Wales devoted to Freda Dudley Ward, knew it was the right rumour about the wrong prince.

Lady Elizabeth knew that this rumour of a royal engagement was yet another signal that she would soon have to come to a final decision whether or not to marry Prince Albert. It was not an easy decision to make. She was twenty-two years old, immensely popular, with a happy family and social life, and numbers of handsome, eligible young men in love with her. For a girl of her age and upbringing, marriage was her only destiny as a career was out of the question; again, with her particularly religious background, the possibility of divorce was not something which she envisaged. Still less would divorce provide a way of escape for someone marrying into the royal family. Lady Elizabeth had seen enough of the Court to understand what marrying into the royal family meant. Apart from the glamour associated with marriage to a royal prince, it offered little that she did not already have – beautiful houses, servants and no money worries. She would, as she well knew, be entering a cage, a large, well-furnished cage but a cage none the less, in which she would be deprived of absolute freedom of choice, and in which she would be observed, her every movement minutely watched whenever she was in public. Royalty watching as a sport was then in its infancy, but Lady Elizabeth knew that, however much royalty mixed with Society, it remained a race apart. As 'Kakoo' Granby, herself soon to be the Duchess of Rutland, put it, 'In those days there was much more of a barrier, they were much more enclosed and they'd never married commoners before.'[38]

On the other hand, the whole destiny of a woman like herself was shaped towards marriage. There is little doubt that she did love Prince Albert, not merely because he was good-looking, athletic and excelled in all the social sports, had a natural elegance and a sense of humour that matched her own, but also because he was very vulnerable, something which would naturally appeal to her. Although, superficially in comparison with his brother, people who did not know him well tended to dismiss him as dull and stupid, people like the Duke of Rutland who did know him well and could afford not to be snobs were less affected by his elder brother's overwhelming charm and thought that Prince Albert was 'a gentleman' where his brother was not. The Duke's daughter-in-law found him not shy when talking to friends; she liked his humour and a quality which she called 'a sweetness about him'. Lady Elizabeth, knowing him better than anyone, saw beyond the agonizing stammer, which still could overcome him, the steadfastness, real goodness and capacity to love, qualities which she thought, rightly, that she could bring out.

In January 1923, however, she still hesitated before committing herself to a life more rigid than she had ever known. Mabell Airlie, an indefatigable Cupid, determined on one last effort to persuade her and invited her to tea. She pointed out how she had given up a free, happy Irish girlhood to marry David Airlie to be subjected first to the Draconian rule of a mother-in-law, then to the dreary following the flag as a soldier's wife, which she had at first hated and then grown to love. This lecture, apparently, worked.

Prince Albert had made up his mind to make one last, and final, proposal. 'This is the last time I'm going to propose to her,' he told the Duchess of Devonshire. 'It's the third time and it's going to be the last.'[39] He had also told his parents of his intention. 'You'll be a lucky fellow if she accepts you,' said King George, who was already captivated. The weekend following the house-party at Firle, Prince Albert was at St Paul's, Walden Bury. On Saturday morning, 13 January, walking with Elizabeth in the wood, he proposed and was accepted. A telegram with a prearranged signal was sent to his anxious parents at Sandringham; it said, simply: 'All right. Bertie.' Two days later, on Monday 15 January, the King recorded in his diary: 'Bertie with Greig arrived after tea and informed us that he was engaged to Elizabeth Bowes-Lyon, to which we gladly gave our consent. I trust that they will be very happy.' 'We are delighted and he looks beaming,' Queen Mary wrote happily in hers. Lady Elizabeth, accompanied by her parents, arrived on 20 January for a formal visit to her new in-laws. 'Elizabeth is charming, so pretty & engaging and natural. Bertie is supremely happy,' an enchanted Queen Mary wrote. Only just over six months before, in August 1922, King George had written apprehensively to his wife that he 'dreaded' the idea of daughters-in-law. Six months later, after more prolonged exposure to his new daughter-in-law at Balmoral, he had totally surrendered: 'The better I know & the more I see of your dear little wife the more charming I think she is & everyone fell in love with her here,' he told his son.

Prince Albert could hardly bring himself to believe that he had achieved the one thing in life that he had set his heart on. Replying to Mabell Airlie's letter of congratulations, his language was ecstatic:

How can I thank you enough for your charming letter to me about the wonderful happening in my life which has come to pass, and my dream which has at last been realized.

It seems so marvellous to me to know that my darling Elizabeth will one day be my wife. We are both very, very happy and I am sure always will be. I owe so much to you and can only bless you for what you did.[40]

To him Elizabeth was, and always remained, as he wrote to his daughter Elizabeth on her wedding day a quarter of a century later, 'the most wonderful woman in the world'.

Prince Albert and Lady Elizabeth were married on 26 April 1923 in Westminster Abbey, the historic church in which they would one day be crowned. It was the first marriage of a royal prince to be celebrated there for 500 years and Lady Elizabeth was the first 'commoner' legitimately to marry into the royal family, but, apart from being conducted by two archbishops and having a heavy royal attendance, their wedding was virtually indistinguishable from any other similar Society occasion. The King had let it be known that he was 'anxious that the arrangements should be of as simple a character as possible and that no unnecessary expense shall be incurred'.

Prince Albert was in the new dress uniform of the Royal Air Force, the first royal bridegroom to wear the uniform of the new Service. Lady Elizabeth wore a dress of ivory-coloured chiffon moiré, embroidered with silver thread and pearls, with sleeves of specially woven Nottingham lace and a train of old *point de Flandres* lace lent by Queen Mary, a tulle veil and a simple orange blossom wreath. There were eight bridesmaids as specified by royal etiquette: Queen Mary's two nieces, Lady Mary and Lady May Cambridge, four friends of the bride, the first two of whom were later to become her ladies-in-waiting, Lady Mary Thynne, daughter of the Marquess and Marchioness of Bath, and Lady Katharine Hamilton, daughter of the Duke and Duchess of Abercorn, while the third, Miss Betty Cator, daughter of a Norfolk landowner and Sandringham neighbour, was to become her sister-in-law as the wife of Michael Bowes-Lyon; then there was the Hon. Diamond Hardinge, sister of Alec Hardinge, and the bride's two young nieces, Elizabeth Elphinstone and Cecilia Bowes-Lyon. The wedding was filmed but not broadcast, because the Archbishop of Canterbury feared that people might listen to it in public houses. The wedding breakfast at Buckingham Palace lasted for one and a half hours and featured classic royal banquet food christened by the royal chef, Gabriel Tschumi, with appropriate names: *Consommé à la Windsor, Suprême de Saumon Reine Mary, Côtelette d'Agneau Prince Albert, Chapons à la Strathmore* and Duchess Elizabeth strawberries. The wedding cake, donated by Prince Albert's friend and collaborator in the IWS, Sir Alexander Grant, was nine feet high and made to a design chosen by the couple on a visit to the McVitie & Price biscuit works in March. Prince Albert was determined that the IWS should be represented at his wedding and among the guests were thirty boys from IWS member firms; through the generosity of Sir Alexander slices of cake identical to the wedding cake were to be distributed to poor children in London and various cities throughout the United Kingdom.

The royal couple's 'known wishes' as far as wedding presents were concerned had been characteristically practical, bearing in mind the large white elephant of a house, the White Lodge, Richmond Park, which had been designated as their future home. They had asked for furniture and the Worshipful Company of Pattenmakers had responded with a tallboy in English oak with shelves and drawers loaded with rubber boots, shoes and galoshes; the Metropolitan Police had given a dinner service. The royal family had been practical in their own fashion, presenting the new Duchess of York with the kind of jewellery befitting her new royal role. The King gave her a suite consisting of tiara, necklace, brooch, ear-rings and hair ornaments of diamonds and Persian turquoises, plus an ermine cape, the Queen presented her new daughter-in-law with a sapphire and diamond necklace with matching bracelet, ring, brooches and pendant, while Queen Alexandra's present was a necklace of pearls and amethysts. Prince Albert gave his bride a diamond and pearl necklace with a matching pendant, while she gave him a platinum and pearl watch-chain. The Prince of Wales's present was characteristic, a fur wrap and 'a luxurious motor car'.

The wedding was the bride's first experience of the public ceremony which would attend the rest of her life. For both of them it was an ordeal demanded of them by their position; for the public it was an excuse for celebration and jollification in a dismal period. However, there was a faint suggestion of 'second best' hovering in the air. *The Times*, then the unquestioned voice of the Establishment, reminded everyone that a more important marriage remained to be settled: 'There is but one wedding to which [the public] look forward with still deeper interest – the wedding which will give a wife to the Heir to the Throne, and, in the course of nature, a future Queen to England and to the British peoples. . . .' Prince Albert was perfectly happy that it should be so. He had no desire to share his brother's limelight. He had married to make his own, essentially private, life with his wife.

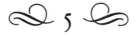

THE YORKS

'His Royal Highness has touched people profoundly by his youth, his simplicity and natural bearing, while the Duchess has left us with the responsibility of having a continent in love with her. The visit has done untold good. . . .'

Sir Tom Bridges, Governor of South Australia, to King George V,

1927

Even on his honeymoon, Prince Albert thought of his parents, now quite alone. 'I do hope you will not miss me very much,' he wrote to his mother, 'though I believe you will as I have stayed with you so much longer really than the brothers.' He received in return an ostensibly charming letter from his father, in which King George's feelings and preoccupations were transparent. Bertie, the King wrote, as if still surprised that his son had managed to pull off such a coup, was indeed a lucky man to have such a charming and delightful wife as Elizabeth. He hoped that they would be 'as happy as Mama & I are after you have been married for 30 years, I can't wish you more. . . . I miss you very much [he continued] & regret your having left us, but now you will have your own home which I hope will be as happy as the one you left.' However, the King could not refrain from revealing his underlying preoccupation, his relations with his eldest son:

You have always been so sensible & easy to work with & you have always been ready to listen to any advice & to agree with my opinions about people & things, that I feel we have always got on very well together (very different to dear David . . .).

The Prince might well have reflected on reading this that he had had little alternative but to listen to his father. It had left its scars; ten years later, discussing the tyrannical behaviour of Sir George Sitwell with his son Osbert, it touched a chord: 'He sounds just like my father!' he told Sitwell; 'Won't listen to a word you say. Always knows better. There's no doing anything with them when they're like that!'[1] Never one to shower his sons with praise, King George grudgingly granted that Prince Albert had done well in his efforts to shore up the family firm. 'By your quiet useful work you have endeared yourself to the people,' he wrote, 'as shown on Thursday by the splendid reception they gave you.' Confidently and, as it turned out, accurately, he predicted their joint future: 'I am quite certain that Elizabeth will be a splendid partner in your work and share with you & help you in all you have to do.'

The Yorks spent the first part of their honeymoon at Polesden Lacey, an opulent, slightly vulgar mansion in the suburban Surrey countryside within easy reach of London. The choice of Polesden may not have been so much theirs as the insistent offering of its owner, Mrs Ronald Greville, whose feelings about royalty were very different from Lady Strathmore's. For her the appetizing qualities of social morsels were in exact ascending proportion to their social rank; royalty was the ultimate delicacy, to be lured along her red carpets and gulped up with avidity at the end. Cecil Beaton called her 'a galumphing, greedy, snobbish old toad who watered at her chops at the sight of royalty'.[2] Short, plump and exceedingly rich, 'Maggie' Greville was a woman of strong will and character who loved the trappings of wealth and power and knew how to use them. Her money came from her father, a self-made brewer, William McEwan, who consoled himself after the death of his first wife with a woman variously described as his housekeeper, his cook and the wife of his day-porter. Maggie was their daughter. Her money bought her a handsome, well-born husband, the Hon. Ronald Greville, and with him the entrée into royal society since he was an intimate of Edward VII and also of the Hon. George Keppel, husband of King Edward's mistress, Alice. Thoroughly materialistic, she could be wittily and cruelly malicious. Harold Nicolson called her 'a fat slug filled with venom', while Lady Leslie said she would sooner have an open sewer flowing through her drawing-room. Her god-daughter, Sonia Keppel, however, asserted that she had a kind heart; indeed, her servants loved her and she treated them with an indulgence that she did not extend to her guests, although her two butlers, Boles and Bacon, were notorious for their drunken exploits. On one occasion when Austen Chamberlain and his daughter were dining, Mrs Greville, noticing that one of the pair of butlers was more than usually intoxicated, scribbled a note on the back of a place card, 'You're drunk. Leave the room at once,' and handed it to him. The butler placed the note on a salver and presented it to Chamberlain, who put on his eye-glass, studied it and sat in stupefied silence for the rest of the meal.[3]

Prince Albert knew the house well, having often spent a 'Saturday to Monday' there. He had first visited it in 1919 with his father, mother and Princess Mary, and in 1920 had been one of a house-party of nineteen including the Maharajah of Kapurthala, Edwina Ashley, Lord Londonderry, Lord Derby's daughter, Lady Victoria Bullock, and her husband Malcolm, the Duke of Argyll, the Hon. Victoria Cadogan and Grace Vanderbilt. The following July the grandees had included the Duke of Alba and the millionaire Sir Harold Wernher. Polesden Lacey was neither grand nor historic in the sense that the other great houses where the Prince stayed were. Although it had originally belonged to Richard Brinsley Sheridan, it had been rebuilt in 1821 to the design of Thomas Cubitt, the developer of Belgravia, and its interior substantially remodelled in 1906 by

Mewes and Davis, the architects of the London Ritz. Embellished with panelling from demolished English churches and Italian palaces, and furnished with antiques bought from London dealers, its atmosphere, rather like Sandringham, was reminiscent of an extremely luxurious Edwardian hotel.

The Yorks were to be frequent guests of Mrs Greville's when she entertained lavishly both at Polesden Lacey and at her London house, 16 Charles Street, decorated with eighteen-carat gold scroll work and superb French furniture. Osbert Sitwell, a frequent guest and one of the few intellectuals whom Mrs Greville invited across her doorstep, said of both her houses that they possessed an unobtrusive luxury of life and background that he had never encountered elsewhere. The guests tended to be as solid as the furniture: English and European royalty, maharajahs, the Aga Khan, ancient English names, great and established wealth, and successful politicians. There were no Bohemians and the Americans would have names like Astor or Vanderbilt: it was a setting in which Prince Albert felt at home, with people whom he met at Court or in the great London houses. The Yorks liked Mrs Greville, as royalty tend to like people who are rich enough to entertain them well and without fuss, secure enough (despite private reverence) to remain themselves and not be intimidated, and bright enough to amuse them. Prince Albert, like many shy people, liked forceful characters and liked to be amused. 'I shall miss her very much,' Elizabeth wrote to Osbert Sitwell on Mrs Greville's death in September 1942, '. . . she was so shrewd, so kind and so amusingly *un*kind, so sharp, such fun, so naughty . . . altogether a real person, a character, utterly Mrs Ronald Greville and no tinge of anything alien.'[4] Maggie Greville left £1½ million; all her jewellery, including a diamond necklace that had belonged to Marie Antoinette and a famous set of rubies, she left 'with my loving thoughts' to Elizabeth, then Queen, and £20,000 to Princess Margaret.

One name never appeared on Mrs Greville's guest list, that of the Prince of Wales. He did not like her and thought her parties boring, representing as they did the traditional side of life from which he was constantly trying to escape. He would have agreed with the elegant aesthete, Kenneth Clark, in his summing-up of the Greville guest-list, 'stuffy members of the government and their mem-sahib wives, ambassadors and royalty'. He preferred the brighter society surrounding Mrs Greville's detested rival as a hostess, Lady Cunard. Emerald Cunard, born Maud Burke in San Francisco in 1872, had married in 1895 the shipping magnate, Sir Bache Cunard, twenty years her senior, and moved to England. Tiny and birdlike, with a darting wit and a gift for a jewelled phrase, Emerald was highly intelligent and well-read and fitted perfectly into cultivated London Society. George Moore adored her and she had been the mistress since 1911 of Sir Thomas Beecham (Mrs Greville liked to refer to Emerald as 'the Lollipop', Beecham's name for his favourite pieces of light music). This was enough to earn her the disapproval of Queen Mary, as Chips Channon wrote: 'The Court always frowned on so brilliant a salon: indeed Emerald's only failures were the two Queens [Queen Mary and, later, Queen Elizabeth] and Lady Astor and Lady Derby.' Lady Astor disliked what she regarded as social-climbing Americans less blue-blooded than herself, while Lady Derby, wife of 'the King of Lancashire', was a representative of the traditionally minded upper echelons of English Society, who disliked Americans and regarded wit and brilliance as something alien and untrustworthy. Emerald was a mistress of quick repartee; when Somerset Maugham refused to come to one of her evening parties because 'I have to keep my youth,' she retorted, 'Then bring him with you.' When she died she was bitterly mourned by people like Nancy Mitford and Diana Cooper, who wrote to Channon, 'our beloved, dazzling, bright, fantastic Emerald, dying. I cannot believe it'.[5] Characteristically, her last words were to order champagne for her doctor and her maid. Almost her only quality in common with Mrs Greville was a weakness for royalty – in her case the Prince of Wales – and she, more than any of the other hostesses, was to promote – one might even say exploit – his relationship with Mrs Simpson.

The Yorks lived a low-profile social life. They were not 'smart' in the sense that the Prince of Wales's friends were, the people who danced every night to Ambrose at the Embassy Club, where the Prince had his own table and Thursdays were like a glamorous private party. Indeed, they hardly rated a mention in the diaries of the time kept by Chips Channon, Harold Nicolson, Robert Bruce Lockhart, Victor Cazalet and others. 'They were rather a prim and proper set compared with the one I was in,' a member of the Prince of Wales's circle remembered. 'Her vocation was to look after him and be a good wife and then she had her children ... nightclubs didn't attract her. They went and stayed with a lot of people in the country and of course he loved shooting. . . .' Where the Prince of Wales and his friends went ski-ing in Kitzbühel and St Moritz in winter, spent summers at Biarritz or, increasingly, in the South of France, and sporting and gambling weekends at Deauville, the Yorks never went abroad except on duty. Prince Albert preferred hunting in the shires, where he rented houses in Northamptonshire for the winter season, Old House, Guilsborough, Thornby Grange and Naseby Hall, where he kept hunters and usually hunted with the Pytchley. There were endless shooting weekends with friends and late summer grouse-shooting and stalking in Scotland. Elizabeth preferred fishing; despite coming from a family of expert shots, she sometimes found shooting days trying.

They were not fast and fashionable, but they enjoyed Society and liked to be amused. Osbert Sitwell wrote of Prince Albert that he had 'a delightful gaiety about him and threw himself into what was going on'. Elizabeth was a natural actress and mimic and their weekend parties often involved dressing-up and clowning around; one photograph, dating from the days when they still saw a good deal of the Prince of Wales, shows Elizabeth as Popeye with battered hat and pipe. Among their friends were couples like Lord and Lady Plunket. Terence Plunket was a handsome, amusing, Anglo–Irish aristocrat, an excellent raconteur and a talented portraitist, who executed caricatures of a professional standard of his friends. Like Prince Albert he was an excellent tennis player and, like

Elizabeth, a keen fisherman. His wife Dorothé was half-American, the daughter of 'Diamond Joe' Lewis, who had made a fortune in South Africa with 'Solly Joel' and lost most of it, and his American actress wife Fannie Ward, who was Cecil B. de Mille's leading lady and played principal boy on the stage for the last time at the age of fifty-five. Dorothé herself was a beauty, petite and blonde, with large violet-blue eyes arched with dark eyebrows. She had been married to Jack Barnato, a First World War air ace, son of one of 'Diamond Joe's' fellow South African adventurers, 'Babe' Barnato. Jack Barnato had married Dorothé when she was twenty and died a year later of influenza in 1918 leaving her £900,000. Dorothé was a gifted dancer, who often danced for charity at her friends' balls, and regularly featured in Society columns. The Plunkets went everywhere: they were very often with the Yorks at London parties and country house weekends. They were on their way to a huge party to be given for them by William Randolph Hearst in California in the spring of 1938 when they were both killed in a plane crash, leaving three small sons. 'We both felt so sad over the ghastly tragedy of Dorothé and Teddy, as you know what intimate friends of ours they had been for many years,' Elizabeth wrote to Circe Londonderry. 'They both gave so much happiness to so many people of all kinds and sorts; their going does leave a terrible blank.... Those dear little boys make one's heart *ache*.'[6] The youngest boy, Shaun, was her godson; years later the eldest, Patrick, became equerry to George VI and subsequently to his daughter.

The Yorks were happy in each other's company. Duff Cooper saw them at the theatre just before Christmas 1926, describing them to his wife, Lady Diana, as 'such a sweet little couple and so fond of one another. They reminded me of us, sitting together in the box having private jokes, and in the interval they slipped out, and I found them standing together in a dark corner of the passage talking happily as we might....' Elizabeth and Duff later became friends; witty and well-read, he was exactly the kind of man she liked. She secretly broke the rules against royalty indulging in partisan politics to support him in the St George's by-election in March 1931 against the combined might of the anti-Baldwin, pro-Imperial Preference Press Lords Rothermere and Beaverbrook, by sending up a busload of her servants from the country to vote for him. Duff Cooper would send her copies of his biographies of Haig and Talleyrand and of books of the moment which might interest her, for Elizabeth, unlike her husband, was a great reader. Osbert Sitwell was another writer who used to send her books. '... I was amazed at the number of modern books she had found time to read in her crowded existence,' he wrote; '... she is highly appreciative of the arts and literature.'[7] Prince Albert did not share his wife's literary and artistic tastes. Like the Prince of Wales he was not much interested in books beyond the 'shockers' published by the Crime Club to which even the cultivated Prime Minister, Stanley Baldwin, was addicted. He was a slow reader; the only book his staff ever heard him discuss was *The Empty Tomb and the Risen Lord*, a serious reconstruction of the Resurrection story by the Rev. C.C. Dobson published in 1923.

The Yorks' determination to enjoy life was somewhat hampered by the King and Queen's choice of their first home – White Lodge in Richmond Park. It was also relatively unmodernized and not very much changed since the birth there of the Prince of Wales in June 1894. For Queen Mary it held charms as the house of her childhood, but for a young couple who liked dancing, the theatre and seeing their friends, it was far from being an ideal home. It was a very large house, with two Palladian fronts built by Queen Caroline, wife of George II, curved wings and a positive hamlet of outhousing. The handsome architecture, however, was not enough to compensate for the failure of the Ministry of Works, supervised from afar by Queen Mary, to modernize it. When the subsequent tenants, Lord and Lady Lee of Fareham, saw it for the first time they were horrified:

We were greatly surprised, on exploring White Lodge, to discover under what uncomfortable and even unsafe conditions ... the Duke and Duchess of York had been living. There was practically no central heating and the rooms in winter were desperately cold; the electric light was inadequate and unsafely installed; the drains were of uncertain date and apparently without system, and there was nothing to show how they were planned or where they went to. Inside the house conditions were equally primitive, and the only downstairs lavatory, which must have been installed at least a hundred years ago, was located *in* the seat of what is now the Secretary's office![8]

There were other drawbacks. After just over one year at White Lodge, the Yorks told Fritz Ponsonby that they found it 'an impossible residence', expensive to run and hemmed in by holidaymakers and sightseers in summer. Ponsonby wrote on their behalf to Sir Lionel Earle at the Ministry of Works on 10 November 1924:

They tell me that it costs them £11,000 a year to live there and that the greater portion of their income is spent in paying for quite unnecessary servants. Whereas in former days Richmond Park was practically in the country, it has been brought very near London by char a bancs and motor cars; the result is that on Saturdays and Sundays the crowd round the house is so great that they hardly dare put their noses outside, and on weekdays there is also a certain number of people always waiting to see them come out and go in, and therefore all privacy has ceased to exist ... the Duke and Duchess of York say that they really cannot go on living there and they have asked me to see whether I cannot obtain for them some residence in London.[9]

'I am amazed to find that the Duke and Duchess of York find they cannot live at White Lodge under £11,000 a year. I can understand it costing them seven, but eleven strikes me as very extravagant,' Earle wrote suspiciously the next day to Sir Warren Fisher at the Treasury, attributing the Yorks' dissatisfaction to another cause. 'I knew from the very start, when White Lodge was allotted to them, that this young couple would never be satisfied and happy there. They are both passionately fond of dancing, and naturally wish to come to London practically every day for this purpose.'[10] There was, it appears, a London housing shortage as far as the younger members of the royal family were concerned, mainly due to the available large houses being underoccupied by elderly royals. Prince Marie Louise and Princess Helena Victoria, grand-daughters of Queen Victoria, occupied Schomburg House, Pall Mall, behind Marlborough House, which was, of course, Queen Alexandra's; Queen Victoria's surviving son, the Duke of Connaught, lived at Clarence House, while two houses at Kensington Palace were taken by her surviving daughters, the Princesses Beatrice and Louise. Earle made discreet enquiries as to whether some tenants of Crown properties might be persuaded not to renew their leases, but without success. By the end of August 1925, Prince Albert, beginning to lose patience, sent Captain Basil Brooke, Comptroller of his Household, to see Earle and press him urgently to do something, but the principal problem was that White Lodge was a white elephant which nobody wanted; the King seems not to have been prepared to provide them with a London house, nor, out of public funds, was the Treasury. Finally in September 1926, nearly two years after the subject was first raised, a happy conclusion was arrived at by which 145 Piccadilly was leased for the Yorks, in return for the leasing of White Lodge to Lord Lee, who saw it as a suitable home for his valued art collection. Even then special legislation was necessary and an altercation arose between Prince Albert and his father on the necessity for an early vacation of White Lodge in favour of Lord Lee. Lee required the house by Lady Day (25 March) 1927; the Yorks, who were due to depart for an official visit to Australia and New Zealand that year, preferred not to move in to 145 Piccadilly until their return. 'The King, however, has told them that they must do the best they can to turn out their things when Lord Lee wishes to have possession of the house,' Ponsonby wrote to Earle from Balmoral on 27 September 1926. The Prince was digging in his toes, as a weary Ponsonby wrote again to Earle from Sandringham on 15 October:

The Duke of York seems to think that he should have official intimation of the date by which he is expected to turn out of White Lodge. He has made very heavy weather over this change and dislikes very much the idea of its taking place while he is in Australia, but it has been pointed out to him that it will be really more convenient to have the change made while he is away, because 145 Piccadilly can be got ready for him by the time he gets back. I have arranged for his personal knick-knacks, his clothes and also all the Duchess' dresses, etc., to be locked up in Buckingham Palace, whilst the servants are to go on board wages. The Queen has promised to help in any way she can. . . .'[11]

For the first four years of their married life, including the birth of their first child, therefore, the Yorks had no real home of their own, escaping as often as they could from White Lodge to rented houses in Northamptonshire for the hunting in winter, while for the summer of 1924 Princess Mary and Harry Lascelles lent them Chesterfield House as a base in London.

Their first child, Princess Elizabeth, was born at 17 Bruton Street, the new home of her Strathmore grandparents, no doubt because White Lodge was perhaps considered too remote from the centre of London for what turned out to be a difficult birth. The Princess was born by Caesarean section on Wednesday, 21 April 1926, at 2.40 a.m. 'Such a relief and joy,' Queen Mary wrote in her diary, 'at 2.30 we went to London to 17 Bruton Street to congratulate Bertie & ... saw the baby who is a little darling with a lovely complexion and pretty fair hair.' The Queen was enchanted, but not overly so; 'I wish you were more like your little mother,' she said. Prince Albert was ecstatic: 'You don't know what a tremendous joy it is to Elizabeth and me to have our little girl,' he wrote to his mother a few days later. 'We always wanted a child to make our happiness complete, & now that it has happened, it seems so wonderful & strange. I am so proud of Elizabeth at this moment after all that she has gone through during the last few days.... I do hope that you & Papa are as delighted as we are, to have a grand-daughter, or would you', he wrote, 'have sooner had another grandson [Princess Mary's son, George, had been born on 7 February 1923]? I know Elizabeth wanted a daughter.' No one minded the Yorks' first child being a girl since no one seriously considered the possibility of her succeeding to the throne.

Indeed, the Yorks' choice of Elizabeth for the baby's name was influenced by her mother's name rather than by any conscious wish to hark back to England's great Queen, Elizabeth 1. Nor, apparently, did they consider the name of Britain's most recent reigning Queen, Victoria. She was to be christened Elizabeth Alexandra Mary after her mother, her grandmother and her great-grandmother. 'I hope you will approve of these names,' Prince Albert wrote to his father. 'We are so anxious for her first name to be Elizabeth & there has been no one of that name in your family for a long time.' 'Your family' the Prince had written, not, it should be noted, 'our family'. In his own mind he had established his own identity apart from his parents; he and Elizabeth were a separate family unit on their own. 'I have heard from Bertie about the names,' King George wrote to Queen Mary; 'he mentions Elizabeth, Alexandra, Mary. I quite approve & will tell him so, he says nothing about Victoria. I hardly think that necessary.'

One of the baby's namesakes, Queen Alexandra, was no longer there to see her second great-grandchild. The eighty-year-old Queen had died suddenly of a heart attack at Sandringham on 20 November 1925. Despite her deafness and increasing frailty, she had still taken a public part in the London season, appearing, slim, dressed often in her favourite Parma violet, a toque with a heavy fishnet veil concealing her age, at functions like polo at Hurlingham, the Royal Tournament and occasional Buckingham Palace garden-parties. When she was at Marlborough House, her devoted son visited her almost every day, and occasions such as her birthday and wedding anniversary had always been punctiliously celebrated with family luncheons. Prince Albert was hunting in Leicestershire when he heard of his grandmother's heart attack on 19 November; she died before he reached Sandringham. The Edwardian era at the Big House, which had lighted his life as a child, was no more.

Princess Elizabeth was born just before the General Strike, called on 3 May by the TUC in support of the miners, appeared to bring Britain to the brink of revolution. In the grim weeks that followed, the existence of the baby Princess seemed the only bright spark in a dark world. On 14 May, the day after the strike ended, Mabell Airlie, bearing a bottle of Jordan water sent from Palestine for the child's christening, had to struggle to make her way through the crowds waiting outside 17 Bruton Street. 'There was', she said, 'such a crowd in front of the house that the baby had to be smuggled out of the back when she went out to take an airing.' Prince Albert told her that there were always a few people waiting to see his daughter, 'but never so many as that day'.[12] Wearing the heavy cream satin and lace robe first worn by Queen Victoria's eldest daughter, which her father too had worn at his christening, the five-week-old Princess Elizabeth was christened on 29 May in the gold, lily-shaped font specially brought up from Windsor to the private chapel in Buckingham Palace. Her godparents were the King and Queen, Princess Mary, the Duke of Connaught, Elizabeth's sister, Lady Elphinstone, and Lady Strathmore. 'Of course poor baby cried,' Queen Mary noted. In fact, she cried so much during the ceremony, Mabell Airlie recalled, that her old-fashioned nurse dosed her well from a bottle of dill water 'to the surprise of the modern young mothers present, and to the amusement of her uncle, the Prince of Wales'. It was the last time Princess Elizabeth would ever make a scene in public.

White Lodge had just one advantage as far as Prince Albert was concerned, room to play tennis. He saw to it that whatever else did not work, the lawn tennis-courts were put in order and he and Elizabeth often played before breakfast. He liked to play with the professionals like the South African, 'Lizzie' Lezard, and, on one occasion in 1921 when Big Bill Tilden visited London, he invited him to play three sets with him at Buckingham Palace. His most regular partner or opponent was Louis Greig, who had partnered him when they won the RAF doubles competition on 8 July 1920. His passion for tennis, however, or perhaps Greig's over-enthusiasm, led him to a public disaster. June 1926 being the jubilee year of the Wimbledon Lawn Tennis Club, he and Greig entered for the men's doubles championship. The committee, delighted with the royal entry, wanted them to play on the centre court, but the Duke of York preferred one of the outer courts away from public attention. A compromise was reached with the match scheduled for Court Number Two. The Prince and Greig were drawn against two veterans, A.W. Gore and H. Roper Barrett, who were fifty-eight and fifty-two years old respectively. Gore had a remarkable record, having won the singles title in 1899, 1901 and 1908 and the doubles title with Roper Barrett in 1909. He also had the distinguished record of having been a singles finalist in seven Wimbledon finals. Roper Barrett had won the doubles in 1909, 1912 and 1913 and was non-playing captain of the British Davis Cup team from 1924 to 1939. A spectator remembered the occasion: 'The crowd was in very close round the court.... The Duke of York was very nervous and couldn't play at all, at times lashing at the ball with his racquet. The crowd began muttering and someone made the well-meaning suggestion to the left-handed Prince, "Try the other hand, Sir." '[13] The Prince and Greig lost to the more experienced players in straight sets, 1–6, 3–6, 2–6. Afterwards, the Prince confessed to the Wimbledon referee, Frank Burrow, that he feared the Wimbledon standard was too good for him, although the women's champion, Suzanne Lenglen, who saw the match, said that she considered that, 'with plenty of practice', he would have 'the makings of a champion'. But, where tennis and golf were concerned, the Prince never learned to master his temperament, too easily losing his temper and becoming discouraged. The Wimbledon experience had been a traumatic one; he never played tennis in public again.

There was a distinct cooling in the relationship between the Prince and Greig, the man who had looked after him so devotedly for so many years. The relationship had naturally changed on his marriage; the Prince's love for and reliance upon his wife left no room – or need – for anyone else. Greig ceased to be Comptroller of the Prince's Household, his place being taken by Captain Basil Brooke, RN, and on the Yorks' wedding day he was made a Commander of the Royal Victorian Order, the order which is in the King's own gift and which is, on the whole, reserved for royalty, courtiers and royal servants; a knighthood came later, in 1932. The CVO was not, perhaps, an over-generous reward for a man whom everyone, even those who at Court did not like him, admitted had been 'entirely un-self-seeking in his devotion'. It was not so much that, as Greig told the King's biographer, he had 'put steel' into the Prince, but he had, as one courtier said, 'given him confidence, jollied him along, got him to do things when he felt he couldn't'. This was a role which the Duchess now filled. 'It's always awkward when an intimate relationship cools,' said one courtier, 'and perhaps Louis Greig wasn't very tactful about it.' Some of the courtiers were snobbish about him because he came from a different background from the charmed circle of interrelated, impeccably bred families who traditionally served the sovereign. Not that this would have mattered to either of the Yorks, who, like most royalty, were far less snobbish than their courtiers. Something, however, happened; hearsay has it that it arose from the tennis match; something, it seems, that Greig is held to have said derogatory to the Duke of York, was maliciously repeated in that centre of male locker-room gossip, White's Club, which reached the ducal ear. 'I remember – although I hardly knew Louis Greig – thinking it was unfair at the time. But they were very sensitive to criticism and that was that,' a friend said.

Greig remained a member of the royal Household, holding a succession of royal appointments: Gentleman Usher in Ordinary to King George V, 1924–36, Extra Gentleman Usher to King George VI, 1937–52, Extra Gentleman Usher to Queen Elizabeth II, 1952–3, and Deputy Ranger of Richmond Park (a delightful sinecure which included a Grace and Favour house), 1932–53. An energetic, popular figure with a huge range of contacts, he had an active and interesting life beyond the royal circle, and, having married into a well-known City family, the Scrimgeours, he had several City directorships. He liked to be in the centre of things, to be in the know, to fix things and to do favours for people, for he was naturally a generous and kind-hearted man. He was a go-between in all sorts of situations including political ones. After the Second World War Greig was, among other things, a member of the exclusive Royal Yacht Squadron and for several years chairman of the All-England Lawn Tennis Club. He died in March 1953, just over a year after the man who, at one time, could have been called his 'protégé'. Greig undoubtedly did well out of his royal connection, but he deserved his honours and successes for all that he did for the future King of England as a young man.

The Yorks' marriage was in every sense a partnership. Elizabeth was totally committed to support and encourage her husband and to give him the confidence he lacked. The central difficulty for Prince Albert was his stammer, consciousness of which accentuated his shyness to the point of inhibition, and which seriously affected the public perception of his capabilities. Robert Hyde wrote that his 'faulty speech ... caused him anxiety, amounting at times almost to mental torture,' adding that on occasion, when leaving a group of workers or one of his camps, 'he would feel that he was expected to wave his hand and wish them "goodbye" or, as the Prince of Wales would have done, the less formal "Cheerio". But at the last moment he would be overcome with diffidence and for the next ten minutes feel miserable and angry with himself for his omission.' In the future, when similar occasions occurred, his wife would whisper, 'Wave, Bertie, wave!' Her extraordinary social graces, the radiant smile, the ability to make everyone feel that he or she alone was the only person who interested her, supplemented her husband's deficiencies in that area, making their joint public functions run on oiled wheels.

Their first public tour of duty as Duke and Duchess of York was in a sense a 'family' one to the Balkans, now regarded by the Palace and the Foreign Office as Prince Albert's 'sphere'. The King, perhaps tired of 'Cousin Missy's' repeated solicitations of support, had not insisted he should accept when invited to be godfather to King Alexander of Serbia's son in Belgrade on 21 October 1923, followed by the wedding of Alexander's uncle, Prince Paul of Serbia, to Princess Olga of Greece, the next day. The Foreign Office, however, coming to life again after the August holiday period, thought differently. The Yorks were on holiday at Holwick Hall, a Strathmore property in County Durham, when the Foreign Office suddenly insisted that the Prince should go to Belgrade. Prince Albert was furious; now that he was a married man he felt that he should not be subject to the last-minute decisions of ministers. 'Curzon should be drowned for giving me such short notice ... he must know things are different now,' he wrote to Greig on 24 September 1923. To Belgrade, however, the Yorks went to stay in a palace overcrowded with Prince Albert's royal European relations, or rather the Greek–Balkan branches. 'We were quite a large family party & how we all lived in the Palace is a mystery,' the Prince wrote to his father. 'We were not too comfortable & there was no hot water!!' As godfather to the baby Crown Prince Peter, his quick practical reactions were an asset when the aged Patriarch of the Serbian Orthodox Church dropped the six-week-old child into the font full of water. His godfather rescued him and handed him back to the Patriarch, and then had to carry the furious infant on a cushion three times round the font preceded by a deacon and clouds of incense. 'You can imagine what I felt like carrying the baby on a cushion,' he wrote to his father. 'It screamed most of the time which drowned the singing & the service altogether. It was made as short as possible, which was lucky & the chapel was of course over-heated as they were frightened of the baby catching cold.' Prince Albert was to take his responsibilities as 'Koum' (the Serbian word for godfather) to the future King Peter II very seriously, involving himself as protector in the young man's troubled career.

The next day the Yorks attended the marriage of Prince Paul of Serbia, son of Prince Arsène Karageorgevic and Aurora Demidoff, heiress to a fabulously rich Russian family, to the beautiful Princess Olga of Greece, daughter of Prince Albert's cousin, Prince Nicholas of Greece, and the Grand Duchess Helen Vladimirovna of the Russian imperial family. Both the Yorks already knew Prince Paul as a friend: at Oxford he had been one of the 'Cranborne Set' headed by a childhood friend of Elizabeth's, 'Bobbety' Cranborne, heir to the Marquess of Salisbury, and which included, among others, Gage and Chips Channon. When Princess Olga was expecting their first child in August 1925, the Yorks lent her White Lodge, and the ties between them were to become even closer a decade later when Princess Olga's sister, Princess Marina, married Prince George, Duke of Kent. The Duchess of York was a great success with her husband's royal relations. 'They were all enchanted with Elizabeth, especially Cousin Missy,' Prince Albert wrote fondly to his parents. 'She was wonderful with all of them. . . .'

It was to be the same story on their next official visit, this time to Northern Ireland in July 1924. In a letter to his father Prince Albert described their reception by the people of Ulster as

astounding. . . . There is no other word to describe the wonderful enthusiasm of the people of Belfast. They turned out in the streets at any time of the day & night, & the noise they made cheering was quite deafening. One could feel all the time that they were really genuine about it, & that they were pleased to see us. . . . We were received in the same wonderful way wherever we went even in the poorest parts. . . .

With touching pride he referred again to Elizabeth: 'Elizabeth has been marvellous as usual & the people simply love her already. I am very lucky indeed to have her to help me as she knows exactly what to do & say to all the people we meet. . . .'

The Northern Ireland visit was followed that winter by the Yorks' first experience of the British Empire on what was really a prolonged holiday in Kenya, Uganda and the Sudan from December 1924 to April 1925. The Prince's diary contains the customary accounts of 'weird' native dances, half-naked Nubian wrestlers wearing belts with bells and dangling monkey tails and not much else, and an endless procession of wild animals, shot or spotted. Of perhaps greater relevance to the future King–Emperor was a long talk with the Governor of Kenya, Sir Robert Coryndon, who clearly intended that his complaints about officialdom should reach the highest circles. Careful of the constitutional proprieties, Prince Albert retailed his opinions to his mother in the certainty that his letter would be shown by her to the King. Describing Kenya as 'a wonderful country', he wrote:

I am certain people at home have no idea what its possibilities are & what its future one day is going to be. Everything is so new & utterly different to other parts of the Empire, & being so young it should be made gradually by the best people we can produce from home. By this I don't mean the settlers who are a very nice lot & for the most part real gentlemen, but the official side of the life of Kenya. I have had several talks with the Governor Sir Robert Coryndon & he is sorry to have to say that things are not quite as they should be owing to lack of first hand & personal knowledge of the officials at home. Ormsby-Gore [Under-Secretary for the Colonies, and chairman of the Parliamentary Committee which had visited East Africa in 1924] ... I understand has gone home with very different ideas to those with which he came out. I know you won't mind me telling you this [he added] but I feel it is an important thing for this vast country to be better understood.

When it came to the public side of his life, however, Prince Albert was still hampered by his stammer. One of his principal objects in wanting to return to England in 1919 had been, as he told his father, to get treatment for his stammer with a new Italian speech therapist. This had certainly helped. Lord Crawford had written of him in the summer of 1920 that he had 'overcome' his speech hesitation but, while he now performed adequately or even well at the kind of occasion for public speaking to which he had become accustomed, such as charity dinners for the IWS, prize-givings and so on, he was now faced with a new ordeal, the microphone and, perhaps for him the ultimate nightmare, public broadcasting. Arriving home on 25 April, Prince Albert had succeeded his elder brother, who left for a tour of southern Africa on 27 April, as President of the British Empire Exhibition at Wembley Stadium, the largest arena in the country. The Exhibition was due to close on 31 October 1925 and Prince Albert would have to make the closing speech in the vast arena, before microphones relaying his words not only to the thousands of people present but to a global audience of ten million people. Among the listeners would be his severest critic, his father, who himself had been heard on the air for the first time when his speech opening the Exhibition the previous year had been broadcast.

'I do hope I shall do it well,' Prince Albert wrote anxiously to his father, confessing his fears and pleading for understanding. 'But I shall be very frightened as you have never heard me speak & the loud speakers are apt to put one off as well. So I hope you will understand that I am bound to be more nervous than I usually am.' It is a letter which makes pathetic reading. On the day, the Prince stood there, a lone figure upon whom all eyes were focused. His jaw muscles working, he forced himself to complete the speech, but at times no sound came out as he struggled to form the words. It was a horrifying ordeal for him. 'Bertie got through his speech all right, but there were some rather long pauses,' the King wrote to Prince George. To Prince Albert, to his family and, indeed, to all those who heard him, the Wembley speech seemed to demonstrate that the King's second son was unfit for public life.

Fortunately among the people present at Wembley on 31 October who heard Prince Albert's agonizing, halting speech was the one man who was able to help him, a forty-five-year-old Australian speech therapist named Lionel Logue. Logue turned to his son and said of the Prince, 'He's too old for me to manage a complete cure. But I could very nearly do it. I'm sure of that.' Logue, like many other therapists, had come to speech therapy through dealing with shell-shocked ex-servicemen who experienced speech difficulties after the First World War. In 1924 he had left Australia with his wife and three sons and set up a consulting office in rented rooms on the second floor at 146 Harley Street. Eileen Macleod, a founder member of the Society of Speech Therapists, when sounded out as to whether she might help with the Duke of York's speech problem, recommended Logue, feeling that a man would be of more help in a problem which she, like Greig, believed stemmed to a considerable degree from the Prince's treatment by his father, and notably King George's impatience with his left-handedness as a boy. Logue, she thought, as an Australian, would not be overawed by royalty and would be better able to treat the Prince on an equal basis. She was to help him as a consultant. An appointment was arranged through the Duke's Private Secretary, Patrick Hodgson, and on the afternoon of 19 October 1926, Prince Albert went to Logue's Harley Street consulting-room for the first time. Logue's notes of that first meeting have been much-quoted:

He entered my consulting-room at three o'clock in the afternoon, a slim, quiet man with tired eyes and all the outward symptoms of the man upon whom habitual speech defect had begun to set the sign. When he left at five o'clock, you could see that there was hope once more in his heart.

The Prince's official biographer, Wheeler-Bennett, explained, almost certainly correctly, the Prince's depressed attitude:

... the disillusionment caused by the failures of previous specialists to effect a cure had begun to breed within him the inconsolable despair of the chronic stammerer and the secret dread that the hidden root of the affliction lay in the mind rather than in the body.

Logue had a dual approach to the Prince's problem inspiring him mentally with confidence by telling him that he could be cured, that success depended upon his own efforts, and convincing him that he was not, as stammerers fear and feel that they are, 'different' from other people, i.e. that he was a perfectly normal person with a curable complaint. Physically he concentrated on relaxing the tension which caused the muscles to spasm and prevented speech from flowing by teaching the Prince to breathe correctly, to develop his lungs through exercises and to control the rhythm of his diaphragm. The Prince had to do these exercises at home for an hour every day lying on the floor, to gargle with warm water and to stand by an open window intoning the vowels in a 'fairly loud voice', each sound to last for fifteen seconds. Logue devised tongue-twisters, which included some of the consonants that the Prince found difficult but were so ridiculous that they made him laugh: 'Let's go gathering heathy heather with the gay brigade of grand dragoons', or, 'She sifted seven thick-stalked thistles through strong thick sieves'. Logue thought it essential that they should meet 'on equal terms' because he regarded an easy personal relationship as part of the treatment. The weekly consultations took place at 146 Harley Street or at his small flat in South Kensington. The Duchess of York took great interest in her husband's treatment and often accompanied him to Harley Street; in public he would always look to her for reassurance and her look and her smile would encourage him on. When, as King, he had to broadcast, she would always be there, helping him to write the speeches to eliminate difficult consonants or rehearsing. Her help was invaluable but, according to Logue, the key factor was the Prince's own courage and determination to fight his private nightmare and overcome it. 'He was the pluckiest and most determined patient I ever had,' he later said of him.[14] Logue's treatment made an instant, marked difference. The Prince wrote to his father:

I have been seeing Logue every day & I have noticed a great improvement in my talking, & also in making speeches which I did this week. I am sure I am going to get quite all right in time, but 24 years of talking in the wrong way cannot be cured in a month.

I wish I could have found him before, as now that I know the right way to breathe my fear of talking will vanish.

On 6 January 1927 the Yorks left for their first major imperial tour, embarking on HMS *Renown* bound, via the Caribbean and the Pacific, for Australia and New Zealand. The ultimate object of the tour was to open the new Parliament buildings at Canberra, which had recently been created as Capital of the Commonwealth of Australia, and the visit had been requested by the Australian Premier, Stanley Bruce, in June 1926. Bruce, doubtless hoping to get the Prince of Wales, had requested the presence of one of the King's elder sons, and, having heard Prince Albert stuttering in public on several occasions during the Imperial Conference of 1926, was privately worried that he might do the same in Australia. For Prince Albert, representing his father on his first imperial mission, there was, despite the new confidence inspired in him by Logue's treatment, always the old fear of invidious comparison between his public performance and those of his father and brother. Twenty-seven years earlier King George, then Duke of York, had performed the same ceremony in Melbourne and only seven years before the Prince of Wales had visited Australia, exciting the usual outpourings of rapturous public enthusiasm. Prince Albert was very conscious of his responsibility: 'This is the first time you have sent me on a mission concerning the Empire, & I can assure you that I will do my very best to make it the success we all hope for,' he wrote to his father from *Renown*.

King George was on the alert to spot any defects; studying photographs of his son's reception at Las Palmas, he quickly made his criticisms known: 'I send you a picture of you inspecting Gd. of Honour (I don't think much of their dressing) with yr. Equerry walking on yr. right next to the Gd. & you ignoring the Officer entirely,' he wrote on 25 January. 'Yr. Equerry should be outside and behind, & it certainly doesn't look very well.' Patiently the Prince replied, explaining that he had already finished inspecting the guard and, walking back to join the Duchess, was giving a message to his equerry. Many sons would have been irritated by the royal nit-picking, but Prince Albert, sharing his father's interest in ceremonial and his consciousness of the importance of getting things right on public occasions, understood. 'It was an unfortunate moment for the photograph to be taken,' he commented tactfully.

He could afford to take his father's criticism calmly as the constant private shadow of his stammer was lifting. Logue's treatment produced an almost instant improvement, which was particularly noticeable on this tour only two months after he first consulted the therapist.

'Your teaching, I must say, has given me a tremendous amount of confidence,' he wrote to Logue on 25 January. 'You remember my fear of [the loyal toast to] the King. I give it every evening at dinner on board. This does not worry me anymore.'[15] For the first time in his life he found he was able to make a speech in public without hesitating. 'I had to make 3 speeches the first morning,' he wrote to Queen Mary from Rotorua in New Zealand on 27 February 1927, 'the last one in the Town Hall quite a long one, & I can tell you that I was really pleased with the way I made it, as I had perfect confidence in myself & I did not hesitate at all. Logue's teaching is still working well, but of course if I get tired it still worries me.' But he depended enormously on his wife, whose charm disguised his shyness, and was horrified when she fell ill with tonsillitis at Christchurch in the South Island after a triumphant tour of the North Island, leaving him to complete their New Zealand visit alone. Convinced, with some justification, that the real success of the tour was the Duchess, he thought of cancelling it and returning to Wellington with her. But he had to go ahead with the plans and the fact that he managed to carry them out without her reassuring presence contributed to his new confidence.

Confidence was the key word in all his letters to Logue at this time: 'I have ever so much more confidence in myself and don't brood over a speech as in the old days,' he wrote from Sydney, Australia. 'I know what to do now, and the knowledge has helped me over and over again.' In Melbourne he addressed thousands of ex-servicemen on Anzac Day on 25 April, and at Canberra on 9 May, after opening the door of the new Parliament House with a golden key, he made a speech in front of an audience of 20,000 people. The speech outside was his own idea; the original plan having been that he should simply open the door while the Royal Proclamation was read out. Bruce, who had had such qualms about the Prince's ability to carry out his duties, was agreeably surprised: '. . . he even insisted that he make a brief speech in addition to his address at the opening ceremony in the Senate Chamber'.[16] Inside the building, despite a temperature of 80 degrees caused by the arc lights installed for the cameramen, Prince Albert delivered his speech from the throne without hesitation. 'I was not very nervous when I made the Speech, because the one I made outside went off without a hitch, & I did not hesitate once,' he wrote to his father. 'I was so relieved as making speeches still rather frightens me, though Logue's teaching has really done wonders for me as I now know how to prevent & get over any difficulty. I have so much more confidence in myself now, which I am sure comes from being able to speak properly at last. . . .' To Harry Batterbee, the Dominions Office official who accompanied him on the tour, the Prince admitted, however, 'I was much too afraid to be afraid. . . .'[17] The trip was a huge success; spectacularly so for the Duchess of York, but also quietly for her husband. 'His Royal Highness has touched people profoundly by his youth, his simplicity and natural bearing,' Sir Tom Bridges, Governor of South Australia, wrote to the King, 'while the Duchess has left us with the responsibility of having a continent in love with her. The visit has done untold good and has certainly put back the clock of disunion and disloyalty 25 years as far as this State is concerned.'

The Yorks arrived home on 27 June 1927, welcomed back on Portsmouth quayside by the three Princes, while at Victoria Station, as a signal mark of honour, the King and Queen waited to greet them in a ceremony meticulously stage-managed by King George. 'Frock-coat & epaulettes, without medals & riband, only stars' were to be worn, he instructed his son. 'We will not embrace at the station before so many people. When you kiss Mama take yr. hat off.' At last, at the age of thirty-one, with his new confidence and the improvement in his speech, the Prince found that his relationship with his father was becoming a more adult one. At Balmoral in September that year the Prince found that he could actually make his father listen. 'I have been talking a lot with the King, & I have had no trouble at all,' he told Logue. 'Also I can make him listen, & I don't have to repeat everything over again.' His father was impressed. 'Delighted to have Bertie with me,' he wrote to Queen Mary; 'he came yesterday evening, have had several talks with him & find him very sensible . . .', adding a refrain that was already becoming familiar, 'very different to D[avid]'.

The problem of 'D' was to come very much to the fore in the following year, when the King's serious illness in November 1928 highlighted the fragility of his health and the possibility that the Prince of Wales might succeed to the throne. The Prince seemed born to be King, gifted with looks, charm and the common touch; he was adored as no royal prince had ever been before him. Only the King suspected, and the Prince's Household knew, the extent to which his character had deteriorated under the pressure of this adulation, that he was spoiled, self-indulgent and self-opinionated, irresponsible and an arrested adolescent in mentality. One of his staff attributed his character defects to a glandular change at puberty when, as has been noted, 'something went wrong with his gland'. His brothers apparently testified that 'from then on his letters changed'.[18] He became 'devoid of all personal loyalty and affection. . . . There was something horribly abnormal about him.' Lascelles thought it was the lack of any spiritual dimension, telling Harold Nicolson that the Prince was 'like the child in the fairy story who was given everything in the world but they forgot his soul. He had no spiritual or aesthetic side at all. He did not know beauty when he saw it and even the beauty of women was only apparent to him when they were the sort of women who excited his particular passions. His love of his garden was merely because it was a form of exercise ... he only liked big game shooting because it made him sweat. He was not really interested in anything at all.'[19]

It is doubtful whether Prince Albert knew this. He was, of course, aware of the gulf which divided the Prince of Wales from his father and their disagreements on everything from trouser turn-ups to weekends. He blamed his father a good deal for this rift, telling his biographer that his father was 'impossible' when they were young men and that 'he really went for David'. This was borne out by several other witnesses: Lady Oxford described the King as 'horrible' to his sons, criticizing the Prince of Wales for his clothes and Prince Albert for his stammer, while Lady Elcho said he was 'quite impossible, cross and jumpy, very jealous of the Prince [of Wales] and all the others' and refusing to ask any of the Princes' friends to the Palace.[20] Being a deeply conventional man himself, Prince Albert accepted without question the Prince of Wales's dominant position in the hierarchy of the younger royal family, although disapproving of some aspects of the Prince's rebellion against tradition. Discussing the question of decorations to be worn at balls and small dances with Lord Londonderry he wrote that he would talk to his brother and get him to 'settle what should be done at small dances', but 'he is rather difficult on these matters and has rather different ideas about them from anyone else. We ought to conform to what he does really, but this is often difficult knowing that he is in the wrong, or at least out of order with what has been done on a similar occasion previously.'[21]

In a manner characteristic of royalty, the Prince's mind fastened on such matters as his brother's unconventionality in the wearing of decorations as a fault. There is no hint in his correspondence of any criticism of the Prince of Wales on larger issues or of character defects which already seriously put into question his suitability as material for a future King–Emperor. Had he really comprehended this at an earlier stage, the whole issue of the Abdication would have come as less of an appalling shock. For the Prince of Wales's entourage, however, their employer's reaction to the news of his father's dangerous illness at the end of November 1928 was the final proof of an egotism having reached the point of insensibility to the demands of public responsibility or family duty. The golden-hearted charmer 'full of fun and rags with everyone', as one of them described the Prince, whose abundant vitality had enchanted them all in the early 1920s, was turning into a difficult, obstinate charge whose impulses they could not control and whose lapses they had to struggle to conceal. The older members of the Prince's Household, like his Comptroller, Admiral Halsey, attributed the decline in the Prince's morals to the influence of his boon companion, Fruity Metcalfe, whom he described as '... not *at all* a good thing for HRH ... an excellent fellow, always cheery and full of fun, but far, far too weak and hopelessly irresponsible. He is a *wild, wild*, Irishman.'[22] The Prince could be forgiven for wanting some relaxation from the endless public duties he was asked to perform on these repeated world tours, but by 1927 when he visited Canada and the USA his fondness for nightclubs, drinking and womanizing was more than the more sober and critical member of his entourage could bear. Early in August 1927, Alan 'Tommy' Lascelles, then the Prince of Wales's Assistant Private Secretary, asked for an interview with the British Prime Minister, Stanley Baldwin, who had been touring the Dominion with the Prince of Wales and Prince George. He told Baldwin that, in his considered opinion, 'the Heir Apparent, in his unbridled pursuit of wine and women, and whatever selfish whim occupied him at the moment, was rapidly going to the devil, and unless he mended his ways, would soon become no fit wearer of the British Crown'.[23] Finding, to his surprise, that the Prime Minister agreed with him, Lascelles then went so far as to say that sometimes when the Prince was riding in some point-to-point race, he 'couldn't help thinking that the best thing that could happen to him, and to the country, would be for him to break his neck'. Baldwin's response was, 'God forgive me, I have often thought the same.'

The Prince of Wales, however, did not mend his ways. For Lascelles, the final straw was 'his incredibly callous behaviour when we got the news of his father's grave illness'. The Prince was at the end of a safari holiday in Kenya en route to South Africa, when they began to receive cypher telegrams from Baldwin reporting the King's serious illness and begging the Prince to come home at once. The Prince came in as Lascelles was deciphering the last one received. 'I don't believe a word of it,' he said. 'It's just some election dodge of old Baldwin's. It doesn't mean a thing.' Lascelles later recalled:

Then for the first and only time in our association, I lost my temper with him. 'Sir,' I said, 'the King of England is dying; and if that means nothing to you, it means a great deal to us.' He looked at me, went out without a word, and spent the remainder of the evening in the successful seduction of a Mrs Barnes, wife of the local Commissioner. He told me so himself next morning.[24]

Prince Albert it seems knew nothing of this; the Prince's loyal staff would not have told him. The King had, indeed, almost died of a serious bronchial infection complicated by a general infection of the blood; on 21 November he felt unwell and by the afternoon of 12 December he was unconscious. On 2 December Prince Albert was appointed a member of the Council of State to deputize for the King during his illness, with the Queen, the Archbishop of Canterbury, the Lord Chancellor, Lord Hailsham, and the Prime Minister, Stanley Baldwin. The Prince of Wales, also appointed a member, was now officially summoned home. Two days later Prince Albert wrote to his brother, by then en route to London, giving details of the King's illness and reporting, 'There is a lovely story going about which emanated from the East End, that the reason of your rushing home is that in the event of anything happening to

Papa I am going to bag the Throne in your absence!!! Just like the Middle Ages....'

The King's convalescence was long and punctuated by two relapses; hardly surprising perhaps, considering that within four days of arriving at the house in Bognor by ambulance from London on 9 February, he was already allowed to resume smoking. In May another abscess formed on the site of the first operation; it burst at the end of the month and the King not only received the new Prime Minister, Ramsay MacDonald, but also attended a public Thanksgiving Service for his return to health, with an open wound in his back. 'Fancy,' he teased his doctors, 'a Thanksgiving Service with an open wound in your back!' It was not until November 1929 that his old friend and cousin, Albert Mensdorff, the former Austrian Ambassador, was able to record that he was back to his old self again: 'He was in a good mood and cursed as in earlier days.'[25] He was not, however, the same man; his illness, according to his biographer, 'left him delicate and older than his sixty-four years'. His prolonged and dangerous illness had not been without its effect on the public; people became aware of how nearly they had lost their sovereign and consequently of the qualities they valued in him. He had only just over five years to live.

The King's illness actually caused a rapprochement between him and his eldest son. Lady Lee recorded in her diary for 5 January 1929 that Lady Mount Stephen, one of Queen Mary's closest friends, told Molly Hudson 'that the Prince of Wales ... said to her, "You know I have never got on with my father, but when, on getting back, I found him a little, shrunken old man with a white beard, the shock was so great that I cried"'. Three months later, on 23 April, she noted that her husband had had an 'interesting talk' with Louis Greig, 'who told him that there had been a real rapprochement between the King and the Prince of Wales. That the Prince had said, "and I now feel for the first time that I have a father", and that the King acknowledged that the Prince had been a real help and comfort to him during his long illness....'[26]

As far as Prince Albert was concerned, there were few clouds on the horizon. He got on extremely well with his elder brother; the Prince of Wales frequently dropped in at 145 Piccadilly and the brothers often played golf together. There was an element of brotherly rivalry in their game; when Prince Albert succeeded his brother as captain of the most historic of golf clubs, the Royal and Ancient at St Andrew's, in the playing-in ceremony of 24 September 1930 he took pains to demonstrate his superiority at the game, somewhat to his brother's chagrin. Traditionally, the captain 'plays himself in' with an inaugural drive from the first tee, an occasion which has been called 'the most nerve-racking shot in golf' since it has to be executed to the accompaniment of a deafening explosion from a small cannon nearby and in front of hundreds of spectators and a number of expectant caddies lining the fairway in the hope of being the first to retrieve the ball, thus winning the traditional prize of a golden sovereign. In 1922 the Prince of Wales, arrayed in a multicoloured Fair Isle sweater, and fortified by a breakfast dram of whisky, drove off at 8.30 a.m. 'Before the early morning crowds, with a bunch of caddies lined up a decent way down the course in the hope of retrieving my ball and so earning a golden sovereign,' he later recalled, 'I made so bad a tee shot, when the traditional cannon was fired, that I had the humiliation of seeing them all run a long way towards me before the first of them reached the ball.'[27] As often, the Prince's memory was not quite accurate. His shot was rather worse, the ball came off the shank of his club and shot off fifty yards to the right bouncing against some iron railings, whereupon a local club-maker hopped over the railings, retrieved the ball and gained the sovereign to the fury of the caddies running frantically back down the fairway. When his turn came in 1930, Prince Albert was determined to demonstrate that there were some things he could do better than the Prince of Wales. His brother noticed that for a few months before Prince Albert was due to make his inaugural drive, he had been ducking their regular golf games together: 'Only later did I discover that he was devoting his leisure to practising assiduously with his driver.' To the dismay of the caddies who, in the words of the local newspaper, stood 'disloyally close' to the tee, Prince Albert executed a magnificent drive of over 200 yards straight down the fairway. The elder brother retained a lifelong passion for the game, despite not being very good at it, a deficiency for which in later life he compensated by mild cheating. Prince Albert, however, found golf too bad – or *vice versa* – for his temper and gave it up in favour of gardening, a more soothing pursuit.

By the early 1930s, after a decade of happy marriage, Prince Albert's life had taken on a settled quality which he might reasonably have expected to have lasted with minor variations for his remaining years. Since their arrival back from Australia in 1927, the Yorks had lived in their London home, 145 Piccadilly, a handsome, south-facing, stone-fronted house near Hyde Park Corner looking across Green Park to Buckingham Palace. From 1931 they also had a country house, the Royal Lodge, in Windsor Great Park. The Royal Lodge had originally been George iv's dream house, designed for him by Sir Jeffrey Wyatville who had worked for him on Windsor Castle, and was intended, rather like the Prince of Wales's Fort Belvedere, to be a refuge from the public gaze. George iv's successor, William iv, and his Queen, Adelaide, demolished most of the house, whose cost had aroused unfavourable comment from a hostile House of Commons. Only Wyatville's chapel and great saloon were left, with a charming octagonal pavilion added by Queen Adelaide. By the time the Yorks first saw it in September 1931 the house was dilapidated and inconvenient, the proportions of Wyatville's saloon spoilt by partitions. None the less, they both loved it on sight. 'It is so kind of you to have offered us Royal Lodge,' Prince Albert wrote to his father, '& now having seen it I think it will suit us admirably.' He had committed a solecism which King George was quick to correct. 'I am so pleased to hear that both you and Elizabeth liked *the* Royal Lodge & would like to live there. . . . I hope you will always call it *the* Royal Lodge by which name it has been known ever since George iv built it,' he replied. Gradually the Yorks transformed the house, restoring the saloon to its original proportions as the central drawing-room and adding two wings on either side, which included two bedrooms for themselves on the ground floor. Characteristically Prince Albert's was an austere room, neat and tidy like a sailor's cabin ready for inspection, furnished simply with a hard bed, a simple dressing-table and one bookcase on which was laid out a few personal mementoes, while his wife's was decorated in her favourite colour, grey blue, the large double bed covered in blue silk with lemon pleating, while the furniture and fitted cupboards were of white apple wood.

At the Royal Lodge Prince Albert became a passionate gardener, spending energetic weekends clearing shrubbery and designing new planting with the help of Eric Savill. He became an acknowledged expert on rhododendrons and on 27 May 1935, after visiting the Countess of Stair at Lochinch Castle in Scotland, wrote her a letter using botanical Latin terms, 'the language of rhododendrons'. It was a long letter, a labour of love which must have required a botanical dictionary and, perhaps, a consultation with Savill in order to produce such passages as this:

As to my visit, I am overjoyed Eclecteum (to be chosen out) and Aberrans (wandering) Cyclium (round) so many Erastum (lovely) and Arizelum (notable) gardens in so short a time, has left me Charitostreptum (gracefully bent) with a Recurvum (bent back), and somewhat Lasiopodum (woolly footed). I must say I am filled Coeloneurum (with impressed nerves) at all the Agetum (wondrous) & Aperantum (limitless) beauties of the gardens Cyclium (round) Lochinch....

It was an enduring passion; the 1947 Chelsea Flower Show, the first to be held after the Second World War, had at his inspiration the finest display of rhododendrons and azaleas in the show's history, and by the time he died the gardens at the Royal Lodge had increased from fifteen acres to ninety.

The Royal Lodge compensated the Prince for having to give up his hunters in the autumn of 1931. Faced with the economic depression and the abandonment of the Gold Standard, the King ordered £50,000 cut from the annual Civil List and Prince Albert, finding his £25,000 curtailed, sold his string of hunters. 'It has come as a great shock to me that with the economy cuts I have had to make my hunting should have been one of the things I must do without,' he wrote to Ronald Tree, Master of the Pytchley. 'And I must sell my horses too. This is the worst part of it all and the parting with them will be terrible.' The King, too, glumly contemplated cutting down on his sporting activities, 'I am going to give up the shooting in Windsor Park as I cannot afford it,' he told Prince Albert. The Prince of Wales, who had already sold his horses and concentrated on golf, had other expensive hobbies and was furious when telephoned by his father at a nightclub in Bayonne, where he was enjoying himself with his new love, Lady Furness, and ordered to give up £10,000 a year. Prince Albert, however, now had his garden and his family to concentrate upon.

The arrival of Princess Margaret Rose, born at Glamis on 21 August 1930, completed the family. The Princess was a trial to officialdom even before she was born. The Home Secretary, J.R. Clynes, anxious to show that a Labour politician and former trades union leader could be as punctilious about protocol as any well-born Tory, instead of waiting for a definite summons, hastened northwards when misinformed by the doctors that his presence would be required early in August. He arrived on 5 August and was kindly taken in by Mabell Airlie at neighbouring Cortachy Castle. Prince Albert was embarrassed and a little irritated by the Home Secretary's precipitate arrival. 'I feel so sorry for Mr Clynes having to be here so long,' he wrote to the King on the 10th, 'I always wanted him to come up when he was sent for, which would have been much simpler.' Clynes's early arrival was probably also prompted by his companion, Mr Harry Boyd, the Ceremonial Secretary at the Home Office, who, Mabell Airlie discovered, was absolutely obsessed

with the fear that because the Duchess of York had decided to have her baby at Glamis there might be some impression that the affair was going to be conducted in 'an irregular, hole and corner way', as he put it. 'Just imagine if it should occur in the early hours of the morning and the Home Secretary could not get to Glamis in time,' he exclaimed agitatedly, pacing up and down the sitting-room at Cortachy. 'This child will be in direct succession to the Throne and if its birth is not properly witnessed its legal right might be questioned. . . .' He produced a book which he had brought with him from the Home Office with passages marked in red ink giving an account of the birth of the son of James II and Mary of Modena, who had been rumoured to have been substituted for a girl by means of a warming-pan. 'We must not risk anything of that sort,' said Boyd,[28]

The royal accoucheur, Sir Henry Simpson, kept Boyd on tenterhooks by announcing that the birth could not take place later than the 11th; by the time ten days had passed the Ceremonial Secretary was frantic, sitting up all night by the specially installed telephone line to Glamis. In the event the Home Secretary and his frantic minion arrived at Glamis with half an hour to spare and to signal by their official presence that no changeling had been smuggled in.

Clynes and Boyd were not the only people kept on tenterhooks by the late arrival of Princess Margaret Rose; this time everyone, including her parents, had been hoping for a boy. The King, after his serious illness in 1928, was ageing rapidly; the Prince of Wales was thirty-five and still showing no signs of wishing to marry; and Prince Henry and Prince George were both bachelors. The Yorks, apparently hoping for a boy, had not settled on a name when the Princess was born and the King then, unaccountably, objected to their first choice, Ann, which after all had been the name of a Queen of England. In the royal family his word was law and even his indulged daughter-in-law had to submit. 'I am desperately anxious to call her Ann Margaret,' she had written to Queen Mary, but 'Bertie & I have decided now to call our little daughter "Margaret Rose" . . . as Papa does not like Ann. I hope you like it. I think that it is very pretty together.'

By the time Princess Margaret arrived, she was already destined to be relegated to second place to her elder sister, 'Lilibet', as she was known in the family,

who was the King's favourite grandchild. To Princess Elizabeth her grandfather
was far from being the explosive, rather frightening figure that he represented
for everyone else and for her Lascelles boy cousins. He would get down on the
floor and play with her as he had never played with his own children; even her
stately grandmother, Queen Mary, reported herself as playing in the garden and
making sandpies with her grand-daughter. On Christmas Eve 1928, when she
was two and a half, Princess Elizabeth was allowed to stay up to hear Christmas
carols and when she heard 'Glad tidings of great joy I bring to you and all
mankind', she called out excitedly, 'I know who Old Man Kind is!' The presence
of his adored grand-daughter cheered the King's convalescence at Bognor after
his illness that 1928–9, and in London each morning after breakfast, when he
had fitted a cigarette into his holder and inspected the weather, the King would
take up a pair of field glasses and train them on 145 Piccadilly where Princess
Elizabeth would wave to him from the windows.

Princess Elizabeth was not only the favourite of her grandparents but the
darling of the world's press. 'It is extraordinary how her arrival is so popular
out here,' Prince Albert had written to his mother during their Antipodean tour.
'Wherever we go cheers are given for her as well & the children write to us
about her.' It was the beginning of that identification of the public with the
royal family as a family which was to be such an extraordinary feature of the
twentieth century. 'I am four and a half months old and I should like a
photograph of Princess Betty' was typical of the letters which Elizabeth's parents
received on their tour. Everywhere her parents went they found enormous
interest in their daughter, and often disappointment when she did not accompany
them. 'The only thing I regret is that we have not got Lilibet here,' Elizabeth
wrote to Queen Mary from Edinburgh, where Prince Albert was to act as Lord
High Commissioner to the first General Assembly of the reunited Church of
Scotland in May 1929:

I fear that it has been a very great disappointment to the people. Not that they would
have seen her, but they would have liked to feel that she was here. In the solemn
old Assembly, the Moderator mentioned in his welcoming address 'our dear Princess
Elizabeth', which is, I believe, almost unique. It almost frightens me that the people
should love her so much. . . .

If the new arrival had been a boy Princess Elizabeth might have faded
somewhat out of the picture, but instead the birth of another girl only reinforced
her elder sister's position. A wax image of Elizabeth on her pony featured in
Madame Tussaud's, a popular song was composed for her and in Antarctica
Princess Elizabeth Land was named after her. All this was not lost on Princess
Elizabeth herself. Out with her grandmother on one of those educational
expeditions which were to be such a feature of Queen Mary's relationship with
her grand-daughters, she horrified the Queen by displaying crowd-pleasing
tendencies. The Princess was wriggling impatiently in her seat and her grand-

mother asked her if she would prefer to go home. 'Oh no, Granny,' said the little girl. 'We can't leave before the end. Think of all the people who'll be waiting to see us outside.' Such vulgar and unroyal instincts Queen Mary, brought up in the stern traditions of Queen Victoria and the German Courts, thought should be instantly suppressed. She told her lady-in-waiting to take the Princess out by the back way and home in a taxi.[29]

Prince Albert was already intensely proud of his eldest daughter. Talking to Osbert Sitwell one night at Polesden Lacey, the conversation turned to Princess Elizabeth. 'He said,' Sitwell recorded, 'giving me at the same time a very direct look, to see if I understood the allusion he was making to Queen Victoria, "From the first moment of talking, she showed so much character that it was impossible not to wonder whether history would not repeat itself."'[30] Nevertheless, perhaps because of his own experiences of childhood and the great inequality of status in his own position in relation to his elder brother, he was anxious that his younger daughter should not be made to feel second best. The Yorks were absolutely determined that their family life should be the happy and united experience which Elizabeth had known and Prince Albert had so grievously missed. 'They were so determined to be a happy family together that although Princess Margaret was four years younger than her sister they treated them as if they were the same age,' a family friend said.

The Yorks' happy family-orientated life at this time was observed from early 1932 by an acute and later indiscreet insider, the children's governess. Marion Crawford, known as 'Crawfie', who joined the ranks of the Yorks' affectionately nicknamed employees – 'Bobo' Jean Macdonald, Princess Elizabeth's nurserymaid who became her dresser and lifelong confidante, and 'Alla' Clara Knight, who had been Elizabeth Bowes-Lyon's nurse and became Princess Margaret's. Crawfie was twenty-two, a bright graduate of the Moray House Training College in Edinburgh with aspirations towards becoming a child psychologist when she joined the royal Household. She arrived on a month's trial in March 1932 and stayed for seventeen years, devoting her life to Lilibet and Margaret as a trusted royal servant until in 1950 she committed the ultimate crime of writing a book about her employers, *The Little Princesses*. Ostracized by the Court, the once-loved and trusted Crawfie became a non-person; her name is not even to be found in the indexes of officially authorized royal biographies such as Wheeler-Bennett's *King George VI* or Dorothy Laird's *Queen Elizabeth the Queen Mother*. She married a fellow Scot, Major George Buthlay, and retired to Aberdeen, refusing to talk any more about her royal experiences. When she died there in 1987 not one member of the royal family either attended her funeral or even sent a wreath.

But in the spring of 1932 she was the Yorks' personal choice for their children's governess. Prince Albert, in particular, had become impressed with her when he met her tutoring his sister-in-law's children in Scotland. Crawfie found the Yorks easy employers:

No one ever had employers who interfered so little. I had the feeling that the Duke and Duchess, most happy in their own married life, were not over concerned with the higher education of their daughters. They wanted most for them a really happy childhood, with lots of pleasant memories stored up against the days that might come out and, later, happy marriages.[31]

At that time there was no definite prospect that the seven-year-old Elizabeth might become Queen of England; her parents had no ambitions of producing a new Elizabeth as cultivated as her namesake, the Virgin Queen, who wrote effortlessly in Latin and Greek at the age of sixteen. All they wanted were two nice, well-behaved, upper-class girls. The Duchess had had virtually no formal education; having learned to read as a child from her mother, she had taught her own children the same way, reading them Bible stories on Sunday mornings, fairy stories and, as she told Cynthia Asquith, '*Alice, Black Beauty, At the Back of the North Wind, Peter Pan,* anything we can find about horses and dogs. . . .'

Their grandfather's only stipulation was that they should be taught good handwriting. 'For goodness' sake,' he told Crawfie, 'teach Margaret and Lilibet to write a decent hand, that's all I ask you. None of my children could write properly. They all do it exactly the same way. I like a hand with some character in it.'[32] This was a somewhat disingenuous instruction on the King's part, since the handwriting of his three elder sons closely resembled his own, a boyish, unformed, scrawling copperplate with carefully looped 'l's', 'y's' and 'g's', and it was he, after all, who had chosen their tutor, Mr Hansell. Only Prince George, who had escaped earlier from Hansell wrote with an elegant, rounded hand, showing some individuality. Queen Mary, characteristically, had constructive criticisms to make of Miss Crawford's well rounded curriculum, which included singing, drawing, music and dancing, reflecting her own interests and what she considered suitable for a royal child 'Her Majesty felt that genealogies, historical and dynastic, were very interesting to children and, for these children, really important,' the governess recorded The Queen also suggested they should be taught the physical geography of the Dominions and India; on Princess Elizabeth's fourth birthday she had given her a set of building blocks made from fifty different woods from various parts of the Empire, following the tradition of instructional card games which she had played with her own children.

The Yorks in these early years placed more emphasis on fun—games of Snap, Happy Families and Racing Demon after tea, and romps after the children's bathtime when they would join them on the nursery floor. Then, according to Crawfie, 'arm in arm, the young parents would go downstairs, heated and dishevelled and frequently rather damp. . . . The children called to them as they went, until the final door closed, "Goodnight, Mummie, goodnight, Papa."'[33] Fun included horses and riding in Windsor Great Park in a family party led by their father. It also included dogs: their father's yellow labradors and, from 1933, the famous corgis, now a royal trademark. The first of this stumpy-looking, uncertain-tempered Welsh breed, Rozavel Golden Eagle, known as

'Dookie', became an object of dread to the Household, being all too prone to snap, but this did not deter the Yorks from acquiring another Corgi, Jane, and founding a dynasty. Photographs of the Yorks with their horses and dogs set a new royal style, healthy, open-air, informal, ordinary, far removed from the regimented ranks of Prince Albert's immediate ancestors.

These family snaps contrasted sharply with the photographs of sophisticated bathing-parties round the Prince of Wales's pool at Fort Belvedere, the out-of-town retreat which he acquired in 1930. Fort Belvedere, familiarly known as 'the Fort', was to become notorious as the rendezvous for his weekends with Wallis Simpson and the refuge to which he retreated when the Abdication crisis broke. Described by Diana Cooper, a frequent weekend guest, as 'a child's idea of a fort', the house was an eighteenth-century castellated folly belonging to the royal family on land bordering Windsor Great Park near Sunningdale. Wyatville and George IV had had a hand in it as they had had in the Royal Lodge; it had battlements, cannon and cannon-balls, 'all the little furnishings of war', as Lady Diana put it. The house, like the Royal Lodge, had been neglected, the gardens and woods surrounding it untidy and overgrown. With the help of his mistress, Freda Dudley Ward, the Prince of Wales had modernized and decorated the Fort, adding bathrooms and a swimming-pool. The main feature of the house was a charming, octagonal drawing-room in which the Abdication would be signed. Like Prince Albert, the Prince of Wales became an enthusiastic gardener and would summon his brothers over at weekends to help him clear the shrubbery.

The Yorks were the Prince of Wales's near neighbours at the Royal Lodge and saw a good deal of him during the years before the advent of Wallis Simpson. Although they did not move in the same smart international set, share his quick dashes across the Channel in his private plane piloted by his pilot, Edward 'Mouse' Fielden, go yachting on the Riviera and dance every Thursday night at the Embassy Club in Bond Street, where the Prince of Wales had 'his' table, they remained close on a family basis. Like the rest of the royal family their major preoccupation as far as the Prince of Wales was concerned was to find him a suitable wife. One evening it had seemed that their hopes would be realized. The Yorks were entertaining a woman friend to dinner when the Prince of Wales rang up and asked the three of them round to York House. When they arrived there, there was practically nobody else, except for the beautiful Princess Marina of Greece. 'He danced with her the whole evening,' the Yorks' friend recalled. 'He never danced with anybody else ... the whole time, an hour or two or three. I could see that the Duke and Duchess of York were thrilled. Then Freda Dudley Ward arrived back next day and that was the end of that.'[34] Princess Marina, who later married Prince George, might have been Queen of England. She was the only really suitable woman after Rosemary Leveson-Gore to whom he ever seems to have been attracted, his preference being for married women.

Freda Dudley Ward had been the chief female influence on the Prince's life

since she became his mistress in the spring of 1918. Half-American, she was the
daughter of a rich Nottingham lace manufacturer; King George, who naturally
disapproved of his son's liaison with a married woman, used to refer to her as
'the lace-maker's daughter'. Small, chic and very much 'in Society', Freda Dudley
Ward was generally popular and regarded by most people as the one steadying
influence in the Prince of Wales's life. He had not, however, been physically
faithful to her for years and in the summer of 1929 he met the American
Society beauty Thelma Morgan Furness. Thelma, twin sister of Gloria Morgan
Vanderbilt, had already been married twice, her present husband being Mar-
maduke, Viscount Furness, a philandering shipping magnate several years her
senior. She had Spanish blood and a beauty described as 'hothouse' and 'mag-
nolia-like' by Cecil Beaton, but, despite her exotic looks and the fast life which
she and her twin Gloria had led, she was a simple soul, empty-headed but good-
natured, gay and given to chattering. The Prince of Wales, however, did not
like intellectual women. 'The Prince was not a man for abstract ideas or
ponderous thought; nor was he interested to any extent in the theatre, books or
art,' she later recalled of their affair. 'Our talk was mostly about people we knew
or had known, and about places we knew and liked. . . .'[35] After a romantic safari
together in the spring of 1930, which ended with the Prince falling dangerously
ill of malaria, they began their affair in earnest, dining and dancing at the
Embassy, Ciro's or the Kit-Kat and, at weekends, living in domestic bliss at the
Fort. There is something rather pathetic about the Prince's longing for a
domestic centre to his life and his attempt to create it, with Thelma, at the Fort.
'Our life was quiet, even domestic,' Thelma recalled. 'He pottered in the garden,
pruned his trees, blew on his bagpipes.' Thelma taught him needlepoint, hoping
that it would provide an alternative to his late-night drinking. 'The hand that
holds the needle cannot hold the brandy snifter!' she remarked to a friend.
Thelma's father, Consul Harry Hays Morgan, read aloud to the couple from the
novels of Scott and Dickens as they busied themselves with their needlework.
It was all very cosy; the Prince called Thelma 'Toodles' and the symbol of their
love was teddy bears.

   The Yorks accepted Thelma and got on well with her, often coming over to
the Fort at weekends from the Royal Lodge. On one occasion the Prince of
Wales had received a shipment of gramophone records from the United States.
Inspecting them Prince Albert said, 'Come on, David, let's see if they really are
unbreakable as the label says.' The two brothers went up to the terrace like two
schoolboys, chucking the records in the air and watching them crash down on
to the flagstones, until Prince Albert discovered how to throw them so that they
would curve back like boomerangs. 'While the brothers roared with laughter,
the Duke had us ducking and dodging like rabbits,' Thelma remembered.
'Unfortunately the records didn't break, and the game went on until we all fled
inside. They followed us in and continued their sport in the drawing-room until
one of the Prince's most treasured lamps was bowled over by a direct hit and
only by the greatest good fortune survived unscathed. The Prince then called a

halt.'[36] One winter weekend, Virginia Water, the lake near the Fort, froze over for the first time in living memory. All four brothers, the Duchess of York, Thelma and another woman guest were walking beside it when someone suggested that they should all go skating. Neither the Duchess nor Thelma had ever been skating before, but skates were produced for them and they were led protesting on to the ice. Prince Albert found two kitchen chairs for them to cling to and they made their way round in gales of laughter. 'The lovely face of the Duchess, her superb colouring heightened by the cold, her eyes wrinkled with the sense of fun that was never far below the surface, made a picture I shall never forget,' Thelma later wrote. '... I remember thinking at the time that if I ever had to live in a bungalow in a small town, this is the woman I would most like to have as a next-door neighbour to gossip with while hanging out the washing in our backyards.'[37] A photograph of this time shows a summer house-party beside the swimming-pool at the Fort; all the men and the women, with the exception of the Duchess of York (who is primly clad in hat, frock and twin rows of pearls), are wearing bathing suits. They include Elizabeth's friend and lady-in-waiting, 'Tor-tor' Gilmour, Prince Albert, Lord Louis Mountbatten, Prince Gustav Adolf and Princess Sybilla of Sweden, and Princess Ingrid of Sweden. Thelma, looking sultry and out of place beside this array of princes, princesses and earls' daughters, her 'raven tresses' unfashionably long and her figure unfashionably voluptuous, is sitting curled like an odalisque, at the Duchess of York's feet. It was, perhaps, the last summer of her reign as *maîtresse en titre*, and in the Simpson years at the Fort the Yorks would be conspicuous by their absence.

❦ 6 ❦

THE YEAR OF
THREE KINGS

'After I am dead the boy will ruin himself in twelve months.'
King George v to Baldwin, 1935

THE year 1936 was to be the most traumatic of Prince Albert's life. Within the space of twelve months he was to experience his father's death, his brother's abdication and his own accession to the throne in the most painful circumstances.

Prince Albert was first made aware of a new woman in his elder brother's life in the early summer of 1934: in the last week of March that year, Mrs Ernest Simpson had replaced Lady Furness as the object of the Prince's affections. Prince Albert had already met Wallis Simpson the previous year when, in the absence on business of her husband, Ernest, she had been staying at the Fort for the weekend at the invitation of her great friend, Thelma Furness. The skating-party at the Fort in which the Yorks took part, described by Thelma in her memoirs, took place on Saturday, 28 January 1933. The fifth member of the party, whose name Thelma did not mention, was, in fact, Wallis Simpson. It is doubtful whether she made any great impression upon her future brother-in-law. To him she seemed no more than an agreeable American woman; she was not well known at that time, nor was the Prince in love with her. She was not beautiful, nor as noticeably chic as she later became. She was small, thin, angular, dark-haired, with a high brow over large and lovely eyes and a square, mannish jaw; her worst features were her hands, which were large and ungainly and her high-pitched, harsh voice; her principal attractions were her vivacious personality and gift for a wisecrack. The Yorks may have liked her, most people did; unfortunately, none of the three who were to become such bitter enemies left any record of their first meeting.

It is unlikely that they met again for some time. They did not move in the same circles and, at the time they met in 1933, Ernest Simpson's shipping business had been badly hit by the financial depression. The couple had to struggle to keep up social appearances in their modern flat in Bryanston Court –

'we really can't do but the very minimum entertaining – one dinner per month – and of course can't go to any of the shows [Society events] that are on Ascot, Aldershot etc.... I must refuse as the tickets are four guineas and lunch one guinea a day ...', Wallis wrote to her aunt Bessie Merryman, on 30 May 1933.[1] Within nine months the woman who could not afford the price of a ticket to Ascot joined the Prince of Wales's Ascot house-party at his expense, once again without her husband. In August, with her aunt as chaperone, she was part of a small party comprising the Prince's Household and Gladys Buist, the wife of his equerry, Colin, who was also a friend of Prince Albert's, at a rented villa in Biarritz, followed by a much talked-of cruise with Lord Moyne on his yacht.

By now Prince Albert would have known a good deal about Wallis Simpson, not all of it accurate. The view which the royal family took of her was that she was a common – in every sense – adventuress, a woman of no birth or fortune. In American terms, however, her breeding was impeccable: her father, Teackle Wallis Warfield, came from a well-known Baltimore family; her mother, Alice Montague, from a distinguished Virginia line. Although claiming to have been born on 19 June 1896, recent research shows that she may have been born one year earlier, seventeen months before her parents were married on 19 November 1896; perhaps because of this, she was never baptized, although a baptismal record was later falsified.[2] Her parents were penniless – her father died of tuberculosis when she was two years old and her mother at one time ran a boarding-house – and she learned through bitter experience that money brings security. She had led an independent life for a woman of her time since parting from her alcoholic pilot first husband, Winfield Spencer, in 1922, first in Washington, where she had had an affair with a well-known Argentinian diplomat, and in Peking and New York. She was a social adventuress who liked the good things of life and knew how to get them, mostly through friends who were a great deal better off than herself. According to reports, she had shown social-climbing tendencies early, naming her dolls after Mrs Astor and Mrs Vanderbilt, the leaders of New York Society. She had married Ernest Simpson in July 1928, as she told her mother, partly because she was fond of him, partly because he was kind and because she needed security: 'I can't go on wandering the rest of my life and I really feel so tired of fighting the world all alone and with no money.'[3] Ernest Simpson, unkindly described by Harold Nicolson as 'a good-looking barber's block', was half-British, half-American and a passionate Anglophile, who had turned down the opportunity of becoming an American citizen in order to join the Brigade of Guards as an officer in the First World War. Indeed, on first meeting the Prince of Wales in January 1931, he had (somewhat pathetically in view of what was to happen) remarked to Wallis, 'You Americans lost something that is very good and quite irreplaceable when you decided to dispense with the British Monarchy.'[4]

Prince Albert now saw her as a threat, not because he imagined for one moment that his brother might ever consider marrying her, nor even because, as a middle-aged divorcee married to a second husband, she was not a suitable 'friend' for the Prince of Wales. Thelma Furness had been, after all, on her third husband, while Freda Dudley Ward had a husband living. The strength of his – and the royal family's – reaction to Wallis Simpson as early as the autumn of 1934 was primarily due to the nature of her relationship with the Prince of Wales, as reported by Prince George, who lived with his brother at York House and also had his own room at the Fort. Where Thelma had pandered to the Prince's whims, Wallis dominated him utterly. Where people outside the royal family saw her as a good influence, stopping him drinking so much, smoking in the wrong places and generally making him behave as the Prince Charming he could be and now so rarely was, the royal family in general thought his public adoration of her dangerous to the prestige of the throne. The brothers, Prince Albert and Prince George in particular, disliked her influence over him and resented the way in which she had cut him off from them. Two years later, shortly before the Abdication, Prince George, who had been the closest of anyone to the Prince of Wales, told Thomas Dugdale, the Prime Minister's Private Secretary, that, 'since Mrs Simpson had entered the King's life, neither he nor his brothers had ever seen him as in days gone by and that he had talked to him that morning [8 December 1936] for a longer time than he had enjoyed for over two years'.[5]

Prince George had redeemed himself as the 'black sheep' of the family by becoming engaged to the eminently suitable Princess Marina of Greece in late August 1934. The Yorks had been aware of the possibility of Princess Marina as a bride for Prince George since the previous summer, when the Princess had arrived for a holiday in England with her sister, Princess Olga, and her brother-in-law, Prince Paul of Yugoslavia, and Prince George had been in regular attendance. Prince Paul had acted as the matchmaker by inviting Prince George to stay at Bohinj, his summer house in the Slovenian mountains, when Princess Marina was there in the second half of August 1934. The engagement came as a great relief to everyone; since escaping from the Navy in 1929 Prince George had fulfilled all his father's fears of getting into bad company; he adored Society and low-life nightclubs and spent the early 1930s making up for lost time. Tall, handsome and, as one Society beauty recalled, '*pourri de charme*', George was offered plenty of opportunities for straying from the strait and narrow way which his father would have had him tread, and he seems to have crossed every borderline. Following his elder brother's example, he had a string of affairs with aristocratic girls, at least two of whom, Poppy Baring and Lois Sturt, he had shown signs of wanting to marry. Although well-born, the girls' 'fast' reputations had doomed them in the sight of the King. Prince George, it seems, was open to any experience. The Prince of Wales introduced him to the world of showbusiness and the theatre and he became an intimate of the high Society bisexual, and in some cases exclusively homosexual, set. There were rumours of encounters with an Argentinian diplomat, an Italian aristocrat and Noël Coward. On 28 April 1932 Bruce Lockhart recorded via Randolph Churchill (neither of whom, it must be said, the most reliable of witnesses) that 'there has been a scandal about Prince George – letters to a young man in Paris. A large sum had to be paid for their recovery.'[6] On one occasion he had even been arrested by the police in company with a known homosexual in a louche nightclub, the Nut House, and held in the cells until his identity was discovered. Potentially more dangerous for Prince George was the drug addiction which he picked up in the same London circles in which many of the smart set sniffed cocaine. Drug-taking was fairly common in some circles in the 1920s and 1930s; when the Prince of Wales visited the Muthaiga Club in 1929 cocaine was openly offered round at dinner even before the loyal toast was drunk and in the Prince's presence. Prince George was introduced to cocaine and morphine by an American girl, Kiki Whitney Preston, but his addiction can hardly have been serious since a short course of seclusion in the country under the surveillance of the Prince of Wales and Freda Dudley Ward cured him and he never subsequently reverted.

It could be said that both his father and his elder brother could be blamed in almost equal proportion for Prince George's misdeeds. The King had forced him into a naval career which he hated and for which he was quite unsuited, simply because he was determined that he should have one son in the Navy. Prince George became his brother's running mate at precisely the moment when the Prince of Wales was behaving at his worst, notably on the Canadian and South American tours. Perhaps his family should not have worried; Prince George, his mother's favourite son, had inherited several of her characteristics, not only her taste for collecting, but also her legitimist outlook and her feeling for Family in the royal sense of the word. Not for nothing did Prince George bear a resemblance to the young George III; he could be very 'royal' if crossed and part of Princess Marina's attraction for him certainly lay in her exotic royal blood.

Princess Marina, at twenty-seven, was one of the most beautiful women in Europe and descended from two exceptionally good-looking royal blood lines, the Greek (or rather Schleswig-Holstein-Sonderburg-Glücksburg) and the Russians. Queen Mary, an expert on royal breeding, remarked on the excellent domestic qualities of the Greek royal family. She told Lady Airlie:

> The women of that Danish family make good wives. They have the art of marriage. Look at Queen Alexandra, could any other wife have managed King Edward as well as she did? No bread and butter miss would be of any help to my son, but this girl is sophisticated as well as charming. . . . Theirs will be a happy marriage.[7]

Princess Marina inherited her dark beauty, fine bone structure and family pride from her mother, the Grand Duchess Helen Vladimirovna, and her chic from the family of her father, Prince Nicholas of Greece, nephew of Queen Alexandra. When she arrived at Victoria Station in September 1934, the British crowd, having expected, as Prince George told Prince Paul, 'a dowdy princess – such as unfortunately my family are – . . . could hardly believe it and . . . shouted "Don't change – don't let them change you!" '[8] The couple were ideally suited; Princess Marina, artistic herself, was wise enough to recognize her husband's talents and allowed him to take charge of all the refinements of their life together, furniture, decor, even the food and wine for dinner-parties. According to Freda Dudley Ward, a great friend, Prince George was 'very in love with Princess Marina'.

The Duke and Duchess of York gave an eve-of-the-wedding luncheon at 145 Piccadilly for Princess Marina and Prince George (created Duke of Kent by the King on 12 October 1934) on 28 November. The pleasure in the occasion had been somewhat spoiled by the appearance of Wallis Simpson at the pre-wedding reception at Buckingham Palace the previous evening. As they had followed the King and Queen into the ballroom, they could not help but notice Mrs Simpson among the guests lining the way for the royal family. As Prince Paul told her when introduced by the Prince of Wales, she was wearing the 'most striking gown in the room', violet *lamé* designed for her by Eva Lutyens with a vivid green sash, no doubt intended to match the emerald and diamond jewellery given to her by the Prince. The Prince of Wales introduced her to his parents, who, concealing an inner indignation, behaved with impeccable manners, impressing their future daughter-in-law, 'with Their Majesties' great gift for making everyone they met ... feel at ease in their presence'. At least that was how the Duchess of Windsor was to recall the episode in her memoirs; privately, at the time, she wrote to her aunt of 'the excitement of the Prince bringing the Queen up to Ernest and self in front of all the cold jealous English eyes'.[9] In fact, the King later told his Private Secretary, Clive Wigram, of his 'fury' that the Prince had 'smuggled Mrs Simpson into the Palace' and then had the effrontery to introduce her to himself and the Queen. This feeling, according to Wigram, was shared by other members of the royal family, which undoubtedly included the Yorks. They did not enjoy seeing Mr and Mrs Simpson in some of the best seats in Westminster Abbey for the Kents' wedding, but at least they did not know that in return for a gift of £50 from a friend, Betty L. Johnston, she had arranged to get her into the Buckingham Palace reception.[10]

There was nothing Prince Albert could do in the face of the Prince of Wales's increasing infatuation except hope that it would pass. He knew from past experience that nothing he could say would influence his brother against doing anything he wanted to do and that to oppose him would only increase his obstinacy in doing it. One factor, however, increased his own resentment of the affair and, therefore, of Wallis Simpson, and that was his concern that worry over the relationship was seriously affecting his father's health. In February Wallis Simpson, without her husband, went with the Prince of Wales for ten days' ski-ing at Kitzbühel, followed by visits to Vienna and Budapest; 'suggestive stories', as the King's Secretary put it, filtered back to Buckingham Palace and, worse still, in the United States the Hearst press was in full cry after the royal romance with comments about the jewellery the Prince had given Wallis Simpson. Gossip about the Prince of Wales's affairs in London Society was nothing new, but the appearance of comment in black-and-white newsprint was a different matter. Anything which appeared in American newspapers would be

'Gangan': Queen Victoria with her great-grandchildren, 1899. From left to right: Princess Mary, Prince Edward, Prince Henry (on her lap) and Prince Albert (seated in front)

Edward VII as Prince of Wales

Queen Alexandra outside Sandringham Kennels with her three eldest grandchildren. From left to right: Prince Albert, Prince Edward and Princess Mary. Painting by Fred Morgan and Thomas Blinks

The Duchess of York's boudoir at York Cottage, 1897

The Prince and Princess of Wales with their
children, 1906. From left to right: Princess
Mary, Prince Henry (seated), Prince
George (standing on chair), Prince John
(in the Princess's arms), Prince Edward
and Prince Albert

Prince Albert aged two

rk Cottage. Prince Albert was born in his mother's bow-fronted, first-floor bedroom on the extreme left

rom left to right: Prince Edward and Prince Albert with their tutor, Mr H. P. Hansell, at Sandringham,
11

ABOVE: *Louis Greig, portrait drawing by a fellow prisoner of war at Halle camp, November 1914*

LEFT: *Prince Albert as a midshipman in 1914*

RIGHT: *'Coaling': Prince Albert (second from left) and shipmates dressed for the job, HMS* Cumberland *1913*

BELOW: *Jutland. Unpublished letter from Prince Albert describing the battle to Mrs Godfrey-Faussett, dated 11 June 1916*

H. M. S. "Collingwood"
4th Battle Squadron
c/o G. P. O.

June 11th 1916.

Dear Mrs Faussett,

Very many thanks for your letter. It was very kind of you to have written to me. I am quite all right and feel very different now that I have seen a German ship filled with Germans and have seen it fired at with ones guns. It was a great experience to have gone through and one not easily forgotten How and why we were not hit or damaged beats me, as we were being fired at a good part of

Prince Albert in the Officers' Mess at Cranwell

The Prince of Wales and Prince Albert in France, 1918

Lady Maureen Stanley

Mabell, Countess of Airlie

Phyllis Monkman

Mrs Ronald Greville in 1891, by Carolus-Duran

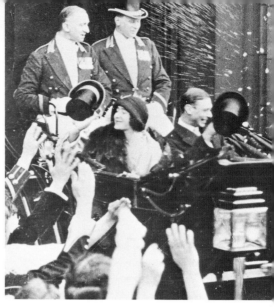

The Duke of York and Lady Elizabeth Bowes-Lyon at the time of their engagement in January 1923

The Duke and Duchess of York leaving Buckingham Palace after their wedding on 26 April 1923

The Duke and Duchess of York on their honeymoon at Polesden Lacey, 1923

The wedding of Prince Paul of Serbia and Princess Olga of Greece in Belgrade, 22 October 1923. Among those present are from left to right: standing, Princess Marina of Greece, Prince Andrew of Greece, Queen Elisabeth of Greece, the Duke of York, King George of Greece (behind the Duke of York), Crown Prince Carol of Romania, half-obscured by King Alexander of Serbia (later Yugoslavia), King Ferdinand of Romania, Prince Arsène Karageorgevic (father of Prince Paul); seated, Princess Nicholas of Greece, Queen Sophie of Greece, Princess Olga, Prince Paul, Queen Marie of Romania, the Duchess of York. Princess Ileana of Romania and the bride's sister, Princess Elisabeth, are seated on the ground in front

The christening of Princess Elizabeth at Buckingham Palace, 29 May 1926. Standing from left to right: the Duke of Connaught, King George V, the Duke of York, the Earl of Strathmore. Seated from left to right: Lady Elphinstone, Queen Mary, the Duchess of York with Princess Elizabeth, the Countess of Strathmore, Princess Mary

read across the border in Canada, considered at the time to be Britain's principal Dominion. Stories about the heir to the throne openly parading his married mistress and lavishing jewellery upon her would, Prince Albert and his family feared, damage the prestige of the Crown. They understood, as members of the Prince of Wales's set in London Society did not, that the vast middle-class conscience across the Empire would find the affair offensive.

There was now an additional reason why the prestige of the Crown vis-à-vis its imperial role had become of more vital importance. In 1931 the Statute of Westminster had granted autonomy to the self-governing Dominions, Canada, Australia, New Zealand, South Africa, Newfoundland and the Irish Free State. It officially marked the end of the 'forward' imperial policy symbolized by Disraeli's creation of Queen Victoria as 'Empress of India' and the renunciation by Britain of her imperial mission. It was the real beginning of decentralization and disengagement on the part of the old imperial power, which was to accelerate almost to its conclusion in the reign of George VI. The Statute of Westminster emphasized the role of the Crown as the link of Empire, 'inasmuch as the Crown is the symbol of the free association of the members of the British Commonwealth of Nations, and as they are united by common allegiance to the Crown', the wording of the Statute ran. The corollary of this new aspect of the monarch as the freely acknowledged sovereign of the autonomous Dominions was to have crucial relevance in the Abdication crisis; any alteration in the royal succession or title, the Statute stated, shall 'require the assent of the Parliaments of all the Dominions, as of the Parliament of the United Kingdom'. This enhancement of the symbolic role of the Crown made the image of the monarch and his personal behaviour even more important in an age when the expansion of the communications media could convey that image more immediately and to a wider audience than ever before. The Empire was still the major preoccupation in Britain among all classes and, as it began to dissolve, so British statesmen clung even more firmly to the imperial idea in its new context. The Crown more than ever before became the symbol of that idea and the fate of the monarchy inextricably linked to Britain's new imperial role.

Prince Albert, with his deep interest in the Constitution, the monarchy and its symbolic significance, understood this very well as his elder brother did not and would not. 'My private life is my own affair' had always been his inevitable response to criticism of his personal behaviour. The personal aspect of the British Crown was brought out strongly in that year by the world-wide response to King George V's Silver Jubilee celebrations, which began with a Thanksgiving Service at St Paul's Cathedral on 6 May 1935, the twenty-fifth anniversary of King George's accession. The royal family drove to St Paul's in open carriages, observed by Chips Channon from a vantage-point in St James's Palace: 'the Yorks in a large landau with the two tiny pink children. The Duchess of York was charming and gracious, the baby princesses much interested in the proceedings and waving'; then the Kents, 'that dazzling pair'; and, finally, 'the

Prince of Wales smiling his dentist's smile and waving to his friends, but he still has his old spell for the crowd'. The star of the whole show, however, was Queen Mary 'in her white and silvery splendour'. 'Never', Channon recorded, 'has she looked so serene, so regally majestic, even so attractive. . . . Suddenly she has become the best-dressed woman in the world.' From Buckingham Palace that evening the King broadcast to his people, a simple affecting broadcast (written for the occasion by his friend the Archbishop of Canterbury) which he delivered in his fine English voice:

I can only say to you, my very very dear people, that the Queen and I thank you from the depths of our hearts for all the loyalty and – may I say so? – the love, with which this day and always you have surrounded us. I dedicate myself anew to your service for all the years that may still be given me.

Every evening during that week crowds gathered outside the Palace to sing 'For he's a jolly good fellow' and, when the King and Queen drove out round the East End, their reception was tumultuous. Returning to the Palace on Thursday evening, the King said to Archbishop Lang, in genuine surprise at his subjects' warmth, 'But I cannot understand. I am quite an ordinary sort of fellow,' to which the Archbishop somewhat unflatteringly replied: 'Yes, Sir, that is just it.' The Archbishop's chaplain and secretary, Alan Campbell Don, commented on the way in which the new medium of broadcasting had projected the personal image of the King: 'the people have come to see in the King just one of them – for which in large measure we have to thank the invention of wireless which can project a man's personality through the ether'.[11]

The nature of the image which King George presented did not escape the foreign envoys and press representatives in London during that week. The French Ambassador, René Corbin, reported to the Quai d'Orsay: 'during the course of the years, he [George v] has become not only the King, but the Father of his peoples and to the loyalty has come to add the warmth of love. That is the secret of the personal and living emotion which to-day fills the heart of this Kingdom and Empire.' Corbin followed this up by making a very important point, the very real, even if symbolic, significance of the Crown to the Empire:

In the course of the great silence which followed the King's broadcast, the foreign observer could not but be struck by the cohesion and power which the family of the British Democracies draw from their attachment to the Crown, considered at the same time as a paternal force and the symbol of unity. . . .[12]

The French envoy in Berlin, François-Poncet, observed the same reaction in the German press. The *Deutsche Allgemeine Zeitung*, hailing George v as 'father of the nation', remarked that 'the Sovereign of Great Britain was much more than a King of England – he was the head of a world Empire and it was the personality of George v that had made it possible'.[13] On a lesser note it was reported that such was the goodwill generated during Jubilee week in London that although the buses and tubes, which normally carried twelve million, transported a record fourteen and a half million, the only complaint was by one woman of having her behind pinched on an escalator.

'I suppose never in our history have we been so blessed!' MP Victor Cazalet, commented. 'Materially. Politically. No strikes. Trade good. Politics quiet, Empire united.' Behind the euphoria of the Jubilee, however, Prince Albert was aware of the extreme concern of the King and his advisers about the Prince of Wales's behaviour. At Whitsun that year, Cazalet, who was on friendly terms with all the royal family, noted in his diary after a long talk with the Prince of Wales, 'Mrs Simpson has complete control. He never leaves her and she can make him do anything and talk to anyone. K[ing] & Q[ueen] very worried. Think P[rince] of W[ales] will throw away all prestige of throne....'[14] Prince Albert knew that at Easter 1935 Clive Wigram had gone over from Windsor to the Fort to warn the Prince of Wales that his father's health was precarious and that when the Prince succeeded to the throne he would find that 'the middle-class Nonconformist section would not tolerate a Sovereign keeping company with another man's wife, however innocent their relations might be'. The Prince had replied with the formula he always used, that his private life was his own affair. The King's reaction had been to instruct Wigram to give orders to the Lord Chamberlain that Mrs Simpson was not to be given invitations to any of the Silver Jubilee functions nor to the Royal Enclosure at Ascot. Six days after the Jubilee Thanksgiving Service at St Paul's the King himself had a long and serious talk with the Prince of Wales about the future if he became King, deploring the fact that he had never married. The Prince had replied that he could never marry as such a life had no appeal to him. When the King flatly accused him of keeping Mrs Simpson as his mistress, the Prince, according to Wigram's diary account, 'was very annoyed and gave the King his word of honour that he had never had any immoral relations with Mrs S.' Disingenuously, the Prince attributed his break with Thelma Furness to his obedience to his father's wishes rather than his passion for Wallis: 'He had broken with Lady Furness, whom he now called a "beast", as the King had asked him to do, but Mrs Simpson was quite different and "made him supremely happy".' He begged the King to believe she was not his mistress and that she should be invited to the Jubilee ball and to Ascot. Wigram then recorded:

The King said that if HRH would give his word of honour that his friendship with Mrs S. was absolutely a clean one, then the King would naturally believe the word of HRH. To this HRH gave his word and the King said that he would arrange for invitations to be sent to Mr and Mrs S.[15]

And so, to the mortification of the royal family, Mr and Mrs Simpson were invited to the State ball on 14 May where, as if to underscore his point to his family, the Prince of Wales, after opening the ball with his mother, danced the next dance with Wallis as if she were the most important woman there. Although her diamond tiara was borrowed from Cartier, the rest of her jewellery was provided by the Prince: 'I have lovely diamond clips as a Jubilee present,' she boasted to her aunt. On 17 June Wallis was at Ascot, this time without her husband, as the star of the Prince's house-party, composed of his Household and, for one night, Emerald Cunard. The King, unusually for him, broke the tradition of a lifetime and retired to Sandringham in the second week in June, perhaps to avoid the spectacle of Wallis Simpson on his son's arm at Ascot. The Yorks, however, did go, perhaps unhappily aware that in the United States the Hearst press was already hinting at a Simpson divorce because of the Prince's affair with Wallis. They could not avoid seeing Mrs Simpson as she was invited everywhere, to the Londonderrys', the Dudleys', Lady Weymouth's, Lord Moyne's, or, as she put it, 'All the very best titles come across whereas no one noticed Mrs Simpson before'

Prince Albert was made more miserable by the feeling that Wallis was corrupting his brother, accepting not only jewellery but also money from him. It was obvious to anyone that the frequency and style of the Simpsons' entertainments could hardly have been achieved on Ernest Simpson's depressed income from his shipping business. Worse than all this, however, was Prince Albert's suspicion that his brother had lied to his father over the nature of his relations with Wallis. According to Wigram's diary account of the interview in May 1935: 'Halsey and the Prince's staff were horrified at the audacity of the statements of HRH. Apart from actually seeing HRH and Mrs S. in bed together they had positive proof that HRH lived with her.'[16] The Prince of Wales always denied both then and later that he had ever been Wallis's lover, successfully suing one author who described him as such and threatening to do the same to his brother's official biographer if he did not drop the word from his book. His motive was almost certainly to protect Wallis's honour. However badly he may have behaved towards other people, towards her he was always the paladin of medieval romance. An additional motive may have been to avoid any suggestion that the Simpson divorce had been collusive and that Wallis was anything other than the injured party. The couple took great pains to cover their tracks; after 1 January 1935 Wallis no longer signed the Visitor's book at the Fort, as the Duke of Kent pointed out to Walter Monckton, the Prince's friend, legal adviser, and Attorney-General to the Duchy of Cornwall.[17] According to the Manuscript Journal of Sir Donald Somervell, Attorney-General at the time of the Abdication and after, investigations by the King's Proctor, Sir Thomas Barnes, which he had authorized, revealed nothing:

Barnes interviewed countless people, members of the crew of the yacht [the *Nahlin*, on which Edward VIII and Wallis were to make their famous cruise in July 1936], servants, hall porters. Barnes became convinced they would get nothing. If they had committed adultery they had done so discreetly and had not publicly indulged in familiarities which normally indicate cohabitation. . . .

Except, it would seem, at the Fort, where the Prince's Household, according to Wigram's diary entry, had positive proof that he had lived with her. 'Lived with' was the contemporary phrase for having sex with, and the meaning of

Wigram's account is not only that the Prince and Wallis had been seen in bed together, but that there was evidence of a physical sexual act having taken place. Either the Prince was lying or his senior staff was guilty of a vicious piece of slander in telling Wigram this, which, given the character of a man like Halsey, normally extremely protective of the Prince, seems highly unlikely. It was, moreover, straining credulity to its limits to accept that a man like the Prince of Wales, who was known for the quantity, if not the quality, of his sexual encounters, should not have gone to bed with this woman with whom he was so passionately in love. The fact that such an encounter would have been adulterous would not have given him the slightest qualm; a large proportion of his previous mistresses had been married women. Lady Diana Cooper, who was very much a member of the inner circle of the friends of Wallis and the Prince of Wales, and who was a guest on the *Nahlin* in July 1936, told Harold Nicolson a year later that she did not believe that 'the King had no physical relations with Mrs Simpson before the marriage. She says', Nicolson noted in an unpublished section of his diary, 'that on the "Nahlin" they had cabins detached from all the other cabins and communicating with each other.'[18] It is hard to see what other interpretation than that they were, indeed, sleeping together could be put on a note of 'Friday night' (5 June 1936) from the then King at the Fort to Wallis in Paris. After telling her now much he is missing her, he writes: 'WE [private code for Wallis and Edward] have just had a lovely long talk but that is a poor substitute for holding tight and making drowsy. No and not making own drowsies either as we have had to do far too often lately.'[19] While it is true that the physical side of their relationship was not the most important part of Wallis's attraction for the Prince, that he found in her a soul mate and, to use Winston Churchill's romantic phrase, she became 'as necessary to his happiness as the air he breathed', the fact remains that in denying that she was his mistress before their marriage he was almost certainly not telling the truth.

If Wigram knew that the Prince of Wales was not telling the truth in May 1935, then it is certain that Prince Albert knew it too. In his eyes, and this explains much of his subsequent actions and attitudes after the Abdication, Wallis Simpson was a social predator who had bewitched and degraded his brother for her own ends. It was evident to everyone that the keynote of their relationship was Wallis's 'domination' of the Prince, underlined by such incidents as this which took place at the house of a childhood friend of the royal family, 'Poots' Butler, née van Raalte, wife of Prince George's equerry Humphrey Butler.

THE PRINCE: 'Have you got a light, darling?'
WALLIS: 'Have you done your duty?'
Little man gets on his haunches, puts up his hands and begs like a dog. She then lights his cigarette. Horrible to see....[20]

While this little scene was intended to be a joke, it was hardly the kind of behaviour the royal family welcomed in the presence of witnesses.

Meanwhile, the Yorks continued to follow the traditional pattern of their lives, which, at the close of the London season, paralleled the King's. They spent a week in brilliant sunshine at Cowes early in August, then returned home to the Royal Lodge to help settle in a redundant shipworker from Sunderland whom they had taken into their employ. 'He told me that you could pick a bunch of flowers in any of the shipyards in Sunderland,' the Duchess wrote to a friend.[21] They then travelled north to Scotland for a week grouse-shooting on the estate of millionaire J.P. Morgan, followed by a visit to Glamis, where Prince Albert went shooting with his brothers-in-law. From Glamis at the end of August they settled at Birkhall on the Balmoral Estate. While Prince Albert spent his days in the open, shooting and stalking 'on the hill', the Duchess occupied herself reading and writing to her literary friends, Duff Cooper and Osbert Sitwell among them.

There could have been no greater contrast between the Yorks' quiet family holiday with their children at Birkhall and the two-month vacation which the Prince of Wales was taking with Wallis in Europe. First he rented the Marquess of Cholmondeley's villa, Le Roc, on the Riviera at Golfe Juan, for a party which included the Prince's equerry, Sir John 'Jack' Aird, a tall, witty Guards officer, his friends the Buists, Lord Brownlow and his beautiful wife Kitty, Lord Beaverbrook's sister-in-law, Helen Fitzgerald, and her 'boyfriend', another friend of the Prince's, and the glamorous, rich racehourse owner, the Earl of Sefton, all of whom were described by Wallis as 'très chic'.

Très chic, too, were the people they mixed with: Lady Mendl, the most expensive and sought-after Society decorator; the Earl and Countess of Portarlington; Daisy Fellowes, a legendary Society figure, daughter of the Duc Decazes and a Singer sewing-machine heiress; the Duke of Westminster, named Bendor after a racehorse and one of the richest men in the world; and Winston Churchill. Lord Louis Mountbatten turned up on his destroyer with the King of Spain's eldest son, the Prince of Asturias. They spent four days in Corsica on the Duke of Westminster's yacht, then travelled to Budapest, Vienna and Paris, where Wallis, helped by her friend, ex-model 'Foxy' Gwynne (who later married Sefton) bought clothes at half-price from Mainbocher. The trip took on a semi-official tone as Wallis and the Prince lunched at the British Embassy with Pierre Laval and the French Cabinet. They dined with Elsie Mendl and the Prince, this time without Wallis, lunched with the French President. It was, Wallis wrote somewhat disingenuously to her aunt, 'a most successful and popular visit for him as he had never been in Paris so long and the King was most pleased with his efforts'. No doubt the King would have been more pleased had the Prince not been so publicly accompanied by Mrs Simpson; possibly, too, he may have equated the unaccustomed length of the Prince's stay in Paris with Mrs Simpson's visits to couturiers. Fortunately he did not know that the Prince smuggled Wallis's Mainbocher clothes back in his private plane. Wallis's 'spoils' from her visit to Paris were obvious to everyone in their circle. Lady Diana Cooper, after dining at the Fort on 6 October, could hardly wait to ring Chips Channon early next morning with the news: 'Mrs Simpson was glittering, and dripped in new jewels and clothes. . . .'

At Balmoral, however, the Prince of Wales/Mrs Simpson affair cast a dark shadow over the royal family's holiday. On 5 September the King had a conversation with Eric Savill, who was in charge of Windsor Park and the adjacent Crown Lands. Savill told him that he had recently been approached by the Prince of Wales, who wished to acquire Fort Belvedere from the Crown as his personal property, giving as his reason the somewhat implausible one that, according to Wigram's report of the conversation, 'the day may come when a republic will be declared in this country and he will have nowhere to live unless Belvedere is his own private property'. It may well be that the old King saw through this elaborate excuse; after all the Prince knew that under his father's will both Sandringham and Balmoral would pass to him on his father's death as private family property. Moreover, the King pointed out, if a republic were to be declared, then the Prince would certainly not be able to live in England and his private property would very probably be confiscated. Meanwhile, since Belvedere was not private family property but part of the Crown Lands, it could not be sold without the sanction of Parliament and the passing of a Bill to allow Crown Lands to sell it. To put a final stop to any such scheme, he also told Savill that any such Bill would have to provide that, on the Prince of Wales's death, the property would have to pass to his successor on the throne and could not be bequeathed to any private individual.[22] This was intended to warn the Prince of Wales off the plan since the King clearly suspected that his son intended to either give or leave the Fort to Wallis. The King was far from strong, with bouts of sleepiness during the day and restlessness at night, even needing the occasional administration from oxygen tanks kept in his bedroom. He worried a great deal about the Simpson situation as his old friend, the Archbishop of Canterbury, at Balmoral for his annual visit, reported to Alan Campbell Don. 'Things look very black – an hour yesterday in the garden with the King outpouring his troubles,' Lang wrote on 20 September.[23] Lang also discussed the King's anxiety when he lunched with the Yorks at Birkhall.

The royal family suspected that the Belvedere scheme had something to do with Wallis; they were well aware that this relationship was different from the Prince's previous attachments. When Lang tried to reassure the King by remarking that the Prince had had 'friendships' before, King George replied that this was far more serious than the others. They do not, however, seem to have contemplated as an explanation of the Fort Belvedere scheme that the Prince of Wales was envisaging an eventuality that he might have to give up his family inheritance in order to marry Wallis. But, by the end of a two-month holiday with Wallis, unencumbered either by husband or chaperone, he seems to have come to a determination that marriage was his ultimate goal. Inside the wedding ring which he was to give to his wife on the occasion of their marriage at Candé was inscribed not only the date of their wedding but also '18-10-35', implying that they entered into an 'engagement' on 18 October 1935.

In contrast to the Prince of Wales's secret pledge to Wallis, the engagement of Prince Henry to Lady Alice Montagu-Douglas-Scott was publicly announced in August. Prince Henry, created Duke of Gloucester by his father in 1928, was now an officer with a crack cavalry regiment, the Tenth Hussars; his bride was the younger sister of his fellow officer and best friend, Lord William Scott. At thirty-five Prince Henry, with his round pink face and prominent blue eyes, was the most Hanoverian-looking of all the children of King George and Queen Mary. Lacking the social graces of his elder and younger brothers, he was good-natured, convivial, fond of whisky, horses and country life in general, and perfectly content with the life of an ordinary cavalry officer; the summit of his ambition was to be colonel of his regiment. His bride came of a Scottish family which was even richer and grander than Elizabeth Bowes-Lyon's; Lady Alice had royal blood through King Charles II's eldest illegitimate son, James, Duke of Monmouth, and close royal associations. Her father, the Duke of Buccleuch, had been on *Bacchante* with King George as a cadet, her grandmother on her father's side had been Mistress of the Robes to Queen Alexandra, while her maternal grandmother, the Countess of Bradford, had been lady-in-waiting to Queen Mary when she was Duchess of York. Her father was a great landowner both in Scotland and in England, with a number of houses, two of which, Drumlanrig in Dumfriesshire and Boughton in Northamptonshire, could well be described as palaces and contained some of the finest collections of paintings, books, manuscripts and works of art in Britain. Lady Alice, however, had been brought up in a simple, family atmosphere, loving horses and outdoor life; she was desperately shy and found fashionable Society both boring and terrifying. Despite being a daughter of one of Britain's richest dukes, she had to borrow suitable clothes from her sister Angela when invited to Balmoral with her mother on the occasion of her engagement. She none the less fitted perfectly into the royal family. Queen Mary was particularly delighted by her son marrying such an eminently suitable girl whose grandmothers she had known so well, and she was popular, too, with the Yorks. 'The Duchess of York and the future King George VI were always an immense support,' Princess Alice was to write in her memoirs.

The Gloucesters were married in the private chapel at Buckingham Palace on 6 November 1935. The wedding was a quiet family affair since the bride's father had died of cancer on 19 October; Princesses Elizabeth and Margaret Rose were bridesmaids, dressed by Hartnell in Kate Greenaway dresses specially shortened at the King's order because 'I want to see their pretty little knees'. At the signing of the Register the King made 'unfavourable comments' on the quality of the pen and Queen Mary, on asking the history of Archbishop Lang's Primatial Cross, was disappointed to hear it was not an antique. The happy couple failed to cut the over-royal and too stiff icing on the cake with the traditional officer's sword, which visibly irritated the King. The Gloucesters, having been instructed that the Kents' foreign honeymoon the previous year had been considered 'extravagant', were told to spend theirs quietly in England and went hunting from Boughton and woodcock-shooting in Northern Ireland. The King's diary entry for their wedding day had read, 'Now all the children are married but David.' Earlier that year, however, he had been heard by a lady-in-waiting to remark, 'I pray to God that my eldest son will never marry and have children, and that nothing will come between Bertie and Lilibet and the throne.'

It was agonizingly obvious to Prince Albert as autumn deepened into the winter of 1935 that his father was, as his doctor, Lord Dawson, told the Prime Minister, Stanley Baldwin, 'packing up his luggage and getting ready to depart'. The death on 3 December of his favourite sister, Princess Victoria, was a heavy blow to the King; overcome with grief, for the first time ever he cancelled his State Opening of Parliament; he was never to appear in public again. It was a family Christmas at Sandringham as usual that year, the Yorks and their children, the Kents with their first child, Prince Edward, born on 9 October, and the Gloucesters, the accident-prone Prince Henry having broken his collar-bone hunting. This year it was not the usual happy occasion. The King looked thin and bent; he was sleepy during the day, restless and breathless at night, when the handyman used to carry up the oxygen tanks in the early hours. The Prince of Wales was restless, snatching surreptitious calls to Wallis and all too clearly longing to get back to her.

The year 1936 did not open promisingly for Prince Albert: Elizabeth caught influenza and then developed pneumonia. She was still ill and weak at the Royal Lodge when, on 16 January, he received a summons from his mother to go back to Sandringham. The message was characteristically low key; a small house-party had arrived, but the King had retired to his bedroom feeling too unwell to go downstairs. 'Most worrying,' the Queen confided to her diary; 'I sent for Bertie to help me with the party.' It should be noted that the Queen did not send for her eldest son, who had no other official commitments and was at the Fort, but for Prince Albert, despite the fact that his wife was very ill and it was, therefore, extremely inconvenient for him to leave her and go to Sandringham. Prince Albert, however, knew that his mother would not have sent for him unless it was a case of urgency and left for Norfolk. He found his father very drowsy, dressed in a faded old Tibetan dressing-gown, a relic of an Indian visit, sitting in his chair in front of the bedroom fire, sleeping or staring out at the square tower of Sandringham Church visible through the bare trees. It was obvious that death would only be a matter of time. Princess Mary was there and, on Friday the 17th, the Prince of Wales arrived in his private plane, having received a cautious note from his mother the previous afternoon while out shooting in Windsor Great Park, 'I think you ought to know that Papa is not very well,' suggesting that he should 'propose himself for the week-end'. Lord Dawson and Clive Wigram arrived that evening.

For Prince Albert and his mother, their pain at the King's approaching death was greatly increased by anxiety about the future. The Queen told Wigram on the evening of his arrival that both she and Prince Albert had been 'horrified' to hear from the Prince of Wales that their beloved Sandringham was regarded by the Prince of Wales only as a 'hobby' (of his father's, presumably). Wigram, attempting to calm her fears, had replied that 'everyone was rather keyed up and not responsible for their thoughts or words'. On Sunday, while Prince Albert was absent, they discussed it again and the idea of a joint-stock company with the Prince of Wales and the Duke of York both contributing to the upkeep of the estate was put forward. Wigram, in his own words, was appalled at the prospect of 'dishonouring the memory' of King George by breaking up his cherished estate and told the Queen he thought that the expenses, then running at the huge sum of £50,000 a year, could be reduced. The Queen then confided to Wigram that she was dividing up the late Princess Victoria's jewellery between the Duchesses of York, Gloucester and Kent, but giving nothing to the Prince of Wales, 'who might pass them on to Mrs Simpson'.[24]

On Sunday 19 January Prince Albert and the Prince of Wales motored up to London, where they parted, the Prince of Wales in strict order of personal priority visiting Wallis at her flat before having tea with the Baldwins at No. 10 Downing Street to discuss arrangements for the succession. Baldwin, as he told his confidant, Tom Jones, was perfectly aware of where the future King had been before calling at Downing Street. Having spoken to Halsey and to the Prince of Wales's Private Secretary, Godfrey Thomas, he was under no illusion as to the problems he might have to face. 'When I was a little boy in Worcestershire reading history books,' he told Jones, 'I never thought I should have to interfere between a King and his mistress.' Prince Albert, deeply anxious, went down to the Royal Lodge to see his family. His wife was still very ill and it was with that additional worry that he returned to Norfolk on Monday 20 January with his brother in his private plane. Prince George had arrived the previous day, Prince Henry being ill in bed with laryngitis at Buckingham Palace. So too, uninvited, had the Archbishop of Canterbury, much to the annoyance of the Prince of Wales, who disliked and distrusted him and even tried to persuade Lord Dawson to tell him to leave.

On that Monday the formal arrangements for the King's passing, even to the timing of his actual death, were completed. That morning the King, too feeble to do more than make his mark on a document, held his last Privy Council to authorize a Council of State to exercise his authority. Wigram ordered his coffin, while Dawson obtained the permission of the family for the peaceful termination of the King's life. The King's doctor orchestrated the King's end; that evening, as the family were at dinner, he sat down with Wigram and composed the bulletin which was to warn Britain and the Empire that their sovereign was dying. Taking a Sandringham menu card, Dawson wrote a phrase that was to be remembered by millions: 'The King's life is moving peacefully to its close.' He then took it to the family at dinner for their approval and it was telephoned through to the BBC for the evening broadcast.

The whole episode of the euthanasia of King George V ushered in a new era of awareness by the Palace of the importance of the media to the monarchy. Dawson later admitted that the moment of the King's death was timed for its announcement to be made in the respectable morning papers, and *The Times* in particular, rather than 'the less appropriate evening journals'. He even telephoned his wife in London to advise *The Times* to hold back the morning's edition as the announcement of the King's death was to be expected. After dinner the Prince of Wales and Prince Albert, assisted by Wigram, drew up plans for the funeral. The date and arrangements for the Accession Council and Proclamation of the new King had already been agreed. That night, however, the old King lingered on; Dawson, seeing that his condition of 'stupor and coma' might last for many hours and could easily disrupt all arrangements, therefore 'decided to determine the end and injected ... morphia gr. 3/4 & shortly afterwards cocaine gr. 1 into the distended jugular vein. ... In about $\frac{1}{4}$ an hour – breathing quieter – appearance more placid – physical struggle gone.' Prince Albert and his family had left the room at this point, the only witness of Dawson's administration of the fatal drug being the King's regular nurse, Sister Catherine Black, who, Dawson admitted, was 'disturbed by this procedure'. Prince Albert later returned with the family to watch his father die almost imperceptibly. 'Intervals between respirations lengthened, and life passed so quietly and gently that it was difficult to determine the actual moment,' Dawson noted.[25] The moment of death was given as 11.55 p.m. and broadcast by the BBC at 12.15 a.m. In the late King's bedroom at Sandringham Prince Albert saw his mother, guardian of the royal tradition to the end, take his brother's hand to kiss it in homage to the new sovereign. The reign of Edward VIII had begun.

It was Prince Albert, however, who was to inherit his father's mantle and tradition in the sense that he represented the dignified, dutiful and domestic life which his father had established as the pattern for the British monarchy. The new King's first actions were symbolic of his determination to break with that tradition. He called himself Edward after his grandfather in whose gallantries, according to his uncle Athlone, he had always as a boy taken 'an unhealthy interest'. When Athlone tried to discourage him the young Prince would inevitably ask, 'But, Uncle Algy, wasn't my grandfather very popular with everyone?' 'It was all right in his time,' Athlone riposted, 'but nobody would stand it today!'[26] Even before his father died, he had given the order to change the clocks on the estate from Sandringham to Greenwich Time.

Through the next twelve months, which were to see the crisis of the British monarchy and crucially affect his own future, Prince Albert was to be little more than an anguished spectator in the developing drama as he saw his brother distancing himself more and more from his family. Even during the sad days at Sandringham as his father lay dying, there had been pointers to an unsettled future – the matter of preserving Sandringham itself, the minor question of the clocks, the tension between the Prince of Wales and his father's old friend, the Archbishop of Canterbury, the patent anxieties of Wigram. It was as if battle lines were already being drawn between the old tradition and the new, between the family, the 'old' Court which, indeed, included most of the new King's

Household, and the Church on the one side and on the other the new King with all the powers of his personality and of his immense mass popularity, his well-known obstinacy and his fixed ideas of the 'new', and, as the power behind the throne, the woman who seemed to dominate the King to the exclusion of everyone and everything else. Prince Albert's fears and those of his family were emphasized by a photograph of the Proclamation ceremony in the courtyard of St James's Palace. Glimpsed through a window looking down on the heralds who were officially proclaiming him were the new King, grave-faced, in dark suit and tie, and, seated in the place of honour in front of him, a woman in a chic hat and furs. The newspaper caption beneath the photograph did not mention her name but she was, of course, Wallis Simpson, watching the proclamation of, as, confused by the Latin numerals, she put it to her aunt in a curious but indicative slip, 'Edward XVIII'.

Prince Albert, who had been closest of all the brothers to his father, must have been surprised at his elder brother's extreme reaction to his father's death. Just before King George died, the Prince of Wales, according to Wigram's diary account, 'became hysterical, cried loudly, and kept on embracing the Queen', while Dawson noted that when he signified 'that death had arrived' the Prince of Wales left the room crying aloud, although he returned later, stood for a while by his father's bedside and said, 'I hope I will make good as he has made good.' He would have attributed it perhaps to feelings of guilt; having literally hated his father while he was alive and being conscious of how much anxiety he had caused him, the new King was suffering a natural reaction. Prince Albert could not know that the hysteria was caused by panic; his brother was locked in a personal crisis made far more difficult for him to resolve now that his father was dead. Edward VIII's Household came to believe that he had intended to elope with Wallis before his father died, thus resolving the situation with a *fait accompli*. Two days after the Abdication Lascelles told Harold Nicolson that 'from "internal evidence" they suspect that he had decided to run away with Mrs Simpson before the King died. They were to do a bunk in February.'[27] A note written three weeks before his father's death by the Prince of Wales to Wallis on New Year's Day 1936 seems to indicate that this was, indeed, what he was contemplating ('Oh! my Wallis I know we'll have Viel Gluck to make us *one* this year').[28] But as King he could not so easily do what as Prince of Wales he could have done, and was probably envisaging doing: marry Wallis and give up his rights to the succession. He had left it too late and now the trap had closed on him.

The real significance, therefore, of his brother's hysterical grief at their father's death and a more unpleasant episode over the reading of King George's will escaped Prince Albert at the time. He accompanied the new King up to London on the morning of 21 January for the Accession Council at St James's Palace, returning the next day, 22 January, for the reading of the will by the King's solicitor, Sir Bernard Bircham. Wigram left a memorandum of the scene describing how King Edward became extremely upset, 'much perturbed', as Wigram put it, when he learned that his father had left him a life interest in Sandringham and Balmoral and their contents but without a personal money bequest. Wigram and the solicitor

tried to explain that the late King felt that his eldest son, as Prince of Wales for 25 years, ought to have built up a nice surplus out of the Duchy of Cornwall and that there was no necessity to provide for him. King Edward VII never left his eldest son any money, for the same reason. However, we failed to comfort the new King. He kept on saying that my brothers and sister have got large sums but I have been left out. [It was rumoured that King George V left each of his children £1 million.]

It was most unfortunate that King Edward VIII was not reasonable. As a matter of fact it was discovered later that he had tucked away over a million sterling. I tried to assure His Majesty that he would be very well off and there was no reason why he should not save money from the Civil List and the Privy Purse as his father had done. His Majesty continued to be obsessed about money.[29]

It was another pointer to the future; on 10 December 1936, the eve of the Abdication, King Edward would make a strenuous attempt to get his father's will reversed and later a bitter quarrel over the financial settlement between them would take place with Prince Albert as his successor. The scene made by the new King on 22 January was a symptom of his inner insecurity about the future and his fear that he might find himself without the huge financial cushion of the Civil List and the Privy Purse.

All this remained below the surface as the family, united for a brief space by mutual grief, carried out the obsequies of King George V. The brothers walked behind their father's coffin on his last journey from Sandringham Church to the ornate little railway station at Wolferton, the scene of his arrivals and departures over the last fifty years. The grim snow-laden clouds had cleared and the day was just the kind on which the late King had loved to go out shooting, sunny, crisp and dry; his white shooting pony, Jock, led by a groom, was part of the cortège. As the coffin reached the far end of Sandringham drive, Prince Albert later told Lord Crawford, an immensely high pheasant flew across the procession, almost exactly above the dead monarch, a tribute which King George would have much appreciated.[30] Omens were not lacking on that day. As the coffin, followed by the two elder brothers walking bareheaded and abreast, approached Westminster Hall where the late King's body was to lie in state, the jewelled Maltese cross atop the imperial crown broke loose and tumbled glittering into the gutter. 'A most terrible omen,' Harold Nicolson wrote. Less portentous, but perhaps equally relevant, was the comment of Walter Elliot MP, who heard Edward VIII's reaction, 'Christ! What's going to happen next?' 'That', Elliot remarked to his fellow MP, Robert Boothby, 'will be the motto of the new reign.'[31]

For the Yorks 1936 was the unhappiest year of their lives. The death of the old King had left a vacuum where the centre of family and Court life had been. The Duchess wrote to Lord Dawson on 9 March:

I miss him dreadfully. Unlike his own children I was never afraid of him, and in all the twelve years of having me as a daughter-in-law he never spoke one unkind or abrupt word to me, and was always ready to listen, and give advice on one's own silly little affairs. He was so kind, and so dependable. I am ... suffering from the effects of a family break-up – which always happens when the head of a family goes. Though outwardly one's life goes on the same, yet everything is different – especially spiritually and mentally.[32]

For all the years of Prince Albert's life and, for the last twelve years, of his wife's, the immutable, steady rhythm of King George and Queen Mary's life together, the dignity, history and tradition which as King and Queen they personified, had, in Helen Hardinge's words, been 'the force which gave our world its powerful sense of security and solidness'. In their place were King Edward and 'Queen Wallis', Bryanston Court and Fort Belvedere. At tea with the Brownlows on 12 February, Chips Channon, the Saint-Simon of Edward VIII's brief reign, found the 'new Court' with Wallis 'very charming, gay and vivacious', wisecracking about Court mourning: 'She said she had not worn black stockings since she gave up the Can-Can. ...'[33]

The new Court floated on the glittering surface of London Society; its principal, self-appointed acolyte was Emerald Cunard. The parties she gave at her house in Grosvenor Square assembled the most amusing, smartest people in London. Like Channon, another expatriate American from a wealthy Chicago family who had married a British fortune, in his case, a Guinness heiress, Lady Honor, daughter of Lord Iveagh, she saw Wallis Simpson as a gold-plated passport to Court. It was even later rumoured that she envisaged herself as holding the most prestigious Court post a woman could hold, as Mistress of the Robes to Queen Wallis. Indeed, Emerald's flattery of Wallis and the King went beyond all bounds. 'Little Mrs Simpson is a woman of character and reads Balzac,' she said of Wallis, who, whatever else she was, was no intellectual, while her usual form of addressing the King was 'Majesty Divine'.[34] To Chips she said:

The King is Mrs Simpson's absolute slave, and will go nowhere she is not invited, and she, clever woman, with her high-pitched voice, her chic clothes, moles and sense of humour is behaving well. She encourages the King to meet people of importance and to be polite; above all she makes him happy. The Empire ought to be grateful.

She, more than any other London hostess, promoted Wallis socially, which was to earn her a blacklisting after the Abdication. (Noël Coward was heard to scream on receiving yet another invitation from Emerald: 'I am sick to *death* of having "quiet suppers" with the King and Mrs Simpson.') Lady Cunard was the most conspicuous but far from the only flatterer. Her rival hostess, Sibyl Colefax, a woman of infinitely less wit and brain than Emerald but possessed of a kinder and more loyal heart, was one of the three women in London Society whom Wallis regarded as a genuine friend. Sibyl wrote her assiduous letters in her notoriously illegible hand, declaring fulsomely that she had 'grown every month more full of delighted admiration for not only your immense wisdom & lovely common (so miscalled!) sense, but also for your unfailing touch of being exactly right in all judgements & in all kinds of moments in life at every angle'. The eccentric and often formidable Margot Oxford told her she had 'every quality to be liked – you are very natural, very kind, never pretend to know what you don't know (a rare quality believe me) & a genuine desire to help the man you love in his very difficult task'. Diana Cooper's verdict was that she was 'good and kind and lovable – what more can one be?'[35]

But, while London Society as a whole did not as yet see the King's liaison with Wallis Simpson as a threat to the fabric of the Constitution and Empire, the old Court, the royal family and, even more, the courtiers, the core of the royal Household, were beginning to get increasingly anxious about the new King's behaviour. 'Though outwardly one's life goes on the same, yet everything is different – especially spiritually and mentally,' the Duchess of York had written to Dawson from the Duke of Devonshire's house, Compton Place, at Eastbourne, where she was convalescing. 'I don't know if it is the result of being ill but I mind things I don't like more than before....' On the surface and at the outset the new King's attitude towards Prince Albert as his heir presumptive seemed impeccable; he appeared anxious to associate him publicly with his reign in the minds of the nation. One of his first official acts had been to order the inclusion of the Duke and Duchess of York after the sovereign and Queen Mary in the prayer for the royal family, which concludes every service of the Church of England. In doing so, he was characteristically cutting through the pettifogging objections of the Church based on the precedent that in the days of William IV and the early reign of Queen Victoria, when there was no direct heir of the body, no mention was made in the Privy Council Orders of an heir presumptive. On 27 January Wigram had written on his behalf to the Archbishop of Canterbury, 'The King especially wishes me to tell you that HM hopes you will arrange for Albert Duke of York and the Duchess of York to be included by names in the Prayer for the royal Family, in spite of the precedent of nearly a hundred years ago.'[36] He also determined that Prince Albert should see certain secret telegrams and papers.[37] Appreciating his brother's interest in tradition and ceremonial he appointed him to the committee entrusted with arrangements for his Coronation and, indeed, never attended a meeting of the committee without him, even though the latter's presence was not always strictly necessary. As a member of the Coronation committee, however, the Prince was aware of the King's instructions that Mrs Simpson should be accommodated during the ceremony in a special place above the Altar (immediately dubbed by courtiers 'the Loose Box'). He was also commissioned by his brother to report on economies to be made at Sandringham, probably as part of a family agreement that the King would not, as he had threatened to as their father lay dying, sell the estate. The report, according to Wheeler-Bennett, which Prince Albert drew up with the help of Lord Radnor, was 'a remarkable example of clarity and common sense', which would have done credit to his efficient great-grandfather,

Prince Albert, and set forward a programme of retrenchment, most of which he would carry out himself during his own reign.

This, however, was the limit of the consultation between King Edward and his brother. Their relations during the summer were to become increasingly strained. Even as Prince of Wales, Edward had been notoriously averse to advice from anyone; now, *Time* magazine reported, he saw the principal advantage of his new ground-floor office at Buckingham Palace (which had been Wigram's ante-room) as having French windows into the garden through which he could escape the latter's lectures. There was only one person whom he consulted and whose advice he would accept unreservedly; as Wallis wrote to her aunt on 30 January in a phrase which would have infuriated Prince Albert, she was 'the only person he has to really talk things over with normally'.[38] As the unique consultant to the King—Emperor, however, Wallis had several important drawbacks. She was full of goodwill and anxious to help her lover do his job to the best of his ability; she was an exceptional hostess, an economical house-keeper, a woman of practical common sense and social tact. She would have made a wonderful wife to a successful businessman, politician or diplomat. But of the British monarchy and Court, of its powers and their limitations, its history and its traditions, she knew nothing. As her opponent, Stanley Baldwin, told Harold Nicolson a year after the Abdication, he considered 'Mrs Simpson to be an admirable woman within her circle of conscience, but to have no conception of proportions outside that circle'.[39]

Prince Albert, longing to help his brother, was cut out; later his wife was to write of his elder brother's 'change of heart and character during the last few years' and to complain of how 'he used to be so kind to us'. The core of the new King's Household remained the same men who had worked for George v and were to work for George vi representing a continuity which they saw as threatened by Edward viii and Mrs Simpson. Clive Wigram, who had received a peerage in the Jubilee Honours of 1935, was now sixty-three and had been in the royal service for nearly thirty years, having joined the Court as Assistant Private Secretary to Lord Stamfordham in 1910. The son of an official in the Indian Civil Service, he had been educated at Winchester, where his chief claim to distinction had been as a cricketer. Bluff and chauvinist, he was once heard to exclaim after a series of visits by foreign ambassadors to Windsor, 'On hearing them, I thank God more and more that I am an Englishman.' 'His horizon is limited', his fellow courtier Fritz Ponsonby wrote of him, '. . . and his political views are those of the ordinary officer at Aldershot.' George v's biographer has called him unjustly underrated'; he was, none the less, a selfless and loyal royal servant. Wigram had found it necessary to lecture Edward on his behaviour while his father was still alive; by the time the new reign opened he was intensely suspicious of his sovereign and, regarding himself as the standard-bearer of the essential traditions of the British monarchy as handed down by his late master, hostile to everything which Edward represented.

His second-in-command, Alexander Hardinge, who was soon to replace him as the King's Principal Private Secretary and to inherit his self-imposed role as guardian of the Crown, playing a significant part in the Abdication crisis, was, although a far more intelligent man than Wigram, cast in the same mould, born into the English governing class and an honourable example of the men who cemented the Empire and oiled the wheels of the Court. His great-grandfather, Henry Hardinge, the first Viscount, was Governor-General of India; his grandfather was a soldier who had fought with distinction in the Crimean War; his great-uncle Arthur had been equerry to Queen Victoria and his father Charles Hardinge, the 1st Lord Hardinge of Penshurst, had had a brilliant career as a diplomatist, royal confidant and Viceroy of India, and had made an aristocratic marriage to the daughter of Lord Alington, a millionaire landowner and racing magnate, who also happened to be a close friend of Edward VII and Queen Alexandra. The Hardinges were a serious family and Alec himself showed early signs of an unusually intense sense of responsibility, not to say priggishness, when while a schoolboy at Harrow he refused to go with other boys on illicit trips because it might have been bad for his father's reputation (Hardinge senior was then British Ambassador at St Petersburg). His father had begun to train him early for what turned out to be his future profession, teaching him the art of letter-writing by making him copy out his official letters during school holidays. When the First World War broke out he had joined the Grenadier Guards, been severely wounded and awarded the Military Cross for gallantry. In 1921, the year of his marriage to Helen Cecil, he was made Assistant Private Secretary to George V and learned his profession under first Stamfordham, who died ten years later, and then Wigram. By the time Edward VIII came to the throne he had been in the royal service and a part of George V's Court for fifteen years, deeply ingrained with its traditions and outlook. Although he was the same age as Edward, and had served in the same regiment during the war, the two men could hardly have been more different, and when Edward's former Private Secretary, Godfrey Thomas, who declined to carry on his duties, recommended Hardinge, he must have done so in the hope that Hardinge would prove to be a steadying influence and keep the new King in line. Naturally shy, serious-minded and a workaholic with an over-developed sense of duty and propriety, Hardinge was, in fact, the last man who could have achieved any sort of influence over the King, who later came to regard him as an enemy. Chips Channon, hearing of him at second hand via Emerald Cunard in December 1935, reported that he was already critical of the heir to the throne: 'I think the Court is dead and out-of-date.... Alec Hardinge ... though quite young, has taken on the Court "colour". He very much criticised the Prince of Wales and his entourage.' 'It is high time such dreary narrow-minded fogies were sacked,' Channon declared, 'as, indeed, they will be, in the next reign.'[40] But, instead of being sacked in the next reign, Hardinge found himself in the all-important role of Private Secretary.

The third member of Edward VIII's official secretariat was his former Private Secretary as Prince of Wales, Tommy Lascelles, who had resigned from his service in 1929, unable to stand any more of the Prince's irresponsible behaviour. When invited in 1935 by Wigram to become an Assistant Private Secretary to George V, he had hesitated on the grounds that the King might die and he might find himself again in the unpleasant position of serving the son, and it had only been on Wigram's hearty assurance that the King would last a long time yet that he had accepted. Like everyone else who had worked for Edward, he had a residual affection for the man and a strong disapproval of his manners as a Prince.

Through these three (Helen Hardinge was an old friend of the Duchess of York) and other sources, such as Louis Greig, Prince Albert was well aware of what was going on at his brother's Court and of the extent to which Wallis's influence was making itself felt. Neither Halsey nor Fruity Metcalfe received the appointments in the new Household to which their long service and absolute devotion might have entitled them. Halsey, who had spoken out about the King's relationship with Wallis, was summoned on the King's accession only to be told deliberately: 'You will have been wondering what post there was for you & I want to tell you there will be none.'[41] There were dismissals and sackings among the royal servants on the grounds of economy, an excuse which could hardly be used when the King, instead of using flowers from the royal gardens, ordered quantities from Constance Spry's London shop to decorate his apartments. Even those friendly towards the King, like Victor Cazalet, could hardly help commenting on his curious double standards, '... sympathising with the miners and so on, while on the other hand wanting everything that a rich, idle bachelor desires in material pleasures – lavishing jewels on his mistress while getting rid of his father's servants'.[42]

It was, no doubt, this last aspect of things, the blatant discrepancy between Edward's economies at Court and his conspicuous expenditure on Wallis, which aroused much of the royal family's indignation. Indeed, the steady stream of jewels lavished on Wallis by Edward as Prince of Wales became a cascade after he became King. That spring Edward's presents of jewellery to her totalled £16,000 (c. £400,000 in today's money), including a stunning ruby and diamond bracelet specially ordered from van Cleef and Arpels in Paris inscribed 'Hold Tight 27.iii.36'. 'He is very rich now,' Wallis commented to her Aunt Bessie. In June, Edward presented Wallis for her fortieth birthday with a ruby and diamond necklace to match, also purchased from van Cleef and Arpels in March. The combined effect of necklace and bracelet could hardly escape comment. 'At supper at Emerald Cunard's', Channon wrote on 27 July, 'Mrs Simpson was literally smothered in rubies....'[43]

The courtiers complained of his slapdash methods of conducting business, comparing them unfavourably with his father's orderly procedures. Helen Hardinge's diary for March 1936 abounds in critical entries: on 13 March: 'Nothing but a ghastly conversation [with two old members of the Household] about how awful the new King is', and on 27 March: 'Confusion in the King's affairs because he's so unpractical'.[44] It was difficult to contact the King during the day because he was still living at Fort Belvedere, although he kept an office at Buckingham Palace. He did not like being disturbed with business at the Fort and officials could only go there on specific invitation and were sometimes left hanging about for hours without being given anything to eat. Since the King himself did not eat lunch, he did not see why other people should and he was deeply inconsiderate of his staff's private and official lives. They might be settling down for dinner when the King would suddenly decide it was time to do some work and would start telephoning. It was, said Helen, quite usual for him to ring Alec five times in the course of an evening. Edward started full of good intentions, throwing himself wholeheartedly into his work, reading through the papers in the official red boxes sent by the government departments and, to prove his industry to his staff, initialling every paper he read. 'This', according to Helen Hardinge, 'turned out to be a mistake because it later showed how short a time that system lasted and illustrated how little official reading he was doing.' As time went by and he became more and more absorbed in his passion for Wallis to the exclusion of everything else, State papers were half read by him or not at all, to the despair of his secretaries whose job it was to see that they were returned to their respective departments in good time and in good order. The King's nonchalant attitude towards the red despatch boxes containing State papers for his perusal was well known, 'mostly full of bunk', was how he described them to Wallis, and there were stories of papers returned marked with the rings of cocktail glasses. As a result, and also because Wallis was rumoured to be a security risk with Nazi links, for the first and last time in history Foreign Office papers were screened before being sent to the King. Three days after the Abdication Lascelles was to tell Harold Nicolson that,

nobody would ever know what they had had to endure during the last year. The King refused to have regular hours and would escape from Thursday to Tuesday to Belvedere where none of them were allowed to go. Then even when he did come he shut himself up at Buckingham Palace with Mrs Simpson. 'The Lady is still there,' the footmen would say to the private secretaries who would have to wait till 8.15 before getting at the King who would then be too bored to listen to what he was saying.[45]

There were more serious grounds for complaint against Edward VIII, of which few people outside the Court and Whitehall were yet aware. Not only was he impatient of tradition, which in some cases was to give deep offence, but he seemed to be both ignorant and careless of his constitutional powers and their limits. Many of the incidents were trivial, such as the case of the debutantes whose presentation was halted when the King, seizing upon the pretext of a shower of rain, cancelled the remainder of the ceremony in Buckingham Palace Gardens, or when the Privileged Bodies representative of the Law, the Church, Science, the Arts, the senior Universities, the Jewish Board of Deputies, the Society of Friends, the Bank of England and the City of London, accustomed to presenting their loyal addresses separately, were told that they would be received all together or not at all. On a lesser note, the King perturbed the

British car industry by ordering a Canadian Buick for his personal use in place of his father's traditional Daimler.

Edward's lack of understanding of his constitutional position extended most obviously into an area in which he was completely uninterested, the affairs of the Established Church of England. As King he was also Supreme Head of the Church with the right to appoint its bishops, but his ignorance on the subject had already been made manifest two years before his accession. At a dinner in the Stationers' Hall on 15 November 1934, the Prince of Wales had asked the Archbishop of Canterbury about the possibility of unfrocking the eccentric Bishop of Birmingham, Dr Barnes, for his views on disarmament. 'Who appoints the bishops?' he asked. 'Such ignorance on the part of the Heir to the Throne is really rather depressing,' Dr Don commented. 'He takes no interest in ecclesiastical affairs.'[46] In the week after his accession he was still unsure, asking Lang, who called on him at Buckingham Palace the day after King George's funeral, 'whether it was the case that he appointed bishops?'[47] The Church of England was regarded as part of the essential fabric of England, the fate of the monarchy and of the Protestant religion having been indissolubly bound together since Henry VIII had rejected the supremacy of the Pope in 1534 and substituted himself as juridical Head of the Church. The Kings of England have retained the title 'Defender of the Faith' originally granted by the Pope to Henry VIII for writing a pamphlet in defence of papal supremacy, and they have traditionally been regarded as such by the Church. Even today, regular attendance at church on Sundays is expected of the Queen and her family. But in 1936, to the mortification of the clergy and members of the Established Church, and indeed of all religious denominations, Edward VIII, Defender of the Faith and Supreme Head of the Church, did not go to church on Sundays nor did he take communion. As Archbishop Lang put it in a letter to Bishop Barnes, 'he [the King] has in this respect ... a constitutional position not merely as an individual but as the representative of the nation'.[48] Ironically, it was King Edward's failure to attend church regularly which was to bring down upon his head the strictures of the obscure Bishop of Bradford, Dr Blunt, whose words, misinterpreted as a reference to Mrs Simpson, opened the floodgates to public discussion of the affair.

Prince Albert had, as Baldwin told Harold Nicolson, 'always been bothered by Edward VIII's lack of a religious sense'; indeed, Baldwin later told Victor Cazalet that 'he had never met a person who had absolutely *no* spiritual or religious background to the same degree'. This lack of religious dimension in Edward widened the gulf in understanding between him and the Yorks, who were possessed of genuinely religious feeling and could not understand how he could contemplate marriage to a twice-divorced woman. Edward himself asserted that he had 'a profound faith in God', but, as a friend remarked, it was a God who kept on dealing him trumps – inferring that the relationship was very much on Edward's terms rather than the Almighty's. To Edward, religion, like ritual and ceremony, was something that was all right for the older generation and unnecessary for the new, which was why, when it came to the crunch, he rejected Baldwin's advice which he regarded as outmoded and based on the values of another generation. Baldwin, talking about the Abdication at lunch with Cazalet on 26 February 1937, told him that 'the King always took the line – well, of course you and Mrs Baldwin are a different generation. I understand your feelings and realize you can't understand the modern view.'[49]

Last, but by no means least, when it came to Edward's relations with the Church, of which he was head, was the Church's attitude to divorce. Quite simply divorce was frowned on, as indeed it still was at Court and in England at large. Lord Halifax, a fervent High Churchman, indulged in long moral discussions as to whether or not he should sit next to a divorced woman at dinner. Social convention regarded adulterous affairs as infinitely preferable to divorce; Edward, with his straightforward attitudes, saw this as hypocritical. Hypocritical it may have been, but, as Head of the Church and pillar of society, he was bound to abide by its rules. Divorce as far as a member of the royal family was concerned was simply unthinkable, and remained so for at least another generation as his niece Princess Margaret's ill-fated romance with Group-Captain Townsend was to show.

While Edward VIII was still viewed by the general public at large as 'the man born to be King ... the most widely known and universally popular personality in the world', as the Home Secretary, Sir John Simon, was to put it in his memoirs, among the inner circle who knew the truth his kingship was regarded with apprehension from the start. Neville Chamberlain, then Chancellor of the Exchequer and future Prime Minister, who was present at King Edward's Accession Council, had written to his sister Hilda on 25 January: 'I do hope he "pulls up his socks" [a curious choice of phrase given Edward's fanatical chic] and behaves himself now he has such heavy responsibilities for unless he does he will soon pull down the throne.'[50]

On 1 March, St David's Day, the King made his first broadcast (which he pronounced 'broadcairst' in his by now much-noted American accent) to the Empire, promising his peoples that, 'although I now speak to you as King, I am still that same man who has had that experience and whose constant effort it will be to continue to promote the well-being of his fellow men. ...' These were unexceptionable sentiments but, Wigram told Lord Crawford, the King, when drafting the broadcast with Sir John Simon, 'had tried to interpolate a sentence about the realisation of Indian aspirations, which would in effect have conceded Dominion status', and that it was only with difficulty that Simon had managed to get the phrase excluded. 'All goes to show', Lord Crawford commented on 17 March, 'that we have to deal with a very opinionated man who probably feels much more resentment than anybody knows at the restraints and restrictions which have surrounded him hitherto.'[51]

The fact that the King, constitutionally supposed only to act on the advice of ministers, was prepared off his own bat to introduce a major, extremely controversial Empire policy initiative, caused the utmost consternation in government circles. He had already upset the Foreign Office; as Bruce Lockhart noted on 12 February after a conversation with Rex Leeper, 'the new King has not begun well – in foreign affairs at least. He would not see King Carol when, because of pro-German tendencies in Rumania, it was important to keep Carol on our side. . . . The King has also been interfering in small matters, and Rex is anxious.'[52] There were difficulties over his proposed itinerary for his cruise with Wallis on the *Nahlin* in August; Edward wanted to board the yacht at Venice, which would have delighted Mussolini against whom sanctions had recently been imposed by England as a member of the League of Nations in protest against the Italian seizure of Abyssinia. The Foreign Secretary, Anthony Eden, had to go round to Buckingham Palace to explain to Edward why it was inadvisable to go to Italy. The King was not pleased and responded sarcastically with a snide remark about the League of Nations, telling Eden that he was not sure which the Foreign Secretary seemed to be most afraid of, 'that I might be jeered by the Italians because my Government had imposed sanctions on Italy which would be bad for British prestige; or that I might be cheered by the same people as a friend of Italy, which would have offended the faithful supporters of the League of Nations'.[53] The King's apparently favourable attitude towards dictators, and towards Nazi Germany in particular, was a source of concern to Eden in the face of the disturbed international situation. Early in February at a diplomatic reception at Buckingham Palace the King had made his pro-German sympathies abundantly clear by holding up the reception line to talk in fluent German to the German Foreign Minister, Constantin von Neurath, and continuing the conversation in another room, a mark of favour which was reported world-wide, even in the American press. That autumn an exasperated Eden told the Czech leader, Jan Masaryk, how worried the Government was by the King's increasing intervention in foreign affairs, remarking that if things went on in this way he would have to abdicate.[54]

Eden's remark may well have been prompted by the King's independent attitude on Anglo–German relations and the unconstitutional lengths to which he was prepared to go in order to further Anglo–German friendship. As Prince of Wales he had criticized the Foreign Office to the German Ambassador, Leopold von Hoesch, for being 'too one-sided' in their approach to negotiations with Germany over the Naval Agreement in March 1935, making it clear 'his complete understanding of Germany's position and aspirations'.[55] In June that year a speech he made to the British Legion advocating friendship with Germany had earned him a dressing-down from his father for mixing in politics and expressing views contrary to official Foreign Office policy. In conversation with his friend von Hoesch at Ascot later that month, the Prince had been unrepentant, expressing himself as convinced that his frank and direct methods achieved better results than 'the timidity and hesitation ... characteristic of politicians'. In conversation with his cousin, Charles Edward, Duke of Saxe-Coburg and Gotha, a grandson of Queen Victoria through his father, Leopold, Duke of Albany, educated at Eton but now a member of the Nazi Party, Edward, now

King, made it quite clear that his conception of his powers was hardly a constitutional one. In a secret report sent to Hitler and Joachim von Ribbentrop at the end of January 1936, the Duke of Coburg wrote:

To my question whether a discussion between Baldwin and Adolf Hitler would be desirable for future German–British relations, he replied in the following words: 'Who is King here? Baldwin or I? I myself wish to talk to Hitler, and will do so here or in Germany.' The King [Coburg added] is resolved to concentrate the business of government on himself. For England, not too easy. The general political situation, especially the situation of England herself, will perhaps give him a chance. His sincere resolve to bring England and Germany together would be made more difficult if it were made public too early. For this reason, I regard it as most important to respect the King's wish that the non-official policy of Germany towards England should be firmly concentrated in one hand [the King suggested that this should be carried on between Ribbentrop and himself through a confidant of Ribbentrop's to be stationed in London] and at the same time brought into relations of confidence with the official policy.... The King asked me to visit him frequently in order that confidential matters might be more speedily clarified in this way. I promised – subject to the Führer's approval – to fly to London at any time he wished.[56]

There is evidence, too, from captured German documents that the King put pressure on the Government against going to war over Germany's take-over of the Rhineland in March 1936. When the crisis broke, Hoesch contacted the King as a result of which, the Ambassador reported on 11 March, the King issued 'a directive to the Government ... that no matter how the details of the affair are dealt with, complications of a serious nature [i.e. war] are in no circumstances to be allowed to develop'.[57]

When the German documents were discovered in 1945, the sections dealing with the ex-King's ideas on European politics and the Third Reich were considered so potentially damaging that the British Government persuaded the US Government to withhold publication of them (see pages 425–7). They were, however, public knowledge in informed circles at the time, as was the fact that both the King and Mrs Simpson were under security surveillance. Rumours that Wallis was a Nazi agent spread and have never been entirely dispelled although there is no concrete evidence to support them. While Wheeler-Bennett told a friend that he was sure that Ribbentrop made use of Wallis, Baldwin, who had seen the secret service reports, told Osbert Sitwell after the Abdication that no evidence had been found to connect her with the Nazis but that she was 'a paid agent' of the Hearst Press, sworn enemies of the British Empire.

The point at issue in 1936 was not that the King was pro-German – a very considerable section of English society at the time was favourable to Germany – or that he was obviously naive and cocksure in his opinions on foreign policy, but that he was prepared to ignore the fundamental principle of constitutional monarchy that the King cannot act against the advice of his ministers and should only act on that advice. Even before the establishment of a constitutional monarchy, a distant ancestor, Charles I, had been beheaded for infringing what were seen as the constitutional rights of subjects; since then the theme of British history had been the long struggle of Parliament to confine the sovereign within constitutional limits, to remove any real executive power and to turn him or her into a symbol whose potency derived from the paradox that he could do no wrong because he could actually do nothing at all. It was this feeling that the King could not be relied upon to keep to the rules, that he did not even understand them, which was eventually to produce a consensus among politicians that he must go.

There is no evidence that Prince Albert shared these official preoccupations to anything like the same degree. He was never to take his brother's undoubted pro-German leanings as seriously as the authorities did. He was, quite simply, used to them, dating as they did from Edward's visits to his German relations in 1913. He was inured to his brother's doing things differently. His principal worry was the damage which the King's relationship with Wallis could do to the monarchy. He was afraid, as the Lord Chamberlain, Lord Cromer, told Crawford, 'that something must happen sooner or later which may produce an open scandal'. The British press had hitherto maintained silence on the subject, which was freely discussed in the American and French newspapers. It was, therefore, particularly worrying that his brother seemed to be increasingly determined to bring it out into the open by forcing Wallis on official attention.

On 28 May an official announcement in the Court Circular section of *The Times* and *Daily Telegraph* came as a particular shock. The names of Mr and Mrs Ernest Simpson appeared as guests at a dinner given by the King the previous evening at York House. It was the King's first official dinner and the other guests were the Prime Minister and Mrs Baldwin, the Mountbattens, the Duff Coopers, Emerald Cunard, Admiral of the Fleet Sir Ernle Chatfield and Lady Chatfield, the Wigrams, the King's equerry, Lieutenant-Colonel the Hon. Piers 'Joey' Legh and his wife Sarah, and the American aviator, Charles Lindbergh, and his wife Anne. The object of the dinner, Wallis recorded in her memoirs, was, as the King declared to her, to introduce his Prime Minister to his future wife. It was noted that Wallis was very obviously acting the part of hostess and was 'very active and pleasant in looking after the guests'. The Prime Minister was surprised to see that the two most prominent positions at table (apart, of course, from sitting next to the King) were given to Wallis and Emerald Cunard, who sat at each end as if they were members of the family. It was, however, the King's defiant gesture in putting the announcement in the newspapers against the advice of his staff which particularly upset his family, so much so that Queen Mary went so far as to raise the subject when she showed Lady Airlie the offending Court Circular notice. As usual, the family blamed Wallis and not Edward. 'Queen Mary said that the King had only sent the list to the Court Circular at the last moment and at her [Wallis's] request.' It was on this occasion that Queen Mary, with 'bright spots of crimson burning on her cheekbones', said, 'He gives Mrs Simpson the most beautiful jewels,' and added, 'I am so afraid he may ask me to receive her.'[58]

On 9 July Prince Albert and his wife found themselves in the awkward position of being guests of honour at the King's second official dinner where Wallis was again present, this time without her husband. Again the guest list appeared in the Court Circular, making it seem as if the Yorks condoned the presence of Mrs Simpson in that context. It was again an evening of sonorous official names: the Marquess of Willingdon, a former Viceroy of India, and his formidable wife; Earl Stanhope, Under-Secretary of State for Foreign Affairs; Sir Samuel Hoare, First Lord of the Admiralty, and his wife, Lady Maud Hoare; Sir Philip Sassoon, Under-Secretary of State for Air; Sir Edward Peacock, a director of the Bank of England and Receiver-General of the Duchy of Cornwall, and Lady Peacock; Captain David Margesson, the Government Chief Whip; Winston and Clementine Churchill; the Hardinges; and Wallis's friends, Diana Cooper, Margot Asquith and Sibyl Colefax. While the Duchess of York sat in the place of honour on Edward's right, Wallis again sat at the head of the table with Sibyl Colefax taking the place previously occupied by Emerald Cunard. It was on this occasion that Samuel Hoare, apparently meeting the famous Mrs Simpson for the first time, while admiring her 'sparkling talk' and 'sparkling jewels in very up-to-date Cartier settings', found that she was 'very American with little or no knowledge of English life'.

The King's dinner on 9 July has gone down in history for a loaded exchange between Churchill and the Duchess of York overheard and recorded by Helen Hardinge. Churchill's subject was the unfortunately topical one of George IV and his secret wife, Mrs Fitzherbert. The Duchess was patently not in the mood for that particular subject. 'Well, that was a *long* time ago,' she said repressively. 'The Duchess had a sort of warning expression on her face that would have deterred anyone less obsessed by his own powers of oratory than Churchill,' Helen Hardinge recalled in an interview forty years later. But Churchill, absorbed in the train of his own thoughts, went on to the royal civil wars between the Houses of Lancaster and of York – which could have been taken, and undoubtedly was by the Duchess, as reference to the estrangement between the King, who was about to use his title as Duke of Lancaster on his Mediterranean cruise with Wallis later that month, and the Yorks. 'That was a very, *very* long time ago,' she said. 'The Duchess of York's second answer to Churchill was very emphatic, verging on sharpness, which was quite unlike her,' Helen Hardinge said. 'Even Churchill could not mistake her meaning.'[59]

The possible parallels between the present situation and that of Geoge IV, Edward's great-great-uncle, and Mrs Fitzherbert, were certainly in the minds of the principal participants at the dinner. Helen Hardinge had been present at an informal dinner-party given by the King at which most of the other guests came from his weekend house-party at the Fort including Wallis, but also her husband, Ernest, and Mary Kirk Raffray, an old friend of Wallis's, now with Wallis's knowledge and approbation Ernest's mistress and, indeed, his future wife. Helen Hardinge was, of course, unaware of this, but she did notice that the King and Mrs Simpson were 'in teasing mood' and they made some apparently joking references to 'matching' Mr Simpson with Mrs Raffray. In the circumstances of the royal dinner-party, however, it was hardly a joke in the best of taste or one that the anxious courtiers (the Wigrams also were there) would have appreciated, the continued presence of Ernest as Wallis's husband being their only insurance against a future which none of them liked to contemplate. Later the guests had walked in the Grand Corridor, lined with portraits of Edward's ancestors. Helen Hardinge recalled:

Gradually the story of George iv and Mrs Fitzherbert seemed to detach itself and as a theme made its way into the conversation. And as we wandered among the paintings that night, perhaps because of the hints and talk about them, their presence became very real. . . . Our little group bristled with unspoken confidences about the present, as we discussed the personal affairs of George iv.[60]

At the Fort, according to one witness, a *Life of Mrs Fitzherbert* was seen with the chapter relating to her marriage to the then Prince of Wales marked.[61]

Churchill, too, had a particular reason for his obsession with the Mrs Fitzherbert theme. Walter Monckton had very recently consulted him on the question of Mrs Simpson's projected divorce and the King's recklessness in relation to her. In his notes, Monckton merely places the interview as somewhere round the end of June. It was, in fact, on 7 July, two days before the dinner at York House, and the question was therefore very much in the forefront of Churchill's mind. Although Monckton had assured him that the King had no thought of marrying Mrs Simpson but would like to see her free 'as his possessive sense' was strong, Churchill had advised against divorce 'because people would say that an innocent man had been divorced because of the King's intimacies with his wife'. He stressed that Monckton should make it plain to the King how important it was that his friendship should not be flaunted in the eyes of the public, and particularly that she should not be invited to Balmoral. 'I deprecated strongly Mrs Simpson going to such a highly official place upon which the eyes of Scotland were concentrated and which was already sacred to the memories of Queen Victoria and John Brown . . . .', Churchill noted in his account of the Abdication written at the end of December 1936.[62]

Churchill had touched on a raw nerve in referring to the royal wars of York and Lancaster. Wallis had not only cut the King off from his brother, but she also seemed to take pleasure in mocking the Yorks in their absence and humiliating them when she met them by demonstrating her hold over Edward. According to a statement by Baldwin in the Beaverbrook Papers, the King, Wallis and their circle 'treated the Yorks badly, making fun of him and laughing at his fat wife'.[63] For Prince Albert the regular golf with his brother was over; Wallis absorbed every minute of the King's leisure. On the few informal moments when they did see each other, the presence of the women made it a strained occasion. Edward, with Wallis and the house-party from the Fort, was trying out a new acquisition, an American station-wagon and, on impulse, drove up to the Royal Lodge to show it to his brother. Accounts of the incident appear both in the Duchess of Windsor's memoirs and in those of the Yorks' governess, Marion Crawford (although it was omitted from the British edition of the latter's book). 'Mrs Simpson', reported the naturally partisan Crawfie, '. . . appeared to be entirely at her ease; if anything, far too much so . . . she had a distinctly proprietary way of speaking to the new King. I remember she drew him to the window and suggested how certain trees might be moved, and a part of the hill taken away to improve the view.' Since Wallis was well known for her discretion and social tact, her behaviour on this occasion can only have been designed to irritate. The Duchess, however, was too cool a hand to show her feelings and her good manners remained unruffled, or, as her future sister-in-law put it, 'her justly famous charm was highly evident'. The two charmers , King and Duchess, carried on the conversation while Prince Albert said little and limited himself to admiring the car. 'I left with a distinct impression that while the Duke of York was sold on the American station-wagon,' the Duchess of Windsor was to write, 'the Duchess was not sold on David's other American interest. . . .'[64]

The Yorks were not invited to Emerald Cunard's or to Sibyl Colefax's lunches and dinners for the couple; people who were conspicuously partisans of the Yorks were cut by Edward or publicly snubbed by Wallis. In August 1935 Hugh Lloyd Thomas, a friend of the Prince of Wales, reported that the Prince 'will not have Mrs Greville in his house or go to hers'.[65] Her principal crime in the Prince's eyes was that she was a great friend of the Yorks, and particularly of the Duchess, and an enemy of Wallis's principal supporter, Emerald Cunard. Another loyal York friend, Hannah Gubbay, was insulted by Wallis in her cousin Philip Sassoon's house because of her friendship with the Duchess of York. The Yorks were so much 'out' of fashionable Society that Harold Nicolson, who went everywhere, did not recognize the Duchess when he sat beside her on a sofa at Maureen Stanley's in February 1936, even though he had, apparently, met her before. Only a few of the traditional aristocrats, like Lady Derby, Maureen Stanley's mother-in-law, and Wallis's fellow-Virginian, Lady Astor, who were friends of the Yorks and the royal family, did not make Wallis welcome. Others, like Ladies Pembroke and Londonderry, took the patronizing view on what Nicolson called 'the Great Simpson question'. As Lady Pembroke told Nicolson at Lady Astor's party on 9 June 1936, since Mrs Simpson was apparently a perfectly decent person, it was the duty of the aristocracy to receive her 'in order that she may learn how decent people behave'; if they cold-shouldered her, 'it will mean that the King (who is extremely loyal) will see nothing but second-rate Americans'.[66] The King, however, was still the King, the apex of the social pyramid, and the loyal friends of the Yorks and of the discarded Freda Dudley Ward were in a small anti-Mrs Simpson minority until in July his public flaunting of his mistress began to turn the tide. On 7 July the Simpson loyalist, Chips Channon, noted: 'The Simpson scandal is growing, and she, poor Wallis, looks unhappy. The world is closing around her, the flatterers, the sycophants, and the malice. . . .' The King's 'tactlessness' in publicly flaunting his relationship was beginning to offend people and to worry his friends like

Monckton and Churchill, causing a change in the social climate towards the couple and towards Wallis in particular. The appearance of Wallis's name in the Court Circular on 27 May had shocked many people. Due to the extreme self-censorship of the British press, this was the first appearance of her name in the newspapers, alerting a wider circle than had hitherto been in the know as to what was going on. It was followed by another reckless gesture on Edward's part. Prevented by the six-month period of Court mourning for his father from attending the races at Ascot in June, he none the less sent Wallis in his car as if she were an official consort. On 13 July, three days after the publication of the King's dinner guest list for 9 July, Harold Nicolson saw Ramsay MacDonald, the former Prime Minister, now Lord President of the Council, busy with arrangements for the Coronation: '. . . this brings him to the unfortunate court circulars in which Mrs Simpson's name figures as a guest. He says this is making a bad effect in the country.' 'The people', the former Labour leader told Nicolson, 'do not mind fornication but they loathe adultery,' arguing that 'nobody would mind about Mrs Simpson was she a widow and were the King not so obstinate and tactless. He horrified people by sending her to Ascot in a royal car.'[67]

On 16 July, the old Court and the new had their first—and last—public confrontation at the traditional ceremony of Trooping the Colour on Home Guards' Parade. As the King, on horseback and accompanied by Prince Albert as Colonel of Scots Guards, took the salute, made a short speech from a raised platform and presented the Colours to his Guards, he was watched from specially erected stands by the royal family in the Royal Pavilion—Queen Mary, the Duchess of York and the two Princesses among them. In an adjoining stand sat the new Court, Wallis, Chips Channon escorting Diana Cooper and, next to them, Emerald Cunard. On the way back from the ceremony, an aggrieved Irishman in the crowd threw an unloaded revolver at the feet of the King's horse. For a moment Edward thought it was a bomb; if it had been it would have blown him, Prince Albert and the escorting general to pieces. Suddenly, the royal family seemed very vulnerable.

Tension between the Yorks and Wallis reached its highest point so far at Balmoral in late September. It would be the last time they were to meet socially and, when they did, the disapproval on their side and the dislike on hers were publicly noticeable. The Yorks were at Birkhall as usual when the King returned from his holiday cruise with Wallis on the *Nablin,* which had caused world-wide interest. Holiday photographs of the King and Wallis swimming, strolling hand in hand, lunching, sightseeing and shopping had been emblazoned across the world's front pages except in Britain where Wallis was cut out. Gossip about the couple's behaviour had reached home: how the King had been drunk when getting off the train in Yugoslavia, how he had been rude to Prince Paul because of their cool attitude to Wallis, how in Vienna the hotel register in the porter's lodge had been open for all to see with 'the Duke of Lancaster' and 'Mrs Simpson' signed in.

All this was bad enough, but to Prince Albert and his family, the worst was that Edward, ignoring all advice, had chosen to invite Wallis to Balmoral for his first visit there as King only just over six months after his father's death. One name, for obvious reasons, was not on the guest list for the Balmoral house-party for the first time in twenty-five years, that of Cosmo Lang, Archbishop of Canterbury. The Yorks, however, invited him to spend a night with them at Birkhall at the end of the month, telling him when he left that he must come again next year 'so that the links with Balmoral may not be wholly broken'. There was no doubt who was upholding the standard of the old Court. As it turned out there was nothing shocking about the guest list at Balmoral, which included those members of the aristocracy best-disposed towards Wallis: the Duke of Buccleuch, the Duchess of Gloucester's eldest brother, and his wife Mollie, the King's old friend, the rich, glamorous Duke of Sutherland and his wife, the Duke and Duchess of Marlborough, the Earl and Countess of Rosebery, Esmond Harmsworth, the newspaper magnate who was to play a considerable role in the forthcoming crisis, the Kents, the Mountbattens, the Buists, with Ulick Alexander and Joey Legh in attendance. The only 'foreigners' were Wallis's old friends, Herman and Katherine Rogers (with whom she had stayed at Peking), and Wallis herself.

The King, however, with his by now famous tactlessness and carelessness of appearances, got things off to a resoundingly bad start. On Wednesday 23 September Prince Albert and his wife found themselves deputizing for Edward at the public opening of the new Aberdeen Infirmary, the King having cried off on the grounds of Court mourning some months earlier, although the mourning period had actually ended on 20 July and, as was perfectly obvious to everyone concerned, what applied to one brother as surely applied to the other. The reason for the King's refusal was, however, made blatantly clear when, that afternoon, as his brother and sister-in-law were fulfilling their official engagement on the other side of the city, Edward, thinly disguised by driving goggles, turned up at Aberdeen Station driving his own car to meet Wallis accompanied by Mr and Mrs Herman Rogers. Two days earlier, the Duke of Kent and his pregnant Duchess had been photographed by the Aberdeen *Evening Express* waiting on the platform at Aberdeen for the branch line to Ballater, Balmoral's nearest station. What was good enough for the Kents, however, was not good enough for Wallis. The King, therefore, drove himself sixty miles to Aberdeen, into the centre of a city he had said he could not visit on that day, and where his brother and sister-in-law were at that very moment carrying out a public engagement on his behalf. The result was a headline on the front page of the Aberdeen *Evening Express*: 'HIS MAJESTY IN ABERDEEN SURPRISE VISIT IN CAR TO MEET GUESTS', juxtaposed with a photograph showing the Duke and Duchess of York performing their official duties in the city.

Scotland was outraged, the Yorks no less so. Nor were they pleased to hear that Wallis was installed in the suite of rooms always used by Queen Mary during the twenty-five years in which she had been Queen of England. For the Roseberys and other guests, the visit was 'a nightmare' with 'W[allis] going out of her way to assert her power and vex the Family', sending the King out of the room to order champagne while she was playing bridge, showing them round the house and saying 'this tartan's got to go', 'suggesting improvements to the royal plate & the placing of furniture'. The servants, no doubt upset by rumours of forthcoming changes and the sackings already made at Wallis's behest, were so edgy that the guests noticed it. According to the Roseberys, 'All her judgements were acclaimed by him [the King] with ecstatic admiration. He frequently handed her state documents to read in full view of the whole party.'[68]

At a dinner-party at the Castle on 26 September, three days after the Aberdeen incident, the Duchess of York made her feelings about Wallis's pretensions absolutely clear. As she entered into the drawing-room ahead of her husband, not Edward but Wallis came forward to greet her. Court etiquette decrees that royalty should be greeted only by the official host or hostess, which in this particular case should clearly have been the King. Either Wallis was ignorant of this convention or, perhaps more likely in view of her previous behaviour with the Yorks, it was, as an observer put it, 'a deliberate and calculated display of power'. According to one account, the Duchess recognized it as such. Walking straight past Wallis and ignoring her attempted welcome, she said, 'as if to no one in particular, "I came to dine with the King." ' The Duke of York looked 'embarrassed and very nervous', the account went on, 'and the King, looking rather startled, abruptly broke off his conversation and came forward to greet his brother and sister-in-law'.[69] At dinner, the Duchess's official royal status was acknowledged as she sat at the King's right hand, Prince Albert being placed between Princess Marina and the Countess of Rosebery. Wallis sat at the head of the table, but it was the Duchess of York who, without a glance at Wallis, led the women from the table at the end of dinner. The Yorks left as early as they decently could.

In return Edward excluded the Yorks entirely. At the beginning of the reign he had consulted Prince Albert over the changes at Sandringham; now he made his own changes at Balmoral without even mentioning them to his brother. Prince Albert was saddened and hurt. 'David only told me what he had done after it was over,' he wrote to Queen Mary from Glamis, 'which I might say made me rather sad. He arranged it all with the official people up there. I never saw him alone for an instant.' On 13 October, the day on which he was writing sadly from Glamis to his mother about his deteriorating relationship with his brother, Wallis moved into a dreary villa in Felixstowe, a small seaside town in Suffolk, to comply with the residence requirements for her divorce in the county. On 19 October Prince Albert and his family took the night train for London, where a bombshell was awaiting him in the form of unwelcome news from Alec Hardinge.

Hardinge told him that he had had definite news that Wallis was divorcing her husband, that the petition was set for 27 October, that he had discussed the matter with the Prime Minister and others at a house-party at Cumberland Lodge that weekend, and that Baldwin had been to see the King on Tuesday 20 October to warn him of the scandal aroused around the world by his 'friendship' with Wallis, and to ask him to prevent the divorce going ahead, a request which the King had refused. Hardinge, taking a much graver view of the situation than, as yet, the Prime Minister seems to have done, warned Prince Albert that 'it might end with his brother's abdication'. Prince Albert was 'appalled and tried not to believe what he had been told'.[70]

He was appalled for several reasons, primarily because, whatever happened, the monarchy must be damaged and his family name dragged through the mud; and secondly, because the possibility now arose that he might have to take over from his brother and do so under the worst possible circumstances. Having seen at first hand his brother's passion for Wallis and her demonstrable power over him, and having come to the unflattering conclusion that she was an adventuress, he could see the dangers that the Simpson divorce presented. He would have agreed with Hardinge that the only way out lay in convincing Edward that marriage with Wallis, as a twice-divorced woman, would be unacceptable to the vast majority of his subjects and that his duty as King lay in his rejecting any such idea. The major problem was that there was nothing either legally or constitutionally to prevent the King marrying Wallis once she was legally free. As the Attorney-General, Sir Donald Somervell, informed Baldwin, the King's marriage would be outside the scope of the Royal Marriages Act of 1772, which required members of the royal family to obtain the sovereign's consent before marrying. It would, however, Sir Donald pointed out, be unconstitutional for the sovereign to marry against the advice of his ministers. Hardinge's dual strategy which, no doubt, he put to Prince Albert, was to get Baldwin to make it quite clear to the King that marriage to Wallis was an unacceptable prospect and, therefore, put the King in the position in which, in order to marry her, he would have to reject his Prime Minister's advice. His second plan was to gather up a weight of evidence demonstrating that such a marriage would be unacceptable to the people of the Empire and thus convince Edward of its impossibility. He was to fail on both counts, firstly because Baldwin was unwilling to drive, or be seen to drive, the King into a corner and secondly because Edward habitually turned a blind eye to any evidence or advice which he found unwelcome or which did not tally with his own opinions or instincts. Finally, all efforts to persuade the King to give up his plan of marrying Wallis were to fail because, in the words of Edward's trusted adviser, Walter Monckton, everyone underestimated the 'strength of the King's devotion and their united will'.

Prince Albert was in the position of a substitute player waiting on the touchline, only that in his case he was extremely anxious that the call to take over would not come. His brother was determined to keep him at arm's length throughout the crisis, nor, on the rare occasions on which they did meet, was it a question of consultation on Edward's part but rather the announcement of *faits accomplis*. Prince Albert, therefore, only learned of the crisis at second hand, principally from Hardinge, who played the most active behind-the-scenes role in the early part of the crisis, and Baldwin, who took charge of the final phase. For a week the Prince remained on tenterhooks awaiting the hearing of the Simpson divorce at Ipswich, while Hardinge mobilized senior Whitehall men to put pressure on Wallis's solicitor, Theodore Goddard, to call off the divorce, wrote letters to Lord Tweedsmuir, Governor-General of Canada, for a sounding of Dominion opinion and attempted without success to persuade the visiting Canadian Prime Minister, William Mackenzie King, to raise the subject with his sovereign. Two days before the divorce, the editor of *The Times*, Geoffrey Dawson, brought to the Palace a copy of a long letter he had received from the United States. Written by a long-time British resident in the United States and signed with a pseudonym, 'Britannicus in Partibus Infidelium', it set out in forthright terms what was being said and written of the King and Mrs Simpson in the States and the infinite harm which was being done to the image of Britain and the monarchy and, for the first time, put forward as the solution the abdication of the King and his succession by the Duke of York. For many years, the writer said, the image of Great Britain in the eyes of the world had been George v. Now, due to 'the poisonous publicity attending the King's friendship with Mrs Simpson . . . the prevailing American opinion is that the foundations of the British throne are undermined, its moral authority, its honour, and its dignity cast into the dustbin. To put the matter bluntly,' Britannicus added, 'George v was an invaluable asset to British prestige abroad; Edward has proved himself an incalculable liability.' The letter culminated with a call for Edward viii's immediate abdication:

It may be presumptuous, and even impertinent, for a person far removed from the centre of things to suggest a remedy; but I cannot refrain from saying that nothing would please me more than to hear that Edward viii had abdicated his rights in favour of the Heir Presumptive, who I am confident would be prepared to carry on in the sterling tradition established by his father. In my view it would be well to have such a change take place while it is still a matter of individuals, and before the disquiet has progressed to the point of calling in question the institution of monarchy itself.[71]

On 27 October, the day of the Ipswich divorce, Hardinge wrote to Dawson thanking him for the letter and expressing his conviction that, when the King saw it, it would 'make the desired impression' on him.[72] The Britannicus letter certainly did not make 'the desired impression' upon Edward; it is doubtful whether, given his closed mind and his overriding passion, anything could. He was aware, through Wallis, of the kind of things that were being said of them in America and in this case no doubt dismissed these charges as being made by yet another stuffy old buffer and the reports as simply the same journalistic farrago of lies, truths and half-truths. However, seeing the idea of his abdication in favour of his brother, who would carry on the tradition of his father, written down in black and white may well have had a subconscious effect. The possibility must always have been in the back of his mind that he might have to abdicate to marry Wallis and, only just under three weeks later at his second meeting with Baldwin, he was to declare that 'he was prepared to go'. In fact, the Britannicus letter was to have an effect quite opposite to that which Hardinge intended. Coming from the source it did – *The Times*, an authority which Edward already regarded with a degree of paranoia – it provided him with additional evidence of a 'plot' or conspiracy, involving the courtiers and the Establishment in the form of the Prime Minister, the Archbishop of Canterbury and the editor of *The Times*, to frustrate his wishes and later to oust him from the throne. Beaverbrook, his supporter, believed it to have been written by *The Times*. Edward himself later pointed the finger at Tommy Lascelles, describing him as 'a traitorous member of his own staff'. Examination of the Dawson archives at *The Times* and in the Bodleian, however, not only reveals the name and address of the author of 'Britannicus', but refutes the suggestion that the letter is other than genuine. The mystery which has grown up around the letter and its authorship is, like so many mysteries connected with the Establishment, directly attributable to the governing passion for secrecy and reveals more about the 'house' traditions of *The Times* than it does about anything else.

On Friday 27 October Wallis was granted a decree nisi on the grounds of Ernest Simpson's adultery at the Hotel de Paris in Bray on 21 July. The name of the woman was not read out in court but, according to Wallis's counsel, Norman Birkett, she was named in the petition and was, presumably, Mary Raffray. Costs were given against the respondent, Ernest Simpson (which Wallis apparently, in accordance with a previous agreement between them, later reimbursed). Walter Monckton (who was not told by the King that he intended to marry Wallis until over a week after the divorce was granted), in an attempt to show that the divorce was not collusive in the ordinary sense and based on genuine evidence of adultery and not on the use of a professional co-respondent, told the Attorney-General that the co-respondent 'was a woman whom S[impson] (whose married life had ceased to have much attraction for him owing to the King) was anxious to marry and had been caught',[73] Wallis was to continue with the fiction that the divorce had not been of her making, telling Victor Cazalet that 'it was not her fault. Simpson had deceived her'.[74] but suspicion that the whole thing had been a 'put-up job' for the King and Wallis's convenience increased the royal family's bitterness about the affair. The British press, operating under a gentleman's agreement arranged by the King and Monckton, simply reported it briefly as if it were an ordinary divorce case and without comment the following day.

That evening, 28 October, the Yorks dined with the Hardinges to celebrate the swearing in of Alec Hardinge as a Privy Councillor. It was a small dinner-party, consisting of the Yorks, Malcolm Bullock, a noted wit and conversationalist, Conservative MP for a Lancashire constituency, with his wife, Lady Victoria, Lord Derby's daughter and Maureen Stanley's sister-in-law, and Osbert Sitwell. Although only one subject, yesterday's divorce, was in the forefront of all their minds, Sitwell later recorded that no one dared bring it up.[75] Later, when Edward began to see the sad saga in terms of a conspiracy against him, he alleged that it was on this occasion that his intriguing Private Secretary discussed his private affairs with the Duke of York, although Sitwell says that he was present from the moment the Duke of York entered the house until he left it and not a word was said on the subject. And there, for the moment, the 'King's matter', as Archbishop Lang called it, appeared to rest. The Yorks, anxious and apprehensive, lived their family life at 145 Piccadilly, the King and Mrs Simpson carried on theirs between Cumberland Terrace, the rented house to which Wallis moved after Bryanston Court, Buckingham Palace and Fort Belvedere. In Downing Street Baldwin waited for an encouraging sign that his lecture of 20 October had produced some reaction from the King. There was none. The 'man in the street' knew nothing of the suppressed drama seething beneath the surface in royal and political circles. The King carried on his public duties with all the charm and panache of which he was capable. At the State Opening of Parliament, an occasion which his father and even his unselfconscious grandfather had always dreaded, he appeared as 'a young, happy Prince Charming', although everybody commented on his accent which came across as a sort of royal Cockney/American hybrid. 'The King's accent is really terrible,' Harold Nicolson wrote. 'He referred to the "Amurrican Government" and ended, "And moy the blessing of Almoighty God rest upon your deliberoitions." '[76] Even Chips Channon was surprised: '. . . he said prog-ress and rowts instead of roots, as I do'. There were rumours that the King's American inspiration, Wallis, watched the ceremony from the Royal Gallery; they were unfounded – as Wallis told Lady Londonderry, she was shopping at Harrods at the time – but they were typical of the fears that were now being voiced in social and political circles. The day before, Channon, his ear as always to the ground, reported, 'all the world is saying that the King intends to marry Wallis, now that her divorce is over. Personally I suspect that this is true. . . .'[77]

The evening of the Ceremony, 3 November, at a 'brilliant dinner of fifteen' at the Channons, Wallis took care to tell Chips that her divorce was 'at Ernest's instigation, and at no wish of hers'. Her line with everyone, even close friends like Sibyl Colefax and Diana Cooper, was to deny that there was any question of her marrying the King. She was tackled by the formidable Lady Londonderry at an evening party at Emerald Cunard's on Friday 6 November, who told her frankly that 'in her view, if the King had any idea of marrying her, he ought to be quickly disabused of the notion, since the English people would never stand for a Queen or King's Consort who had been twice divorced and whose previous husbands were both still living'.[78] The next day Wallis wrote to Lady Londonderry, of whose considerable social influence she was, of course, aware. Talking of herself as 'the innocent victim' of the sensationalist American press, she went on to make a statement which would certainly have surprised the members of the King's Household. 'I have come to the conclusion that no one has been *really* frank with a certain person in telling him how the country feels about his friendship with me, perhaps nothing has been said to him at all. I feel that he should know however and I am going to tell him the things you told me.' Nothing, however, would calm the rumours: 'it is quite true', Channon wrote, 'that the monarchy has lost caste enormously since last January. All the world knows that the King is the slave of an American, who has had two husbands and two divorces....' On 10 November, to everyone's horror, Wallis's name was mentioned for the first time publicly in the House of Commons. During question time the subject of the Coronation came up and McGovern, Labour MP for Shettleston, Glasgow, jumped up and shouted, 'Why bother, in view of the gambling at Lloyd's that there will not be one?' There were roars of 'Shame! Shame!' and he called out, 'Yes ... Mrs Simpson.' '... the truth is that the monarchy has lost ground in a frightening manner,' Channon commented. 'Prince Charming charms his people no more....'[79] Outside the chamber, the lobbies were filled with hunger marchers from Lancashire and South Wales, protesting against the new unemployment regulations, and at the door a queue was singing the 'Red Flag'. Fear of socialism among the upper classes made the possibility of a discredited monarchy even more dangerous. At dinner, three days previously, Honor Channon and Jean Norton, beloved of Edward's champion, Beaverbrook, argued that if the King married Wallis he would have to abdicate immediately, 'for if he did not, we would have unrest, a Socialist agitation and a "Yorkist" party'. Chips, dining at the House of Commons on 12 November, heard 'wild talk ... absurd, unfair abuse of Mrs Simpson'; two days later he told a horrified Prince Paul that 'the House of Commons openly talked of abdication'.

In the first week of November Prince Albert attempted repeatedly to contact his brother and talk the situation over with him. The Duke of Windsor's Abdication archive contains what Queen Mary's biographer described as 'helpful letters from the Duke of York', all to no avail. 'I have been meaning to come & see you but I wanted to see David first,' Prince Albert wrote to his mother on 6 November. 'He is very difficult to see & when one does he wants to talk about other matters.' It was not long, however, before the royal family learned in the clearest possible terms of the King's intention. The King's move was precipitated by a letter from Hardinge, to which the King attributed such importance that he later headed a chapter describing a critical phase of the Abdication crisis as 'The King received a letter'. In it, Hardinge warned the King that he knew for a fact that the silence of the British press was not going to be maintained, that the Prime Minister and senior members of the Government were meeting to discuss what line should be taken and that their resignation should not be excluded, precipitating a general election in which the King's 'affairs' would be the only issue: '... even those who would sympathize with Your Majesty as an individual would deeply resent the damage which would inevitably be done to the Crown, the corner-stone on which the whole Empire rests....' The only solution, he told the King, was that Mrs Simpson should 'go abroad *without further delay*'.[80] It was at this point, in the second week of November, that the second, more active phase of the drama began.

Hardinge's letter, in the words of the historian of the Abdication, Brian Inglis, 'smoked the King out'. It burst like a bombshell into the woolly haven of his lover's cloud-cuckoo land into which he had retreated. With a lover's obsession, Edward focused on the suggestion that Wallis should be sent away. It was to be the only paragraph which he later reproduced in his book. He saw it not as advice intended to avert a serious situation threatening the Crown, the Empire and the Constitution, but as some Machiavellian test of the strength of his love devised by Baldwin and 'nebulous figures around him', using his Private Secretary as a tool.

But what was Mr Baldwin's purpose? Was this a move to test the strength of my attachment? If the real intention was to try to induce me to give Wallis up by pointing at my head this big pistol of the Government's threatened resignation, they had clearly misjudged their man. I was obviously in love. They had struck at the very roots of my pride. Only the most faint-hearted would have remained unaroused by such a challenge.... This was not the crisis of a Prince; it was the crisis of a King. And because it was not my nature to watch and wait, I resolved to come to grips at once with Mr Baldwin and the nebulous figures around him.[81]

This curious paragraph, written after the event and with all archival material available, illustrates in a nutshell the key to the Abdication crisis. Edward was a man obsessed – 'insane' was the word used of him not only by Baldwin and Wigram but by friends and sympathizers such as Chips Channon. Not one of the letters shown him by Hardinge, including the Britannicus letter, not one word of warning or supplication spoken to him by men whom he knew to be his friends, such as Godfrey Thomas, Joey Legh and Ulick Alexander, nor any consideration of country and Empire, nor of the traditions and responsibilities of his family, weighed with him for an instant compared with this impugning of his love for Wallis. And so, like one of Tennyson's Knights of the Round Table, he sallied forth to fight for his lady love. 'I decided to have it out with the Prime Minister,' he wrote. At 6.30 p.m. on the evening of Monday 16 November Baldwin went to Buckingham Palace at the King's invitation to hear his sovereign declare that he intended to marry Wallis as soon as she was free, whether the Government approved of it or not. If they approved, he would marry her and be a better King in consequence; if not, he was prepared to abdicate. Baldwin, fortified by the opinions of the Dominion leaders which he had received from unofficial soundings, attempted to persuade him that the throne was the one link uniting the Empire and that a shock like this might lead to its breaking-up. The King, Baldwin told his family that evening, 'simply could not understand and he [SB] could not make him'.[82] He described the peculiar exaltation of the King's mood as he spoke of Wallis: 'The King's face wore at times such a look of beauty as might have lighted the face of a young knight who had caught a glimpse of the Holy Grail.' Back at Downing Street Baldwin asked Somervell to start work drafting an Abdication Bill (this was apparently done on 24 November) and retired shaken to bed. 'David', he told the Chief Whip, Captain Margesson, 'I have heard such things from my King to-night as I never thought to hear.'

After dinner, without warning, the King went round to his mother at Marlborough House. The Duchess of Gloucester, who was staying at the time, recalled:

He was in a great state of agitation and asked his mother if I could leave the room as he had a very serious family matter to discuss. Queen Mary was discernibly angered by this request, but with many apologies asked me to go.... Afterwards they [the Queen and Princess Mary, now the Princess Royal] came to fetch me. They were very upset. 'I'm so sorry,' the Queen apologised again. 'It was so rude of us sending you away, but David has told us some distressing news which you will know all about in due course.'[83]

For Queen Mary it must have been the most horrifying conversation of her life. She and the Princess Royal had listened sympathetically as Edward told them of his passion for Wallis; it was hardly news to them, after all. But when he told them he was prepared to abdicate in order to marry her, they were, in the words of her biographer, 'astounded and shocked'. To Queen Mary, as her son well knew, 'the Monarchy was something sacred and the Sovereign a personage apart'; ordinary human feelings did not come into it. To her, the choice seemed clear: he must give up Wallis or give up the throne, and, in reality, there should be only one choice, give up Wallis. In Edward's account, 'The word "duty" fell between us'; the trouble was that their interpretation of it differed so widely that there was an unbridgeable gulf between them. To her, his duty was to stay on the throne; to him, since he felt himself unable to function as King without marrying Wallis, his ultimate duty was, if necessary, to leave it. To her, the sacrifice should be his love; to him, it should be his throne. The King then asked his mother and sister to receive Wallis as his intended wife; both refused. Enough has already been said to illustrate the springs of Edward's action; Queen Mary's was best put in her own words in a letter written eighteen months later in July 1938:

You ask me in your letter of the 23rd of June to write to you frankly about my true feelings with regard to you and the present position and this I will do now. You will remember how miserable I was when you informed me of your intended marriage and abdication and how I implored you not to do so for our sake and for the sake of the country. You did not seem able to take in any point of view but your own.... I do not think you ever realised the shock, which the attitude you took up, caused your family and the whole Nation. It seemed inconceivable to those who had made such sacrifices during the war that you, as their King, refused a lesser sacrifice.... My feelings for you as your Mother remain the same, and our being parted and the cause of it, grieve me beyond words. After all, all my life I have put my Country before everything else, and I simply cannot change now.[84]

Prince Albert heard the news first-hand from Edward the following day. It is not difficult to imagine his reaction of utter horror and despair at the prospect which was now becoming ever more certain. Like every other member of the royal family he knew what it meant to be King. The nightmare possibility which had haunted the back of his mind since Hardinge's warnings three weeks before was turning into reality. The only account we have of the interview is Edward's – one brief mention in *A King's Story*, published in 1951 – 'Bertie was so taken aback by my news that in his shy way he could not bring himself to express his innermost feelings at the time....' Eleven years later in June 1962 he published a somewhat fuller version:

My brother came to the Palace next day at my summons.

We met in a small room off the garden. I gave him the upshot of the encounter [with Baldwin the previous evening] adding, 'It looks to me now, the way things are shaping up, that I shall probably have to go.'

Although [the Duke of Windsor continued] I had never discussed my personal problems with him, he was not without sources of information of his own.... He had, however, the tact never to bring up the matter, counting on me to do so in due course. [This was not exactly the case; as Prince Albert's letter of 6 November to his mother showed, he had certainly tried to discuss the matter and failed only because Edward 'always wants to talk about something else'.]

At that moment he must have realised for the first time that the succession was about to pass to him.

'Oh,' he said, 'that's a dreadful thing to hear. None of us wants that, I least of all.'

'I'm afraid there's no other way,' I said. 'My mind is made up.'

The ties between us had always been close. His feelings towards me then were very warm. Whatever the outcome, he said, he and I must stay in touch; we were brothers, before anything else.[85]

In his earlier memoirs, *A King's Story*, the Duke of Windsor went on to say that, although 'Bertie in his shy way ... could not bring himself to express his innermost feelings at the time', he did so a few days later in a letter. 'He wrote that he longed for me to be happy, adding that he of all people should be able to understand my feelings; he was sure that whatever I decided would be in the best interests of the country and the Empire.'[86]

Was the King bluffing? Although he was certainly telling the truth as far as his determination to marry Wallis was concerned, it does not seem from the evidence that he thought at this time that abdication would be necessary in order to do so. It has generally been assumed that Edward summoned Prince George later on the Tuesday, 17 November, in order to inform him of his decision to marry Wallis, but, according to Chips Channon, this was not the case. At midnight on 3 December, in the final week of the Abdication crisis, just as Channon, arrayed in lederhosen, was about to leave for a costume ball at the Austrian Legation, the Duke of Kent rang him from his neighbouring house in Belgrave Square and asked him to come round. Channon found Prince Paul and his wife Princess Olga with the Kents. Later when the party broke up Prince George went home with Channon, his wife Honor and their friend Jean Norton, where they 'talked and deplored' until after four in the morning. Prince George said he loved the King more than anyone, how the King ignored him, how he had not even seen him since the Balmoral visit until the evening in our house at our now historic dinner on 19 November. The King had rung him on the telephone before dinner that evening to say he was going to marry Wallis, and the Duke of Kent had not known whether to congratulate him or not.... And he [the King] had only rung him because he knew he would meet him at our dinner....[87]

Prince Paul's version, told to Channon in August 1939, differs slightly from the first in making it a personal interview, not a telephone call, but he confirms the date as the 19th, not the 17th, and adds some illuminating detail. Lunching in the silver and blue rococo dining-room at Belgrave Square, Prince Paul told Channon it always reminded him of 'our famous Edward VIII dinner-party a few days before the Abdication trouble began':

He re-told the story today, of how the then King had sent for his brother, the Duke of Kent, on that famous Thursday, having himself only just come back from his triumphant tour in Wales; he began by saying that he wanted his brothers to know, before they met that evening at 'Chips' Dinner Party', that he was going to marry Wallis. The Duke of Kent gasped, 'What will she call herself?' 'Call herself?' the King echoed. 'What do you think – Queen of England of course.' 'She is going to be Queen?' 'Yes and Empress of India, the whole bag of tricks.' The King was cock-a-hoop, gay, happy and confident. That was Thursday evening 19 November, at about 7.30 p.m. The Duke, flabbergasted, rushed home to dress and tell his wife and Princess Olga about it.[88]

The important point of Prince Paul's account is that it shows the King, *only three days* after his conversation with Baldwin on Monday 16 November, as confident that he would marry Wallis and make her 'Queen of England ... Empress of India, the whole bag of tricks'. The clear inference to be drawn from this is that he believed, once again, that he could 'get away with it', marrying Wallis on his own terms and making her Queen whatever his family or the Government thought of it. The threat of abdication at this stage was no more than that, just a threat, designed to underline the seriousness of his intention and, if possible, to silence opposition. Everyone remarked on the King's state of euphoria at Channon's dinner-party in honour of Prince Paul and Princess Olga on the evening of 19 November. Victor Cazalet, sitting next to Wallis, noted, 'HM in great form.... Every few minutes he gazes at her & radiance fills his countenance such as make you have a lump in your throat....' One reason for his euphoria was that he now saw their marriage as certain; on the day of her divorce he had presented her with a magnificent emerald ring; the stone, weighing 19.77 carats, was one of the greatest emeralds in the world which had once belonged to the Great Mogul. One of two sold by Cartier after splitting up the original huge emerald, it had been bought by Edward for a special price of £10,000 (c. £250,000 in today's value), and inscribed 'We are ours now 27 X 36'. The second reason for his high spirits was the wonderful welcome he had received on his tour of South Wales, from which he had returned that day, which he had taken as confirmation that he still held the inalienable affection and support of his people. On Armistice Day, 11 November, he ordered from van Cleef and Arpels Wallis's Christmas present, two huge jewelled quills, one set with diamonds, the other with rubies. Exactly one week later Edward stood before the twisted derelict wreck of the Bessemer Steel Works at Dowlais in South Wales, where a few years before 9,000 men had been employed. Moved by the sight of hundreds of unemployed steel workers singing an old Welsh hymn among the ruins, he uttered the famous words, 'Something must be done to find them work.' The next day, touring an impoverished housing estate at Pontypool, he had pledged, 'You may be sure that all I can do for you I will. . . .' That evening he left for London to join Wallis at the Channon dinner, where, according to Chips, 'the room seemed to sway with jewels' and the King told Honor 'he approved of splendour'.

Prince Albert would certainly have been told by Prince George and/or Prince Paul of what Edward had said about making Wallis Queen. Prince Paul and Princess Olga, who were then in London on an official visit, were very much on the 'family' side, which had earned Prince Paul a sharply regal put-down from the King at the Channon dinner. The King had, in fact, refused to invite Prince Paul to anything during his visit, so that, Eden complained to Harold Nicolson on 23 November, Prince Paul had been forced to falsify his official communiqué in order to conceal this omission. The principal reason for the King's rudeness was, apparently, the couple's coolness towards Wallis on their Yugoslavian holiday. Prince Albert, however, saw things from a rather different angle than his infatuated brother, who was by now quite out of touch with reality. He had several meetings that week with Queen Mary, and on the 19th, the day of the dinner, saw Baldwin, who at that time, according to the Prime Minister's own account to Thomas Jones, was under the impression that 'the King had agreed to go quietly' if necessary in order to marry Wallis, and his talk would, therefore, be on the basis of abdication being a possible contingency. He saw his brother again on 24 November, by which time Lord Harmsworth had put forward as a possible solution a morganatic marriage between the King and Wallis. Morganatic marriage between a reigning sovereign and a person of non-royal birth was recognized in continental Europe. Under its provisions the wife would not share the royal rank of her husband, nor would their children, although legitimate, have the right to succeed their father. To Wallis, too, it seemed a sensible compromise and that weekend at the Fort she persuaded the King, whose first reaction to the idea was one of distaste, to consider it. Such a marriage would require legislation as there was no provision for it under English constitutional law. Harmsworth was, therefore, deputed to put the proposal to Baldwin; when this did not evoke an immediate response, the King took the initiative and summoned him to a meeting on 25 November. Neither Prince Albert nor his brother left any record of their conversation on the 24th, but one may imagine that, since the morganatic proposal had been put to Baldwin the previous day, it formed at least a part of the subject of their talk. Prince Albert clearly saw abdication as on the cards at this point, as he wrote to Godfrey Thomas the following day, 'If the worst happens & I have to take over, you can be assured that I will do my best to clear up the inevitable mess, if the whole fabric does not crumble under the shock and strain of it.'

There were now, indeed, signs that a constitutional crisis was developing. There was mischief-making by Baldwin's enemies, the press lords; on Monday Rothermere's *Daily Mail* published a leader headed 'The King Edward Touch', referring to the King's pledge to South Wales, contrasting the King's concern with the Government's lethargy and mendaciously asserting that the King had already summoned his ministers and called for action. Beaverbrook, summoned by the King, arrived back in England on the 26th. The *Mail* article raised the spectre of a King's party in opposition to the Government and the involvement of the monarchy in politics, as Geoffrey Dawson was quick to point out in the leading article in *The Times* the next day. It was not difficult for Baldwin to envisage an alliance of the popular press and the two most charismatic politicians of the day, Churchill and Lloyd George, both his enemies, against him. It is significant that on the morning of the day on which he was scheduled to have an evening meeting with the King, Baldwin invited Attlee, leader of the Labour Opposition, Sinclair, the Liberal leader, and Churchill, his most vocal opponent within the Conservative Party, to Downing Street, to ask them whether, in the event of his resignation and that of his Government, they would support him. Attlee and Sinclair pledged loyalty and said they would not form a government if asked to do so by the King. Churchill apparently assured Baldwin that, 'though his attitude was a little different, he would certainly support the Government', but as he was already known as the King's friend, Baldwin and his confidant, Neville Chamberlain, did not believe him. Chamberlain noted that Churchill was 'moving mysteriously in the background and, it is suggested, expressing willingness to form a Government if there should be any refusal on our part to agree'. Baldwin was now suspicious of the King as his subsequent behaviour showed. He told the meeting of the inner Cabinet of senior ministers that afternoon that 'the King had now swung round and had taken up the position that he would contract a morganatic marriage to be legalised by Act of Parliament'. The consensus of the meeting was, according to Chamberlain's diary, 'that we must act cautiously, and find out the attitude of Opposition and Dominions before committing ourselves. S.B. should point out various difficulties but not turn anything down.' Chamberlain added that he had no doubt that if the morganatic marriage were to be arranged, 'this would only be the prelude to the further step of making Mrs S. Queen with full rights'. This would seem to have been Baldwin's opinion too, since by his own account he told the King that evening, 'if he thought he was going to get away with it in that way he was making a huge mistake'.[89]

This third encounter between the King and Baldwin was the crucial point of the crisis, for during it Edward, in Beaverbrook's words, laid his neck upon the block. It remained only for Baldwin to swing the axe. At his own request, the issue of his marriage became a constitutional question. When Baldwin warned him that it was his personal opinion that legislation necessary to make the

morganatic marriage possible would not pass Parliament, Edward clearly did
not believe him. He was still counting on his enormous popularity to carry him
through. Baldwin offered to consider the proposal formally if the King wished,
warning, 'It will mean my putting it formally before the whole Cabinet and
communicating with the Prime Ministers of all the Dominions. Do you really
wish that, Sir?' Edward answered that he did. He was thus binding himself to
accept the advice of his Government, whatever that advice might be, or precipitating a constitutional crisis of the first magnitude. According to the Marquess of Zetland's minute of the Cabinet meeting two days later at which the
proposal was formally considered, Baldwin believed that the King might stick
to his line whatever happened and provoke the Government's resignation:

. . . his [the King's] present intention seemed to be to refuse to withdraw from his
position. It was pointed out, at the Cabinet, that this might involve the resignation
of the Government and that in this case it would give rise to a Constitutional issue of
the first magnitude, viz, the King versus the Government. It seems that the King has
been encouraged to believe that Winston Churchill would, in these circumstances, be
prepared to form an alternative Government. If this were true, there would be a grave
risk of the country being divided into two camps. . . . This would clearly be fraught
with danger of the most formidable kind.[90]

Prince Albert was due on 29 November to take the night train to fulfill a
long-standing engagement at Edinburgh, where he was to be installed as Grand
Master Mason of Scotland in succession to his elder brother, who had held the
office as Prince of Wales and relinquished it when he became King. The
possibility that he might soon have to succeed his brother in another, far more
difficult, office was in the forefront of his mind, as he wrote to his Private
Secretary, Sir Eric Miéville, that evening: 'I hate going to Scotland to do what I
have to do as I am so worried over this whole matter. I feel like the proverbial
sheep being led to the slaughter.' He knew now that the critical phase of the
crisis had begun. On the morning of the 27th Hardinge had visited him, no
doubt to discuss the consultation with the Dominion Prime Ministers, which,
at the King's request, Baldwin was about to undertake. Unlike his brother, he
can have had few illusions as to what the response would be. The Government
set particular store by the reaction of Canada, 'the eldest child of the Commonwealth' as Baldwin called the Dominion. The King owned a ranch in Alberta,
the 'EP', and was Canada's idol. But Canada, as the United States's next-door
neighbour, was also the best-informed of all Edward's Dominion of his affair
with Wallis, and Hardinge had recently received a letter from Lord Tweedsmuir
which made Canadian opinion on the subject clear:

Canada is the most puritanical part of the Empire and cherishes very much the Victorian standards of private life. . . . She has a special affection and loyalty for the
King . . . [which] is strongly felt particularly by the younger people . . . and they
are alarmed at anything which might take the gilt off their idol. Canada's pride has
been deeply wounded by the tattle in the American Press. . . .[91]

Prince Albert, who, as he noted in his diary, was kept informed throughout, would have been shown the text of the telegrams which were to be sent out at 1.04 a.m. on the morning of 28 November to the Prime Ministers of the dominions of Canada, South Africa, Australia, New Zealand and of the Irish Free State. It was on the response of these leaders of Empire opinion as much as on that of the elected Government of Great Britain that, it was thought, the King's future would depend. Opinion against the King within the Cabinet was hardening meanwhile, prompted by moral disapproval of the King's proposed marriage and deep suspicion of the manœuvres of Beaverbrook and Churchill. On 30 November, Ramsay MacDonald, who as Lord President of the Council was in a position to know, told Harold Nicolson that both the Cabinet and the Privy Council were determined that the King should abdicate, 'but he imagines that the country, the great warm heart of the people, are with him'. 'I do not think so,' Nicolson commented. 'The upper classes mind her being an American more than they mind her being divorced. The lower classes do not mind her being an American but they loathe the idea that she has had two husbands already.'[92] On the same day Chips Channon, who had friends, notably Jean Norton, in the Beaverbrook circle, wrote: 'There is no hope for the King ... and it looks almost certainly as if the Yorks will succeed,' commenting with resignation, 'Honor and I will be out of the royal racket having backed the wrong horse.' And, the next day: 'things are moving in favour of the Yorks, and from a realistic point of view I must confess that this seems the best solution'.

The exchange of telegrams between Baldwin and the Dominion Premiers, the text of which has recently been released by the Public Record Office, is one of the key episodes of the crisis. The manner in which the position was put to the Premiers and their response makes nonsense of the King's subsequent claims that he was 'jockeyed off' the throne by an Establishment conspiracy. The views expressed by the Dominions, which were to be echoed by the majority of the British public, were also to be, in King George VI's view, the justification for his position vis-à-vis Wallis, as Duchess of Windsor, which was that as she had publicly been declared by the majority as unfit to be Queen or even morganatic wife of the King, she was not fit to be a member of the royal family. In the long battle with his brother over making Wallis a Royal Highness, the key phrase in the King's view was that to do so 'would make nonsense of the Abdication'.

The text of the telegrams gave a fair résumé of the position since Baldwin's first meeting with the King on the subject on 20 October:

I felt it my duty recently informally to broach matter with the King and to give him warning of the grave consequences which existing state of affairs might produce, especially in event of then pending divorce suit being proceeded with. Another opportunity of raising matter with him occurred when I was summoned by him for an interview on 16th November after grant of decree *nisi*. HM told me in course of that interview, speaking informally, of the fixed intention which he had of marrying Mrs Simpson. He appreciated, however, he said, that idea she should become Queen and that her children should succeed to the Throne (as unless otherwise provided by legislation must be position of

King's wife) was out of the question; he told me therefore he contemplated abdication and leaving succession to the Duke of York.

The King informed Queen Mary and his brother(s) subsequently that above course of action was contemplated by him. I should add that in my opinion there is not any possibility of dissuading the King from this marriage if decree is made absolute and such a course does not therefore appear to form one of the practicable alternatives in front of us.

On the 25th November I returned for a further talk with the King on which occasion HM outlined to me and asked my view on a new proposal which had been put to him from some outside quarter. It is assumed in this proposal also that Mrs Simpson cannot be Queen but it contemplates that marriage between the King and her should not necessitate his leaving the Throne. The suggestion in this proposal is that an undertaking on his? (or her) side that although his wife would reside with him in Buckingham Palace she would not be treated as Queen nor would appear on any state occasion, and he would agree further that it would be proper, when marriage was announced, that there should be introduction of legislation for purpose of fixing the lady's position as the wife of the King but not as Queen and of amending the Act of Settlement so as to bar issue of marriage from succeeding to the Throne. A necessary part of suggested arrangements would be that on their side the Governments would undertake to acquiesce in the marriage on this (these) condition(s) and would be responsible for any legislation required to put it into effect.

While promising that I would consider the above suggestion I informed His Majesty that there was not in my view any chance that such an arrangement would receive the approval of Parliament here. I reminded the King of the very important factor that position in relation to Dominions, whose assent would be equally essential, was also to be considered.

At this point Baldwin could not refrain from inserting what he thought to be a necessary caveat: 'I think it, moreover, very probable that such an arrangement if it were agreed to now would prove to be temporary and that pressure would later on be brought to bear with a view to the wife of the King being given her position as Queen.' He then put three alternatives to the Premiers for their opinion:

In my consideration of the question it would be very helpful to me if as soon as possible I could have your personal view and what in your opinion would be view of public opinion in your Dominion regarding three following possibilities:–
(i)   Marriage of His Majesty to Mrs Simpson, she to become Queen.
(ii) King's marriage to Mrs Simpson without his abdication but on basis that she should not become Queen and accompanied by necessary legislation.
(iii) A voluntary abdication by King in favour of Duke of York carried out as above.[93]

Mackenzie King of Canada, in a telegram despatched at 12.45 a.m. on the morning of 30 November, replied rejecting course (1) outright, and giving it as his view that Parliament and Canadian public opinion would be unfavourable to course (2), and that his Government would be as unwilling as the Government of the United Kingdom to assume responsibility for legislation required to put such an arrangement (the morganatic marriage) into effect. With regard to course (3), he cabled:

On the assumption mentioned in your message, namely that the King's intention to marry Mrs Simpson is fixed and unalterable, a voluntary abdication by the King in favour of the Duke of York, as suggested by His Majesty in your interview with him on November 16th, would appear to me to be the honourable and right course for the King to pursue. It would, I believe, be so viewed by our Parliament, and by Public Opinion in Canada, while occasioning deep regret that such a step had become necessary.[94]

At 12.12 a.m. on 3 December Baldwin telegraphed the opinions of the Dominion Prime Ministers to Mackenzie King. They amounted (with the exception of New Zealand which still havered on the brink of condemnation, their Premier never having even heard of Mrs Simpson, and the Irish Free State which replied that it was really not their affair) to a resounding 'No' to proposals 1 and 2 of the 28 November telegram. The Dominions would not accept Mrs Simpson as Queen, nor would they countenance the morganatic proposal. Australia, whose tough response had been anticipated through the decisive stance of the High Commissioner in London, Mr Bruce, and which was led by a Catholic Premier, Mr Lyons, was the most hostile to the King, going so far as to declare that abdication was now the only solution, whether he married Mrs Simpson or not. Their replies are worth quoting as significant of Empire opinion on the monarchy and its unifying importance to the British Commonwealth:

Prime Minister of the Commonwealth of Australia states that Commonwealth Government are profoundly disturbed by news. His Majesty is extremely popular throughout Australia but there is widespread condemnation of marriage to the lady in question. In their opinion proposal that she should become Queen cannot be considered while alternative proposal that she should occupy ?an anomalous position as wife but not as Queen ...s countenance [?runs counter] to best Popular conception of Royal Family. He fears a weakening of loyal ties would result from marriage unless it were preceded by abdication.

He feels that course (3) [Abdication] would be a solution which would fully repair prestige of Monarchy which has been gravely shaken by recent events. He has mentioned that he himself has been so greatly disturbed that he doubts whether he and his wife would have felt able to attend the Coronation and that he considers a continuance of present situation would be in highest degree disastrous. He is convinced that succession of Duke of York would be hailed with deepest relief and satisfaction throughout Australia. It would be felt that domestic traditions of late Monarch which were very greatly valued throughout the Commonwealth would be fully presided over (?preserved) and that in other respects by Duke who with Duchess had made themselves popular everywhere in Australia would be thought likely to prove a worthy successor to his father.

In a subsequent message Prime Minister of the Commonwealth of Australia has expressed his strong view that situation has now passed the possibility of compromise i.e. that even if His Majesty now drop(?s) proposal of marriage nevertheless abdication should take place since in Mr Lyon's [*sic*] view public confidence in Australia is now so shaken that no (?other) course is possible.

The Prime Minister of the Union of South Africa felt:

Public marriage under all the circumstances might make His Majesty a liability instead of an asset to Commonwealth. Marriage without right of succession would not improve matters now and would raise fresh troubles later if there were issue. To peoples of the Union abdication would be a great shock where the marriage under the circumstances would be a permanent wound.

De Valera of the Irish Free State made it plain that the 'position of the Irish Free State in whole matter is one of detachment. If they had same interest that we have they would certainly consider person in position of His Majesty should be above reproach.' At first sight he had favoured course (2) 'on assumption that divorce was a recognised institution in England', but if public opinion would not stand for it, then 'he supposes there would be no alternative to course (3)'.[95]

With the Dominions' rejection of the morganatic proposal, which was formally turned down by the Cabinet on 2 December, it looked as though the final point had been reached: the King must renounce Mrs Simpson or give up the throne in order to marry her. Press silence was about to break, leaving no room for further manœuvring. On 1 December, the Bishop of Bradford, Dr Blunt, recently returned from a Lambeth conference entitled 'Recall to Religion', had taken it upon himself to recall the King to his Christian duties in an open address. The innocent man of the cloth insisted that, although he had seen some American press cuttings about the affair, he was primarily concerned not with the King's adultery but with his churchgoing and only wished to take the King to task for not going to church on Sundays. Since, however, informed opinion was thinking of nothing else but the King and Mrs Simpson, it was immediately interpreted as a reference to the affair and consequently as the opening of the breach in the wall of public silence. By the evening of Monday 1 December the Press Association had picked it up; by the 2nd it was published in the provincial papers led by the *Yorkshire Post*, and it was clear that the national dailies would follow suit no later than the 3rd. For Baldwin, the 'Blunt instrument', as the Bishop's address came instantly to be known, was a heaven-sent opportunity to bring the King to his senses by showing him what was being said about him and Mrs Simpson in black and white. For, when Baldwin went to the Palace on 2 December to inform the King of the Cabinet decision on the morganatic proposal, he found him still convinced that his domestic popularity would carry the day. The Prime Minister took with him the Dominion replies and even showed him Lyons's last telegram declaring that there was now no alternative to abdication. The King's response was that 'there were not many people in Australia'. The King, who had spent the weekend in isolation at the Fort where Wallis, sick with nerves as she might be, was the dominant influence, was, however, still unaware of the real state of public opinion. He was utterly shocked by an article in the *Birmingham Post*, saying plaintively, 'They don't want me,' as he showed it to Baldwin. Baldwin, although later describing Edward in Parliament as 'behaving like a great gentleman', actually described him afterwards to his Private Secretary, Major Dugdale, as 'ill-tempered and petulant ... very angry about Bishop Blunt, whose utterance he clearly thought had been inspired by No. 10'.[96] The King asked Baldwin about Parliament and when the Prime Minister replied that the answer there would be the same as the Dominions' had been, he persisted, saying that Parliament had not been consulted. Baldwin replied that he had made soundings which indicated that 'the people would not approve of your marriage with Mrs Simpson' and put forward the three alternatives which, as he saw it, had faced the King since the beginning: 1) to give up the idea of marriage; 2) to marry contrary to the advice of ministers; 3) abdication. 'To all arguments based on responsibility towards his people, the King did not react, not feeling any responsibility which should dictate or influence his conduct,' Baldwin said later. By Edward's own account, he told Baldwin, somewhat ambiguously in one sense, 'Whether on the Throne or not, Mr Baldwin, I shall marry; and however painful the prospect, I shall, if necessary, abdicate in order to do so.' The interview ended with the customary eulogy of Wallis, which by now fell upon somewhat tired ears: 'Wallis is the most wonderful woman in the world.' 'Well, Sir, I hope that you may find her so,' Baldwin replied. 'Whatever happens, I hope you will be happy.'

Prince Albert arrived back in London on the morning of Thursday 3 December, the day on which the crisis took on a new, confusing and potentially dangerous turn. Although he had been kept informed of the progress of the negotiations between Baldwin and his brother, the results of the Dominions consultation and the rejection by the Cabinet of the morganatic proposal, no one, however, seems to have thought to warn him that, as he was travelling south from Scotland, Fleet Street's presses were rolling out the long-suppressed story of King Edward and Mrs Simpson. When he alighted at Euston Station that morning he was, in his own words, 'both surprised & horrified to see that the posters of the Daily Press had the following as their headlines in block letters "The King's Marriage".' He hastened to see Queen Mary to discuss this latest disagreeable turn of affairs and then saw his brother, in the presence of Walter Monckton. The King, he said, 'was in a great state of excitement', saying 'he would leave the country as King after making a broadcast to his subjects & leave it to them to decide what should be done'.[97]

This new departure was the King's and Wallis's counter to Baldwin's ultimata of the previous day and was, in effect, nothing less than an utterly unconstitutional attempt to appeal to the people over the heads of their elected representatives. The idea almost certainly emanated from Wallis, who never, then or later, understood the principles of a constitutional monarchy. It was based on the conviction that the King's popularity would carry all before it and that, given time to reflect, the country would choose the King rather than Baldwin. That this conviction showed the couple to be utterly out of touch with reality and was, in fact, baseless, was to be demonstrated over the following days when the idea of a King's party was briefly floated but fizzled out in the face of the massive disapproval of the majority. Baldwin having warned the King that she was in danger, Wallis left the country that day, 3 December, and, escorted by Lord Brownlow, fled across France to refuge with the Herman Rogers at Lou Viei near Cannes. That same day, before she left England, she wrote a quick note of instructions for the King: 'Be calm with B[aldwin] but tell the country to-morrow I am lost to you but Perry [Brownlow] and myself can discreetly manage. We will let Bateman [the private switchboard operator at Buckingham Palace] know [i.e. their whereabouts].'[98]

Baldwin later said that he 'had felt all along that he was fighting against Mrs Simpson', and there is considerable evidence to show that hers was, indeed, the ultimate will. 'What Mrs Simpson wanted was the what the King wanted,' Beaverbrook, one of the King's closest advisers at the time, was to write in his account of the Abdication, while Monckton, who spent the entire ten days at the Fort with the King prior to the Abdication, later confided to Victor Cazalet that 'he would have gone for *her* more if he had it [the Abdication crisis] over again'.[99] It was this feeling, that Wallis, rather than the confused and besotted King, was calling the shots and prolonging the crisis, which contributed to the hardening of the royal family's attitude towards her. The intention was still that they should marry and the King remain on the throne. The idea behind Wallis's flight was to defuse the situation, as the King later told Cazalet in an intimate talk *à trois* in Paris just over a year later.

When Baldwin saw the King on the evening of 3 December, Edward made it clear that, despite Baldwin's advice, he had not given up the morganatic marriage idea and repeated to him what he had told Prince Albert earlier, that he proposed to go abroad the following Sunday. Before doing so he wanted to broadcast to the people explaining his position and that of Mrs Simpson and handed him a copy of his proposed text, which Baldwin summarized in a 'Most Immediate. Secret and Personal' telegram in the early hours of 5 December to Mackenzie King:

By ancient custom King addresses his public utterances to his people and on this occasion is talking as a friend to British men and women within or without his Empire.... His Majesty has tried to (serve) this country and Empire for last twenty years and is not forgetting Dominions and dependencies beyond the seas who have always shown him such open-hearted kindness. It was never his intention to hide anything but time has now come for him to speak. He could not go on bearing heavy burdens resting on him as King unless he could be strengthened by a happy married life and he is firmly resolved to marry woman he loves when she is free to marry him. Neither Mrs Simpson nor he has ever sought to insist she should be Queen. All they desired was that their married happiness should carry with it a proper title and dignity for her befitting his wife. He now feels that it is best to go away for a while so that his hearers may reflect calmly and quietly but without undue delay on what he has said. Broadcast would conclude 'Nothing is nearer to my heart than that I should return but whatever may befall I shall always have a deep affection for my country and for you all.'

At the same time he told the Canadian Prime Minister that he proposed pre-empting the possibility of a campaign in favour of the morganatic marriage proposal by making a statement to the Commons indicating that the Government opposed it. The broadcast proposal was, he thought, unconstitutional and could not be made without the advice of ministers of all the King's Governments.[100]

There was now an atmosphere of deep crisis. After seeing Baldwin, the King went round to Marlborough House, where he told his mother, Prince Albert and Princess Mary 'that he could not live alone as King and must marry Mrs. S —,' Prince Albert recorded in the diary which he kept of events from that day; 'When David left after making this dreadful announcement to his mother he told me to come & see him at the Fort the next morning....'

In fact, he was not to see his brother for four agonizing days. When he telephoned the next morning, Friday 4 December, to make an appointment, the King put him off until the following day, remaining incommunicado, as far as his successor was concerned, until the evening of Monday the 7th, despite his brother's repeated attempts to contact him. He was forced to endure the suspense of waiting through that final crucial weekend to find out whether the outcome he dreaded would happen or not. Prince George and Prince Paul saw him constantly over those days, Princess Olga's diary recording the family emotions, Queen Mary angry, Prince Albert distraught:

Dec. 4th. Day of uncertainty. Georgie and Atinse [Princess Marina] went to see Aunt May [Queen Mary] at 12 – walked in the garden with her – very upset and angry with David.... The Yorks came for a wander, he mute and broken.... Bertie rang up to ask Pacey [Prince Paul] to go round and see them – he stayed nearly 2 hours – he put off leaving till Tuesday.

Dec. 5th [Saturday]: Nothing decided. Many don't want an abdication yet. Others feel, like the family, that he had better go as he can't be trusted to play the game.... Georgie rang David up last night – said he would love to help him and see him. David said perhaps today but didn't let him come.... Aunt May ... very upset, tried to appeal to him in vain.

Dec. 6th: Nothing new. The Cabinet has met twice today and Baldwin has been back and forth to the Fort. David has let nothing out of his intentions. We four drove to Royal Lodge, found Harry and Alice [Gloucester] there also. Bertie in an awful state of worry as David won't see him or telephone.[101]

Prince Albert did not share the feeling of the family, principally his mother, that the King had better go. He dreaded the prospect of kingship, and, although he had taken the precaution of deciding the name under which he would succeed, he continued to hope against hope that it would not happen. Chips Channon, who obtained his information direct from Prince Paul, noted on Saturday: 'The Yorks are staggered and behaving well; he intends to call himself George VI instead of Albert which people will think too Germanic.' But Prince Paul told Channon at dinner on the Sunday evening after having tea at the Royal Lodge that they knew nothing. 'The Duke of York is miserable, does not want the throne and is imploring his brother to stay.' Prince Albert's only source of information now was the Prime Minister. According to Baldwin's biographers, Middlemas and Barnes, the Prime Minister, among his other preoccupations that weekend, spent some time 'in total secrecy', preparing the Duke of York for his unwilling inheritance. Four years later King George VI was to confide to Halifax, then British Ambassador to Washington, that 'he had been to see Baldwin three or four times at No. 10 those last few days without anybody ever knowing. He had gone in somebody else's car to the garden entrance unobserved.'[102]

But Baldwin himself could not yet be certain if and when the King would go and remained, he afterwards said, unsure of the outcome right up to the last moment, Wednesday 9 December. He now thought it vital that the crisis should terminate as soon as possible. On Friday there had been an upsurge of sympathy for the King following on the breaking of the story in the press and a campaign in certain papers in favour of the morganatic marriage. There were fears that a King's party might be formed, fed by the news that the King was consulting Churchill (albeit with Baldwin's unwilling sanction) and the knowledge that he was supported by Beaverbrook. The fears of the Cabinet were expressed by the Secretary of State for India, the Marquess of Zetland, in a letter to the Viceroy, the Marquess of Linlithgow, written on the Saturday, that, if the King refused to come to a decision, the Government might be forced to resign and, since the Labour Party would refuse to come in, Churchill would form a Government which would not survive in the present House of Commons, be defeated and demand a dissolution. Zetland wrote:

And therein lies the supreme danger, for the country would be divided into opposing camps on the question whether or not the King should be permitted to marry a woman ... without making her Queen. The Dominion Prime Ministers are strongly opposed to a morganatic marriage.... On this issue it might well be that the Empire would disintegrate, since the throne is the magnet which at present keeps it together, while there might arise a situation in this country which would not be far short of civil strife.[103]

Baldwin also feared, as he later told Sir John Reith, Director-General of the BBC, that the King might fly out to join Wallis and they had, therefore, arranged that no aeroplane could be available. Although a diminishing crowd of protesters with placards pleading for the King wandered between Buckingham Palace and Downing Street where the Archbishop of Canterbury was booed on Sunday when he went to visit Baldwin, MPs visiting their constituencies during the weekend found the mass of the people, even the wives of the miners who had cheered the King in November, unutterably opposed to his marrying Mrs Simpson.

Baldwin no doubt told Prince Albert that he suspected one thing was keeping the King on his throne, the will-power of Wallis Simpson. This was later confirmed by Walter Monckton, who, after the Abdication, talked freely in the circles in which he moved. Both he and Sir Edward Peacock were at the Fort, witnesses of a series of harrowing telephone calls between the couple which, Monckton said, no one who heard them could ever forget. Sometimes the King would even be reduced to tears. The King himself, whom Churchill on Friday night had found 'under very great strain and very near breaking-point', was by now willing to go and, although on Friday he had told Peacock, who was drafting financial arrangements, that 'it is by no means certain that I shall go', by Saturday he had taken the decision to send Monckton, accompanied by his solicitor, George Allen of Allen & Overy, to tell Baldwin he was prepared to go and to negotiate personal terms. These were to include a financial settlement, a suitable title for Wallis with the rank of Royal Highness, and the assurance that her divorce would go through. Monckton evidently fearing that evidence of collusion might prevent the making of Wallis's decree nisi absolute, actually proposed that, along with a Bill giving effect to the King's wish to abdicate, there should be another making Wallis's decree absolute forthwith. When Baldwin saw the King, whom he found 'very nervous and difficult' that afternoon at the Fort, he promised to put it to his colleagues, but when an informal meeting of Cabinet on Sunday turned it down out of hand as an unholy bargain, Monckton intimated that in that case the King would require time for consultation, even months rather than days. At that Baldwin said firmly that it must be settled by Christmas, and Chamberlain was heard to make the characteristic remark that the delay and indecision were harming the Christmas trade. The majority of the Cabinet had now lost patience with the King; indeed, Monckton later wrote that, as far as negotiations with the Government went, the King had missed the boat on the weekend of the 4th–6th: 'I think there is little doubt that due provision would have been made for an income and title if he had expressed his willingness to go at once.'[104]

On that day, Sunday 6 December, Wallis, alarmed by a telephone call from Chips Channon to the effect that Baldwin was giving the King an ultimatum of a decision by 5 p.m., made what turned out to be her final effort to keep the King on the throne. A long, recently published letter reveals that her ultimate objective was still morganatic marriage without abdication, but in the short term the whole question should be postponed until the following autumn to allow controversy to cool. Her plan was for the King to tell Baldwin that he stood by his original decision to abdicate if necessary to marry Wallis ('this saves you and me in the eyes of the world because naturally if you did not make this clear you would be a cad ... and I would be the woman ... that was turned down'), but that in order not to create a situation in the country, he would not press the issue until October. This would be a 'sporting fair' gesture and 'appeal to the world'. 'No one but Baldwin and the Dominions want you to go,' she assured him, '... back up your people and make an 8 month sacrifice for them. Then they will give you what you want.' He must speak out over Baldwin's head, she told him:

The people in the press are clamouring for a word from you.... You must speak and tell the plan of the Duchess [the morganatic marriage with the title of Duchess of Cornwall or of Lancaster] and my plan. Don't be silenced and leave under a cloud I beseech you and in abdication no matter what form unless you can let the public know that the Cabinet has virtually kicked you out by repressing the two proposals....[105]

On Sunday evening, having waited all day to hear from his brother, Prince Albert rang up the Fort, only to be told, 'The King has a conference & will speak to you later.' The King did not ring back. On Monday morning Prince Albert waited again to hear and then telephoned again at 1 p.m. This time 'my brother told me he might be able to come & see me that evening'. Prince Albert replied that he 'must go to London but would come to the Fort when [the King] wanted me'. He did not, of course, go to London but waited until, as he put it, 'at 10 minutes to 7.0 p.m.' his brother rang to say 'Come & see me after dinner.' Prince Albert replied that he would come at once and immediately went round to the Fort, arriving at seven o'clock.

The King had finally made up his mind. Rather than risk losing Wallis he was prepared to go and as soon as possible. The suddenness of this decision to throw in his hand, despite Wallis's firm solicitations to the contrary, was probably prompted by the arrival at the Fort that morning of Wallis's solicitor in the divorce case, Theodore Goddard. Goddard brought with him the unwelcome news that there might be an intervener making a formal application to the King's Proctor to investigate the Simpson divorce and suggested that he should fly to Cannes to inform his client of this development. The King, fearing that he might frighten Wallis and also suspecting a plot by Baldwin to do precisely that, forbade him to go, but, at Baldwin's instance, Goddard ignored the King's prohibition. The chapter in the King's memoirs dealing with the crucial days of the Abdication week, 8 and 9 December, is headed 'The "Conspiracy" that failed' and refers to attempts by Beaverbrook and Brownlow to get Wallis to renounce marriage to the King and also to a similar plot by Baldwin and Sir Horace Wilson, a leading civil servant and confidant of Chamberlain, with Goddard as their instrument. He had, therefore, determined to pre-empt their efforts by announcing his decision to abdicate. His resolution may even have been strengthened by a telephone call from Wallis during which she read him the text of a press statement she had drafted with Brownlow declaring her willingness 'to withdraw, if such action would solve the problem from a situation that has been rendered both unhappy and untenable'. Brownlow had wanted to strengthen the statement with a declaration that she had no intention of marrying the King, but she had refused. Although the Beaverbrook Press, for obvious reasons, took the line that the Simpson statement meant 'the end of the crisis', none of those closely involved thought it was genuine. Brownlow later told Beaverbrook that he 'had no belief in statement'.[106] Sir Edward Peacock's notes on the episode stated that the King's final wavering over the abdication was due to the insistence over the telephone of the lady that he [the King] should fight for his rights. She kept up that line until near the end, maintaining that he was King, and that his popularity would carry anything etc.... The lady persisted in her advice until she saw that that tack was hopeless. Then she apparently began to think of her own unpopularity, and a statement was suggested, which she issued from Cannes. The King approved, well realising that this would to some extent divert the criticism from her to him, the very thing he wanted.[107]

Goddard's arrival at Cannes did, however, have the effect upon Wallis that the King had predicted; on 9 December Goddard reported to Baldwin's secretary, Dugdale, by telephone, that Wallis was in a 'terrified state of nerves, complete capitulation and willingness to do anything had superseded her former truculent self'. 'The woman will do anything,' he told Dugdale, 'but I can't get any encouragement from your end.' 'Goddard thought he could have changed the face of history,' Dugdale commented, 'Mrs Simpson's volte face came too late.'[108]

At the Fort that Monday evening the King told his brother of his final intention to abdicate. Prince Albert wrote in his diary:

The awful and ghastly suspense of waiting was over. I found him pacing up & down the room, & he told me his decision that he would go. I went back to Royal Lodge for dinner & returned later. I felt once I got there I was not going to leave. As he is my eldest brother I had to be there to try & help him in his hour of need.

According to the Duke of Windsor's memory of that day, he asked Prince Albert to the Fort 'to discuss the disposition of family property, heirlooms and so forth, for, in the process of stepping down from the Throne, I should also abdicate, for legal purposes, the position of Head of the House of Windsor'. Prince Albert's diary is silent on the subject of their discussions but, instead of remaining on at the Fort, he left his brother with Prince George, who had arrived that night, and went up to London with his wife.

From then on as head of the family and prospective King–Emperor, the strain on Prince Albert was almost intolerable. The crisis had been going on now for almost a month since the King had first announced to his family that he intended to marry and to abdicate if necessary. To make things worse, the Duchess was ill with influenza and could not support him as she usually did. The responsibility that had been his brother's now fell upon him and, at the same time, the disagreeable necessity of taking decisions on family business matters. On the afternoon of Tuesday 8 December, he saw Monckton, who, he noted, 'was not allowed to see me before', adding baldly, 'he told me all the facts'. 'The facts' presumably included the actual abdication procedure and a résumé of the negotiations which Monckton had been carrying on with Baldwin the previous weekend. Prince Albert then went to tell Queen Mary what he had learned from Monckton, and then down to the Royal Lodge, where he informed Prince Henry. While talking to his brother he received a call from Monckton summoning him 'urgently' to the Fort to meet the King and the Prime Minister.

He arrived at the Fort, simultaneously with Sir Edward Peacock, at about

6.30 p.m. to find the Prime Minister, Dugdale, Monckton and the King's other legal adviser, George Allen, already there, from which it could be deduced that the terms of the abdication had been under discussion. Prince Albert's diary is again silent as to what took place between the time he arrived and the hour at which they sat down to dinner, but, since he had been summoned over 'urgently' by Monckton, it would seem likely that it was to talk over points that had already been under negotiation and were to be raised again the next day. While the King was changing for dinner, Prince Albert and Prince George, who had been at the Fort all day, talked to Baldwin, reassuring him that he had done all he possibly could and that neither he nor they could prevail on Edward to change his mind. According to the Prime Minister the King, that evening, had refused to discuss anything, 'but had merely walked up and down the room saying – "This is the most wonderful woman in the world." '[109] Both brothers had been surprised and shocked by their brother's calm. 'How can he let the Empire down and not mind?' as Princess Olga put it. 'He was very calm about it all – except about her,' Prince George told Prince Paul, '. . . he never broke down and wouldn't think either of the future or of what he was giving up – only of her.'[110]

To his family, Edward's attitude seemed callous and irresponsible. It was, perhaps, one of the things that they resented most about the whole episode. As the new Queen was to write, 'I don't think we could ever imagine a more incredible tragedy, and the agony of it all has been beyond words. And the melancholy fact remains still at the present moment, that he for whom we agonised is the one person it did not touch.'[111] At dinner that night at the Fort, after he had irrevocably announced to his Prime Minister that he was giving up the throne for Wallis, the King was at the top of his form, 'smiling cheerfully, completely calm and outwardly without a care in the world', as Dugdale put it. Baldwin described him to the Cabinet next day as 'happy and gay as if he were looking forward to his honeymoon', which, in a way, he undoubtedly was. Prince Albert, Dugdale noted, 'was very silent'.

For the future King, too, the die was now cast; the dinner that night was, in his own words, 'one that I am never likely to forget'. Knowing 'the final and irrevocable decision' Edward had made, they were all, he said, 'very sad'. At the time he felt only warm feelings towards his brother, admiring him as much as he ever had. 'My brother was the life & soul of the party,' he wrote, and, according to Dugdale who was sitting opposite him, he said at least twice, 'Isn't my brother wonderful, isn't he wonderful? No-one could carry off this dinner as he can!' And to Monckton, who was sitting beside him, he whispered, '& this is the man we are going to lose'. 'One couldn't, nobody could, believe it,' he recalled. Dugdale, according to his wife, was 'depressed by the dullness of the Duke of York' that evening in contrast to the brilliance of his brother. Baldwin reassured him, telling him that the future King was very like his father as a young man and where King George v had appeared 'most uninspired and dull' compared with his father, 'by perseverance, reliability, example to his people, and a sense of duty did he gain for himself the much loved position he held when he died'.[112]

Prince Albert returned sadly to London where, to add to his troubles, the Duchess was still ill. Inexorably now the wheels were in motion which were to propel him to an office which he had never wanted, a responsibility which he knew and dreaded, and what was to be a bitter separation from the brother he loved. That morning, Wednesday 9 December, he was to see Monckton and Sir Edward Peacock, always known to the brothers as 'E.R.P.', on his brother's business. The two lawyers went first to 10 Downing Street, where they discussed the abdication procedure and the possibility of intervention in the divorce suit, and touched on the financial settlement for the ex-King. Monckton and Peacock found Baldwin, Chamberlain and Simon in an unforgiving frame of mind. 'All three Ministers said that if His Majesty went to Mrs S. or did anything to emphasise that side of things before the Civil List was passed, he would not get a penny, because Parliament would refuse to pass it.'[113] They then went to 145 Piccadilly to 'explain the immediate situation to the Duke of York'. He agreed to his brother's retaining royal rank after his abdication and gave permission for him to live in Fort Belvedere 'if and when he was allowed to return to England'.[114] Later that morning he saw Baldwin and then his lawyer, Sir Bernard Bircham. The subject of his meeting with Bircham was almost certainly what was to become the vexed question of the terms of George v's will, by which Edward, as eldest son and quite apart from his position as King, had a life interest in Sandringham and Balmoral which would now have to be transferred to Prince Albert as the new head of the family. Prince Albert had already seen his mother early that morning and, no doubt, informed her of what had been discussed at the Fort the previous evening; at lunchtime, by previous arrangement, Queen Mary and the Princess Royal, Prince Albert and the King met in the privacy of the Royal Lodge away from the hordes of photographers and journalists who now besieged the Fort, Marlborough House and 145 Piccadilly. Queen Mary's characteristically unrevealing diary entry for the meeting read: 'Rather foggy day. At 1.30 with Mary to meet David (on business) at the Royal Lodge – Back before 5 – Georgie and Marina dined.'

Family business took up a great deal of that day, most of which Prince Albert spent at Fort Belvedere in a meeting with Edward and their two respective solicitors. The Duke of York's account reads:

After this [the meeting at the Royal Lodge between Edward and Queen Mary] I went to the Fort where D & I, Bircham & Allen ... had a talk. I had to stop it as it involved too much (& had a word with W.M.[onckton] who had just returned from No. 10). I then had a long talk with D but could see that nothing would alter his decision. His mind was made up. I motored up to London with W.M. (much to our mutual surprise) as D had been very suspicious previous to my talk with him, & we were able to discuss what we liked in confidence.

'I had to stop it as it involved too much,' the Duke of York wrote of the Fort Belvedere meeting; despite the protracted meetings over these last days, matters between him and his brother were not finalized before Edward left the country and remained to bedevil their relations over the following year. It had been an exhausting and emotionally draining day; it was late when he arrived in London with Monckton and went to Marlborough House to report to his mother. There, by his own account, he broke down and 'sobbed like a child' on her shoulder. Years later Queen Mary told Harold Nicolson, 'that the present King had been appalled when he succeeded. He was devoted to his brother and the whole Abdication crisis made him miserable. He sobbed on my shoulder for a whole hour – there, upon that sofa.' Both the new King's mother and his wife were to find it impossible to forgive either Edward or Wallis for the suffering which, as they saw it, their selfishness had inflicted on him. While he was with his mother a message came from Downing Street that he and his two younger brothers would be required at ten o'clock the next morning, 10 December, to witness Edward's Instrument of Abdication. Both he and his mother knew that Monckton, Hardinge and Lascelles were at Downing Street for a meeting chaired by Sir John Simon to finalize arrangements for the King's Message to Parliament and the Instrument of Abdication, and, clearly anxious to find out what was happening, they summoned Monckton from the meeting. 'Bertie arrived very late from Fort Belvedere and Mr Walter Monckton brought him and me the paper drawn up for David's abdication of the Throne of this Empire because he wants to marry Mrs Simpson!!!!!' Queen Mary wrote, expressing her horror in a shower of exclamation marks. 'The whole affair has lasted since 16 November and is very painful. It is a terrible blow to us all and particularly to poor Bertie.' The Instrument read:

I, Edward the Eighth of Great Britain, Ireland and the British Dominions beyond the Seas, King–Emperor of India, do hereby declare my irrevocable determination to renounce the Throne for Myself and for My descendants, and My desire that effect should be given to this instrument of Abdication immediately.

Queen Mary expressed her feelings about it to Monckton in one short phrase: 'To give up all that for this.'

It was after midnight when an exhausted Monckton left Marlborough House, bearing the draft documents for the King's approval. Sir Edward Peacock was there, having informed Edward of the Cabinet's decision that he must be absent from England for a period of not less than two years. He had seemed to agree, but later he was to chafe under this restriction, and the question of his return to England was to form a vexed question on the list of grievances against his brother. Business matters occupied even what should have been a dramatic and emotional day on Thursday 10 December. Before driving over to the Fort to witness his brother's Instrument of Abdication, Prince Albert had a private meeting with Wigram in preparation for what was intended to be a final settlement of family matters between himself and his brother. Afterwards, in the octagonal drawing-room at the Fort, with Prince Henry and Prince George (the latter, to the King's amusement, arriving late as usual), Monckton, Peacock and Ulick Alexander, he was 'present at the fateful moment which made me D's successor to the Throne.... It was a dreadful moment & one never to be forgotten by those present.' Perhaps his mother's comment echoed in Bertie's mind – 'To give up all that for *this*.'

Prince Albert spent all morning and afternoon of 10 December at the Fort until he could bear the tension no longer and left for the Royal Lodge. But the Duchess, ill in bed at 145 Piccadilly, was not there to soothe him and he found 'I could not rest alone.' Meanwhile, Baldwin in the House of Commons was moving consideration of the King's Message (i.e. the Instrument of Abdication); he was generous in his references to the King and included a message which Edward had specifically asked him to do, of friendship and support for his brother, the Duke of York; he did not, to Edward's lasting resentment, mention the other message he had been given by the King, intended to absolve Wallis of responsibility for the Abdication. The speech was received in awed silence.

Returning to the Fort at 5.45, Prince Albert attended what he described as 'a terrible lawyer interview' and Monckton as 'a general settlement of the money affairs'. Present were his brother, Monckton, Alexander, Bircham and Allen. All Prince Albert recorded of the meeting was that 'E.R.P. was a very great help' and that it 'terminated quietly & harmoniously'. Frances Donaldson, quoting Peacock's notes (now officially closed), cites his report:

The discussion threatened to become heated as sentiment and legal fact were getting rather mixed [Peacock wrote] so I intervened to shift this, then had a short talk with the Duke of York and Bernard Bircham alone. I removed the technicalities which were perplexing the Duke & stated directly & simply what I believed would be his desire should certain eventualities occur. I said that if I was right I was sure the question re B[almoral] and S[andringham] could be settled to his & everybody's satisfaction.... He agreed.[115]

Now, with the publication of parts of Wigram's diary, it is revealed that the subject of the meeting was a rerun of the emotional scenes which had taken place at the reading of King George v's will in January.

The King, Wigram recorded, 'made an impassioned speech pointing out how badly off he would be', and asking that the will be altered so that he might fully benefit from it as the eldest son. With seemingly equal fervour Wigram intervened to say that 'King George would turn in his grave if he thought that his eldest son was not willing to give effect to his wishes'. Abdication, he emphasized, had not been contemplated, and naturally not provided for, when the will was drawn up, and he repeated what had been intended concerning the opportunities of saving money available to the sovereign but not to his brothers and sister. The party split up into groups in separate rooms, and eventually a few minor alterations to the will were agreed upon and signed by the King and Prince Albert in the presence of others.[116]

Edward's financial future was no doubt at the forefront of his mind since Monckton, before returning that afternoon to the Fort from delivering the Abdication documents to 10 Downing Street, had discussed with Baldwin and Chamberlain the possible provision that Parliament would make for the King after his abdication. Monckton's biographer states that at this meeting 'both of them took the view that a substantial provision was probable'. Monckton, as a seasoned negotiator, can hardly have regarded this as totally satisfactory; and opinion based on parliamentary reaction in the future could hardly be considered a concrete commitment, particularly given the previous hardening of opinion against the King evident in the Cabinet and the country over the past few days. A proposal drawn up by Hardinge, under which the ex-King would receive £25,000 a year, in return for which he would promise not to return to England without consulting the King and the Government, was currently on the negotiating table. For a man accustomed all his adult life to a far larger income, and, moreover, a man who had spent vast sums of money on Wallis and made over to her a considerable financial settlement, £25,000 a year was hardly a huge sum. Edward was giving up the throne of England and his position as eldest son of the House of Windsor with, as yet, no concrete settlement. Like most rich men, he discounted what he had already accumulated (in Wigram's opinion 'well over a million sterling'); he was now angry, emotional and uncertain about his financial future. Fortunately for him, however, at this juncture, neither his brother nor Wigram knew of the huge savings he had made and, when they did find out later, were outraged not only at his deviousness in concealing this, but that Edward, while refusing to live up to his responsibilities as head of the House of Windsor, was equally unwilling to suffer the financial consequences of his decision. In their view, he wanted to have his cake and eat it.

Arriving back in London from the Royal Lodge after dinner, Prince Albert was greeted by a large crowd outside 145 Piccadilly, 'cheering madly'. 'I was overwhelmed,' he said simply. It brought home to him forcibly that next day he was to become King. His feelings at the prospect were expressed in the phrase which he was to use in his account of the Abdication to describe Friday 11 December, the day of his accession, as 'that dreadful day'. Much of the morning of the dreadful day, before he technically and formally replaced his brother, was occupied by discussions as to his brother's title on Abdication. Monckton gave details of his interview:

I pointed out that the title 'His Royal Highness' was one which Abdication did not take away, and one which would require an Act of Parliament for its removal. The King, for himself and his successors, was renouncing any right to the Throne but not to his Royal Birth which he shared with his brothers. The Duke saw the point and was ready to create his brother Duke of Windsor as the first act of the new reign.[117]

The problem was not necessarily simple as there was no precedent for a voluntary formal abdication of the throne in British history. James II had fled (leaving Windsor curiously enough on 11 December) without formally abdicating and had, therefore, continued to call himself King, despite the existence of a successor on the throne. That morning Wigram, an ever-present figure at these critical meetings, accompanied by Sir Claud Schuster, Clerk of the Crown and Permanent Secretary to the Lord Chancellor, came for consultation:

... Schuster wanted to ask me what my brother King Edward VIII was going to be known as after his abdication. The question was an urgent one, as Sir John Reith was going to introduce him to the air that night as Mr Edward Windsor. I replied: That is quite wrong. Before going any further I would ask what has he given up on his abdication? S. said I am not sure. I said, It would be quite a good thing to find out before coming to me. Now as to his name. I suggest HRH D of W[indsor]. He cannot be Mr E.W. as he was born the son of a Duke. That makes him Ld. E.W. anyhow. If he ever comes back to this country, he can stand & be elected to the H. of C. Would you like that? S. replied No.

As D. of W. he can sit and vote in the H. of L. Would you like that? S. replied No. Well if he becomes a Royal Duke he cannot speak or vote in the H. of L. & he is not being deprived of his rank in the Navy, Army or R. Air Force. This gave Schuster a new lease of life & he went off happy.

This interview demonstrated a very clear perception of constitutional implications on the part of the future King, which from his account appears clearer than that of the representative of the highest law officer in the land. He had thought the situation through very carefully. It certainly seems probable that a parallel suggested by Bernard Shaw's *The Apple Cart* lay behind his question to Schuster as to whether he would welcome the idea of the ex-King standing for election to the House of Commons. Just seven years before, in 1929, Shaw's play had posed a situation in which a king, if he did not wish to take his minister's constitutional advice, threatens to resign and put himself forward as a commoner for a seat in the House of Commons at the next election, a solution which Shaw hinted at in an *Evening Standard* article during the crisis. No doubt the recent threat of a King's party the previous weekend had brought the possibility of such an eventuality to the forefront of official minds. Given the nature of the soon-to-be Duke of Windsor and, indeed, some of his subsequent actions, it was not an entirely baseless fear.

Prince Albert confirmed his decision that day by pencilling in in his own hand a last paragraph to a typewritten draft of the Declaration to be made at his Accession Council the following day. It read: 'furthermore, My First Act on succeeding my brother [to the throne – deleted] will be to confer on him [the title of HRH the Duke of Windsor from this date – deleted] a Dukedom & he will henceforth be known as HRH The Duke of Windsor.'[118]

At 1.52 p.m. on Friday 11 December 1936, Prince Albert, Duke of York, became King George VI of Great Britain, Ireland and the Dominions beyond the Seas. It was a moment which, literally, the King never forgot. Exactly four years later, on 11 December 1940, entertaining Halifax to an informal lunch at Buckingham Palace, the King looked at the clock and said, 'By summer time 1.52. The time to the minute at which I took over four years ago.' He also told Halifax of his secret meetings with Baldwin at 10 Downing Street during the last days of the crisis and how, on the morning of the 11th, he had gone to see Baldwin there and, as he was leaving, said to the Prime Minister, in a whimsical reference to the change that was about to take place in his position: 'I come to see you this morning but you will have to come and see me this afternoon.'[119]

That evening he went to have a final talk with his brother: 'I went to the Fort as King with Harry arriving at 7.0 p.m. All D's servants called me His Majesty. Sir J[ohn] R[eith] wished to announce D as Mr E. Windsor for his broadcast. I put that right. One other matter I settled too.' During these last days, Edward later recalled, they had spoken to each other 'with a frankness recalling the untroubled companionship of our youth', nor did this seem to be an occasion for pompous phrases about the monarchy. Edward assured his brother:

'You are not going to find this a difficult job at all. You know all the ropes, and you have almost overcome that slight hesitation in your speech which used to make public speaking so hard for you.' Words do not come easily to Bertie on occasions of great emotion [Edward continued]. Without his having to tell me so, I knew that he felt my going keenly. At the same time he can be extremely practical. 'By the way, David,' he asked me, 'have you given any thought as to what you are going to be called now?' This question took me aback. 'Why no, as a matter of fact, I haven't,' I replied.

'I shall create you a Duke,' Bertie said. 'How about the family name of Windsor?'[120]

The stage was now set at the Royal Lodge for the final act in the royal family tragedy – Edward's farewell dinner. The guests were strictly limited to the family, Queen Mary, the Princess Royal, the royal brothers and Queen Mary's brother, Algy Athlone, and his wife Princess Alice, who since the beginning of the crisis had been staying with her at Marlborough House. After the dinner, the Duke of Windsor was to make his farewell broadcast from Windsor Castle. There had been a certain amount of nervousness as to what he might say. Baldwin had arranged that Sir John Simon should be consulted in the drafting of any broadcast, and reassured the Canadian Prime Minister in a telegram sent on the evening of 10 December that 'if he does broadcast, message will be unembarrassing from the public point of view as it is being prepared in consultation with people in whose discretion I have complete confidence'.[121] Queen Mary, however, seems not to have shared that confidence and thought it safer that her son should go quietly. She had appealed to Edward not to make the broadcast, an appeal which he rejected and which, he later told her biographer, he much resented. It seems, however, that the Queen had some real grounds for concern, according to a curious story retailed by Baldwin's official biographer, G.M. Young, to the editor of *The Times*. While researching for the biography Young discovered that Churchill wrote the Abdication broadcast:

'But Edward had written his own, and it began "I am now free to tell you how I was jockeyed out of the Throne." Winston made him put it on the fire. . . .'[122] There are good reasons to believe this story; it tallies exactly with Wallis's instructions to Edward in her letter of 6 December: 'Don't be silenced and leave under a cloud I beseech you and in abdication no matter in what form unless you can let the public know that the Cabinet has virtually kicked you out. . . .' If Wallis had had her way, one of the most famous broadcasts in history might have been very different.

The Earl of Athlone recalled that the dinner at least on that night was relatively cheerful. 'It might have been quite a gloomy occasion,' he told Osbert Sitwell. 'I take my hat off to the butler! Pretty flowers and china and all that – the table beautifully set out: beautifully done. Made it quite cheerful.' After the Duke of Windsor left at around 9.30 p.m. to make his broadcast from Windsor Castle at 10, Athlone records the new King making his authority as head of the family quite clear to his brothers: '. . . the new King, dear old boy, fairly went for his brothers, saying, "If *You Two* think that, now that I have taken this job on, you can go on behaving just as you like, in the same old way, you're very much mistaken! You Two have got to pull yourselves together." '[123]

Edward began nervously and, to his listening family, his opening sentence might have been ominous: 'At long last I am able to say a few words of my own. . . .' But he went on to make a broadcast which even his mother found 'good and dignified' and moved many of his listeners to tears. The key sentence was, of course, his reason and justification for abdicating the throne: '. . . I have found it impossible to carry the heavy burden of responsibility and to discharge my duties as King as I would wish to do without the help and support of the woman I love.' He exonerated Wallis, as Baldwin had deliberately neglected to do, 'The other person most nearly concerned has tried up to the last to persuade me to take a different course,' and thanked his family for their comfort and Baldwin 'in particular' for the 'full consideration' with which he had been treated. As he went on his confidence grew; the final sentence 'God Save the King' was almost a shout. When he had finished Edward stood up and, putting his arm on Monckton's shoulder, said in an emotional misquotation of Sidney Carton's famous last words in *A Tale of Two Cities*, 'Walter, it is a far better thing I go to.'[124] It was fortunate that the microphone was not still turned on.

When Reith came into the room after a discreet pause, he thought that Edward and Monckton 'looked as if they had been having an argument'. When the King left to find Wigram, Monckton told Reith he was 'glad I had come in when I did and that I got the King's mind off himself. He said there would be a ghastly reaction in a week or so, and the King didn't in the least realize what he was doing. . . .'[125] It seems probable that Monckton was insisting the King must go back and say goodbye to his family and one could, indeed, question his judgement in thus prolonging this unnatural family gathering in which there was really no more – because there was too much – to be said. Returning to the Royal Lodge, Edward found the atmosphere less tense, 'feeling that what I had said had to some extent eased the tension between us'. It was getting late and the night was foggy, and Queen Mary and her daughter prepared to leave for London; 'and then', ran Queen Mary's account, 'came the dreadful good bye as he was leaving that evening for Austria. The whole thing was too pathetic for words.' As Queen and as mother, it must have been the worst moment of her life. The Princess Royal was in tears, but Queen Mary behaved, as always, impeccably. 'The Queen was magnificently brave throughout,' Monckton wrote, 'and took leave of the King cheerfully. I shall always remember the car starting and the King's bow to his Mother when she left.' As the big black Daimler rolled away into the foggy night, the four brothers and Monckton remained, chatting inanely about every subject under the sun except the unspeakable one of Edward's imminent departure. Eventually, Prince George, at least, could contain himself no longer, bursting out, 'This is quite mad!' But, at the end, the consciousness of an historic royal occasion brought out the correct atavistic response in a ritual parting. 'When D & I said good-bye,' wrote King George VI, 'we kissed, parted as freemasons & he bowed to me as his King.'

At eleven o'clock on the morning of 12 December, as the former King was still on his way to exile, King George VI read out a declaration at his Accession Council:

I meet you to-day in circumstances which are without parallel in the history of our Country. Now that the duties of Sovereignty have fallen upon Me I declare to you My adherence to the strict principles of constitutional government and My resolve to work before all else for the welfare of the British Commonwealth of Nations. With my wife and helpmeet by My side, I take up the heavy task which lies before Me....

For the new King–Emperor and head of the House of Windsor it was a solemn public promise, the words of which were carefully and deliberately chosen. To the Prime Minister he wrote: 'I hope that time will be allowed me to make amends for what has happened.'

CONSECRATION

'There is no doubt that the King and Queen have entered on this task with a real religious sense.'

Harold Nicolson, May 1937

A T forty-one, the new King, George VI, faced a situation unique in the annals of his family's history. For the first time there had been no stately progression from one reign to the next, the carefully worded bulletins recording the deteriorating health of the dying monarch, the traditional funeral rites, the springing of enthusiasm at the opening of a new reign. George VI's predecessor, as he wryly told his Minister of War, Leslie Hore-Belisha, was 'very much alive' and in exile, conjuring up parallels in the historically minded of 'the King over the Water', Bonnie Prince Charlie and the '45, and appearing, notably in American eyes, if not as an alternative to his brother, at least as the rightful King. The comparison between the two brothers, between Edward superstar and the shy, relatively unknown King George, cock pheasant and ugly duckling, would always be there. Moreover Edward, in the eyes of his family and of the majority of his subjects, had deserted his post, staining the family escutcheon and tarnishing the image of the monarchy. It was up to the new King, his brother, to put that right.

There was an undercurrent of doubt, occasionally voiced in the press, in Society and on the Stock Exchange, that he would not be mentally and physically up to the job, and to the strain of the Coronation ceremony in particular. King George's past history of ill-health and, above all, his speech hesitation were all too well known. His small, slim stature and fine-boned features gave him a somewhat fragile appearance. But his looks belied his athleticism, while the determination that had won him his wife and the courage with which he had largely mastered his stammer had led his father to say 'Bertie has more guts than the rest of them put together.' While lacking his brother's public relations skills, the crowd-pulling, flashing charm, he had what his brother so noticeably had not – self-discipline and integrity. As *Time* trumpeted in a pre-Coronation report, 'George VI is sound in that in which King George V was most sound and King Edward VIII by no means sound – Character....' George VI had many of his father's good qualities, an innate sense of decency and duty, a capacity for hard work, common sense and sympathy for his fellow human beings, and some of his faults, including violent fits of temper, known as the King's 'gnashes', an inheritance which probably also owed something to the 'breezes' of his maternal grandfather, the Duke of Teck. He was unusual for a 'royal', as his courtiers were happily to discover, in his consideration for themselves and their families. His parents, although kind in themselves, had been extremely demanding towards their staff. Servants and more particularly courtiers in their eyes should have few human feelings and no physical failings; minor ailments, physical weakness and tiredness were not permitted to exist. Queen Elizabeth as King George's widow, the possessor of an extremely strong and tireless constitution, later developed this 'royal' lack of understanding to a marked degree, but King George vi, perhaps because of his own experiences of physical suffering and feelings of inferiority, was more truly humane than any of his family.

Moreover, having lived in closer proximity to his father for longer than any of his brothers, he, more than any of them, 'knew the ropes' of kingship and as King he had also one considerable advantage over his predecessors and, indeed, most of the British ruling class, a thorough knowledge of the working and living conditions of the working class in industry. He was well acquainted with British trade unionism and familiar with its leaders, a knowledge which was to prove invaluable later in his reign in dealing with the post-war Labour Government. Lastly, he had a secure happy family image which amply fulfilled the constitutional expert, Walter Bagehot's requirements for monarchy. Writing in the reign of the new King's great-grandmother, Bagehot declared: 'A *family* on the throne is an interesting idea . . .', adding in a passage which was particularly relevant to the recent crisis, 'We have come to regard the Crown as the head of our *morality*. We have come to believe that it is natural to have a virtuous sovereign, and that domestic virtues are as likely to be found on thrones as they are eminent when there.'[1] And in Elizabeth he had a wife whose talent for public relations was superior even to that of her brother-in-law, the Duke of Windsor.

But all these qualities were far from being widely known or appreciated early in 1937 and rumours of his incapacity circulated constantly. Archbishop Lang unintentionally may have fuelled the fire when, in an attempt to promote the new King in his offensive Abdication Broadcast of 13 December 1936, he actually succeeded in pointing up George vi's main public deficiency:

In manner and speech he [King George vi] is more quiet and reserved than his brother. (And here I may add a parenthesis which may not be unhelpful. When his people listen to him they will note an occasional and momentary hesitation in his speech. But he has brought it into full control, and to those who hear it it need cause no sort of embarrassment, for it causes none to him who speaks.)

The whole passage was unnecessary and the last sentence actually untrue; the hesitations which still dogged the King's public speaking were naturally a source of anxiety to him and any speech or broadcast which passed off without a hitch was an occasion for celebration and self-congratulation. One might say that the

King showed the understanding side of his nature in not giving the Archbishop a sharp rebuke for his tactless intervention; his therapist, Lionel Logue, is recorded as having been 'exasperated' at the Archbishop's remarks and afraid that they would have an adverse psychological effect on his patient when he came to face the crucial ordeal of the Coronation ceremony and broadcast on 12 May 1937. With friends like Archbishop Lang, it might be said, who needed enemies?

As Coronation Day approached the rumours multiplied. On 8 March *Time* reported that the King, apparently a 'paid subscriber' to the news/gossip magazine *Cavalcade*, contacted the editor of the magazine through a close friend,

suggesting a denial be printed of rumours circulating on the Stock Exchange that another mild epileptic fit had been suffered by His Majesty. This denial, since it came virtually from the honest King–Emperor himself, could be accepted as the nearest thing possible to the lowdown on a matter of utmost interest to British businessmen in view of the approaching Coronation in which they have many millions at stake. But between the business-like King–Emperor and his business subjects stand the Gentlemen of England. The printed denial in *Cavalcade* was pounced upon, its excision forced.

Another friend of the King's, Robert Hyde, whose heart was perhaps better than his head, also felt compelled to speak out in public in his defence. At an Industrial Copartnership Association luncheon shortly before the Coronation, he told the guests that in his long association with the King he had never

found any evidence of those shortcomings, of physical and mental weakness, which notorious gossip has attached to him. Those of us who have watched him for the past twenty years conquering that hesitation in his speech which filled him with real anguish have only been filled with admiration.... Those of you who hear this gossip, do not heed it; it is unkind, unworthy and untrue.

The whispering against the King, according to his biographer, amounted to allegations that his frail health would not stand up to the ordeal of the Coronation, that the order of service had been shortened to the barest minimum and even that there would be no Coronation at all. Even if he did succeed in going through with the ceremony, it was said that the King would never be able to undertake the arduous duties that would fall to him, that he would never be able to speak in public, and that he would be a recluse, or at best a 'rubber stamp'. The rumours were widespread enough to be mentioned by the *Daily Sketch* in a leader marking the King's first anniversary of his accession on 11 December, which described the gossip as not merely 'idle' but also 'purposeful'. It seems likely that some of the stories – which still circulate today – originated with partisans of the ex-King, unable to forgive the supplanting of their idolized 'Majesty Divine', drawing fuel from the King's stutter and the history of epilepsy in his family represented by his dead brother, Prince John. Rumours of 'falling fits' were current in Britain and America, where they persisted until the King's visit to the United States in 1939 demonstrated his physical fitness.

Denigration of the King when he was Duke of York had become a habit among the smart set that surrounded Edward VIII; it persisted among the defeated 'Cavaliers' (Chips Channon's phrase) after the Abdication, and this rumour was one of those handed down to a younger likeminded generation as insider knowledge and an enjoyable sneer against the successful, respectable 'Roundheads'. On a less scandalous plane, even such a respected expert on royalty as Dermot Morrah, followed by authors Denis Judd and Robert Lacey, hinted that at the time of the Abdication it was considered passing over the Duke of York in favour of the Duke of Kent, a ludicrous suggestion in view of Kent's scandalous past and one for which, according to Baldwin's biographers Middlemas and Barnes, who have seen all the now closed Abdication papers, there is no documentary evidence whatsoever. The Duke of York's apparent isolation from events over the final weekend of 4–6 December and his brother's reluctance to see him, which Lacey sees as possibly caused by indecision as to whether York or Kent should succeed the King, was only apparent and the hiatus was due to the confusion of the negotiations between Baldwin and the King that weekend and uncertainty as to whether and when he might abdicate.

The King was certainly aware of the rumour that he suffered from 'falling fits', i.e. epilepsy, and, well informed as he was (if *Time*'s story is true, *Cavalcade* was the nearest thing to a news magazine available at the time), he also knew that many people feared he was not up to the job. Comparison with his father and elder brother weighed heavily upon him and he was, in fact, himself unsure of his ability to stand the strain. The tension of the Abdication crisis when he broke down and sobbed for an hour on his mother's shoulder no doubt left him mentally and physically exhausted. Evidence of this appears in the correspondence leading up to the decision, announced on 9 February 1937,[2] that he would not visit his Indian Empire to hold a Durbar in the cold weather that year. Plans for a Durbar in line with the splendid ceremonies held to celebrate his father's accession in 1911 had been announced in King Edward VIII's one and only speech at the Opening of Parliament outlining government plans for the official and legislative year. In an initial audience with the Secretary of State for India, the Marquess of Zetland, King George expressed willingness to follow his brother's plan for the Durbar, but by January he was evidently hesitating, despite enthusiastic assurances from Indian officials, notably the Viceroy, the Marquess of Linlithgow, of the 'deep respect and regard in which the Crown is held' in India and of the importance of the Durbar in dissipating 'any unsettling effects which the King's abdication could have produced'.[3]

But on 18 January Zetland told Linlithgow that he had had a talk with Baldwin on his return from a stay at Sandringham the previous weekend and that 'both the King and Baldwin are apprehensive of the strain of an Indian visit on top of a summer burdened with Coronation festivities....'[4] In a conversation with Zetland at the end of the month Wigram denied that fear of the hostility of the nationalist Congress Party (which had recently passed a resolution forbidding Congress officials to attend ceremonies relating to the King's Coronation) had weighed on the King's mind, stressing that the King's feelings were that 'he felt that he could not undertake it so soon after his accession; that he was overwhelmed with the magnitude of the task which had been thrust upon him and that he must have more time to settle down'. Wigram added that the King's medical advisers were against 'a programme involving nervous strain both in anticipation of and during an Indian visit so soon after the burden of the coming summer'.[5] Publicly the reason given in the official statement on 9 February was that 'the duties and responsibilities which he [the King] has undertaken on acceding to the Throne in unexpected circumstances make it impossible to contemplate a prolonged absence from Great Britain during the first year of his reign. His Imperial Majesty', the statement added, 'looks forward to visiting India for the purpose of holding a Durbar at a later date.' The King's official biographer dubs this as a 'clear and incisive decision', an example of 'that pragmatic common sense, that ability to take first things first, which was so invaluable an asset to the King'. He makes no mention of the consideration which came first in the mind of the King and his advisers, the simple doubt as to whether he could stand up to the strain.

A disappointed Viceroy wrote that the Indian nationalist party attributed the postponement of the Durbar plans principally to the recent success of the Congress Party at the polls (elections being held in preparation for provincial autonomy under the 1935 Act), but from the correspondence it is clear that anxiety about the strain on the King rather than fear of Congress hostility was the principal reason for postponement. Zetland told Linlithgow that the British press had accepted the public reason as valid, 'at least by papers of repute', but the postponement of the Durbar visit merely increased speculation about the King's mental and physical health. Two days after the statement the *News Chronicle* referred to the postponement having given rise to 'a crop of rumours that the King's health is causing grave concern to the Cabinet and the royal entourage'. Under a banner headline 'Whispering against the King', the political correspondent alleged: 'There is a malicious whispering campaign in Britain directed against the King'; the scandal-mongers, who included 'famous Mayfair hosts and hostesses, prominent stockbrokers and some politicians', might find themselves being charged with treason. The Durbar postponement, the fact that the King did not broadcast the customary royal Christmas message, his rare public appearances, even the fact that the parliamentary debate on the regency bill centred on the question of the 'capacity' of a monarch to rule, all fuelled the rumours.

For the King, the Coronation service, which was to be broadcast to millions, would be the crucial test. It can hardly have helped the King's confidence to find that his secret fears about his own abilities were shared by his confidential advisers, such as Wigram, his doctors, and the Archbishop of Canterbury. Baldwin told Zetland that he had advised the King to 'stay at Sandringham as long as possible'. Lang and the Duke of Norfolk, hereditary Earl Marshal in charge of royal occasions, had agreed with Reith of the BBC that the Coronation ceremony should be broadcast from Westminster Abbey for the first time, but had turned down the BBC's proposal for televising the ceremony with an apparatus on a small platform above the reredos, 'which would be camouflaged as stone with some Gothic ornament by the Office of Works', and another concealed behind a tomb. Television was then in its infancy; a memorandum by Lang of 13 January 1937 records that 'inasmuch as the results of this Television could only be seen by a limited number of people within about 25 miles of London who happened to have the necessary apparatus in their houses, the Earl Marshal and I both considered that it was not worth while to have Television'. There was, however, in the Archbishop's eyes, another cogent reason for not televising the ceremony; a pencilled note in his hand reads 'no possibility of censoring'.[6] This did not apply to filming; the Archbishop and the Earl Marshal were to censor the film of the Coronation on the evening after the ceremony. Lang was clearly nervous that a live television broadcast might reveal incidents embarrassing to the King, who could suffer from muscular spasms in his cheeks and jaw when struggling to enunciate a word.

Indeed, nervousness about the King's public performance on this crucial occasion and particularly about his speech is evident in Lang's correspondence on the preparations for the coronation, in which he, as chief officiating priest, was intimately concerned. Interfering and officious as ever, he apparently recommended a new speech therapist to treat the King in preparation for the event. Lord Dawson, the King's chief medical adviser, replied on 25 March that he thought any such change inadvisable:

The difficulty I see in introducing anybody new to the King at the present time seeing that he has considerable confidence in Logue, for myself, I think it is quite likely that broadcasting itself, if only the King will begin practising efforts while he is at Windsor [for Easter], will have a good effect on the King's speech. He thinks so himself, and has himself suggested that Logue, whom he knows well, should be with him.[7]

A memorandum by Lang of 25 April records that he and Wigram had agreed not to let anyone but Logue see the King because 'it would only increase his self-consciousness and nervousness.'

Lang's suggestion was probably prompted by the King's poor performance at the ceremony held to present to him the Church's Loyal Address from Convocation at Buckingham Palace two days before. Although, at the King's request, two paragraphs of the address referring to the change of sovereign were cut out ('. . . HM preferred . . . that nothing should at this late stage be said about that . . .', Dr Don wrote), unspoken comparisons with his brother may have affected him. 'The King was evidently rather nervous and his stammer when reading his reply was very apparent. This unfortunate impediment will be a lasting drawback to him—for Edward VIII was such an excellent speaker,' Don commented.[8]

The King's own fears centred on the live broadcast he would have to make from Buckingham Palace in the evening after the ceremony on Coronation Day. Tommy Lascelles told Reith in January that 'the King was more fussed about his Coronation Day broadcast than anything else', suggesting it might be pre-recorded, with the implication that hesitations might be edited out. Reith turned this down saying the King should decide 'whether the deception mattered' and that, in any case, he would have to go through the motions of broadcasting at the time. But Reith, too, was concerned that the Coronation broadcast should be a success and instructed the BBC's engineer in charge of outside broadcasts, Robert Wood, to 'make a good broadcaster' of the King. Wood, a microphone expert, was to help him minimize the effects of his stammer. Wood and the King began rehearsals with the King standing at a high ledger desk because Logue believed that standing helped him speak more clearly. Later, Wood managed to make him sit at ease at a desk, but at this stage he still had to win the King's trust. 'It was hard for the King too,' Wood wrote in his memoirs, 'because you could see how he had suffered all his life because of his impediment and you could not help but feel sorry for him. . . . Little by little I helped him with tone formation and lip formation, and showed him how he could let the microphone do the work.'[9]

The King had what Harold Nicolson described as 'a fine English voice', strong and resonant; in a very English way he pronounced his 'r's as 'w's. He eventually became, in Wood's words, 'a master of the microphone' and a very good broadcaster. At the beginning, however, his delivery tended to be monotonous; he spoke slowly and carefully with a rhythmic emphasis developed to carry him along in breathing phases with pauses – Logue called them three-word breaks – between and there was always the lurking fear that he would stop. There was something touching about hearing that manly voice hesitate and then go doggedly on, even forcing himself sometimes to repeat words two or three times in order to be able to carry on. Normally Logue and Wood would go carefully through the script checking words that might trip the King up; right into the early 1940s he was still to have problems with initial 'c's and 'g's, and, according to Wood, during the war he used to have great difficulty with words with double 's's such as 'oppression' and 'suppression' which unfortunately came up a good deal. ' . . . the King struggled without let-up,' Wood recorded. 'I was full of admiration for his perseverance, his resolution.'

The Coronation service presented a particular difficulty; the words of the service were laid down as a traditional rite and the King's responses could not be altered to eliminate difficult passages. With Logue, according to Reith, very much in charge, Wood in attendance and the Queen always very much involved, the King worked hard. On 5 May with Reith a tall, sardonic rather intimidating presence, the King went through his speech twice completely, it being recorded and then played back. There was also an intermediate attempt when he coughed and spoilt 'the bloody record'. The King, Queen, Logue and Reith listened to the first attempt in the King's bedroom which, Reith noted, was quite a small room in which the only remarkable thing was a glass case containing about one hundred jewelled cigarette cases. 'There were a good many stutters so they tried again,' he remarked. But when the real occasion came to do it live even Reith was pleased. 'King got through much better than at rehearsals and really did quite well,' he recorded. There was one puzzling pause at the beginning when the listening millions thought the King's stammer had got the better of him. In fact, this was due to a slight hitch in the carefully planned arrangements by which the King, who had been waiting for the Queen in a room outside the studio, was supposed to walk to the broadcasting room as the national anthem was being played and take his place at the microphone as it finished. For some reason the anthem took less time than expected and the King arrived a few seconds late at the microphone. But it was a triumph. In the words of *Time*, the King's voice was 'warm and strong' and he did not stammer as he delivered the first ever Coronation broadcast at the end of a day which must have seemed the longest of his life:

It is with a very full heart I speak to you tonight. Never before has a newly crowned King been able to talk to all his peoples in their own homes on the day of his Coronation ... the Queen and I will always keep in our hearts the inspiration of this day. May we ever be worthy of the goodwill which I am proud to think surrounds us at the outset of my reign. ...

The Coronation is the single most significant ceremony of a sovereign's life, transforming him or her from an ordinary mortal to a powerful symbol, half-man, half-priest, in a solemn ritual whose history goes back over a thousand years and whose significance is far older. No man or woman could fail to be affected by it; for George VI in particular, whose interest in ritual and sense of history was very strong, it was to have an extraordinarily strengthening, confidence-giving effect. For both him and the Queen the religious significance of the ceremony, in which they were to dedicate themselves before God to the service of their people, was very strong. Cosmo Lang, an intrusive presence throughout, who saw this as an occasion for asserting the cause of Religion over the Worldliness represented by the late King, held a private meeting with them at Buckingham Palace on the evening of the Sunday before Coronation Day, at which they all knelt in prayer:

I prayed for them and for their realm and Empire, and I gave them my personal blessing. I was much moved and so were they. Indeed there were tears in their eyes when we rose from our knees. From that moment I knew what would be in their minds and hearts when they came to their anointing and crowning.

During the ceremony itself, a kind of religious exaltation came upon the King; he later privately told Lang, as the Archbishop noted in an unpublished passage, 'that he felt throughout that Some One Else was with him'.[10] Ramsay MacDonald reported to Harold Nicolson on 27 May that the King had told him 'that for long periods at the Coronation ceremony he was unaware of what was happening'. 'There is no doubt that they have entered on this task with a real religious sense,' Nicolson commented.[11]

The underlying emotional tension was there all through the ceremony. Lady Alexandra Metcalfe saw the King's jaw muscles working 'all through the

Coronation', as, a few weeks later, she was to see the Duke of Windsor's do exactly the same at the rehearsal on the eve of his wedding at Candé.

Nervousness and a sense of occasion did not, however, prevent the King from enjoying the comical aspects of the ceremony and the rehearsals leading up to it. On 4 May he entertained Reith with an amusing account of that morning's rehearsal at the Abbey with the Archbishop of Canterbury and the Dean of Westminster cannoning into each other and tripping over things. There were some farcical episodes in the run up to the ceremony; just under a week beforehand it was found that the enormous Bible presented by the University Presses was so heavy that the Bishop of Norwich, whose job it was to carry it in the procession, would undoubtedly have collapsed under the weight, and a smaller one was hastily ordered to replace it. Serious correspondence took place between Gerald Wollaston, Garter King at Arms, the expert on heraldry and ritual, and the Archbishop on the question of who and what should be used to dry the holy oil with which the King was to be anointed. Eventually Wollaston decided that the Dean of Westminster should do it but 'He seemed not altogether to like the idea of the cotton wool for the drying, and thought a fine cambric material would be best.'[12]

The actual ceremony was something of a case of the King keeping his head when all about him were losing theirs and his own account of it is, among other things, an amused catalogue of blunders by peers and priests. The royal day started with a rude awakening at about 3 a.m. by the testing of loudspeakers on Constitution Hill, one of which, the King noted, 'might have been in our room'. 'Bands and marching troops for lining the streets arrived at 5.0 a.m. so sleep was impossible,' he went on. 'I could eat no breakfast & had a sinking feeling inside. I knew that I was to spend the most trying day, & to go through the most important ceremony of my life. The hours of waiting before leaving for Westminster Abbey were the most nerve racking.' At last the golden State Coach first used by George 11 in 1726 set out in pouring rain from Buckingham Palace for Westminster Abbey, where a symbolic ray of sunlight struggled through the clouds as it drew up at 11 a.m. The Queen's procession, which started before the King's, was held up by a fainting Presbyterian chaplain. The Abbey was so full that nowhere could be found to take him, and there was some delay before he could be removed and the procession start up again. 'I was kept waiting, it seemed for hours due to this accident,' the King wrote.

'Finally came the King looking rather strained but quiet and dignified,' Don recorded, 'with the Bishops of Durham and Wells on either side. (These two claiming the place of honour as their predecessors have done since the day of Richard Coeur de Lion).' But the Bishop of Bath and Wells, he said, was an awkward mover and Durham 'fidgety'. Later, by the King's account, the two prelates did worse. The King knelt, 'supported' by the Bishops whose job it was to hold the Order of Service for him, at the altar to take the Coronation oath, but 'When this great moment came neither Bishop could find the words, so the Archbishop held his book down for me to read, but horror of horrors his thumb covered the words of the Oath,' the King wrote. Confusion and clumsiness were not confined to the clerics; the nobility also fumbled their tasks. The Duke of Portland carrying the Queen's Crown and the Marquess of Salisbury bearing the King's both got their Garter chains entangled in the fringes of the cushions on which the crowns rested as they presented them to the Archbishop to be placed on the altar. 'My Lord Great Chamberlain [the Earl of Ancaster] was supposed to dress me,' the King went on, 'but I found his hands fumbled & shook so I had to fix the belt of the sword myself. As it was he nearly put the hilt of the sword under my chin trying to attach it to the belt.' (Later the King joked with Ancaster's daughter, Lady Priscilla Aird: 'I wouldn't choose your father as a valet.')[13]

Even the supreme moment, the placing of St Edward's Crown, the Crown of England, on the King's head, was fraught. As the King said, the Crown weighed seven pounds 'and it had to fit'. 'I had taken every precaution as I thought to see that the Crown was put on the right way round, but the Dean and the Archbishop had been juggling with it so much that I never did know whether it was right or not.' According to the Archbishop, the King had been very anxious in discussions before the ceremony that the Crown should be put on the right way round and so it had been arranged that a small piece of red thread should be inserted as a marker under one of the principal jewels in the front. But when the Dean brought the Crown to the Archbishop, the thread was missing: 'some officious person must have removed it'. The King then rose from the ancient Coronation chair first used in 1307, within it the Stone of Scone, allegedly the stone upon which Joseph of Arimathea had his vision and brought from the Holy Land. As he turned to move towards his throne, 'I was brought up all standing, owing to one of the Bishops treading on my robe. I had to tell him to get off it pretty sharply as I nearly fell down....'

Fortunately none of the bungling was apparent to the guests in the Abbey, who included Chips Channon, invited in his capacity as Member of the House of Commons, who was 'dazzled by the red, the gilt, the gold, the grandeur', watching the peeresses as they took their places in the North Transept, a 'vitrine of bosoms and jewels and bobbing tiaras'. He watched as the royalties came in, first 'our own tuppeny Royalties, i.e. the Carisbrookes, Mountbattens, Carnegies etc.', then the 'real Royalties ... the Princess Royal, looking cross, the tiny princesses excited by their coronets and trains, the two Royal Duchesses looking staggering ... Queen Mary, ablaze, regal and over-powering,' was the last to enter before the Queen. By a tradition said to date back to the days of the Plantagenet kings, the widow of the late sovereign does not attend the Coronation of his successor; Queen Mary had deliberately broken with this tradition to signify her active support for the new reign. She had been deeply involved as a consultant over the arrangements for the Coronation and she was not going to miss the occasion. Glittering on her bosom was her eldest son's Garter Star, which she had asked to borrow for the ceremony.

The family ghost at the feast was, of course, the Duke of Windsor. The first monarch to listen to his successor's Coronation, he sat beside the radio at the borrowed Château de Candé in Touraine, knitting a dark blue sweater for Wallis. As the Queen came in, 'dignified, smiling and much more bosomy', according to her old friend Channon, musing upon the days when he and the rest of the 'happy group', Prince Paul, Gage and others, had been 'a little in love with her', no one could help thinking what it might have been like had the thin, angular, chic figure of Queen Wallis been in her place. Even Winston Churchill, finally converted, whispered to his wife, 'You were right. I see now the "other one" wouldn't have done.' No one could forget that, had it not been for 'the other one', the Coronation of King George vi would have been the Coronation of King Edward viii. George vi had stepped into his brother's shoes; now he was wearing his crown.

Despite the haunting thoughts in the background and the long shadow of recent events, the Coronation ceremony was both beautiful and moving, its historic ritual obliterating the sad, sordid memories of recent months and elevating the idea of kingship. Queen Victoria's grand-daughter, Princess Alice, Countess of Athlone, thought that of all the four Coronations she had attended 'Bertie's' was 'the most moving'. 'I thought Bertie looked too wonderful as he stood at the altar divested of his robes and wearing only knee breeches and a shirt which suited his fine figure,' she recalled.[14] Another observer found that the King, with his slim figure and high cheekbones, reminded him of a medieval icon, the effect enhanced by a shaft of sunlight catching the King's golden tunic as he sat on the Coronation chair for the crowning.

In one important sense the Coronation of King George vi differed from that of his predecessors who had borne the title 'King of Great Britain and Ireland and Ruler of the British Dominions beyond the Seas'. He was now, separately, King of Canada, Australia, New Zealand, South Africa and Eire, under the provisions of the Statute of Westminster, and this change had to be reflected both in the Coronation oath, the ceremony of recognition (when, after the crowning, the King is recognized by those present as 'The undoubted King of this Realm') and the oath to defend the Protestant faith. Much complicated haggling had taken place between the various Dominions and the Secretary of State for the Dominions, Malcom MacDonald, able son of Ramsay, with South Africa and Eire – as usual – being the most troublesome, before the final forms had been agreed upon. The Coronation oath read out by the Archbishop of Canterbury to King George went:

Do you solemnly promise and swear to govern the peoples of Great Britain, Ireland, Canada, Australia, New Zealand, and the Union of South Africa, of your possessions, and the other territories to them belonging or pertaining and of your Empire of India, according to their respective laws and customs?

This oath is followed in the Coronation rite by a promise to maintain the Protestant faith. De Valera (naturally), Mackenzie King (on behalf of the Catholic French Canadians) and the Catholic Premier of Australia, Lyons, having demanded that this promise should be limited to the United Kingdom, a general profession was made with regard to the Dominions in which the King promised to maintain the 'true profession of the Gospel'.

For all his faults and his precarious health (Lord Dawson sat in the congregation with a syringe at the ready in case the Archbishop should collapse), Lang, with his fine voice and sense of theatre, was the ideal celebrant for such a ceremony and well capable of transmitting its significance. When he administered the oath, he raised his voice and, turning slightly westwards in order to be audible in the Choir where many of the Dominion representatives were seated, recited the words with great emphasis as if to bring home the significance of the King's position as 'Head of the Great Commonwealth of free peoples'. For Lionel Logue, seated with his wife in the Royal Box and proudly wearing the Coronation medal presented to him by the King the previous evening, one of the great moments of his life was when the King looked at him and gave an imperceptible nod, as if to say, 'We did it.'

Outside Buckingham Palace that evening the crowds surged roaring 'We want George' and 'We want the King'. ('The King wants his dinner,' Robert Wood heard King George mutter in an amused aside.) Inside, the King completed the last dreaded hurdle of the broadcast, pinned a Coronation medal on Wood 'as a memento' and, with the Queen, stepped out on to the balcony overlooking the Mall to wave to his people. Opposite, the huge white marble monument to his great-grandmother, Victoria, rose like a stranded ship from the crowds, yet another reminder, as if he needed one, of his great heritage.

The success of the Coronation released a great wave of popular enthusiasm for the new King and Queen, a surge which had been building up over the past weeks. People had been willing King George to succeed and to blot out the past. On the Friday before the ceremony, at a huge Empire Parliamentary Association luncheon attended by some 800 men in morning suits 'and a few Socialists in flannels', parliamentarians, Dominion and colonial dignitaries in London for the Coronation, prolonged applause had broken out when the Speaker of the House of Commons, Fitzroy, turned to the King and said pointedly, 'We have complete confidence in the future of your reign.' That occasion had been the King's first public ordeal close to his Coronation and it had been a nerve-racking one, which he surmounted with some difficulty. 'The King rose, the amplifier was put in front of him, and for a few terrible seconds there was dead silence, as he could not get the words out,' Channon recorded. 'A feeling of uneasiness came over the crowd; but soon the King, controlling himself, read out a short speech of thanks. As he went on he seemed to warm up, and finished in good style, and sat down amidst great applause and relief.' Then, Channon had written of 'the King, faltering, with his halting speech and resigned kindly smile, and everyone pretending that he had done it well'.

After the Coronation there was no need to 'pretend' that the King had done something well; that autumn he even overcame the ordeal of delivering the speech from the throne at the State Opening of Parliament without a hitch. It was a task which had frightened his father and grandfather – George V used to say that he knew of few worse ordeals than being obliged to deliver somebody else's speech, at the same time balancing on his head a $2\frac{1}{2}$ pound gold crown. Even Edward VIII had admitted to feeling apprehension at the prospect of his debut in this ceremony: 'Inevitably, my performance would be compared with that of my father, who was always superb on these occasions,' he wrote. For George VI, comparison with both his father and his brother, whose expert performances were fresh in everyone's memories, would equally be inevitable. 'My father always did this sort of thing so well,' he told Logue, as he sat in his study at Buckingham Palace practising delivering the speech as he would have to do, seated and wearing the Crown. But in the event even the critical Channon admitted that he had acquitted himself well with only the slightest hesitations.

Channon, too, noticed the difference in the King immediately after the Coronation; at the Sutherlands' magnificent ball on 18 May he remarked upon 'how both the King and Queen have gained greatly in presence and dignity'. Chaplain Don, witnessing another public ceremony performed by the King in July, was 'much struck by the King's demeanour – he has found himself and is growing in stature as the months go by – it is as though the charisma of the Coronation had effected a deepening and enlightening of the inner man – he is rising firmly to the calls upon him'. [15] This was partly due, too, to a consciousness of his new-found popularity. Lang, having tea with the King and Queen after his investiture with the Grand Cross of the Royal Victorian Order, found them both 'greatly pleased and encouraged by the enthusiastic reception everywhere accorded to them'. In the East End of London, in the City, at the Naval Review at Spithead (scene of the famously tired and emotional performance by the BBC commentator, Commander Woodrooffe – 'the Fleet's lit up, we're all lit up . . .'), at the Empire Day Thanksgiving Service in St Paul's and on State visits to Scotland (5–11 July) and Northern Ireland (27–29 July), the crowds gave them unmistakable evidence of their popularity, fuelling their confidence in themselves and their ability to perform their new roles.

The Queen had slipped into her new part successfully and with ease; she was a natural actress and had, after all, once played the Winter Queen. It was evident to everyone that, however much she had claimed, perhaps genuinely, that she dreaded being Queen, she was throughly enjoying it. 'Really David,' Wallis wrote waspishly just before Christmas 1936, 'the pleased expression on the Duchess of York's [she refused to give her her new title of Queen] face is funny to see. How she is loving it all.'[16] Harold Nicolson, more charitably disposed towards the Queen than Wallis, gained the same impression when he attended a grand dinner-party at Buckingham Palace on 17 March 1937 in company with Lloyd George, Baldwin, Halifax, the Dukes of Rutland and Buccleuch, the Earl of Ancaster, Sir Montagu Norman, the Governor of the Bank of England, and their wives, and Oliver and Maureen Stanley. There were powdered footmen standing motionless on each fourth step of the staircase leading up to the drawing-rooms:

The dining-table is one mass of gold candelabra and scarlet tulips. Behind us the whole of the Windsor plate is massed in tiers. The dinner has been unwisely selected since we have soup, fish, quail, ham, chicken, ice and savoury. The wine, on the other hand, is excellent and the port superb. When we have finished our savoury the King rises and we all resume our procession back to the drawing-rooms. On reaching the fourth drawing-room the equerries tell us to drop our ladies and to proceed to a drawing-room beyond where the men sit down for coffee and cigars. The King occupies that interval in talking to Baldwin and Lloyd George....

We then pass on into the Picture Gallery, where we are joined by the women and the King and Queen. Maureen Stanley is at once summoned by the King and occupies most of his attention. The Queen then goes the rounds. She wears upon her face a faint smile indicative of how much she would have liked her dinner-party were it not for the fact that she was Queen of England. Nothing could exceed the charm or dignity which she displays, and I cannot help feeling what a mess poor Mrs Simpson would have made of such an occasion. It demonstrated to us more than anything else how wholly improbable that marriage would have been....

Thereafter [Nicolson concluded], the Queen drops us a deep curtsey which is answered by all the ladies present. We then go ... back to the Stanleys' house and have some beer while we discuss the strange legend of monarchy.[17]

Praise showered down upon the Queen from all sides. Although she had put on weight – so much so that Channon remarked on her 'bosomy' look at the Coronation and rumours circulated that she was pregnant again – her poise, charm and warmth captivated everyone who saw her. One of her major advantages both as a woman and as Queen was her ability to make the individual to whom she was speaking feel that they were the one person in the world she wanted to talk to. This was to be of enormous value to her in the factories and the mills as much as at State dinners and Society balls. People felt her warmth and interest and related easily to her. The technique of dealing with crowds and individuals on her public appearances came naturally to her; already she had developed the twirling gesture when waving to crowds which is still her trademark. Breaking with royal tradition, she smiled constantly in public, giving everyone the happy impression that she was enjoying herself, which she very often was. 'I find it's hard to know when *not* to smile,' she admitted to Cecil Beaton. When Ramsay MacDonald, on retiring from public life, had had an audience with the King, he met the Queen shortly afterwards and told her that her husband had 'come on magnificently since his accession'. She had been pleased. 'And am I doing all right?' she asked. 'Oh you ...', Ramsay replied with a sweeping gesture as if words were unnecessary. She had a gift for saying the right thing and took trouble to inject into the conversation an intimate, personal, often lightly teasing note which charmed the person she was talking to. But there was steel beneath the velvet glove, for the Queen had strongly held views and deeply felt convictions, particularly where religion, the family and morals were concerned. She was tough, mentally and constitutionally, but part of her skill was not to let most people see it.

Both of them were conscious of the need to project a new regal image to celebrate the transformation of the Duke and Duchess of York into the King and Queen of England. A young Norman Hartnell, whose name was to become synonymous with royal dressmaking, was brought in to consult over the Coronation and to glamorize the Queen's wardrobe. The King had evidently been studying the royal collections for inspiration and had found it in Winterhalter. The inevitable cigarette in hand, he led Hartnell off to inspect the Winterhalter portraits of royal ladies. 'His Majesty made it clear in his quiet way that I should attempt to capture this picturesque grace in the dresses I was to design for the Queen. Thus it is to the King and Winterhalter', Hartnell wrote, 'that are owed the fine praises I later received for the regal renaissance of the romantic crinoline.' Hartnell designed two crinoline evening dresses for the Queen to be worn at the State banquets for the visits of the King of the Belgians and King Carol of Romania, the first of silver tissue over silver gauze, with a deep *berthe* collar of silver lace sewn with diamonds. The first, Hartnell described as 'the first great dress I designed for any member of the Royal Family, but the second was never worn, someone leaked a description of the dress to the press which was printed the day it was to be worn. The King fell into a royal rage and the dress was abandoned.'[18] The crinolines were ideally suited to the Queen's unfashionably curvaceous figure and were to be a sensational success when she visited Paris a year later. The Queen's new awareness of her appearance and clothes were quickly noticed. Kenneth Clark, Surveyor of the King's Pictures, who had grumbled about her taste in clothes in March 1937, a year later noted after lunching with the royal family that 'the Queen was looking very trim, was wearing more fashionable clothes, and drank only sherry in the morning'.[19]

The King's recently acquired confidence in his abilities and, indeed, in his own health and strength is evident in the correspondence, resumed in August 1937, about the postponed Indian Durbar. The letters between the Viceroy, Linlithgow, Zetland at the India Office in Whitehall and Alec Hardinge, now the King's Principal Private Secretary, reveal the Indian officials reversing their previous position on the desirability of a royal visit to India in the winter of 1938, while the King is increasingly determined to go and stands out for his point of view for as long as he can, against the feeling of his Governments both in London and on the spot.

Circumstances had changed in India since the announcement in February of the postponement of the visit. In July Congress took office and Congress ministries came to power in seven out of the eleven autonomous provinces. Congress Party politicians were opposed to the Federation to be inaugurated under the Act of 1935. On 30 August Linlithgow wrote to Zetland expressing apprehension that the Congress politicians would seize on the propaganda opportunities offered by a royal visit to make trouble. The provincial ministers now in power in Congress provinces would refuse to take part in ceremonies, to attend the person of the sovereign or to vote funds for the visit. 'We can hardly allow His Majesty to commit himself to a visit to India without warning him of what may occur, while—knowing him as well as I do—I cannot but feel that he may not be willing to contemplate any unpleasantness of that sort,' the Viceroy wrote.[20] All of them had in mind the example of the Prince of Wales's visit to India in 1921, which the nationalist politicians had seen as a political move by the Government to win favour for the unpopular Montagu–Chelmsford Constitution and which had resulted in hostile demonstrations.

The King, according to Zetland, had taken this point when discussing the matter with Neville Chamberlain, the new Prime Minister, at Balmoral, and had 'shown himself very sensitive to hostile comment in India'. In a private letter to the Viceroy on 12 September 1937, Zetland continued:

It is unfortunate that Nehru recently discussed the prospect of a Royal visit with representatives of the Indian press and wound up ... with the unflattering observation that if the British Government were anxious to safeguard the King against the possibility of any untoward incident their best course would be to keep him in England. . . .[21]

An increasingly nervous Viceroy canvassed the British Governors as to the desirability of the visit and found that their views on balance were against it. He suggested further postponement on the grounds of the unsettled international situation, 'the only convincing reason which we can at this stage give', and the King's health. As to the first, Zetland minuted beside it that a visit to Canada was under consideration and if it took place instead of an Indian visit would 'knock the bottom out of' this excuse; as to the King's health, he wrote, 'I do not think that this is now a consideration.' It had become abundantly clear that the King's health could certainly stand up to the strain of a Durbar, but, for Indian political reasons, Zetland too was now against the visit taking place: '... owing to proximity to Federation it would provide Congress with the opportunity for demonstrating it as an attempt to make use of the Crown to support a policy to which India was opposed'.[22]

The King, on the other hand, was now increasingly determined to go to India; an extract from Cabinet Conclusions of 20 October 1937 reveals Hardinge on the King's behalf querying the omission of any reference to an Indian visit in the draft of the King's speech at the Opening of Parliament. He said, according to Zetland, that this omission 'would give colour to a rumour that the King did not desire to visit India though the facts were that the King would like to go as soon as he was advised that this could be done with advantage'. Deferring to the King's insistence and overriding the telegraphed preference of the Viceroy for postponement, Chamberlain accepted a sentence suggested by the King – 'I am looking forward with interest and pleasure to the time when it will be possible for me to visit my Indian Empire' – with the proviso that this should not affect the Government's ability to advise on the desirability or not of the visit later that year.[23] The King, although well aware of both Linlithgow's and Zetland's opinions on the subject, continued to press for the visit to go ahead. 'A new factor in the case is the apparent desire of Their Majesties to visit India as soon as we are in a position to agree to their doing so,' Zetland warned Linlithgow in a private letter of 15 November. Hardinge had told a member of

Zetland's staff that 'the King would regard advice adverse to the visit as very disappointing' and that when Zetland had audience of the King 'HM hoped that ... I should not face him with a definite decision adverse to the subject. I gather that he will wish to discuss with me pretty fully the pros and cons and that he will do so with a desire on his part to overcome any obstacles which we see to the proposal....' The King apparently had in mind to hold a Durbar at Delhi primarily for the Indian princes, the military and officials, which need not include the potentially troublesome provincial ministers of the Congress Party.

Zetland was thoroughly disconcerted by the firmness of the royal stance on a subject which he thought had already been decided against, writing cautiously to the Viceroy that 'the rather unexpectedly strong view which appears to be taken by T[heir] M[ajestie]'s themselves must of course be taken into account'.[24] Both of them now took concerted action to counter the King's determination to go ahead. On 19 November the Viceroy telegraphed that Sir James 'P.J.' Grigg, the Finance Member of the Government of India, would prefer not to have to provide for the expenses of a Durbar in 1938–9, while Zetland replied that he still thought the strongest argument against the visit to be the political one. Early in December the Secretary of State returned to the charge against Buckingham Palace with a cogently worded résumé of the pros and cons for the Durbar which politely dismissed the King's idea of limiting it to princes and the military and eliminating the embarrassing political element, stressed his fear of the Crown's being seen to be involved in local politics and brought in the weighty argument of the huge expenditure, £1 million, which would fall exclusively on Central Government in India. 'I presume it may be taken for granted', Zetland concluded, flexing his muscles, 'that if His Majesty decides not to visit India in 1938–9 it will be on the grounds that His Majesty does not feel justified in spending so long a time away from England and that no question of any other Imperial visit will arise.'[25] Despite the whole tenor of Zetland's written opinion being against it, the King was still clearly determined to go if he possibly could, even on a modified scale, if the costs could be kept down. On 14 December Hardinge replied:

The King was keenly interested and his personal inclination is quite obviously strongly in favour of a visit next winter if after further consideration we consider that the risk might be taken. He was, however, as he expressed it, shocked by the estimated cost of a visit and he told me that he thought that the sum mentioned was altogether out of the question. He would himself feel very strongly that he would not be justified in imposing so heavy a burden on the Indian taxpayer, and he begged me to represent this to you and to ask you whether you could not let me have, for his information, a rough indication of the various headings under which the money would have to be spent.[26]

The King wanted further discussion with the Secretary of State and the Prime Minister before taking a final decision around the end of January.

The last round of the battle shows the King fighting a determined rearguard action against his Secretary of State and the Viceroy, much to the former's surprise and exasperation. On 1 February Zetland took the step of advising the King that the next winter would be inadvisable for a visit, primarily on the grounds of expense and the state of the Indian Government budget. The King, he told the Cabinet the next day, had agreed and asked him to draft an announcement of further postponement. The Cabinet then asked Zetland to prepare an announcement to this effect for the King's agreement.[27] But, as a long, rather indignant letter written one week later by Zetland to Linlithgow explained, this was not, as everyone thought, the end of the affair. The King was still reluctant to abandon the project and only capitulated in the end when advised to do so by the Prime Minister, advice which, as a constitutional monarch, he could not ignore:

It is extraordinary how difficult it has been to obtain a final decision from HM on the question of a royal visit. He sent for me last Tuesday the 1st, and discussed the matter with me for rather more than half an hour. I had provided Alec Hardinge with all the relevant facts in advance and the King had had an opportunity therefore of informing himself fully of the views which you and I hold upon the matter. The impression left upon my mind at the end of my audience was that he accepted the advice which I tendered to him and made up his mind, though with a good deal of regret, that a visit next winter was not really practicable.... I showed him the draft of a possible communiqué which I had drawn up. HM read it with care and said that he would like to think it over, and would instruct Hardinge to let me know his considered opinion in due course. I, therefore, felt justified in informing the Cabinet next morning that a decision against a visit next winter had been taken and that HM had asked me to arrange for an official announcement.... Imagine, therefore, my surprise when the Thursday morning I received a message from the PM asking me to come and discuss the question with him. I saw him on Thursday evening and he told me that the King had raised the question with him in the course of an audience.

It seems that the King had thought again, and that it had occurred to him that if the financial difficulty was the chief obstacle to the visit he might persuade the Chancellor of the Exchequer to find the money. Neville Chamberlain told me that he had discouraged this idea but that at the King's request he had agreed to discuss the matter further with me. Neville asked me if the financial difficulty was the only serious obstacle in the way of a visit next winter. I told him that this was not so, and that an equally serious obstacle, though it was one which one could not refer to in public, was the risk that there might be considerable political agitation in progress in India next winter in connection with the inauguration of the federal provisions of the Act. Neville said that if this was so, he accepted our conclusions as final and that he would inform the King accordingly....[28]

The King had lost the battle but still hoped that he had not lost the war, and that postponement really meant only postponement. He insisted on making his own alterations to the draft drawn up by Zetland after discussions with the Prime Minister. The communiqué ran:

HM feels ... that he would not be justified in imposing any additional burden on the existing revenue of India, at a time when the calls on them in connection with the inauguration of Provincial Autonomy are already heavy.... With this consideration in mind and after taking counsel with his advisers, HM has reluctantly come to the conclusion that it would be advisable to wait until the general world outlook has become more settled [at Linlithgow's suggestion 'world' had been inserted between 'general' and 'outlook', thus drawing attention away from the Indian political situation] and the financial prospects more definite before committing himself to an engagement so long in advance.

The last paragraph stressed that the King had by no means abandoned the idea: 'In communicating his decision to the Secretary of State for India, His Majesty has once more repeated his strong desire to visit India and his intention of doing so as soon as circumstances will permit.'[29] 'The King hopes that his visit will not have to wait until Dominion Status has been attained,' Hardinge wrote to Zetland on 3 March 1938, 'for he feels that this would mean relegating it at least to his old age!'

It was a battle which the King did not abandon and was to renew after the Second World War against Churchill and, once more, Grigg. Finally, Indian independence and its subsequent troubles and, curiously in view of the first postponement, his own health meant that he was never to see his Indian Empire.

The King had chosen his title deliberately, to emphasize continuity and a return to the values and traditions of his father's reign. His forty-first birthday had been on 14 December 1936; he had marked it in a special way to show his love and appreciation for his wife by appointing her a member of the most ancient Order of Chivalry, the Order of the Garter. It was characteristic of his liking for symbolism and tradition that he should have done this, as Queen Elizabeth wrote to Queen Mary: 'He had discovered that Papa gave it to you on his, Papa's birthday, June 3rd, and the coincidence was so charming that he has now followed suit, & given it to me on his own birthday.' It was a signal of the importance of Elizabeth in his private and public life, for the reign of George VI was to be a partnership in a very real and unprecedented sense. He had taken care to associate his wife with him in every public speech he had made, at the Accession Council on 12 December, in his message to Parliament and in his New Year's broadcast to the peoples of the Empire and Commonwealth. At Sandringham in particular, where the memories of his father and grandfather were so strong, he was conscious of his responsibility as upholder of the family tradition. He and Queen Elizabeth looked on the task which faced them with a religious sense of self-dedication and sacrifice, as he put it in his New Year's broadcast:

I realise to the full the responsibilities of my noble heritage. I shoulder them with all the more confidence in the knowledge that the Queen and my mother Queen Mary are at my side. . . . To repeat the words used by my dear father at the time of his Silver Jubilee, my wife and I dedicate ourselves for all time to your service, and we pray that God may give us guidance and strength to follow the path that lies before us.

He re-emphasized continuity by reappointing all his father's former servants. In the first week after the Abdication Wigram (who had officially retired in August 1936, leaving, as he put it, his colleagues to 'face a sticky wicket') was appointed Permanent Lord-in-Waiting to the King and for three months from January he was to relieve Alec Hardinge (whose health, never strong since being wounded in the First World War, had been sapped by the strain of the crisis). Hardinge, the activist in the crisis, retained his position as Principal Private Secretary and Tommy Lascelles his as Assistant Private Secretary. Wigram spent the night at Lambeth on 16 December to give his old friend the Archbishop the glad tidings. 'Thus the Court, thank God, will revert to the old well-tried ways, to the infinite relief of all concerned,' was Don's comment.[30] Sir Eric Miéville became Assistant Private Secretary. Ulick Alexander, loyal and discreet Keeper of the Privy Purse to King Edward, retained his post under King George. Other friends and servants of Edward's such as Joey Legh and Jack Aird, who had made their feelings about the Wallis–Edward affair quite plain, were to be taken on by the new King. Legh honourably accompanied Edward into exile in Austria even though he had disapproved of his relationship with Wallis and made his dislike of her quite clear. 'Joey always loathed Mrs Simpson and she hated him because she knew he didn't approve,' a member of Legh's family remembered. After he returned from Austria, the King summoned him and asked him to join his Household as equerry and to stay on in the grace-and-favour house in St James's Palace. 'You've been wonderful with my brother, and I know you've done your best. I want you to come and look after me and show me the ropes,' the King told him.[31] Legh agreed, later becoming the Master of the King's Household and the closest to him of all his courtiers, dying in the royal service at the age of sixty-four. The Duke of Windsor never forgave him for this and, although they were to meet off and on over the years and Legh would be the one to arrange the Duke's visits to the King, the Duke would be noticeably cool and a friendship which had begun in the First World War ended with the Duke's infatuation with Mrs Simpson.

Walter Monckton, the ex-King's trusted confidant and henchman during the last days of his reign, retained the confidence and even the friendship of the new King. 'At the time of the Abdication King George VI told Walter that he wanted to be served by him in the same way as he had served his brother. He was to remain Attorney-General to the Duchy of Cornwall, but more than that, he was to be available at all times to advise the King as a friend,' Monckton's biographer wrote. The King marked his approval of what Monckton had tried to do by making him the first knight of the new reign. He was to be a Knight Commander of the Royal Victorian Order, the order which is reserved as the personal gift of the sovereign. George VI, with the thoughtfulness which was to be characteristic of him, demonstrated the personal friendship and gratitude which lay behind it in an unexpected, informal investiture, as Monckton recalled in his memoirs:

The announcement of the honour to be conferred upon me came out with many others in the New Year Honours, but as I was in the Household it was not necessary for me to attend an Investiture, and the King sent for me on the day of the announcement. I went to his house at 145 Piccadilly, and saw him in a little room on the first floor. I had no idea that he intended to knight me then and there, but after ten minutes' conversation he pointed to a yellow footstool in the background, and said: 'We shall be needing that.' I pulled it out; he told me to kneel on it, and produced a sword. When he tapped me lightly on the shoulder I started to get up. He said: 'No, I haven't done yet,' and tapped me on the other. When I eventually got up he said: 'Well, Walter, we did not manage that very well, but neither of us had done it before!'[32]

Monckton in the future was to be the only real channel of communication between George VI and his exiled brother, a relationship which was destined to be one of extreme turbulence. Monckton managed to remain friends with both sides, although, as he wrote, at times one or the other of the Windsors would show 'signs of mistrust'; he never lost the King's confidence and the King would address his personal letters to him 'My dear Walter'.

The only member of Edward's court to fall victim to the new regime was 'Perry' Brownlow, who, with his wife Kitty, had been, apart from his official position as equerry, social friends and sympathizers of Wallis and Edward and intimates of Lord Beaverbrook. Brownlow, having accompanied Wallis on her flight across France, should hardly have been surprised to find himself *persona non grata* with the post-Edward regime. He was superseded as Lord-in-Waiting by the Marquess of Dufferin & Ava and told that his name could never appear in the Court Circular again. Both Wigram and Lord Cromer, the Lord Chamberlain, denied that the King had dismissed Brownlow and Chips Channon alleged that there was a plot by a 'Court clique' behind the King's back to 'Black List' the late King's friends. None the less, it does seem unlikely that it was done without the King's knowledge or consent. Brownlow had been so closely involved in the final stages of the crisis that his presence at Court would only have provided an unpleasant reminder of an episode which everyone wanted to forget. He was, moreover, a figure of no great stature who was prone to scrapes and errors of judgement. The King, in a humorous reference to the county in which Brownlow's family seat was located, later dubbed him 'the Lincolnshire Handicap'.

The King personally took immediate steps against one other member of his brother's circle, Emerald Cunard. On 16 December Queen Mary wrote a private letter to Prince Paul of Yugoslavia with the instructions 'Please Burn':

The other day in my presence Bertie told George he wished him and Marina never to see Lady Cunard again and George said he would not do so. I fear she has done David a great deal of harm as there is no doubt she was great friends with Mrs S. at one time and generally made a great fuss of her. Under the circumstances I feel none of us, in fact people in society, should meet her. I am sure you will agree one should not meet her again after what has happened and I am hoping that George and Marina will no longer see certain people who alas were friends of Mrs S. and Lady Cunard and also of David's.... I am hoping that for our sake you and Olga will no longer see Lady C.... As you may imagine I feel very strongly on the matter but several people have mentioned to me what harm she has done....[33]

The Queen was clearly writing under great stress, her sentences repetitive, her handwriting sloping and weak, almost unrecognizable from her normal hand which was very like Queen Victoria's and as firm and formed as her own character. 'It [the Abdication] very nearly killed poor Queen Mary,' the new Queen wrote to Victor Cazalet; 'there is indeed such a thing as a broken heart and hers very nearly collapsed.'[34] That Christmas at Sandringham Queen Mary did collapse, retiring stricken to her room from Christmas Eve to New Year's Day.

The King's action in ordering Prince George to boycott Emerald Cunard was backed by his mother, as her presence at the interview with Prince George and her personal letter to Prince Paul indicated. It was also supported by his wife. That this was definitely the case is confirmed by a letter from Queen Elizabeth among Lady Londonderry's papers. As a leader of Society Edith Londonderry was naturally aware of every current, rapid and possible rock in the social landscape. The season of 1937 was Coronation summer and, planning to give a ball at Londonderry House three weeks after the coronation to which she invited the newly crowned King and Queen, she tactfully wrote to Queen Elizabeth checking who might or might not be acceptable. Thanking her for her considerateness in consulting them, Queen Elizabeth replied that Lady Cunard was the only person they felt they did not want to meet at the moment as the bitter experiences of the recent past were still so fresh in their minds.

The King's reaction to the Abdication was less violent than his mother's; three months later a friend was to describe Queen Mary as 'still angry' with her eldest son. His anger against his brother was to come later; now his emotions towards him were a mixture of sorrow, pain and embarrassment, but he clearly shared the natural family feeling that 'other people' had led the late King astray. These feelings were publicly voiced by the Archbishop of Canterbury in a BBC broadcast on 13 December, the first Sunday after the Abdication. The Archbishop, who, in spite of the general suspicion that he was an arch-conspirator against the King, had been largely on the sidelines of the crisis despite a few attempts to intervene, now took this opportunity to vent his pent-up feelings in sonorous condemnatory passages, in which he spoke of the 'tragedy' of the Abdication and referred directly to the late King's way of life and choice of friends:

Even more strange and sad it is that he should have sought his happiness in a manner inconsistent with the Christian principles of marriage, and within a social circle whose standard and whose way of life are alien to all the best instincts and traditions of his people. Let those who belong to this circle know that today they stand rebuked by the judgement of the nation which had loved King Edward.

The Archbishop's broadcast, which was seen, even by those who had not supported King Edward, as vindictive, un-English and an unsporting attempt to kick a man when he was down, evoked a storm of protest. Within twenty-four hours 250 letters, the majority of them vituperative, had arrived at Lambeth

Palace, 'mostly from lower-middle-class homes' the snobbish prelate noted, writing to his old friend Wilfred Parker, Archbishop of Pretoria, that he had also received 'numberless letters of gratitude from really leading and responsible people including the Prime Minister'. 'It is of course an immense relief to me to know now that in the new King and Queen I have very old and intimate friends and that I can now look forward not with misgivings but with joy and thankfulness to the forthcoming Coronation,' Lang added.[35] Indeed, with a characteristic lack of humility he had appointed himself the royal family's spokesman, and he certainly would not have spoken out as he did without knowing that what he intended to say would meet with their approval. He had drafted Queen Mary's Message to the Nation after the Abdication and was on excellent terms with the new King and Queen; a week later when he went to 145 Piccadilly to see them he found them both '*most* friendly and quite charming'. The new Queen confirmed that the Archbishop had given vent to feelings that they could not publicly express when she wrote to Victor Cazalet:

I don't think you need feel the Archbishop failed to express the right thing. *She* [Queen Mary] felt he said exactly what he should and was grateful to him. All the family feels the same. I think the nation vaguely *felt* it, but *he* put the issue clearly and as no one else had the right to do. Nowadays we are inclined to be too vague about the things that matter, and I think it well that for once someone should speak out in plain and direct words, what after all was the truth. . . .[36]

Sir John Reith expressed the general post-Abdication feeling that dangerous new forces which threatened to undermine the traditional stability and virtues of British life had been defeated when he wrote in his diary, after attending Sunday service in his local country church the day after Edward went into exile: 'We felt as if a cloud of depression of which we had been almost physically conscious had lifted. Poor Edward. But thank God he and his ways have passed and there is a new King and Queen. The effect is quite extraordinary. It seemed as if the old England was back. . . .'[37]

Symbolically, King George emphasized this by being seen physically to take over his family heritage. In March he and his family moved into Buckingham Palace, which Edward VIII had always hated – even its particular smell had filled him with a sense of unease, no doubt connected with memories of his father. For the same reasons George VI found it reassuring. Although he never regarded Buckingham Palace as 'home', it was at least familiar territory where he had lived with his parents as a young man until his marriage. He and the Queen now occupied his parents' former apartments on the first floor with the Princesses on the floor above. Leaving the public rooms as they were, the King and Queen had the private apartments redecorated, bathrooms remodelled, dark walnut panelling replaced with painted pine and reproduction chimneypieces discarded in favour of originals. The Queen had her mother's touch for creating a delightful atmosphere in her houses. When Lady Airlie had tea with them at the Palace in the early months of their reign in the Belgian Suite on the ground floor which they were then using, she remarked on how homelike it seemed already. The King smiled proudly. 'Elizabeth could make a home anywhere,' he said.

For Easter 1937, the King and Queen opened up Windsor Castle, the huge fortress–palace dominating the River Thames which more than any other building symbolized the glamour and grandeur of an ancient monarchy. Nearly nine hundred years had passed since William the Conqueror first saw the defensive potential of the site and built a *motte* with keep and wooden palisade on the chalk cliff above the river, and eight hundred since his son, Henry I, established the first royal residence there. All the King's ancestors had lived there, most of them adding to the vast building, galleries, towers, chapels and art treasures for the royal collections. According to Queen Ena of Spain, herself a grand-daughter of Queen Victoria, Edward VIII had been the only sovereign of the House of Windsor never to spend a night there as King. For George VI his occupying the Castle was almost as much a confirmation of himself as King and head of his House as the Coronation service would be.

The King revived the tradition of inviting his ministers to spend a night at Windsor; among the first was Duff Cooper as Secretary of State for War, with Diana, who had so often been weekend guests at King Edward VIII's alternative Windsor. At the Fort in July 1935, Diana Cooper noted, she had occupied a pink bedroom, 'pink-sheeted, pink Venetian-blinded, pink-soaped, white telephoned and pink-and-white maided'. At Windsor on 16 April 1937 the Coopers were ushered down a many-doored musty passage to a suite redolent of defunct royalty:

a sitting-room with piano and good fire, evening papers, two well-stocked writing-tables and thirteen oil-paintings of Royalty ... besides the oils there are about a hundred plaques, miniatures, intaglios, wax profiles etc of the Family in two Empire vitrines, and two bronze statuettes of King Edward VII in yachting get-up and another Prince in Hussar uniform.

Duff's 'very frigid' room, with tapless bath enclosed and lidded in mahogany, led out of the sitting-room and beyond it Diana's 'throttlingly-stuffy' bedroom with nine oil paintings of the family and 'a bed for three hung in embroidered silk', with its own large bathroom with eight more oil paintings of the family, by Muller and dated 1856, a bronze statuette of princess Louise on horseback, and another royal group including two more of Queen Victoria's children, Princess Beatrice and Prince Leopold, with 'Waldie' on the moors. Everything was as grand and formal as it had been in the days of King George V and Queen Mary: 'Dinner at 8.30, ladies leave dining-room with gentlemen at 9.30 but gentlemen don't stop, they walk straight through us to the lu and talks and drinks. Girls gossip until 10.15 when the men reappear flushed but relieved, and at 10.30 it's "Good night".' Through dinner a military band played concealed behind a grille, but it was not all quite the same as it had been when Queen Mary was the hostess. When Diana retired to bed Duff, who had long been an admirer of the Queen's, remained behind for 'an hour's so-called drinking tea with the Queen. She put her feet up on a sofa and talked of Kingship and "the intolerable honour" but not of the [Abdication] crisis.'[38] Diana was impressed by the monarchical splendour. Comparing the two regimes, Fort Belvedere and Windsor, she told Channon, 'that was an operetta, this is an institution'.

The King, with Diana sitting next to him at dinner, was intrigued to hear her declare, 'I'm afraid I'm a Rat, Sir.' He could hardly wait to retail this to Osbert Sitwell, who had coined the name for the deserting supporters of Edward VIII and Mrs Simpson in his verse satire 'Rat Week', written in the last week of the Abdication. Nor could he resist the temptation of conveying to Sitwell that he knew perfectly well that he was the author of 'Rat Week', although it had been anonymously privately circulated. Sitwell, an old friend of the King and Queen, was spending the weekend at Windsor from Saturday to Monday, 23–25 April, when the King summoned him to talk to him, saying casually in the course of the conversation: 'Do you know, someone came down here the other day who sat next to me at dinner, and said "I'm afraid I'm a Rat, Sir"?'

'Rather nonplussed,' Sitwell remarked:

'What a foolish thing to say, Sir. Who was it, if I may ask?'

'Someone you know very well – a person who has said a number of foolish things in her time,' the King observed. 'Can't you guess?'

I could not [Sitwell recalled] and the King then took refuge in the use of initials, for ... all members of the royal family consider initials to be an absolute and impenetrable disguise, absolving the person who employs them from any blame that might be incurred by mentioning a name, but at the same time affording an unmistakable indication of identity. . . .

'D.C. . . . D.C. . . . D.C. . . .,' the King repeated.

Stupidly, I failed to fit the correct names at once to the initial letters – but it proved to have been my old friend, Lady Diana Cooper. . . .[39]

It must have been, indeed, with a sense of wry amusement that the King observed the social effects of the transference of power from his brother to himself. Just one year earlier King Edward VIII and Wallis with Ernest Simpson and his mistress had been wandering through the Great Corridor at Windsor invoking the ghosts of King George IV and Mrs Fitzherbert and he himself had been the ignored, unrecognized Duke of York, the King's younger brother. Now he was King, the focus of the splendour and tradition that Windsor could provide, and people like Diana Cooper could not wait to consign to oblivion the weekends at the Fort ruled by Wallis. For the King it was not so easy to forget about his brother even had he wished to. The Duke of Windsor seemed not to realize the implications of the step he had taken, still less was he prepared to take the consequences. Questions which had arisen at the time of the Abdication remained to be settled and even before George VI was crowned he became involved in increasingly bitter wrangles with his brother, setting the pattern of their future relationship which was to last until his death.

ℒ 8 ℒ

TWO CAMPS

'... the King constantly talks of his brother: it is as if he can't talk of anything else; he seems haunted by him....'

Marie Belloc Lowndes, *Diaries and Letters, 1911–47*

O N 11 January 1937 at Sandringham, less than a month after his accession, George VI confessed to Lucy Baldwin, the homely wife of the Prime Minister, how he needed time to adjust himself to his new station and its duties, and how 'all his life he had been outshone by his brilliant brother....'[1] This basic lack of confidence in himself was to take years to shake off; indeed, it is doubtful if he ever entirely succeeded in doing so. It prompted much of his reaction to his brother, fuelled by a growing distrust of his brother's aims and motives; it was responsible also for the Queen's fierce protectiveness towards her husband where the Duke of Windsor was concerned . The second determining factor in the relationship between the two brothers was Wallis; the family blamed her and her pretensions, although unfit, to be Queen of England or at least the wife of the King, for triggering the Abdication, more than they did Edward for his desertion of duty for her sake. Within a year of the Abdication the King and his brother, despite initial goodwill, were no longer on speaking terms. The events of that year engendered mutual suspicion verging on paranoia and resulted in a long-running family quarrel in which there was to be no forgiving or forgetting. The Duke of Windsor's resentment at what he saw as his family's pettiness and vindictiveness, coupled with his own supremely bad judgement, was to lead him down dangerous paths in a blaze of international publicity, raising suspicions that he was not merely competing with his brother but even contemplating replacing him. The King was, in the words of the novelist, Marie Belloc Lowndes, 'haunted' by his brother; the Duke of Windsor was a family spectre that refused to stay in the cupboard.

According to one account of the Duke's parting with his brother at the Royal Lodge on the night of 11 December, the Duke 'bowed and kissed King George's hand, saying "Thank you, Sir, for all your kindness to me" and in answer to his protest put his hand on his shoulder and said, "It's all right, old man, I must step off with the right foot from the first." '[2] It was, unfortunately for the future of the fraternal relationship, to be the only indication he was to give that he truly understood the transition that had taken place between their relative status and position. It was as difficult for him to break the habit of years as the elder brother, the star of the family, as it was for King George to think himself out of a long habit of deference to his brother even when he thought him wrong.

The trouble began with the telephone calls which a harassed King George, involved in the heavy task of learning his new job, received from his brother, restless, lonely and bored at Enzesfeld, the Austrian Schloss put at his disposal by Eugene de Rothschild and his American wife Kitty. The substance of these calls, which began as brotherly conversations, soon developed into the transmission of Wallis's demands and fears expressed in letters and telephone calls from Cannes. ('It's only after one of them [Wallis's telephone calls]', Fruity Metcalfe retailed to his wife, Lady Alexandra, 'he ever seems a bit worried and nervous.') As a result, the Duke of Windsor's telephone conversations with his brother, in Walter Monckton's words, 'often ran counter to the advice which the King was getting from his responsible Ministers in the Government. This caused him [George VI] trouble which none would understand who did not know the extent to which before the Abdication the Duke of Windsor's brothers admired and looked up to him.' The King found these conversations embarrassing and difficult. 'The Duke of Windsor was particularly quick in understanding and decision,' Monckton wrote, 'and good on the telephone, whereas George VI had not the same quickness and was troubled by the impediment in his speech.'[3] Sometimes he was simply too preoccupied to take his brother's calls. Metcalfe described Edward's dawning realization of the changed situation when, one evening at dinner, he received a message that the King was on the telephone:

He said he couldn't take the call but asked it to be put through at 10 p.m. The answer to this was the [*sic*] HM said *he would talk at 6.45 p.m. tomorrow* as he was *too busy to talk any other time*. It was pathetic to see HRH's face. He couldn't believe it! He's been so used to having everything done as he wishes. I'm afraid he's going to have many more shocks like this. . . .[4]

The principal difficulty which the King had with these telephone calls was, however, the kind of demands which the Duke was now making on him.

What they were can be deduced from Wallis's published letters to the Duke, which, from the letter of 6 December quoted above until they joined each other in France in May, represent a mounting quasi-hysterical tirade against the Duke's family. Her bitterness and frustration was engendered in part by a sense of Paradise Lost, but also by a subconscious feeling that Edward had lost caste and position through his relationship with her. The words 'respect', 'dignity' and 'position' crop up frequently in her letters to him at this time, usually in connection with some slight by his family. On 12 December in her first letter to him after the Abdication, she wrote: 'Above all we want to have a dignified position no matter where we are. . . .' This was in connection with her doubts as to whether the King would grant her the title of Royal Highness, an issue which was to build what the Duke of Windsor himself later called a 'Berlin wall' between himself and his family and cause a deep and lasting bitterness. 'I suppose we will have difficulty about a name for poor me as York [the King] I don't suppose will make me HRH.'[5] In her next letter she brought the subject up again, as the tail end of an explosion of bitterness against Queen Mary's denial that she had received Wallis: '... your mother has placed me in a worse position than ever and practically says she would not accept me. It is plain that York guided by her would not give us the extra chic of creating me HRH – the only thing to bring me back in the eyes of the world.'[6]

She returned to the charge in a particularly bitter letter on 3 January:

I am so distressed over the way your brother has behaved from the first and is certainly giving the impression to the world at large that your family as well as Baldwin and his ministers do not approve of me. I do think now that the deed is done your family should not give out such an impression.... Naturally we have to build up a position but how hard it is going to be with no signs of support from your family. One realizes now the impossibility of getting the marriage announced in the Court Circular and of the HRH. It is all a great pity because I loathe being undignified and also of joining the countless titles that roam around Europe meaning nothing.

This time she blamed Baldwin and the politicians,

whose game it is to have you forgotten and to build up the puppet they have placed on the throne. And they can succeed [she went on] because just as they had for months an organized campaign to remove you – and how cleverly they worked – so they have one to prove they were right in what they did and the first step is to eliminate you from the minds of the people. I was the convenient tool in their hands to use to get rid of you and how they used it!

He had been far too trusting, she told him; perhaps now he realized he couldn't go on being so: 'You must employ their means to accomplish your ends.' She suggested that in a month's time he write a strong letter to the King 'setting forward the reasons for him not to treat you as an outcast and to do something for me so that we have a dignified and correct position as certainly befits an ex-King of England....'[7]

Wallis was shrewd enough to realize that as far as title and recognition as a member of the royal family was concerned, the King held all the cards, nor was she wrong in her suspicion that the attitude of the British Government was hardening against them. Realizing that the Duke's telephone calls were doing more harm than good where the King was concerned, she advised him to write instead. In January the Attorney-General, stung by allegations in the wake of the intervention by Francis Stephenson in the Simpson divorce that the legal officers were involved in a cover-up by failing to investigate evidence of collusion, ordered the King's Proctor to undertake an investigation. According to a note on the Attorney-General's typescript memorandum on the episode, 'A Petitioner who had committed adultery is supposed to disclose this to the court',[8] and had evidence of adultery been uncovered it seems probable that the court could have refused to sanction the Simpson divorce. From Somervell's note, however, it seems that he and the King's Proctor were far from eager to find such evidence; the result would have been 'a first-rate and squalid sensation'. Only small fry were interviewed; those who knew or suspected the truth, such as Halsey and Diana Cooper, were unlikely to come forward, and the general feeling was that 'the King having abdicated to marry' should not be prevented from doing so. None the less, on 6 February a panic-stricken Wallis implored the Duke of Windsor to ask the King to put pressure on Somervell by summoning him to 'simply let him know that anything in the way of holding up my decree absolute would be most objectionable to him'.[9] According to Somervell's journal, Barnes's questioning of hall porters, etc., turned up nothing: 'Their enquiries also confirmed the view that even if divorce had some collusive factors (eg the willingness of Mrs S. that her husband should be unfaithful) was not collusive in the ordinary or any provable sense.'[10] There is no evidence that the King attempted to influence Somervell in any way; it is extremely unlikely that he did so. Whatever his private views on the subject of his brother's marrying Mrs Simpson may have been, as head of the House of Windsor his opinion would undoubtedly have been that any more public scandal should be avoided, as he wrote to the Prime Minister later that year, 'the Monarchy has been degraded quite enough already'.

In mid-February the relations between King George and his brother took a serious turn for the worse in a quarrel over money. Somehow it was discovered that the Duke had been less than frank with his brother at Fort Belvedere on the evening of 10 December 1936 when, after what the then Prince Albert had described as 'a dreadful lawyers' meeting', a financial agreement was signed between them of which the principal ingredient was a promise by the future King to pay his brother an allowance of £25,000 a year 'if Parliament does not make provision for His Majesty [Edward VIII] in the new Civil List, unless the reason for such action on the part of Parliament is due to His Majesty's conduct from that date'. Edward VIII, for his part, had promised not to see Mrs Simpson until the Civil List became law, and to sell to the new King his life interest in Balmoral and Sandringham.[11] At Fort Belvedere, he had pleaded poverty, attempted to get his father's will revised in his favour, as Wigram's diary revealed, and failed to divulge the huge capital he had accumulated as Prince of Wales. At a tripartite meeting in London on 10 February 1937, with Wigram and Bircham representing the King and Monckton and Allen the Duke of Windsor, Sir Warren Fisher, Permanent Secretary to the Treasury, backed by Sir Horace Wilson, a leading civil servant and confidant of Neville Chamberlain, made it plain that the Government would not countenance provision for the Duke of Windsor being made out of the Civil List voted annually for the upkeep of the monarchy. Nor did they wish an annual allowance to be paid by the King to the Duke of Windsor; in view of the Duke's failure to disclose the extent of his private fortune to his brother when he signed the agreement at Fort

Belvedere, the Government had also apparently advised the King that he was, therefore, not bound by the promise he had then made to pay the Duke £25,000 if no provision was made under the Civil List.

The King was upset by his brother's deviousness, but wrote a tactful letter the following day saying that he was 'very disturbed' that the Belvedere Agreement had become known and that it would probably cause trouble and force uncomfortable financial disclosures when the Civil List was discussed. People were still angry about the Abdication – 'a little sore with you for having given up being King'. He was, therefore, asking Monckton to go out and explain things and they hoped that a solution could be arrived at. Monckton had, in fact, written over a month before warning the Duke that there might be trouble over his Civil List pension and that opinion against him was hardening, but the Duke, even as King, had never understood the depth of feeling against his marriage or the hostility of the reaction to his Abdication, still less, isolated at Enzesfeld, his mail tactfully censored by his aides, did he understand it now. He turned angrily on his brother, writing on 21 February:

You now infer that I misled you . . . as to my private financial position. While naturally not mentioning what I have been able to save as Prince of Wales, I did tell you that I was very badly off, which indeed I am considering the position I shall have to maintain and what I have given up. . . . You now ask me to tell you what my private means are, but I prefer not to. . . .[12]

After discussing things with Monckton he offered to rent the King Sandringham and Balmoral for the same annual sum of £25,000 and to pay his quarter share of the pensions granted by his father. 'I am relying on you to honour your promise,' he concluded. It was on that visit that Monckton had the embarrassing task of conveying to the Duke that his telephone calls to his brother must stop, something which can hardly have improved his temper.

The King was by now extremely worried as to the implications for the royal family of a public airing of their finances, which would surely follow any controversy over a pension for the Duke of Windsor. He was being pressured by the Government not to abide by his promise to pay the Duke of Windsor an allowance because, if he made any such provision out of the money allotted to him under the Civil List, it would be deeply resented. The Government implication, as Warren Fisher had made clear, was that the huge capital sum the Duke had accumulated (£25 million in today's money) made it unnecessary, while the manner in which he had concealed it at the time released the King of any obligation to do so. The weight of public opinion was behind the Government; Pierson Dixon, returning on leave from the British Embassy in Ankara, spent five weeks in London in February and was surprised to find that opinion was 'almost unanimously against' the Duke of Windsor: 'few even in favour of a pension of £20,000 (what was promised by the Duke of York when he left). His services as Prince of Wales and his charm apparently forgotten entirely.' The King's solution to placate the Government was to scrap the Belvedere

Agreement until the Civil List had been passed and to draw up a new one later. The Duke refused to trust his brother, forwarding copies of his letters to his solicitor with the contemptuous comment that if published they 'would become world famous for their naivety'. He intended to hang on to the original agreement, he told Allen, and, if necessary, to use his inheritance of Balmoral and Sandringham as a 'stick'.

It has been widely assumed that the King treated the Duke of Windsor in a niggardly fashion over the financial arrangements between them, promising him an annuity of £25,000 a year and then meanly cutting it down to pay certain pensions. The Windsors, it is said, were forced to write their memoirs and various other articles for the press because they were short of money to finance their admittedly luxurious style of life. The comments of those who were intimately concerned in the affair do not bear out this view. Winston Churchill and Lloyd George appointed themselves the Duke's champions and were both involved in negotiations with Chamberlain, then still Chancellor of the Exchequer, in the spring of 1937 over the provision to be made for the Duke. Both Churchill's correspondence and his later comments reveal that he considered the arrangements to be perfectly satisfactory. Both Churchill and Lloyd George, as members of the parliamentary Civil List Committee which would draw up the provision to be made for members of the royal family in the new reign, were in a position to put pressure on the Government and the King if they thought the Duke of Windsor's interests required it. Lloyd George was a violent pro-Windsor, anti-Baldwin partisan. On 16 March, the day on which the King issued his official message on the Civil List setting the parliamentary procedure in motion, Lloyd George had dined at Buckingham Palace, his first meeting with the King and Queen since the Abdication. There he had a long conversation with the King and did not hesitate to tackle him on the question of 'the Duke of Windsor's salary', telling him 'quite bluntly that it would be wisdom to see that he got a generous allowance'. According to Frances Stevenson, Lloyd George's secretary/mistress and later wife, who recorded the occasion in her diary, the King 'cordially agreed with this sentiment, but when D. [Lloyd George] went on to ask him if the Duke had much money saved, he said he did not know what the position was. (This may indicate greater shrewdness than D. gives him credit for.)'[13]

On 24 March Churchill wrote two letters, one to Chamberlain, the other to the Duke of Windsor: the first requesting a meeting on behalf of himself and Lloyd George to discuss the Duke of Windsor's finances before the Civil List Committee met, and asking for private information on the Duke of Windsor's financial situation:

Baldwin mentioned to me that he possessed a large capital sum, which I gather is from £800–£950,000 – a large part of which was at one time settled on the lady, though I believe she has renounced all but £10,000 a year. Besides this I am aware that there is an agreement signed by the present King to pay the Duke £25,000 a year – I presume free of tax. However there has lately been some discussion about this, and meanwhile the

Duke has not yet made over to the King his life interest in Balmoral and Sandringham. Let me say at once that if the signed agreement holds good, that the £25,000 is free of tax, and if the capital sum is what I have been led to believe, these assets would in my opinion together constitute a satisfactory and proper provision.[14]

On the same day he wrote off to the Duke of Windsor, telling him that he and Lloyd George were on the Committee and anxious to see that proper provision was made for him, that he had seen Monckton, that if the Duke had any points to raise would he let him know, and that he hoped to receive 'assurances from the Chancellor of the Exchequer which will make it unnecessary for the matter even to be mentioned in the Civil List Committee, still less in the House of Commons'.[15] Both Churchill on behalf of the Duke of Windsor and Chamberlain on behalf of the King were anxious that there should be no public discussion of the royal family's private finances, but signs of trouble loomed at the first meeting of the Committee on 8 April, when Clement Attlee, leader of the Labour Party, asked for information about the private savings and fortunes of members of the royal family and Leo Amery unexpectedly raised the question of providing for the Duke of Windsor in the Civil List 'as the King's son'. Chamberlain and Baldwin were, according to Churchill, 'disconcerted and said nothing', and Churchill smoothed things over by suggesting that it would be premature to go into extensive discussion at such an early stage. Chamberlain later told Amery 'that opposition to any figure in the Estimate would be vocal in every quarter of the House, and would lead to enquiries into the late King's private fortune which he assured me is substantial, and that it is not true that he is heavily in debt'.[16] Characteristically Churchill took advantage of the threat posed by Attlee's and Amery's interventions to press home his side of the bargain. He wrote to Chamberlain later that day:

Attlee's question about the private fortunes of the Royal Family and Amery's unexpected reference to the Duke of Windsor's position, show how easily we might find ourselves immersed in awkward topics. The best solution would surely be that the King should honour his signature about the £25,000 a year and that the Duke of Windsor should intimate to you that he does not desire to make any request for provision in the Civil List. . . . This could then be stated in public.

If on the other hand a dispute arises about the annuity of £25,000 a year, and if the question about the provision for the Duke of Windsor is raised in the Committee, it seems to me that you will have no choice but to disclose the capital figure mentioned yesterday; and the moment this is disclosed the Labour Party could hardly help drawing the moral of the very large savings which it is possible for Royal persons to make, and to argue that the existing Civil List should be reduced. Thus it seems to me that the King's interest, no less than that of the Duke of Windsor, is directly involved in an amicable settlement of the kind outlined.

I should have thought it would not be a hardship for the King to pay the £25,000 on the assumption that the Civil List is voted at the figure now proposed by you. It is true that it is £36,000 less than the previous Civil List but on the other hand there is the £50,000 a year saving on account of the Duke of York. Thus there is a balance of £14,000, practically the £25,000 he promised to provide for his brother.

Pointing out that any dispute between the two brothers would be 'a disaster of the first order to the monarchy', he hinted that Chamberlain should put these points in his audience with the King that evening.[17]

Chamberlain's private comments on the two statesmen were less than flattering and revealed an extreme suspicion as to the validity of their motives. He told his sister, Hilda:

The Civil List Committee has now been set up and I don't believe that I should have any serious trouble with the Labour Party were it not for Lloyd George and Winston – These two pirates have (for their own purposes) constituted themselves the champions of the Duke versus the King and they are trying to blackmail the latter into regular swindling arrangements by threats of making trouble in Committee. ... I don't mean to let these bandits get away with it. ...[18]

Chamberlain, whose Non-conformist conscience had been shocked by the moral connotations of the Edward–Wallis affair and who shared none of Baldwin's sentimental regard for Edward, determined to set himself up as the defender of the new King and the new reign against the 'piratical' attempts of Churchill and Lloyd George. Armed with the powerful legal expertise of Sir John Simon (referred to by Windsor as 'Sir John Snake'), he went to the King 'to discuss the document he had signed with his brother'. As he suspected, he found it to be a document

showing signs of haste and strain. It was vague and contradictory and it was evident that it must be replaced by something more specific and carefully prepared. I hope the King will set about this soon as we are always liable to trouble in the Com.ee from Winston and Ll G who are hunting together. ...[19]

Wigram, too, was involved: 'I brought Clive Wigram back to town in my car ... I was able to clinch my arrangements with him on the way.'[20] Wigram and Chamberlain separately had interviews with Churchill and Lloyd George the following day and secured their agreement to avoid public discussion of the matter, as Churchill reported to the Duke of Windsor on 30 April, two days after the Civil List was voted in Parliament:

Last Monday I had a visit from Wigram who brought me privately the King's assurance about the financial affair, that 'I could be sure he would not let you down'. ... In consequence of this assurance, which I felt bound to accept, coming as it did directly from His Majesty, neither of us raised the matter on the Civil List Committee, and, as Your Royal Highness may have seen, the Committee has agreed upon its report on terms which seem to me very favourable to the new Sovereigns and their Family, and which certainly leave resources out of which the promised provision can be met. ...[21]

But Chamberlain still took the threat of public discussion of the royal family's finances seriously. Any revelations as to the size of the late monarch's personal fortune and to the amount of money which Edward, as Prince of Wales and Duke of Cornwall, had been able to salt away over the last twenty years would certainly lead to public trouble with the Labour Party over the Civil List and comment in the press. He hoped, he told his sister Hilda in one of the long, confidential letters which he was in the habit of writing to her and to his other sister, Ida, to reach a satisfactory agreement with Churchill and Lloyd George and thus get the Committee through 'without a discussion which would thoroughly discredit the Duke but would not fail at the same time to give another jolt to the Monarchy itself'.

The King himself, now within a month of the ordeal of his Coronation, was extremely anxious that nothing further should happen to shake the position of the monarchy. At the Civil List Committee meetings, Attlee made it quite clear that his party considered that the monarchy had been living in a style 'based upon conceptions of Kingship now out of date and of a society rigidly divided into social classes', that 'great and numerous residences, an army of attendants, a titled entourage and the habitual observance of elaborate ceremonial' were nowadays a hindrance to understanding between the monarchy and a society in transformation. He proposed that there should be a further period of consultation 'to ascertain how best to achieve such changes as would result in increased simplicity' and what provisions should be made from the consolidated fund for royal Household pensions, 'due regard being had to the position of the Duchies of Lancaster and Cornwall and the revenues therefrom'.[22]

The Civil List passed with no mention made of provision for the Duke of Windsor, but the private financial wrangling dragged on until February 1938 with disagreements over the valuation of Balmoral and Sandringham, threats by the Duke of Windsor to prevent the royal family from spending their summer holiday at Balmoral, and other points at issue between the brothers. In the end the King paid the Duke's allowance not from the Civil List, which, under the Act of 1911, had made this provision for the younger sons of King George v, but on interest due on the Crown valuation of Balmoral and Sandringham and from his own private funds from the Duchy of Lancaster.[23] Of the £25,000 originally agreed to, pensions amounting to £4,000 were to be deducted. This reduction, argued by Windsor partisans as evidence of the King's 'niggardly' treatment of his brother, was simply his share of the pensions paid by all the brothers, waived at Fort Belvedere and reintroduced by the Duke himself as a possibility in February. The Windsors' claims of poverty were hard to sustain; the extreme luxury of their life in France before the war with its conspicuous consumption in terms of clothes, jewels, antiques and servants, could only have been borne by a very, very rich man. Helen Hardinge, who, as the wife of Edward's former Private Secretary, was in a position to know, estimated his personal fortune at £1 million and his income at £60,000 annually. Marie Belloc Lowndes, whose sources of information on the royals were exceptionally good, estimated his income in 1939 at £80,000. A typed note in the Beaverbrook archives records that Churchill told Beaverbrook on 20 August 1949 'that D[uke] has income of £100,000 a year from England the charge on the Royal properties and so on, which he collects free of tax....'[24]

It is, therefore, hard to see how the Duke of Windsor can claim to have been shabbily treated. The royal properties were independently valued by experts. In

November 1937 the value of the farms at Sandringham was put at £104,475 at twenty-one years' purchase, a figure to which the King's advisers had agreed, although not necessarily at twenty-one years – 'maybe 22 or even 24 or 25'.[25] As far as reducing the amount to cover pensions for which the Duke of Windsor was liable, it does not seem unjustified. The King continued, for instance, to pay a huge Annual Subscriptions List, which included those of the Duke of Windsor as Prince of Wales.[26] In fact, George VI out of his own pocket paid pensions which morally the Duke of Windsor ought to have paid, among them the ex-King's old friend, 'G' Trotter, who served him for fourteen years from 1921 to 1936 and was then dropped because Wallis did not like him. 'He cast him off,' Lascelles told Bruce Lockhart; 'He did nothing for him, and in the end the old man had to take a job as a shop-walker. . . . Do you know who is paying his widow's pension now? Not the Duke of Windsor, but George VI.'[27] Nor did the Duke do anything for his favourite private detective, Chief Inspector David Storrier, who died in his service and left a widow. The discussion with Lascelles arose when Bruce Lockhart told him that people supposed that the Duke of Windsor was hard up for money because he wrote articles for the newspapers. 'He became quietly indignant,' Bruce Lockhart recorded; '"if you knew what that man had taken out of the country, you would know that he did not need money. . . ."' As early as October 1937 American papers started the rumour that he had been 'jockeyed out of his private fortune'. Dawson of *The Times*, writing to his Washington correspondent Willmott Lewis, said that this was 'almost comically wide of the mark. In that respect at all events he has done very well for himself. . . .'[28]

Sir John Wheeler-Bennett, charged with the delicate task of writing George VI's official biography, found the question of the financial settlement between the two brothers particularly difficult, but not because he would have to defend the King against charges of niggardly treatment of his brother. Bruce Lockhart wrote:

As regards Edward VIII Jack [Wheeler-Bennett] will have to write how, as Duke of Windsor, Edward was inveterately greedy of money and made great demands on his brother, King George VI – demands which the King fulfilled at considerable sacrifice to himself. Jack will have to tell how insistent the Duke was on his demands and how little gratitude he showed when his extravagance was paid for by the King. . . .'[29]

In the end, Wheeler-Bennett, or the royal family, preferred to maintain their policy of silence on the Duke of Windsor and his affairs.

With the King under increasing strain in the run-up to his Coronation, the problems created by his brother loomed very large, among them questions arising from his forthcoming marriage to Wallis after her decree nisi was to be made absolute on 27 April. Wallis was, not unnaturally, concerned that it should be conducted with 'dignity' and gain them the 'sympathy' of the world, something which, since she was in the habit of opening all the hate mail which the Duke was not allowed to see, she was anxious to win over. Wallis craved royal recognition, the one thing which the family was determined not to grant her. She wanted the King's help to avert any trouble with the King's Proctor over the divorce, and for him to give the lead in stemming the current rumours (which were true) that the royal family hated her. She wanted her wedding to be a royal occasion, graced by members of her husband's family, and she wanted to be admitted to membership of the royal family with the granting of the title of Royal Highness upon her marriage. She wanted, too, for the King to use his influence with the Church to produce a bishop to marry them, despite the Church's ruling against divorce. 'If there was one decent bishop your brother should send him to marry us. If not why play with the Church of England? Let's have something else ...', she wrote on 6 February;[30] any religion, it appeared, would do.

In February the King offered the choice of place for the Windsors' wedding between the Château de la Cröe, a lavish villa on the Riviera on Cap d'Antibes, the property of an English magnate named Sir Pomeroy Burton, and the Château de Candé, a Renaissance château in Touraine owned by Charles Bedaux. The Duke indicated his preference for the second, as offering more dignified-sounding surroundings than the Riviera with its café society connotations. Nobody either in the Windsor entourage or at Buckingham Palace bothered to check up on Bedaux, a self-made millionaire with shady connections, whose relationship with the Windsors was to prove disastrous for them and for Bedaux himself. Early in March Wallis took the decision that for practical reasons they should not be married before the Coronation. Everyone's attention would be on the Coronation, she wrote, and 'from the press point of view we would not be properly handled', but once that was over 'they will turn their attention to you'. There was certainly a sense of competing events: '... we have time to watch the other event and make ours perfect. We shall lose trying to do it beforehand and it puts the cards across the channel.'[31] At that time it was still not clear to the Duke of Windsor that his family did not intend to attend his wedding, since on 22 March Wallis wrote to Aunt Bessie that 'George VI has suggested June 4th as a convenient time for him to send a member [of the family] to the wedding.' By the end of the month, having heard nothing further, Wallis appears to have been getting angry with the King, writing to Edward on the 31st of 'your wretched brother' and suggesting the content of the 'straightforward' letter which they were planning Edward should write to the King:

... put in the letter that if he continues to treat you as though you were an outcast from the family and had done something disgraceful and continues to take advice from people who dislike you ... that there would be only one course open to you and that would be to let the world know exactly the treatment you were receiving from the people (family) you had placed in their present position ... you did not expect your brother to slip into your shoes and forget you completely not giving even any small help in the remaking of your life. ... Don't be weak, don't be rude, be firm and make him ashamed of himself – if possible ... 4 months of filthy treatment – rub it in – & the advisers.[32]

The King had no doubt been too busy to consider the question of 'decent bishops' attending the wedding or even whether the royal family should do so, but clearly when he consulted the ecclesiastical authorities on the question he was reminded of his position as head of the Church and the Church's current ruling on the remarriage of divorced persons. In fact, the following month Dr Henson, Bishop of Durham, told Churchill that Mrs Simpson's divorce from her first husband (for incompatibility of temper) was not recognized as a divorce by the Church of England and that a marriage with the Duke of Windsor would, therefore, be doubly bigamous. In April Walter Monckton, entrusted with the delicate task of finding a suitable clergyman to celebrate the Windsor marriage, called at Lambeth where Don reminded him of the recent resolution passed in all four houses of Convocation 'deprecating the use of the Marriage Service in the case of all persons who have a former partner living', which seemed to rule out any clergyman of the Church of England. 'Whether Walter Monckton can prevail on the couple to abandon the idea of a religious ceremony remains to be seen,' Don wrote. 'He is shortly going to see the Duke and will do his best to persuade him to do nothing to raise fresh storms and difficulties but he says that the Duke is the most obstinate man he ever met and, in order to meet Mrs S's wishes for a "dignified" ceremony, may prove troublesome.'[33] When, therefore, Monckton consulted the King about it at Windsor a week later, the King informed him of his decision that no member of the royal family would attend the ceremony and that none of the King's chaplains should officiate.[34]

The King's decision was rightly interpreted by Wallis as meaning she had nothing more to hope from him in making her wedding 'dignified'. As far as she, and therefore the Duke, were concerned, it was now open war. '... now we must protect WE and as we have been turned adrift we have an excellent chance. How stupid two camps. Well who cares let him be pushed off the throne. The minute the family split – danger,' she wrote to the Duke on 21 April.[35] The Duke now sent off the letter to his brother, whom they referred to as 'Mr Temple' (i.e. father of Princess Elizabeth = Shirley Temple, the child star), embodying, as the Duke put it to Wallis, 'all your points which are flawless'. It was a letter which they had been planning to send but now, when they had apparently nothing left to hope for, was the 'spycological [*sic*] moment'. The letter was despatched by messenger from Enzesfeld on 14 April; its contents have not been revealed, but the King's reaction to it may be gauged from his outpouring to Anthony Eden at Windsor a few days later. On 21 April Eden's friend and Secretary at the Foreign Office, Oliver Harvey, noted in an unpublished section of his diary:

AE had been to Windsor for the night and found King much incensed against the Duke of Windsor who was trying to get more money out of him, although he had gone off with something near a million £! When he abdicated it had not been known that he had this sum representing apparently savings in his private account and King George had undertaken to get him a parliamentary grant or to make him an allowance. When this

had been discovered, there was great indignation and it was felt that Edward had put in
some very sharp practice. These savings out of the Prince of Wales's revenues would
normally be used by the King when he came to the throne, and of course this King is
deprived of these into the bargain [i.e. Edward VIII had not only removed revenue which
would normally have been used by the King when he came to the throne, but had also
given a large part of it to Wallis]. Incidentally Edward has already settled the larger part
of the interest on this sum on Mrs Simpson.

There was also indignation over Edward's wish to make Mrs S HRH when they marry
as King George feels that he cannot expect his subjects to curtsey to her. It appears,
however, that according to Sir J. Simon as the D. of Windsor is HRH, the moment she
marries him she must become HRH automatically and there is no stopping it except by
special Act of Parliament.

Finally the D of W wishes to come back again and this King George is most anxious
to prevent as although he is sure his brother would not want to intrigue he feels certain
she would make him....[36]

The King was torn by these private conflicts between his responsibility as
King–Emperor and his private feelings for his brother, whom – as distinct from
Wallis Simpson – he still loved. Wallis, in fact, had sometimes in her letters
taunted the Duke of Windsor about his belief in the King's continuing affection
for him – 'if he is as fond of you as you say he is'. On 18 May, the King was to
write to Churchill thanking him for 'your very nice letter to me' at the conclusion
of the Civil List negotiations and expressly for what he had done for his brother:
'I know how devoted you have been, & still are, to my dear brother, & I feel
touched beyond words by your sympathy & understanding in the very difficult
problems that have arisen since he left us in December....'[37] He was trying to
do his best for his kingdom, his family and his brother in that order and it was
an impossible task. In the month of May, the month of his Coronation, the
question of Wallis's title after her marriage to his brother became acute. Wallis's
decree absolute was due to be granted on 27 April and to be made public on 3
May. On 8 May the date of their wedding was announced; it was not to be 4
June, as apparently the King had suggested, but 3 June, which, being King
George V's birthday, seemed to the royal family an additional affront. On the
same day Wallis by deed-poll reverted to her maiden name of Warfield.

On 3 May, the day the decree absolute was read out in court, Baldwin, who
was due to retire as Prime Minister at the end of the month, had an interview
with the King in the course of which King George told him firmly that he did
not wish Wallis Simpson to be made 'royal' and, therefore, a member of the
royal family upon her marriage. Baldwin replied that from his knowledge of the
Duke of Windsor this would 'greatly annoy' him. The King, however, persisted,
and on the following day wrote a letter to the Prime Minister in which he made
the grounds for his views quite clear. He had, he said, thought a great deal
about the question and to him it seemed that the most important point to be
considered was whether she was a fit and proper person to become a Royal
Highness after what she had done in this country and whether the country

would understand it if she automatically became one on her marriage. He reminded Baldwin that 'in our family' once a person became a Royal Highness they remained so for life whatever happened and that, therefore, in his view and that of all his family, it would be a great mistake to acknowledge Mrs Simpson as a suitable person to become royal.[38]

Baldwin promised the King that he would, as he had over the morganatic marriage proposal, consult the Dominion Prime Ministers as to whether they were in agreement with the Letters Patent in the form which the King wished, i.e. to confirm or restore the Duke of Windsor in his royal rank while specifically excluding his wife or any heirs they might have. Baldwin, however, was congenitally indisposed to undertake any unpopular action and, after having unwillingly but successfully dealt with the ex-King during the Abdication crisis, he was extremely unwilling to enter virtually the same arena again within a few weeks of his retirement. Although he had told the King on 3 May that he would speak to Chamberlain about it, he procrastinated as Chamberlain's diary for 23 May indicated:

I am much vexed by SB's behaviour. The King wants to issue Letters Patent which would prevent Mrs Simpson becoming a Royal Highness. SB doesn't like the idea which he thinks would greatly annoy the D. of Windsor but he is shirking responsibility and trying to put it on me. He promised to sound out the Dominion Ministers but did not do so and told Simon he wanted me to do it. I did it yesterday and they were unanimously in favour of the Letters Patent.[39]

The King's letter and the Dominions' decision were of key importance. It was in many ways a re-run of the Abdication procedure, only that in this case it was the King's initiative and his interpretation of the question which prevailed. The King's decision not to grant Wallis the title of Royal Highness, which would normally have followed upon marriage to a person of royal rank, was to cause a permanent split between himself and his brother. It was, however, one which he never regretted and refused to reconsider; when the Duke brought it up for the last time over ten years later, he replied with a phrase which was extremely significant. To do so, he wrote, 'would not make sense of the past'.

In taking this decision the King was, as is apparent from what Eden told Harvey, going against the legal opinion of one of the sharpest minds in the country, that of Sir John Simon. Most experts argued that, although the Duke of Windsor in abdicating had given up his rights to the succession, his rank of Royal Highness as the King's son was an inalienable birthright already established by Letters Patent of 1917, which had not been revoked and could not, therefore, be 'restored' by Letters Patent of 1937, as the King argued. Stemming from this inalienable birthright was the generally accepted rule that on marriage a wife takes the rank and status of her husband. The King, however, took the view that ultimately legal opinion was irrelevant since his power to act in this way was justified by his position as Fount of Honour, an opinion in which he was later supported by a Labour Lord Chancellor, Lord Jowitt (who had changed his mind on the question since advising the Duke to the contrary in 1937). Moreover, in his view, the Duke in renouncing the succession had also renounced his royal rank and, therefore, that of his wife. In these Letters Patent of 1937 he proposed to 'restore' the Duke's royal rank but specifically to exclude his wife from sharing it. In abdicating, the King argued, the Duke had accepted the expressed view of the people of Britain and the Empire that Mrs Simpson was unfit to be Queen and, therefore, equally unfit to be a member of the royal family. That was, in effect, what the Abdication had been about. To reverse the decision by making Wallis a member of the royal family contrary to publicly expressed opinion would be neither logical nor right. In this view that the people would not understand or accept such a promotion for Wallis he was backed up not only by the Dominion Prime Ministers, but by the Duke's principal English supporter, Churchill. Just over a week before the King had his interview with Baldwin, Wigram had consulted Churchill on this very point. A memorandum among the Churchill Papers entitled 'note of remarks to Lord Wigram', dated 25 April, sets out his views on this as on other points at issue between the royal brothers. 'I do not think that any Government will be found in England which would advise the Crown to take such a step [i.e. the granting of the rank of Royal Highness to the Duchess of Windsor on her marriage]. On the contrary I am sure that they would advise insistently against it. . . .'[40]

The Letters Patent under the Great Seal published on 28 May 1937 therefore declared 'that the Duke of Windsor shall, notwithstanding his act of Abdication . . . be entitled to hold and enjoy for himself only the title, style or attribute of Royal Highness, so however that his wife and descendants, if any, shall not hold the said title or attribute'. The King did not need Baldwin to tell him that this decision would 'greatly annoy' his brother. Handing Monckton the letter conveying it to the Duke, he said wryly, 'this is a nice wedding present'. In Chamberlain's first audience with the King as Prime Minister on 30 May, it was clear that the King was concerned about the effect of the Letters Patent upon his brother when they discussed, according to Chamberlain's diary, 'his troubles with his brother, the wedding and the Letters Patent'. 'The King', Chamberlain added, 'evidently found it a great relief to be able to tell his brother that so far from taking anything away what he had done was to give him a title from which he would otherwise be debarred when he ceased to be in the line of succession.'[41]

The news of his brother's decision burst like a bombshell upon the Duke of Windsor at Candé on the eve of his wedding. Although Wallis herself had repeatedly warned him from the first days of his departure from England that the King would not make her an HRH, to the Duke it was the final slap in the face from his family. He was never able to comprehend his family's attitude to Wallis nor the depths of pain which the Abdication had caused them. Mountbatten, after a visit to them later that year, reported to Harold Nicolson that 'the Duke is still completely unable to comprehend why it is that everybody including Queen Mary did not welcome Mrs Simpson'. Over ten years later, explaining his continued determination to stick by his decision, the King was to recall the great anguish and suffering the Abdication and the resulting estrangement had caused him, something, he wrote, which the Duke had never seemed to understand.[42] The Duke, as always, had thought only of Wallis throughout the crisis. Writing to Wallis's Aunt Bessie on 22 December 1936, he told her that the experiences Wallis had been going through had been 'ghastly' and 'That thought as you know was the only one that really worried me.'

The Duke of Windsor apparently did not initially blame his brother for the decision. Rather pathetically, he simply could not bring himself to believe that 'Bertie' could do such a thing to him. According to Wallis, he exclaimed, 'I know Bertie. I know he couldn't have written this letter on his own. Why in God's name would they do this to me at this time!' Who then did he mean by 'they'? Twenty years later he blamed principally Sir John Simon, whom he accused of writing it 'probably with the help of someone in the Palace secretariat [i.e. Hardinge or Lascelles] and God knows who else. . . .' While Sir John Simon may well have helped draft the Letters Patent as, indeed, he had the Abdication Bill, it is clear from the Eden evidence that he advised the King that what he was doing had no basis in law. Moreover, the Home Secretary would certainly not have taken the initiative over this, which was, after all, primarily a royal family matter. The Duke of Windsor's line after his abdication was always to present 'Bertie' as a cypher without a mind or will of his own. 'My brother just took a piece of paper that was handed to him and copied it. It was not an idea he'd have thought of himself,' he went on. Other people, notably Monckton, always anxious to be charitable and fair to both brothers, followed Edward in this line.' 'If the King had been left to himself', he said, 'I feel confident that he would not have assented to this course because he knew the effect he would have on his brother.'[43] Their inference was that the King was unduly influenced in this matter by the undoubted hostility of the Palace secretariat – Wigram, Hardinge and Lascelles – and of certain members of the Government, presumably Chamberlain. The evidence does not bear this out.

The Duke, as usual, was underestimating his brother when he said, 'It was not an idea he'd have thought of himself.' It was exactly the sort of point which the King, with his legitimist outlook and interest in questions of title, would be capable of thinking out himself. He had, after all, at the time of the discussions over the Duke's own title, shown himself more *au fait* with the constitutional implications than the experts from the Lord Chancellor's Office, and it had been he, not they, who had pointed out the dangers implicit in not granting his brother a royal dukedom. His letter to Baldwin of 5 May, and Chamberlain's subsequent comment about the Letters Patent, show the King as taking the initiative against Simon's and Baldwin's advice. Certainly it was a decision which he would have taken in consultation with his family; as he told Baldwin, the feeling of 'I and my family and Queen Mary' had been that it would be a great mistake to acknowledge Mrs Simpson as a suitable candidate for royal rank. Wallis always liked to depict the King as 'run' by the royal ladies, which was ironical in view of their similar feelings about herself and the Duke. 'York guided by her [Queen Mary] would not give us the extra chic of creating me an HRH,' she had written in December, while in February she blamed the King's neglect of his brother on 'the wife who hates us both'. Later she liked to wisecrack that the British monarchy was 'a matriarchy in pants': 'The King's wife runs the King and the King's mother runs the King's wife.' The theme of the dim, dull, weak, hen-pecked 'Bertie' runs through both the Windsors' memoirs and was, indeed, freely expressed by them in conversation when presenting the Duke as so much better an occupant of the throne.

From the moment that the King denied Wallis the title of HRH, the situation became, as Wallis put it, 'two camps', with open competition and publicity-seeking on the Windsor side, and increasing dismay and suspicion on the part of the King. Indeed, the 'two camps' aspect was emphasized and the social world divided into those who curtseyed and bowed to the Duchess of Windsor as if she were a Royal Highness and those who refused to do so. The Duke of Windsor made it clear from the start that he wished his wife to be treated in accordance with his rank, even by close friends or old acquaintances. When Countess Munster, owner of Wasserleonburg, the castle in Austria which the Windsors rented for their honeymoon after leaving Candé, was there to greet them when they arrived, she said, 'Wallis, how well you're looking.' There was a cold glare from the Duke. 'The Duchess, you mean,' he corrected her. Dining at Somerset Maugham's villa in the South of France, whose house-guests in-cluded such friends as Harold Nicolson, he deliberately referred to Wallis as 'Her Royal Highness'. As usual in the social world, people's reactions were minutely noted and fears of their repercussions exaggerated. Diana Cooper, reported as having curtseyed 'very low' to the Duchess of Windsor on meeting her in Paris, was subsequently panic-stricken when not invited to a ball at Windsor. Was it, she asked her friends, because she had curtseyed to Wallis or because Duff was no longer a minister? The new American Ambassador to the Court of St James's, Joseph P. Kennedy, who regarded himself as a particular friend of the royal family, ordered his wife Rose if possible not to accept the US Ambassador William C. Bullitt's invitation to dinner in Paris for the Windsors when she happened to be there on her own, and if she did so on no account to curtsey, 'because we're in with the other lot'.[44]

One aspect of the 'two camps' situation which had now developed between himself and the Windsors did cause the King anxiety. As he had confessed to Eden in April, he knew that the Duke of Windsor wished to return to England, which he was 'most anxious to prevent as although he is sure his brother would not want to intrigue he feels certain she would make him'. The truth was that the King, despite all the evidence of his and the Queen's popularity, was still unsure of himself. He felt, as he had told Mrs Baldwin, that he needed time to develop his capabilities for his new job and he now clung to the fact that his brother, or Monckton on his behalf, had at the time of the Abdication, prom-ised that he would not return to England for two years.

It seems probable that the King's raising of the subject with Eden on 21 April was a direct result of the 'straightforward' letter he had received from his brother under instruction from Wallis on 14 or 15 April, and that among her 'flawless points' was an express statement of their intention of returning to England. To add to the King's distress, the Kents, apparently, were backing the Duke's return and 'were also being tiresome'. When the King asked Eden for his advice on this, Eden told him that 'he should take a very firm line'. Indeed, the Government reaction seems to have been much the same as the King's, for five days after the Eden interview Churchill, in his already quoted memorandum to Wigram, repudiated a suggestion that the Government should revive a proposal of Hardinge's made at the time of the Abdication that the Duke of Windsor should promise not to return to England within a stated period of time in return for his pension, and that this should be inserted into the private financial settlement between the King and his brother in the form of a clause requiring the Duke of Windsor to promise not to return to England without the King's permission. This ministerial advice had, apparently, gone too far for the King, who, although anxious about the prospect of his brother's premature return, would have seen the suggestion as dishonourable. 'Moncton [*sic*] showed me your Royal Highnesses' correspondence with the King,' Churchill wrote to the Duke of Windsor on 30 April, 'and I was very sorry that the Ministerial advice had caused both you and the King so much distress. It is painful to see how much hard feeling there is in some quarters....'[45]

Churchill's objections to the proposal were put to Wigram in the strongest terms:

I understood that the allowance, apart from certain business elements, was a matter of family affection arising out of the King's promise to the Duke before the latter's abdication. It is altogether a personal and brotherly affair. It would not be right for Ministers to advise the King to make the payment of this allowance contingent upon the Duke not returning to England without the King's permission. Such advice would tend to involve the King in what might become very distressing publicity. Above all Ministers should not advise that such a condition should be presented to the Duke through the lawyers. The Duke would have no option but to refuse to receive such a communication; for otherwise he would put himself in the position of bartering his right to his native land for pecuniary advantage....

It was stated to Parliament by the Attorney-General during the passage of the Abdication Bill that no condition of exile followed voluntary abdication. As this declaration preceded the abdication, it must stand as a formal and solemn pledge both to Parliament and to the late King....

Churchill, however, stressed that although he deplored the ministerial initiative, he too was against the Duke of Windsor's early return: '... far from advising the Duke to return at the present time, I would urge him most strongly to allow several years to pass before taking up his residence in England.' In his opinion, 'The great and growing popularity' of the King and Queen would soon make the thought of competition between King and ex-King no longer a factor, and then the conditions for the Duke's return would be more favourable.[46]

In the summer of 1937, however, 'the thought of competition' undoubtedly existed in the mind of the King, the Government, the press and the Windsors themselves. On 3 June at the Château de Candé, the protagonists of what Churchill called 'one of the great loves of history' celebrated their wedding. The occasion, the finale of a tragi-comedy which had shaken the British Empire, was something of an anti-climax. Lady Alexandra Metcalfe, a guest at Candé for the wedding at which her husband Fruity was to be best man, wrote that, but for the press hordes at the gate, 'one might be attending the wedding of any ordinary couple'. '... try with all one's might & main when looking at her one can't register that she can be the cause of the whole unbelievable story. One almost begins to think there is nothing incredible, unique or tragic about it as they are so blind to it all.'[47] Wallis had done her best to make the occasion chic, if it could not be splendid. She was dressed by Mainbocher in long, ice-blue crêpe satin, with a tight, long-sleeved jacket with tiny buttons, a halo straw hat with tulle and, as everyone remarked, a magnificent sapphire and diamond bracelet. The flowers were done by Constance Spry and Cecil Beaton was there to take photographs for *Vogue*. There was even a clergyman, the Rev. R.A. Jardine of Darlington, who had volunteered his services, but who sadly later turned out to be a publicity-seeker making capital from the Windsor connection. Only seven English people attended the wedding of the man who six months earlier had been the idolized King–Emperor, and only the bridegroom's obvious emotion and simple dignified manner gave what Lady Alexandra Metcalfe called 'the sad little service' the dignity Wallis had longed for. The love, it seemed to observers, was noticeably one-sided. 'If she occasionally showed a glimmer of softness, took his arm, looked at him as though she loved him one would warm towards her, but her attitude is so correct,' she wrote. 'The effect is of a woman unmoved by the infatuated love of a younger man....'[48] Cecil Beaton, too, felt the lack of romance. Wallis, he thought, was 'today especially unlovable, hard and calculating and showing an anxiety but no feeling of emotion'. Her face, he noted, had broken out in spots and she was not looking her best. Prince Charming, too, faded under the photographer's professional scrutiny:

His expression though intent was essentially sad. Tragic eyes belied by impertinent tilt of nose. He has common hands, like a little mechanic's, weather-beaten and rather scaly and one thumb nail is disfigured. His hair at forty-five [in fact, forty-three] is as golden and thick as it was at sixteen, his eyes fierce blue do not seem to focus properly, are bleary in spite of their brightness and one is much lower than another. Whether or not he will be pleased with my photographs I cannot tell for they will not be flattering to him, accustomed to highly retouched pictures taken many years ago....[49]

After the ceremony Monckton took the new Duchess aside and warned her that this was a marriage that must not fail:

I told her that most people in England disliked her very much because the Duke had married her and given up his throne, but that if she made him, and kept him, happy all his day, all that would change; but that if he were unhappy nothing would be too bad for her. She took it all very simply and kindly, just saying: 'Walter, don't you think I have thought of all that? I think I can make him happy.'

Wallis kept her side of the bargain; from the Duke's point of view it was to be the perfect marriage.

The King carried out his duties that Coronation summer with his brother still very much on his mind. The Windsors had retired to Wasserleonburg for a protracted honeymoon, but the King was not allowed to forget them. Reports of the first Garter Service which he held as King at St George's Chapel, Windsor, on 14 June, a ceremony which meant a great deal to him, showed some sections of the press only too keen to bring the Duke of Windsor to the fore, some devoting their coverage 'mainly to the absence of the Duke of Windsor' and their photographs showing the accidental fall of a member of the escort. In Wigram's view some of them 'used the occasion as propaganda for the Duke of Windsor'.[50] In July there were acrimonious exchanges over the financial settlement, which was still not finalized.

The prospect of the Windsors' marriage raised the question of the official attitude to be taken towards the Duke and Duchess of Windsor by His Majesty's diplomatic representatives. Prompted by the imminent publication of Wallis's decree absolute and the subsequent emergence of the Duke from his Austrian exile, the two Ambassadors most nearly affected, Sir Eric Phipps in Paris and Sir Walford Selby in Vienna, had applied to the Palace for guidance from the King as to 'what attitude to adopt to the Duke and Duchess of Windsor after their marriage, what His Majesty's wishes were regarding their entertainment, either official or private, or their participation in official ceremonies of any kind'.[51] There were, after all, no British precedents for dealing with a voluntary ex-King. On 1 May Hardinge, on the King's behalf, forwarded their queries to the Foreign Office. 'The King realises the problem may face representatives at short notice and therefore they should be instructed in advance,' he wrote to Sir Robert Vansittart. His Majesty wished the Foreign Office to submit their suggestions. Three days later Vansittart, having consulted Eden, replied cautiously, virtually passing the buck back to the Palace. In the case of official receptions when the Windsors' were present in a foreign capital, Vansittart wrote, HM representatives should seek special instructions as to whether they should be invited, and in the case of private functions the representatives should take their own decisions with the option of asking for advice.

What I think we ought to avoid, if we can, is a situation in which the Duke might ask an Ambassador or representative to put him and his wife up for a visit .... Misconceptions might be created if [the representative] did, particularly if any interviews or contact with political personages took place during the stay....

As a general line Eden feels that a representative should treat the Duke of Windsor and his wife rather as they would a member of the Royal Family on a holiday, but that if anything were contemplated which might give to the visit a more serious aspect, our representatives must necessarily refer home.

Since Eden was aware from his visit to Windsor that the royal family had not been pleased by what they considered Sir Walford Selby's over-friendly attitude towards the Duke of Windsor while he was in Austria, he was determined that the final decision should come from the Palace.[52] The King did not reply to this missive for four months; Hardinge was later to give as a reason for the delay the fact that the question of whether or not the Duchess of Windsor should be a Royal Highness had not been settled at that time. Since, however, the Letters Patent were published on 28 May, some reply might have been expected to follow not long after. That it did not do so indicates that the King regarded this as an important question which he would prefer to consider at leisure, a leisure which the frenetic pace of the Coronation summer with its public and private functions and State visits did not permit. He also, no doubt, found it a painful and embarrassing problem with which he would prefer not to have to deal.

By the time the King and Queen finally reached Balmoral on 30 August, the need for a decision had become acute, at least as far as Phipps and Sir Geoffrey Knox in Budapest, both facing imminent visits by the Windsors, were concerned. On 31 August Vansittart wrote to Hardinge at Balmoral pressing him for an answer[53] and, on 2 September, Hardinge relayed the King's considered opinion at length:

The most important point, in HM's opinion, is that HRH the Duke of Windsor and the Duchess should not be treated by HM's representatives as having any official status in the countries which they visit. For this reason it seems to the King that, except under special instructions, HM's representatives should not have any hand in arranging official interviews for them or countenance their participation in any official ceremonies.

Private entertaining, on the other hand, should be left to the discretion of the representative on the spot, subject to the limitation that the Duke and Duchess should not be invited to stay as guests in the Embassy or Legation concerned.

HM takes it that in the ordinary course the Duke will inform HM's representative that he will arrive in the country or in the capital on a certain date. The usual safety measures should automatically be put into operation. A member of the Embassy staff, other than the Ambassador or Minister, should meet HRH at the station, & it should be ascertained if HRH & the Duchess would wish to be entertained at the Embassy in an absolutely private & informal way. Should this be desired care should be taken in the invitation of guests as the Duchess of Windsor should be placed on the right of HM's representative on every occasion. . . .

Again, if the Head of State asks what attitude he should adopt, he should be told that there is no objection to his issuing a purely private & unofficial invitation to the Duke and Duchess should he wish to do so, but that anything of an official nature should be avoided. If any invitation to an official ceremony were contemplated, HM representatives should refer home for instructions. . . .[54]

These instructions have been put forward as examples of extraordinary pettiness on the part of the King, but they were more or less in line with Eden's suggestion in May as to treating the Windsors as if they were 'members of the Royal Family on holiday'. In the King's view, since the Duke of Windsor had no official position and would, therefore, not be on an official visit to any foreign capital, the Eden line was the correct one. The instruction that many of his diplomatic representatives found hard and, in cases where they were friends of the Duke's, downright embarrassing, was that no official of the first rank should meet the Duke on arrival. The King, however, stressed that the most important point was that the Windsors 'should not be treated by HM's representatives as having any official status in the countries which they visit': the preliminary protocol of meeting on arrival should, therefore, be in line with the others. The King's instructions to his diplomatic representatives were soon seen to have an extremely acute relevance and to have been based on a shrewd understanding of his brother's character. He knew that his brother could not long resist the temptation to step back into the limelight.

On 29 September a copy of a telegram sent by Sir Walford Selby in Vienna caused as much consternation at Balmoral as the original had at the Foreign Office. Selby had just received a letter dated 20 September from the Duke of Windsor informing him that he intended visiting Germany 'in order to see what is being done to improve the living and working conditions of the labouring classes in several large cities', the visit to commence from 11 October.[55] On the same date, Victor Mallet, temporary head of the British Embassy in Washington in the absence on leave in England of the Ambassador, Sir Ronald Lindsay, telegraphed Vansittart asking him to pass on to Lindsay the information that he had just opened a letter addressed to Lindsay by the Duke of Windsor, with the same date and containing much the same language as that addressed to Selby, only this time the Windsors' destination was to be the United States where they intended to arrive on 6 November. Eden and the Prime Minister were outraged and their opinions forwarded by Vansittart to Hardinge for the King's perusal. Vansittart, rabidly anti-German, scribbled a postscript to Hardinge on 1 October:

Personally, I think these tours, prearranged without a word to us, are a bit too much. And I hope our minions abroad will be instructed to have as little as possible to do with them. If we are expected to assist we are entitled to be consulted and to have a chance of dissuasion. The direct approach to our minions, without our knowledge, is hardly fair.[56]

Hardinge replied: 'I entirely agree with what you say about these tours, & I feel strongly that nothing should be done to make them appear other than what they are i.e. private stunts for publicity purposes – they can obviously bring no benefits to the workers themselves.'[57]

Every piece of information filtering through the Foreign Office to Balmoral made the projected tours sound worse. Sir George Ogilvie-Forbes, in charge at the Berlin Embassy and a friend of the Duke's, discovered that an embarrassed

German Foreign Office knew nothing of the Windsors' visit and that it had been arranged through a private approach to Hitler, who had welcomed the idea and put the notorious Dr Ley, Chief of the (Nazi) Labour Front, in charge of it. From Paris Phipps warned that the Duchess had told him they would be entertained by Hitler[58] and, further, that he had heard reports from François-Poncet of the excitement of the top Nazis over the visit:

François-Poncet says that Ribbentrop has been displaying feverish activity over the trip to Germany of the Duke of Windsor; he declares that Ribbentrop believes HRH will some day have a great influence over the British working man & that every effort will be made during the visit to make HRH even more pro-German than he is already supposed in Germany to be....[59]

From Balmoral on 6 October Hardinge, on behalf of the King and following suggestions from Vansittart,[60] sent instructions to Ogilvie-Forbes that only an official junior to himself should be present at the Windsors' arrival, that members of the Embassy should not accept invitations 'from whatever source' connected with the tour, have no part in arranging any official engagements or interviews and do no private entertaining on the Windsors' behalf, although 'individual member (i.e. Ogilvie-Forbes himself) might accept the Duke's invitations'.[61]

Furthermore the King, through the Foreign Office, now knew that the organizer of these tours was Charles Bedaux, the Windsors' host at the Château de Candé. In fact, as early as 14 September, Victor Mallet in Washington had picked up through a friend in the State Department the information, which he passed on to the Foreign Office, that Bedaux had recently visited a US Legation concerning a trip to the United States which the Duke of Windsor was to make 'to investigate working-class conditions'.[62] Bedaux was a buccaneering character of considerable personal charm who had once joined the Foreign Legion, emigrated to America at the age of twenty, and achieved fame and fortune through his invention of the Bedaux system, a form of time and motion study for industry which the American Congress of Industrial Organization dubbed 'one of the most completely exhausting, inhuman "efficiency" systems ever invented'. By the time he met the Windsors, Bedaux had established a glittering list of American client firms and was intent on establishing himself in Europe and the Far East. His efforts to restore his German company, suppressed by the Nazis in 1933, had led him into various intrigues and was only finally achieved by the means of large bribes, principally to the revolting Dr Ley. It can reasonably be assumed that one of Bedaux's motives in promoting the Windsor tour in both Germany and the United States would have been to gain commercial advantage by their reflected prestige. There is no evidence as to whether or not the Duke of Windsor knew any of this at the time; he was fascinated by Bedaux, as very rich men who have never earned a penny in their lives are often intrigued by self-made men. All that he, and the King, certainly did know in September 1937, was that Bedaux had strong Nazi connections and that the trip was to be undertaken under the aegis of Ley (described by Count Galeazzo Ciano,

Mussolini's son-in-law, and the Italian Foreign Minister, as a 'drunkard who used to live in a Cologne brothel').[63]

The manner in which the German visit was organized was certainly evidence of the Duke's continuing desire for the limelight, his pro-German and even more pro-Nazi tendencies and, at best, his poor judgement. For the King it was also a sign of how his brother was prepared independently to undertake initiatives against the wishes and policy of the King and his Government. Indeed, Monckton, who had not been consulted over the tours, told Cazalet that the Duke had admitted to him that 'he did not tell him about Germany because [he] would have told the King'.[64] Both the King and Queen, however, were far more upset by the implications of the Windsors' projected tour of the United States. On 3 October the Duke of Windsor issued a press communiqué from Wasserleonburg, which as Lord Crawford commented, 'almost read like a challenge to our Sovereign':

In accordance with the Duke of Windsor's message to the press last June that he would release any information of interest regarding his plans or movements, His Royal Highness makes it known that he and the Duchess of Windsor are visiting Germany and the United States in the near future for the purpose of studying housing and working conditions in these two countries.[65]

On 8 October Sir Ronald Lindsay arrived at Balmoral for high-level discussions about the Windsor tour of the United States. The reason for the summons was the Ambassador's ideas on how he should treat the Windsors, which certainly did not accord with the views of the King or the Foreign Office. Lindsay had written to Vansittart on 3 October, saying that, although personally the prospect of the visit filled him with horror, he thought it of great importance that no impression should be given that 'the *visit to America in itself* is in any way disapproved' and suggesting, therefore, that he should invite the Windsors to stay at the Embassy, present them at the White House and give them a large 'Belshazzar' (banquet). He argued that the huge publicity which would inevitably accompany the tour would focus interest on the British Embassy attitude. Vansittart forwarded Lindsay's ideas to Hardinge, commenting that he was doubtful about the first two as they would give the impression of an official visit.[66]

At Balmoral Lindsay found, as he later told his brother, Lord Crawford, the King and Queen in a

state of extreme nervousness about it [the Duke of Windsor's visit to Washington] or rather about all the Duke's activities – his theatrical appeals to popularity and these visits of inspection – perfunctory and no doubt pretty insincere, but none the less evidence of his readiness to bid for popularity. Hitherto he has been quiet and has shown no desire to study housing conditions in France and Austria – and now he wants to go to Washington....[67]

Lindsay found himself arguing till midnight against the combined forces of the King, the Queen and Lascelles. The two men put it to Lindsay that 'the Duke was behaving abominably – it was his duty not to embarrass the King – he had promised not to – and he was dropping bombshell after bombshell, and this was the worst of all'. They told Lindsay that the Duke 'was trying to stage a come-back, and his friends and advisers were semi-Nazis'. 'He was not straight – he hadn't let the King have an inkling of his plans, and the first news of them was a letter from him to the King's own agent. He had not been countenanced by any of the King's people abroad so far, and how could he be put up in the King's own house in Washington?' The Queen skilfully reinforced her husband's position by taking a different tack:

while the men spoke in terms of indignation, she spoke in terms of acute pain and distress . . . all tempered by affection for 'David'. 'He's so changed now, and he used to be so kind to us.' She was backing up everything the men said, but protesting against anything that seemed vindictive. All her feelings were lacerated by what she and the King were being made to go through. And with all her charity she had not a word to say for 'that woman'. . . .

Lindsay, describing the scene at Balmoral, followed it up with a comment which went straight to the heart of the matter:

It interested me to notice that really the King does not yet feel safe on his throne, and up to a point he is like the medieval monarch who has a hated rival claimant living in exile. The analogy must not be pressed too far because I don't think George wanted the throne any more than Edward, and if he is there it is owing to a sense of duty which Edward lacked, and not owing to a love of power which one sometimes thinks Edward may have after all. But in some ways the situation operates on the King just as it must have done on his medieval ancestors – uneasiness as to what is coming next – sensitiveness – suspicion. . . .[68]

Lindsay was not far wrong in his surmise that the King, instinctively perhaps, thought in those terms. He had been bred and brought up as a member of the royal family, steeped in the history of the British monarchy by Queen Mary, and once before he had made a reference, even though humorous, to such competition between rival princes in his letter to his brother during his father's serious illness in December 1928, retailing the story that 'your rushing home is that in the event of anything happening to Papa I am going to bag the Throne in your absence!!! Just like the Middle Ages. . . .'

For the King, a major factor in the equation between himself and his brother was Wallis; as he told Eden that spring, he did not think his brother on his own would intrigue, 'but she will make him'.

How far were the King's suspicions justified? Most less-involved observers, such as Lindsay and Monckton, thought that it was more a case of both Windsors wanting to have their cake and eat it, and to show the world that he had not lost caste by giving up the throne for her. The Duke missed the stimulation of public admiration which he had so long enjoyed. He was not devoid of personal vanity; in his days as Prince of Wales he had carefully gone through newsreels of his tours with the editors in order to present himself in the most favourable light. He was a man of no intellectual or spiritual resources, no interests beyond his wife, gardening and golf, who had been used to life and travel at the highest level. 'In fact he wants to gad about and dance as he has been doing for the last ten years,' as Crawford unkindly remarked. When, however, to this harmless vanity and restlessness was added his basic irresponsibility, his refusal to take advice from anyone but his wife, and his bitterness and resentment against his brother, the mixture could become dangerous. All his adult life up till the Abdication he had been protected from the consequences of his actions by a loyal and devoted staff; now he was virtually on his own and, moreover, open to manipulation by men like Bedaux and the Nazis. It was a path which in future years was to lead him very close to treason.

The King's suspicions about his brother's desire to stage a come-back in the public eye and to set himself up in a leading role were confirmed by subsequent reports from his diplomatic agents in Berlin and Washington. On 17 October Ogilvie-Forbes reported to Eden, in a letter which was seen by both Hardinge and Lindsay, the contents of a conversation he had had at dinner with his American opposite number, Prentiss Gilbert, during the Duke's visit to Berlin. Gilbert told him that Bedaux had approached him with a view to obtaining from the United States Government official recognition of the forthcoming visit and, he understood, the treatment of the Duchess as royalty. Bedaux apparently hinted that the United States Government, rather than himself, should pay for a special train for the Windsors from New York to Washington and attempted unsuccessfully behind Gilbert's back to get Frances Perkins, Roosevelt's Secretary for Labour, to send an invitation to the Duke. Gilbert gained the impression that Bedaux was 'running' the Duke and probably paying the expenses of his tour outside Germany, including a visit to Sweden 'to a Swedish millionaire whose name he did not know and who was interested in World Peace through Labour reconciliation'. Bedaux then said that 'it was intended that HRH should take up this line and even went so far as to express the opinion that HRH might in due course be the "Saviour" of the Monarchy!'[69]

At the end of November Lindsay, back in Washington, was shown two letters on the subject of the Duke of Windsor and the Peace Movement written by Bedaux in August and September, which he forwarded to Hardinge. According to Bedaux, Labour was to be rallied to the cause of capitalism by a Peace Movement headed by the Duke of Windsor:

A world-wide peace movement must have as its task to raise humanity's level of life's enjoyment ... labour must be well-treated and this must be done quickly in order to safeguard the principle of private ownership and individual reward which is the keystone of lasting peace.... The Duke of Windsor ... has always been concerned with the lot of the working man and he has now become an expert on sociological questions: but he is not satisfied with this, and plans to widen his knowledge by a personal study of living and working conditions in many lands. No better leadership for such a movement could be found than in the Duke of Windsor.[70]

The kernel of this idea appears to have come from the 'Swedish millionaire' mentioned by Prentiss Gilbert, and to have been first put to the Duke in May via a Swedish–American named Colonel Robert Solbert, who had written to the Duke at Candé inviting him 'to head up and consolidate the many and varied peace movements throughout the world', and that the Swedish millionaire, Axel Wenner-Gren, was prepared to put up the financial backing for it. Bedaux had replied on the Duke's behalf that he was 'very interested' in leading such a movement and intended soon to study working and housing conditions in many countries.[71] The Duke did not go to Sweden to meet Wenner-Gren, the fifty-eight-year-old founder of Electrolux, a man who had amassed a huge fortune and world-wide interests and, like many such men, consequently regarded himself as uniquely qualified to solve the world's problems (and help himself at the same time). He was to meet him three years later when Wenner-Gren was already, like Bedaux, under suspicion of being actively pro-Nazi. The idea of leading an international peace movement continued to appeal to the Duke of Windsor, who, or so it would appear from Bedaux's remarks to Gilbert, saw it as a potential launching-pad for himself as a possible alternative to his brother.

Only a man as politically naive and, indeed, insensitive as the Duke of Windsor could have thought of making a tour of United States labour conditions under the auspices of a man like Bedaux, whose name, in the eyes of organized labour, was synonymous with capitalist oppression, and preceding it with a Nazi-sponsored tour of Germany in the company of Dr Ley, who had suppressed free German trade unions, and including a meeting with Hitler, rightly regarded as 'the world's most ferocious foe of democracy'. In the end, the King's and the Foreign Office's fears about the Duke's tour of the United States proved to have been unnecessary as the tour collapsed under the weight of American condemnation of his German visit. Reaction against it was particularly strong in Wallis's home town, where the Baltimore Federation of Labour passed a resolution condemning the Duke's tour on precisely those grounds and adding, in words that might have been penned by Hardinge or Vansittart, expressions of disbelief that labour conditions in Baltimore 'are to be studied by one who while resident here in no way showed the slightest concern nor sympathy for the problems of labor or the poor and needy'. The Duke, disconcerted, telephoned Lindsay to ask 'if Bedaux were the only source of difficulty'.[72] Bedaux fled from America, whence he was only to return in 1943 under armed guard to face an indictment for treason and communicating with the enemy, and the Duke of Windsor cancelled the trip on the eve of departure, partly as a result of a ludicrous mix-up when he thought he was talking on the telephone to the American Ambassador in Paris, William C. Bullitt, who was encouraging him to go in a spirit of anti-British mischief, when he was actually speaking to Sir Eric Phipps, the British Ambassador, who naturally advised him in the opposite sense. A senior Palace official, probably Lascelles, commented angrily after the crisis: 'what is really wanted is that the public should cease to take him seriously, and realise the truth – that his mental and moral development just stopped dead when he was about 15, and that though a sad figure, he is no longer a particularly interesting one'.[73]

The episode left its scars, increasing the intense suspicion with which many influential people in British public life regarded the ex-King. Lindsay wrote that on this point 'the Palace secretaries are extremist, the Foreign Office still more so. All are seeing ghosts and phantasms everywhere and think there are disasters round every corner.' At Court Wigram, Hardinge and Lascelles certainly were hostile to the Duke of Windsor, as now, due to the Duke's own actions, were Eden and Vansittart, a former friend of the Duke's who particularly disliked his dealings with the Nazis. Reports of the ex-King's come-back plans continued to filter through. On 28 December Phipps passed on in confidence to Eden a story that he had heard from Sir William Tyrrell, the former Ambassador, to the effect that

some time ago a special correspondent of the "Daily Herald" [the Labour newspaper] came over here to interview the Duke of Windsor. Tyrrell was shown an account of the interview, in which it was stated that HRH said that if the Labour Party wished, & were in a position to offer it, he would be prepared to be President of the English Republic. Tyrrell urged Greenwood [deputy leader of the Labour Party and editor of the *Herald*] to have this left out of any published account of the interview ... this Greenwood promised to do, & I understand that, so far, the interview has not seen the light of day....[74]

In November Horace Wilson, the most influential man in Whitehall, told Monckton that the only real worry as far as the Government was concerned was that the Duke's return to England might be exploited by extremist groups, which he undoubtedly meant to include Sir Oswald Mosley's fascist blackshirts, who had supported Edward VIII over the Abdication.[75]

The King, however, according to Monckton, was not an extremist as far as his brother personally was concerned, despite his anger at his behaviour over the German and American tours, and their continuing private disputes. He was, perhaps, the Duke's only friend at Court or in Whitehall, for the evidence is that the Queen, fierce on her husband's behalf, would not forgive the Duke for the suffering he had caused over the Abdication nor the wrong he had done. On one point alone he remained adamant, even obsessed: he did not want his brother to return to England. In November the Government renewed their suggestion that the Duke's allowance should be conditional on his remaining abroad and, according to Monckton, the King wrote to the Duke saying he could only give him permission to return on the advice of ministers. 'K[ing] v. nervous about W[indsor] & his possible popularity,' Victor Cazalet noted after dining with Monckton, when the latter told him 'the whole Windsor story'. 'Otherwise v. friendly towards him & wants people to go & see him.'[76] It was hard for the King to forget the experience of years dinned into his memory, of his brother's almost magical crowd appeal, the way in which his charm could light up a room. With his intimate knowledge of his brother's character, he knew him, or thought he did, to be selfish, headstrong and irresponsible, but not wicked or dangerous. Perhaps he clung to the remnants of the memory of how 'David' was before the golden years of adulation spoiled him. But he was now the King, and he was not prepared to let his brother wreck things for him. It was in part a reaction spurred by his ingrained inferiority complex, in part a sense of what was due to the family and the monarchy.

His brother, not surprisingly, did not see it in the same light. He never had. Three weeks after his conversation with Monckton, Cazalet dined alone with the Windsors and talked until 1.15 a.m. on the same subject – the Abdication. Cazalet's comment was: 'She never grasped what it was all about. He never saw it in the perspective everyone else did.' Edward VIII's perspective in December 1936 had been focused on one aspect alone, Wallis Simpson. It had not changed. Cazalet found him, as Monckton had said he would, 'very bitter about HRH'. 'He is not on speaking terms with the King,' Cazalet continued. 'He said, "If people want me to be Buddies with my brother he must recognize his sister in law – I want to be – I did everything I could during that last week not to make [a] King party. I want to help him. If he will grant me this – we never want to see them again. . . ." '[77]

$$\mathcal{Q}\,9\,\mathcal{Q}$$

BULWARK AGAINST
DICTATORSHIP

'... the liberties of the people and the integrity of the Empire are deeply rooted in Constitutional Monarchy, and the ancient usages, ceremonies and traditions centring upon the Crown, have become, even more than in former times, a bulwark against dictatorship, and the symbol of the union of all the members of the British Commonwealth of Nations. . . .'
Resolution of the Select Committee on the Civil List, 26 April 1937

THE King had, in truth, little real reason to feel insecure on his throne by the autumn of 1937. He had surmounted the public ordeal of the Coronation, establishing his image as King in the minds of millions who saw the ceremony on film. He had made himself known in the United Kingdom by official visits to Scotland and Northern Ireland, acclaimed with enthusiasm wherever he and the Queen went. From Balmoral on 10 August Hardinge reported to his friend, Sir Hughe Knatchbull-Hugessen, HM representative in Nanking, that Their Majesties were in the very best of health and spirits and 'very happy to think that the Coronation summer has passed off with what everyone acknowledges to have been unqualified success'. Certainly, he added, the King and Queen had made no effort to spare themselves, and the 'astonishing' receptions given to them everywhere showed that this was appreciated. 'The Coronation year', he concluded, 'has been a great personal triumph for them. . . .'[1]

The King had, moreover, made a good personal impression on members of his Government, like Anthony Eden, and public servants like Sir Ronald Lindsay, men who had known him before merely by sight and, it must be said, dim reputation. Eden, who had seen the King briefly in March to discuss the Coronation, when he found him 'very keen and taking great interest and much more self-assured', told Harvey after his interview at Windsor in April, when they had discussed the King's problems with his brother, that he had been 'very impressed by the King'. He was equally impressed by the Queen, 'who has great character and common sense and encourages the King'. Lindsay, after his momentous conversations with the King at Balmoral in October, reported to his wife:

The King is lithe, brown, and walks like a mountaineer, the very picture of health. He talks a great deal and you would never think he could be tongue-tied before a crowd except for an occasional and momentary check noticeable to anyone on the look out for a stammer. He talks quite well and vigorously ... I should say he was an almost exact repeat of his father both in manner and in mind, though not in appearance, and he made a good impression on me, much better than I had expected.[2]

The comparison with George v, often glibly made, was, however, a deceptive one. Whereas they shared many of the same characteristics and outlook on life, George vi could by no stretch of the imagination be called a family tyrant, as his father undoubtedly had been, nor could the life of Queen Elizabeth as Queen Consort have been described, as Queen Mary's was, as 'dignified slavery'. Where George v confided everything to his valet, Howlett, and to his mentor, Lord Stamfordham, his son was wary of courtiers and opened his heart only to his wife and, to a much lesser extent, his two trusted Prime Ministers, Chamberlain and Churchill. George vi was a more complex, less outgoing and more thoughtful character than his father; the communication problems which he had suffered in his earlier life had made him observant of others and accustomed to listening to them. George v had chatted unrestrainedly and often inconsequentially to anyone with whom he happened to be in conversation, so much so that Queen Mary had had to dismiss a lady-in-waiting given to asking the King indiscreet questions to which he too readily responded. George v had listened to his Prime Ministers, but not to ministers of lesser rank. Eden, who served as Foreign Secretary to both monarchs, told Bruce Lockhart that George vi liked to listen and rarely talked during an audience whereas George v talked all the time. The first time Eden had audience of George v, the King had 'talked without stopping for half an hour before Eden had a chance to speak, then scarcely had he begun before the King pushed the bell to summon the equerry. ' "The Band can play now," the King told the equerry. Anthony was completely bowled out.'[3] George v, brought up in an unconfined family atmosphere by two notable extroverts, his father and his adoring mother, had an open, trusting attitude towards his fellow men; his two elder sons, influenced by their mother's impenetrable reserve and their father's constant criticism, and perhaps also by the tales told upon them by their father's confidants, were more reserved.

The Duke of Windsor, curiously, attributed this wariness on the part of himself and his brother to his father's explicit instructions, which were no doubt intended to produce an outward correctness of manner rather than the deep-rooted inhibition which seems to have been the result: ' "Remember who you are," my father used to say to me and my brothers when we were growing up, and indeed, he never stopped saying so until he died.' The King was not suggesting that the Princes were actually different from other people, but that they should conduct themselves as if they were:

We were never to forget that we were examples of a special kind of behaviour. People were watching us. Our lives were under the surveillance of some who might not be understanding of ordinary human frailties.... It was excellent advice ... but it had its drawbacks.... One learned to be withdrawn, wary, non-committal, and, above all else, to keep one's emotions under a tight leash.[4]

Both brothers were, as a result, notably wary of confiding in their staff. Where George V would always send for Stamfordham after seeing a government minister and tell him exactly what had passed, so that Stamfordham could then write a memorandum and send it to the King for approval, 'George VI, keeping his own counsel, would never tell his Secretaries exactly what had passed at interviews, passing them off with a phrase and never going into details of the conversation.'[5] The Duke of Windsor's secretary, Dina Wells Hood, remarked on her employer's exceptional secrecy and wariness with his employees, while even Walter Monckton, who acted as the Duke's secretary as well as his legal adviser during the last days of the Abdication crisis, was never told everything. Both George VI and his elder brother only really trusted their wives.

There were several reasons for the distance at which George VI kept his courtiers, apart from the effects of his father's early training. One of them was his determination to work hard, come to his own conclusions and to be his own man. When he joked with Lloyd George about de Valera calling him 'the instrument of the Government', he intended to show Lloyd George, his brother's partisan who liked to propagate exactly that view, that he knew what was being said of him.[6] People had underestimated him all his life because of his shyness and his stammer; now he was going to show them what he was really capable of. The King's determination to make up his own mind and to do his own homework instead of accepting his Secretary's marked-up briefs was to be a major source of friction between himself and his Principal Private Secretary, Alec Hardinge. Beyond that there was a feeling that, although inspired by loyalty to the throne and the monarchy, the royal servants, notably Wigram and Hardinge, had in the active roles they had assumed during the Abdication crisis, perhaps presumed too much and, in the case of the King's relations with his brother, were continuing to do so. The Duke of Windsor's acid droplets of warnings about Hardinge may have had their effect. Neither the King nor the Queen wanted to be 'run' by their courtiers, and in that minor respect the events of the Abdication had left a sour taste.

The King – unlike his elder brother – recognized his own inexperience in affairs of State, in domestic politics and on the increasingly threatening front of foreign affairs, and consequently his need for good advice. He was to establish exceptionally close working relations with his Prime Ministers, notably Chamberlain and Churchill.

Neville Chamberlain had replaced Baldwin as Prime Minister upon the latter's retirement, on 30 May 1937. Chamberlain, at sixty-eight, was almost the complete opposite of 'SB', for whom he had considerable liking not untinged with contempt. Where Baldwin had cultivated the easy-going image of the likable

English countryman, John Bull with his pipe and slippers and his roots in the soil, Chamberlain was corvine in appearance, thin with a shock of white hair, dark eyebrows over piercing eyes and a curving beak of a nose. Where Baldwin was lazy, Chamberlain was painstaking and energetic; where Baldwin was liked or tolerated by the political opposition whom he saw it as his mission to placate, Chamberlain was loathed. He never suffered political fools gladly and would rip a Labour opponent apart with the cutting edge of his sarcasm for indulging in what he saw as 'sob-stuff' sentimentalism. He had few real friends even on his own side; his temperament was reserved, even repressed, and he seemed cold to outsiders. His only real confidantes were his wife and his two sisters. But he was capable of warmth; he had deep underlying passions for Shakespeare and for music, for birds, trees, flowers and the reflective pleasures of angling. And when he unbent, he had charm; his integrity and self-confidence won him the loyalty of people as disparate as Lord Halifax, Chips Channon and the royal family.

Chamberlain had become involved in the King's private business even before he succeeded as Prime Minister, when Baldwin had left him to deal with the delicate question of the Civil List and the settlement between the King and the Duke of Windsor. When Halifax visited him on his deathbed in November 1940, Chamberlain proudly described his relationship with the King and Queen who had just visited him. 'He felt that he had been in a sense their Godfather – or something like it,' Halifax noted in his diary. '[He said] "SB left a good deal of all that to me" – with a chuckle.'[7]

Chamberlain deliberately set out to make friends with the King and ended by winning the trust of the entire royal family. He had been acquainted with and liked the Queen when she was Duchess of York, describing her to Hilda as 'the only royalty I enjoy talking to, for though she may not be an intellectual she is always natural and moreover appears always to be thoroughly enjoying herself'.[8] He was decidedly prejudiced in favour of the new sovereigns, writing approvingly after a Court ball in April 1937 that it was 'a most brilliant spectacle. The King and Queen looked very happy as they danced together.... Some few people remembered the Duke of Windsor and fervently thanked Heaven that he was out of the way and replaced by Sovereigns whom everyone could respect.'[9] He determined from the outset of his premiership to get to know the King, expressing the hope when he 'kissed hands' that the King 'would let me come and see him fairly often and he said "Yes because we hardly know one another, do we".... He has repeated this several times to various people and I want him to realise as soon as possible that I am not really an alarming person....'[10] On 26 June he told his sister Hilda, 'I went to see the King yesterday at my own suggestion, nominally to tell him about the Imperial conference but really to get on to more intimate terms with him. I like him very much and find him easy to talk to....'[11] In August he had a long conversation with the King before the latter left for Balmoral: 'I managed to get in another talk with the King which lasted for $1\frac{1}{4}$ hours. He is a bit tired but pleased with the way things are going and is evidently gaining in confidence all the time.'[12]

On his first visit to Balmoral in the last week of August 1937 he fished with the Queen and shot with the King, picnicked with them on Loch Muick and drove with them accompanied by Pierpont Morgan through the woods ending with a raid on the gooseberry bushes at Abergeldie, 'the Queen diving under the net and thoroughly enjoying the gooseberries'. 'I learned from the Household that the King and Queen were very pleased with their PM as a guest,' he boasted to his sister Ida,[13] while his thank-you letter to the King underlined what he clearly felt to be a new intimacy and friendship:

One makes more progress in getting to know a man who is staying in the same house and with whom one converses on any topic as it comes up than one does in fifty official interviews, and my four days at Balmoral have made me feel that my relations with Yourself and the Queen will henceforth be on a new footing. I need hardly say how greatly I value this approach to intimacy and how helpful it will be to me as head of Your Majesty's Government.[14]

At Balmoral King and Prime Minister discussed the increasingly threatening international situation, which had developed from November 1936 until the late summer of 1937 while British political interest had been inward-looking, absorbed first with the trauma of the Abdication then the euphoria of the Coronation. While the Italian Foreign Minister, Ciano, forged agreements with Hitler at Berchtesgaden, Germany signed the anti-Comintern pact with Japan and fascist soldiers entered Spain, the attention of British ministers had been focused on one thing alone, King Edward's desire to marry Mrs Simpson. The European political situation now occupied centre stage and of this complicated and dangerous labyrinth King George knew little more than the average Briton. He had had no time as yet to familiarize himself with the subtleties of the situation; finding Eden, his Foreign Minister, 'difficult to talk to', for guidance he was rather to rely on Chamberlain, who, to Eden's discomfort, was playing an increasingly interfering role in foreign affairs.

Perhaps Chamberlain's greatest and most significant fault in this arena was a businessman's arrogant belief that he could solve anything personally and by pragmatic means. With his roots in the rich commercial soil of Birmingham and a great political heritage – his father, Joseph Chamberlain, had been one of the most charismatic politicians of the late Victorian age and his brother Austen (who died in March 1937) had also been an outstanding political figure – he was filled with self-confidence in his own abilities. A startlingly successful political career late in life had implanted in him a taste for power. Unfortunately he was also narrow-minded, stubborn and incapable of understanding that foreign policy in general, and the European situation in particular, required a wider and deeper knowledge than that which he possessed. He despised the Foreign Office (as he came increasingly to despise Parliament when it opposed his policy of appeasing the dictators) and increasingly bypassed his Foreign Secretary. Within just over six months of becoming Prime Minister he had dispensed with one major obstacle to his policy of reasoning with Hitler, the rabidly anti-German

Vansittart; within ten, he had forced out Eden, the obstacle in his path of rapprochement with Mussolini.

Unfortunately for Britain and for himself, Chamberlain's policy of appeasing the dictators rested on the fundamentally false premise that Hitler and Mussolini were reasonable, straightforward men. There was nothing essentially wrong with the idea that Britain should go to all reasonable lengths to preserve the peace of Europe and to prevent a repetition of the war of 1914–18, which was still a nightmare in the back of everyone's minds. As Churchill had written to his wife on 8 March 1935: 'If the Great War were resumed – for that is what it would mean in two or three years' time or even earlier – it will be the end of the world.'[15] If Hitler had been the man Chamberlain and the men of appeasement imagined him to be, then perhaps he would have been satisfied with a settlement which would not only wipe out the objectionable terms of the Versailles Treaty but bring within the Reich all the German-speaking peoples. Nor was there anything wrong in attempting to detach Italy from Germany, had Mussolini been a different type of man than he was. Friendship with the controlling power in the Mediterranean was certainly desirable for Britain's maintenance of her communication with her Empire in India and the Far East. Moreover, everyone – not least the dictators – recognised that in 1937 Britain was neither ready nor willing to fight a war. Like everyone who had fought in the First World War, the King shared the universal feeling of 'never again', that peace must be maintained at almost all costs. And, like many other people and influenced particularly by his father, he had a deep-rooted fear of 'Bolshevism', of which the most obvious opponents in their own countries as well as in Spain were the two fascist powers.

On Sunday, 20 February 1938, Eden handed in his resignation to the Prime Minister, the outcome of three months of disagreements between the two men over Chamberlain's approach to the dictators. The King was spending the weekend at the Royal Lodge when he learned of the impending resignation of his Foreign Secretary from the Sunday morning newspapers of the Beaverbrook–Rothermere press. In the confusion surrounding Eden's resignation no one had thought to advise the King of what might happen. He had been told by Hardinge of the unusual summoning of a Cabinet meeting on the Saturday and he was aware of the differences of opinion between Chamberlain and Eden, but no one had bothered to keep him informed of what was going on. It was humiliating to have to learn of the resignation of his Foreign Secretary from Lord Beaverbrook's newspaper and an infringement of his constitutional rights as sovereign, whose threefold duty it is to advise, to encourage and to warn his Government in moments of crisis. The King was furious and demanded that machinery should be set up to ensure that this never happened again. Hardinge arranged with Sir Maurice Hankey, Secretary of the Cabinet, that it should be the Secretary's responsibility for reminding the Prime Minister to keep the King informed of any impending crisis, or if he could not, to get in touch direct with the King's Private Secretary. At the King's own suggestion the system by which he had to wait to receive the final copy of Cabinet Conclusions was changed so that a draft copy of the minutes could be sent to him at the same time as to the Prime Minister.

The King saw Eden on 22 February, when the ex-Foreign Secretary came to surrender his Seals of Office. He was courteous and sympathetic and delighted Eden by tactfully telling him 'that he had great sympathy for his point of view and did not think it would be long before he saw him again as one of his senior ministers'. It is unlikely that these were the King's real feelings and, in this case, Eden was perhaps fortunate that he was dealing with George VI rather than George V. The King was by now a firm supporter of Chamberlain; he scarcely knew Eden, did not share his artistic and aesthetic tastes, and had not found him personally so forthcoming as the Prime Minister. He later complained to one of the Dominions Prime Ministers that 'he had not been able to establish personal relations with Mr Eden, whom he found it difficult to persuade in conversation to depart from his brief'. The immediate causes of Eden's resignation were varied and complex, and it is improbable that the King knew more about them than most of Eden's colleagues did at the time. The overall cause, however, he certainly would have understood: that Eden disagreed with the Prime Minister's policy of appeasing the dictators and was, therefore, taking the honourable way out.

The King, moreover, found himself more in sympathy with Eden's successor, Edward, Viscount Halifax, who was destined to play a large part in his reign, first as Foreign Secretary, then as Ambassador to Washington through the war years. Halifax's background as a sporting aristocrat was one with which the King felt at home, while his wife, Lady Dorothy, daughter of the 4th Earl of Onslow, was lady-in-waiting to the Queen. Later they were to become personal friends; the King would write to him as 'My dear Edward' and – a signal mark of favour – appointed him Chancellor of his cherished Order of the Garter; after the King's death Halifax erected a memorial monument to him on his Yorkshire estate, Garrowby. Halifax, who followed Chamberlain's foreign policy lead unquestioningly, was equally incapable of comprehending the nature of the dictators. He was essentially a patrician Englishman, born into a world of great possessions: his mother, daughter of the Earl of Devon, could count three Courtenay Emperors of Constantinople among her ancestors; his father was descended from Tory Yorkshire squires and the great Northumbrian Whig clan of Lord Grey of the Reform Bill. Halifax himself, although born with an atrophied left arm and without a hand, was a great sportsman, an excellent rider and passionate about hunting. Spectacularly tall, when he moved he 'could be graceful and grave and shy simultaneously, like a tall water-bird wading in the shallows'. He had had a brilliant career, both at Oxford – where he took a First in Modern History, was elected a Fellow of All Souls in 1903 and Chancellor of the University in 1933 – and as Viceroy of India from 1926 to 1929, where he had succeeded in making a friend of Gandhi. Like other Englishmen of his generation and upbringing, including his friend, Geoffrey Dawson, the editor of *The Times*, another sporting Yorkshire squire, Fellow of All Souls and leading apostle of appeasement, Halifax was more attuned to the Empire than to Europe and, as Foreign Secretary, in the words of his biographer, 'It was at once evident that he did not ... find the study of foreign affairs a matter of absorbing interest. ...' He was a man of enormous personal charm, of which he was quite aware, and not entirely to be relied upon when political expediency came into play; alluding to both his High Church views and his slipperiness, Churchill nicknamed him 'Holy-Fox'.

Halifax's patrician background and his lack of psychological insight led him to regard men like Hitler and Hermann Göring, Commander-in-Chief of the German Air Force, as figures of fun, not to be taken seriously; the Nazis, he thought, were only dangerous because of their inferiority complex. He met both men when he was invited to Berlin in November 1937, ostensibly for the purpose of attending an international hunting conference. Of Göring who entertained him among the vulgar splendours and looted treasures of Karinhall, he wrote that he was

frankly attractive: like a great schoolboy, full of life and pride in what he was doing, showing it all off, and talking high politics out of the setting of green jerkin and dagger. A modern Robin Hood: producing on me a composite impression of film-star, gangster, great landowner interested in his property, Prime Minister, party manager, head game-keeper at Chatsworth.[16]

Halifax's visit to Germany in November 1937 was to have a most unfortunate effect upon Hitler's perception of English statesmen in general and the pliability of the Chamberlain Government in particular, fitting neatly into what with hindsight can be seen as a ghastly sequence of events leading Europe towards war. When he arrived in Berlin on 17 November to be greeted by the Ambassador, Nevile Henderson, with anxious advice to go as far as possible in meeting the Führer's point of view, he did not know that his visit coincided with a psychological point at which Hitler, content that what he called the preparatory stage of his plans for Germany had been arrived at, was about to raise the ante drastically in his game with the democracies. On 5 November, at a secret meeting in the Reich Chancellery, Hitler disclosed some of his secret thoughts to an inner circle of powerful men: Field Marshal von Blomberg, the War Minister; Colonel-General von Fritsch, Commander-in-Chief of the Army; Admiral Raeder, Commander-in-Chief of the Navy; Göring and von Neurath, the Foreign Minister. Germany's future, Hitler declared, could only be safeguarded by acquiring additional *Lebensraum* in Europe; the immediate objectives were to safeguard her eastern and southern flanks by annexing Czechoslovakia and Austria. Her two 'hate-inspired antagonists' were Britain and France; 'Germany's problem', Hitler concluded, 'could only be solved by means of force, and this was never without attendant risk.'[17] Hitler's calculation that the attendant risks were becoming increasingly affordable was to be encouraged by the tenor of his conversations with Halifax at Berchtesgaden.

Halifax had never read *Mein Kampf*, in which Hitler had first defined his policy of *Lebensraum*, and from which he never substantially deviated. It is doubtful whether he had even seen a copy until the Queen sent him one almost exactly two years later. He had very little idea of what Nazism was about and continued to regard its leaders as harmless figures not devoid of a certain charm. The crucial point of his visit was his meeting with Hitler on 19 November at Berchtesgaden. Halifax, arriving by car at the foot of a flight of steps, saw only a pair of black patent shoes and silk stockings and was about to mistake Hitler for a footman until saved by the urgent muttering of von Neurath, '*Der Führer, der Führer.*' Indeed, the gulf between the two men was exemplified in a photograph taken for the occasion, in which Halifax, a willowy, aristocratic figure impeccably and soberly dressed in the English gentleman's winter overcoat with bowler hat and rolled-up umbrella (an item which was to become almost a symbol of appeasement after Munich), tactfully positioned on the step below the Führer, poses with the squat, unmistakably plebeian dictator in uniform jacket and dark trousers, the Iron Cross dangling from his breast and the swastika arm-band encircling his left arm.

The result of the Berchtesgaden meeting were worse than Eden and Vansittart had feared. Eden's minute of his instructions to Halifax and Henderson had read:

I have spoken to Lord Halifax and Sir Nevile Henderson together. The former will listen and confine himself to warning comments on Austria and Czechoslovakia. I have impressed on Sir Nevile Henderson the need for doing all we can to discourage German intervention in these two states. We must keep Germany guessing as to our attitude. It is all we can do until we are strong enough to talk to Germany.

Unfortunately Halifax's version of 'warning comments' can scarcely have been interpreted by Hitler as such; he spoke of 'possible alterations in the European order which might be destined to come about in the passage of time'. Halifax recorded:

I said that there were no doubt other questions arising out of the Versailles settlement which seemed to us capable of causing trouble if they were unwisely handled, e.g. Danzig, Austria, Czechoslovakia. On all these matters we were not necessarily concerned to stand for the *status quo* as today, but we were concerned to avoid such treatment of them as would be likely to cause trouble. If reasonable settlements could be reached with the free assent and the goodwill of those primarily concerned we certainly had no desire to block them.[18]

Hitler no doubt placed his own interpretation upon these cautious remarks; the democracies were unlikely to use force to prevent him achieving his immediate objectives. Two days later, on 21 November, at an assembly of the Nazi Old Guard at Augsburg, Hitler repeated ominously in public something of what he had said in secret on 5 November: 'I am convinced that the most difficult part of the preparatory work has already been achieved. ... Today we are faced with new tasks, for the *Lebensraum* of our people is too narrow.'[19]

On 12 March 1938, as Chamberlain pursued negotiations for an Anglo–Italian agreement, Hitler annexed Austria, sending an emotional message to Mussolini, who had not lifted a finger to prevent it: 'Thank you, thank you. I shall never forget, never, never. . . .' Chamberlain's faith in Hitler was slightly shaken, but he still had hopes of Mussolini. On 16 April an agreement, known as the 'Easter Accords', was signed in Rome between Britain and Italy. In return for the small concession of an Italian promise to withdraw their volunteers from Spain, the British Government recognised 'de jure' the Italian conquests in Africa.

With Austria swallowed up by Germany, it was obvious that Hitler's next target would be Czechoslovakia. On 24 March Chamberlain, in a statement to the House of Commons, made it clear that there was nothing he would, or could, do to prevent it. He was not prepared to risk an unwinnable war with Germany for the sake of preserving the integrity of Czechoslovakia, nor would he support Britain's democratic ally, France, in any such course. 'I have, therefore,' he said, 'abandoned any idea of giving guarantees to Czechoslovakia, or the French in connection with their obligations to that country.'

Four days later Hitler held a meeting with Konrad Henlein, leader of the three and half million German minority in Czechoslovakia and the lever which the Führer intended to use to upset the Czech Republic. At this meeting it was agreed that Henlein's policy should be constantly to put forward demands to the Czech Government that he knew could not be fulfilled, thus maintaining a continuing atmosphere of tension. The first of Henlein's outrageous demands was issued on 24 April 1938; three days later Sir Eric Phipps warned Halifax that the French had information that 'Germany meant to settle the question of Czechoslovakia this summer at the latest', and might attack as early as May. As a result of this the French Premier, Edouard Daladier, and his Foreign Minister, Georges Bonnet, hurried to London to persuade their British allies of Hitler's real intent to destroy the integrity of Czechoslovakia, only to find Chamberlain and Halifax resolute in their determination not to risk war over Czechoslovakia. Together the allies determined on what Halifax's biographer called the 'ignoble' policy of putting pressure on the Czech Government to yield to Henlein's demands.

On 2 May Hitler, having put all these events in train, embarked on a State visit to Italy to which he had committed himself on the occasion of Mussolini's visit to Berlin the previous September. Accompanied by every top- and middle-ranking Nazi and hanger-on who could squeeze on to the four special trains provided, he progressed like the German Emperors of the past through the major Italian cities. A Roman triumph was put on for him at Rome, where a new railway station was built for him so that he could glimpse the Colosseum and approach the Italian seat of government, the Campidoglio, by the Imperial way through the Forum. Bundles of *fasci* and gigantic eagles decorated his route and all the resources of Cinecittà contributed to a spectacle worthy of Cecil B. de Mille. Behind the scenes Ribbentrop produced a draft German–Italian treaty of alliance for Mussolini to sign, but as yet the Italian dictator was unwilling formally to commit himself. Hitler's visit to Rome, with its display of showy uniforms, polished jackboots, goose-stepping and stiff-armed salutes, was, however, an ominous demonstration to the democracies of the sympathy – and similarities – between the two fascist regimes.

It was against this background of simmering European trouble and fascist threat that the King and Queen undertook their first major State visit to their European democratic ally, France, in the summer of 1938. The visit had been planned before the resignation of Eden and before Chamberlain had warned the world that he would not support Czechoslovakia or France in fulfilling her treaty pledges to that country. The royal visit was designed to bolster up an alliance that was, indeed, fragile on the political level. In April Daladier, in England with his Foreign Minister to cobble together a plan for coercing the Czechs, had visited Windsor. His impressions had not been good; less than a year later at luncheon with the anti-British American Ambassador in Paris, Bullitt, he told him he had found

Chamberlain a desiccated stick; the King a moron, and the Queen an excessively ambitious woman who would be ready to sacrifice every other country in the world in order that she might remain Queen Elizabeth of England . . . he considered Eden a young idiot and did not know . . . one single Englishman for whose intellectual equipment and character he had respect. He felt that England had become so feeble and senile that the British would give away every possession of their friends rather than stand up to Germany and Italy.[20]

In the last week of May, however, there had been a war scare over Czechoslovakia which had brought the allies together in a brief spasm of firmness. Fear of war hung like a thundercloud on the horizon; the French people seized upon the visit of the English sovereign and his Queen as a tangible symbol of the solidarity of the democracies. For them it was, too, a symbol of national reconciliation after the bitter political quarrels of the recent past, an occasion for celebration, as the British Ambassador put it, to 'produce a healthy effect upon Hitler, Mussolini and Co., who like to think that the streets of Paris are running in blood. . . .'[21] Memories of 1914–18 were still vivid. 'France will never forget that a million soldiers of the British Empire sleep beneath her soil,' declared *L'Information* when the visit was officially announced in February. Even children were aware of the significance of the visit; a questionnaire, put to children between the ages of eight and twelve in the Paris region, produced a positive reaction to the word 'anglais' or 'britannique' and a majority of children responded affirmatively to the question 'Are the English our friends?' Questioned as to the motives of the visit, the children replied 'so that in war time they will come and help us' . . . 'for peace' . . . 'to see that there won't be a war' . . . 'to ask if there will have to be war' and 'to show Hitler and the Duce that we too have friends'.[22]

The King and Queen were aware of the great responsibilities of their role as central figures in this European spectacular in which each official *tableau* would be set against a background of political hopes and fears, of a longing for everything to be a success, a counterpoint to the aggressive, fantastic displays of Hitler and Mussolini. For them also the visit had a great significance as their first State visit abroad as sovereigns representing their country in the capital where Edward VII had been loved as the founder of the Entente Cordiale. The visit had been due to begin on 28 June when, five days before, on 23 June, Cecilia Strathmore died suddenly at Glamis. The Queen was, privately, devastated. It was some time before she could bring herself to reply to the deluge of letters of condolence which she received, including one very personal, friendly note from Chamberlain, written as soon as he heard the news in the lull of a House of Commons debate. Elizabeth answered touchingly and personally:

I have been dreading this moment ever since I was a little child and now that it has come, one can hardly believe it. She was a true 'Rock of Defence' for us, her children, & Thank God, her influence and wonderful example will remain with us all our lives.

She had a good perspective of life – everything was given its *true* importance. She had a young spirit, great courage and unending sympathy whenever or wherever it was needed, & such a heavenly sense of humour. We all used to laugh together and have such fun.

You must forgive me for writing to you like this, but you have been such a kind friend and counsellor to us during the last year.....[23]

She did not allow private grief to come before public duty. The state visit was postponed until 19 July; the Queen's official couturier, Norman Hartnell, and his workroom achieved miracles designing and fitting a new wardrobe in the alternative Court mourning colour, white, and the Queen was with the King when they left Dover to cross the Channel in the Admiralty yacht, *Enchantress*. The King had just recovered from a bout of gastric influenza and may still have been suffering the after-effects. Diana Cooper reported that just before the *Enchantress* sailed, a small boy shot off to purchase a hot-water bottle for His Majesty. The French Ambassador in London, Corbin, described him as being 'rather preoccupied' before his departure, but whether that may have been the prospect of a series of rich French banquets on a recently recovered stomach, or intelligence reports of an assassination plot by a Catalan anarchist cell known as 'the Dwarfs', was impossible to tell. On 18 July, the day before the King's departure, Scotland Yard received via the French Embassy further confirmation on 'the Dwarfs'' plot and warning of a second plot by another Spanish anarchist, Ramon Ferdandez, who was alleged to be planning to bomb the royal train from the air.[24] The French Cabinet also feared the possibility of an *attentat* against the King and Queen on the part of the Gestapo.

These threats were taken seriously; the last royal visit to France had ended tragically only four years before with the assassination of King Alexander of Yugoslavia in 1934. French security for the visit was consequently extremely heavy. In Paris no one was allowed into any house along a route taken by Their Majesties without a pass issued by the Prefecture of Police and no member of the public was allowed on any roof overlooking the route. The entire police force was mobilized and supplemented by 9,000 officers and men of the reserves;

the streets were lined with a double row of troops and *gardes mobiles,* some 20,000 men. Outside Paris there was a soldier stationed every 100 yards along the route taken by the royal train, every bridge, culvert and level crossing was guarded, stations were closed to the public and three aeroplanes with orders to force down any aircraft appearing in the vicinity circled above the royal train all the way. None of this could obscure the extraordinary welcome the royal couple received wherever they went. Groups of people gathered at vantage-points along the route taken by the royal train, waiting for hours for a moment to cheer and wave flags as the train passed. At the 'sumptuously decorated' Bois de Boulogne Station, which had been constructed for the occasion, 10,000 pigeons were released as the King and Queen emerged to drive to the Foreign Ministry, where apartments had been specially renovated and decorated for them at an estimated cost of some 12 million francs.[25] Both the Government and the Municipality of Paris had spent considerable sums decorating public buildings and streets, shops and stores were elaborately decorated, and in the side streets and poor quarters the flags of both nations and photographs of the King and Queen appeared in thousands of windows. The principal buildings were lit up at night and on the Seine floodlit fountains played in front of the royal apartments in the Quai d'Orsay, while 'fanciful representations of the Loch Ness monster and his family' were moored near the Pont Neuf, presumably a tribute to the Queen's Scottish origins.

Royalty fever had begun to grip the country in general, and Paris in particular, even before the King and Queen's arrival, tapping latent roots of royalism. Provincials crowded into Paris and the atmosphere, the British Minister reported, was not unlike that of Coronation Day or George V's Jubilee. Even the communist newspaper, *L'Humanité,* extended the hand of friendship in the warmest and most complimentary terms, 'although taking care to draw a distinction between the "real England"'—presumably represented by Their Majesties—'and the Conservative administration of Mr Chamberlain'. A special number of *L'Illustration* recalled that Queen Elizabeth was descended from the Kings of Scotland, who had given France the '*charmante* Mary Stuart' as Queen and that she had '*de notre sang dans les veines*'. The King was described as being easy, friendly and approachable: 'Nobody has a more simple natural and easy style of approach than the King of England,' the magazine declared. 'The handshake which he gives one, frank, energetic, with *je ne sais quoi* of spontaneity and sympathy, puts you at once at your ease, however modest your social station might be. . . .'[26]

The public occasions of the visit were carefully orchestrated between War and Culture—the inauguration of the Britannia monument marking the disembarkation spot of the first British troops to land in France in 1914 on 19 July, the laying of a wreath by the King at the tomb of the Unknown Soldier on 20 July, a visit to the Military Hospital and a review at Versailles on 21 July and, on 22 July, the unveiling by the King of the memorial to the Australian dead at Villers-Bretonneux, evocations of blood shed together in the all-too-recent past, being interspersed with artistic celebrations. Since February French commentators had been contrasting the peaceful nature of the Franco-British entente with the aggressive aims of the Axis; afterwards they were to underline further the contrast between the glorious fêtes which had accompanied the royal visit with 'the blaring military parades of the totalitarian powers'.

The arrival of the King and Queen released a tidal wave of enthusiasm and patriotism that had been building up over the past months. Feelings of patriotic, royalist pride and fervour were not confined to the French. The Dowager Duchess of Rutland remembers standing with the Winston Churchills, Diana Cooper and Venetia Stanley on the balcony above the staircase at the Opéra watching the King and Queen come up the staircase preceded by two footmen carrying twenty-branched candelabra of tall white candles, the King slim and handsome in evening dress and decorations, the Queen radiant in diamonds and the white Winterhalter crinoline designed for her by Hartnell. 'I felt proud of my nation,' she said. 'The French went mad about the King and Queen. Winston was like a schoolboy he was so delighted. . . .'[27] At Malmaison two old ladies in tears begged Diana Cooper for her place on the royal path: 'You see her all the time,' one said. 'If only we had a King,' said the other.

The most beautiful and evocative of all the fêtes was given at Versailles on the 21st, where the President and Madame Lebrun gave a luncheon for 260 people in the Galerie des Glaces. Each guest had thirteen glasses by his or her place for the thirteen wines to be served, which, according to Diana Cooper, had all been bottled on the birthdays of presidents or kings. Thirteen is an unlucky number in many countries and for many people who were present it was difficult not to hear the echo of ghostly voices prophesying war. The Galerie des Glaces had not been used for such a function since the Peace Conference which closed the First World War. That afternoon, as the royal party looked down from the chapel galleries on a *tableau* of the Comédie Française to the strains of Monteverdi and sunlight streamed through the windows, the angry noise of aeroplane engines drowned the music—a flypast of the French Air Force which had been scheduled for the morning but postponed because of mist. That morning 50,000 troops of the French Army had passed in review before the King and Queen, the President of France and his guests, including Churchill, invited as a special guest of the French Government. Everyone had taken comfort from the spectacle of the military might of Britain's ally, even Churchill, as Halifax recalled. 'Even now', he wrote in his memoirs, 'I can recapture the strength of emotion with which Churchill, who was looking on, spoke of the French Army as the bulwark of European freedom. . . .'[28] Less than two years later that bulwark, in which so much trust had been placed, would crumble before the German armies and Hitler himself would visit Paris for the first time, not as a tourist but as a conqueror.

Hitler and Mussolini were the spectres at the feast. Both democratic Governments were anxious that this public display of the Entente Cordiale should not be taken as a deliberate threat to the dictators. The King's speech on his first night in Paris at the banquet at the Elysée Palace made this quite clear. 'Our entente has nothing exclusive about it,' he said, 'our friendship is not directed at any other power. . . .' Behind the scenes Halifax was taking further steps down the road of appeasement, persuading the unwilling French ministers, Daladier and Bonnet, to agree to the sending of Lord Runciman to 'investigate' the areas of disagreement between Henlein and the Czech Government. On stage and in the limelight the *coup de foudre* between the King and Queen and the French people reached its climax on the last night, when the royal couple appeared several times on the balcony of the Foreign Ministry, summoned by the cheers of a huge crowd estimated at over 10,000. Diana Cooper and her English friends left the banqueting halls of the Quai d'Orsay to join the clamouring crowds below 'I can never forget it,' she wrote. 'To the French the Royal Visit seemed a safeguard against the dreaded war. That at least is what they told me but I could see nothing to allay my fears. . . .'[29]

The immediate success of the royal State visit in demonstrating the unity of France and the strength of the Anglo–French alliance was not to withstand the strain of Hitler's war, although some of the warmth of feeling which it evoked survived in the Anglo–French undercover co-operation during the war and in the spontaneous outburst of the Liberation. But while the political benefits proved in the long term to have been illusory, no one could deny that it had been a personal triumph for the King and Queen, whose 'gracious and kindly personalities . . . [had been] so largely responsible for making the occasion the triumphant success it undoubtedly was,' the chargé d'affaires, Ronald Campbell, wrote to Halifax on 1 September. Both of them had been surprised and moved by their reception, as the King said in his farewell message to President Lebrun: 'Nor, M. le President, shall we ever forget the warm and affectionate welcome given to us by the men and women of your country, for it has touched us deeply and we are truly grateful. . . .' Arriving back in London at Victoria Station they were greeted by cheering crowds. Corbin reported that they were 'visibly happy at the success of their trip' and that the Queen had told him that she and her husband had had 'a marvellous experience'.[30] '. . . it was the wonderful *warmth* of feeling which struck Their Majesties as being the most remarkable thing about the truly remarkable visit to Paris,' the Queen's lady-in-waiting, Lady Katharine Seymour, wrote to Helen Hardinge's mother, Lady Milner, editor of the *National Review*. 'The Queen said these sentiments were expressed by all the people wherever Their Majesties went, and that it was almost a *personal* affair, and so unlike the reception usually given by one country to another.'[31] For the Queen, it had been an heroic effort, coming so soon after the death of her mother. She was still missing her mother, Katharine Seymour wrote, 'especially since her return from France', although, she said, 'she is far too brave to mention her loss'.

At the end of July the King went to Cowes to visit the Royal Yacht Squadron. Unlike his father and grandfather, the King did not enjoy sailing; his father's old yacht, the *Britannia*, had been taken out to sea and scuttled after his death.

'Cowes week' in the first week of August, traditionally an important part of the royal calendar between racing at Goodwood in the last week of July and arrival at Balmoral in time for the 'Glorious twelfth', was not George VI's idea of sporting amusement any more than was the family passion for racing. At Cowes he and his family joined the royal yacht *Victoria & Albert* for a gentle holiday cruise up the eastern coast of England to Scotland and Balmoral. Britain was enjoying a heat-wave and the sea was smooth when the *Victoria & Albert* dropped anchor off Southwold in Suffolk for the King to make his annual visit to the Duke of York's Camp; the King was rowed ashore to be greeted by an army of half-naked boys – many of them with legs and arms painted violet. The boys from the factories and mines, whose skins were totally unused to the sun, had had to have their sunburn treated by painting with picric and vaseline. After a meal of roast lamb, gooseberries and custard, followed by the usual speeches and camp ceremonies, the King was rowed back to the royal yacht, where the Queen and the two Princesses could be seen standing at the deck-rail. It was to be the last camp at Southwold; the Duke of York was now King and the little East Anglian town suffered the same fate as the previous site, victim of its own success and the enormous popularity and curiosity of the Duke of York's Camps. The next year the camp would be held in the privacy of Balmoral and it would be the last one.

While the King and his family relaxed at Balmoral in August and September, Hitler's plans for disturbing the peace of Europe were nearing fruition. The saga of the September crisis over Czechoslovakia and the subsequent Munich agreement with Hitler makes sad reading. The inexperienced King, bewildered by the crisis and appalled by the impending prospect of a general war, anxiously supported Chamberlain's misguided efforts to maintain peace, which only succeeded in making war ultimately more certain. In the King's defence it must be said that his principal sources of information on the crisis, Chamberlain and Halifax, men whom he liked and trusted, were entirely convinced that appeasement was the only alternative to war; indeed, only one member of the Chamberlain Cabinet, Duff Cooper, opposed the Prime Minister's policy. Churchill and Eden were in the wilderness and regarded by the Court (but, in Eden's case, not by Hardinge) and, indeed, the majority of the House of Commons with suspicion as war-mongers. The King knew, too, of the parlous and still unprepared state of Britain's defences, and that Britain was not ready for a war which, in the first instance, it was feared would result in immediate bombardment of London with heavy civilian casualties. As Churchill put it succinctly in a letter to Lord Moyne: 'Owing to the neglect of our defences and the mishandling of the German problem in the last five years, we seem to be very near the bleak choice between War and Shame. My feeling is that we shall choose Shame, and then have War thrown in a little later....'[32]

On 3 September 1938, one year to the day before the outbreak of the Second World War, Hitler's final plans for the crushing of Czechoslovakia were drawn up to be put in motion from noon 27 September. Hitler had, therefore, already set an upper limit to the date for the destruction of Czechoslovakia more than three weeks before the venomous tone of his speech at the annual Nazi rally at Nuremberg on 12 September galvanized the democracies into flurried action. 'Developments seem very slow,' Chamberlain had written to the King on 6 September, who was, therefore, quite unprepared for the renewed crisis and was still at Balmoral when he received a letter from Chamberlain, dated 13 September, written in the aftermath of the Nuremberg speech. In this letter the Prime Minister warned the King that intelligence reports indicated that Hitler intended to attack Czechoslovakia that month, but that the British Ambassador at Berlin, Sir Nevile Henderson, 'steadily maintained that Herr Hitler has not yet made up his mind to violence'. Chamberlain, therefore, proposed personal contact with Hitler to solve the crisis before it got to a critical stage, producing, he hoped, 'an Anglo-German understanding, preceded by a settlement of the Czecho-Slovakian questions'.

The King arrived at Buckingham Palace by night train from Balmoral on the morning of 15 September, the day on which his sixty-nine-year-old Prime Minister boarded an aeroplane for the first time in his life for a seven-hour journey to meet Hitler at Berchtesgaden. Anxious to do what he could to help, the King told Halifax that he had prepared a draft of a personal letter to Hitler, appealing to him as 'one ex-Serviceman to another' to spare the youth of Britain and Germany the horrors of a second world war. Halifax replied that he doubted that the 'ex-Serviceman' aspect would carry any weight with Hitler and put the King off tactfully by suggesting he should refer the idea to the Prime Minister when he returned. Perhaps it was just as well; the boost that such a personal appeal from the King of England would have given the dictator's already monstrous ego would hardly have helped the cause of peace and would, no doubt, have been taken by the Führer as yet another sign that Britain was not prepared to fight.

Chamberlain arrived back in London on 16 September, convinced that the only possibility of a peaceful solution was to force the unfortunate Czechs to yield up the Sudetenland as soon as possible without a fight or even a plebiscite. Daladier and Bonnet came to London to concoct an Anglo-French ultimatum to this effect. The King, who had sent Chamberlain a handwritten letter to be handed to him on arrival at Heston, praised his 'courage & wisdom in flying to see Hitler in person' and pressed him to come and see him as soon as possible. 'I am naturally anxious to hear the result of your talk, & to be assured that there is a prospect of a peaceful solution on terms which admit of general acceptance.' But after a meeting with Chamberlain at 9.30 that evening the King was understandably confused, some subconscious instinct possibly telling him that Britain should have taken a firmer line. 'Everything is in a maze,' he wrote to Lascelles the next day. 'The Cabinet is always sitting, so no news. The French arrive tomorrow & if they won't stand up to Hitler how can we & the World must be told it is their fault and not ours. . . .' In Cabinet on 19 September, Leslie Hore-Belisha expressed it as his opinion that Czechoslovakia would not be able to survive without the Sudeten German areas; Chamberlain, incredibly, replied that Hitler had assured him that he had no designs on Czechoslovakia and that 'he would not deliberately deceive a man he respected'.

Armed with the Anglo–French plan for self-determination in the Sudetenland which had been forced on the Czechs, Chamberlain flew off to Germany again on 22 September, this time to Godesberg on the Rhine where, to his consternation, Hitler (who in any case was not interested in a peaceful solution of the Czech question) told him that it was no longer relevant. When Chamberlain suggested a commission to oversee the transfer of populations where necessary and an international guarantee, in which Britain would join, of Czechoslovakia's independence and security, Hitler declared that he now wanted the evacuation of the Sudetenland by the Czechs by 28 September. After two days' increasingly acrimonious discussion, Hitler graciously told Chamberlain he would extend the deadline to 1 October. When Chamberlain lunched with the King at Buckingham Palace on 25 September, he described his horror at Hitler's aggressive attitude and warned the King that the rejection of Hitler's terms at Godesberg, which the Cabinet had determined, could lead to war. Chamberlain had been inclined to give Hitler what he wanted without an argument, but, even for Halifax, this had been too much and on the 26th, pushed by Halifax, he announced that he would make a last appeal to Hitler to settle the affair by negotiation, together with a warning that, if France fulfilled her treaty obligations, Great Britain would come to her aid. The King again suggested a personal appeal from himself to Hitler and showed Chamberlain the draft of a telegram which he intended to send. Chamberlain turned it down. That evening, despite the presence in Berlin of Chamberlain's intermediary, his confidential aide, Sir Horace Wilson, Hitler delivered at the Sportpalast a speech of such frightening hatred against the Czechs that everyone who heard it was convinced there must be war. That day Hitler issued an ultimatum to Wilson: he must have Czech acceptance by 2 p.m. on 28 September.

Chamberlain, however, did not give up, as the King told Queen Mary on the evening of the 27th, while trenches were being dug in Hyde Park and the population of London fitted with gas-masks:

The latest news is ... the Prime Minister has just sent a telegram to Hitler & Beneš [President of Czechoslovakia] suggesting that they should get into touch with each other & to propose that Hitler should occupy Asch & Egerland on Oct. 1st. That an International Commn. should then arrange for the rest to be handed over peacefully by Oct. 10th.

Beneš has been told, as he well knows, that his country will be overwhelmed anyhow, & that it would be wise for him to take this course.

If Hitler refuses to do this then we shall know at once & for all that he is a *madman*.

It is all so worrying this awful waiting for the worst to happen....

That evening Wilson's report of his acrimonious meeting with Hitler that day seemed to have ended even Chamberlain's hope of a settlement; the King again offered to send Hitler a telegram. Again, Chamberlain, this time convinced that Hitler in his present exalted ugly mood would merely publish it with an insulting reply, turned the offer down. That night, weary and defeated, Chamberlain broadcast to the nation, speaking in a thin and exhausted voice of 'How horrible, fantastic, incredible, it is that we should be digging trenches and trying on gas-masks here because of a quarrel in a far-away country between people of whom we know nothing.' It was hardly a clarion call by a national leader to a just war, but the majority of his listeners, remembering the horrors and the deaths of 1914–18, could respond to Chamberlain's feelings.

By the 28th, 'Black Wednesday', everyone believed that the worst would, indeed, happen. They did not know that late on the night of the 27th, Chamberlain had received a conciliatory message from Hitler, or that the Prime Minister had replied suggesting he should come immediately to Berlin for a four-power conference and at the same time written a personal letter to Mussolini to intervene. In the hour before his ultimatum expired Hitler came to a decision to agree to Mussolini's suggested four-power conference on condition that Mussolini should be present in person and that the conference should be held at once, either in Munich or Frankfurt. Mussolini accepted, choosing Munich. Soon after 3 p.m. having received Mussolini's confirmation, Hitler sent an invitation to Chamberlain and Daladier. The message reached the British Prime Minister, via Halifax in the Peers' Gallery, as, tired and haggard, he was recounting the gloomy sequence of recent events to the House of Commons. The effect was electrifying as Chamberlain, his face lit up with joy and relief, announced: 'Herr Hitler has just agreed to postpone mobilization for twenty-four hours and to meet me in conference with Signor Mussolini and M. Daladier at Munich.' It seemed to be a last-minute reprieve on the brink of war. Queen Mary, watching from the Ladies' Gallery with the Duchess of Kent, went straight from Westminster to describe the scene to the King as 'dramatic', 'wonderful'; she herself, she said, had been too moved to speak.

The following day Chamberlain flew to Munich to sign the 'piece of paper' which he was to flourish at the welcoming crowds at Heston airport on his return the next day. He had an ecstatic welcome, not least from the King, who had wanted to go to Heston to greet him in person but had had to content himself with sending a welcoming note via his Lord Chamberlain, asking him to come straight to Buckingham Palace, so that he could 'express to you personally my most heartfelt congratulations'. King and Prime Minister appeared on the balcony of Buckingham Palace to the delight of wildly cheering crowds; later from the window of Downing Street, Chamberlain, with Disraeli's words after the Congress of Berlin in mind, spoke of bringing back 'peace with honour', a phrase which was to haunt him (and which he had at first refused to use): 'This is the second time in our history that there has come back from Germany to Downing Street peace with honour. I believe it is peace for our time.'

In fact, the Munich agreement was not substantially different from the Godesberg memorandum which the Cabinet had rejected earlier. The result was the dismemberment of Czechoslovakia, as General Jodl wrote in his diary on the night of the agreement: 'The Pact of Munich is signed. Czechoslovakia as a Power is out. . . .' On 1 October the Germans marched into the Sudetenland. Czechoslovakia lost her fortifications and 11,000 square miles of territory. President Beneš, who had dared to stand up to the Nazis, was forced into exile and within a month the new regime had ceded further territory to Poland and to Hungary. In Germany Hitler's prestige rose to new heights.

'Yesterday was a great day,' the King wrote to Queen Mary on 1 October. 'The Prime Minister was delighted with the result of his mission, as we all are, & he had a great ovation when he came here.' Not everyone, however, was delighted. Winston and Clementine Churchill with Lord Cecil of Chelwood seriously discussed marching to Downing Street at the head of like-minded supporters to hurl a brick through the Prime Minister's windows, and Cecil coined a bitterly mocking paraphrase of Chamberlain's proud use of the old adage, 'If at first you don't concede, fly, fly and fly again.' Duff Cooper resigned immediately, to be received kindly by the King, who was 'frank and charming. He said he could not agree with me, but he respected those who had the courage of their convictions.' In the Commons the Labour Party and the Conservative Opposition, the 'Glamour Boys' followers of Eden and Churchill, voted against the agreement and Churchill made a most powerful speech on what he called 'the abandonment and ruin of Czechoslovakia', describing it as a disaster of the first magnitude for Britain and France. 'It must now be accepted', he warned, 'that all the countries of Central and Eastern Europe will make the best terms they can with the triumphant Nazi Power.' The day would come, he prophesied, when Hitler might choose 'to look westward' and then Britain and France would bitterly regret the loss of the Czech Army, which would have required thirty German divisions to defeat it. There could never, he said, be peace between British democracy and the Nazi Power. The Western democracies had been found wanting – 'This', he said, 'is only the beginning of the reckoning. . . .'[33] *The Times*, which had first floated the idea of sacrificing Czechoslovakia to Hitler in a leader of 7 September, now mocked Churchill for prophecies which 'made Jeremiah appear an optimist'.

Feeling over Munich ran high in Society and in the country at large with great bitterness between the two sides. For the present the pro-Munich faction was by far the majority; Chamberlain, fondly caricatured as 'the man with the umbrella', and temporarily as popular as that other man with an umbrella – Charlie Chaplin – was deluged with heart-felt letters of gratitude, presents of umbrellas, flowers and fishing-rods from all over Europe. President Roosevelt sent a hearty cable, 'Good Man', and the Kaiser, a voice from another war, wrote to his cousin Queen Mary, describing the British Prime Minister as 'inspired by Heaven and guided by God'. Queen Mary sent it on to the King to be shown to Chamberlain and then deposited it in the Royal Archives with a letter in which she ardently backed the Prime Minister against his critics in the House of Commons. 'I am sure you feel as angry as I do', she told her son, 'at people croaking as they do at the PM's action, for once I agree with Lady Oxford who is said to have exclaimed when she left the H of Commons yesterday, "He brought home Peace, why can't they be grateful?"' From Munich to the day of his death, the King and the royal family were to be loyal friends to Chamberlain.

The most that can be said for Chamberlain's policy at Munich is that it did win Britain a breathing-space in which to prepare for war, but that it was dishonourably gained at the expense of a smaller country. It was, however, no more than a breathing-space and in the end the sacrifice of Czechoslovakia proved to have been in vain and, indeed, when war eventually came, to have made the situation worse for the Allies, as Churchill predicted. It made war more likely because Hitler – and Mussolini – became convinced that the democracies would not fight and that there was, therefore, no limit to the demands that they could make on them. The King, and even more the Queen and Queen Mary, were 'Munichois' to the core, convinced that Chamberlain had been right in his efforts to save peace. The King supported Chamberlain's policy objective for the future, which he noted down after a long conversation with the Prime Minister on 19 October, in terms which suggest that the King had pressed Chamberlain to rearm as much and as quickly as possible: 'The PM agreed with the King that the future policy must be the cultivation of friendly negotiations combined with intensified rearmament. One must be strong in order to negotiate. . . .' Chamberlain apparently was so satisfied with the results of his personal initiative with Hitler, that he contemplated a repetition in future. 'At times', he told the King, 'the old diplomacy fails, and personal interviews with dictators are called for.' The King noted also that, in Chamberlain's view, both the United States and Soviet Russia should be 'left alone' by Britain, a cardinal error, and that the Anglo–Italian negotiations should be pursued.

The King and Queen were still at a snowy Sandringham in the first month of the New Year when Chamberlain, accompanied by Halifax, left for Rome in a further attempt at appeasing the dictators. It is hard to see what the British Prime Minister hoped to achieve by this personal pilgrimage to Mussolini; in the event, its only result was to reinforce the Italian dictator's contempt for the democracies and his conviction that Britain would not fight. Mussolini had already decided to accept Ribbentrop's proposal made at Munich to turn the anti-Comintern alliance into the Pact of Steel between Italy and Germany with the adhesion of Japan. He was in close touch with the Japanese Ambassador as Ciano recorded in his diary: 'The Ambassador is very favourable to the Alliance, which he considers an aggressive instrument by which to obtain from Great Britain "the many things she owes us all".'[34] Furthermore, Mussolini's shopping list for 1939 would have shocked Chamberlain had he seen it, including as it did 'Settling accounts with France', which included annexing Corsica and Djibouti, making Tunisia an Italian protectorate and gaining a foothold in the Suez Canal administration. Albania, too, was included: 'Albania, liquidation by agreement with Belgrade. . . .' Munich had convinced Mussolini that he had nothing to gain from friendship with Britain, which would certainly have to oppose his plans for an extension of the Italian Empire at the expense of France, or for his Balkan ambitions in an area in which in abandoning Czechoslovakia to her fate Britain had clearly shown her powerlessness and lack of interest. Only friendship with the all-conquering Hitler could bring him the booty which his power-hungry soul craved. Chamberlain, he had decided, 'must be accorded a not too enthusiastic welcome', and he was enraged when crowds in the popular quarters of the capital cheered the old man with the umbrella who had saved the peace.

Against this unpromising background Chamberlain and Halifax arrived in Rome by train on 11 January. Ciano noted that these two soberly dressed English gentlemen might have come from 'another world'; another observer, noting the contrast between the two English statesmen and the peacock uniforms of the fascists, thought that they looked 'like undertaker's mutes'. As far as Mussolini was concerned, fine feathers did make fine birds. 'These men are not made of the same stuff as the Francis Drakes and the other magnificent adventurers who created the Empire' was his verdict, to which he added the not unperceptive comment, 'These, after all, are the tired sons of a long line of rich men, and they will lose their empire.'[35] When the visit ended with nothing accomplished, Ciano telephoned Ribbentrop to assure him that it had been no more than a '*grande limonata*' (big lemonade – big nothing).

If Ciano's diary is to be believed, it would have been wiser if Chamberlain and Halifax had stayed at home. The impression which the Italians gained from their discussions was 'the profound uneasiness which dominates the British attitude to Germany'. German rearmament, he said,

weighs upon them like lead. They would be ready for any sacrifice if they could see the future clearly. This sombre preoccupation of theirs has convinced me more and more of the necessity for the Triple Alliance. Having in our hands such an instrument we could get whatever we want. The British do not want to fight.

In view of what Mussolini and his fascists really thought of the British Prime Minister, it is all the more pathetic to find Chamberlain writing to the King an eight-page, fascinated account (including a long physical description) of the dictator, who made a very good impression upon him. 'Both Halifax and I were favourably impressed with Mussolini,' he told the King. 'Talking with him is a much pleasanter affair than with Hitler. You feel you are dealing with a reasonable man, not a fanatic, and he struck us both as straightforward and sincere in what he said.'[36] Unlike Hitler, he continued, Mussolini had a sense of humour, although he did have some faults. 'He feels at home reviewing his troops or his sports organisations, or declaiming to the crowd from a balcony but in polite society he is not altogether comfortable and his manners are not too good. He walked about at receptions with both hands in the pockets of his evening trousers.' Chamberlain's conclusion showed that his visit to Rome, far from opening his eyes to the true nature of the regime and its leader, had merely confirmed his blinkered belief in the rightness of his policy. '... I feel confident', he concluded, 'that the personal contacts we have established will tend to keep Mussolini on the rails and to confirm him in the belief that it is worth his while to keep the peace. . . .'

Chamberlain's disillusionment with the dictators was not long in coming. On 14 March German troops entered what remained of independent Czechoslovakia; on the evening of the following day Hitler, accompanied by Keitel, Ribbentrop and Himmler, was in Prague and on 16 March, speaking from the ancient Hradschin Castle overlooking the capital, Hitler dissolved the Czech State and announced the German Protectorate over Bohemia and Moravia. Nor was that the end: the next object to be swallowed by Germany was the city of Memel, demanded from and surrendered helplessly by the Lithuanian Government on 21 March. Then on the same day Ribbentrop reopened the question of ceding Danzig with the Poles and three days later an agreement with Romania established German dominance in that mineral-rich Balkan country.

Chamberlain had, at last, had enough. On 17 March at Birmingham, in a speech which had been intended to be a celebration of his seventieth birthday, he warned the dictators that, if Britain's liberty were challenged, he would fight. The King's response to this major switch in policy was to send an enthusiastic letter of support: 'The Queen and I listened to your speech last night with great interest,' he wrote on 18 March, '& I am glad that it has been so well received all over the world. . . .'[37] On 31 March Chamberlain went further. In response to rumours of an imminent German attack on Poland, he gave the Polish Government the public guarantee which five months later would lead to Britain's declaration of war on Germany.

Imminent European war provided the backdrop to the two most important State visits the King and Queen were to make before the conflict. On 5 May 1939 they sailed from Southampton in the Canadian Pacific liner, *Empress of Australia*, for what was to be their first, and for the King only, visit to the Dominion of Canada and the United States. For the royal couple it was to provide an opportunity of establishing themselves on the international stage; two years later the Queen was to tell Mackenzie King, the Canadian Prime Minister, 'that tour made us', speaking of it as 'coming at just the right time . . . for us'.[38] It was also intended to forge links across the Atlantic which were to prove of vital importance after the outbreak of the Second World War. 'Of the warmth of their reception', wrote the King's official biographer, 'they were never for a moment in doubt.' This was not precisely true, even as far as the Dominion of Canada was concerned, still less so in the case of the United States; isolationists in both countries regarded the royal tour with suspicion as an attempt by the Chamberlain Government to drag them into war on Britain's side.

Mackenzie King had issued the invitation to visit Canada when he was in London for the Coronation and the Dominion Prime Ministers' Conference, hoping that a visit by the King and Queen would cement the cracks in Canadian unity, threatened by a French Canadian separatist movement among the large, minority, French-speaking population. From the British point of view the reinforcing of Canadian loyalty to the Crown, shaken and shocked by the Abdication, was of primary importance. And, as always, there was the Windsor factor; the King and Queen were not known in Canada where the ex-King had once been universally adored.

The invitation to visit the United States had been the personal initiative of President Franklin D. Roosevelt, whose motives for issuing it were primarily related to the European situation. Convinced that sooner or later Britain would have to stand up to Hitler, he had been dismayed by Chamberlain's policy of appeasement and his snubbing of Roosevelt's offers of help, and, like most Americans who were not isolationists, appalled by Munich. As Roosevelt's son Elliott put it, 'As a practitioner of the arts of persuasion, Father wanted the welcome he planned for the King and Queen of England to act as a symbol of American affinity for a country whose present political leadership he did not trust.'[39] Like Chamberlain, Roosevelt believed in the power of personal diplomacy; he was, moreover, according to his son, 'fascinated by kings and queens, half-amused, half-impressed, by the pomp and pageantry that enveloped royalty'. Having met George v, whose salty naval humour he shared, he was curious to see how George vi was shaping up and to establish personal contact with him. Indeed, his first inclination had been for a private, unofficial visit, with the King and Queen slipping unostentatiously across the border from the Canadian tour to see the New York World's Fair and to spend three or four informal days at the Roosevelt's country home, Springwood, at Hyde Park on the Hudson River. The informal, private nature of the visit was designed to avoid arousing isolationist ire and also to give the President full opportunity of exercising his famous charm upon the King. Indeed, when, on a visit to Canada in August 1938, Roosevelt learned that the King and Queen would definitely be going to Canada the following year, the President wrote a personal letter to King George, dated 25 August 1938, written on an informal man-to-man basis and suggesting that both the American Ambassador in London, Joseph P. Kennedy, and the British Ambassador in Washington, Sir Ronald Lindsay, should be kept out of the arrangements.[40]

Lindsay, however, aware of Roosevelt's great domestic unpopularity, was alive to the danger that if the King and Queen's visit were seen as a private Roosevelt family party, it might rebound unfavourably on them. Lindsay felt that it would do more good if the visit were made official and included Washington and Congress on the itinerary. He made this clear to the President when handing him the King's friendly but noncommittal reply to Roosevelt's invitation. Roosevelt was annoyed; returning to the charge he wrote again to the King saying that he agreed with the Ambassador that 'it would probably be advisable' for Their Majesties 'to pay a visit to me at the Capital, but,' he added resentfully, 'I think that Lindsay should not call the visit to Washington "the principal part of the plan". I say this to you quite frankly because he does not even refer to your coming to stay with Mrs Roosevelt and me at Hyde Park.' He went on to make a direct, personal, punchy appeal to the King, over the head of his diplomatic representative:

I know you will not mind my telling you that in my judgement, to the American people, the essential democracy of yourself and the Queen makes the greatest appeal of all. Probably the official visit to the Capital should be made, and also a visit to New York but if you could stay with us at Hyde Park for two or three days, the simplicity and naturalness of such a visit would produce a great effect. . . .[41]

The President's diagnosis of the reaction of the American people was to turn out to be absolutely accurate. Further to emphasize the apolitical nature of the King's American visit, Mackenzie King was to accompany the King to the United States as minister-in-attendance, instead of Halifax, whose presence would at once have raised suspicion of political discussions behind the scenes.

From the King's point of view, the prospect of visiting the United States was a fraught one. He would be the first reigning British sovereign to do so since the former colonies had rebelled against his great-great-great-grandfather, George III. Since that date the population of the United States had been swelled by a number of ethnic groups with grievances against the British—the Irish, the Jews (because of recent policy on Palestine) and, to a lesser extent, the Italians and Germans. Isolationist feeling was strong, particularly in the Midwest; the Arms Neutrality Bill was before Congress and the visit could have been regarded as an attempt by the British to influence the outcome. Moreover, in the United States, far more than in Canada, the 'Windsor factor' was a potent consideration. The Duke of Windsor's hugely successful American tours as Prince of Wales were still remembered and, while his image had been somewhat dented by the previous year's German visit and the fiasco of the cancelled Bedaux trip, there was still a strong groundswell of sentiment in the couple's favour. Wallis was, after all, an American and, although the majority of the American upper class thought (as Lindsay had reported the previous year) much the same as their British counterparts about Wallis and Edward, they were widely regarded as the modern Romeo and Juliet. They still had fervent and vocal partisans among the population at large, particularly in New York. On 21 December 1936 *Time,* reporting US opinions on the Abdication, had zeroed in on 'the masses'' reaction to a news film on the subject, shown at Manhattan's 'No. 1 newsreel theatre', the Embassy in Times Square. According to the news magazine, the audience reaction had been as follows to the appearance on screen of:

Prince [*sic*] Edward (*cheers*); Mrs Simpson (*cheers*); her first husband Commander Spencer, USN (*boos*); her second and present husband Mr Simpson (*cheers & boos*); the Archbishop of Canterbury (BOOS); new Crown Princess Elizabeth (*boos*); new King George & Queen Elizabeth (*boos!*); Prime Minister Baldwin (PROLONGED CATCALLS AND BOOS!); King Edward & Mrs Simpson bathing in Mediterranean (CHEERS!).

Moreover, since early 1938 with the publication of a book *Why Edward Went,* the theory, in which the Windsors themselves now seem to have believed, that

Edward was pushed off the throne by an Establishment conspiracy, was gaining ground.

On 18 January 1939, while arrangements for the forthcoming tour were being finalized, Don Wharton, executive editor of *Scribner's*, forwarded to Geoffrey Dawson at *The Times* a parcel containing information about the Windsors and the proposed royal visit to the United States, which the King's Private Secretary, Sir Eric Miéville, to whom Dawson forwarded it, described as 'unpleasant'.[42] The papers which Buckingham Palace had found so unwelcome included a bundle of material referring to an organization called 'the Friends of the Duke of Windsor in the United States', which had come into existence the previous year 'to appreciate and defend him and urge his qualification as an international leader in the cause of human welfare and world peace', and a copy of the invitation to the annual dinner to be held in New York on 20 January, the anniversary of his accession. A press release for the dinner repeated the speakers' suggestions that an international office be created for the Duke of Windsor, presumably as the head of a Wenner-Gren-like peace and welfare movement, and reiterated the theme that Edward had been forced off the throne by traditionalists because of his humane and democratic tendencies. The 'Friends', according to the information Wharton sent with the package, were a collection of unknowns, none of whom had even met the Duke of Windsor. They included a New York matron with Stuyvesant in her name, various clergymen of different denominations, a 'President of the Arab League', an unknown actress and a Dr Har Dayal, who was described as a 'philosopher, author and lecturer of India'.

The motley 'Friends' hardly represented a threat to the royal couple and were of little interest beyond providing evidence of the ex-King's links with peculiar peace movements and the continuing power of his name as a figurehead. Buckingham Palace did, however, take seriously an article by Josef Israels II printed in *Scribner's*, entitled 'Selling George VI to the United States', and it was to this article that Miéville particularly referred as 'unpleasant'. Israels's opening line read:

If a public relations counsel had the power to choose from scratch which British personalities he would drop into the American scene for the greatest British profit, they would not have been King George and Queen Elizabeth. The important fact about the United States is that a large part of the country still believes that Edward, Duke of Windsor, is the rightful owner of the British throne, and that King George VI is a colorless, weak personality largely on probation in the public mind of Great Britain, as well as of the United States.

Stories were current, Israels said, of

George's alleged epileptic seizures, his speech impediment and an impression that he is of poorer royal timber than has occupied England's throne in many decades.

As for Queen Elizabeth, by Park Avenue standards, she appears to be far too plump of figure, too dowdy in dress, to meet American specifications of a reigning Queen. The living contrasts of Queen Mary (as regal as a woman can be) and the Duchess of Windsor (chic and charmingly American) certainly does not help Elizabeth....

Israels's message was unmistakable – the personal success or failure of the King and Queen in America was critical: '... the difference between apathetic acceptance of the product and its enthusiastic purchase by the American people will be the difference between success and failure of British–American relations during the next critical international period you expect to face during the next few years.'[43]

The North American tours were, therefore, seen as a public test of the King and the Queen even before they had begun. Four days after the King and Queen sailed for Canada, the Duke of Windsor broadcast an appeal for world peace directed at America from the famous First World War battlefield of Verdun. It was, as Mr Israels would have put it, another public relations disaster for the Duke, although on a more minor scale than the visit to Germany. Although sincerely felt and moving in its language, speaking of 'the presence of the great company of the dead' as 'a soldier of the last war whose earnest prayer is that such cruel and destructive madness shall never again overtake mankind', it was widely seen as a gesture of appeasement or, at its worst, yet another attempt to steal the limelight from his brother just as that brother was en route for an all-important visit to North America. The BBC refused to broadcast it and Edward's erstwhile champion Beaverbrook hastily ordered a leader inserted into the *Daily Express* the morning of the broadcast, hoping perhaps to deflect the Duke from his purpose as he had tried in vain to dissuade him from going to Germany. The King was on his way to America, he told the Duke, therefore, 'Any word spoken to the United States at present should have come from him.' If the Duke was determined to appeal for peace, then he should have at least waited: 'Such an appeal would have been uttered more appropriately after the King's peace mission to the Dominion had been brought to a conclusion.'[44]

What made the Duke do it? Did he see himself as the leader of an international peace movement, in the role in which the 'Friends' and Wenner-Gren had cast him? Did the speeches of the 'Friends', of which he undoubtedly received copies, provide the germ of an idea which the clear advance of war that spring turned into a firm determination to action? There is no doubt that Edward's experiences in the First World War were, together with his passion for Wallis, the most formative of his life. Like thousands of his generation he could not forget them nor could he bear the thought that they might be repeated only a generation later. Headstrong, accustomed to getting his own way and, it must be said, utterly inconsiderate of his brother, he brushed aside the thought that, although 9 May might be the anniversary of the Battle of Verdun, it was also the moment when his brother was irrevocably embarked on an important mission.

The Duke's own explanation of his broadcast is worth quoting. He was adamant – and unrepentant – that the idea was only his, although what he says might seem to suggest that late-night conversations with representatives of fascist states had some part in it.

The idea was mine. I was not without my own sources of intelligence at the time. The German, Italian and Spanish Ambassadors [in Paris] were all good friends of mine. So was Bill Bullitt, in the American Embassy. And I still had one or two lines into Whitehall, even though my own Ambassador was hardly forthcoming. From these and other sources, I became convinced that Europe was headed down the slippery slope to war. Only the Americans had the influence to arrest the slide. That was why I decided to aim my appeal at them.[45]

The Duke's biographer has charitably suggested that the Duke was a 'sucker' for the plans of Fred Bate of the NBC, an old regular of Wallis's Bryanston Court circle, who organized the broadcast. This may be partly so, but it is hard not to suspect that there was a decided intent on the part of the Windsors to upstage the King and Queen before they arrived in America and to draw attention to the Duke as an international figure of equal importance.

The Windsors were particularly bitter with the King and Queen that spring, mainly because of their strenuous resistance to the Duke's attempts to return to England with, if possible, some kind of official post. Walter Monckton had been sent to England to negotiate this in August and September the previous year. Arriving to spend the night at Balmoral, Monckton spoke to Chamberlain, who was also a guest, before seeing the King. He found Chamberlain not averse to the idea of the Duke's returning

to be treated as soon as possible as a younger brother of the King who could take some of the royal functions off his brother's hands. The King himself, though he was not anxious for the Duke to return as early as November 1938 (which was what the Duke wanted) was not fundamentally against the Prime Minister's view. But [noted Monckton], I think the Queen felt quite plainly that it was undesirable to give the Duke of Windsor any effective sphere of work. I felt then, as always, that she naturally thought that she must be on her guard because the Duke of Windsor, to whom the other brothers had always looked up, was an attractive, vital creature who might be the rallying point for any who might be critical of the new King who was less superficially endowed with the arts and graces that please.[46]

The Duke, however, wrote to Chamberlain making it plain that he did not intend to give up; in November Chamberlain asked the Gloucesters, en route back home for Kenya, to stop off in Paris to see the Windsors and test public reaction to their meeting. The result, according to the Duchess of Gloucester's memoirs, was a flood of vituperative letters which she found 'quite upsetting'. Chamberlain himself called briefly on the Windsors and reported back to the King on the interview, which no doubt further concerned the question of the Duke's return. The Duke, apparently, then had planned to return in the spring of 1939, but was asked to postpone it in view of the royal tour of North America. Writing angrily to Lord Beaverbrook about press speculation as to the cause of the postponement, the Duke of Windsor said,

Of course, you now know as well as I do, that it is for no other reasons than for fear lest the attitude my mother and sister-in-law seem likely to adopt towards my wife may provoke some controversy in England and adverse criticism of them in America, that I have been advised to postpone our projected visit to England this spring until after the King and Queen's official visit to Canada and the United States. In accordance with the policy of playing my brother's game, I have agreed to another postponement, but, believe me, for the last time. . . .[47]

It may be doubted whether the Verdun broadcast was really in line with 'the policy of playing my brother's game'; the Duke's feelings towards the King at the time were very far from fraternal. On 9 May, the day of the broadcast, Ambassador Bullitt, who was on extremely friendly terms with the Windsors, reported to the President from Paris, warning him not to raise the subject of his brother with the King: 'About a month ago the Duke of Windsor wrote to Queen Mary that Bertie had behaved toward him in such an ungentlemanly manner because of "the influence of that common little woman" the Queen, that he could have no further relations with Bertie. . . .'[48]

The King's feelings about his brother's broadcast are not on record; no doubt they were as icy as the waters of the North Atlantic through which the *Empress of Australia* made her way towards the fog-shrouded Newfoundland coast. The foghorn sounded continuously as the ship edged through an ice field at much the same latitude as the *Titanic* when it struck the iceberg in April 1912. The Queen wrote to Queen Mary:

For three & a half days we only moved a few miles. The fog was so thick, that it was like a white cloud round the ship, and the foghorn blew incessantly. Its melancholy blasts were echoed back by the icebergs like the twang of a piece of wire. . . .

We very nearly hit a berg the day before yesterday, and the poor Captain was nearly demented because some kind cheerful people kept on reminding him that it was about here that the Titanic was struck, & *just* about the same date. . . .

The King told his mother that he had found the whole experience most interesting and that at least it had given him two extra days' rest: 'I should not however have chosen an ice field surrounded by dense fog in which to have a holiday, but it does seem to be the only place for me to rest in nowadays!'

On 17 May the King and Queen stepped ashore at Wolfe's Cove, Quebec, the first reigning British monarchs to set foot in the New World as the attendant American press was quick to point out. The French-speaking crowds received them with a reserved curiosity, impressed above all with the Queen, whom they had only seen in photographs when she never looked her best and whose 'plump and dowdy' reputation as Duchess of York had preceded her. '*Qu'elle est charmante!*' they exclaimed and – still more surprised – '*Qu'elle est chic!*' US fashion experts, poring over the news photographs of the Queen, were, according to *Time*, 'pleasantly surprised at the Queen's style'. It was the quiet beginning to a tour which was to become a personal triumph for the royal couple just as their Paris visit had been. At Quebec the Catholic Cardinal Villeneuve gave the King's hand 'a lingering fatherly patting' and was deeply impressed by his simplicity and friendliness and by the speech he gave in 'unhesitating French' (preceded by one in 'slightly stammering' English). The King and Queen both nervously

picked at their food – lobster tails, followed by grilled chicken – both refusing
the Grand Marnier soufflé, to the consternation of their fellow guests who
thought they should follow the royal example and were greatly relieved when
the royal footmen indicated that they should go ahead. The King was clearly
longing for a cigarette and, as soon as Mackenzie King had finished toasting
the royal couple in Veuve Clicquot '28, he lit up before a waiter could get to
him with a match. Next day, en route for Montreal, they boarded the royal train,
a silver, blue and gold twelve-car streamliner with royal bedrooms connected
by a sliding panel, gold-plated telephones, a lounge car, offices and bedrooms
for the staff and party. At Montreal, the royal charm captivated even the mayor,
M. Houde, an Italophile fascist, and a member of the royal staff reported to the
Governor-General, Lord Tweedsmuir (the former John Buchan), that the scenes
of welcome 'were as impressive as those at the Coronation'. The Apostolic
Delegate told Tweedsmuir that the chief French nationalist leader in Quebec
said 'after this they might drop the subject for Quebec had gone madly imper-
ialist'.[49] At Ottawa the Governor-General gave a garden party at which the
genteel of the capital became, in Tweedsmuir's words, 'wildly enthusiastic' and
'cheered the whole time like children at a school feast'. It was amazing, he said,
to see 'great bodies of French ecclesiasts, headed by the Archbishop, shouting
"*Vive le Roi* and *vive la Reine!*" '

That evening, 100,000 people packed into the central square cheered the King
and Queen when they appeared on the floodlit balcony after a parliamentary
banquet, but the event which set the whole tour alight occurred the next day at
the unveiling of the War Memorial in Connaught Square by the King.
Tweedsmuir described the scene to Hardinge:

The King spoke admirably and clearly, as he has done each time since he landed. After
the ceremony the Queen said to me that she wanted to go down among the veterans,
and I thought, knowing what excellent fellows they are, that it would be worth chancing
it. A most extraordinary scene followed. The King and Queen, and my wife and myself,
were absorbed in a crowd of six or seven thousand ex-soldiers, who kept the most perfect
order among themselves, and opened up lanes for Their Majesties to pass through. There
was no need of the police, and indeed the police would have had no chance. It was a
wonderful example of what a people's king means, and it would have been impossible
anywhere else in the world. One old man shouted to me, 'Ay, man, if Hitler could see
this!' It was extraordinarily moving because some of these old fellows were weeping.

In the afternoon there was a great send-off at the station, and another highly emotional
scene when the band played 'Will Ye No Come Back Again.'

The capacity of Their Majesties for getting in touch with the people [Tweedsmuir
concluded] amounts to genius. It is the small unscheduled things that count most, and
for these they have an infallible instinct.[50]

At Toronto, meeting the world-famous Dionne quintuplets, there was another
spontaneous incident, when Cecile rushed over to kiss the Queen, who, obviously moved, went down on her knees to gather her into her arms, while quin
Yvonne, seeing the King on his own, went over and took his hand, engaging

him in brisk French conversation about the brass buttons on his naval uniform. Even the hard-boiled US press were impressed; their reports of the huge popularity and easy democratic charm of the King and Queen did a great deal to heighten the warmth of their reception when they reached the United States.

The Governor-General was enchanted. 'Our monarchs are the most remarkable young people,' he wrote to Stair Gillon on 26 May. 'I have always been attached to the King, and I realise now more than ever what a wonderful mixture he is of shrewdness, kindliness and humour. As for the Queen, she has a perfect genius for the right kind of publicity, the unrehearsed episodes here were marvellous.'[51] The King, exhilarated by the love and enthusiasm emanating from the crowds, and experiencing the adrenalin surge of mass popularity, was enjoying himself as he had never thought he would in similar circumstances. To Tweedsmuir's dismay, he insisted on staying up late talking into the night after an exhausting day's engagements. 'He will never go to bed early,' he wrote to a friend; 'there were several things that Neville Chamberlain wanted him to talk to me about, and we had very confidential talks about general politics and possible appointments. . . . I have a very deep respect not only for his character, but for his brains.'[52] To Stanley Baldwin he wrote on 19 June, after the King and Queen had finally departed for home: 'The King has a remarkable flair for political questions, and his judgement, especially after his talks with the President, seemed to me very shrewd.'[53]

The verdict of *The Times* correspondent, J.A. Stevenson, in a private letter to Dawson, was that

The royal tour has been an unqualified success from start to finish and Their Majesties did a first-rate job and achieved a great personal triumph. If I had not seen it with my own eyes, I would not have believed that they could have evoked such demonstrations of loyalty and personal affection from a people normally so inarticulate and unemotional as the Canadians are. But they combined regal dignity in their public appearances with a democratic friendliness in their private contacts.

The royal staff, however, earned few plaudits; the servants, in particular, failed to stay the course. The King's barber, weighing sixteen stone, fell out of his bunk on the royal train on top of the Queen's hairdresser, weighing nine. The king's valet became ill on arrival in Canada as did the Queen's 'second maid', who had to be hastily replaced by a housemaid from the Governor-General's household. The press accused the royal Household, with certain exceptions, of snobbishness, confirming the generally held view of the British upper classes. 'I do not think', Stevenson wrote angrily to Dawson, 'there was a single person on the pilot train who did not resent the disdain with which the entourage treated us. [The Earl of] Airlie was an honourable exception and I presume Tommy Lascelles was extremely busy . . . [but] as for [George F.] Steward the so-called press liaison officer he attained the highest flights of inefficient pomposity.'[54] The *Times*'s man's view of the Household was shared by George

Dixon of the New York *Daily News*. 'Equerries', he wrote, '. . . always seem to bring out the beast in me.'

But Dixon and the other US reporters on the pilot train which accompanied the royal train across Canada were captivated by the King and Queen. British readers, he wrote, could have no idea of the punishment the royal couple endured on their gruelling trip, never with a chance to relax, always on parade, but 'Their Majesties took those parades like real soldiers'. And, he told them, after swapping cracks with the King at Banff, 'your King has a terrific sense of humour'. Also at Banff was John Barry of the Boston *Globe*. The King asked Barry where he lived. 'I'm from Boston,' said Barry. 'You remember we'd trouble with another George there once.' The King smiled disarmingly, 'Oh yes,' he said. 'I think I've heard about it. Something about tea, wasn't it?'[55]

Mackenzie King sent Tweedsmuir an euphoric cable from Victoria, British Columbia, on the last leg of the visit to Western Canada: 'Words cannot begin to describe triumphal nature of royal tour to date It has surpassed all expectations in almost every particular Each day has seemed more wonderful than the last. . . .'[56] The Governor-General in a personal letter to the British Prime Minister summed up what he saw as the real effects of the royal tour of Canada in shoring up Canadian unity and guaranteeing the Dominion's loyalty in the coming conflict.[57] 'The Royal Visit has ensured that there will be no neutrality for Canada,' Stevenson assured his editor.

The thermometer stood at 94° on the morning of 8 June 1939 when the King and Queen stepped out of the royal train at Washington Union Station to be greeted by the President and Mrs Roosevelt. It was not only an historic meeting but also a personal occasion to which both men had been looking forward for months. Perhaps no President of the United States could have been better fitted to get on with King George VI than Roosevelt, the thirty-second President. Twelve years older than the King, Franklin Delano Roosevelt came from patrician stock, the East Coast American aristocracy to whom the Atlantic, even in the days of the steamship, was only a pond and Europe a holiday home. His father shot and hunted with English dukes and mixed with European aristocrats at German spas. For all his democratic ways and beliefs, Roosevelt was deeply conscious of his aristocratic background; a dozen lines of *Mayflower* descents converged in him and he, like his mother, could name every one of them. At Harvard one of his interests had been research into his family's genealogy. But his belief in democracy and the welfare of the people had been fostered at Groton, the select boarding-school which he had entered the year after King George was born, and at which the celebrated headmaster, Endicott Peabody, had instilled into his pupils the ideals of service and the development of a 'manly Christian character'. Like George V he had a passion for the Navy, collecting naval prints, books, manuscripts and pamphlets (and also stamps); he had served in the Navy Department and briefly, like George VI, on board a warship during the First World War and, like George VI, he had had first-hand experience of the devastation of war in France. Although, unlike the King, his happy family background and the love and admiration which had been lavished on him by his parents had produced in him a brimming self-confidence, he knew what it was like to experience and to overcome serious illness. In the summer of 1921, his thirty-ninth year, he had contracted severe poliomyelitis, which had left him crippled and in a wheelchair. King George saw a man with a handsome leonine head and wasted legs no thicker than a man's arm, who was still overflowing with vitality, humour, charm and ideas. What he could not see was the subtlety and princely capacity for detachment that lay beneath.

Eleanor Roosevelt, the President's wife and cousin, towered beside her husband, dwarfing the King and Queen. A remarkable woman and a personality in her own right, she wrote her own newspaper column, 'My Day', and was a tireless and idealistic worker for a number of causes. She had regarded the royal tour with a certain amount of amused detachment, leaving most of the details to her husband, which was just as well, since, according to her son Elliott, her homespun notions of hospitality extended to the scrambled eggs she prepared for all seasons and square dancing in the East Room of the White House after such a simple supper. The White House food was notoriously bad. Particularly, since she was largely indifferent to material needs herself, she had been amused by the elaborate five-page list sent by Bill Bullitt from Paris with the details he had gleaned from the French State visit as to the needs of Their Majesties and their Households down to the last tooth-glass and hot-water bottles for the ladies-in-waiting, tissue paper and 'light muslin cloths' for the Queen's dresses and a 'large solid table' on which His Majesty's valet could clean the King's shoes. Their Majesties always had an early morning cup of tea at 8 a.m., followed at 9.15 by breakfast, on trays and prepared separately by their own servants, the King having tea, toast, fruit, bacon and eggs, the Queen tea, toast and fruit. They liked tea to be ready for them whenever they returned. 'Moreover, when they come back about midnight, ham sandwiches should always be prepared' and fruit available. The King brought his own liquor and spirits. Bullitt's list of newspapers which were or were not liked by Their Majesties, although hardly relevant to the United States, was a revealing one: 'For Their Majesties: *The Times, The Telegraph,* the *Daily Sketch.* . . . Should never be produced: *Daily Mirror, Sunday Pictorial, Daily Mail* (read, however, by some of the Household and the servants), *News of the World, Daily Express.*'[58] Lascelles, who had visited Washington earlier to make arrangements, had passed on such vital information as that the King did not like suet puddings or capers, and that protocol required the King to be served precisely thirty seconds before the Queen. At the White House, where the Queen's bedroom had formerly been Abraham Lincoln's study, a last-minute inspection of the prints donated by a friend of the family for the occasion had revealed, among harmless scenes from Queen Victoria's family life, a depiction of General Burgoyne surrendering at Saratoga. It was hastily removed.

The two-day visit taking place as it did in the heat and humidity of a Washington summer and at the end of the long Canadian tour was a real test for the King and Queen, the focus of interest in the nation's capital. The 100 top Washingtonians, crammed into the President's reception-room at Union Station, saw a King who was 'young, fit and earnest', although they noted that his 'smiling muscles' stood out rigidly and that he was smaller than they had expected, dwarfed by the towering Sir Ronald Lindsay. The Queen they saw as 'crisp and bonny', 'the perfect Queen: eyes a snapping blue, chin tilted confidently, two fingers raised in greeting as girlish as it was regal'. Her long-handled parasol, an object that had not been seen publicly in Washington since the days of the previous President Roosevelt, seemed 'out of a story book', but as she wore what was described as an 'unselfish' off-the-face hat, it failed to save her fair Scottish complexion from sunburn. Some 60,000 people ('mainly government employees and blacks, the principal elements of the population,' according to the French Ambassador) lined the royal route from Union Station past the Capitol down Pennsylvania Avenue to the White House, 500 of whom collapsed in the heat as did sixty Girl Scouts waiting to be reviewed at the White House.

The King felt instantly at ease with the President as he sat beside him chatting as they drove in an open carriage to the White House. Eleanor Roosevelt was fascinated by the Queen's gracious manner and the way in which she bowed right and left, apparently with real interest, 'actually looking at people in the crowd so I am sure many of them felt that her bow was really for them personally'. Afterwards she discovered that the cushion upon which the Queen sat had springs which made it easier to keep up the continual bowing. At the end of a long day, which included a diplomatic reception at the White House, a drive round Washington and a garden-party at the British Embassy, Mrs Roosevelt was impressed by the way in which the King and Queen in some 'miraculous way' managed to change for dinner and appear looking completely unhurried. '... the Queen never had a crease in her dress or a hair out of place. I do not see how it is possible to remain so perfectly in character all the time,' she commented. 'My admiration for her grew every minute she spent with us.'[59]

Both Roosevelts were particularly impressed by the King's knowledge of and interest in the American Government and, close to both their hearts, the New Deal welfare agencies. At the garden-party, watching journalists were impressed when the King instantly said, on being introduced to South Carolina's senior senator, 'Cotton Ed Smith?' At the same party the Texan Vice-President, John Nance 'Cactus Jack' Garner, showing off his democratic manners, slapped the King on the back in greeting and later, according to Secretary Ickes, 'pawed' him; the King endured it with good humour and good manners. The Queen, her face and arms flushed and slightly swollen with sunburn, suffered visibly but none the less, according to an observer, 'she did not cease to smile or, like the King, to do her duty with as much conscientiousness as good grace'. After a White House banquet at which, according to Elliott Roosevelt, the White House cooking 'lived down to its reputation', there was an all-American 'musicale' evening arranged by Mrs Roosevelt, with cowboy ballads ('whoopee, Ti Yi Yo, Git Along, Little Dogies'), folk songs by the Coon Creek girls from

Pinchem Tight Hollow in Kentucky, square-dancing, 'These Foolish Things' by crooner Kate Smith, and some magnificent negro spirituals by Mrs Roosevelt's protégée, Marian Anderson. The following day included a visit to the Capitol, where, according to *Time*, the King 'endured an ordeal of Klieg lights and Congressional crudeness as 74 Senators and 352 Representatives trotted by in 25 minutes', while New York's Sol Bloom mispronounced their names and Patton of Texas addressed speeches of welcome to 'Cousin George' and 'Cousin Elizabeth', followed by lunch on the presidential yacht on the Potomac and a visit to Washington's home, Mount Vernon.

For the King, the most interesting part of the day was a visit to a Civilian Conservation Corps camp at Fort Hunt, on which he was accompanied not by the President, who could not manage the walking involved, but by Mrs Roosevelt. The boys were drawn up in two lines, the King stopping to speak to every other boy, the Queen to the intervening ones. The King, Mrs Roosevelt remembered, 'asked really interested questions, such as whether they were satisfied with their food, what they were learning and whether they thought it would help them to obtain work and, lastly, how much they were earning'. He had previously described the Duke of York's Camps to the Roosevelts, telling them how, referring to boys from the depressed mining areas, he 'had been deeply troubled to find that many boys had no conception of doing a full day's work, because they had never seen their fathers do a day's work, many of Great Britain's miners having been on the dole for years. . . .' The King was concerned about the effect of their fathers' long-term unemployment upon the boys and 'wanted to set up something as useful as the ccc camps in Great Britain'. When they had reached the end of the second row, the camp commandant suggested that, although the boys had prepared their barracks and mess hall for his inspection, the King might not feel up to crossing the field in the broiling sun. The King responded, 'If they expect me to go, of course I will go.' The Queen, heroically, followed across the field with Mrs Roosevelt where the King made a thorough inspection, looking at shelves of supplies, examining the undersides of furniture when he heard the boys had made the things themselves, looking into pots and pans on the stove, and in examining the menu. 'Finally we trudged back across the field', Mrs Roosevelt recalled, 'and when we reached the bulletin board [featuring ccc camps across the country and pictures of their work] . . . the Queen murmured gently in my ear that the heat had made her feel very peculiar and did I think she could return to the car. I assured her that no one would mind and we went back and sat in the car while the King examined every picture.'[60]

En route back to Washington they stopped at Arlington Cemetery, where the King laid a wreath at the Tomb of the Unknown Soldier and at the Canadian Cross, and then on to tea on the White House Lawn. This function had been organized in response to the King's particular request to meet the heads of all the government agencies contributing to national recovery under the New Deal. Eleanor Roosevelt had been charged by her husband to introduce each agency head to the King with a brief outline of the work they were doing and then give them three minutes with the King before taking them over to the Queen. 'I had rather dreaded trying to engineer this', Mrs Roosevelt wrote, 'and wondered how I was going to condense the introduction into a brief enough explanation, but I soon found that my explanation could be very short, for the King seemed to know at once, as I spoke the name, what that person was doing, and he started right in with the questions.' She was so impressed with the King's knowledge that she later asked him how he knew what work every person in the US Government did: 'He told me that before he came he had made a study of the names and occupations of everyone in the government; that the material had been procured for him, and was part of his preparation for this trip to Washington.'[61] The King's honesty and seriousness appealed to Mrs Roosevelt, as she told a friend: 'Both [the King and Queen] interested me & I think he feels things more than she does & knows more. She is perfect as a Queen, gracious, informed, saying the right thing & kind but a little self-consciously regal.'[62]

After dinner at the British Embassy (before which the Queen had made a special point of appearing to the eight-year-old daughter of the President's aide, Harry Hopkins, to sparkle in white crinoline and diamonds as the little girl's vision of a 'Fairy Queen'), they left that night for New York. Although it had been feared that this might be the toughest part of the tour – a major part of the population of Manhattan and Brooklyn, Jews, Irish, Italians and Harlem West Indians, could be said to have grievances against the British – by the day of their arrival the King and Queen were popular in advance. 'Our nation today welcomes King George and Queen Elizabeth,' trumpeted the *New York World Telegram*. 'They are greeted by the American people not merely as representatives of another great democracy, or as royalty, but as two great human beings who have won that distinction in their own right. . . . We like them. And we hope they like us.' Reporting the royal arrival at the Battery the *New York Daily Mirror* put it punchily: 'so these were their Majesties. A blondish, tired-looking man and a cute, cuddly, home-looking girl in an ice-blue ensemble. The man bowed stiffly; the girl beamed warmly. That smile let loose the works. Wow! Zowie! Hey!' Cheering crowds greeted them at vantage-points as they drove with the mayor, Fiorello La Guardia, down the magnificent new West Side highway to Central Park and along the East River to the World's Fair site on Flushing Meadows. There was even some ticker-tape and, to the British officials' relief, not a squeak of Irish protest. According to the *New York Times*, for sheer numbers the crowds were unprecedented and 'similarly we can recall no parallel for the steady warmth of the greetings'. It was a tiring day of motorcades, presentations, inspections; a prolonged visit to the Exhibition was followed by a drive to Columbia University on Morningside Heights. By this time the King and Queen were at last showing signs of exhaustion and moving like automatons. Newspaper woman Inez Robb wrote that at times the muscles in the King's lean cheeks convulsed 'as if he were gritting his teeth to stick it out and see it through in the British tradition' and that the Queen was flushed with fatigue. But in public relations terms it had been worth it. 'We said we liked them, much, when they came,' the *New York World Telegram* wrote on 12 June, 'and hoped they would like us. We like them even better after watching them take the hurdles of our hospitality. No matter what our future opinions may be about the British Empire ... there will be forever only affection for the charming pair who visited us, smilin' through.'

Hours late, after a ninety-mile drive up the Hudson River, during which the King had insisted on stopping and telephoning the Roosevelts at intervals along the way, they arrived at the Roosevelt home, Hyde Park. This twenty-four-hour visit to his family home was the moment which the President had been planning since the idea of extending the royal tour from Canada had first occurred to him; when he intended to get to know the King, to impress upon him his own ideas for international relations and to gain first-hand, up-to-date knowledge of the thinking of the British Government. It was typical of Roosevelt's *modus operandi* to make what for him was the most important part of the tour appear – which it also was – as a kindly, hospitable gesture of consideration for two tired people who were also friends. As Mrs Roosevelt put it, 'My husband always loved taking people he liked home with him. I think he felt he knew them better once they had been at Hyde Park.'[63]

He had fought to keep Hyde Park on the King's itinerary against the reservations of Lindsay and the representations on political and social grounds of well-connected Republican ladies, who had seen to it that their adverse comments came to the ears of the British Foreign Office. One emphasized that the Hyde Park visit to the home of a President so unpopular and suspected of trying to drag America into an European war would rebound disastrously on the royal couple.[64] Another claimed to have just spent ten days with the President's mother in New York and that Sara Roosevelt was anxious about the visit which 'all New York thought preposterous'. Hyde Park itself, the lady wrote, was totally inadequate:

There is no proper arrangement for secret service men and police even in ordinary times. The house has no proper suites and rooms etc., and the service represents a scratch lot of negroes and white, English and Irish. The Footman is a lout of a red-haired Irishman, and should only be carrying wood and coals and polishing shoes....[65]

As it turned out the Roosevelts did have trouble with the servants over the royal visit, but it came not from the loutish Irish footman but from James, Sara Roosevelt's English butler. The President had decided to send up two black butlers from the White House to help out the Hyde Park staff during the royal stay. Shortly afterwards James came to her and told her he would like to take his annual holiday from a certain date. 'Oh, but James,' she replied aghast, 'that's just when Their Majesties are going to be here.' 'Madam,' the butler answered, drawing himself up, 'I cannot be a party to the degradation of the British monarchy.' In the absence of James, the two White House servants, unfamiliar with the house, caused a serving table to crash resoundingly during the royal dinner and, tripping over an unseen step, to send a tray of after-dinner drinks, glasses and ice, spinning over the floor to the feet of the Queen. This was not the only occasion when the legendary snobbery of British upper servants caused problems for the Roosevelts. The King's valet found the standard of food and drink at the White House far below that to which he was accustomed, while the Queen's dresser, asked by a White House usher if she would relay a message from the Queen to a lady-in-waiting, drew herself up icily and replied, 'I am the Queen's maid.'[66]

The King and Queen felt immediately at home in the family country-house atmosphere of Hyde Park. The President got things going on the right footing by having a tray of cocktails waiting for the couple when they arrived hours late and weary from New York. 'My mother', the President told the King, 'thinks you should have a cup of tea; she doesn't approve of cocktails.' 'Neither does my mother,' said the King and gratefully took one.

After dinner the King, the President and Mackenzie King had a long talk about the international situation; later the following afternoon Roosevelt and the King had a further conversation. The King was so impressed with what the President told him that he took careful notes of it afterwards and kept these notes with him in a despatch case which he carried throughout the war. The King himself was extremely well briefed on American attitudes from a thirty-four-page document entitled 'Vade Mecum 1939', which had been prepared for him by F.R. Hoyer Millar of the Foreign Office. This included such headings as 'New Deal, President, Congress and Public Opinion', which left the King with no illusions as to the hostility with which the President's domestic policies were regarded by 'the capitalistic classes', and an accurate precis of Roosevelt's two terms, his achievements and his mistakes. The King had learned how the great record of Roosevelt's first term as President had not been consolidated in his second, partly through the President's failings as an administrator and his blunder in attempting to pack the ultra-conservative Supreme Court with nominees favourable to his New Deal legislation. The business world and the southern Democrats of his own party regarded him with suspicion and he had largely lost control both of Congress and his party. The entire domestic political outlook was dominated, the King was told, by the 1940 presidential election, which the Republicans appeared confident of winning, although they had no worthy candidate and it was not yet known if Roosevelt would run again. The King had been made aware of the divided state of US public opinion as regards the European situation and that, although emotionally American public opinion was strongly on the side of the democracies, politically 'there is any amount of neutral thought'. There were still, Hoyer Millar warned, many Americans who actively disliked, even hated, Britain because of unpaid war debts, Irish grievances, psychological dislike of Englishmen and inferiority complexes, but increasingly among the educated classes the feeling was voiced that if Britain were involved in a war, America was bound to come in sooner or later and that it was of capital importance to America that the democratic powers should win 'because a Nazi world would not be worth living in'. The document detailed the President's stand on the European situation, his apparently inbred prejudice against Germany and his courage in revealing his feelings to the American public, warning them of the dangers and preaching the necessity of military preparedness, and his success in educating his people 'in a new school of thought on foreign affairs'. There followed an analysis of the present state of Anglo–US relations, improved by the granting of Dominion status to Ireland and by the firm line recently taken on Czechoslovakia, although resentment of Britain's attitude over Munich and the *Anschluss* had left a suspicion that 'we may rat again'. Several pages were devoted to the complexities and possibilities of the proposed revision, then before Congress, of the Neutrality law which would have a major effect on America's ability to supply Britain with arms in the event of war, and the powers of the President under the Constitution. The survey, largely favourable to Roosevelt, concluded with some less than flattering observations on the US congressional representatives and a tribute to Roosevelt's Secretary of State, Cordell Hull.[67]

The King was, therefore, far from being at a disadvantage in high-level, informal discussions with the Prime Minister of Canada and the President of the United States, both several years his senior in age and political experience. From the King's notes, in the first conversation the President talked expansively and generally of the friendship between the USA and Canada and of his plans for the defence of the Canadian Pacific seaboard. More specifically, he mentioned one of his favourite plans for circumventing the US Neutrality Act, which was to become a vital reality on the outbreak of war, whereby aeroplane parts could be shipped from the US to Canada and assembled there for transport to Britain. He heartened the King with assurances of how he and Cordell Hull were working to turn American public opinion 'on the right tack' towards aid for the democracies. In the second conversation they spoke of the European situation 'in a general way', with Roosevelt expressing the vain hope that 'France & Italy would get together', and the question of loans to Romania. The King found the President 'definitely anti-Russian' – 'I told him so were we but if we could not have an understanding with her, Germany would probably make one,' the King recorded prophetically. Roosevelt was, he noted, 'terribly keen' about the idea of safeguarding the western hemisphere through a US naval patrol in the Caribbean, using British West Indian bases in return for relieving Britain of this responsibility. (This idea was to be partially realized in the Anglo–American Destroyers for Bases deal of September 1940.) He was also misleadingly optimistic as to the likelihood of America entering the war if Britain were attacked. 'If London was bombed USA would come in,' the King recorded.

Those two late-night conversations with Roosevelt at Hyde Park were the King's first experience of talking world politics with a world leader, and he found it a heady one. Exhausted as he was, he was still prepared to talk far into the night at 1.30 a.m. when the President, playing a fatherly role, leaned forward from his chair to place a hand on the King's knee. 'Young man,' he said, 'it's time for you to go to bed....' But even then the King did not want to go to sleep; upstairs on that Saturday night he called Mackenzie King into his room to talk over what had been said and to tell him how he felt about his new-found friend, the US President. Later the Canadian Prime Minister wrote to Roosevelt telling him how the King had enthused about the warmth shown to him and the Queen on their US visit, how much they had been taken by the family charm of Hyde Park and the friendliness of the Roosevelt family, and above all how much he had appreciated his talks with the President:

He told me that he had enjoyed his talks with you more than with anyone else, that he found it easier to carry on a conversation with you than with almost any one, and that he had appreciated beyond words the welcome you had given him and the frank and open way in which you had talked over many matters.... For yourself personally his admiration could not have been greater.[68]

From that weekend at Hyde Park on, the King felt that he had a 'special relationship' with the American President.

Next day, Sunday 11 June, the Roosevelts and their guests attended St James's Church, Hyde Park, followed by a picnic at the President's Hilltop Cottage. The King took off his tie, ate hot dogs, drank Ruppert's beer and took home movies of the Indian storyteller and singer who performed at the picnic. Afterwards the President 'whizzed the Royal pair round the estate in his Ford with manual brakes and gearshift, giving Scotland Yard palpitations'. Then he and the King had another swim, the King, according to the President's son, James, arrayed in a dark-blue bathing-suit which, with its 'vestigial remnants of arms and legs', looked like a genuine relic from the era of his grandfather, Edward VII. As they left for the journey back to Canada and home, the royal couple stood waving on the rear platform of the train; as it pulled out the people gathered on the banks of the Hudson suddenly began to sing 'Auld Lang Syne'. 'Good luck! All the luck in the world!' the President yelled, as his wife thought how 'incredibly moving' the scene was in the evening light. Four days late the King and Queen, amid scenes of great emotion, boarded the liner *Empress of Britain* at Halifax to return home. 'I nearly cried at the end of my last speech in Canada,' the King wrote, 'everyone round me was crying.' They had been travelling for over a month, traversing 10,000 miles (1,000 of them in the US) and had been seen by an estimated 15 million people.

The King and Queen had made an excellent impression in the United States not only on the President, who described them to his cousin Nicholas Roosevelt as 'very delightful and understanding people [who] know a great deal not only about foreign affairs in general but also about social legislation',[69] but also on American public opinion. With very few exceptions, such as the irredeemably isolationist *Chicago Tribune*, the press was enthusiastic. 'The British sovereigns have conquered Washington,' Arthur Krock wrote in the *New York Times*, 'where they have not put a foot wrong and where they have left a better impression than even their most optimistic advisers could have expected.' Even the isolationist Father Coughlin felt moved to describe them as 'lovely personalities'.

Politically there was to be no immediate benefit to Britain from the King's visit to the United States; President Roosevelt was to lose his battle with Congress to amend the Neutrality Act, and, when Britain declared war on Germany in September, the President could do no more than issue a declaration of neutrality. Perhaps the best assessment of the importance of the visit was the measured judgement of Henry Stimson, Secretary of State under Hoover, who wrote to Lindsay that 'the trip will have a quiet solid influence.towards a good understanding on both sides of the Atlantic which can hardly be overestimated'.[70]

Personally, however, the North American tour had a great impact upon the King, both in his confidence in himself and his ability to do his job and in his general outlook, broadening his view of the world. 'There must be no more high-hat business,' he said to one of his advisers during the tour, 'the sort of thing that my father and those of his day regarded as essential as the correct attitude – the feeling that certain things could not be done.'

It also enormously raised his standing in his own country. The people of Great Britain were immensely proud of their King and Queen's success, giving them what *Time* described as a monster welcome home. Off the Isle of Wight a destroyer brought Princess Elizabeth and Princess Margaret to join their parents, whom they had not seen for seven weeks. The King had arranged a special homecoming luncheon on board at which they sang his favourite 'Under the Spreading Chestnut Tree' (with actions) and the popular 'Lambeth Walk'. From the port of Southampton along seventy-eight miles of railway to Waterloo Station in London the railway was lined with people cheering and waving flags, while the crowds along the route from the station to Buckingham Palace made it seem like Coronation Day all over again. There was a sense of relief that the King and Queen were back safely in these dangerous times. Even the hardened members of Parliament, crowded on to a specially allocated space in Parliament Square, lost their heads, as Harold Nicolson described:

... the bells of St Margaret's began to swing into welcome and the procession started creeping round the corner. They went very slowly and there were the King and Queen and the two princesses. We lost all dignity and yelled and yelled. The King wore a happy schoolboy grin. The Queen was superb. She really does manage to convey to each individual in the crowd that he or she has had a personal greeting ... she is in truth one of the most amazing Queens since Cleopatra. We returned to the House [of Commons] with lumps in our throats.[71]

Fifty thousand people crowded into the Mall and in front of Buckingham Palace waved flags, handkerchiefs, umbrellas and even handbags. As the King and Queen disappeared into the Palace they began to sing 'God Save the King', 'Land of Hope and Glory' and 'For He's a Jolly Good Fellow'. Then the chants of 'We want the King', 'We want the Queen', began until the royal family came out on to the balcony overlooking the Mall, smiling and waving for five minutes before they went inside again. The crowd continued cheering and singing until just before 9 p.m. the King and Queen stepped out again. It was, the *Daily Mirror* enthused, 'the greatest of all homecomings, the closing scene of the greatest royal day since the Coronation'.[72]

At the Guildhall the next day, 23 June, the King, filled with new-found confidence and real emotion, made the speech of his career so far. 'I have never heard the King – or indeed few other people – speak so effectively, or so movingly,' Lascelles wrote to Mackenzie King. Speaking of British institutions founded on ideals of liberty and justice, of the Crown as head of a Commonwealth of Nations and a potent force for promoting peace and goodwill among mankind, the King obviously experienced such emotion that people felt he might break down, a feeling that made the speech even more effective. The experiences of the past weeks culminating in this major occasion, Lascelles thought, had made the King a first-class public speaker. He was, perhaps, not quite that yet, but he moved his hearers (including such expert orators as Winston Churchill and Cosmo Lang) as, his fine English voice breaking with real feeling, he spoke of liberty and peace against a background of threatening war.

❧ 10 ❧

THE KING AT WAR

'The ... King lived through every minute of this struggle with a heart that never quavered and a spirit undaunted; but I, who saw him so often, knew how keenly, with all his full knowledge and understanding of what was happening, he felt personally the ups and down of this terrific struggle and how he longed to fight it, arms in hand, himself.'
Churchill to the House of Commons, 11 February 1952

THE Second World War was to project the image of the King as the unifying symbol of his people as no peacetime experience could have done. From the moment when, six hours after the declaration of war on Germany on Sunday, 3 September 1939, he donned uniform to broadcast to the Empire, he became the focus of an intense loyalty and identification on the part of millions. He, with the Queen and Winston Churchill, were to be seen as the spirit of an embattled Britain and her Empire.

War had seemed probable but not inevitable when the King returned from Canada in June. The probability had added the emotional edge to the North American farewells, the inevitability was something which many people, not least among them the King guided by his Prime Minister, had been unwilling to contemplate. On 22 July the King embarked for his last summer holiday of the peace with his family on the *Victoria & Albert*. They were accompanied by Lord Louis Mountbatten and their first port of call was to be the Royal Naval College at Dartmouth, where Mountbatten's eighteen-year-old nephew, Prince Philip of Greece, was a cadet. For the thirteen-year-old Princess Elizabeth it was to be a momentous meeting with her future husband. Only the young Prince's uncle and the Princesses' governess seem to have noticed the impression he made. 'Philip came back aboard V & A for tea and was a great success with children,' Mountbatten noted with satisfaction in his diary. The King, who was more interested in comparing records in the College punishment books with the Rear Admiral commanding Yachts, seems not to have noticed anything, although he is reputed to have roared, 'Damned young fool!', when the young Prince, rowing furiously in the wake of the royal yacht, was the last of the college cadets to obey the order to turn back.

The King had continued to receive reassuring messages from his Prime

Minister to the effect that Hitler understood that Britain 'meant business' and that, therefore, the German dictator was unlikely to risk a major war for Danzig. In July Chamberlain had dismissed a suggestion by the King that they use Philipp of Hesse, a royal relation married to a daughter of the King of Italy, who moved in Hitler's circles and often acted as an emissary between Hitler and Mussolini, 'to convey to Hitler that we are in earnest'. The idea, inspired by a conversation between Hesse and the Duke of Kent in Rome, came to nothing and the King did not press it. He was also aware that Chamberlain was more immediately concerned with fending off attempts to force Churchill and Eden into the Government, putting pressure on Lord Camrose to call off the press campaign in the *Daily Telegraph* for Churchill's inclusion, and indeed refusing to postpone the adjournment of Parliament for the summer recess because he feared Churchill would mount an attack upon him. Chamberlain had enlisted the royal family's moral support against this 'intrigue' and, apparently, had succeeded. At a Buckingham Palace dinner on 17 July for Prince Paul of Yugoslavia, which both Chamberlain and Churchill had attended, Chamberlain had gloated that Churchill looked 'very depressed', which he attributed to the failure of his plot; 'I sat between the Queen and the Duchess of Kent at the dinner', he told his sister, 'and neither of them left me in any doubt about their sentiments.'[1] Early in August 1939 Chamberlain left for a fortnight's salmon-fishing in Scotland.

At Balmoral the King was enjoying what was to be the last of the Duke of York's Camps, which opened on 5 August. The boys were camped beside the River Dee only a few hundred yards from the castle, and on most evenings the King would walk down to the big marquee for sing-songs after supper, particularly his favourite 'Under the Spreading Chestnut Tree' in which he took an enthusiastic part. Starting early in the morning, dressed in kilt, tweed jacket, open-necked cricket shirt and long stockings with the skean-dhu, he would climb his beloved 'hill', the 3,000-foot Lochnagar, with groups of boys from the camp. Going at 'a tremendous pace' he would question the fitter boys who could keep up with him about their lives at home and at school, with the less fit straggling several hundred yards behind. It was on these occasions that his love of nature showed. 'One thing in particular struck me,' a boy recalled. 'The King was intensely aware of everything around him. He pointed out birds and animals and views, never growing tired of answering all our questions.' At the top, the King sat down to a picnic lunch with the boys, then led them down the mountain by a different route, reaching Balmoral Castle in the evening. At the end of the day, one boy wrote, he seemed as fresh and full of enthusiasm as he had been at the start. On 9 August the King broke off his Balmoral holiday to inspect the Reserve Fleet at Weymouth. Echoing his Prime Minister's optimism, he wrote to Queen Mary on his return to Scotland: 'It is wonderful the way in which all the men have come for duty at this time & I feel sure it will be a deterrent factor in Hitler's mind to start a war. . . .' Writing to his sister from Lochmore, not far away on the same day, Chamberlain's letter was entirely devoted to the subject of salmon-fishing.[2] The last month of peace had precisely twenty-one days left to run.

On 22 August the King heard the news that the German–Soviet Pact had been signed; his immediate reaction was to order Hardinge to write to the Foreign Office suggesting that he send a personal friendly message to the Emperor of Japan: 'His Majesty ... feels that, when dealing with Orientals, direct communication between Heads of State may be helpful.' Informed by Chamberlain on the 23rd that Parliament had been summoned for the following day, he left immediately for Buckingham Palace, leaving the Queen and the Princesses at Balmoral. On 25 August, recognizing the immediate dangers of a German attack on Poland, the Government signed a formal treaty of alliance with the Polish Government. As appeals for peace from King Leopold of the Belgians, President Roosevelt and the Pope flooded in, the King was desperately anxious to take any initiative he could to avert war. At a meeting with Chamberlain on the 27th he offered to make a personal appeal to Hitler, but was politely put off. At Buckingham Palace the King dined alone with his brothers, Kent and Gloucester, as strange emissaries came and went, frantic telephone calls were received from Rome with offers from Mussolini and Ciano to intervene, and Hitler pretended to consider negotiation with Poland. The British Ambassador in Egypt, Sir Miles Lampson, calling at Buckingham Palace on 29 August, found the King 'in admirable form' and confident of peace, speaking of Hitler's disruption of his sporting season at Balmoral rather as his father had done on the outbreak of the First World War. 'He had never had so many grouse up there as this year. He had got 1,600 brace in six days and had been much looking forward to this week's shoot. It was utterly damnable that the villain Hitler had upset everything. HM thought that there would now be peace and that this time Hitler's bluff had been called.'[3]

However, on the previous day, 28 August, all international train traffic ceased and the pound began to slide on the New York Stock Exchange. Arrangements were made for the royal family and the various departments of government to move to selected locations in Worcestershire and Gloucestershire, a country house near Worcester, Madresfield, home of the Earl and Countess Beauchamp, being rented for the King and Queen in the name of the French Ambassador. At the National Gallery Kenneth Clark and Lord Lee of Fareham had put into operation the plan they had worked out during the Munich crisis to transport 2,000 paintings to three secret hiding-places. On the 31st it was announced that three million mothers and children would be evacuated the next day from places of danger. 'It is odd to feel that the world as I knew it has only a few hours more to run,' Harold Nicolson wrote in his diary.[4]

In the early morning of 1 September German troops crossed the Polish frontier. Chamberlain, at last accepting the inevitable, invited Churchill to join his Government. On the evening of 2 September the House of Commons assembled, expecting to hear the Prime Minister announce that Britain's ultimatum to Hitler, sent that day to withdraw behind the Polish frontier or accept the declaration of war by Britain and France, would expire at midnight. Instead, when Chamberlain got up to speak at 7.45 p.m., in a voice which betrayed 'some emotion as if he were sickening for a cold', he referred only to the possibility of further negotiations due to the Italian proposal for a conference to discuss a possible German–Polish settlement. The House could not know that this was only partly true, that the Italians had already decided (and told Halifax so) that the situation was hopeless, or that the real reason for Chamberlain's hesitation was difficulties with his French allies over the timing of the expiry of the ultimatum. 'The House was aghast,' Leo Amery wrote in his diary. 'For two whole days the wretched Poles had been bombed and massacred, and we were still considering within what time limit Hitler should be invited to tell us whether he felt like relinquishing his prey!' 'You speak for England, Arthur!' Amery shouted at Arthur Greenwood to rousing Conservative cheers. The temper of the House was for war, Churchill later recorded, 'more resolute and united than in the similar scene on August 3, 1914, in which I had also taken part'.[5] The Anglo–French ultimatum received no reply from Hitler. From eleven o'clock on the morning of Sunday 3 September, Great Britain and France were at war with Germany.

That day the King began a diary which he was to keep until January 1947. He also was thinking of the day twenty-five years before, when his father was sitting in just the same place writing in *his* diary, 'Please God ... protect dear Bertie's life':

At the outbreak of War at midnight of Aug. 4th–5th 1914, I was a midshipman, keeping the middle watch on the bridge of HMS 'Collingwood' at sea, somewhere in the North Sea. I was 18 years of age.

In the Grand Fleet everyone was pleased that it had come at last. We had been trained in the belief that War between Germany & this country had to come one day, & when it did come we thought we were prepared for it. We were not prepared for what we found a modern war really was, & those of us who had been through the Great War never wanted another. . . .

For the King, as for most of his generation who had experienced that war to end all wars, that feeling was the reason why he had supported Chamberlain in his efforts to maintain the peace. In the evening Chamberlain came to the King to mourn the collapse of his hopes; at 6 p.m. the King broadcast to the Empire, appealing to 'my people at home and my peoples across the Seas' to stand 'calm and firm and united' in a war that was not of his country's making.

The King was now, as Head of State and Commander-in-Chief of the Armed Forces of Great Britain and the Empire, a war leader, but, as he was well aware, for all his high-sounding titles, he had no more real power actually to affect the course of the war than he had had as midshipman on board HMS *Collingwood* in 1914. It was, however, still his duty to advise, to counsel and to warn and the use which he made of this duty, together with the closeness and mutual respect which developed between him and his wartime Prime Minister, meant that his influence was more than merely symbolic. He had huge access to information – he was for instance to be one of the very few privileged to see 'Ultra', the secret information from the Enigma decrypts which resulted from the breaking of the enemy codes – which his naval and air experience helped him to understand. As Churchill was later to say of him in tribute, 'I made certain he was kept informed of every secret matter; and the care and thoroughness with which he mastered the immense daily flow of State papers made a deep mark on my mind.' He kept a chart of aircraft production and losses at Buckingham Palace, which was updated monthly by the office of the minister concerned. He spoke daily to politicians, civilians involved in the war effort, soldiers, sailors and airmen in order to keep abreast of developments on the home and overseas fronts. He knew key people in various areas personally and received information direct from them. He was also particularly involved in Anglo–American relations. 'The King took a very great interest in things – people talked to him and he could make his points,' Lieutenant-General Sir Ian Jacob, Military Assistant to the War Cabinet, recalled. 'Churchill was a tremendous monarchist and therefore he took his duty to the King very seriously. He would not give way on something he thought important, of course, if they were at odds but he would certainly give full attention to everything the King said.'[6]

This, however, was in the future. Until the German *blitzkrieg* at the end of the 'phoney war' in May 1940 and the bombing of British cities gave him an active role, there was little the King could do. 'I wish I had a definite job like you,' he wrote wistfully on 23 October 1939 to Mountbatten, then captain of the *Kelly* and commander of the 5th Destroyer Flotilla. 'Mine is such an awful mixture, trying to keep people cheered up in all ways, and having to find fault as well as praising them.'[7] He was, however, soon to be given the opportunity to exercise his constitutional right to advise, counsel and warn in that first winter of the war when a bitter and potentially dangerous quarrel broke out between the generals of the British Expeditionary Force in Northern France and the Secretary of State for War, Leslie Hore-Belisha.

The King was kept extremely well informed on the progress of affairs at the BEF: the Commander-in-Chief, General the Viscount Gort, VC, reported to him by letter, while Alec Hardinge, as an ex-Guards Officer, was an old friend of Gort's and also corresponded with his Chief of Staff, Lieutenant-General Sir Henry Pownall. Moreover, the Duke of Gloucester was somewhat unhappily acting as Chief Liaison Officer between Gort's HQ and the French armed forces under the Supreme Commander, General Gamelin, and writing regularly to his brother. It was no secret among the well-informed that Gort, known to his intimates as 'Fat Boy', a brave, popular officer whose brain the brilliant Alan Brooke compared with that of a 'glorified boy-scout', heartily disliked his political chief, Hore-Belisha, under whom he had previously worked as CIGS, the operational head of the Army, at the War Office. It was an attitude widely shared by the plethora of generals at Gort's GHQ in France and particularly so by Pownall. That this was partly due to the prevalent anti-Semitism of the officer class is evident from the contemptuous references to Hore-Belisha in Gort's private correspondence, where he refers to Hore-Belisha as 'Horeb' or 'Belli', and in the diaries of Pownall, who used the East End term 'Ikey'. Hore-Belisha, then generally regarded as a rising political star, having made his name as Minister of Transport, was intelligent, dynamic and full of ideas. The Army already owed him a good deal. He had sacked top generals (earning their undying hatred), built barracks, increased recruitment and generally made living conditions for the troops more bearable. At a time when the Army was treated as the Cinderella of the Services, he had fought hard for his meagre share of defence budgets and had backed Pownall when, as Director of Military Operations and Intelligence at the War Office, he had warned at the time of the *Anschluss* that sooner or later British troops would have to fight on French soil. But his undisguised political ambition, an unfortunate passion for self-publicity and a penchant for unilateral decision-making had made him loathed and distrusted by the most powerful figures at the War Office, including not only Gort, as CIGS, but also the principal civil servant, Sir James Grigg, one of the toughest of the Whitehall mandarins. Dislike and distrust of their political chief was, therefore, simmering among the General Staff officers at GHQ even before Hore-Belisha visited the BEF on 18–20 November 1939 and criticized the Force for lack of progress in building up concrete defences. 'What he wants is the *réclame* of having built a Belisha line greater and stronger than that of Maginot,' Pownall noted scornfully.[8] This was the genesis of the great 'Pill-Box Row', which was to prove to be Hore-Belisha's undoing.

Two days before Hore-Belisha arrived in France the Duke of Gloucester returned to England on 16 November, despatched by Gort to make arrangements for the King's forthcoming visit to the British and French Armies in France. The Duke's biographer is anxious to deny any suggestion that Prince Henry was involved in an intrigue against Hore-Belisha, but since he spent some time with his brother, including a day's shooting at Sandringham on 20 November, it seems highly unlikely that they did not discuss the situation at GHQ. In any case, in the unlikely event of Prince Henry having maintained a discreet silence, the King was very soon enlightened by means of Pownall, another emissary from Gort, who arrived in London on 22 November, ostensibly also to discuss the King's visit, but in reality to make contact with the power points in London. Pownall's first call was at Buckingham Palace, where, he recorded, he discussed with Hardinge 'pretty frankly the virtues and failings of Hore-Belisha at the War Office, of CIGS [Gort's successor, General Sir Edmund 'Tiny' Ironside] and various other generals. . . . The King at least must not be deceived.'[9]

The King's next intimation of simmering trouble came from General Ironside, who had been on a fact-finding mission on 30 November to discover if there were any basis to Hore-Belisha's continuing allegations. Ironside's audience with the King on his return from France had been engineered by Pownall and 'Boy' Munster, another well-connected Gort aide. According to Ironside, the King was angered by what he had heard 'and distressed by the offence evidently given to his army in the field'. He instructed the CIGS to enquire what effect it had had on Gort personally and 'spoke gravely' to the Prime Minister. This may have been Ironside's impression, but according to Chamberlain's own account the King merely 'observed that he would like me to see the CIGS on his return [from France] and though he said no more something in his manner indicated that he had reason for the suggestion'.[10] The Prime Minister, therefore, saw Ironside on 4 December, receiving, as he reported to the King, 'a very reassuring account of the line'.

That day the King, accompanied by the Duke of Gloucester, embarked from Dover on his own visit to France. At Gort's uncomfortable headquarters, the Château Dewase in Arras, the King had ample opportunity to learn the details of the great 'Pill-Box Row'. Pownall had 'several useful conversations' with Hardinge, who also accompanied the King. Pownall noted with satisfaction:

Both the King and Hardinge are under no illusions about Hore-Belisha and realise that he must go. We did not fail to keep them fully informed of all the details of H-B's recent disgraceful behaviour, and there's no doubt we have the Palace on our side against him. The King, when I sat next to him at dinner, went so far as to ask me who, in my view, should replace H-B at the War Office. I told him M[alcolm] Macdonald [*sic*] & he seemed to like the idea.[11]

On his return to London the King spoke to Chamberlain about his visit to France, not only, as is evident from a letter he was to write to Queen Mary, to reassure him that all appeared to be well with the BEF defences, but also to discuss a change at the War Office. His representations were followed up by a deputation to Chamberlain from two of the most powerful men in Whitehall, Sir Horace Wilson and Sir Edward Bridges, Secretary to the Cabinet, who advised him that in their view Hore-Belisha's continued tenure of the War Office 'would give rise to serious discontent in Whitehall'. After the Prime Minister had made his own visit to Gort's HQ on 15 December, he returned convinced that the King's fears were grounded. He did not, however, tell the King what he had in mind. 'He had had good talks with Gort, but he is not thinking of removing Hore-Belisha from the War Office,' the King wrote to the Duke of Gloucester from Sandringham on 3 January. Two days later he received the news that Hore-Belisha had suddenly and sensationally resigned.

There were rumours that the King was responsible, prompted by a 'cabal' of the General Staff using the Duke of Gloucester. 'The Crown decided to intervene dramatically, and sent for the PM ... the PM, startled by the King's complaint, gave in', Channon, who was both a Chamberlain aide and a friend of Hore-Belisha, wrote the next day. Two days later, he put it more bluntly: '... it has now leaked out that the King himself insisted on Leslie's resignation....'[12] Pownall, the most active member of Channon's 'cabal', expecting Hore-Belisha to be reprimanded not removed, had come to the same conclusion: 'Some extra pressure must have come on him [Chamberlain] in that interval *whether from other members of the Cabinet or from the Palace, I don't know. I rather fancy the latter* [this section is heavily inked out in the original manuscript].'[13]

From an examination of Chamberlain's private papers, it is perfectly clear that the King did no more than alert his Prime Minister to the troubles between the BEF and the Secretary of State, something which he was not only constitutionally entitled but also bound to do. Chamberlain did not tell the King what he had in mind, although, at the beginning of the first week in January, having already decided to offer Hore-Belisha the Ministry of Information, he sounded out colleagues – principally Halifax but also Churchill, the leader of the Opposition, the proprietor of the *Daily Telegraph*, Lord Camrose, and even the British Ambassador in Washington, Sir Ronald Lindsay – as to the effect in America of Hore-Belisha being a Jew, and he fixed an appointment with Hore-Belisha for the afternoon of 4 January. To his consternation, after the Cabinet meeting on the morning of the 4th, Halifax told him that he was now opposed to Hore-Belisha at the Ministry of Information because 'it would have a bad effect on the neutrals both because H.B. was Jew & because his methods would let down British prestige'. A harassed Chamberlain wrote to his sister:

If I had known earlier of the strength of Edward's views, which were I suspect inspired by Cadogan [Sir Alexander, Permanent Under-Secretary at the Foreign Office] at the last moment . . . I should have left H.B. alone. Having to make up my mind at 1.45 with the appointment in a hour, I decided to offer the Board of Trade which had been suggested both by Edward and Sam [Hoare]. It came as a complete surprise to H.B. and it was evidently a shattering blow. . . .[14]

It was equally evident that Chamberlain was losing his grip. Wracked by gout, his nerves and confidence shattered by the collapse of his hopes for peace and within under a year of death from cancer of the stomach, he was no longer the unflappable man of business. He must have known that while the post of Secretary of State for Information would have been acceptable to Hore-Belisha, that of President of the Board of Trade, a junior office without a seat in the Cabinet, would not. Concerned about Hore-Belisha's potential for trouble and hostile press coverage, which was already representing the resignation as a victory for Army brass-hats over a popular, democratizing minister, Chamberlain wrote the King a long letter on 8 January asking him not only to soothe Hore-Belisha's wounded feelings when he came to give up his seals of office at the Palace the following afternoon but to suggest to him 'in his own interest as well as in that of the public' that he should keep quiet as far as the press campaign was concerned.[15]

The King, according to Hore-Belisha's diary, did not take up Chamberlain's suggestion of a heavy-handed 'warning-off'. Showing a better instinctive judgement than his Prime Minister, he was aware that such an approach could be counter-productive and that soothing a wounded spirit by a simple, friendly attitude could effect a great deal more. By Hore-Belisha's own account he succeeded: 'This is a sad moment,' he told Hore-Belisha as the ex-Minister handed him the red box containing his seals of office.

I said: 'Not at all, Sir. It has been a privilege to serve you and I have tried to do what I could for the Army.'

HM said: 'You have and how quickly you have done it. No man could have done more.'

By this time we were sitting by the fire. HM said: 'You wanted to introduce conscription earlier – before you doubled the Territorial Army?'

I said that was so

He spoke of his camp for boys. I said universal service brought all classes together, in the same way as his camp was intended to do....

During the last half-hour interview HM expressed his regret at my departure and his last words were: 'I hope very much, and I have no doubt, that I shall be handing you back seals again.'[16]

The resignation of Hore-Belisha, triggered by mutual distrust between the Minister and the generals, was symptomatic of the nervous unsettled atmosphere which prevailed as the 'phoney war' dragged on. Defeatism was rife; in the House of Lords Crawford noted that the defeatists pleading for peace and forgiveness had been the most prominent in debate. Various peace feelers had been put out; on 7 November King Leopold of the Belgians and Queen Wilhelmina of the Netherlands, warned of an imminent German attack (which was, indeed, planned but postponed), had issued a joint offer as mediators for peace to the King, the President of France and Hitler. The British Government rejected it, but increasingly the cause for which the country thought it had gone to war in September, the defeat of Hitlerism, seemed to be being forgotten. The King, worried by the evident disunity, issued a rallying cry in his Christmas broadcast, which was to be the most famous he ever made. He reminded his listeners that

true peace is in the hearts of men, and it is the tragedy of this time that there are powerful countries whose whole direction and policy are based on aggression and the suppression of all that we hold dear for mankind.... I believe from my heart that the cause which binds together my peoples and our gallant and faithful Allies is the cause of Christian civilization....

The King spoke live, as he was always to do until his last broadcast, dressed in the uniform of Admiral of the Fleet, sitting in front of two huge microphones on a table at Sandringham. The broadcast was an ordeal for him, as was evident from his frequent hesitations; on one occasion with great determination he even went back a phrase and began again. At the end he was speaking with slow, deliberate phrasing, but his peroration was to ring round the world:

A new year is at hand. We cannot tell what it will bring. If it brings peace, how thankful we shall be. If it brings continued struggle we shall remain undaunted. In the meantime I feel that we may all find a message of encouragement in the lines which, in my closing words, I should like to say to you:

'I said to the man who stood at the Gate of the Year, "Give me a light that I may tread safely into the unknown." And he replied, "Go out into the darkness, and put your hand into the Hand of God. That shall be better than light, and safer than a known way." '

May that Almighty Hand guide and uphold us all.

The New Year, 1940, was to bring war with a vengeance. On 9 April, the Germans occupied Denmark and attacked Norway; by the end of the month King Haakon had embarked on a British warship and it was evident that the Allied, principally British, Expeditionary Force there had been a failure. On 8 May, after a two-day debate on the conduct of the Norwegian campaign, Conservatives and Opposition joined together to defeat the Government of 'the men of Munich'. Chamberlain's future as Prime Minister was still in the balance when, at 3 a.m. on the morning of 10 May, Hitler's ground and air forces invaded Holland, Belgium and Luxembourg in a concerted assault stretching from the North Sea to the Moselle. That afternoon Chamberlain, faced with the absolute refusal of the Labour Party to join with him in a National Government, went to Buckingham Palace to offer the King his resignation and the – to both men – unpalatable advice that there was no alternative to Churchill as his successor.

The King was genuinely sorry to see Chamberlain go. He had shared the general feeling of frustration during the 'phoney war': 'everything we do or try to do appears to be wrong, & gets us nowhere,' he had written in his diary in mid-March and, aware of the growing swell of criticism of the conduct of the war which focused on Chamberlain and what the newspapers called the 'Tired Men' of his Cabinet, had attempted, in vain, to persuade Chamberlain to bring younger and more dynamic men into the Government. When Chamberlain sent him a list of proposed Cabinet changes in the last week of March, the King, foreseeing that they would not be enough to satisfy the critics, had gently tried to suggest that they should be more drastic. He had written on 25 March:

I cannot help feeling a little apprehensive of the criticism which might arise if there was not a leavening of younger men in such a War Cabinet. I expect you have probably thought of this aspect of the matter already, but I felt it would be a pity if it were to have a damaging effect in the reconstituted Government as a whole.[17]

Chamberlain had not accepted his advice. Apart from strengthening Churchill's position by making him Chairman of the Military Co-ordination Committee set up to co-ordinate the war effort of the three Services, the 'Tired Men' had simply been shifted around to new places. 'There is no new blood coming in,' the King had commented gloomily in his diary. When the crisis had broken, six weeks later, over the Norway debate, the King had offered to help by speaking to Attlee and attempting to persuade him, on patriotic grounds, to join a National Government. Chamberlain had refused and, indeed, it is extremely doubtful if the royal intervention would have succeeded. Bitterness against Chamberlain ran too deep. The King, in his partisanship for Chamberlain, had not wished to recognize that the Prime Minister's critics had a case. 'It is most unfair on Chamberlain to be treated like this after all his good work,' he had written on

9 May, the day after the Commons vote had made Chamberlain's position untenable. 'The Conservative rebels like Duff Cooper ought to be ashamed of themselves for deserting him at this moment.' In their interview of 10 May he told Chamberlain frankly 'how grossly unfairly' he thought he had been treated. 'The King was as nice as possible,' Chamberlain wrote to his sister the next day.

The King's loyalty to Chamberlain and suspicion of his successor was shared by his family – Queen Mary even going so far as to write to her lady-in-waiting, Lady Cynthia Colville , whose son Jock had been Chamberlain's Private Secretary, saying how much she hoped Jock would remain with Chamberlain 'and not go on with the new Prime Minister'. A week later Chamberlain received a letter in the Queen's upright, decorative handwriting:

I must write you one line to say how deeply I regretted your ceasing to be our Prime Minister. I can never tell you in words how much we owe you. During these last desperate & unhappy years, you have been a great support & comfort to us both, and we felt so safe with the knowledge that your wisdom and high purpose were there at our hand. I do want you to know how grateful we are, and I know that these feelings are shared by a great part of our people....

Chamberlain's farewell broadcast on the evening of the 11th announcing his resignation had, she told him, reduced the future Queen of England to tears: 'My eldest daughter told me, that she and Margaret Rose had listened to it with real emotion – In fact she said "I *cried*, mummy." '[18]

The King remained a loyal friend to Chamberlain, who, as Lord President of the council, was a member of Churchill's Government until forced out by his deteriorating health. They continued to have what the King described to his mother as their 'talks', which were important to the King who had still not come to terms with Churchill. At the beginning of August, in the midst of the worries and anxieties of the war, he found time to write a personal letter to Chamberlain recovering from an operation. 'I have always had a dread of operations myself,' he wrote, hoping that Chamberlain would be able to get some rest. 'I wonder how you have stood the strain so well, carrying on your work amidst so much uncalled for criticism. But I really do think the people of the other side [the Labour Party], now that they are in the Government, have begun to realise & understand the magnitude of the task you did without their help....'[19] By the end of September Chamberlain knew that he was dying of inoperable cancer; Churchill, who was already thinking of substituting Eden for Halifax and bringing in Beaverbrook, needed his place and on 4 October Chamberlain's final resignation from the Government was announced.

There was little public sympathy as Chamberlain noted bitterly in his diary. The King, however, wrote a letter which Chamberlain described as 'kind and understanding' and one 'which I shall always treasure':

You were my Prime Minister in the earliest years of my reign, & I shall ever be grateful for your help & guidance during what was in many ways a very difficult period. For me too it will always be a pleasure to recall our many & intimate talks together. I have sympathized with you very much in seeing your hopes shattered by the lust & violence of a single man; & yet, as I told you once before, your efforts to preserve world peace were not in vain, for they established, in the eyes of the civilized world, our entire innocence of the crime which Hitler was determined to commit. For this alone, the country owes you a debt of gratitude.

The last entry in Chamberlain's diary read proudly: 'This day [14 October 1940] the King and Queen drove here from Windsor to see me and spent about $\frac{1}{2}$hr with us. It was a characteristic bit of kindness and sympathy.'[20] Less than a month later he was dead. 'I am very sad about poor Mr Chamberlain,' the King wrote to Queen Mary, '& I know that I have lost a trusted friend. When he was PM he really did tell me what was in his mind, & what he hoped to do. I was able to confide in him. . . .'

Within the year, the King would be able to establish an even closer relationship with Churchill, who was to confide in him more than any of his other Prime Ministers. In May 1940, however, Churchill was very much the King's second choice. He had suggested Halifax to Chamberlain as his successor, but having been told that Halifax was not enthusiastic over the prospect principally because, being a peer, he would have found it difficult to carry on business in the House of Commons, the King conceded, as he wrote in his diary, 'that there was only one person whom I could send for who had the confidence of the country & that was Winston'. The King's official biographer went so far as privately to describe the King as 'bitterly opposed' to Churchill's appointment.[21] He had not forgotten Churchill's behaviour as a last-ditch supporter of King Edward during the Abdication and shared the widely held view of him as a dangerous political maverick. On the day of Chamberlain's resignation, 'Rab' Butler told the Prime Minister's Private Secretaries, Colville and Dunglass, that Churchill was 'the greatest adventurer of modern political history'.[22]

Inviting Churchill to become his Prime Minister on the evening of 10 May, the King succeeded in concealing his true feelings with the family habit of banter when in difficulty. According to Churchill, the King seemed in an almost playful mood:

His Majesty received me most graciously and bade me sit down. He looked at me searchingly and quizzically for some moments, and then said, 'I suppose you don't know why I have sent for you?' Adopting his mood, I replied, 'Sir, I simply couldn't imagine why.' He laughed and said, 'I want to ask you to form a Government.' I said I would certainly do so.[23]

It was the beginning of a great wartime partnership, not unmarked by occasional tussles or even jealousy over matters which the King regarded as within his sphere when Churchill bulldozed his way through Palace sensibilities. The joking manner in which the King had received Churchill was indicative of the fact that he could still not take him seriously as a political leader. 'I cannot yet think of Winston as PM,' he wrote in his diary the following day. '. . . I met Halifax in the garden [of Buckingham Palace][24] & I told him I was sorry not to have him as PM.' Halifax also reported the meeting in his diary, noting that the Queen, deeply loyal to Chamberlain, spoke 'very strongly about H[ouse] of C[ommons] behaviour'. The King, he said, was clearly apprehensive of Churchill's administrative methods.[25] A month later the King was not much happier with his new Prime Minister when Halifax went to see him after tea at Buckingham Palace: 'He was funny about Winston and told me he did not find him very easy to talk to. Nor was Winston willing to give him as much time, or information, as he would like.'[26] When Halifax saw the King again a fortnight later he was still dissatisfied with Churchill, complaining 'a good deal of the difficulty of making contact with Winston'.[27] Both the King and Queen still missed Chamberlain and his habit of going to the Palace regularly once a week to explain the situation in a careful, unhurried way. They were reported as 'a little ruffled by the off-hand way in which he treats them. Winston says he will come at 6.00, puts it off by telephone till 6.30 and is inclined to turn up for ten hectic minutes at 7.00.' But both of them already, Colville said, 'appreciate Winston's qualities, and see that he is the man for the occasion', while 'Winston, however cavalierly he may treat his sovereign, is at heart a most vehement royalist'.[28]

The Tuesday luncheons between the King and his Prime Minister, when the two men would help themselves from a side-table and talk things over in private, were started on 10 September and eliminated these early misunderstandings. The King's minor irritations were soon submerged by admiration for Churchill's qualities as a war leader, which he so outstandingly demonstrated in the high summer months of 1940. Moreover, an element in the King's wary attitude towards Churchill had derived from his support of the Duke of Windsor; but in July 1940 Churchill's firm stance vis-à-vis the Duke changed all that (see pages 434–6). At this early stage, however, the King felt the need to demonstrate to Churchill that he intended to assert his prerogative. Among the names raised by the incoming Prime Minister as his choice for ministerial posts in his Government was that of the King's *bête noire*, Lord Beaverbrook. Within hours of Churchill's triumphant return to the Admiralty, with tears of emotion in his eyes and a sense of relief that at last he held the power to change the course of history, a handwritten letter arrived from Buckingham Palace:

My dear Prime Minister,

I have been thinking over the names you suggested to me this evening in forming your Government, which I think are very good, but I would like to warn you of the repercussions, which I am sure will occur, especially in Canada, at the inclusion of the name of Lord Beaverbrook for aircraft production in the Air Ministry. You are no doubt aware that the Canadians do not appreciate him, & I feel that as the Air Training Scheme for pilots & aircraft is in Canada, I must tell you this fact. I wonder if you would not reconsider your intention of selecting Lord Beaverbrook for this post. I am sending this round to you at once, as I fear this appointment might be misconstrued.

I hope you will understand why I am doing this, as I want to be a help to you in the very important & onerous office which you have just accepted at my hands.

The King was making it clear that Churchill could not expect an absolutely clear run and that his sovereign had every intention of exercising his royal constitutional duties. Personally he had no reason to love Beaverbrook for his part in the Abdication, when the mischief-making Canadian newspaper magnate had supported King Edward principally in pursuit of his well-known penchant for causing trouble and his equally well-known vendetta against Baldwin. Like many people the King thought Beaverbrook's great qualities of vision and dynamism vitiated by his restless passion for intrigue and manipulation of people and situations, and his moral unscrupulousness. But 'the Beaver' was an indispensable crony and comrade-in-arms with whom Churchill could fight again, as he loved to do, the political and military battles of the First World War over glasses of brandy late into the night. And in this particular case Churchill needed Beaverbrook's dynamism in a vital post, aircraft production.

Churchill, equally determined that he should appoint whom he chose, ignored the King's advice. It may have been at this time that the King and Queen had the unpalatable experience of meeting Beaverbrook at a private dinner-party given by Maureen Stanley, who mischievously placed the press lord next to the Queen. The King leant across the table to say aloud to his wife, 'Well, you'd never have guessed this was going to happen, would you?' 'It was extraordinary that Maureen didn't warn them,' a fellow guest commented, 'but I suppose if she had they wouldn't have come. Beaverbrook was slightly subdued, rather staggered, everybody was....'[29]

The King was on stronger ground for his next round with his Prime Minister. Towards the end of May Churchill put forward for the great honour of Privy Counsellor the name of his closest disciple, the astonishing Brendan Bracken, whose mysterious and unconventional background excited all sorts of rumours, even that he was Churchill's illegitimate son. Behind a physically unattractive appearance, an unruly mop of wiry red hair, thick glasses and a reputation for abrasive ruthlessness, lay an encyclopaedic brain and an unsuspected heart of gold. Lonely, unpopular, devoted to Churchill, he was, as described by Jock Colville, 'a bright comet sweeping across the skies, afraid of nobody, jolting Churchill out of melancholy or intemperate moods, and proving a strikingly successful Minister of Information, in contrast to his three predecessors.'[30] An entry in Colville's diary for 1 June reads:

The PM wants to make him a Privy Councillor. The King has caused Alec Hardinge to write and expostulate. Winston, however, who is nothing if not loyal to his friends, has taken up the cudgels vigorously and, in his reply, complains that it is indeed hard if his most loyal supporter, who has stood alone with him in the wilderness prophesying the wrath to come, is to be refused this honour. I suppose Winston will get his way, but it is clear that the King has a mind of his own.[31]

The King whom Halifax described as 'much surprised and not a little disturbed at being invited to make Brendan Bracken a PC', objected on the understandable grounds that the honour of a Privy Councillorship was traditionally reserved 'for those who have attained high office in, or rendered long service to, the State'. Apart from having a brilliant career in financial journalism and becoming Member of Parliament for Paddington at the age of twenty-nine, Bracken could certainly not have been said to have qualified under those terms. His only real qualification was, as Churchill unashamedly pointed out in an emotional reply, his role as disciple and comforter to Winston Churchill. 'I should have thought that in the terrible circumstances which press upon us, and the burden of disaster and responsibility which has been cast upon me after my warnings have been so long rejected I might be helped as much as possible,' Churchill replied resentfully.[32] Few people knew better than the King the strain under which Churchill was working. The following day Hardinge reported in the most sympathetic terms that His Majesty had agreed to make Bracken a Privy Counsellor: 'The last thing that His Majesty wants to do is to create difficulties for you when you are bearing such an overwhelming burden of responsibility and anxiety – indeed his sympathy for you is beyond measure.'[33]

Meanwhile at Buckingham Palace the King, already host to King Haakon of Norway (known in the family as 'Uncle Charles'), had received another royal refugee, Queen Wilhelmina of the Netherlands. At 5 a.m. on 13 May the King was told by the duty police sergeant that the Queen of the Netherlands was on the telephone. At first he did not believe it, but 'went to the telephone & it was her. She begged me to send aircraft for the defence of Holland. I passed this message on to everyone concerned, & went back to bed. . . .' Later that day he received another telephone call from the Queen, this time from the North Sea port of Harwich where she had arrived on a British destroyer. Wilhelmina insisted that she be returned to Holland at once and that immediate British military aid be sent. Embarrassed, the King had to explain that, in the present threatening circumstances, neither was possible, and at 5 p.m. he went in person to meet her at Liverpool Street Station. 'She told me that when she left The Hague she had no intention of leaving Holland, but force of circumstance had made her come here. She was naturally very upset, & had brought no clothes with her.' The sixty-year-old Queen had gone to the Hook of Holland to find a ship to take her to the south, where her troops were still holding out against the Germans. Undeterred by the German bombing of the port, she boarded an elderly British destroyer, HMS *Hereward*, which happened to be alongside the quay, and asked to be taken to Flushing. Subsequently the Admiralty ordered the *Hereward* back to Britain on the grounds that the approaches to Flushing were mined and so the brave Queen found herself an unwilling refugee in London. The following day the Dutch Army surrendered.

Across the channel the situation of the BEF and their French allies had developed rapidly and alarmingly since 10 May. The British and French command strategy had been based on the certainty that the main German attack would come on the northern front between Namur and Antwerp. Instead, on 13 and 14 May seven German divisions broke out of the Ardennes, crossing the Meuse and driving westwards outflanking both the Maginot Line and the advancing Allied Armies to the north. By the evening of the 15th the French Ninth Army was in full retreat; there were no further defensive positions or troops in reserve between the Germans and Paris. Furthermore, there was now the distinct possibility that the Germans, by executing a pincer movement, could cut off the BEF from the sea. On 15 May the French Premier, Paul Reynaud, telephoned Churchill with the stunning news that 'the battle was lost' and 'the road to Paris was open'. Churchill flew to Paris to find the French High Command 'beaten already', while outside the windows of Reynaud's office in the Quai d'Orsay smoke rose from the burning archives. 'Where is the strategic reserve?' Churchill asked Gamelin. The General shrugged his shoulders, 'None.' That day the French and British Armies were given permission to withdraw from the trap into which they had advanced. On 19 May Gort decided that in order to save the BEF from destruction he might have to retreat upon Dunkirk and ordered Pownall to telephone the War Office to advise them of this. In London Chamberlain was already examining the consequences for Britain of the fall of Paris and somewhat inadequate plans were laid for the defence of government offices in Whitehall by Bren guns should the German try to capture them.

The King was not yet aware of the desperate situation of his troops in France. He was not told of Gort's warning to the War Office on the 19th. Nor did he realize that Churchill's response to Gort's message – an order to march southwards and take up station on the left of the French Army – was totally unrealistic and could have led to the destruction of the BEF. On the 21st Ironside, who had gone to France to deliver Churchill's orders and had had a chance to talk over the situation with Gort, returned to the Prime Minister with a gloomy assessment of the morale of Billotte and Blanchard, the generals with whom the BEF was supposed to be co-operating in the new offensive, while at the same time Sir John Dill at French HQ at Vincennes with General Weygand, who had replaced Gamelin as Supreme Commander of the Allied Forces, and General Georges, sent in an optimistic despatch which was entirely without foundation. That evening Churchill went to Buckingham Palace at 7 p.m. with a confused report. It was, he told the King, difficult to know what the situation was since telephone communications with France had almost totally broken down. The Germans, it seemed, were thrusting towards Boulogne. He proposed flying to France the next day to meet Weygand at Vincennes to co-ordinate a Franco–British offensive.

The King was by now extremely anxious. The war had already touched his family – his cousin, Lord Frederick Cambridge, having been reported missing in action. Since the Duke of Gloucester had returned from France on the 20th (having been bombed twice en route), the King was now aware of the serious situation facing the BEF and less liable than Churchill to be carried away by the castles in the air painted by Weygand. The report he received from the Chief of the Air Staff, Air Marshal Sir Cyril Newall, of a Chiefs of Staff meeting with Churchill on the evening of the Prime Minister's return from France, so alarmed him that he summoned Churchill to Buckingham Palace at 10.30 p.m. that same night when he heard for the first time of the possibility of evacuation. 'He [Churchill] told me that if the French plan made out by Weygand did not come off, he would have to order the BEF back to England,' the King wrote in his diary that night, 23 May. 'This operation would mean the loss of all guns, tanks, ammunition, & all stores in France. The question was whether we could get the troops back from Calais & Dunkirk. The very thought of having to order this movement is appalling, as the loss of life will probably be immense.'

Knowledge of the potential danger in which Britain now stood added force to the words of the broadcast which the King delivered the next day, Empire Day, 24 May 1940, for which he and Logue had been anxiously rehearsing for the past days. He had been worried that the speech might have been overtaken by events and the carefully rehearsed text have to be modified and, therefore, more difficult for him to deliver. In the end, he was able to broadcast it as it had been originally written. 'The decisive struggle is now upon us,' he had told his listeners. '. . . it is no mere territorial conquest that our enemies are seeking. It is the overthrow, complete and final, of this Empire and of everything for which it stands, and after that the conquest of the world.' It made a deep impression on his listeners and even he was content as well as relieved. 'I was very pleased with the way I delivered it, & it was easily my best effort,' he wrote, adding, 'How I hate broadcasting.'

The following day the King received formal notice in a letter, dated 25 May, from his cousin, King Leopold III of the Belgians, that the Belgian Army was exhausted and could retreat no further westwards to support the BEF. Leopold, who, under the Belgian constitution, occupied the difficult position of being both actual Head of the Government and in a real sense Commander-in-Chief of the Armed Forces, also informed him that in spite of all the advice he had received to the contrary, he considered it his duty to his army and his people to remain in Belgium to share their fate. With it he sent a short personal note to '*mon cher Bertie*': 'I am convinced I am acting in the best interests of my country. We were very moved by your impressive speech yesterday evening. I also have an entire faith in the future. May God bless you [tr.] *Affectueusement à toi et à la chere Elizabeth.* Leopold.'[34]

Leopold's decision to remain in Belgium and surrender with his armies was to earn him general condemnation and Churchill's deep resentment. It was Churchill's policy to keep Heads of State or of Government of countries overrun by the Germans as 'free Allied governments' in London, both for propaganda purposes, as a focus for free fighting forces, and, not the least importantly, in order officially to appropriate any funds which might lie outside the captured country. Conversely it was Hitler's design to keep them there, by force, if necessary – in Queen Wilhelmina's case the special Kommando parachute team ordered to capture her missed her by only half an hour. Constitutionally bound as he was to follow his Government's policy, the King's reply, drafted by Halifax in consultation with Chamberlain, expressed 'grave concern' at Leopold's decision, putting it to him that he could do more for his country giving his authority to a united Belgian Government than remaining as a German captive, even a hostage. It was to no avail. On the evening of 27 May Leopold opened peace negotiations with the Germans and on the following morning surrendered with his army.

From that moment the Belgian King was to be made the scapegoat for what became an Allied rout. At 7 p.m. on 26 May Gort, convinced that Churchill's offensive plan would result in the destruction of his force, commenced Operation DYNAMO, codename for the evacuation of the BEF through Dunkirk. King George was horrified by the news of the Belgian surrender, which he thought would make the evacuation of the BEF 'almost impossible'. Indeed, a week earlier General Alan Brooke had written in his diary on the evening of 23 May, 'Nothing but a miracle can save the BEF now....'[35] But the miracle did come: on the evening of 24 May Hitler ordered Guderian's XIX Panzer Corps, some of which were a bare fifteen miles from Dunkirk, to halt their advance. It was not resumed until the morning of 27 May, providing a crucial breathing-space which enabled the BEF and part of the French First Army to withdraw inside the Dunkirk perimeter and organize their defences. Fortunately the sea was calm, making evacuation from the beaches in small boats possible. Crucial, too, was the British spirit *in extremis*. The British, as so often in their history, galvanized by disaster, succeeded in snatching the BEF – a propaganda victory – from the jaws of defeat. From 26 May to 5 June, under the direction of the Royal Navy, a motley fleet of 887 vessels ranging from naval ships to fishing boats, motor cruisers and sailing dinghies ferried over 300,000 men (240,000 British troops and 85,000 French, the Admiralty's final total being 338,226 of Allied troops landed in England, a few thousand having sailed directly to French ports) across the Channel, while in the air the RAF fought a heroic battle with the Luftwaffe. Between 25 May and 5 June 394 German planes were destroyed for the loss of 114 aircraft of the RAF – a superiority of substantially more than three to one.[36]

The King was concerned to find out the truth of the charges of betrayal levelled by the British and French allies at the Belgian King and his army, begun by Paul Reynaud in a vitriolic broadcast on 28 May, the morning of the Belgian surrender, and taken up by the British propaganda organs and the press, notably the *Daily Mirror* which accused the 'traitor King' of stabbing the gallant BEF in the back. Their accusations were publicly repeated by Churchill in the Dunkirk debate on 4 June, when he charged Leopold with having 'suddenly, without prior consultation ... surrendered his army and exposed our whole flank and means of retreat'. Brigadier Davy and Admiral Keyes, the two British liaison officers at Leopold's Quartier-Général, were warned on their return on 28 May to make no public statements about their mission, but both of them were summoned separately to Buckingham Palace where they were able to tell the King the truth – that these charges were without foundation.

The Belgians had not withdrawn leaving the British flank exposed, nor had the King surrendered without warning the Allies. Gort, in fact, had begun the evacuation of the BEF on 26 May without telling either the Belgians or the

French. The French did not learn of the evacuation until the morning of 28 May, when Blanchard visited GHQ; the Belgians only found out on the 29th. Nor did Leopold surrender suddenly and without warning as Churchill alleged. On 26 May he sent messages to Weygand, Blanchard and Gort that the Belgian Army was nearing the end of its resistance, and on the 27th he repeated that message to Gort via Keyes, while on the same day Davy had personally given Pownall the same information. Keyes later sent the King a full dossier on his mission exonerating the conduct of Leopold and his army, using documents which he had concealed from an MI6 officer who had arrived at his house on the day of his return demanding that he hand them over. The King, Keyes was later told, was privately 'furious' at the way in which Leopold was being used as a scapegoat.

King George knew the whole truth about the BEF and the Belgians; he had, after all, also heard the BEF's case from both Pownall, who arrived in London on 28 May, and Gort, who followed on 31 May. He could not publicly disagree with his Government's propaganda line, but privately, when it came to matters within his own sphere, he refused to allow punitive action against Leopold. When it was suggested that the Belgian King's appointment as Colonel-in-Chief of the 5th Royal Inniskilling Dragoon Guards should be revoked, he turned it down, ordering that Leopold should continue to receive all the honours, privileges and respect due to him. He also refused to consider a proposal that Leopold's name should be struck off the Roll of Knights of the Order of the Garter or that his Garter banner in St George's Chapel at Windsor should be taken down.

While the King privately deplored the campaign of denigration against Leopold, he did, however, agree with Churchill that the Belgian King had made an error in allowing himself to be captured by the Germans. He knew, as Leopold had told him in his letter of 25 May, that he had done it in what he saw as the best interests of his country, not only because as Commander-in-Chief he could not desert his army, but as Head of State he thought he could protect his people better from the consequences of the German occupation by staying. But as a result of this decision Leopold was to be a hostage of the Germans, to suffer charges of collaboration and to be involved in a bitter quarrel with his Government which ended in his abdication after the war. Six months after Dunkirk, when sitting with Roosevelt's aide, Harry Hopkins, in the air-raid shelter at Buckingham Palace during the Blitz, the King, according to a memorandum by Hopkins,

expressed a good deal of sympathy with the King of the Belgians. It was perfectly clear that he felt that the King had had two responsibilities – one as Commander-in-Chief of the Belgian Army and the other his job as King, and that he had got the two jobs mixed up. He apparently had little or no criticism of him as Commander-in-Chief of the Army, but as King he thought he should have left the country and established his government elsewhere.[37]

Similarly, the King showed great sympathy for Gort, the other scapegoat for the disaster which had overwhelmed the BEF in May 1940. On the morning of Gort's arrival from France he sent for him, invested him as Knight Grand Cross of the Bath and shortly afterwards appointed him, with Dill, as Aide-de-Camp General. They were almost the only public tributes that Gort received; he was not allowed to publish his *Despatches* until the autumn of 1941 for fear of antagonizing the French and even then only in a version bowdlerized by the Government. In Gort's case, as in that of Leopold, the King refused to be led by the majority view. There were many reasons for the rout of May 1940 which could hardly be laid at Gort's door, and although he undoubtedly made mistakes, his decision to ignore Churchill's orders and retreat had saved his force from total destruction. In April 1941 when Gort was offered the Governorship of Gibraltar, the King said firmly that he was glad the Secretary of State for War, David Margesson, had made it clear to Gort that this appointment did not bear the usual significance of the end of his military career, but was prompted by the 'possibility of future developments in the area'.

On 31 May, as troops were still being ferried from the Dunkirk beaches, the King told Hugh Dalton, Minister of Economic Warfare, that the date for Hitler's invasion of Britain was, according to the latest information, 1 August. The Dunkirk operation ended on 3 June and, on the following day, Churchill, speaking in the House of Commons, made his famous promise to the world that Great Britain would fight the invader on the beaches, 'we shall never surrender'. Britain's only remaining European ally, France, was clearly doomed, despite Churchill's stalwart personal attempts to stiffen the French leaders' morale. 'I had to remind Winston', the King remarked humorously to Dalton, 'that he is only PM in England and not in France as well!'[38] On 14 June the Germans entered Paris unopposed, the sixth European capital to fall under their rule in nine months. Great Britain and the Empire now stood alone against Hitler.

The King felt a sense of elation now that the Anglo–French alliance, which had been under intolerable strain, had snapped, a feeling which he shared with many of his subjects. 'Personally I feel happier now that we have no allies to be polite to & to pamper,' he wrote to Queen Mary on 27 June. It was an opinion shared by Eden, who, as Secretary of State for War, had, with Churchill, had to bear most of the brunt. Asked by the King why he was in such excellent spirits, Eden replied, 'Now we are all alone, Sir. We haven't an ally left.' At a Privy Council meeting at Buckingham Palace, Halifax remarked to Dalton on how wonderfully cheerful the King seemed 'when he must feel that all his Empire may be crashing about his ears'.[39]

Hitler's attack on Britain in the late summer of 1940 brought the war to the home front and at last gave the King the active role he had longed for. Action and the adrenalin effect of war and danger revitalized him. Both he and the Queen, seeing themselves as symbols of British resistance to the enemy, were buoyed up by a wave of emotional patriotism as Britain stood alone facing the threat of invasion.

The King flatly refused a ministerial suggestion that the Princesses should be sent to Canada for safety. A number of mainly upper-class children had already been evacuated to Canada and the United States. Churchill was of the same mind: 'I strongly deprecate any stampede from this country at the present time,' he minuted on 18 July. The Princesses were actually taking an avid and sometimes bloodthirsty interest in the war. 'Isn't it grand about Sylt?' they had exclaimed excitedly to their mother after the British bombing raid on the island in March.[40] Princess Elizabeth gave up her German lessons and began reading American history. In October she broadcast to the children of the Empire in the high clear voice which was so like her mother's. Plans had been made as early as May 1939 for the Government and the royal family to move to the Worcester area in the case of invasion, but they were never to be put into operation. Throughout the war and the Blitz the King and Queen remained working in London during the day and sleeping at Windsor at night. Evacuation from the country was simply not to be considered. 'I should die if I had to leave,' the Queen told Harold Nicolson. She was taking instruction in firing a revolver every morning. 'I shall not go down like the others,' she said in a veiled reference to the other European royals, which was a little unfair to the unwilling refugee Queen Wilhelmina. The King had been practising rifle shooting in the gardens of Buckingham Palace since June and, he told Halifax, now always carried a rifle in the car with him as well as a revolver. 'I reminded him that he had given Dorothy and me permission to walk through the Gardens, and what time would he, therefore, be practising,' Halifax commented.[41]

Royal security was, however, far from watertight, as King Haakon discovered when he asked the King what would happen if a team of German parachutists dropped in the grounds as they had at Queen Wilhelmina's palace in May. King George pressed the alarm signal to alert the Coates Mission, a hand-picked body of officers and men from the Brigade of Guards and the Household Cavalry, who, equipped with armoured cars for a quick getaway, were supposed to stand ready day and night to protect the royal family. Nothing happened. Apparently, when the officer of the guard telephoned the police sergeant on duty at the Palace, he was told that he knew nothing about an attack. Eventually alerted by an equerry, a party of Guardsmen appeared at the double and proceeded to thrash the Palace shrubbery 'in the manner of beaters at a shoot rather than of men engaged in the pursuit of a dangerous enemy'. During the Blitz, the royal air-raid shelter at Buckingham Palace was the house-maids' former sitting-room in the basement, furnished with hefty buttoned Victorian settees, *fauteuils* and ornate tables, among which stood, somewhat incongruously, pails of sand, a spade and a hand pump for dousing fires. Things were not a great deal better at Windsor, where no high-level plan for defending the castle against parachutists seems to have been in existence until the King asked the new Commander-in-Chief Home Forces, Alan Brooke, to lunch to discuss the situation. It was by then 13 October, by which time the invasion scare was over, so much so that the King was contemplating going to Sandringham, which, being near the exposed East Coast facing Germany, was an area of maximum danger.

But the inveterate British spirit of amateurishness even in war was complemented by a surging patriotism which affected everyone, even intellectuals like Harold Nicolson, and which focused on the King and Queen as well as upon the bulldog figure of Winston Churchill. Nicolson met them at a private luncheon on 10 July at which Gort was also present. As usual, he was bowled over by Elizabeth's charm, but now he was impressed, too, with the King. He wrote to his wife, Vita:

What astonished me is how the King is changed. I always thought him rather a foolish loutish boy. He is now like his brother [Windsor]. He was so gay and she so calm. They did me all the good in the world. . . . Gort was simple and modest. And those two resolute and sensible. *We shall win.* I know that. I have no doubts at all.[42]

On 1 August Hitler issued his directive 17 aimed at establishing 'the necessary conditions for the final conquest of England' and ordering the intensification of air and sea warfare 'against the English homeland'. On the day Hitler issued his directive King Gustav of Sweden wrote to the King proposing a conference 'to examine the possibilities of making peace'. The King received this letter on 2 August, the day on which German bombers dropped leaflets detailing Hitler's peace proposals over southern England. The King was irritated by the King of Sweden's initiative, writing in his diary:

How can we talk peace with Germany now after they have overrun & demoralized the peoples of so many countries in Europe? Until Germany is prepared to live peaceably with her neighbours in Europe, she will always be a menace. We have got to get rid of her aggressive spirit, her engines of war & the people who have been taught to use them.

The King was, in any case, displeased with his fellow monarch, not only for his neutrality but also for his behaviour to his uncle by marriage, King Haakon of Norway. King Haakon, who had arrived at Buckingham Palace as a refugee with his son, Crown Prince Olav, on 10 June, had himself, to the dismay of the British Government, attempted to negotiate a partition of his country between German occupied and free Norway before leaving. Sir Alexander Cadogan noted in his diary for 5 June 1940: 'King of Norway sent tiresome message. Prepared to do a "Leopold". Drafted reply urging him not to be an ass or a traitor. Got it approved by W.S.C. [Churchill] and Neville [Chamberlain]. Halifax about [it] at Palace.'[43] A few days later, having received no reply from the Germans who no doubt preferred to have the whole of Norway as a Nazi fief under the notorious Major Quisling, King Haakon had accepted the Foreign Office advice and left on a British warship from Tromsö.[44] Two weeks later George VI heard that the King of Sweden was 'intriguing with Hitler to depose Haakon and put in the grandson [three-year-old Prince Harald, son of Gustav's niece by Olav] with a Regency'.[45] Summoning Cadogan to the Palace at 10 a.m. on the morning of 25 June, the King asked him to draft a firm reply to the King of Sweden.

George VI was at the beginning of an expanding role as trouble-shooter with the monarchs of Europe.

It was the shared experience of the Blitz on London in September 1940 which more than anything forged a bond between the King and his people. Just as his father after twenty-five years on the throne discovered his own popularity on his Jubilee drives through the East End of London, so just over five years later George VI on his visits to that same East End, now reduced to rubble, found real and immediate contact with his subjects in a way which royalty do not normally experience. The Battle of Britain entered its second phase in the last week of August. From 24 August to 6 September 600 enemy aircraft were over Britain each day. There was an invasion scare on 1 September and again over 7–8 September. But instead of invasion came the Blitz. On the clear night of 7–8 September, more than 200 German bombers struck London; by dawn on the 8th more than 300 Londoners had been killed and 1,337 seriously injured. It was just the beginning: after three days the death toll had tripled; by mid-September Churchill told the House of Commons that 2,000 civilians had been killed and about 8,000 injured by bombing, four-fifths of them in London alone. In just one week at the end of the month no less than 1,300 out of 1,500 civilian deaths were Londoners. At first it was the working-class areas round the London docks which took the brunt of the bombing. At Westminster MPs worried about the feeling in the East End, where there was said to be much bitterness; fortunately, as Harold Nicolson put it from the viewpoint of the Ministry of Information, the Germans subsequently 'smashed about Bond Street and Park Lane and readjusted the balance'. Euan Wallace, Senior Regional Commissioner for Civil Defence in London, accompanying the King on a visit to the bombed areas of the East End – Shoreditch, Bethnal Green, Stepney, Poplar, Bermondsey, Southwark and Lambeth – on the morning of Monday 9 September, after a night of devastation, remarked not only on 'the welcome given to the King by everybody and the evidence of cheerfulness as well as courage and determination', but that 'the King was evidently most interested and talked to all and sundry. He insisted on carrying out the programme to the full. It is almost impossible to believe that he is the same man who took the oath before the Privy Council less than 4 years ago.'[46] The real community of feeling with the people, however, came after the Germans bombed Buckingham Palace, a deliberate policy decision made by Göring, who personally took over the direction of the Blitz on 7 September.

On 9 September a random bomb had fallen on the north side of the Palace but it did not explode, and the King calmly continued to use his study directly above it. It exploded in the early hours of the 10th, shattering the windows on all floors, including the King's study, and demolishing the swimming-pool. On their arrival from Windsor that morning the King and Queen moved to apartments overlooking the inner courtyard. They were soon to discover what it meant to be bombed in earnest. On the evening of 13 September the King recorded in his diary the experience of that day:

We went to London & found an Air Raid in progress. The day was very cloudy & it was raining hard. We were both upstairs with Alec Hardinge talking in my little sitting-room overlooking the quadrangle.... All of a sudden we heard an aircraft making a zooming noise above us, saw 2 bombs falling past the opposite side of the Palace, & then heard 2 resounding crashes as the bombs fell in the quadrangle about 30 yds away. We looked at each other, & then we went out into the passage as fast as we could get there. The whole thing happened in a matter of seconds. We all wondered why we weren't dead. Two great craters had appeared in the courtyard. The one nearest the Palace had burst a fire hydrant & water was pouring through the broken windows in the passage. 6 bombs had been dropped. The aircraft was seen coming down the Mall below the clouds having dived through the clouds & had dropped 2 bombs in the forecourt, 2 in the quadrangle, 1 in the Chapel & the other in the garden. There is no doubt that it was a direct attack on the Palace.

The King was shaken; he had had a narrow escape from death. For several days afterwards, as he privately admitted in his diary, he suffered a shock reaction: 'I quite disliked sitting in my room on Monday and Tuesday. I found myself unable to read, always in a hurry, & glancing out of the window....' Moreover, despite the Queen's public declarations of being glad to be able to look the East End in the face, he was privately furious and outraged at what he suspected to be an attack upon himself by a member of his own family. As an airman himself, he was well aware of the difficulty of executing a bombing raid on a specific building in good visibility, let alone in the daring and dangerous manner in which this particular raid had been executed, by diving through rain clouds and flying low under the cloud, aiming straight up the Mall at the heart of the Palace. To him, the affair suggested detailed local knowledge, and the man he suspected, unfoundedly, was a young cousin twice-removed, a son of the Infante Alfonso, 5th Duke of Galliera and of Princess Beatrice, known in the family as 'Baby Bee', youngest daughter of Queen Victoria's son, Prince Alfred, Duke of Edinburgh and Saxe-Coburg. Alfonso, a general in the Spanish Air Force, whose son was a pilot in the Italian Air Force, had as recently as July been seeing the Duke of Windsor in Madrid. The Germans, as the King's intelligence information had revealed to him, were anxious to see his elder brother back on the throne. Could this attack be part of a plot to kill him and replace him with his brother? In the murky world of the Nazis no plot was too extreme to consider. Only in July Ribbentrop had attempted to mastermind the kidnapping of the Duke of Windsor from Portugal for that very object. No evidence has been found to support the King's suspicions; a more likely candidate as the royal bomber would have been another relation, Prince Christopher of Hesse, a Nazi pilot in the Luftwaffe. The King kept his own counsel. 'Baby Bee's' lease of the King's Cottage, a substantial Georgian grace-and-favour house at Chiswick, was terminated and granted instead to the retiring Archbishop of Canterbury, Cosmo Lang. Nor did Churchill, to whom the King does not seem to have confided his suspicions of family betrayal, take the bombing of Buckingham Palace lightly. 'This', he said, 'shows the Germans mean business.'

The bombing of Buckingham Palace had tremendous propaganda value in a sense quite opposite from that intended by Göring. As the King realized, recording in his diary, 'I feel that our tours of bombed areas in London are helping the people who have lost their relations & homes & we have both found a new bond with them as Buckingham Palace has been bombed as well as their homes, & nobody is immune.' It was heart-rending and time-consuming. *Time* magazine calculated that the King spent a third of his working day out touring the blitzed areas in London and throughout the country. 'Never in British history', it declared, 'has a monarch seen and talked to so many of his subjects or so fully shared their life.' Lord Woolton, Minister of Food, who accompanied the King and Queen on some of their tours, left a graphic account of the devastation of the bombed streets: 'We motored through miles of streets in which all of the windows had been broken, doors blown off, and there were huge areas in which houses had been completely wrecked, and it seems to me impossible that anybody should live in these places again. . . .'[47] On 11 October Woolton took the King and Queen round the communal feeding centres in Peckham and Lambeth:

The Queen asked me about the morale of the people who had been bombed: when we were coming through a very slummy district a crowd gathered round the carriage and called out 'Good luck' and 'God bless you' and 'Thank yms for coming to see us'. I knew the district and had been there only a week before. I said, 'You asked me about morale. All these people have lost their homes.' The Queen was so touched she couldn't speak for a moment: I saw the tears come into her eyes and then she said, 'I think they're wonderful.'

Woolton was impressed by the way the King and Queen handled the situation, 'I was very greatly impressed by the simplicity of both of them. They were so easy to talk to and to take round, and fell so readily into conversation with the people whom they were seeing, without any affectation or side. They were, in fact, very nice people doing a very human job.'

They were both moved by what they saw and experienced in those autumn days of the Blitz, the King so much so that he determined to reward civilian gallantry with decorations equivalent to the Victoria Cross for servicemen in action. They were to be named the George Cross for conspicuous gallantry and the George Medal for devotion to duty among the Civil Defence Services and the civilian population as a whole. Both the purpose and the design of the medal were very much the King's work. Medals and decorations were a passion which he had inherited from his grandfather, Edward VII, and he now owned a superb personal collection. Perhaps because he cared so much about it, his broadcast on the evening of 23 September announcing the institution of the awards was one of his finest. 'There will always be an England to stand before the world as the . . . citadel of hope and freedom,' he declared. 'Let us then put our trust, as I do, in God and in the unconquerable spirit of the British people.' On 27 September, with the Queen and Euan Wallace, he toured the sites of recently exploded land mines in Hendon, Wembley and Ealing. He was moved by the courage of the bomb disposal squads and furious with the petty-mindedness of the War Office in refusing them suitable rewards for their gallantry. As Wallace noted in his diary:

The King is very angry that the War Office will not recognise bomb disposal officers as being eligible for military decorations on the ground that they are not 'working in the face of the enemy'. He wanted to give Lt Davies the vc and said some things about the generals at the War Office which would have surprised them.[48]

Over the war years the King, often accompanied by the Queen, travelled over 52,000 miles of railway track to inspect men and women in the Services and key war industries and the victims of German bombing raids on towns like Coventry. On the clear moonlit night of 14 November 1940, Air Raid Precaution wardens on duty at Windsor Castle saw wave after wave of enemy aircraft flying over the castle heading northwards. That night of the full moon, in Operation MOONLIGHT SONATA, 300 planes dropped 543 tons of bombs on Coventry, devastating the city centre including its ancient cathedral, killing nearly 507 of its citizens and injuring more than 420. (The Germans themselves invented a new word, 'Coventrated', to describe such destruction.) On 16 November the King went to Coventry by car – the devastation was too great for the city to be reached by train. Normally, however, he travelled by the royal train, which he used as a headquarters and mobile home, working, eating and sleeping on it to avoid the disruption which would have been caused by a royal descent on a local hotel or landowner's house in war conditions. The train, part of which had been built for Queen Victoria, had been overhauled just before the war and was extremely comfortable. The royal carriages had air-conditioning, inter-communicating telephones and electric fires. The King and Queen each had their own coach with drawing-room, dining car, sleeping cabins and accommodation for maid and valet. The train was armoured with bullet- and splinter-proof steel, but in one respect harked back to the strict days of the King's great-grandmother: sleeping accommodation for the ladies-in-waiting and all other women passengers was at one end of the train, while that for the men was at the other with the royal coaches, through which no one was allowed to pass, acting as a chastity belt in the middle. One thing about the train was not luxurious – the food. Lady Hambleden, who frequently accompanied the Queen as lady-in-waiting, prudently took her own tin of biscuits with her to ward off hunger pangs. 'The food was Spartan ... they were very ration-minded.'

Once when they were going off to Liverpool to board the train for some inspection tour, there was an air raid. 'I think, Sir, we ought to go down to the cellar,' Lascelles quietly suggested. But after about ten minutes the King got very impatient and, instead of sending someone else, dashed upstairs himself to see what was happening. 'Really, it must be over by now.... Ridiculous bombs....' Of course everybody followed him and from the Palace the party drove 'like bats out of hell' through the darkened streets to Liverpool Street, where everybody was picking themselves up after a bomb had fallen nearby. 'The King got into the train calmly as if it was a perfectly ordinary event.' The King was brave, even fatalistic in the face of potential physical danger. Once, when someone mentioned the possibility of an attack being made on him during the tours he said, 'Well, it's no use worrying because if someone wishes to kill me there's nothing to stop them. Because if they don't mind being caught themselves and they wish to kill me, they can. So what's the point of worrying?'[49]

The King found physical danger easier to deal with than his own private phobias, which could make his public duties nightmarish. He suffered from a fear of heights, which made flying an uncomfortable experience. On one occasion he had to inspect a lighthouse, forcing himself to climb the winding steps to the top, an irrationally frightening experience for people who suffer from vertigo. He was sweating with nerves by the time he reached the top, but he did it. 'He could have got out of doing that because he was the King,' a courtier said, 'but just because he was the King he went ahead and did it. He never ducked doing anything unpleasant.' Worse still for a man who was by the nature of his job the focus of all eyes on huge public occasions, his particular phobia which he managed to conceal from all but his closest courtiers, but never entirely to overcome, was what one described as 'a kind of claustrophobia that he couldn't bear taking reviews ... he just couldn't bear it just like some people can't stand lifts'. Even when he had to review the guard in the quadrangle at Windsor he would get into a nervous state beforehand. The worst occasion was undoubtedly to be before reviewing the Eighth Army troops in North Africa in the presence of Montgomery and the other generals. When the time came for the King to leave his tent to take the review, he suddenly began to grit his teeth and mutter, 'I can't, I can't.... I'm not going to do it.' The equerries were ashen as Joey Legh told him calmly, 'Well, Sir, I'm afraid you've got to do this. You've come all this way and you've got to....' Still gritting his teeth, the King repeated, 'No, I'm going home, I'm going home....' Legh said, very quietly, 'Well, all right Sir, you'll have to swim.' There was a dreadful pause, then suddenly the King smiled, seeing the humour of the situation. 'Give me my cane,' he said and got up, went out and did it perfectly.[50] Curiously situations like these did not reproduce themselves when the King was surrounded by crowds in bombed streets, when he found it easy to talk to people and to put them at their ease. Nor was it the same on naval or troop inspections at close quarters. Once, inspecting a ship's company on the quayside, he demonstrated his formidable royal memory, stopping in front of a sailor and saying, 'I know your face. Weren't you on the same ship as I was at the Battle of Jutland?' 'Yes, sir,' the man replied.

The King and Queen played their parts as symbols of national resistance and hope consciously and with skill. The King appeared always in uniform, the striking and becoming midnight-blue uniform trimmed with gold of an Admiral of the Fleet set off his lean figure and fine features. With his high cheekbones and delicate bones without an ounce of extra flesh, the King was highly photogenic. Cecil Beaton, who took many photographs of the couple, described him as 'looking extremely handsome, like a carved wooden effigy, in his naval uniform'. The Queen, to her chagrin and that of Beaton, was not. Photographs of the Queen showed up her principal deficiency, her plumpness, and did not reflect the beauty of her skin and eyes, nor the magnetism of her charm. Carefully she discussed the image to be presented with the royal couturier, Norman Hartnell. 'One of the essential elements of a majestic wardrobe is visibility,' he pronounced. 'As a rule, ladies of the Royal Family wear light-coloured clothes because such colours are more discernible against a great crowd, most of which will be wearing dark everyday colours.' The war, he wrote in his stately autobiography, brought 'a new dress problem to the Queen':

What should she wear when visiting bombed sites? ... How should she appear before the distressed women and children whose own kingdoms, their small homes, had been shattered and lay crumbled at her feet?

In black? Black does not appear in the rainbow of hope. Conscious of tradition, the Queen made a wise decision in adhering to the gentle colours, and even though they became muted into what one might call dusty pink, dusty blue and dusty lilac, she never wore green and she never wore black. She wished to convey the most comforting, encouraging and sympathetic note possible....[51]

The Queen had a talent for public relations that amounted to genius and a quick appreciation of what made a good news picture. Lord Woolton recorded:

At one [communal feeding] centre, a very dirty child in its mother's arms grabbed at the Queen's pearls and a photographer ran round and tried to get a picture. He was just too late because the Queen had moved away. I was standing behind her and murmured 'Your Majesty, you've broken a pressman's heart': without showing the slightest sign that she had heard, she moved back into position for the baby again to play with her pearls, and so that the press man could take his photograph.[52]

High heels, a face-revealing hat (another royal tradition according to Hartnell) and hyacinth blue crêpe was hardly the ideal outfit for the dust and rubble of a bomb site, but her public appreciated it. 'Oh, ain't she lovely; ain't she just *bloody* lovely!' was the reaction of a crowd of East End women as recorded by her husband's biographer. The Queen, with the stamina of a showbusiness trouper, had learned to smile through dust and tedium as her husband's consort in his factory-visiting days, enduring in a cloud of industrial particles hours of conversation with besotted dignitaries whose politics were not to her liking. The courage and spirit of the women in the Blitz did move her, however. Talking to some East End women who had been bombed out of their homes, she heard them repeat, 'As long as we've got our hubbys and our children safe nothing else matters.' 'Only human relationships are important now,' she commented.[53]

The King and Queen were anxious to show that they shared the problems faced by their people. The Queen rummaged through storerooms and bedrooms at Windsor to find extra furniture for people who had lost all their possessions in the bombing of their homes – she collected no less than sixty suites. As the Battle of the Atlantic between the German U-boats and the supply convoys from Canada and the United States began to have a severe effect on supplies, and every ounce of effort had to be directed towards home production, the King instituted stringent economies at Buckingham Palace and Windsor. Buckingham Palace had been one of the first major establishments to introduce fuel economies in the autumn of 1941; a year later it was intensified. In line with newsreel campaigns showing large men apparently wallowing happily in minute amounts of bath water, the King ordered that every bath in Windsor and Buckingham Palace be painted with a black or red line at the five-inch level, and every bathroom to display a notice calling for attention to the need for fuel economy. Only one light was allowed in each bedroom; all other bulbs were removed – a considerable hardship given the vast size of most of the rooms. No central heating was in use at either palace and no fires were lit in bedrooms except on doctor's orders. When Mrs Roosevelt visited in the autumn of 1942, she was appalled by the cold the King and Queen endured. The King was suffering from a severe cold, to which she soon fell a victim, and they both sniffed and sneezed in chorus. The President's wife, who had come with an inadequate supply of handkerchiefs, had shamefacedly to resort to tissues. At Windsor the number of boilers in operation was reduced so that on certain days of the week there was no hot water supply in some of the residential parts of the castle and hot water had to be fetched from the kitchen as it had in the days of the early Georges. The Big House at Sandringham was shut up, and when the family came to Sandringham they used Appleton, a smaller house nearby which Edward VII had given to his daughter, Queen Maud of Norway. At Windsor, the famous herd of deer was drastically reduced from 1,000 head to a breeding nucleus of 100 and fenced in in an area unsuitable for cultivation, while 1,500 acres of parkland were ploughed up for cereal crops and heads of wheat rippled beneath the equestrian statue of George III, whose nickname was Farmer George. The King was depicted standing proudly in front of a huge porker, a member of his herd of Large White Pigs, fed entirely on swill from the castle kitchens. Even the horses from the Royal Mews were made to work for their living; Noah, one of the famous Windsor Greys, was photographed in tandem with another horse from the royal stables drawing not a royal carriage but the Windsor mowing machine. As part of the war effort, the Princesses collected tinfoil, rolled bandages and knitted socks for the Forces and contributed from their pocket money to the Red Cross, the Girl Guides and the Air Ambulance Fund.

In November 1940 the King as 'one of our hardest workers' received the gold medal of the TUC Congress from the chairman of the TUC General Council. 'That means I can attend any TUC, does it?' asked the King. 'Yes, sir,' replied George Gibson. Frederick Marquis, Lord Woolton (the King characteristically had refused to let him have the title Lord Marquis), as Minister of Food from April 1940 to November 1943 and Minister of Reconstruction from 1943 to May 1945, naturally saw a good deal of the King on the home front. Woolton, as a successful middle-class Liverpool industrialist, found the King knowledgeable on the working-class front and understanding of the huge problems of reconstruction resulting from the Blitz. As early as October 1940 Woolton could see the problems which would confront the country as soon as the war was over:

We are all telling them now that they are heroes for the way in which they are standing up to bombardment – and it's true: I think they will keep on being heroes, but when the war is over they will demand the rewards of heroism: they will expect them very soon, and no power on earth will be able to rebuild the homes at the speed that will be necesary. I'm afraid there will be grave discontent.[54]

Woolton contrasted the Prime Minister's lack of interest in the subject unfavourably with the King's. It was not until the day after Christmas 1940, when the first period of the Blitz was over, that Churchill summoned Woolton to Chequers to discuss the subject. The King – and the Queen – apart from their tours of communal feeding centres showed an immediate practical interest. When Woolton proposed an emergency service of workers to deal with Blitz conditions, the King showed his paper to the Queen and suggested she might be able to help. Women were to be specially enlisted to act with other services and specifically to 'go into streets that had been blitzed and where people were still in their homes, and ... help them taking food and kindliness and information and encouragement'. Their practical sympathy was intended to supplement the work of the wvs, whose authoritarian attitudes and bossy manner had caused antagonism in the working-class areas. Woolton suggested to the Queen that they should be called Queen's Messengers, because 'I think food and kindliness indicate the things that Your Majesty means to the people of this country – practical sympathy....' 'Do you really think the people think of me like that, because it is so much what I want them to think,' the Queen asked, ' – and it's true. It's what I try to be.'[55] The Queen was extremely skilled at projecting herself in the image which she perceived that people wanted. Women in particular saw her as a cosy, approachable figure – and here her plumpness as well as her charm helped – the sort of woman with whom they could imagine having a cup of tea and a giggle over jam-making at the Women's Institutes. It was not, of course, an entirely true picture, for the Queen was sophisticated, shrewd and tough, an aristocrat through and through, but there was enough truth in it – her genuine interest in people, her ability to make them feel at home with her and the strength of her patriotic feeling – to make that image entirely credible. She was also a superb actress with an innate sense of timing and of the importance of a gesture, the twirling hand in greeting, the head cocked slightly to one side as she listened when people talked to her, and, above all, the radiance of her smile. Gone were the days when royalty were not supposed to smile in public, but none of them were ever to match the quantity nor the quality of the Queen's smiles. When Cecil Beaton complimented her on her ability to smile naturally at photographers she said, revealingly, 'I find it's hard to know when *not* to smile.' She had the star's trick of looking fearlessly into the camera and looking on it as a friend. Her sensitivity to people gave her the ability to adapt herself perfectly to her audience, from East End women to sophisticates like Harold Nicolson: 'I think', he wrote in an unpublished passage in July 1940, 'the real secret of her charm is that she is perfectly conscious of the dignity of her position and yet somewhere at the back she is amused by it. One always feels that at any moment she may burst into giggles. . . . [56]

The King, unlike his wife, had no gift for small talk and only smiled when something amused him, which it did more often than people suspected. Despite his shyness, he, too, could make people feel at home, helped by his very un-royal considerateness. Woolton had a private meeting with the King after a Privy Council meeting in March 1942 during which he had been in such discomfort after an attack of colitis the previous night that he had hardly been able to stand through it.

After the meeting the King took me to his room: he immediately said that I didn't look very well, and pulled up an easy chair for me to sit in. He talked very intelligently about the food situation, and very frankly about my colleagues! He spoke of [Ernest] Bevin — and mentioned in passing that when he (B) sat in the chair in which I was sitting he bulged all over the sides. He said that B had no understanding of the mind of the people, adding 'Neither has the Prime Minister'. The King has been brought up to do the industrial side of the royal job, and he knows more about the working man than the Minister of Labour [Bevin].[57]

The King's quality of honesty got through to people in the same way as his wife's charm. *Time*, reporting in the summer of 1941, wrote that one of the country's most popular songs of the spring had been 'The King Is Still in London' and more recently 'The Day I Met His Majesty The King', the words of which ran:

> He just smiled at me as if he'd known me all his life,
> The day I met His Majesty the King.
> He talked and we spoke
> Just like two ordinary folk
> The day I met His Majesty the King. . . .[58]

Thus, the King made his indelible mark as a symbol of British resistance on the home front. He could have no comparable impact on the specific fortunes of war overseas. He did, however, see himself as having a key political role to play in sustaining the Atlantic partnership between Great Britain and America. The emergence of the United States and the Soviet Union as superpowers as a result of the war was the major foreign policy revolution of his reign, and while atavistically the King regarded the Russian leader as an ogre, he felt that he had established a personal relationship with the President of the United States which he would maintain to a lesser extent with his successor, Harry S. Truman. The relationship between the King and Roosevelt changed and was to some extent overshadowed when the colossal figure of Churchill entered the transatlantic partnership. But the King and the President could correspond on a Heads of State basis to which Churchill, for all his talents, could not aspire. At the end of the President's life, when he wanted to overrule Churchill on a point, Roosevelt was heard to threaten to appeal to the King. The King was fortunate in that both Roosevelt and Churchill had an inherent reverence for the office of sovereign, but the manner in which he filled that office won him the personal respect, and even affection, of both. The King also saw it as his role to represent Britain to America in a wider sense, to the generals, soldiers, admirals and airmen, as well as the envoys and politicians who crossed the Atlantic. His visit to the United States had had a great impact upon him; he now felt, rightly or wrongly, that he understood Americans. He also felt, as he told the President's representative, Harry Hopkins, in January 1941, that 'he was sure from the last visit that he knew what was deeply embedded in the President's mind'.

He had begun his correspondence with the President while Chamberlain, who despised and discounted the United States as a world force, was still Prime Minister, writing on 2 April 1940 to suggest a post-war international welfare organization. On 1 May both he and the Queen had received handwritten letters from the President and Mrs Roosevelt, 'to tell you and the Queen how very much you are in our thoughts'. 'Always', Roosevelt had written, 'I want you and your family to know that you have very warm friends in my wife and myself over here. . . .' The Queen was so moved that she had responded with a thirteen-page letter in her own hand. 'I can honestly say that our hearts have been lightened by the knowledge that friends in America *understand* what we are fighting for,' she wrote on 11 June 1940. The King replied on 26 June, after the fall of France, backing up Churchill's plea for naval vessels, 'As you know, we are in urgent need of some of your older destroyers to tide us over the next few months', he urged the President. The result was to be the Destroyers for Bases Agreement, finalized on 2 September 1940; about which the King wrote the President a grateful letter on 5 September, reminding him that the germ of this idea had come up in their conversation in Hyde Park – 'how far off all that seems now!'[59]

The King had eventual reservations about the Destroyers for Bases Agreement, whereby fifty veteran First World War American destroyers were transferred to the Royal Navy in return for ninety-nine-year leases for the establishment of American naval, air and sea bases in Newfoundland, Bermuda, the Bahamas, Jamaica, Antigua, St Lucia, Trinidad and British Guiana. By the end of the year the scale of US intervention in the Caribbean, and the local protests it aroused, touched his position as Head of the Empire. After reading a paper by the Secretary of State for the Colonies, George Lloyd, he was, as he noted in his diary, 'much disturbed over it, as the USA is asking for more facilities than were originally agreed to, & wishes to fortify & have garrisons in Bermuda & Trinidad'. Although he realized that Roosevelt had to make aid to Britain as clearly worthwhile as possible in the eyes of the isolationists, he was determined that the question of sovereignty over the islands should not arise. 'The Americans have got to understand that in leasing the bases the question of Sovereignty does not come in. These islands are part of the British Colonial Empire & I am not going to see my West Indian subjects handed over to the US authorities,' he minuted to Hardinge on 30 December.

The King, like Churchill, hoped and believed that America's entry into the war on Britain's side could not be long delayed. In the treasured memorandum from Hyde Park he had recorded that, if London were to be bombed, 'America would come in'. The Blitz came and the King waited for the result of the presidential election of 1940, hoping that if Roosevelt won, he would bring America into the war. On 11 November 1940 he sent, via the new British Ambassador to Washington, Lord Lothian, a handwritten letter of congratulations to Roosevelt: 'In these grave and anxious days it is a great relief to feel that your wise & helpful policy will continue without interruption,' he told the President.[60] The President's idea, however, was to provide any aid necessary for the defeat of Germany short of actually going to war. The eventual outcome of this was to be Lend-Lease; the immediate result was the mission of Harry Hopkins to London as the President's personal representative.

On 30 January 1941, the King and Queen entertained Hopkins to luncheon at Buckingham Palace. They already knew him from their White House visit and were well aware of his particular importance as a link with Roosevelt. Frail, wracked by chronic ill-health, often drinking more than was good for him, Hopkins, in Churchill's words, 'burned with the flame of democracy'. He was more than merely the President's personal representative, he was his mouthpiece, the interpreter of his will, the selfless defender of his interests. Ostensibly there to discuss with Churchill what practical help America might be able to offer, his private brief was also to gauge Britain's capacity and, above all, will to resist. Roosevelt wanted to hear, from someone he trusted completely, whether the defeatist reports of his Ambassador, Kennedy, had any basis, 'to see whether British morale was really as bad as Kennedy pretended'.[61]

Hopkins had been favourably impressed with the King and Queen in Washington. As he told Churchill at Ditchley shortly after his arrival, in his opinion 'the astounding success' of their US visit 'had made America give up its partisanship of the Windsors'. After lunching at Buckingham Palace he recorded for the President the substance of a long conversation with the King and Queen:

The King ... asked me about my trip to Scapa Flow with Halifax, and I told him the details of the amusing incidents including the firing of the UP gun, and about the bomb landing five feet from me instead of on the enemy. He told me that the Prime Minister had failed to tell him of this incident. I told the King the reason for that was that the Prime Minister didn't think it was funny and I did!

The three of us had lunch together in the next room. We discussed at length their visit to America a year ago last May, and it was perfectly clear that the President made a great impression on both of them.

I told the King how much the President enjoyed meeting them, how dear friendship was to him personally, and how great his pleasure was in receiving personal messages from the King. I urged the King, whenever he was of a mind, to send the President appropriate personal notes because I believed that that was one of the ways to keep our two countries closely related during these trying times.

The Queen [who had already endeared herself to Hopkins in Washington by her kindness to his daughter Diana] told me that she found it extremely difficult to find words to express her feeling towards the people of Britain in these days. She thought their actions were magnificent and that victory in the long run was sure, but that the one thing that counted was the morale and determination of the great mass of the British people.

The King discussed the navy and the fleet at some length and showed an intimate knowledge of all the high-ranking officers of the navy, and, for that matter, of the army and air force. It was perfectly clear from his remarks that he reads very carefully all the important dispatches and, among other things, was quite familiar with a dispatch which I had sent Sunday night through the Foreign Office.

He thinks very highly of the Commander-in-Chief of the military forces and, as with everybody else, has great confidence in Churchill. He discussed quite freely with me the great difficulties this country would have if anything should happen to Churchill.

If ever two people realized that Britain is fighting for its life it is these two. They realize fully that this conflict is different from the other conflicts in Britain's history and that if Hitler wins they and the British people will be enslaved for years to come. . . .

The King won Hopkins's loyal heart by talking 'at great length about the President' and his 'obvious deep interest in the defeat of Hitler'. The air-raid alarm had gone off just as the three sat down to luncheon, but they ignored it until, as they reached the coffee and port stage, a bell rang. At this, the King got up saying, 'That means we have got to go to the air-raid shelter,' and they retired to the Palace air-raid shelter sitting-room, which Hopkins described as 'a small lighted room with table and chairs', where they talked for a further hour 'about Washington and America's relationship to the war'. The King asked Hopkins about Wendell Wilkie (the non-isolationist Republican who had been Roosevelt's opponent in the recent presidential election) and his forthcoming visit, and seemed, Hopkins recorded,

greatly pleased that I was sure Mr Wilkie and the President would see eye to eye in regard to the President's foreign policy.

The King expressed the great hope that somehow the President and Churchill could get together personally in the near future. He believed that it might be arranged.

When I emphasized the President's great determination to defeat Hitler, his deep conviction that Britain and America had a mutuality of interest in this respect, and that they could depend on aid from America, they were both very deeply moved. . . . The King on his part told me how greatly he appreciated the President's speeches and said he was sure from the last visit that he knew what was deeply embedded in the President's mind. He told me to tell the President how much beloved he was by the people of Britain and asked that I give up to the President his warmest expressions of thanks and appreciation and a personal word of friendship.[62]

The King's appreciation of the importance of relations with the United States came out in his interview with Halifax at Windsor on Christmas Eve 1940. Lord Lothian had died earlier that month and Churchill, seizing this opportunity, which he had long contemplated, of replacing Halifax as Foreign Secretary with Eden, had offered Halifax the job as his successor. The King took particular pains to persuade the reluctant Halifax that, as he put it in his diary, 'the post of my Ambassador in USA was more important at this moment than the post of Foreign Secy. here'. Halifax, who saw the appointment for what it was, a demotion and a skilful manœuvre by Churchill, retorted that the British Government would be very flattered if the US Secretary of State, Cordell Hull, arrived in London as Ambassador, but would hardly change its policy as a result. 'I said no,' the King recorded, 'but Roosevelt has got to be helped by us to "get over" his policy of Aid to Britain which is going well now, but should we suffer a disaster F.D.R.'s opponents would do their best to counter it. I think he understood this.' When Halifax arrived in Chesapeake Bay aboard the *King George V* on 24 January 1941, Roosevelt did him the signal honour of sailing out to meet him on the presidential yacht, invited the Ambassador and his wife to tea and afterwards drove them to the British Embassy. After a rocky start Halifax, contrary to general expectation, was to prove an extremely successful Ambassador and for the King an invaluable source of information on American affairs, his long lucid letters providing first-hand illustration of the American domestic political background, enlivened by snippets of insider gossip. 'The Lease-Lend Bill flounders along in the Senate,' he wrote to the King on 7 March 1941, 'what the President a few days ago called "that disgusting spectacle on the Capitol"....'[63]

The King had written personally to Roosevelt on 14 February to thank him for the courtesy he had shown in going to meet Halifax, and when the new US Ambassador, John G. Winant, arrived on 1 March he went down to Windsor station to meet him, 'the first time in the history of Great Britain that a King had gone to meet an Ambassador', as Winant recorded. Winant was very pro-British and had consistently advocated help to Britain; he had been in Britain at the time of Dunkirk and had done his best to counteract Kennedy's defeatist line by sending back contrary reports. Tall, with Abraham Lincoln looks – craggy features, dark piercing eyes under bushy eyebrows – and an almost inaudible voice, he was to be extremely popular in London, although less so with Churchill, who had more in common with the cosmopolitan Averell Harriman, Roosevelt's special emissary. Winant for his part found the Prime Minister a reactionary. 'Winant thinks Winston out of touch with what younger England is thinking for after the war,' Halifax was to note in his secret diary early in 1942.[64] The King liked Winant, although finding him taciturn on social occasions. 'The Winants are both very silent people,' he noted after entertaining them to luncheon on 25 April. Like every American from Eisenhower down who met the King during the war, Winant was surprised by the quality of the King's knowledge of the current situation. 'We talked', the Ambassador recorded of his first meeting with the King in *A Letter from Grosvenor Square*, 'about men in the government and the present state of the war. Then and afterwards when I met him I found him to be completely informed on the day-to-day progress of the armed forces, and on any other subject that concerned his people.' He was also taken aback by the phenomenal royal memory: 'He remembered meeting me on a previous occasion and picked up a conversation where we had left off more than two years ago.'[65]

In the spring and early summer of 1941, after the passage of the Lend-Lease Bill in March, the King earnestly hoped for American help in the Battle of the Atlantic, where, if the German U-boats succeeded in preventing the convoys getting through with supplies, the outcome of the war might well be decided. 'The spirit of the people is wonderful, but we have all got to stand a great deal more strain this summer, I am afraid,' the King wrote to Halifax from Sandringham on 14 April.[66] 'The Balkans and Libya are our latest worries, added to the Battle of the Atlantic. The latter is much the most important and that is where the USA can help us by doing her own convoy work. But will she?' That month Roosevelt instituted a patrol system whereby US warships and planes could 'trail' the merchant convoys and report the presence of raiders to the British; he also extended eastwards the security zone and patrol area in which US patrols would operate. It was something, and the King was pleased. 'The new American patrols, which have just come into force, are going a long way to solve our difficulty of escorting convoys,' he wrote in his diary on 25 April. But by the end of May the situation for Britain and the Empire looked bleak. On one night, 10 May, German bombing killed more than 1,400 civilians, destroyed 5,000 houses and made 12,000 people homeless. In the Atlantic in April and May British, Allied and neutral merchant shipping losses amounted to 296,418 and 136,260 tons. The sinking of the huge German battleship *Bismarck* on 27 May had provided the only ray of light for Britain in what Churchill himself described as 'the worst days' of the war so far. But on that same day the evacuation of the BEF from Crete began, a disastrous blow to British military prestige – a wag quipped that from now on the initials of the BEF stood for 'Back every Friday'. With the capture of Crete the Germans now had a stepping-stone towards Suez, the lifeline of the British Empire in the East, and North Africa, where Rommel had now retaken all of Cyrenaica won by Wavell, threatening Egypt and nullifying the only success the British Army had hitherto enjoyed.

Still Roosevelt, besieged by the pro-British interventionist views of his closest advisers like Hopkins and Harriman, on the one hand, and the isolationists on the other, did not respond. He had already gone beyond the legal limits in aiding the British and, as Halifax had warned the King on 16 May, domestically he was in a difficult position, 'there is much bitter criticism of him and suspicion cutting across the main issue'.[67] The King, anguished by the situation and encouraged by a ringing speech from the President on 27 May, decided on a personal appeal to Roosevelt in a four-page, handwritten letter dated 3 June 1941.

Buckingham Palace

My dear President Roosevelt,

It is some time ago since I last wrote to you, & in doing so now, I would like to tell you how much your last speech of May 27 has encouraged everybody in this country to carry on, knowing that the immense potential industrial strength of your country is behind us.

I have read with great interest all that you have said & done during the past months since you have been re-elected President, & I have been so struck by the way you have led public opinion by letting it to [sic] get ahead of you....

He referred back to their talks at Hyde Park:

After so many years of anxiety, when what we wanted to happen seemed so far off from realisation, it is wonderful to feel that at last our two great countries are getting together for the future betterment of the world. I do thank God it was possible for the Queen & me to come to America in those few months before war broke out in Europe, a visit which gave us the chance to meet you & so many Americans. I can assure you that we both have a very real affection in our hearts for the people of the United States....

Among the advantages which Britain still had during these dark days were, the King put it to Roosevelt, the 'truly remarkable ... spirit of the people under the strain of terrible & indiscriminate bombing' and Winston Churchill, 'indefatigable at his work, with his many & great responsibilities ... a great man, & has at last come into his own as leader of his country in this fateful time in her history'. Lastly, the King stressed the personal note: 'As I know you personally I would like to feel that I can write to you direct. So many communications between Heads of State have to go through "official channels" & I hope that you will be able to write back to me in this personal way....'[68]

Roosevelt did not reply, nor, apparently did Eleanor Roosevelt answer a similar personal letter from the Queen. The King was deeply hurt, not only as Head of State, but on a personal level. He had remembered with warmth the fatherly and frank way with which Roosevelt treated him, and had carried his notes of the President's words with him as if they were tablets of stone. The President's silence sowed seeds of doubt about Roosevelt in the King's mind, seeming like a small but wounding personal betrayal. When, having perhaps comforted himself that the letter had gone astray as a previous one had, he discovered that the President had, indeed, received his letter, he could not conceal his feelings, as Victor Cazalet reported to Halifax on 17 July:

I told the King how much you had said the President enjoyed getting his letter, to which the King answered in a loud voice, 'Oh, so he's got it, has he?'

I then said that you had told me about it and that the President was full of it, etc., laying it on perhaps a little thick but you know how it is with royalty! To which he said, 'Oh, it is about five weeks since I wrote it and I never had any acknowledgement yet.'

The Queen then chipped in here and said, 'I also wrote to Mrs Roosevelt and I have never had an answer.' The King then said, 'The last letter I wrote to him got lost somehow in the diplomatic bag and never reached him at all!'[69]

Roosevelt's failure to reply to the King could probably be ascribed to two reasons, the first being that Roosevelt 'didn't want to know' about further appeals to help Britain in her days of crisis in early June 1941, when, short of declaring war on Germany, there was virtually nothing more he could do. Halifax had warned the King earlier that the President would not declare war unless Germany forced him into it, and even the torpedoing of a US merchant ship, the *Robin Moor*, did not move him. Roosevelt was convinced, probably correctly, that he would not get a declaration of war passed in Congress, and, rather than risk a major defeat, he sat tight, waiting for events to unroll. The second reason was that he no longer set such store by personal communication with the King now that he was in correspondence with Churchill, whose personality and reputation fascinated him. The first question he had asked Wendell Wilkie on the latter's return from Britain earlier that year had not been about Britain but about Churchill: 'Is he a drunk?'[70]

The King was not to write another long, personal letter to Roosevelt until March 1942, when his Empire found itself once more *in extremis*. In the interval Roosevelt and Churchill had established personal contact at the highest level at their first face-to-face meeting at Placentia Bay early in August 1941 after the German attack on Russia had changed the face of the war, a contact which was to become even closer when America entered the war in December that year after the Japanese attack on Pearl Harbor. The King had always pressed for a meeting between Churchill and Roosevelt; in 1941 he sent with the Prime Minister a graceful note of introduction, which Churchill handed to the President on 9 August: 'This is just a line to bring you my best wishes, and to say how glad I am that you have an opportunity at last of getting to know my Prime Minister. I am sure you will agree that he is a very remarkable man. . . .' The President for his part sought to make amends for his previous deficiency as a correspondent by sitting down two days later to write a friendly letter to the King: 'I have had three delightful and useful days with Mr Churchill. . . . It has been a privilege to come to know Mr Churchill in this way and I am very confident that our minds travel together, and that our talks are bearing practical fruit for both nations.' He wished, he said, that the King could have been present at Divine Service on 'your latest battleship' – the *Prince of Wales* – attended by hundreds of British and American sailors together. 'We think of you both often,' the President wrote, 'and wish we could be of more help – But we are daily gaining in confidence in the outcome – We know you will keep up the good work.'

The King had reservations about the public outcome of the Placentia Bay meeting, a joint declaration of war aims under the high-sounding title of the Atlantic Charter, promising self-government, equal trading opportunities and economic collaboration towards an improved standard of living. He feared a repetition of the situation after the First World War when America had withdrawn from Europe. 'The USA had deserted us after the Great War in Europe & might easily do so again if she does not come in & feel the effects,' he told

David Margesson. 'The joint statement said all the right things, but how are we going to carry them out?' he wrote to Queen Mary. 'Most of the peoples of Europe will have forgotten that they ever had a Govt. of their own when the war is over. America and ourselves will have to feed them in Europe for years & years.' It might have been equally pertinent for the King to object to the pledge to self-determination which certainly had a bearing on his Empire. Churchill, despite having telegraphed Attlee at the time that 'it would be most imprudent on our part to raise unnecessary difficulties', certainly had reservations about the application of the self-determination pledge, although he seems to have kept them to himself. In his report to the King at lunch on 19 August, his comments were reassuringly optimistic. 'F.D.R. told him that at the moment he would not declare war but that he would wage war with us, against Germany, as evidenced by taking over all convoy work to Iceland,' the King recorded in his diary.

W. was greatly taken by him, & has come back feeling that he knows him. He had several talks with him alone, when W. put our position to him very bluntly. If by the Spring, Russia was down & out, & Germany was renewing her blitzkrieg here, all our hopes of victory & help from USA would be dashed if America had not by then sent us masses of planes etc., or had not entered the war. F.D.R. has got £3,000,000,000 to spend on us here. On the general situation W. told me the Atlantic was much better, he thought Japan would remain quiet.

But it was the Japanese, not the Germans, who were to strike the blow which knocked America off its neutral fence, when they attacked the US Pacific Fleet at its base at Pearl Harbor, Honolulu, on the morning of Sunday 7 December 1941. On 8 December the United States and Great Britain, the latter reacting to the Japanese attack on Malaya, declared war on Japan; three days later the European Axis powers, Germany and Italy, declared war on the United States, thus unilaterally bringing about the results for which the King and Churchill had been hoping for so many months.

The King's distrust of Churchill had long since been replaced by a warm admiration and friendship. 'He tells me, more than people imagine, of his future plans & ideas & only airs them when the time is ripe to his colleagues & the Chiefs of Staff,' the King wrote to his mother on 2 February 1943 of his relationship with his Prime Minister. As early as October 1940, a month after the private Tuesday lunches at Buckingham Palace had started, when they served each other from a side-table, talking freely as no servants were present, Queen Mary had written to her sister-in-law, Princess Alice, that 'Bertie' was seeing a lot of the Prime Minister and they had learned to like each other. Churchill fed the King with information, wanting him to be thoroughly informed and to understand everything. The King was flattered and fascinated and he responded by giving Churchill his friendship and absolute support.

There were moments when Churchill unwittingly bulldozed through the royal sensibilities, occupying the limelight which the King and Queen thought should be theirs. In June 1942 Victor Cazalet had a long talk at the Palace with Mrs Greville, still, in the last year of her life, on intimate terms with the King and Queen. 'K[ing] and Q[ueen] feel Winston puts them in shade,' he noted in an unpublished passage of his diary. 'He is always sending messages for Nation that [the] King ought to send. . . .'[71] Some weeks later, dining with the Halifaxes over from Washington and Tommy Lascelles, the conversation turned to the same subject: 'We talk of K. & how Winston quite unconsciously has put them in background. Who will tell him?'[72] There was, perhaps, a small element of rivalry between them. A few years later, when discussing Churchill's refusal to let him go to the Far East late in 1944, the King said: 'Do you know why he wouldn't let me go? Because I would have had the Burma Star [medal] and he wouldn't!'[73] The King liked to demonstrate his superior knowledge of such matters as industrial conditions to sympathetic listeners like Woolton, and he would complain, as everyone else did, of the punishing late hours inflicted by Churchill on his advisers and colleagues and of the sometimes woolly decisions taken late at night. He liked, too, to tease Churchill by stealing a march on him as on the occasion of one of their Tuesday luncheons in 1943, when he produced a bottle of French wine of the 1941 vintage and would not tell him how he got it. (It had been flown from France by the former Captain of the King's Flight, 'Mouse' Fielden, then engaged with 161 Squadron on secret operations in France.)

These, however, were minor points of a developing friendship. Churchill had greatly admired the King's courage when the Palace had been bombed – it was not generally known then how close his escape had been – and how the King had made light of the episode. They also shared many of the same feelings: almost simultaneously with the news of Pearl Harbor on 10 December 1941 they learned of the sinking by the Japanese off Malaya of the two British battleships *Repulse* and *Prince of Wales*, the latter being the ship on which the Prime Minister had travelled to Placentia only a few months before. Both King and Prime Minister had been in sombre mood at their weekly Tuesday lunch on the 9th, when Churchill revealed the extent to which the US Pacific Fleet, upon which British security in the Far East had depended, had been crippled: 'The Prime Minister came to lunch. He gave me the latest news from America which was dreadful,' the King wrote that day in his diary. 'In Pearl Harbor 3 US battleships were sunk & 3 seriously damaged. There are now only 2 effective US ships in the Pacific. A very serious situation for our ships P of W & Repulse who are out there. . . .'

The King was touring industrial South Wales when he heard that his fears for the two British battleships had been realized. 'I thought I was getting immune to hearing bad news, but this has affected me deeply, as I am sure it has you,' he wrote to Churchill, the 'former naval person' who had twice served as First Lord of the Admiralty. 'There is something particularly "alive" about the big ship, which gives one a sense of personal loss apart from consideration of loss of power.' To that other 'former naval person', President Roosevelt, whom he knew would be deeply wounded by the disaster to his Navy, he sent a cable of sympathy: 'My thoughts & prayers go out to you and to the great people of the United States at this solemn moment in your history when you have been treacherously attacked by Japan. We are proud indeed to be fighting at your side against the common enemy.'

Churchill was to be in need of the King's friendship and support in the early months of 1942 as the news from the battlefronts all over the Empire worsened and disaster followed upon disaster. On 15 February at Singapore 85,000 British soldiers surrended to an enemy force vastly inferior in numbers. It was, as Churchill later called it, 'the greatest military disaster in recent history'. Only three days before British pride had received a slap in the face nearer home when three German warships, *Scharnhorst*, *Gneisenau* and *Prinz Eugen*, escaped from the British blockade in Brest and sailed up the English Channel in broad daylight to the safety of their home ports, bringing down the entire force of six Swordfish aircraft and four Hampden bombers sent to intercept them. 'I am very depressed over the loss of Singapore and the fact that we were not able to prevent the 3 German ships from getting through the Channel,' the King wrote to Queen Mary the day after the fall of Singapore, associating himself with the use of the first person plural with the experience of his Prime Minister. 'We are going through a bad phase at the moment, and it will take all our energies to stop adverse comment and criticism from the Press and others.' The King was worried enough to instruct Hardinge to sound out opinion, and was reassured to find that 'Winston is the right, & indeed the only person to lead the country through the war', although he recorded there was also a general feeling that as Prime Minister and Minister of Defence Churchill was overburdened. Knowing his man, however, the King predicted, rightly, that Churchill would not give up being Minister of Defence. At lunch on Tuesday the 17th he found that Churchill was in truculent, fighting mood, resenting the criticism. 'He was very angry about all this, & compares it to hunting the tiger with angry wasps about him.' 'I do wish people would get on with the job & not criticise all the time,' the King wrote loyally to his uncle Athlone.

Churchill did, however, agree to reconstruct his Government, giving up the leadership of the House of Commons to Eden and bringing Stafford Cripps and Oliver Lyttelton into the War Cabinet. Attlee became Deputy Prime Minister and, to Churchill's regret and the King's relief, Beaverbrook resigned. The changes were announced on 19 February, a week before the debate in the House of Commons which ended in the Government winning a vote of confidence. 'I am glad Winston has been prevailed upon to make them [the changes] before and not after the debate,' the King commented in his diary on the 19th. 'The House of Commons wants Winston to lead them; but they don't like the way he treats them. He likes getting his own way with no interference from anybody and nobody will stand for that sort of treatment in this country.' To Halifax he wrote:

I have been having a worrying time of late with all the criticism of Winston and his methods. I know the country is behind him as their leader in these difficult times before us. The reorganisation of the Government which he has done should have a good effect, if only the Press would play fair and give them a chance to get results. I hope Winston will let Cripps, Eden and Lyttelton help him; he has confidence in them....[74]

Shuffling Cabinet Ministers, however, could not conceal the dismaying perception becoming general in higher circles that the King–Emperor's Empire was tottering and the King's armed forces had apparently lost the will and capacity to fight to win. At lunch with the King on 24 February, Churchill confided his fears: 'Burma, Ceylon, Calcutta and Madras in India and part of Australia may fall into enemy hands,' the King noted of their conversation. Moreover, he feared losing the U-boat war in the Atlantic, where the Germans had suddenly changed their Enigma-machine code and their most secret signals carefully monitored and decrypted at Bletchley since the summer of 1941 became unreadable once more and were to remain so for nearly a year. Tuesday lunches between the King and Churchill continued to be dominated by bad news through March and April 1942. In North Africa the British forces under General Auchinleck, appointed the previous June by Churchill in place of Wavell, made little headway. Of the military forces engaged against the Germans, it was embarrassingly true that only the Russians, whose armies Western experts had rated as weak, were actually winning engagements. The King had declared 29 March, Palm Sunday, a National Day of Prayer. The reaction of Churchill, who was present when the Archbishop of Canterbury suggested the idea to the King, is said to have been, 'If we can't bloody well fight, we'd better pray.'[75]

Earlier that month Churchill had shown the King a long telegram from President Roosevelt with a survey of American plans for the war expressing interest in opening up, as Stalin had requested, an Allied second front in Europe that year to take the pressure off the Russians, who were bearing the brunt of the fighting against the Germans. The arrival in London of a succession of high-ranking Americans for the planning of this operation was to give the King a heightened personal role in Anglo-American relations, since he received them all at Buckingham Palace or Windsor and Churchill saw to it not only that he was fully briefed on all developments but also attended the high-level working dinners at Downing Street. On 11 March the King sent a long, handwritten letter to the President thanking him for the generosity of his plans for aid, particularly in shipping. 'Shipping is our one great obstacle in retarding our immediate aims, but though it will take time & great effort on all our parts to prepare, the final issue, i.e. Victory is without any doubt to be with us.'[76]

The King sent the letter via his brother-in-law, David Bowes-Lyon, the closest to the Queen of her family and also a friend of the King's. Bowes-Lyon's mission in Washington was to set up a Political Warfare Executive (PWE) organization in the States, with his office in the British Embassy in Washington and another in New York; the King's letter was also one of introduction to the President. Bowes-Lyon's royal and social connections were to be of great assistance in

Washington, where his ostensible job was to keep American and British propaganda in step. He operated at high level using his contacts and charm in the White House, at the State Department and with the American propaganda and subversion organizations, owi and oss. They were also to arouse a good deal of jealousy in the intricate and intriguing world of the intelligence and secret services. He acted closely with Halifax and was to provide the King with an additional source of inside information in the American capital. 'I like David very much,' Halifax noted in his diary after a private luncheon with Bowes-Lyon on the eve of his departure for London in May, 'and I should think he was thoroughly useful in telling the King and Queen things they might not otherwise know.'[77] Bowes-Lyon was, indeed, useful; he took with him a letter from Halifax to the King in which, among other things, he warned the King of the intrigues of Beaverbrook, who had recently been in Washington, for the removal of Sir John Dill, in Washington as Churchill's special emissary with the American Chiefs of Staff. Dill, no favourite of Churchill's, was, Halifax told the King, invaluable in Anglo–US military relations, having 'made for himself a remarkable position here; he is completely trusted by the President and US Chiefs of Staff'. On 15 May, a few days after Bowes-Lyon's arrival back in London, Halifax noted in his diary: 'Telegram from Winston saying Dill is to stay on.'[78]

On 8 April Hopkins and General Marshall arrived in London with the American plan for opening up a second front to 'give maximum support to the Russians', with a combined land and air offensive by Great Britain and the United States involving an assault on beaches between Le Havre and Boulogne envisaged for 1943. On 10 April the King lunched at 10 Downing Street with Churchill, Hopkins and Marshall and invited them to lunch at Buckingham Palace the following Wednesday. On 14 April at Churchill's invitation he dined at 10 Downing Street, again to meet Hopkins and Marshall with the Chiefs of Staff, Alan Brooke, Admiral Sir Dudley Pound and Air Marshal Lord Portal, Mountbatten and Lord Ismay, Secretary to the Committee of Imperial Defence. Brooke recorded in his diary:

After dinner heated discussion as to possible future of German plans. I propounded possible German move through Eastern Mediterranean with sea and airborne attack against Cyprus and Syria. I suggested this might be alternative if Germany did not feel strong enough to attack in Russia. The King very interested, and resulted in good argument with Winston.[79]

In May the King was intrigued to meet the Soviet Foreign Minister, Molotov, who had come to London to negotiate the Anglo–Soviet Treaty as a prelude to the second front. The King received him on 22 May, and, perhaps thinking of his father's firm refusal to shake the hand of a representative of the regime that murdered his cousin, the Tsar, wrote to his mother, describing Molotov. '... he looks a small quiet man with a feeble voice, but is really a tyrant. He was quite polite,' he told Queen Mary, explaining how the Russians had wished with this treaty to gain recognition for their annexation of the Baltic States and Poland. Eden, backed up by Winant, had refused to agree to such a legitimization of Soviet frontiers and had offered instead a mutual assistance pact, signed on 26 May. By July, however, the Anglo–American allies had decided on a North African landing, Operation TORCH, rather than the major invasion of Europe in 1943 for which Stalin had been pressing. Bravely, Churchill (who, unknown to anyone but his doctor, had suffered a mild coronary on 26 December 1941) decided that it was his duty to bear the unpalatable message personally to Stalin, assessing the military situation in North Africa en route. On the eve of his Prime Minister's departure the King sent him a letter in his own hand, describing his journey as 'epoch-making' and stressing that he must take care of himself on such a stressful journey:

I shall follow your journey with the greatest interest & shall be more than delighted when you are safely home again.
     As I have told you before, your Welfare means a great deal not only to the United Nations, but to me personally. With my very best wishes to you in your new venture.
     Believe me,
     Your very sincere and grateful friend,
     George RI.[80]

'Always Sir you are vy. good to me,' Churchill replied that same day in a letter which, written as it was in his own hand in the midst of the turmoil of departure, illustrates the importance he attached to it: '. . . I trust indeed and pray that this journey of mine will be fruitful. . . . Yr Majesty's faithful & devoted servant, Winston S. Churchill.'[81] Churchill left Moscow on 16 August. 'As a bearer of unwelcome news', the King telegraphed to him the next day, 'your task was a very disagreeable one, but I congratulate you heartily on the skill with which you have accomplished it. The personal relationship which you have established with Stalin should be valuable in the days to come. . . .'[82] The plans for Operation TORCH could now proceed.
     Just one week later the King suffered a personal tragedy. On 25 August 1942 he was picnicking in vile weather, low mist, rain and a chill east wind, with a shooting-party which included his brother Harry on the moors near Balmoral. At that moment not far to the north-east his brother, the Duke of Kent, was a passenger in a Sunderland flying boat W4026 en route for Iceland, where he was due to inspect RAF installations. Flying far too low at 700 feet through the dense mist known locally as 'haar', at about 1.30 p.m. the aircraft hit the top of a gentle hill below Eagle's Rock on the Duke of Portland's Langwell estate and careered down the farther slope, engines at full tilt, scoring a deep scar on the moorland before bursting into a fireball. The King, for some reason, was not told of his brother's death until dinner that night, when Archie Sinclair, Secretary of State for Air, telephoned Balmoral. His sister-in-law, the Duchess of Gloucester, having had a 'nightmare drive through the fog' the previous night, was

sitting next to him when the message came for the King to take an important call:

We were all left in silence at the table, each one of us, and particularly Queen Elizabeth, suspecting something awful had happened. The King came back and sat in silence. I could feel he was in deep distress and soon the Queen caught my eye, signalling me to rise with her and lead the ladies from the room. In the drawing-room we all assumed the news must be of Queen Mary's death.... Then the Queen left us and came back with the King who told us that it was the Duke of Kent who had been killed....[83]

Deeply shocked, the King went back to Windsor for the funeral four days later at St George's Chapel. 'I have attended very many family funerals in the Chapel', he wrote in his diary, 'but none ... have moved me in the same way.... Everybody there I knew well but I did not dare to look at any of them for fear of breaking down....' Two weeks later, accompanied only by Joey Legh, he forced himself to visit the crash site on a desolate Scottish hillside:

I motored to Berriedale & walked from there to the site of the Sunderland crash where George was killed.... The remains of the aircraft had been removed, but the ground for 200 yds long & 100 yds wide had been scored & scorched by its trail & by flame. It hit one side of the slope, turned over in the air & slid down the other side on its back. The impact must have been terrific as the aircraft as an aircraft was unrecognisable when found. I felt I had to do this pilgrimage.

He comforted himself by writing of his brother that 'He died on Active Service', but like many other wartime aeroplane crashes this was a tragic accident which should never have happened. The pilot, an Australian named Flight-Lieutenant Frank Goyen, had nearly 1,000 hours in ocean patrols to his credit, his first pilot who sat beside him was the Commanding Officer of 228 Squadron, Wing-Commander T.L. Moseley; the remaining crew including a second pilot, a navigator and seven other men – engineers, radio operators and gunners – were all experienced. Although many theories were advanced for the crash, including sabotage, the most likely explanation was pilot error due to disorientation in the bad visibility. One poignant aspect of the tragedy was that, as the King wrote sadly in his diary, 'The war had brought him out in so many ways. Always charming to people in every walk of life....' The Prince, on the verge of middle age, had at last settled down after years of wildness and insecurity, supremely happy in his marriage, with three children, a daughter and two sons, the youngest of whom, Prince Michael, had been christened at Windsor only three weeks before. Before the war he had been designated Governor-General of Australia; characteristically he had already planned and ordered the decor of Government House in Canberra. Then war broke out and he had swapped his naval job at the Admiralty for the uniform of the RAF. The King had relied on his charm and ambassadorial talents to fulfil important missions, such as a visit to Canada to inspect the air training schools which were turning out pilots for the defence of Britain, and to the United States where he visited aeronautics laboratories and aircraft factories, toured Washington and charmed the Roosevelts. To Louis Greig the King wrote, 'I shall miss him & his help terribly.'

The King did what he could to help his widowed sister-in-law, Princess Marina. It was typical of his kindness and sensitivity that he realized that only one of her immediate family could help her in her misery. Her sister Elisabeth known in the family as 'Woolly', married to a pro-Hitler German aristocrat, Count Toerring-Jettenbach, was clearly out of the question, but Princess Olga was in exile in Kenya. The King swiftly took the decision to send for her, persuading Churchill to allow it on compassionate grounds. The King visited his sister-in-law several times at Coppins, the Kents' country house in Buckinghamshire, while Princess Olga was there, and Queen Mary, heroically restrained in her grief at the death of her favourite son, did what she could to comfort her. He and the Queen, after the death of the Duke of Kent, had, however, little in common with their sister-in-law. Princess Marina was very conscious of her royal and imperial blood and, like all the descendants of the Greek – and, therefore, Danish – royal families, she was exceptionally close to her immediate relations, just as Queen Alexandra, her great-aunt twice removed, had been in her day. Like Alexandra she had been poor, but unlike Alexandra it had been the poverty of exiled royalty with all its concealed humiliations of dependence upon the bounty of the rich and the social-climbers. And so she was proud in a way that the more secure Windsors were not. Like the Duke of Windsor, regarding herself as 'real' royalty, she looked down with pride not unmixed with concealed annoyance at the dominance of the commoner Queen. It may, or may not, have been true that she referred to her sisters-in-law, the Queen and the Duchess of Gloucester, as 'those common little Scottish girls'. Beyond her own relations her friends were the people who had been her husband's, artistic, amusing people like Noël Coward, not the traditional English and Scottish grandees of the royal circle. Princess Marina, a European in her background and upbringing, had never really become Anglicized, nor did she become absorbed into the British royal family in the same way that her sister-in-law, the Duchess of Gloucester, did.

With the death of the Duke of Kent, the King had now only one brother to help him with public duties, the Duke of Gloucester, who, despite his many qualities, was the butt of unkind jokes. As recently as June 1942 a motion intended as criticism of the conduct of the war after the latest military humiliation, this time at Tobruk where 33,000 British troops surrendered to a German force half that number, had failed when the House of Commons collapsed with laughter at the suggestion put forward by Sir John Wardlaw-Milne, the mover of the motion, that the Duke of Gloucester should be Commander-in-Chief of the British Army. The King had been anxiously trying to find a suitable job for his brother, but making him Commander-in-Chief of the Army was not one he had considered. Prince Henry, a genial soldier not overburdened with brain, was certainly not the man to save the British Army in its darkest days. His own reaction to the Wardlaw-Milne incident was 'What impertinence on part of

Wardlaw-Milne without asking anybody & me in particular.' Gloucester was overseas at the time, representing his royal brother in the Middle East and India, after an uncomfortable time as second in command of the 20th Armoured Brigade, having been demoted from major-general to colonel in order not to embarrass the commanding officer, a brigadier. As the King's brother it was difficult for him to be what he would have liked to be, an ordinary cavalry officer. Although he was a genial figure, well liked by his junior officers, one of whom described him as 'a real chap' and 'a soldier's man', he was not suited to the higher levels of the Army. He had hated his time as liaison officer at Gort's GHQ in France in 1939, where brilliant staff officers like Pownall and 'Boy' Munster looked down on him as stupid and wrote and said rude things about him referring to his drinking and his braying laugh.[84] Comments by Pownall on the subject have been heavily inked out in the manuscript of his diaries. Gloucester was not, however, too stupid to be aware of this and later surprised Alan Brooke by his bitterness. Staying with the Gloucesters in March 1941, Brooke reported: 'I was interested to find how bitter he was about his treatment by Gort at GHQ in France. Apparently there was a great deal of friction towards the end.'[85] At the time, Prince Henry had told a fellow officer in France that Gort's headquarters was 'so abysmally dull the port only went by once' and he had to go and stay with a cavalry squadron to find himself in sympathetic company.[86]

Brooke himself was sympathetic towards Gloucester, although embarrassed by the tentative attempts by the King and Gloucester himself to place him at the War Office or on Brooke's personal staff. The King was very fond of his brother and felt responsible for him; as the Duchess of Gloucester later wrote, Prince Henry was 'devoted' to the King and 'relied greatly upon his good advice'. The death of the Duke of Kent made the question of suitable employment for his only surviving brother even more urgent for the King. Only two days later, having travelled down from Balmoral for his brother's funeral, Gloucester called on Brooke, 'suggesting that I should give him some employment connected with me!' The following day, 28 August, Brooke was summoned to Buckingham Palace at 12.30 a.m. to see the King, where they discussed the journey he had recently undertaken with the Prime Minister to Cairo and Moscow. 'We also talked about the death of the Duke of Kent', Brooke recorded, 'and the fact that he [the King] wanted me to find some form of employment for the Duke of Gloucester. This will not be very easy, however he no longer suggests a command.'[87] On 15 September the Duke himself returned to the charge, asking for employment at the War Office. 'Not an easy job!' Brooke commented tersely. The Duke of Gloucester had one advantage over his brothers in that he did not share their nervous temperament, but as a royal brother his disadvantage was that he lacked their charm and, even more importantly, the royal memory for names and faces which wins so many hearts. 'He couldn't remember the chaps in his own regiment when he saw them,' a fellow officer recalled. The Duke of Windsor, who was fond of jokes at Prince Henry's expense (the Windsors customarily referred to him as 'the Unknown Soldier'), used to say that he was tone-deaf and only recognized the national anthem if everyone stood up. By October the King had given up the idea of the War Office for his brother. Prince Henry, Regent Designate until the majority of Princess Elizabeth in April 1944, was until then assigned the tedious job of inspecting units, hospitals, factories and civil defence units on the King's behalf. Eventually the King found a solution: the Duke of Gloucester took up the job for which the Duke of Kent had been destined when war broke out and was appointed Governor-General of Australia in November 1943.

That autumn Eleanor Roosevelt, armed with one of those friendly man-to-man letters to the King at which her husband was so adept, was among the stream of American visitors to London in the run-up to Operation TORCH. 'I wish much that I could accompany her, for there are a thousand things I want to tell you and talk with you about,' the President wrote. 'I want you and the Queen to tell Eleanor everything in regard to the problems of our troops in England which she might not get from the Government or the military authorities. You and I know that it is the little things which count but which are not always set forth in official reports.'[88] Mrs Roosevelt was there at the Queen's invitation, to observe the part played by British women in the war effort and with a brief from her husband to check up on the welfare of US troops stationed in Great Britain. The King and Queen hoped that she would put the case for wartime Britain in her own country, where many people still saw the British as idle, aristocrat-ridden and wallowing in inherited wealth. In the event, Mrs Roosevelt was much impressed and somewhat disconcerted by the austerities of life at Buckingham Palace, where she spent two nights. The King and Queen showed her to her rooms, explaining that she could only have a small fire in the sitting-room in her huge suite and one in the outer waiting-room; all the window panes had been broken in the bombing and replaced with wood and isinglass and 'one or two small panes of glass'. She later discovered that her rooms were the most comfortable in that 'blitzed place' and normally occupied by the Queen. Mrs Roosevelt, noting that wartime restrictions on heat, water and food were as strictly observed at the Palace as any other home in Britain, wondered at the painted black line in her bathtub showing the minuscule amount of water allowed. The food, although served on gold and silver plates, would have shocked the King's grandfather. Dinner consisted of fish croquettes with potatoes (fishcakes) as a starter, followed by cold ham and chicken with 'a kind of jellied pâté' and salad, two green vegetables including the 'inevitable' brussels sprouts, pudding, a savoury and fruit.

On her arrival she had family tea with the King and Queen and the two Princesses around a set table, finding the future Queen of England to be 'quite serious and a child [she was sixteen] with a great deal of character and personality. She asked me a number of questions about life in the United States and they were serious questions.' At dinner she sat between the King and Churchill, finding the latter 'not easy to talk to, which was my experience in Washington'.

'Sometimes,' she commented, 'I think by the end of the day there has been a little too much champagne because he repeated the same thing to me two or three times. . . .' According to her son Elliott, who was then stationed in England, she preferred the King to Churchill, whose views she regarded as 'antediluvian'; later in her visit, dining with the Churchills at Downing Street, they disagreed over Loyalist Spain, and when Clementine Churchill supported Eleanor, Churchill lost his temper. She got on better with the King, as long as they avoided 'international', presumably colonial, subjects. 'In all my contacts with them I have gained the greatest respect for both the King and Queen,' she later wrote. '. . . the fact that both of them are doing an extraordinarily outstanding job for their people in the most trying times stands out when you are with them, and you admire their character and their devotion to duty.'[89]

The planning of TORCH also brought General Dwight D. Eisenhower, designated as Supreme Allied Commander of the Expeditionary Force, to England. It was the beginning of a long and warm relationship between him and the royal family, initiated when Eisenhower spent forty-five minutes in private conversation with the King at Buckingham Palace on 12 July 1942. Eisenhower, according to his military Boswell, Captain Harry C. Butcher, found the King 'to be most personable and very much "in the know" as to current and prospective plans for Allied operations'. The King told Eisenhower of an incident earlier that year when Wigram had told him that two high-ranking American officers had expressed a wish to see Windsor Castle on a Sunday when it was closed. The King and Queen had volunteered to stay indoors and not embarrass the visitors, but when the day came the King had forgotten his promise and, as it was such a fine day, the entire family went to have tea in the garden where Wigram normally brought distinguished visitors. Suddenly they heard Wigram's voice, pointing out flowers in his curious idiom, 'Here's a lusty little fellow' and 'Here's a bright little chap', and looking up they saw just over the crest of the hill four heads – one very tall. The King instantly remembered his promise, knowing that if Wigram saw them he would terminate the tour; he exclaimed, 'This is terrible, we must not be seen,' so on their hands and knees the family crawled to the garden wall and escaped through a door into the castle. The two American officers were Eisenhower and his towering deputy, General Mark Clark.[90]

Three months later the King gave Eisenhower and Clark a farewell audience, during which he surprised Clark by knowing all the details of a hazardous mission the American had made to North Africa to contact the local Vichy French commanders preparatory to the launching of TORCH. 'I know all about you,' the King told him. 'You're the one that took that fabulous trip. Didn't you, by the way, get stranded on the beach without your trousers?' The King, Clark recalled, had obviously read the cable in which he reported on his mission and said he had 'thoroughly enjoyed your statement that you were forced to hide in an "empty repeat empty wine-cellar"'. 'He was kind enough to compliment me on a trip "well done",' Clark wrote, 'and as we left there was real emotion in his voice as he said, "Good-bye and God-speed".[91]

North Africa was then very much in the forefront of the King's mind. Six days earlier General Bernard Montgomery's long-awaited assault on the German position at El Alamein had begun. By 5 November what Montgomery described to Brooke as a 'terrific party and a complete slogging match' was over; by the evening of 6 November 30,000 prisoners, 350 tanks and 400 guns had been taken in the western desert, Rommel and the remnants of the Afrika Korps were in full retreat, four German and eight Italian divisions had ceased to exist and General Alexander, Churchill's eventual choice to replace Auchinleck, cabled the Prime Minister, 'Ring out the bells'. For the King, El Alamein was the first relief from three years of anguish at the failure of his armed forces, the first sign that the enemy was not invincible. 'A victory at last, how good it is for the nerves,' he wrote in his diary, pinning Alexander's telegram to the relevant page.

On 5 November the King sent his Prime Minister a generous tribute, a letter written in his own hand and addressed to 'My dear Winston':

I must send you my warmest congratulations on the great Victory of the 8th Army in Egypt. I was overjoyed when I received the news and so was everybody else. In our many talks together over a long period I knew that the elimination of the Afrika Corps, the threat to Egypt, was your *one* aim, the most important of all the many other operations with which you have had to deal.

When I look back and think of all the many arduous hours of work you have put in, and the many miles you have travelled, to bring this battle to such a successful conclusion you have every right to rejoice; while the rest of our people will one day be very thankful to you for what you have done. I cannot say more.[92]

Churchill replied in a moving letter:

No Minister in modern times ... has received more help and comfort from the King, and this has brought us all thus far with broadening hopes and now I feel to brightening skies.

It is needless to assure Your Majesty of my devotion to Yourself and Family and to our ancient and cherished Monarchy – the true bulwark of British freedom against tyrannies of every kind; but I trust I may have the pleasure of feeling a sense of personal friendship which is very keen and lively in my heart and has grown strong in these hard times of war.[93]

The King, however, was not happy with the situation in North Africa after the Allied landings in November 1942 and the Casablanca Conference in January 1943. He had very much disliked the deal which the Americans had made with Admiral Darlan to bring over the Vichy French forces in North Africa and, when he had said goodbye to Eisenhower and Clark, had dropped heavy hints of his feelings about Darlan, remarking that 'no one trusted him and that he had shifty eyes'. Darlan was known to be deeply anti-British and as Vice-President and War Minister in the Vichy Government tainted with collaboration, while General Giraud, who under the American deal was to be the principal military commander of the post-landing French forces, although heroic and anti-German had no personal following. General de Gaulle, whom Roosevelt and his personal representative in North Africa, Robert Murphy, disliked and distrusted, was conspicuously left out of the arrangements and, on the not unjustified grounds of security leaks among the Free French in London, was not even told of the landings until after they had taken place. The King – and British public opinion – found it hard to accept that de Gaulle, who had stood alone with Britain in 1940 and refused to knuckle under to the Vichy compromise with the Germans, should be treated on the same level, or even worse, than Frenchmen who, whatever their undoubted loyalty to France, had preferred to treat with the enemy. Fortunately for de Gaulle's future, Darlan was shortly removed from the scene by an assassin in Algiers on Christmas Day 1942.

The King was well aware, however, that the Americans were continuing to support Giraud and were prepared to drop de Gaulle if he refused to compromise with him. He knew, too, that Churchill was ambivalent towards de Gaulle and suspected that he was prepared to sacrifice him to the all-important end of maintaining good relations with Roosevelt. The King, however, was not given to ambivalence. He was prepared for a slight tussle with his Prime Minister if necessary. Before meeting Churchill he talked to Henry 'Hal' Mack, the Foreign Office representative on Eisenhower's staff, and did not care for what he heard. 'The whole position in N. Africa is an enigma to me,' the King wrote in his diary. 'PM has come back even more anti-de Gaulle than when he left.... He now talks of breaking him ...', Oliver Harvey, Mack's superior at the Foreign Office, wrote in his.[94] When Churchill raised the subject of de Gaulle, the King was prepared. In his account of their lunch on 9 February, when Churchill reported personally on Casablanca, he wrote:

He [Churchill] was furious with de Gaulle over his refusal to accept F.D.R.'s invitation to meet him & Giraud. The latter made friends with F.D.R. & got on well. I warned W. not to be too hasty with de G. & F.Fr.Nat. Comee [Free French National Committee].... I told W. I could well understand de G's attitude, & that of our own people here, who do not like the idea of making friends of those Frenchmen who have collaborated with the Germans.

The King remained uneasy about the political aspects of the Allied plans and anxious that the Allies should not continue in this equivocal manner in their forthcoming assault upon Italy. 'I feel we must have a cut & dried joint plan for this & that we must be firm & not deal with any of the Fascist regime or Mussolini's people, or any kind of quisling,' he wrote in his diary on 16 February. On that day Churchill, who should have been lunching with the King, was in bed with pneumonia, but the King's anxiety over the North African situation overrode his usual considerateness. Having heard further bad news from Eisenhower, who was proposing to postpone the Sicily operation and whose lines had been broken by Rommel, and frustrated by his inability to talk the situation over with Churchill, he wrote him a long, critical letter instead:

My dear Winston ...

I do not feel at all happy about the present political situation in North Africa. I know we had to leave the political side of Torch to the Americans, while we were able to keep Spain and Portugal friendly during the time the operation was going on. Since then I feel the underhand dealings of Murphy with the French in North Africa, and his contacts with Vichy, have placed both America and this country in an invidious position. I know we had to tread warily at the start, but is there nothing we can do now to strengthen [Harold] Macmillan's and Alexander's hands in both the political and military sphere, to make the two French sides come together.

It looks as if the US Forces have had a sound defeat last week, which will not help them in French eyes, and as if we shall have to do all the fighting there. The state of affairs, according to the telegrams I have seen, looks as if it was deteriorating.

Now I hear that from the American point of view the date of Husky [the Allied invasion of Sicily] will have to be postponed to the later one, whereas we can plan for the earlier one, which will be an aggravation of our difficulties in preparing the operation. . . .

This fact will throw out all our careful calculations for convoys and escorts, and will upset our import programme again. I should not think of bothering you with these questions at this moment, but I do feel worried about them, and I would like an assurance from you that they are being carefully watched. I cannot discuss these vital matters with anyone but yourself.

Churchill took the King's anxiety seriously. Summoning the CIGS to his bedside to check the text before he sent it, despite his fever, he dictated a seven-page rebuttal defending Murphy and the Americans against the King's charges, and attacking de Gaulle, whose insolence he blamed for his difficulties with Giraud and the Americans. Eisenhower had been ordered to put forward Operation HUSKY to its original date, while as to the military situation, although he was not entirely happy with it, Montgomery would counterattack and the Americans recover.

The King was reassured, but not completely so. He continued to be pro de Gaulle and to attempt from time to time to modify Churchill's hostility towards him. He also summoned Alan Brooke to the Palace on 25 February to hear the CIG's assessment of the military situation. Brooke spent an hour with the King: 'He asked me all about the military situation and took the greatest interest in all details,' Brooke recorded. By then, the battle in Tunisia had already taken a turn for the better, the Americans having re-taken the Kasserine Pass on 24 February. British reading of the German Army's Enigma code enabled Alexander and Montgomery to forestall planned German offensives, as the King learned when he drove down to lunch with the convalescent Churchill at Chequers on 8 March. There was a complete reconciliation. 'The two of them talked hard in the room next to the office, and we could hear the two tongues wagging like mad!' one of Churchill's secretaries wrote. 'When the King left for London Churchill insisted on accompanying him to the door in spite of instructions to the contrary. . . .'[95] By 25 March the King could feel confident enough of the outcome of the battle in Tunisia and the clearing of the German forces from

North Africa to plan a visit to the Allied Forces there and sent Hardinge to the War Office to discuss it. 'The King', Brooke noted, 'is very keen to go out. . . .'

On 11 June, under the sobriquet 'General Lyon', the King, accompanied by Hardinge, Legh and 'Mouse' Fielden, left Northolt aerodrome in the four-engined York bomber which was luxuriously fitted out for Churchill's use. Sir James Grigg, Secretary of State for War, Archie Sinclair, Secretary of State for Air, and Louis Greig accompanied him in a separate plane. It was his first journey out of England since December 1940 and the fact that the King of England could now fly from the beleaguered home country to North Africa symbolized that the tide of eventual victory had turned in the Allies' favour. It should also have been a celebration of the Anglo–American partnership that had turned, *pace* the Russians, defeat into victory. That it did succeed in being so was a tribute to the quick thinking and determination of Harold Macmillan, recently appointed Minister Resident to Allied Force Headquarters, and to the good relations which the King already had established with Eisenhower and the other American commanders.

The King arrived in high spirits on 12 June to be greeted by Eisenhower. 'He was buoyant and friendly with General Ike,' Eisenhower's British woman driver and intimate friend, Kay Summersby, reported, 'the first to admit his downright excitement at getting out of embattled England for the first time since the war started.' Eisenhower, according to Captain Butcher who was also present, was 'fond of the King', whom he thought of as 'democratic', and from the airport at Maison Blanche into Algiers the two men talked about the Tunisian campaign and the coming invasion of Sicily, the King, according to Summersby, displaying 'a unique familiarity with even the most technical points, obviously up to date on all developments'.[96] Macmillan, summoned to meet the King at his villa, requisitioned from a rich French wine merchant and, the King noted, 'like all French houses, [with] very erratic and defective plumbing', discovered to his dismay that the visit had been badly planned. He found the King 'very tired from his journey and had not slept at all' and consequently experienced 'a good deal of difficulty in getting him to agree to the various items'. Macmillan thought the real trouble was the courtiers whom he described as 'deplorable', meaning not so much Legh ('does his best, and, although looking half-witted, is not so'), but Hardinge ('beyond the pale . . . idle, supercilious, without a spark of imagination'). '. . . his whole attitude towards the trip', Macmillan commented, 'makes one wonder why he advised the King to undertake it at all.' Macmillan, to whom successful co-operation with the Americans was a primary objective, was surprised to find the royal party somewhat reluctant to undertake this part of the plan:

At first the view was that HM had come to see his own armies, not the American. Alec seemed rather to favour that extraordinary idea! However, after a bit we persuaded them that they were wrong and that such an attitude would be an absolute disaster. Actually [he added], General Lyon was merely tired and feverish. I do blame Alec, because he just doesn't seem to live in the modern world. . . .

It was only after some time that Macmillan succeeded in getting the first two days, including a visit to the American Army entailing a two-hour flight each way and a gruelling programme of reviews, agreed. Hardinge, who was responsible for the organization of the visit, its objectives and programme, clearly had quite failed to grasp its significance. This, together with other stresses and strains in the Palace relationships, was to cost him his job.

At dinner, however, the King, who had had a bath and a sleep, was 'in excellent form' as he entertained Eisenhower, Naval Commander-in-Chief, Admiral Cunningham, Grigg, Macmillan and their aides. 'He was very good with Eisenhower,' Macmillan noted, 'who was himself in excellent shape – interesting, amusing, not too shy or too much at ease – in fact the real natural simple gentleman which he is.' After dinner the King took the General apart and presented him with the GCB 'with a few very well-chosen phrases'.[97] The next day, Sunday 13 June, after church service with the Royal Navy at the dockyard, the King held a slightly more tricky entertainment, a lunch for the two rival French Generals, Giraud and de Gaulle. For this Macmillan was primarily responsible, Churchill's advice having been 'in rather governessy terms' that the French should not be invited to lunch with the King unless they were 'behaving well'. ' "Were they?" asked George VI. "No Sir," replied Macmillan. "Some have resigned; others are threatening resignation. I can't say they are behaving well." Nevertheless he urged the King to hold the lunch on the grounds that "it may do good, and it can do no harm".' The King laughed and, at the lunch, according to Macmillan, he 'did very well and spoke good French to both generals who were on his right and left'.[98] It was, he later told his biographer, 'a great success'. After lunch the King, visiting a convalescent camp for Eighth Army soldiers near the sea eight miles outside Algiers, was surrounded by 500 half-naked troops singing 'For he's a jolly good fellow' and cheering him to the echo.

Monday was the turn of the American forces. Security surrounding the King's visit had been so tight that General Clark at the Fifth Army training camp at Oran had been told to prepare a demonstration for the British War Minister and 'a special visitor'. The 'special visitor' was, of course, the King, who flew out to the camp in the York with his fighter escort for an exercise scheduled to take place at one o'clock in the afternoon of the blazing North African summer. On arrival, the King, no doubt looking forward to a chance to get inside out of the sun, asked Clark the name of the hotel where they were going to lunch, only to be told that they were to lunch in the open. The meal, as Clark admitted in his memoirs, was not a great success. Although he had chosen a shady spot, the flies were so bad that a man had to be stationed behind the King flapping with a towel to keep them away and the food, presented in GI mess kits, was hot beef stew, which Grigg spilled over his trousers. Even after lunch there was an awkwardness when they came to pose for photographs. Clark was exceptionally tall and even under normal circumstances would have dwarfed the King, but unfortunately on this occasion he happened to be standing at the King's left on a hump

that made me tower even still more definitely over His Majesty, who was standing in a little depression.

'Would you', the King asked before the picture was taken, 'mind swapping places with me? You're so tall that I'd like to stand on the hump. You can take the rut....'

However, the King was deeply interested by the mock street-fighting exercises which the GIS put on in a specially constructed village; hand grenades were exploded and demolition charges knocked down buildings to give verve and realism to the proceedings. 'He departed in a pleasant mood,' Clark wrote, 'and I felt that perhaps the afternoon's exercises had made up for the difficulties we had had at luncheon.'[99] Next day, 15 June, at Macmillan's suggestion, the King gave a garden-party at his villa in Algiers. About 180 British and American officers and civilians were invited, the band of the Royal Marines played and 'it was a *tremendous* success.... HM did very well and was most gracious to everybody. The Americans were really delighted, and letters about it will reach every distant part of the USA,' Macmillan recorded.[100]

Meanwhile, the King moved on to Tripoli on 19 June to visit the Eighth Army and its controversial commander, General Montgomery, whose talent for fighting the Germans was only equalled by his ability to infuriate the Americans from Eisenhower down and, indeed, his own senior colleagues in AFHQ, with his boastfulness and outspoken criticism. The King had been treated to Montgomery's views on the North African situation and the plans for HUSKY a month before when Montgomery, returning to London as the triumphant conqueror of Rommel, had had tea on 18 May with the King, Queen and Princesses at Buckingham Palace. During that visit Montgomery had been mobbed and cheered by crowds wherever he went as if he had been a British film star, but on his return to Algiers he had had to face a severe dressing-down and a lecture on Anglo–American relations from his hero and protector, Alan Brooke, who attempted to 'make him see the whole situation and the War as a whole outside the Eighth Army orbit'. It was after this visit with the King to Montgomery's HQ that Brooke said to the King, 'I used to think he would like my job, but I don't think he does now.' 'No,' the King replied, 'but I sometimes wonder about mine!'[101]

Shortly after his arrival at the aerodrome of Castel Benito on 19 June the King conferred upon Montgomery the accolade of knighthood which he had earned at Alamein. 'The King is to stay with me at my HQ and my cook is very excited,' Montgomery had written to a friend three days earlier. In fact, Montgomery himself was tremendously excited and flattered by this, the first visit paid by the King to an army commander in the field in the Second World War.[102] He had been, as he recorded in his diary, anxious about the King's safety 'as enemy parachutists were at large, and Tripoli itself was full of Italians. I confined all civilians to their houses during the visit; on the second day, 21

June, I opened fire in Tripoli on suspicious people trying to break out. . . .'[103] During his four-day visit the King stayed at Montgomery's Army HQ camp west of Tripoli, occupying the captured caravan that had belonged to the German Field Marshal Messe. 'He is a most delightful person', Montgomery wrote of the King, '& he likes people to be quite natural with him. . . .' Among Montgomery's 'natural' habits was going to bed early; he would be in bed by 9.30 at night, King or no King. The King, who liked to stay up late discussing things, was no doubt disconcerted by this first experience of his General's inflexible rule; on later visits, as in Normandy the following year, he learned to expect it.

For the King, however, the most moving part of his trip was his visit to Malta across the sea which Mussolini had once claimed to be Mare Nostrum. Malta's endurance of a fourteen-month siege from June 1941 to September 1942 had been one of the most famous episodes of the war and on 15 April 1942 the King himself had bestowed on the island and its people the George Cross for valour. The King had been determined to make the tribute of a personal visit, despite the risks. Sicily, still in Axis hands, was only sixty miles to the north, the Italian fleet and the Italian Air Force were still under Axis control, and the last raid on Malta from the Italian mainland was to take place in October 1944, well over a year later. Nothing had been announced beforehand but the King was determined, if possible, to carry out his plan, and at dinner on his first evening in Algiers he had tackled Admiral Cunningham on the subject. 'I had set my heart on that', the King later wrote to Queen Mary, '& it was not difficult to persuade the Naval & Air C-in-C's of its importance or its effect on the Island itself. . . . I knew there was a risk in any case but it was worth taking. . . .'

On the night of 19 June the King, accompanied by Cunningham and Macmillan with the rest of his party, left the harbour of Tripoli, still half-blocked by sunken ships, on the cruiser *Aurora* for Malta. It was bright moonlight and, according to Macmillan, neither on that night nor on the return trip on Sunday night, did any of the naval officers on board sleep at all. At 8.15 the following morning the King, a slim figure in white naval uniform, stood alone on a special platform constructed in front of the bridge as the *Aurora* slowly made her way into the Grand Harbour at Valletta, a slow passage lasting at least three-quarters of an hour with all the cliffs and forts filled with troops, sailors, airmen and civilians, thundering out a tremendous welcome. He wrote to his mother on 26 June:

I shall never forget the sight of entering the Grand Harbour at 8.30 a.m. on a lovely sunny day, & seeing the people cheering from every vantage view point, while we were still some way off. Then later, when we anchored inside, hearing the cheers of the people which brought a lump to my throat, knowing what they had suffered from six months constant bombing. . . .

Through streets filled with cheering crowds the King drove to the Palace to hand the Governor, Lord Gort, his Field Marshal's baton. 'Flowers, flags, confetti – and all the people, usually led by their clergy, with religious banners and emblems outside each church and crowding every square,' Macmillan wrote. 'Considering that they had only been told in the early morning, I don't know where they found the flags and how they had time to decorate the streets....'[104] The King drove all over the island, from town to town, village to village. 'In each village the population gave me a great reception & I found the profusion of flowers which they threw into the car was quite detrimental to my white uniform,' he wrote. The *Aurora* sailed at 10 p.m. into another moonlit night.

The King returned to London from Algiers on 25 June, sunburned, exhausted and thin – with the heat and the constant stomach upsets from which all the party intermittently suffered he had lost a stone. But the fact that the trip had taken place at all was a harbinger of things to come. The Mediterranean was no longer an Axis sea; the King had crossed from North Africa to Malta twice in thirty-six hours in a cruiser escorted by four destroyers without seeing a hostile ship or aircraft. Just under two weeks later Operation HUSKY began. The high quality of German resistance and the rather less impressive quality of Allied co-operation in the campaign were indications of problems to come, but on 3 September 1943, four years to the day after Britain had declared war upon Germany and approximately three years and six months since the Germans had expelled the BEF ignominiously from the Continent, British troops landed on the Italian mainland. Three days later, on 9 September, the US Fifth Army under General Clark landed at Salerno. It was by no means the end of the war, but it was the beginning of the end.

The return of the Allied forces to the European mainland was to culminate in Operation OVERLORD, the Normandy landings on D-Day, 6 June 1944, which represented the high-point, indeed the last peak, of Anglo–American co-operation. Nine months before the King had had very serious doubts about the strategical wisdom of OVERLORD, inspired by a long talk with the South African leader, Field Marshal Jan Smuts. Smuts's view, with which the King agreed, was that it would be more sensible to consolidate the ground so far won in Italy and to strike towards the Balkans, rather than to make a hazardous assault on the heavily defended West Wall within easy communication of Germany itself, merely to please the Russians. 'I agree with Smuts about all this,' the King had written in his diary on 13 October 1943. 'If you have a good thing [i.e. Italy] stick to it. Why start another front across the Channel.... The Russians do not want us in the Balkans. They would like to see us fighting in France, so as to have a free hand in the east of Europe.' The King had invited Churchill and Smuts to dine with him to discuss the possibility before the Prime Minister met Roosevelt and Stalin at Tehran. '... I have always thought that your original idea last year of attacking the "under belly of the Axis" was the right one,' he wrote to Churchill:

The present situation as we know has turned out even better than we could ever have hoped for last year & would it not be possible to carry on there.... Italy is now at war with our enemy Germany; Roumania & Hungary are trying to get into touch with us.

What we want to see is Greece & Yugoslavia liberated; then Turkey may come in with us. . . . Let this country be the base from which all bombing operations will take place in an ever increasing intensity on Germany [the King added].

Churchill, however, had agreed at the Quebec Conference in August that OVERLORD should be the primary US–British ground and air effort against the Axis in Europe, setting the target date for 1 May 1944. Whatever his private reservations about OVERLORD and his preference for a strike towards the Balkans through the Dodecanese as the King and Smuts suggested, he was realistic enough to know, as he told the King in his letter accepting the royal invitation to dine, that he had no chance of getting Roosevelt and Stalin to agree.

On 15 May the King, with Churchill, Smuts, the Chiefs of Staff and over 150 commanders of land, sea and air units participating in D-Day attended a high-level presentation of the final plans for OVERLORD at Montgomery's old school, St Paul's. A huge plaster relief, 'the width of a city block', of Normandy and the Cotentin beaches showing the terrain, formed the background to explanations of the plan by the principal commanders. Montgomery, wearing built-up shoes and brandishing a pointer, traced the manœuvres of 21 Army Group, which was to be faced by his desert antagonist, Rommel, and predicted the German reaction to the landings. He told his audience:

We shall have to send the soldiers into this party 'seeing red'. We must get them completely on their toes; having absolute faith in the plan; and imbued with infectious optimism and offensive eagerness. Nothing must stop them! If we send them into battle in this way – then we shall succeed.

Closing the proceedings, the King made an impromptu speech – 'absolutely first class ... quite short, and exactly right,' Montgomery commented – and ended by asking God's blessing on OVERLORD. He then passed down the front row, shaking hands with the distinguished guests, pausing to speak to Eisenhower, the Supreme Commander. 'Your Majesty,' Eisenhower told him in his deep Kansas voice, 'there will be eleven thousand planes overhead on D-Day, and OVERLORD is backed by the greatest armada in history. It will not fail.'[105]

The run up to D-Day featured a battle of wills between the King and Churchill, in which the King handled his Prime Minister with considerable skill. At lunch on Tuesday 30 May the King discovered that the Prime Minister had laid plans with Admiral Ramsay, head of Naval Operations for OVERLORD, to watch the first day's bombardment from a cruiser, HMS *Belfast*, and even to tour the beaches. Churchill did not tell the King that neither the Admiral, nor Eisenhower, the only other authority to be informed, had been enamoured of the idea. The King, who had been thinking for some time of doing exactly the same, seized on the idea and suggested he should go too. The two were to talk to Ramsay about it the following Thursday. 'It is a big decision to take on one's own responsibility,' the King wrote in his diary on 31 May. 'W. cannot say no if he goes himself, & I don't want to have to tell him he cannot. So? I told Elizabeth about the idea & she was wonderful as always & encouraged me to do it.' Lascelles, however, was appalled at the thought of King and Prime Minister committing themselves to this dashing exploit on the same warship in the thick of a major invasion. Reluctantly, the King himself had come to the same conclusion, writing to Churchill the next day that he thought 'the right thing to do is what normally falls to those at the top on such occasions, namely, to remain at home and wait.... I don't think I need emphasise what it would mean to me personally, and to the whole Allied cause, if at this juncture a chance bomb, torpedo, or even a mine, should remove you from the scene,' he added persuasively. 'Equally, a change of Sovereign at this moment would be a serious matter for the country and Empire. We should both,' he went on, 'I know, love to be there, but in all seriousness I would ask you to reconsider your plan. Our presence, I feel, would be an embarrassment to those responsible for fighting the ship or ships in which we were, despite anything we might say to them.' Touchingly, he concluded, 'The anxiety of these coming days would be very greatly increased for me if I thought that, in addition to everything else, there was a risk, however remote, of my losing your help and guidance.'

Churchill, however, was determined to go and Lascelles's rather less subtle approach, pointing out that no Prime Minister could go abroad without his sovereign's consent, only made him more obstinate. The King argued with Churchill without avail, noting with some exasperation in his diary: 'I am very worried over the PM's seemingly selfish way of looking at the matter. He doesn't seem to care about the future, or how much depends on him.' He was not going to give up, nor was he prepared to stand on his constitutional dignity and jeopardize his friendship with Churchill by refusing him permission to go. He wrote yet another letter, this time both imploring him on the grounds of fair play not to go and advising him that it was his duty not to:

I want to make one more appeal to you not to go to sea on D Day. Please consider my own position. I am a younger man than you, I am a sailor, & as King I am the head of all three Services. There is nothing I would like to do better than to go to sea but I have agreed to stop at home; is it fair that you should then do exactly what I should have liked to do myself? You said yesterday afternoon that it would be a fine thing for the King to lead his troops into battle, as in old days; if the King cannot do this, it does not seem to me right that his Prime Minister should take his place....

Grumpily and ungraciously, Churchill complied; not, as he pointed out in his reply, because as Prime Minister and Minister of Defence he could not go where he considered it necessary without the consent of the Cabinet, but simply because the King asked him to. 'Since Your Majesty does me the honour to be so much concerned about my personal safety on this occasion, I must defer to Your Majesty's wishes,' he wrote, adding, unfairly and somewhat waspishly, '& indeed commands.' In his diary the King was anxious to set the record straight. 'I was not raising any constitutional point,' he wrote. 'I asked him as a friend not to endanger his life & so put me & everybody else in a difficult position.' It was, perhaps, better for their future relationship that they did not go at the same time as rival stars upstaging one another. In the event, Churchill got to Normandy first, making a day trip on D-Day + 6 – 12 June – to Montgomery's beach-head where he landed and lunched at the General's headquarters. The next day he reported to the King at their Tuesday luncheon, later giving the King formal permission to visit the beaches, which the King did on 16 June, driving ashore in a DKW amphibian to be met by a 'very enthusiastic' Montgomery, with whom he lunched in his caravan at his tactical HQ. The King greatly enjoyed his day which, as Lascelles wrote to Ismay, had only one unfortunate sequel arising from Montgomery's mania for publicity. He gave permission for some fifty reporters and photographers to attend the small ceremony at tactical head-quarters when the King presented decorations to some few officers and men. The censor remissly allowed these reports through and the precise route from the beaches to the General's headquarters was thus revealed.[106]

The King returned not to Buckingham Palace, but to Windsor. On 15 June, the night he had left London en route for Normandy, Hitler had launched his new secret weapon, the VI flying bomb, and life in London became as unpleasant – and perhaps more dangerous – as it had been during the months of the Blitz. Over 500 civilians were killed during the first week, sixty of them in the Guards Chapel within yards of Buckingham Palace. At the Palace windows were regularly blown out by the blast and replaced with squares of talc; for the next few weeks the King's Tuesday luncheons with Churchill were held in the basement air-raid shelter. The King, fascinated by this new technical phenom-enon, visited anti-aircraft batteries and fighter squadrons to see for himself what results were being achieved against the flying bomb. The figures were not entirely reassuring. At one battery the success rate was only two out of five, which the King hoped was not because his presence had made them nervous. Two RAF fighters were seen to be 'left standing' by one bomb as it sped towards London. The King found the 'stiff upper lip' heroism of the fighter pilots intimidating. 'I find it so difficult to talk to them', he wrote, 'as they will never say what they have done, and they have all got stories to tell.'

The King, like Churchill, was longing to be in the front line. Exhilarated by his visit to the Normandy battleground, he went on to tour the Italian front from 23 July to 3 August. His visit was well timed: 'Alex [General Alexander] told me that he was particularly glad I had come out just at this moment as the troops rather feared that their campaign had been put in the shade by the Press ever since the landing in Normandy,' he recorded. He spent a week with Alexander at his caravan HQ on the eastern shore of Lake Bolsena, behaving, according to Alexander, as if he were on holiday, very relaxed and enjoying it all. Alexander was amused to find that the King, who occupied the General's own caravan, was 'not at all satisfied with my simple comforts, and had fresh lighting installed and a small extra tent attached to the caravan. He also brought a bath made of some sort of rubber stuff – I think it came from a barrage balloon. It was an excellent bath and when he left he gave it to me.'[107]

The King flew to Naples, where he stayed at the Villa Emma, where Nelson had first met Lady Hamilton. Security was so tight that a party of notables, including Sir D'Arcy Osborne, the Ambassador to the Vatican, arriving to join the King after dinner, were suspected of being journalists and sent away. However, according to Macmillan, they were eventually retrieved and a 'very merry evening' ensued until quite late. The monarch, Macmillan noted on his arrival, was in excellent form, although he had the slightly embarrassing task of explaining to him that if the King of Italy or his son sent any message or asked to see him, he should not reply without consulting his ministers. Earlier that year, Macmillan and his American colleague, Robert Murphy, had had a difficult time with King Victor Emmanuel III, whom the Americans were determined to dislodge, on account of his connections with fascism, in favour of his son, Umberto, Prince of Piedmont. Macmillan had formed a high opinion of the Italian sovereign's eel-like qualities: 'old age has not deprived this monarch of any of his subtlety in negotiation and ingenuity of mind,' he had written of this interview in his diary on 10 April 1944. He could not exclude the possibility that Victor Emmanuel might attempt to embroil King George in some way and he would have been even more nervous had he known that the King of Italy had, without consulting the Allies, moved to Naples that month.

On Monday 24 July George VI attended a magnificent luncheon in his honour in the huge banqueting hall of the former royal palace of Caserta, a vast building on a far grander scale than either Buckingham Palace or Windsor Castle. He then flew north to Marcianise to meet Alexander. He spent two nights at General Sir Oliver Leese's Tac HQ in splendid hill country overlooking Arezzo and the enemy positions beyond. Tremendous effort had been put into making the King's two caravans palatial: the bedroom was furnished with gilt Louis XVI *fauteuils* with flowered satin seats, bowls of pink and white carnations and chintz curtains, the sitting-room with red chairs and red gladioli. The bathroom boasted the General's large marble bath reposing on a tiled floor 'liberated' from Arezzo. 'Seldom', Leese wrote to his wife, 'can a reigning monarch have sat in his bath, watching a bombardment of enemy positions a few thousand yards away, to the strains of a Grenadier Guards' Band playing behind his caravan!' The caravans were surrounded by a specially constructed rock garden with '8 Army' proudly picked out in blue stones and the royal lavatory, in a green sentry box, had a walnut seat and a paved and tiled floor. Strategically placed behind it was a dug-out in case the Germans should be tactless enough to shell the site at a difficult royal moment.

The King drove up winding roads in the General's open Humber, propped up on rugs so that he was easily visible to the troops stationed informally in groups along the roads, but 'with officers among them to keep going spontaneous and continued cheering'. The King stopped several times along the route to speak to the men before arriving at the HQ, where he and Alexander dined on whitebait from Lake Trasimene, geese from the HQ flock and corn on the cob. There were pipers round the table and in the background the Grenadier Guards' Band, a curious spectacle in that wild, wooded country. The King stayed talking till midnight, making the band play 'Lili Marlene' three times. The next day they drove towards Florence, the King 'amazed' at the progress the troops had made fighting through the extremely difficult wooded and enclosed country and tangled and rugged hills. At Lake Trasimene the King inspected a Polish contingent of about 1,000 men looking splendid, Leese recorded, as they marched past with their famous Prada step rather like the Prussian goose-step. The Polish Generals Sosnkowski and Anders came back to dine while a Polish band played Polish songs, including one particularly lively folk tune from Lwow. General Anders sang the verse and they all, including the King, joined lustily in the chorus.[108] Later the King went on to visit units of the US Fifth Army, commanded by his old acquaintance General Clark, preparing to cross the Arno on the Cecina sector, making a tour of inspection in an open command car with Clark and his irrepressible cocker spaniel, Pal, sitting on the seat beside him.

On 31 July the King flew back to Venafro, near Naples, where he reviewed the Canadian Corps, lunched with the officers and presented the VC to Major J.K. Mahony, a newspaperman from Vancouver, for gallantry during the Canadian Corps' thrust through the Gustav and Hitler lines. Accompanied by Macmillan the King drove to Cassino to meet Alexander, who took them on a tour of explanation of that protracted and painful battle. 'This was a great treat,' Macmillan recorded, 'and His Majesty seemed very pleased. He was in excellent form and most genial.' After a picnic tea they drove back to Naples where the King entertained Macmillan and his wife, Lady Dorothy, to dinner with Legh and Admiral Cunningham.[109] Macmillan visited the King at the Villa Emma on business the next day with telegrams on Greek, Yugoslav, Turkish and Italian affairs. 'He was in excellent form and (as usual) I was impressed by his retentive memory and his detailed knowledge of what is going on.' Macmillan contrasted the King's 'good and sensible judgement' when talking quietly in private with his occasional behaviour in company, a characteristic of the nervous and shy. '(When excited by company, he is sometimes rather wild in his talk.)' He was immensely amused, Macmillan said, by an incident which had taken place early that morning. The picket-boat which patrolled all night outside the Villa Emma had arrested a suspicious-looking couple who were fishing from a small boat just off the villa in the early hours, about 5.30 or 6 a.m. These proved to be the King and Queen of Italy; the Queen protested vigorously and the noise woke up the King of England, who put his head out of the window and called for silence. Finally the Queen produced a visiting card of *Alice in Wonderland* proportions declaring her to be S.M la Regina d'Italia and gave it to the naval lieutenant in charge of the patrol. The young officer's report, accompanied by the Queen's card, amused the King enormously and he kept the card as a souvenir. That night, the King invited Macmillan to an after-dinner showing of, appropriately, Churchill's favourite film, *Lady Hamilton*, with Laurence Olivier and Vivien Leigh. 'His Majesty very happy,' Macmillan recorded, the implication being that the King, as was his wont in congenial company, had been enjoying more than a glass or two of his favourite whisky.[110] The King left the following day at noon from Pomigliano airport, 'in the highest spirits till the end', Macmillan who saw him off reported. 'It has been a really happy and successful visit.'

By the end of August the Battle of Normandy was over, a momentous victory which seemed to herald the end of the war as the Allies drove across the Somme and the Meuse, heading eastwards towards Germany. On 24 August the King, taking a brief holiday at Balmoral, sent Montgomery a congratulatory message: 'Ever since you first explained to me your masterly plan for your part in the campaign in western France, I have followed with admiration its day to day development. I congratulate you most heartily on its overwhelming success.'[111] On 31 August the King promoted Montgomery to Field Marshal, a unique honour granted as it was to a general still on the field of battle. Montgomery, it seems, was already looking forward to a visit from the King or even to have suggested it, for on 22 August Lascelles wrote to him from Balmoral thanking him for his 'attractive suggestion' but saying there was no chance of the King taking 'the trip in question' before the end of the month. Montgomery's promotion was announced on 1 September, the same day on which the Supreme Commander, General Eisenhower, took over from him as C-in-C Allied Ground Forces, and by the time the King arrived on a visit to Montgomery's 21 Army Group HQ at Eindhoven on 11 October, the British had suffered a disaster in the airborne operation at Arnhem, codenamed MARKET GARDEN, the Allied thrust eastwards had split and slowed down, and a resentful, critical Montgomery was quarrelling bitterly with his American colleagues over the future command and conduct of the campaign.

The King spent six days staying in Montgomery's own caravan, a signal honour. Air Marshal Sir Arthur Coningham, New Zealand Commander of 21 Army Group's tactical support aircraft, seized by 'an almost paranoid jealousy' of Montgomery, had attempted to prevent the King's visiting his HQ by sending a message to Lascelles that it would be unsafe to fly into Eindhoven or even to approach it by road. 'Complete and utter nonsense,' Montgomery assured Lascelles on 6 October, Coningham apparently having advised Churchill to halt the King at his own luxurious headquarters at Brussels. This the King absolutely refused to contemplate. According to Lascelles, he 'would rather put the whole thing off if the only alternative was to go and sit in the outskirts of Brussels'.[112] He intended to visit the General in his tactical HQ just as he had in North Africa and Normandy and, when Montgomery cabled Churchill taking full responsibility for the King's safety, he got his way. The King thoroughly enjoyed his visit to Montgomery's HQ, where the spartan Field Marshal, a teetotaller and non-smoker, would retire to bed at his usual hour of 9.30 sharp, leaving his liaison officers to entertain the King and his entourage with intelligence of the day's events. 'To say that this visit was an unqualified success is to put it mildly,' Legh wrote to Montgomery afterwards. '... I can recall no occasion when HM was in better form or enjoyed himself more.'[113] Montgomery himself described the King's visit as 'great fun' – 'he stayed with me as an ordinary soldier guest, with no formality at all. . . .'[114] Although he would not have admitted it to anyone, Montgomery was an avid courtier, pressing upon the King not only his opinions but his printed words and even his diaries, dictated in the third person and typed up by his assistants, despatching them to Buckingham Palace in instalments. When the Field Marshal was in emotive mood, which he frequently was, he deluged the King with letters and documents, as this letter from Lascelles written shortly after the King's visit reveals:

May I answer with one letter yours of yesterday and 2 of 26th? Kit [Colonel Christopher] Dawnay duly delivered to me the 2 secret documents on the campaign, which are now safely in the King's hands. He asked me to thank you particularly for sending the copies so quickly, and to assure you that they will be seen by no eyes but his own. I am also to thank you for the reports on the operations carried out by the Guards. . . .[115]

The 'secret documents on the campaign' almost certainly related to the Field Marshal's disagreements with Eisenhower on the manner of the future advance on Germany, of which the King was certainly aware when he met Eisenhower at HQ Hodges' First Army near Liège on 14 October and lunched with him there. Seated opposite the King was the forward-thrusting, gung-ho General George Patton, whose boasting was of a legendary order almost on a par with Montgomery's. Spotting the famous pearl-handled pistols at the General's belt, the King could not resist asking him if he had ever shot anyone with them.

'Oh yes,' replied Patton promptly, adding, 'Really, not these pistols. These are the ones I carry socially. I carry my fighting pistols when I'm out on campaign.'
   'How many men have you killed in war?' asked the King.
   Without batting an eye, George said, 'Seven, Sir'. This was too much for Eisenhower. 'How many did you say, General Patton?' he asked.
   Instantly he replied, 'Three, Sir.'
   'Well, George,' Eisenhower said, 'I'll let you get away with that.'[116]

The King, Eisenhower recorded in his memoirs, was popular with all the American forces. 'He liked the simple life of a soldier and was perfectly at home with all of us.' The King, with his eye for things sartorial, admired the American battledress, the cloth of which was vastly superior to the rough, prickly variety used by the British Army. A month later, Eisenhower forwarded a length of it to Buckingham Palace as a present for the King.[117]

The weather was too bad for the King to fly home, so he and his party embarked on what Lascelles described to Montgomery as 'one of those unstable Hunt class destroyers' for a 'beastly' five-hour journey home. Both Legh and Lascelles were seasick, while the King, clad in oilskins, went on the bridge and managed to avoid being ill, Legh reported. He asked after Rommel, Montgomery's spaniel, which had had pneumonia. The dog's namesake, Montgomery's admired adversary, Field Marshal Erwin Rommel, had committed enforced suicide on the 14th of that month because of his suspected involvement in the July plot on Hitler's life. Later on in Germany, Montgomery's troops captured the German Field Marshal's white stallion which Montgomery also named

'Rommel' and presented it as a final victory gift from the men of 21 Army Group to the King. In June 1946, Churchill, having read in the *Illustrated London News* that 'Rommel', in a gesture of insensitivity worthy of ancient Rome, was to be on show in the Victory Parade, sent a letter of protest to the King: 'Naturally I was rather upset by the idea of this poor creature being led in triumph through the streets....' As a result 'Rommel' did not take part.[118]

The King loved being with his troops, escaping from being penned up at Buckingham Palace. After Normandy and Italy he planned an even greater escape, to his 'Forgotten Army' in India and to his cousin, Mountbatten, now SACSEAC (Supreme Allied Commander South-East Asia Command). The King was well aware of the troops' feelings through Mountbatten, and of his cousin's disappointment at the repeated cancellations of offensives in the Far East in favour of the war in Europe. Condoling with Mountbatten on the disappearance of his last project TARZAN, the King had written on 7 January 1944 that he personally saw the logic of finishing the battle for Rome before concentrating on the East adding, 'and so really do you'. The King was convinced that a visit from him would help the morale of his 14th Army, writing to Churchill on 7 November 1944, 'A visit from me would buck them up.' He planned to go in February 1945 but Churchill, aware of the extreme sensitivity of India in American eyes and of political expectations there, was not prepared to face the consequences of a visit by the King–Emperor. The King resented this final obstruction of his desire to visit his troops in the last theatre of the war. Leo Amery, Secretary of State for India and Burma, within whose political sphere it lay, was not consulted as he only discovered after an interview with the King. Amery noted on 20 March:

[The King] began by telling me how cross he was with Winston for not allowing him to go to India in February to see the troops on the ground that this would at once give rise to the idea that he had some big political decision to make. I must say that it is a little typical of Winston to have done this without consulting me.... Personally I should have seen no great objection....[119]

The idea remained very much in the King's mind, however, skilfully played upon by Mountbatten, who knew exactly the terms in which to present a Far Eastern visit. He pleaded on 1 April 1945:

Once we have got Rangoon do *please* come out. You can easily do a flying visit via Delhi without any previous announcement and go on after a day or two straight to Rangoon. It's the one chance you will have of visiting your Indian capital without endless political complications and you have NEVER been there, whereas David, your father and grandfather all visited Delhi (1922, 1911, & 1876).

Rangoon fell on 3 May 1945, but Mountbatten was to preside over the dissolution of the King's Indian Empire without the King–Emperor ever being able to set foot there. The King minded a great deal that he had never been allowed to fulfill this, one of the things that he had been determined to do when he came to the throne. First Grigg and then Churchill had prevented his following, as Mountbatten had so neatly pointed out, in the family footsteps.

'Events are moving very fast now,' the King wrote in his diary on 30 April, the day on which Hitler committed suicide in the Berlin bunker. Four days earlier the Allied Armies had crossed the Rhine and the last V2 silo had been bombed by the RAF after 1,050 of the ballistic rockets had hit targets in England. The end of the war, which, in military terms, was already over, could not be long delayed. On 2 May the German capital surrendered to the Russians. On 4 May Montgomery reported to Eisenhower that all enemy forces in Holland, north-west Germany and Denmark had capitulated with effect from eight o'clock the following morning. The King, having received the news in a telephone call from Churchill from 10 Downing Street, sent Montgomery a message of congratulation on the surrender at Luneberg Heath, its terms indicating to anyone reading between the lines how well informed he was as to Montgomery's disagreements with his Supreme Commander, Eisenhower: 'You have often told me your plans for defeating the Germans opposed to you. You have now done it with a thoroughness which I hope satisfies you as fully as it does me,' the King signalled. 'I send you my heartiest congratulations on your triumph over our enemies and over the many obstacles that you have had to surmount in a campaign that will always be historic.' On the draft of the signal Lascelles had noted: 'If any third party sees it, the "obstacles" are, of course, the rivers Rhine, Elbe, etc.; but Monty will understand that they include SHAEF!'[120] Three days later the instrument of unconditional surrender of the German Armies to the Western Allies and to Russia was signed in a schoolhouse at Rheims by General Jodl on behalf of the German High Command. It was 2.41 on the morning of 7 May 1945; the actual moment for the end of the war in Europe was to be one minute after midnight on 8/9 May.

A last-minute muddle between the Powers as to the timing of the announcement of the end of the war made it all something of an anti-climax. Preparations for VE-Day had been going on for months. Work had been undertaken many months previously for strengthening the balcony on the Mall front in anticipation of its use by the royal family on the great day. For weeks the horses who were to draw the royal carriages on State drives through London had been trained to unaccustomed noise by having the BBC Forces Programme broadcast regularly in their stables. The King had already made a recording of his victory broadcast and filmed it. Loudspeakers had been fixed in place in the Mall, where crowds were gathering in anticipation of a declaration on 7 May, the date on which Churchill wished it to be made. The King returned from Windsor to London on the night of Sunday 6 May and was disconcerted to hear that Stalin and Truman had opted for Tuesday 8 May, so that the actual official announcment of the Allies' victory was made by Count Schwerin von Krosigk from Hamburg on 7 May. Finally, despite further attempts to delay by Moscow, it was agreed that at 3 p.m. on 8 May Churchill should make the formal announcement of the end of hostilities and of the unconditional surrender due at one minute past midnight.

The Duke of York with Princess Elizabeth

The Duke of York at the Wimbledon
Lawn Tennis Championships, June 1926

The Duke of York speaking outside Parliament
House, Canberra, 1927

By the swimming-pool at Fort Belvedere. From left to right: The Hon. Mrs Jock Gilmour, Lord Louis Mountbatten, the Duke of York, Prince Gustav Adolf of Sweden, his wife Princess Sybilla, Princess Ingrid of Sweden, the Duchess of York, Lady Furness

BELOW: *Edward VIII and Mrs Simpson. The cruise of the* Nahlin, *1936*

ABOVE: *The Yorks with daughters and dogs in 1936 (labradors then outnumbering corgis by four to one)*

inley Baldwin   *Alexander Hardinge*   *Walter Monckton*

OVE: *Halifax and Hitler at*
rchtesgaden, November 1937

ABOVE RIGHT: *Neville Chamberlain*

RIGHT: *Alan Lascelles*

The Duke and Duchess of Windsor after their wedding at the Château de Candé on 3 June 1937, flanked by Herman Rogers (on the Duchess's right) and 'Fruity' Metcalfe (on the Duke's left)

The King about to be crowned. Sitting on the Coronation chair and wearing the glove presented by the Lord of the Manor of Worksop, he holds i his right hand the sceptre of State and in his left the ceremonial sceptre bearing the dove of peace

Coronation of King George VI and Queen Elizabeth, 12 May 1937. In the Royal Gallery behind the Kin are from left to right: the Earl and Countess of Strathmore, the Duchesses of Kent and Gloucester, Queen Maud of Norway, Queen Mary, Princess Elizabeth, Princess Margaret, the Princess Royal

LEFT:
The King and President Roosevelt, June 1939

BELOW:
The Blitz: the King and Queen inspecting bomb damage at Buckingham Palace, September 1940

BOTTOM:
The Blitz: the King and Queen with people bombed out of their homes in Sheffield

ABOVE RIGHT: *The royal family with Mrs Eleanor Roosevelt in the Bow Room at Buckingham Palace, October 1942*

ABOVE LEFT: *The King, entering the Grand Harbour of Valletta, Malta, acknowledges the cheers of the George Cross islanders, 20 June 1943*

The King meets Field-Marshal Montgomery's terrier, 'Hitler', in Holland, 15 October 1944

VE-Day, 8 May 1945. The King and Win Churchill on the balcony of Buckingham Pal.

The royal tour of South Africa: the royal family with Field-Marshal Smuts in Natal National Park, March 1947

ABOVE: 'I felt I had lost something very precious': on the balcony at Buckingham Palace after the wedding of Princess Elizabeth and the Duke of Edinburgh, November 1947

The last family outing: at a performance of South Pacific on 30 January 1952. Group-Captain Peter Townsend is sitting between the Queen and Princess Elizabeth

ABOVE LEFT: *The King modelling his own design for Garter trousers; photograph taken by the Duke of Edinburgh at Sandringham, January 1952*

ABOVE: *The last family Christmas at Sandringham, 1951. From left to right: back row, the Duke of Kent, Princess Margaret, Princess Alexandra of Kent, Princess Marina, the Duchess of Kent, the Duke of Gloucester, Princess Elizabeth, the Duke of Edinburgh, the Duchess of Gloucester. Seated: Queen Mary, the King with Princess Anne, the Queen with Prince Charles. Front row: Prince Richard of Gloucester, Prince Michael of Kent, Prince William of Gloucester*

LEFT: *The King's coffin is carried from the train at King's Cross Station, watched by Queen Elizabeth The Queen Mother, the Queen, the Dukes of Gloucester and Edinburgh*

Appropriately, 8 May was a Tuesday, and the King and Churchill lunched together as usual. The King wrote:

We congratulated each other on the end of the European War. The day we have been longing for has arrived at last & we can look back with thankfulness to God that our tribulation is over. No more fear of being bombed at home & no more living in air-raid shelters. But there is still Japan to be defeated & the restoration of our country to be dealt with, which will give us many headaches & hard work in the coming years.

❧ 11 ❧

A NEW WORLD

'During his reign there were developments in the Commonwealth, some of which entailed the abandonment of outward forms which a lesser man might have felt difficult to surrender, but he was essentially broad-minded and was ready to accept changes that seemed necessary.'
Clement Attlee in a tribute to the King, 11 February 1952

THE King was tired, exhausted by the strain of almost six years of war. People listening to his Victory broadcast noticed that his hesitations were worse than usual. 'Today', he had said, 'we give thanks for a great deliverance.' There was an anguished pause before the word 'deliverance' as the old difficulty with the 'g's had reappeared. Harold Nicolson noted that his words were excellent, 'but it is agony to listen to him – like a typewriter that sticks at every third word'. In the film of the broadcast shown a week later the King's tension and exhaustion were only too clear; his face appeared 'wizened and lined', his mouth twitching with his efforts to control his stammer.[1] At the Thanksgiving Service at St Paul's on 13 May, Chips Channon noticed that the King looked 'drawn', although he added enviously, 'he has the Windsor gift of looking half his age'. 'I have found it difficult to rejoice or relax', the King wrote at the end of a fortnight's celebrations, 'as there is still so much hard work ahead to deal with.' By the end of that Victory summer he was to write to his brother, 'I feel burnt out....'

Looking ahead beyond the victory, the King found little to cheer about. In Europe the discovery of the concentration camps had revealed their full horror. Reports coming in from Eastern Europe of torture, summary execution and wholesale intimidation of Poles, Romanians, Yugoslavs and others evidenced how empty the expectations of the Western Allies and the promises of the Russians at Yalta proved to have been. Quite apart from the huge problems of refugees and the homeless in a devastated Europe, in Britain itself people needed housing, clothing and feeding. At least Churchill had not promised the people, as Lloyd George (who died on 27 March 1945) had done, 'a world fit for heroes to live in', but expectations were there – of a better world, of a reward for the hardship and the suffering – without the resources to fulfil them. The King remembered the aftermath of the First World War when his father had feared social revolution.

As the Russians had swept westwards in the last year of the war, fulfilling the King's forebodings of autumn 1943 about their intentions towards Eastern Europe, he had become increasingly concerned about the fate of his fellow monarchs, the Kings of Greece, Yugoslavia and Romania. In his efforts to help his fellow kings as much as he could, he was to find an ally in Churchill, an ardent believer in the monarchical system, often against the Foreign Office who tended to regard sovereigns – even, perhaps, including its own – as an irrelevant nuisance, an attitude expressed in Oliver Harvey's diary when he wrote of King George II of Greece: 'I've always said these countries are better as republics.' The King, not unnaturally, did not share this view. Not only as Head of State but also as Head of the House of Windsor and, therefore, the senior member of the remaining sovereigns of Europe, he regarded himself as standing in a special relationship to them, not only as their relation but as their colleague. Always fiercely protective of his rights as sovereign, he tended to be wary of the Foreign Office, which cherished its Palmerstonian tradition of independence from, and even disregard of, the sovereign, which was to become more marked after the departure of his friend Halifax and his replacement as Foreign Secretary by Eden in December 1940. Indeed, a fierce row had broken out between the King and the Foreign Office within months of Halifax's departure when the Foreign Office successfully intrigued to block the appointment of David Bowes-Lyon as press officer in New York, even to the extent of lying about it to the Minister concerned, Duff Cooper, by saying that the King and Queen opposed it.[2] The King, attributing the Foreign Office action to personal animosity and interministerial intrigue, was furious at this misuse of his name and was only soothed by Halifax, who had originally proposed the appointment, warning him 'how ready ill-disposed Senators would have been to say that we were trying to cash in on the affection felt for the King and Queen by such an appointment'.[3]

The King's complaints about lack of consultation on the part of the Foreign Office frequently related to their dealings with his royal relations of Yugoslavia and Greece. The Foreign Office for their part sometimes felt that the King played too active a part when it came to his fellow Kings. There was some trouble between the King and the Foreign Office over his cousin King George II of Greece, great-nephew of Queen Alexandra, who had lived in exile in London and Cairo since his flight from Greece after the German attack in March–April 1941. The Foreign Office view of the Greek King, if Harvey's diary is to be believed, was that he was stupid, mean, chary of risking his life at the front, pro-German and given to intriguing with the Greek politicians.[4] The King of Greece on his side complained loudly of the Foreign Office attitude.[5] The King tended to sympathize with his cousin to a degree which the Foreign Office regarded as bordering on the unconstitutional. On 19 March 1944, when the King sent Lascelles to the Foreign Office to complain to Cadogan that the King felt Eden did not confide in him enough, Cadogan replied that he would take any opportunity that offered itself to try to remedy his situation but that he 'wasn't going to make one', and riposted by complaining on his side that the King had shown the King of Greece telegrams from Rex Leeper, British Ambassador to the Greek Government, which he ought not to have done.[6] After Churchill's heroic dash to Athens at Christmas 1944 saved Greece from a take-over by communist guerrillas, King George eventually returned to his uneasy throne in September 1946 after a plebiscite in April resulted favourably to the monarchy.

The King felt responsible for other European monarchs, his relations who, like the King of Greece, having faced the Germans, were now confronted with an even more serious threat, that of communism. Churchill had saved Greek democracy and, incidentally, the Greek King by making a deal with Stalin. In May 1944 the Prime Minister admitted to Averell Harriman that Britain had promised a 'hands-off' policy in Romania, which was to be considered a Russian sphere of influence, in return for a similar attitude by Russia towards Greece. Roosevelt, to whom this policy was formally proposed at the end of the month, had warned Churchill against the dangers of establishing post-war spheres of influence, but the British Prime Minister justified it by arguing – as was to be the case with Yugoslavia and Tito – that the Russians were the only power that could do anything against the Germans there. In Romania King Carol, son of 'Cousin Missy', had been forced to abdicate on 6 September 1940, leaving the throne to his son by the Greek Princess Helen, known in the family as 'Sitta'. King Michael, then only nineteen years old, had been left under the tutelage of the pro-Nazi General Antonescu. Five years later the young King played an heroic part in a coup against Antonescu, holding him covered with a pistol while members of his household arrested the dictator's aides. Michael's new Government had declared war against the Axis powers, ending hostilities against the Allies, but it was by then too late to save the country from Stalin. In March 1945, the Russians installed a puppet communist government; Churchill refused to intervene on the grounds that the British could not risk offending Stalin and jeopardizing the recent agreements at Yalta on behalf of a country that had been part of the Axis for most of the war. 'We really have no justification for intervening in this extraordinarily vigorous manner for our late Roumanian enemies,' he minuted firmly to Eden on 5 March, 'thus compromising our position in Poland and jarring upon Russian acquiescence in Athens....'[7] George VI agonized about the fate of his royal relations. 'Poor Michael and his mother Zitta [*sic*] in Rumania have been having a very worrying time from the Russians and again we can do nothing to help them for the moment,' he wrote to Queen Mary on 25 March 1945. He could not agree with Churchill's argument that they deserved no help because they had previously been allied with the enemy. 'I feel so differently towards them, than the attitude taken up by the Government,' he wrote. 'The latter say Rumania was an enemy and is now in the Russian sphere.' Two years later King Michael was forced to abdicate; on his arrival in exile at Lausanne, George VI sent the British Minister at Berne to offer his personal sympathy and to hear King Michael's account of the deliberate humiliations inflicted on him by the Soviet-inspired Government. He remained in touch with the young ex-King, as Michael testified to his biographer: 'King George gave me advice which I have always tried to follow both as a king and a man.'[8]

The King's closest personal involvement with the Balkan royal families had been with Yugoslavia, where he had been forced to watch first his friend, Prince Paul, and then his godson, King Peter, swept away by the fortunes of war. As Regent of Yugoslavia since the assassination of King Alexander, Prince Paul had fallen victim to the pressure of events in the spring of 1941 as Hitler turned to settle accounts in Greece and the Balkans before attacking Russia. Prince Paul had been under constant pressure from the British Government on the one hand and Hitler on the other. George VI, at the behest of his Government, had sent Prince Paul a series of letters and telegrams warning him not to join the Axis pact, backed up by optimistic assessments of Britain's strength and ability to help him. In the face of Hitler's threats, the disunity of his country and the apparent weakness of his military forces, Prince Paul had signed the pact on 26 March 1941. That same evening a coup encouraged by the British had ousted Prince Paul and placed King Peter on the throne, greeted rapturously by British propaganda. Prince Paul was made the villain of the piece; like Leopold he was to be another scapegoat for a British setback. It is hard to see what else he could have done; when Hitler decided to finish with Yugoslavia in Operation PUNISHMENT, Yugoslav resistance lasted precisely twelve days since, as Prince Paul had predicted, the Croats showed little disposition to fight and as a result of the German victory obtained an independent state of Croatia under Ante Pavelić, the murderer of King Alexander. The Anglophile Prince Paul was refused asylum in England and kept under humiliating conditions of house arrest as a political prisoner, first in Cairo and then in Kenya, at the behest of Churchill and the Foreign Office, who referred to him as a 'wretched and treacherous creature' who had 'done his damnedest to stab us and the Greeks in the back'.

The King had learned of Prince Paul's plight through his letters to the Duke of Kent, his intimate friend. He had attempted to help by intervening with Eden in May 1941, suggesting that Prince Paul's children could get no education where they were in Kenya and that they might be allowed to move to South Africa. He had that month been shown a letter from Princess Olga to the Duchess of Kent revealing the real story of the coup, which was that King Peter, far from shinning dramatically down drainpipes to escape what Churchill later called 'the treacherous clutches of the Regent',[9] had spent the day in the company of Princess Olga and knew nothing of the proclamation he was supposed to have signed. Even the broadcast he was supposed to have made was a fake. 'Poor little Peter tried to be brave and sensible, it was heartrending to leave him alone,' Princess Olga wrote in her diary for that day. 'As we parted he cried and begged to go with us....'[10] The King, however, was not entirely convinced that Prince Paul was blameless of all the charges levelled at him by Churchill and the Yugoslav politicians in exile. 'Poor Paul, he has a lot to answer for I am afraid for the present position of the Balkans,' he had written in his diary in September 1941, but he remained personally sympathetic and friendly towards the disgraced Prince. At Coppins, after the Duke of Kent's death, Princess Olga was able to tell him the whole story. 'Bertie has been here twice ...', she wrote to Prince Paul on 25 September 1942. 'Spoke so nicely of you, asked me about our life etc., all of which seemed to touch him....'[11]

Rebecca West's book, *Black Lamb and Grey Falcon*, published that year (1942) repeated the story of Paul's guilt and Peter's heroism and the British press continued to dub Paul 'the quisling Prince'. Churchill, who referred contemptuously to him as 'Prince Palsy', did not relent when he came to write his history of the war where his account of the coup of March 1941 read like a Ruritanian adventure. On 3 March 1946 the *Sunday Times* was to publish an article in which Prince Paul was described as a 'war criminal' and later that month a further article stated that he would be among the accused at the forthcoming trials at Nuremberg. As far as the British public was concerned, Prince Paul was a pro-Axis fascist and an admirer of Hitler. On 23 July 1946 the Foreign Office advised the Palace that it would be 'preferable' if the King on his forthcoming visit to South Africa (where Prince Paul and Princess Olga had been living since 1943) avoided meeting Prince Paul while there. There were 'no objections' to the King meeting Princess Olga, 'for which there are good family reasons', the letter instructed, but the meeting should be private and neither Prince Paul nor Princess Olga should appear at public or semi-public receptions for the royal couple. Meeting Prince Paul, the Foreign Office feared, 'would be likely to give rise to unfavourable comment. It is just the sort of thing that the Russian press finds useful as a pretext for insulting propaganda against us and it might also be misinterpreted in some circles in England.'[12] Publicly the King acquiesced, knowing that the Labour Government, which had been in power since July 1945, was vulnerable to left-wing attack. Lascelles, therefore, arranged via Harold Nicolson that Prince Paul should absent himself from Johannesburg during the royal visit, but privately the King and the Queen were determined not to snub their old friend. When they returned to England the Queen admitted to Nicolson that they had seen Prince Paul 'secretly in the country'. According to Prince Paul's biographer, this sign of faith and loyalty 'changed Paul's life', marking the beginning of his rehabilitation, although he was not to return to England until invited by Queen Elizabeth II and the Queen Mother to attend the King's funeral.

The King's relationship with Prince Paul was based on friendship; with King Peter, to whom he was related through Peter's grandmother, 'Cousin Missy', he had more formal obligations as his Koum, or godfather, since the Prince's christening in October 1924. 'I am his "Koom" [*sic*], a sort of permanent godfather in Serbia,' George VI had written in his diary on 21 June 1941, the day of King Peter's arrival in England as yet another royal refugee from Hitler.

'I held him at his christening. So I must look after him here. Perhaps it was destiny.' Under Serbian tradition his duties as Koum obliged him not only to supervise Peter's education but also to be consulted on his godson's choice of a bride. This role came into play when Peter fell in love with and wished to marry Princess Alexandra of Greece, posthumous daughter of King Alexander and his commoner wife, Aspasia Manos, a powerful personality widely believed to possess the evil eye. Although the King cautiously gave his approval to the engagement, he was less willing to approve a date for the marriage, which was opposed by the King's mother, 'Missy's' daughter, the ex-Queen Marie, and the Serbs of Peter's Government-in-exile. The King felt that Peter's principal objective should be to regain his throne and that after his departure for Cairo in the summer of 1943 he should remain there in readiness for that and not be encouraged to return to London to marry against the wishes of his Serbian followers. He was, however, anxious to do his best for his godson and not to stand in the way of his marriage if Peter was seriously in love, and in February 1944 he made enquiries through the Foreign Office instructing their local representative to gauge the state of Peter's feelings. From Cairo Ralph Stevenson replied that King Peter was physically attracted to Princess Alexandra and fond of her, not deeply in love but feeling in honour bound to her. Marriage in Cairo, he informed the Foreign Office, would be opposed by the Yugoslav Government-in-exile, who insisted that George VI should attend as Koum.[13] The King and the Foreign Office, however, gave their blessing and, after Balkan scenes between the prospective mothers-in-law and their minions, King Peter and Princess Alexandra were married on 20 March 1944 with George VI as their best man.

The remainder of King Peter's story was a sad one; like King Michael of Romania he was to be a victim of what Eden in a Note for the War Cabinet of 1 January 1945[14] called 'the cruel reality' of the Yugoslav situation, where the King's future depended on the wishes of Tito, leader of the communist partisans, backed by the British as the effective force against the Germans. King Peter's Serbian supporter, Mihailović, was sacrificed to this policy and later executed by Tito; King Peter, now an irrelevance, never regained his throne.

The fate of the Kings of Yugoslavia and Romania was just one facet of the changes sweeping Europe in the wake of the disastrous Big Three Conference at Yalta in the Crimea from 4 to 11 February 1945, when Stalin had obtained virtually everything he wanted from a largely powerless Churchill and a failing and capricious Roosevelt, and then proceeded to take everything he had not been given as well. The King had inherited a deep fear and suspicion of Soviet communism from his father; he was bewildered and disturbed by the outcome of Yalta, as this diary entry of 23 February revealed:

I find in my daily reading of Cabinet papers & FO telegrams, besides the daily papers (Press), that it is almost impossible to keep a clear mind on all that is going on nowadays.... The Polish question is by no means settled & Gen Anders who commands the Polish Army in Italy is here now for talks as neither he nor his troops will take the statement about Poland as it is now written. They took an oath to the Polish Govt. in London not to the Lublin Committee. They are fearful of Russia and always have been.

In Rumania the Rumanian Govt. started off well, & Michael was praised after their liberation. Now orders from Moscow have come to work up agitation against them & to form a minority Communist govt.

Stalin, no doubt, after having met Winston, F.D.R. & other people from the Western part of the world appreciates the need for having 2 very useful Allies & is doing his best to be friendly with them, but he has not got enough time in which to teach some of his people on Allied Commissions the same thing. Stalin realises it himself that he must come back into the world, so probably does Molotov, & that making contact with us & with the Americans is not such an antipathy to all his ideas. But can he stop his anti-democratic policy in the Balkans in time? Stalin has put his name to some very important negotiations together with those of 2 very modern & enlightened countries & can he play fair? These negotiations are the foundations of the future peace of the World & will they ever be ratified?

The future peace of the world in terms of the Cold War between Russia and the West was to be the dominant preoccupation of the last decade of the King's reign, but the full extent of Stalin's plans for Eastern Europe had not yet been revealed when one of the principal architects of Yalta, Roosevelt, died suddenly on the afternoon of 12 April 1945 of a massive cerebral haemorrhage at his cottage in Warm Spring, Georgia. To the King it was a great shock; he had retained his affectionate admiration for the President despite occasional bouts of anti-Americanism which Halifax, on a visit to Windsor in July 1944, attributed partly to his being 'heated up by Winston', who had been 'greatly hurt by the reluctance of the American Chiefs of Staff to concur in his strategical ideas'. Halifax again diagnosed the old trouble of feeling that Roosevelt was ignoring him:

I did by best to soothe him and perhaps partly succeeded. I think part of the trouble has been due to the President not answering his letters! And to a feeling that the King had that the President was reluctant to come to England, as he spoke quite sharply about the President's idea of going to Cherbourg. 'Why Cherbourg, when he won't come here?' I was able to tell him that the President had the possibility of a visit here very much in mind which gave him a great of deal of comfort![15]

The King, however, continued to hope and plan for the President's visit, retaining his faith in the President's friendship despite the increasingly widening differences between Roosevelt and Churchill. There is evidence, too, from Halifax's diary that the President, despite his failings as a correspondent, also saw himself as having a special relationship with the King as Head of State to Head of State on a superior level to that which he enjoyed with Churchill. Halifax wrote:

I heard a day or two ago, on very direct authority, the following, for which I do not quote any names because I was told not to, but the evidence for it is very good: A short time before he died, someone had been sent for to see President Roosevelt to discuss some question of production. He told someone his concern afterwards, that when he went in, the President was sitting, staring into space, and apparently completely absorbed in his own thoughts. He only spoke three times (not to the visitor but as if to himself) – 'If Churchill insists on Hongkong, I will have to take it to the King.' This was repeated three times. . . .[16]

This curious episode shows not only that Roosevelt contemplated overriding Churchill by appealing over his head to the King, but also that Roosevelt, for all his sophistication, background and connection with Britain over a considerable period of years, still did not really understand the workings of the British Constitution, attributing to the King more power than he really had. One day Roosevelt had asked Halifax if Hong Kong was a Crown Colony, and if that meant it was a personal possession of the King. Halifax had explained that it was not as simple, generally the case being that Crown Colonies were not self-governing but much more under the control of Whitehall, whereupon Roosevelt said he had an idea about Hong Kong:

At the present time it was likely to become more and more of a political headache for us; China was bound to get more restive about it; American opinion thought it was just a survival of the bad old imperialism; and it would be a good thing all round if we could find some means of taking the sting out of it.

His idea was this: let the King send a telegram to Chiang Kai-Shek, saying how impressed he had been with the Chinese resistance to the Japanese aggressors over the years, and that to mark his admiration of Chinese resistance, he wished to present his Crown Colony of Hong Kong to China as a free gift in perpetuity . . . each evening and dawn the British flag would be raised and lowered saluted by Chinese soldiers, existing British business would be guaranteed its accustomed rights and position under law, and the port of Hong Kong would be declared and remain for all time a free port for the commerce of nations – FDR said this way things could remain the same and 'it would take care of the question for seventy years'. Halifax objected that Chiang's successor might not feel the same way.[17]

At the time of Roosevelt's death the King had been looking forward to welcoming the President to Buckingham Palace in the late summer after the conclusion of the San Francisco United Nations Conference. He sincerely mourned the President, to whom he had looked up as a father-figure whose charm had never ceased to captivate him since their late-night conversations at Hyde Park in June 1939, and whose occasional lapses as a correspondent he had resented all the more because he counted so much on their relationship. Whatever had been the recent strains in the Anglo–American partnership, the King realized what Britain and the world owed to the American President. 'He was a very great man', the King wrote in his diary, '& his loss will be felt the World over. He was a staunch friend of this country. . . .'

'Winston will feel his loss most of all in his dealings with Stalin . . .', the King added. The King was looking forward to meeting the Russian leader himself at the first post-war meeting of the Big Three at Potsdam, as Churchill wrote to inform Stalin on 15 June 1945. The King, he said, hoped to meet Stalin and the

Soviet generals in Berlin on a day when the conference would not be sitting. He would like to be invited to lunch by Stalin at the Soviet Headquarters and would give a dinner that evening in the British sector of the city to which he would invite the leading Russians, President Truman and Americans, and was planning to lunch with Truman the next day.[18] A week later Lascelles wrote to Montgomery, now Military Governor, asking him if he could 'put up' His Majesty for three or four days, during which the King would like to see as much of 21 Army Group as possible, spending one day in Berlin to entertain the Big Three.[19] The idea was dropped, however, apparently on security grounds, for on 1 July Churchill wrote again to Stalin, informing him that 'the King now finds it impossible to make his tour in Germany at the present time, as so many detectives and special service officers will be required for the Conference of the Three'.[20] Instead, the King went to Northern Ireland, no doubt regretting missing the opportunity of seeing Stalin in the flesh. Stalin for his part expressed at least a polite interest in the King. 'He takes a very sensible line about the monarchy,' Churchill told his doctor, Lord Moran, '... he sees it binds the Empire together.'[21]

The King would have to face the distant threat of Stalin and the immediate problems of post-war Britain and the British Empire without Churchill. While the King and Churchill had hoped that the coalition National Government could be continued until the end of the war with Japan, the Labour Party had made it clear at their annual conference that it would not. Offered by Attlee the choice of an election sooner or later, Churchill chose the former, resigning on behalf of himself and the present Government on 23 May. According to constitutional practice Churchill saw the King at noon on 23 May and placed his resignation in his hands. The King recorded:

I did not accept it then. I told him I would see him again at 4.0 p.m. when I would give him my reply. I had to have a Prime Minister in being during those intervening 4 hours in case of emergency especially in war time. When he came at 4.0 p.m. I told him at once that I accepted his resignation & asked him to form a new Government. So he became my Prime Minister for the 2nd time.

The King's decision to ask Churchill to form a second Government was not only a formality but the obvious choice; he was the leader of a party with a majority of 100 over all others in the House of Commons. In the circumstances, however, a general election was inevitable and Churchill chose to dissolve Parliament on 15 June, polling day to be 5 July. The King was not unduly concerned, writing philosophically in his diary on 29 May, after seeing the outgoing Labour and Liberal ministers of the coalition: '... they felt that the time had come to break away. Parliament is 10 years old, and no one under the age of 30 has ever voted, the House of Commons needs rejuvenating.... Thus has ended the Coalition Government which during the War has done admirable work. Country before Party has been its watchword. But now what?' 'The outcome of it [the general election] is uncertain', he wrote on the same day to the Duke of Gloucester, now Governor-General of Australia, 'as no party may secure a clear working majority....'

Polling began on 5 July; the King retired to Balmoral for the voting and counting period, extended to enable all the troops stationed overseas to vote. When the election result was announced on 26 July it was a landslide victory for Labour, the biggest defeat for the Conservative Party since the election of 1906, which had been the nine-year-old Prince Albert's first political memory. The Conservatives lost 160 seats while Labour gained 230, which, with their allies, gave them a huge majority of 180 in the House of Commons. No one, neither Attlee nor Churchill, had expected a government defeat of this magnitude. The King was thoroughly and unpleasantly surprised. Churchill, on his return from Potsdam, had told the King he expected to be returned with a majority of between thirty and eighty seats, but at seven o'clock on the evening of the following day, 26 July, he drove to Buckingham Palace to tender his resignation and formally to advise the King to send for the Labour leader, Clement Attlee, as the next Prime Minister.

It was, the King wrote in his diary, 'a very sad meeting'. His Majesty told Churchill roundly that he thought the people were very ungrateful 'after the way they had been led in the War'. Although Lascelles attempted to comfort the King by telling him that Churchill was not the man that was needed for the task of reconstruction, that it was 'best for Winston and best for the country',[22] and Mountbatten, typically, told the King that he would be able to influence this new Labour lot, the King was deeply moved at losing Churchill, so much so that, five days later, thinking he had not expressed his true feelings fully enough at their last meeting, he sat down on 31 July to write not one but two handwritten letters to his former Prime Minister. 'My heart was too full to say much at our last meeting,' he told him. 'I was shocked at the result & I thought it most ungrateful to you personally after all your hard work for the people.' In his second letter he tried to convey what their partnership had meant to him.

My dear Winston,

I am writing to tell you how very sad I am that you are no longer my Prime Minister.

During the last 5 years of war we have met on dozens, I may say on hundreds, of occasions, when we have discussed the most vital questions concerning the security & welfare of this country & the British Empire in their hours of trial. I shall always remember our talks with pleasure & only wish they could have continued longer.

You often told me what you thought of people & matters of real interest which I could never have learnt from anyone else. Your breadth of vision & your grasp of the essential things were a great comfort to me in the darkest days of the War, & I like to think that we have never disagreed on any really important matter. For all those things I thank you most sincerely. I feel that your conduct as Prime Minister & Minister of Defence has never been surpassed. You have had many difficulties to deal with both as a politician & as a strategist of war but you have always surmounted them with supreme courage....

For myself personally, I regret what has happened more than perhaps anyone else. I shall miss your counsel to me more than I can say. But please remember that as a friend I hope we shall be able to meet at intervals.

Believe me,

I am,

Your very sincerely & gratefully,

GRI

Churchill replied, also in his own hand, that he had read the King's letter 'with emotion'.

It was always a relief to me to lay before my Sovereign all the dread secrets and perils wh. oppressed my mind, & the plans wh. I was forming, & to receive on crucial occasions much encouragement. Yr. Majesty's grasp of all matters of State & war was always based upon the most thorough & attentive study of the whole mass of current documents, and this enabled us to view & measure everything in due proportion.... Yr. Majesty has mentioned our friendship & this is indeed a vy. strong sentiment with me, & an honour which I cherish.[23]

The King found it difficult to break the habit of confiding in Churchill. Almost a year after the election he was still consulting his former Prime Minister. Lord Moran noticed one morning an open letter on a table by Churchill's bed, which bore the familiar red letterheading and large type of the Private Secretary's Office at Buckingham Palace. (The King used black letterhead with his monogram for his personal stationery.) 'The King wants me to look through his speech for the State Banquet to the UNO delegates,' Churchill explained. Attlee had sent the speech to Buckingham Palace, who had sent it on to Churchill.

The relationship he had enjoyed with the King was, indeed, one of the things which Churchill, too, regretted with his loss of power. While waiting for the results of the election he had, Moran recorded, comforted himself with his recollections of this. In three years, he said, he had lunched more than 200 times with the King. No servant had been present and they had waited on themselves. If Churchill had got up to get something for the King, the King would in turn fetch something for Churchill. 'No subject had ever been so honoured,' Churchill said; he wanted no other reward. The King offered him the honour which he regarded the most highly, the Order of the Garter, but Churchill declined it, saying that it would not be suitable for him to accept while leading the Opposition in the House of Commons – 'he hoped he would be able to accept it later'. It was to be eight years before he did so, on the occasion of Queen Elizabeth II's Coronation in 1953.

On 16 July while Churchill, at Potsdam, was still Prime Minister, the first successful atom bomb test was carried out in New Mexico. The King was one of the few people outside Los Alamos who had been told of the experiments, which were being carried on there under the codename TUBE ALLOY; he was later to surprise the US Chiefs of Staff with his technical knowledge of the project. Plans had already been made to use the bomb on Japanese cities; on 23 July

Truman instructed General Spaatz, commander of the US Strategic Air Force, to drop the first bomb as soon after 3 August as weather would permit, and in view of this altered his plans to visit London at the end of the Potsdam Conference intending to go straight home. The King, however, was determined to meet the new American President and suggested that as Truman was returning home on the USS *Augusta*, he should board the warship off the coast of England and spend an hour or so with the President. In the end it was agreed that Truman should fly from Berlin to Plymouth and board the *Augusta* there, where the King could meet him.

The King had heard good reports from Churchill of the new American President, a tough, shrewd, able, down-to-earth New Dealer from Independence, Missouri, the epitome of Middle America and a complete antithesis of President Roosevelt, the cosmopolitan East Coast patrician. 'Watch the President,' Admiral King, US Chief of Naval Operations, had told Moran at Potsdam. 'He is a more typical American than Roosevelt, and he will do a good job, not only for the United States but for the whole world.' And at Potsdam it had been clear how much things had changed since Roosevelt's death. '... when Stalin gets tough Truman at once makes it plain that he, too, can hand out the rough stuff,' Moran wrote. '... [Churchill] ... rubs his eyes to make sure he is not dreaming, chortles, looks very pleased and is quick to give President Truman vigorous and measured support... "if only this had happened at Yalta," the PM said....'[24]

The King, therefore, was prepared to like the President when they met on 2 August 1945. Truman, for his part, wrote in his diary that the King was 'a very pleasant and surprising person'. They had a private talk on board HMS *Renown* in Plymouth Sound, when the King questioned Truman about Potsdam and the atom bomb test. The President told him that he thought Stalin had taken too much for the US and UK liking and would be forced to disgorge some of it at the new Foreign Secretaries' Council in London. 'He was horrified at the devastation of Berlin by our combined bombing,' the King noted. 'He could see that the Big Powers would have to combine for all time to prevent another war.' The King showed the President a sword that had been presented to Sir Francis Drake by Queen Elizabeth I, saying that, although it looked dangerous, it was not properly balanced. They then sat down to what the President called a 'nice and appetising' lunch – soup, fish, lamb chops, peas, potatoes, ice cream and chocolate sauce. At lunch, the King met the new Secretary of State, James Byrnes – 'I liked him, attractive of Irish origin & a great talker' – and Truman's Naval Chief of Staff, Admiral William Leahy. Lascelles, who was there, later reported that Byrnes, 'a chatterbox', began discussing the impending dropping of the atomic bomb in front of the waiters serving lunch. 'As this is Security Silence No. 1 the King was horrified. "I think," he said, "Mr President, that we should discuss this interesting subject over our coffee on deck."'[25] Leahy, who was impressed by the extent of the King's knowledge of TUBE ALLOY, told him he did not think much of the future capabilities of the bomb – 'It sounds like a professor's dream to me. . . . ' 'Would you like to lay a little bet on that, Admiral?' the King asked.

Four days later, on 6 August, the first atomic bomb was dropped on Hiroshima. On the 9th a second bomb destroyed Nagasaki. On VJ-Day, 15 August, when the Japanese Government accepted unconditional surrender, the King, after opening his first peacetime Parliament and receiving, on the balcony of Buckingham Palace, the cheers of the delighted crowds, thought of Churchill whom he would have liked to have had standing on the balcony beside him. 'I wish he could have been given a proper reception by the people,' he wrote in his diary that night. 'The final surrender of Japan was signed in Tokyo Bay on board the uss "Missouri" . . . yesterday,' the King recorded on 3 September. 'Thus has ended the World War which started 6 years ago to-day.'

The King had been twenty-two years old when the First World War ended; he was now, at the end of the Second World War, in his fiftieth year. He had reigned less than a decade, but the six years of war had given him a lifetime's experience of government and world politics. It had also, with the experiences of his industrial work, given him an understanding of the physical circumstances and mental outlook of ordinary men and women, which was invaluable to him in adjusting the monarchy to the temper of the times. Having established the monarchy as a symbol of a united, embattled Britain, he had now to ensure that it was not viewed as a part of the old class structure which the massive vote for Labour in the general election had indicated a general desire to sweep away. His success in getting on with the Labour leaders and in accepting and at least appearing to support the radical social changes they were to effect was perhaps the most important of his achievements as King. He was also, concealing his inner feelings of dismay, to preside over the virtual dissolution of his Empire with dignity. Recognizing that in post-war terms Britain was a second-class power and the Empire an unsustainable illusion, he saw a continuing role for the monarch as Head of the Commonwealth.

Having known most of the principal Labour men as Cabinet Ministers in the coalition National Government during the war was, for the King, certainly a help in lessening the shock of transition between Churchill and Attlee. It was a shock, none the less; the King complained to his brother that he found his new Government 'difficult to talk to' and his new Prime Minister a man of notoriously few words, 'completely mute'. The King did not have his father's capacity for small talk, or rather his habit of chattering throughout his audiences with his ministers and thus preventing them from getting a word in edgeways. Basically, this was a question of background; the King, even in his shy, early days, had always been able to get through an audience with, say Cadogan, by discussing the prospects for the forthcoming partridge-shooting season, at the same time as the ostensible subject of the interview, the new Free French leader, General de Gaulle, whose personality and prospects had seemed to the King in those early days before he came to know and admire the General considerably less interesting and promising than the partridges'. Until Attlee succeeded to power in July 1945, the King's communications with him in private conversation had been limited, according to the Prime Minister's memoirs, to a conversation on pipe construction in 1938. (The King apparently owned a pipe with a self-cleaning device which kept the bowl at the same level, something which greatly interested the then Major Attlee, MP.) Although Attlee had been Churchill's Deputy Prime Minister, he had been completely eclipsed by him in the King's eyes and, indeed, those of the rest of the world, except for the Chiefs of Staff and others who were grateful for Attlee's quiet competence in chairing Cabinet meetings in the absence of the wordy and dictatorial Premier. When the awkward silences of their early meetings were surmounted, the King and the Prime Minister found that they had some experiences in common. Attlee came from a professional middle-class background, had fought as an officer in the First World War and afterwards taken up social work, and particularly boys' clubs, in Limehouse, which later became his parliamentary constituency. To that extent, therefore, they shared a background and a knowledge of the problems and conditions of the urban poor. Quiet, with a shining bald pate and a drooping First World War moustache, Attlee was neither an inspiring nor a prepossessing figure; Churchill was puzzled by his total lack of charisma in comparison with the power of his position. 'He seems to accept without question that Clem is a dim little man, who has been washed up by a tidal wave and left high and dry, with great power which he does not know how to use,' Lord Moran recorded.[26] The King himself, in conversation with Harry Hopkins in January 1941, had given it as his opinion that Attlee had no real power in the Labour Party and was merely a figurehead for Bevin, Herbert Morrison and others.[27] But Attlee was to carry through the most radical changes in British social and economic life and through nationalization of the major means of production – coal, steel and the utilities – transform the industrial base in accordance with socialist principles. He was to set in train the major decolonization of the British Empire. He was also skilful enough to stifle various attempts to dislodge him from the leadership by Stafford Cripps, Aneurin Bevan and Morrison, so that in retrospect he is looked upon not just as a dull man but as one of the wisest and most competent of post-war Prime Ministers.

Although the King never accorded Attlee the signal favour of coming to the head of the stairs at Buckingham Palace to meet him as he had with Churchill, the two men established a solid relationship. The King at times would worry that the Government was going too fast down the socialist road or he would become irritated by Attlee's phlegm in the face of obvious danger signals. He did not welcome many of the changes the Government were effecting in the nation's life, but in Morrison's words, 'he accepted calmly and willingly the changes of political outlook and of personality in the kind of minister he had known throughout his reign'. Morrison wrote that he always found the King 'fair in his observations' and 'meticulously observant of his constitutional position'.[28] Loyally, the King sided with his Prime Minister against Churchill's virulent parliamentary attacks, although he was sometimes worried enough by them to seek reassurance from Attlee. In August 1947, when the Government was proposing emergency powers, denounced by Churchill as 'a blank cheque for totalitarian government', the King wrote to Attlee:

I need not say that I know very well that, so long as you are at the head of any Government, due regard will be given to the rights of Parliament itself, and that Parliament will be offered the opportunity of exercising its proper functions. . . . I know that your attitude towards this supremely important matter is the same as my own.

In the view of Attlee's biographer, one reason why Churchill's fierce attacks on the Parliament Bill for the reform of the powers of the House of Lords failed was because it became known that the King himself had raised no difficulty about it. The King accepted the Prime Minister's argument that nothing had been done about the Lords for thirty-six years, and that apart from a quantitative reduction in the powers of the Lords to 'delay' legislation necessary in the period of the war, the functions of the Second Chamber would be left intact. The King, in the words of Attlee's biographer, 'had already come to trust Attlee as a bulwark against demagogic change'.[29] Attlee repaid the King's trust with an affection which he rarely demonstrated in his public life. Michael Foot wrote:

Only once did I ever see Attlee emotionally affected in public and the occasions for doing so were frequent, dating back to an early morning in San Francisco in May 1945 when his Parliamentary Private Secretary, John Dugdale, and I broke into his bedroom to tell him that the Second World War was over and that we would like a statement from him for the British Labour movement; then he just got back into bed. But when he spoke of George VI's death, tears were in his eyes and voice.[30]

'You will find that your position will be greatly strengthened,' Mountbatten had written shortly after the 1945 election, 'since you are now the old experienced campaigner on whom a new and partly inexperienced Government will lean for advice and guidance.'[31] While this was characteristic Mountbatten hyperbole, he was not the only friend of the King who thought so. After travelling down with the King to Plymouth to meet Truman when they had had a long discussion on Potsdam, and the King showed him all the papers, Halifax noted in his diary, 'He seemed in a very good way and I should fancy will be able to influence our new Labour friends very well.'[32] Certainly the King always proudly proclaimed that he had influenced Attlee over the first of his Cabinet appointments and noted that he had done so in his diary. The King's entry for 26 July 1945 reads:

I then saw Mr Attlee & asked him to form a government. He accepted & became my new Prime Minister. I told him he would have to appoint a new Foreign Secy. & take him to Berlin [to the Potsdam Conference]. I found he was very surprised his Party had won & had had no time to meet or discuss with his colleagues any of the offices of State. I asked him whom he would make Foreign Secy. & he suggested Dr Hugh Dalton. I disagreed with him & said that Foreign Affairs was the most important subject at the moment & I hoped he would make Mr Bevin take it. He said he would but he could not return to Berlin till Saturday at the earliest. . . .

Attlee later denied that the King's intervention had altered his decision as to who should be Foreign Secretary. 'I naturally took into account the King's view which was very sound, but it was not a decisive factor in my arrival at my decision.' Certainly Attlee did not immediately indicate a change of mind; before lunch the following day, 27 July, he gave Dalton the firm impression that it would be he who would be accompanying him to Potsdam as Foreign Secretary, even to the extent of advising him to take a thin suit because of the heat. But at 4 p.m. he rang Dalton, asking him to come to the Cabinet Office, where he told him that he now wanted Bevin to be Foreign Secretary and offered him the Chancellorship of the Exchequer. The most likely supposition is that the King's pressure did cause Attlee to have second thoughts about Dalton as Foreign Secretary, and that he therefore made soundings in Whitehall and at the Foreign Office, where Cadogan was firmly against the idea of Dalton. Dalton had come up against the Foreign Office as Minister for Economic Warfare and was known to have an ungovernable temper, to be violently anti-German, pro-Zionist and possibly favourable towards the Soviet Union. There is no doubt that the King put his point very strongly to Attlee. Lascelles wrote that 'His Majesty begged him to think carefully about this, and suggested that Mr Bevin would be a better choice'. Although the King perhaps took too much of the credit for the decision, it seems likely that his firmly expressed opinion, borne out by that of the Foreign Office, did have a decisive effect. There is no doubt, moreover, that the King was right. Bevin, whom Cadogan welcomed as 'broad-minded and sensible, honest and courageous ... the heavyweight of the Cabinet and will get his own way with them', was to prove to be one of the great Foreign Secretaries of the twentieth century.

The King's overall knowledge and experience of the problems facing Britain and the Government were now longer and more continuous than most of his ministers', and he often could not resist the temptation to show them that he knew better than they did. Morrison, Lord President of the Council, Attlee's deputy when he was abroad and his rival for the party leadership, wrote of the King in his *Autobiography*: 'I was impressed with his up-to-date knowledge; he must have been a most assiduous reader of official papers. On occasion he enjoyed trying to trip up his ministers by asking about some detail of which he had good knowledge but of which they might be ignorant despite the fact that it affected their office.' Morrison, therefore, 'got into the habit of checking up details of such people and matters as I surmised might be the subjects of this friendly contest of knowledge.'[33] The King liked to keep them on their toes, and wished them to be under no illusions that he did not know what was going on. He did not hesitate to criticize some aspects of the Government's programme, telling Attlee on 20 November 1945 'that he must give the people here some confidence that the Government was not going to stifle all private enterprise. Everyone wanted to help in rehabilitating the country but they were not allowed to.' He liked, too, to show off his practical up-to-date knowledge, as when he discussed housing with the Prime Minister: 'I told him I had heard that Local

Authorities had had their plans turned down & were unable to build any houses because they could not get a permit from Health.' Attlee replied that papers he had read showed a good improvement in approved permits to build now. 'But where are the houses?' the practical King asked. Characteristically he was also interested in the clothing situation: 'the PM told me all available suits etc. go to the Demobilised Men, & the Women's clothes stocks are much exaggerated. I said we must all have new clothes & my family are down to the lowest ebb.' The Prime Minister might well have wondered quite how low the royal ebb would have been considered by a working-class family of four, but no doubt was too tactful to say so. To Dalton, as President of the Board of Trade in the previous Government, it seemed that the King's concerns in his department's work focused on the trivial, again reflecting his intense interest in clothes: overalls, the rumour that he was moving the Luton hat industry to Newcastle, the royal theory that utility suits did not actually save any material, and the exorbitant prices charged by shopkeepers for silver boxes and cigarette cases, which made it difficult for him to buy presents for people.[34]

The King did not like Hugh Dalton and made no secret of this, although it seems to have taken Dalton himself, who was preternaturally thick-skinned, five years in Government to realize it. By 1945, however, even he seems to have found the King's manner unenthusiastic towards him, commenting tartly in his diary, after handing over his seals of office as President of the Board of Trade in the last days of the coalition Government in the summer of 1945:

The King has very little to say, and doesn't seem to have focused on any B[oard] of T[rade] problem.... I don't suppose he has ever seen a coupon either for clothes or food. Anyway he really had nothing to say, and made no personal impact on me whatsoever. As nearly inanimate as an animate Monarch could be![35]

The King, in fact, went so far as to tell a later Labour Chancellor, Hugh Gaitskell, that Dalton was the only one of 'your people' that he could not abide. The primary cause of this, Gaitskell discovered, was childhood memories of Dalton's father, the disagreeable old Canon. 'I gathered that the King's dislike of him (I found this was shared by the Queen as well afterwards) really goes back to Windsor days,' Gaitskell noted, 'when Hugh Dalton's father was tutor to King George v, and apparently very like HD in having a loud voice and a bullying manner.'[36] There could have been many other reasons for the King's detestation of Dalton, who was probably the most unpopular man in public life of his day, loathed by a majority from Churchill down to the civil servants who worked for him. 'Keep that man away from me,' Churchill would say, 'I can't stand his booming voice and shifting eyes,' while one of his civil servants described him as 'vain, arrogant, without any understanding of how to handle men'. The King, however, did not dislike him merely for his personal characteristics or even, as Gaitskell divined, just because he himself had, as a child, detested Dalton's father. His aversion, in a characteristically royal way, derived from family tradition and loyalty. Hugh Dalton, the son of a courtier who, as tutor to George v, had been particularly close to him, had become a doctrinaire socialist and, the family thought, a republican. At Cambridge, as a member of the Carbonari, the younger Dalton had indulged in toasts such as 'Damn the King!' George v told the Canon, who had unwisely brought his impudent son to see him, 'Don't ever bring that anarchist son of yours to see me again. I don't care for his ideas.' 'We never understood why he turned against us,' the Duke of Windsor later said. Hugh Dalton had, thereafter, compounded his crimes by selling off royal gifts inherited from his father. Atavistic and loyal, George vi carried on the family tradition; socialism might be understandable and forgivable in some people, but in the son of a royal servant, a man admitted to the inner circle and indulged with the King's confidence as the Canon had been, it was nothing less than betrayal. To him, Dalton was a traitor and a turncoat.

Indeed, the King found the motivation of upper-class socialists difficult to understand. Lord Longford, on being first received by the King on his appointment as lord-in-waiting in 1946 and expecting the usual non-committal royal remark, was startled to hear the King open the conversation with 'Why did you join them?' Longford, a Catholic convert, at first thought the monarch was referring to the Church, then realized it was the Labour Party. Much taken aback he muttered something anodyne. 'I wanted to say, "because I believe that each one of us is equal in the sight of God", but realised this would be too tactless from a subject to a King.'[37] Public-school socialists like Hugh Gaitskell, whose wife Dora did 'not really much approve of royalty' and could hardly bring herself to curtsey to them, saw him as a reactionary. Staying at Windsor Castle in the spring of 1951, Gaitskell, then Chancellor of the Exchequer, recorded in his diary that, as he had always thought, 'the King and Queen are extremely conservative in their views', the Queen particularly so:

The Queen talked as though everybody was in a very bad way nowadays, not happy, poor, dispirited, etc. She did not say this in anger but implied that it could not be helped and that she hoped it would come to an end some day. I got into an argument with her then and implied that not everybody was quite so miserable and perhaps she did not see the people who were happier. I think she resented this.

Mrs Gaitskell, however, got on better with the King,

who drank whisky all evening and talked a great deal. He said to her at one point, 'I wonder what he has got in his box for us?' (meaning me) 'I hope it will not be too terrible.' Dora replied, 'I don't suppose it will be as bad as all that. After all he is rather right wing.' This the King thought a tremendous joke and laughed a great deal at the idea of my being thought right wing.[38]

As an intellectual and a politician Gaitskell did not understand that the King was, in a very real sense, by birth and upbringing (unlike the Queen), conservative with a small 'c' but essentially apolitical. Often, like his great-grandmother, Queen Victoria, he saw himself as representing the essential England, as opposed to the doctrinaire vision of the politicians. It was his duty to get on with the politicians in whom the reality of power reposed, but he could not look at things from their angle. In this context, left-wing and right-wing labels did not have the ideological significance which they had for men like Gaitskell, who, for instance, had instantly assumed, when the King told him that he could not abide one of the Labour leaders, that he must be referring to the left-wing rebel, Aneurin Bevan, the Minister of Health, when the King meant Dalton. In fact, the King had got on perfectly well with Bevan, a fellow stammerer, whose Celtic charm and fluency he found initially easier to deal with than Attlee's laconic Anglo-Saxon attitude. 'I found him easy to talk to,' the King had recorded of their first meeting, when he teased Bevan with a reference to his previous role as a thorn in the side of the Churchill Government. 'I asked him how he liked the responsibility of a Government Dept. instead of criticising it.' When Bevan, as architect of the National Health Service, resigned office in 1951 in protest against Gaitskell's proposed budget introduction of dental charges, the King was unable to understand the ideological reasons for his action. 'He must be mad to resign over a thing like that,' the King told Gaitskell, waving a well-shod foot in his Chancellor's direction. 'I really don't see why people should have false teeth free any more than they have shoes free.' 'He is, of course, a fairly reactionary person,' was Gaitskell's comment.[39]

Earlier, in a private conversation about the budget, the King had asked Gaitskell, ' "Is it going to be the end?" Meaning was I going to propose the confiscation of all large estates or something of the kind. I assured him that I did not think he would feel it was the end....'[40] In his darker moments in the immediate post-war period the King did feel threatened as he saw the experiences of his fellow monarchs abroad, and at home the country estates of his youth disappearing under the weight of Labour taxation. 'Everything is going now. Before long I shall also have to go,' he told Vita Sackville-West in 1948 on hearing that her family home, Knole, had been taken over by the National Trust. Vita's son Ben, after a visit to Windsor that Easter in his capacity as Assistant to the Surveyor of the King's Pictures, reported the King as 'worried much by the prospects of a Republic. He sees everything *en noir*.' The King's fears may have been prompted by a visit that weekend by the unfortunate King Michael of Romania, but there is little doubt that he saw the position of the monarchy in 1945 as to some extent a mirror image of 1918, when his father, too, had feared social revolution. He was extremely careful not to inflame left-wing feeling. Court entertainments were few and far between, as Queen Mary complained to Gaitskell at a Buckingham Palace dinner-party for the Shah of Iran that summer, '... they won't do enough of this kind of thing now'.[41]

The King's sensitivity towards the prevailing democratic spirit and the impoverished state of the country revealed itself in his decision that there should be no state grants to the military leaders of the Second World War as there had been after the First World War. Alan Brooke, who as CIGS might have expected the highest honours, was fobbed off with a barony and had to sell his cherished set of Gould's *Birds of Great Britain* in order to pay for the required robes. Montgomery's demands, as usual, had been the most outrageous; he had immediately put in a request for a fully furnished grace-and-favour house from the King: 'Quite a small house, 7 or 8 bedrooms would be ample.' The King turned him down, and refused another request from the Field Marshal two years later for the use of Walmer Castle, the official residence of the Warden of the Cinque Ports, an honorary office held by Churchill. 'The present Lord Warden has given no indication that he wishes to relinquish it,' Lascelles responded crushingly. 'The houses in the King's gift are all bespoke.'[42]

Democratic, money-saving measues in the King's view were all very well in their place, but not when they touched cherished institutions like His Majesty's Brigade of Guards. On succeeding Alan Brooke as CIGS in 1946, Montgomery had turned his energies towards rationalizing the post-war Army and in his reformist zeal trod on many military toes, including the aristocratic ones of the Brigade, whose early-warning cries of pain were heard at the Palace. In line with the slimming down of the Armed Forces, infantry regiments were to be cut by thirty-one per cent, although the Brigade of Guards was to be reduced by only twenty per cent. None the less, the major-general commanding the Brigade, Budget Lloyd, complained to the King, who summoned Montgomery to the Palace for an explanation. Montgomery came away from the interview as usual convinced that his arguments had carried the day, but Lascelles telephoned him to disabuse him of the impression that His Majesty's silence had signified assent. His Majesty emphatically would not agree. The Brigade of Guards was too close to the throne, linked to it by bonds of service, tradition and the higher ranks of freemasonry. The Duke of Windsor as Prince of Wales had been an officer in the Grenadier Guards, as had the King's brother-in-law Viscount Lascelles, the King was Colonel-in-Chief of the Welsh Guards, and Princess Elizabeth was Colonel-in-Chief of the Grenadiers. The Household Cavalry, the Blues and Royals, both by tradition and in reality meant what their title implied. Stationed within a stone's throw of the royal palaces at Windsor, Wellington and Knightsbridge Barracks, they provided not only ceremonial military protection for the royal family but also social cannon fodder for royal parties and escorts for the two young Princesses. As a result of the King's veto, the Brigade of Guards remained at their pre-war strength of ten battalions.

The King's favourite among his Labour Ministers was undoubtedly his Foreign Secretary, Bevin, whose bulldog English views and earthy sense of humour he shared. The King had become fond of Bevin during the war, when the brilliant, outspoken trades union leader had been Minister of Labour. Bevin's lumbering, shapeless figure in his ill-fitting clothes had been a familiar sight in the corridors of Buckingham Palace, when he would make his way into the King's presence, shake the royal hand with his other hand still firmly stuck in his pocket and sit bulging over the edges of an elegant chair. Bevin tended to make a virtue of his 'call a spade a spade' way of speaking – he once said to the Queen, eyeing the Palace gold plate, 'I like your crockery' – as he did of his deliberately plebeian manners. Lord Woolton, attending a Buckingham Palace dinner for Mrs Roosevelt in October 1942, thought he went too far:

At the other end of the table Bevin was holding the stage and I felt was overstepping the limits of courtesy both to his sovereign and to a very distinguished visitor by the way he was laying down the law. He cultivates the bluff, working-man attitude, but I thought overdid it in the presence of the King and Queen and I noticed in the drawing-room afterwards that whilst he was talking to the Queen the King went over to join them – and Bevin continued to sit as the King joined the group. During dinner he broke one of the liqueur glasses; when he did it the King exclaimed 'Now what have you done' and told him to use one of his other glasses – I thought treating him like a child who doesn't know any better.[43]

The King did not mind Bevin's manners and when others took it upon themselves to object on his behalf he rebuked them. When his new young equerry, Group-Captain Peter Townsend, primly complained that Bevin might at least take his hand out of his pocket when shaking hands with His Majesty, the King told him firmly that the important thing was not his manners but the fact that he was 'a real Englishman. I like him.'

Fond as he was of risqué humour and earthy stories, the King appreciated Bevin's jokes; on being asked whether he would be taking his wife to the Paris Conference the Foreign Secretary replied, 'Taking Mrs Bevin to Paris is like taking a sandwich to a banquet.' More importantly than his humour, the King appreciated Bevin's talents as Foreign Secretary, his robust attitude in the face of Soviet obstructiveness and aggression, his seizing of the initiative in turning an idealistic speech by Marshall in June 1947 into the European lifeline of the Marshall Plan for the economic recovery of Europe, and the part which he played in calling for European co-operation which resulted in the Brussels Pact and eventually in NATO. He liked, too, the opposition which Bevin, the most powerful voice in the Cabinet, put up against the cuts in military spending on defence at home and of the Empire demanded by Dalton to offset spending on the socialist domestic programme.

The year 1947, the eleventh of the King–Emperor's reign, was the moment of truth for post-war Britain. The previous year, 1946, had been a year of full employment and a tidal flood of socialist legislation, but in 1947 things had started to go seriously wrong. The worst winter of the century ushered in an unprecedented fuel crisis. On 28 January, Big Ben struck once and then symbolically fell silent; the next day the Thames froze at Windsor. Coal pits were blocked by snow, ports frozen up. By the end of the first week in February electricity cuts of five hours a day were imposed on the country; unemployment rose to $2\frac{1}{4}$ million and production fell. The weather improved in mid-March, but by then the damage had been done; the fuel crisis was succeeded by a financial crisis. The dollar credits on which the British Government had been surviving were almost exhausted, and on 5 June Dalton told the Cabinet that if the present rate of drawing upon them were to continue, they would have run out by the end of the year. On 20 August he was forced to announce the suspension of the convertibility of the pound, a serious blow to Britain's international credibility. Suspension of the convertibility of the pound brought home the unpleasant fact that Britain was no longer a world power; she could not afford her Empire. War had hastened the progress of imperial disintegration already evident before 1939; post-war ideology, coupled with the common-sense realization that Britain no longer possessed the necessary resources in men and money, accelerated it to a point of centrifugal force. In that year, the King–Emperor stood in Windsor Great Park looking sorrowfully at a plantation of trees, each representing a colony of his Empire. 'This is Singapore,' he said pointing to one. 'There is Malaya ... Hong Kong is over there. They have all been lost to the Empire Plantation. Burma, too, over there. The time may soon come when we shall have to cut out the Indian tree – and I wonder how many more.'[44] The Victory parade on 8 June 1946, over which the King had presided, had been the swansong of his Empire.

On 1 February 1947, in the teeth of the fuel crisis, the King, with the Queen and the two Princesses, sailed from Portsmouth on his Navy's newest battleship, HMS *Vanguard*, on what was to be his last imperial tour. The South African tour had been planned the year before for the twin purpose of helping Britain's friend, Field Marshal Smuts, for whom the King had a deep admiration, to win votes in the face of the threat of the Nationalist Party in the forthcoming election, and to give the King a much-needed holiday with his family. When it came to leave, however, the King did not want to go, feeling, as he told Queen Mary, that he should be at home with his people, 'having borne so many trials with them'. Indeed, he offered to return but Attlee refused, chiefly on the grounds that to cut short the King's tour would magnify the crisis in international eyes. The King worried, none the less, as the Queen wrote to Queen Mary: 'This tour is being very strenuous as I feared it would be & doubly hard for Bertie who feels he should be at home. ... We think of home all the time. ...'

All the signs were that the King's health was under strain during the tour, despite the long sea voyage which had preceded it. He had had no respite from crisis since the end of the war, the three weeks' sea voyage out on *Vanguard* was to be his only chance to relax. The weather was rough for some days from the outset; the King, a seasoned sailor, stayed in his cabin and slept. Signs of tension and irritation were never far from the surface. When the French battleship *Richelieu* (which the King's Navy had tried so hard to sink at Oran in July 1940) was late in taking up her escort station off the French coast, His Majesty 'fretted' at the delay, even more so when the unfortunate French sailors lining the decks in his honour, thoroughly soaked by the heavy seas, failed to deliver the expected salvo as a royal salute and only a puff of white smoke emerged. When they reached South Africa, the tour was a two-month marathon, most of it (thirty-five nights) spent in the aptly named 'White Train'. They also motored or flew hundreds of miles. The King was on show all the time, as the object either of Boer curiosity – not all of it friendly – or of adulation from tribespeople as his great-grandmother's 'reincarnation'. His profile was described as 'fine as if etched on a postage stamp' and he lost seventeen pounds in weight. The Queen was at her heroic trouping best, smiling, waving, charming the crowds, never at a loss for conversation; the King, according to an observer, was 'more restrained (not unnaturally) and perhaps partly due to a natural shyness and over-fatigue'. Princess Elizabeth remarked to someone that both 'Mummy and Pop were just about done in but that she and Margaret were enjoying every moment of it. . . .'

There was barely concealed political tension; the Nationalist Party remained aloof. At the presentation of addresses of welcome by the members of the Senate and House of Assembly in Cape Town on 17 February, it was noted that only eleven Nationalist members of the House of Assembly out of a total of forty-six put in an appearance and not one Nationalist senator. The right-wing Nationalist press, described by the British High Commissioner, Sir Evelyn Baring, as 'unrelenting in its hatred of the British connexion', either ignored the visit or wrote abusive articles. While the pro-Government newspapers reported the enthusiasm with which the royal family was generally greeted, the Nationalist *Die Burger* commented disapprovingly on the mingling of 'Europeans and non-Europeans' in the crowds, lingered pointedly on the fuel crisis and mocked the King's pronunciation of an Afrikaans sentence at the opening of Parliament. Southern Rhodesia, a loyal British colony, was less complicated territory. The King opened the Rhodesian Parliament, attended two *Indabas*, inspected the view from Cecil Rhodes's hill-top tomb, visited Northern Rhodesia and 'gazed spellbound' on the Victoria Falls. In Swaziland they were given a performance by 15,000 warriors of the traditional dance known as the 'Inexplicable Mystery', after they had been greeted with the traditional salutation, a deafening whistle. Sir Evelyn remarked as a 'notable feature' of this occasion that 'no European police or Administrative officers interfered in any way with the dance', contrasting it with what had happened in Zululand where the Zulu warriors had been forbidden to carry spears, a very large number of white policemen had been present and 'Europeans attempted to organise the Zulu dance with the result that the Zulu themselves lost enthusiasm'. The comparison between the two events, one in British High Commission Territory, the other in the Union, was not lost on black South Africans. Dr Moroka, a member of the Union Natives' Representative Council, wrote an article in a paper named *Bantu Welfare* 'comparing the freedom with which His Majesty mixed with his African subjects in the High Commission territories with the proceedings in the union where, according to the writer, he was kept away from Africans and everything was done to underline the idea of white supremacy'.[45]

Reports show that the King himself was unhappy about this. A correspondent of Lady Milner, writing on Senate, Cape Town, paper, commented:

Several little incidents have occurred which tend to show that the King was getting a little restless under the regimentation imposed upon him. Tired to death of being ordered about and sleuthed by Afrikander policemen wherever they moved, so much so that one of his staff remarked to me, 'Are they never going to allow them loose among the people?'

The *Cape Times* reported that once when on a country ramble the King was heard to say, 'Well, mother, we've shaken off the Gestapo at last.' Unfortunately, he didn't know that there was a reporter lying nearby in the long grass.

'Another very indicative incident', Lady Milner's correspondent reported, occurred at the State banquet in Pretoria, when the official in charge of the microphone neglected to switch it off after Smuts had made his speech and sat down. The following exchange then occurred between the King and the Field Marshal:

SMUTS: You are to follow me now, Sir.
KING: I'll speak when I've had my coffee and the waiters have left the room.
SMUTS: They're waiting for you now in England, Sir.
KING: Well, let them wait. I have said I will speak when the waiters have left the room.
PRINCESS ELIZABETH: Can't we be heard?
A MAN'S VOICE: No.
Shortly after the King rises and speaks. On resuming his seat:
SMUTS: That was very good, Sir.
KING: Well, I suppose now I may have my coffee.[46]

There were also untoward episodes. One day the royal family had to drive, through torrid heat, 120 miles through the mining towns of the Rand, where hundreds of thousands of black miners and their families lined the route, pressing forward, waving and shouting with enthusiasm as the open royal Daimler passed. The King was tired and on edge, a victim of classic crowd claustrophobia. To his equerry's horror, he began to fire instructions at the driver, unsettling him in difficult conditions. Behind him the Queen was doing her best to soothe the King, and the Princesses, knowing the form, were trying to make light of things. The atmosphere in the car became so tense that Townsend turned round and shouted at the King, 'For Heaven's sake, shut up or there's going to be an accident.' There was, but not the kind that Townsend envisaged, yet in its way far more upsetting:

It was as we entered Benoni. First, I saw a blue-uniformed policeman, ahead of the car, come racing towards us, with a terrible, determined look in his eyes, which were fixed on something behind us. I turned, to see another man, black and wiry, sprinting, with terrifying speed and purpose, after the car. In one hand he clutched something, with the other he grabbed hold of the car, so tightly that the knuckles of his black hands showed white. The Queen, with her parasol, landed several deft blows on the assailant before he was knocked senseless by policemen. As they dragged away his limp body, I saw the Queen's parasol, broken in two, disappear over the side of the car. Within a second, Her Majesty was waving and smiling, as captivatingly as ever, to the crowds. . . .

What had happened, however, was not an attempted assassination but a heart-breaking exhibition of loyalty. Crying 'My King! My King!', the man had, clutched in his hand, a birthday present of a ten-shilling note – a huge sum for him – for Princess Elizabeth, soon to be twenty-one. This tragic vignette was the result of police paranoia, but the tension in the Daimler certainly contributed to the Queen's tigress-like defence. The King was immediately concerned, asking

Townsend to find out if the man was all right. 'I hope he was not too badly hurt. . . .' He was also contrite and, with considerable magnanimity of soul, sent for his equerry to apologize: 'I am sorry about today,' he said, 'I was very tired. . . .'[47]

The King felt that he was part of a sideshow, a totem in a travelling circus, marking time to Jan Smuts's tune when what really mattered was happening at home. James Cameron, among the numerous press crew travelling on the White Train, was also struck by the King's tension, as he reported:

The King kept saying that he should be at home and not lolling about in the summer sun; never was a man so jumpy. . . . One evening he called some of us Press people along to his dining car, ostensibly because he had a communication to make, but more probably to relieve the deadly boredom. . . . We found him behind a table covered with bottles of all sorts of dedication. 'We must not f-forget the purpose of this t-tour,' he said. '. . . trade and so on. Empire co-operation. For example; South African b-brandy. I have been trying it. It is of course m-magnificent, except that it is not very nice. But,' he said triumphantly, 'there is this South African liqueur called V-Van der Humm. Perhaps a little sweet for most. But, now, if you mix half of brandy with half of Van der Humm. . . . Please try.

Cameron gave a moving picture of a man longing to escape from his trammels, but within the framework of a freedom which was all that a King would be allowed. One evening the King ordered the train to halt beside a beach near Port Elizabeth. Police appeared and roped off a large crowd of onlookers into two halves:

Down the path from the Royal Train walked a solitary figure in a blue bathrobe, carrying a towel. The sea was a long way off, but he went. And all alone, on the great empty beach, between the surging banks of the people who might not approach, the King of England stepped into the Indian Ocean and jumped up and down – the loneliest man, at that moment, in the world.[48]

Two of the best-informed American political commentators, Walter Lippmann and Stewart Alsop, saw the royal tour of southern Africa not in terms of black and white or British v. Boer but as representing a definite shift in British colonial policy from India and the Far East to Africa. The military correspondent of the *New York Times*, Hanson Baldwin, put it in terms of world strategy, arguing that Europe was now too vulnerable as a base in the age of the atom bomb and the ballistic missile. South Africa, far from the military and economic threat posed by the superpowers, might be the answer for Britain, which could also develop her mineral resources – 'exploitation of this . . . might conceivably restore the British pound to its historic position as the arbiter of world destinies. None of the Dark Continent's potentialities – as a military base, political capital, and economic reservoir – has been lost on the British. . . .' Walter Lippmann saw this as a shift in British policy away from the doctrine of Anglo–American solidarity held by Churchill and Truman, towards a new power-grouping between the two superpowers, headed by the British. He wrote:

The Royal Family did not go to South Africa in order to escape the cold weather in England but to mark and to promote the change in empire and the revolution in imperial strategy. In South Africa, which is a rich and undeveloped land, Britain may find the means of becoming, despite the liquidation of the Indian and Near Eastern empires, an independent Great Power in the world.[49]

Similar possibilities had occurred to members of the King's entourage, as a letter from Lascelles to Ismay indicates. The King's tour had been followed by a similar tour of southern Africa by Montgomery in his role as CIGS, after which he sent a top-secret personal report for transmission to the King. Lascelles told Ismay:

I was much impressed by it. He works out, in his clear dogmatic way, the general idea that took root in my own mind after our South African trip – that the co-ordination and intensive development of all the British territories in Central and Southern Africa is going to be of vital importance in the coming East v. West struggle ... & to the whole future of the Empire.... I was so much impressed by it that I've suggested to the King that he ought to get Monty down to Sandringham towards the end of next month and talk it all over with him. It is the kind of sphere in which the Sovereign could do a lot: and later on, it might provide a field in which Dickie's undoubtedly great talents could be further utilized.[50]

Earlier that month Attlee had given an interview to C.L. Sulzberger of the *New York Times*, in which he revealed his thoughts to be tending in the same direction, telling Sulzberger that he 'believed the world tended to sell Great Britain short as a power', and pointing out that not only did Britain have the secret of atomic fission, 'but also influenced the vast imperial importance of Africa'.[51] Although the King's visit was not undertaken with the avowed intention of switching British colonial ideas from the East towards Africa, it was seen as a pointer to the future.

By the time the King returned to London at the beginning of May, events in India had moved rapidly towards the transition of power. For the King, the loss of India, the country which he had so much wanted to visit, was undoubtedly the most painful, although he had come round to the view that, given the inter-communal tensions and resultant massacres, the sooner independence for India was negotiated the better. Britain did not have the forces to act as umpire and policeman between the Hindu and Muslim communities while their leaders wrangled over the alternatives of co-operation or partition. A luncheon at Buckingham Palace on 5 December 1946, when he sat between the rival leaders, Nehru and Jinnah, had convinced him that the outlook for their co-operation was extremely poor, although he still hoped for a satisfactory political solution. On 8 December he saw Attlee about it:

I told him that I was very worried over the breakdown of the Indian leaders' talks, & that I could see no alternative to Civil War between Hindus & Moslems for which we should be held responsible as we have not enough troops or authority with which to keep order. The PM agreed ... Nehru's present policy seemed to be to secure complete domination by Congress throughout the Govt. of India. The Muslims would never stand for it & would probably fight for Pakistan which the Hindus dislike so much. The 2 main political parties in India had no real will to reach agreement among themselves; the situation might so develop as to result in Civil War in India, & there seemed to be little realization among Indian leaders of the risk that ordered govt. might collapse. We have plans to evacuate India, but we cannot do so without leaving India with a workable Constitution. The Indian leaders have got to learn that the responsibility is theirs & that they must learn how to govern.

Attlee's solution was to cut through the Gordian knot by sacking the Viceroy Wavell, whom he now regarded as 'defeatist' and 'lacking the finesse', as he told the King, to carry both Indian parties with him. Wavell's sacking was to some extent unfair; it was certainly ungracious since Attlee carried on negotiation with his successor for two months before informing Wavell he was to be replaced. His choice of Mountbatten as the last Viceroy was, however, inspired. The King's reaction was warm approval, with the reservation that Mountbatten must be given a clear brief: 'Lord Mountbatten', he told Attlee on 17 December, 'must have concrete orders as to what he is to do. Is he to lead the retreat out of India or is he to work for the reconciliation of Hindus and Muslims?' Mountbatten sailed for India on 20 March 1947, armed with a declared date for British withdrawal from India, not later than 1 June 1948, to obtain a unitary Government for British India if possible within the framework of the British Commonwealth, and, if not, to leave the Indians to work out their own salvation.

The King had already arrived in South Africa by the time Mountbatten left, but to Wavell, created an earl but justifiably wounded by Attlee's treatment, he sent, via Lascelles, a typically kind message. Lascelles wrote:

For me to say how highly His Majesty values your services to the Crown in India, both as Commander-in-Chief and as Viceroy, seems to me, even though I write under orders, almost an impertinence; it would also be unnecessary for I am sure you know it already. What you may not know, perhaps, is how fully the King has understood, all through these recent years, the immense difficulties with which you have had to cope ... no man who is so comprehensively well informed as His Majesty could fail to realize that, in all the history of British rule in India, there has never been a Viceroy with a harder task ... than fell to your lot.

One thing especially The King charged me to say to you; on the purely personal side, he is very grateful indeed to you for the extremely generous references which you have made, in private and in public, to the appointment of Dickie Mountbatten as your successor.... The King feels that you have done a great deal towards giving him a good start, and is very grateful to you.

The first stage in the negotiations was over by 20 May, when Mountbatten arrived back in London with the news that the Muslim and Hindu leaders had failed to agree on the basis of a unitary government for India and that partition was, therefore, on the table. Moreover, in view of the inter-communal tension, Mountbatten and the British Government had come to the conclusion that the date for the devolution of power must be brought forward. Mountbatten stayed with the King at Buckingham Palace during the week in which he put the latest plan to the Cabinet. By the time he left London on 30 May, it had been agreed that two self-governing Dominions of India and Pakistan should be established, with the right to decide whether or not they remained within the Commonwealth. The decisions were made public on 3 June, when Mountbatten announced at a press conference that the date for the transfer would be 15 August, then only just over two months away. On 18 July the Indian Independence Bill became law.

The King, although kept closely informed by his cousin, had no active role in the drama of the transition of power in India, beyond urging Mountbatten 'to do what he could to see fair play for the [Indian] Princes', an instruction which the Viceroy interpreted very loosely. The King felt that he had inherited a moral responsibility for the Princes from Queen Victoria, who, in return for the loyalty of most of them during the Indian Mutiny, had promised in 1858 to 'respect the rights, dignity and honour of Native Princes as our own'. By 1947 the Native princes numbered some 565 separate States ranging in size and importance from petty principalities to entities like Kashmir or Hyderabad, with a bewildering variety of standards of government and administration. The British Government, in framing its India Act of 1858, had not envisaged a transference of power, least of all in the conditions of confusion, haste and demagoguery existing in the summer of 1947. The Congress Party, under whose sway the greater number of the Princely States would come, saw their future as part of India and no business of the British. Attlee, the India Office and the British Government's man-on-the-spot, Conrad Corfield, Political Adviser to the Princely States, thought that Mountbatten was hardly acting in the Princes' interests in making a deal with the Indian leaders on their behalf before independence. Attlee, having promised in Parliament that the Princely States would decide their own future, sent the Viceroy a telegram telling him he was going too far, but backed down when Mountbatten protested that he was doing his best. The bargain struck with the Indian leaders was that the Princely States would adhere to the Indian Union for the purposes of defence, foreign affairs and communications, retaining their remaining rights and their privy purses. In return for this, Mountbatten had agreed to use his influence to persuade the princes to adhere; something which Corfield regarded as unethical and unwise: 'he had agreed to use his influence as the representative of the paramount power to recommend a bargain which could not be guaranteed after independence. . . .'[52] Mountbatten, naturally, put it to the King in the best possible light: 'If I can get all the States in on the wonderful terms I have been able to obtain for them, I shall have carried out your instructions to do what I could to see fair play for the Princes,' he wrote on 3 August.[53]

The Viceroy did not hesitate to use the King's name in his efforts to push the Native rulers into adherence. Pointing out that adherence now meant joining a Dominion with the King still at its head, he wrote to the Maharaj-Rana of Dholpur:

I know that His Majesty would personally be grieved if you elected to sever your connection with him whilst he was still the King of India now that it has been made clear that this would not involve you in accepting to remain within a republic if this was unacceptable to you when the time came.

Determined to deliver the Princes as a package to independent India he was none too scrupulous about the way he chose to do it. One minister of a Princely State told Corfield that, after an interview with the Viceroy on the subject, 'he now knew what Dolfuss felt like when he was sent for to see Hitler: he had not expected to be spoken to like that by a British officer: after a moment's pause he withdrew the word "British" '.[54] Walter Monckton, negotiating on behalf of his old friend and client, the Nizam of Hyderabad, ruler of India's largest State, called Mountbatten's methods 'intolerable blackmail', 'an exhibition of power politics' and 'an exact replica of those in which Hitler indulged'.[55] Monckton made his views known in London: 'It is horrible that we should have encouraged the Rulers to believe in our promises up to such a short time ago and should then leave them without the resources to stand comfortably on their own feet,' he wrote to Leo Amery. 'It is still worse that they should feel that, in spite of their loyalty, they are being left at the mercy of those who have proved in the past to be our enemies and theirs.' The King, however, took the *realpolitik* view: 'I am so glad', he wrote to Mountbatten on 13 August, two days before Independence, 'that nearly all the Indian States have decided ... to join either one or other of the Dominions. They could never have stood alone in the World.'[56]

On 15 August 1947 the King lost the 'jewel' in his imperial Crown and the initial 'I' [Imperator] which Disraeli had bestowed on his great-grandmother not quite seventy years before. Queen Mary, who had a special place in her heart for India after her two visits there, took it especially hard. On the back of the envelope of the first letter the King wrote to her after Independence, she noted, 'The first time Bertie wrote me a letter with the I for Emperor of India left out, very sad....' The Crown of India made for George V to wear at the Durbar in 1911, at a cost to the Indian Revenues of £60,000, remained with the other Crown Jewels in the Tower of London for the time being, but the King agreed that if either India or Pakistan should in future secede from the Crown, the Crown of India should be vested in some Indian authority. The King did, however, ask for one memento of the Raj, the last of the Union Jacks which had been flown day and night above the Residency in Lucknow since the siege during the Indian Mutiny. He wanted it to be hung with other historical flags and banners at Windsor.

There is no indication available of what were the ex-King–Emperor's real feelings on the passing of the Indian Empire, which had figured so largely in British history for more than 100 years. His official biographer gives no hint; the relevant files at the India Office will be closed until well past the end of the century. No doubt he accepted Mountbatten's view that there was no alternative. The aftermath of Independence must none the less have caused him pain. The break-up of the Indian Army caused untold bitterness and an estimated 200,000 people died in inter-communal massacres on the partition of the Punjab. The truth was that the British had long since lost control, 'we have the responsibility without the power', as Wavell had said bitterly. While some people saw it as a shameful scuttle, others – including probably the King – were grateful that at least it had been well stage-managed. Harold Nicolson wrote:

This great surrender of power is represented as a brilliant triumph. I quite see that Dicky Mountbatten has managed with great firmness and skill to turn a disaster into a very honourable retreat. But to lose 400 million citizens as if it were some tremendous acquisition will be regarded by foreigners as a proof of our outrageous hypocrisy. It is not that. We do not desire to deceive others; we wish only to comfort ourselves. . . .[57]

The King comforted himself with the concept of the New Commonwealth which was to replace the old Empire; a free association of largely self-governing nations for which the Crown, as before, would provide the link. It was an idea to which his daughter as Queen Elizabeth II was to cling as one of the principal *raisons d'être* of the Crown she inherited from her father. It was something to which she had publicly dedicated herself in a broadcast speech delivered during the royal tour of South Africa on 21 April 1947, her coming-of-age. 'I should like', she had said in her high girlish voice, 'to make that dedication now. It is very simple. I declare before you all that my whole life, whether it be long or short, shall be devoted to your service and the service of our great Imperial Commonwealth to which we all belong. . . .' Her father still firmly believed that the monarchy had a role to play outside the United Kingdom and was prepared to do his utmost to maintain it.

There is evidence that the King, therefore, minded deeply, not so much the gradual and accelerating dismemberment of his Empire, as the departure of member States from the Commonwealth and allegiance to the British Crown. Burma had been the first to go in June 1947, when the Burmese Constituent Assembly declared Burma to be a sovereign republic outside the British Commonwealth, a decision which was formalized with the passage of the Burma Independence Act on 14 November. The year 1948 was to see the final departure of Eire, which the King minded a great deal more, with the repeal in September of the External Relations Act, the last formal link with the Crown. At a party at Buckingham Palace on 26 October 1948, the King and the Queen had made a determined personal effort to stop the Irish breakaway. The King and Queen took John Dulanty, the Irish Minister, aside. 'Why leave the family?' they said to him. Dulanty afterwards told Harold Nicolson:

The King was distressed by the whole business. He had been so glad to see relations with Eire improving; he had looked forward to the day when he would visit Dublin; now it was impossible. Was it any personal fault in himself? Dulanty assured him that 'even the angel Gabriel' could not have prevented it. 'Well, whatever we are,' said the Queen, 'we are not two angel Gabriels.'[58]

The Republic of Ireland was formally declared on Easter Monday 1949 – symbolically at the Dublin Post Office, scene of the Easter Rising thirty-three years before – marking the formal, final ending of the country's troubled relationship with the British Crown. In January that same year, the new Indian Constitution declared India to be a sovereign democratic republic, but, unlike Ireland, the Indian leaders had indicated willingness under certain conditions to remain within the Commonwealth. Huge efforts were to be made to accommodate her which were to result in a new formulation of the King's position in relation to the Commonwealth. India was prepared to acknowledge the King as Head of the Commonwealth, but not as King of India, therefore allegiance to the Crown was no longer to be regarded as essential for membership of the Commonwealth and the Crown would become simply a symbol of association. This inevitably meant a change in the King's title, a subject in which the King took the keenest interest. The title 'Head of the Commonwealth' was to be inserted, the more pointed word 'Kingdoms' dropped in favour of the vaguer 'Realms'. In Canada, Australia and New Zealand, the King was still King and Defender of the Faith; in Ceylon, Pakistan and South Africa he was to be King but dropped Defender of the Faith; while as far as India was concerned, he was to be Head of the Commonwealth. It was a clever compromise, retaining for the Crown the form, if not the substance, it had historically enjoyed, and giving the King the role that he was determined to maintain in an intercontinental association of States for which he and his successors were to be the unifying symbol.

12

THE HOUSE OF WINDSOR

'... the King and Queen and their two daughters provide one of the very best examples of English family life. A thoroughly close-knit and happy family all wrapped up in each other. . . .'

Alan Brooke, January 1944

AFTER almost a decade on the throne, the King remained essentially a private, shy man, dependent on his family for happiness and support to an unprecedented degree. He still looked for encouragement on public occasions and even large private social functions to his wife, whom he described to his elder daughter as 'the most marvellous person in the World in my eyes'. He had not got over his dislike of public functions. 'Oh my God!' he would exclaim with mock exasperation. 'How I hate being a King! Sometimes at ceremonies I want to stand up and scream and scream and scream.'[1]

Like the wild game which he so industriously pursued in the countryside round his homes, the King only appeared as his real self in his natural habitat, his family circle. There the high spirits which he rarely showed to outsiders came out. One member of a neighbouring family who frequently saw the King on holiday at Balmoral remembered him like this:

He had a fine sense of humour and was an incorrigible practical joker frequently employing almost school-boy pranks. The door of the bedroom ajar usually meant books lodged on top of it – not always appreciated by the older generation. . . . Apple-pie beds were not unknown. Generally, in Scotland at any rate, everything was very informal and he fully expected his practical jokes to be returned against himself.[2]

Sometimes his capacity for seeing the funny side of things got the better of him, even on formal occasions. At the opening of the controversial New Bodleian Library building at Oxford in 1946, there was a moment of great embarrassment when the specially made silver key with which the King was trying to open the door snapped in his hand. There was a stricken silence, when the voice of the public orator came across clearly, 'Art revenging herself'; the King burst into laughter and at that all the undergraduates, crowded round the Sheldonian opposite, just yelled and yelled. The King had inherited his father's liking for salty jokes; he was fond of after-dinner stories in all-male company and knockabout comedy, particularly The Crazy Gang and the popular comedians of the 1940s, Tommy Trinder and Tommy Handley of the classic radio show *ITMA*. According to the actors who went down to Windsor by royal request to do shows, often at the estate workers' York Club, the King had a fine touch in telling stories, often of a distinctly bar-room kind. 'After the show he'd ask us, "Have you heard any good stories lately?" And then he'd tell the best, get Tommy Trinder asking if he could write them down. . . .'[3]

The young often found the King easier than the Queen, as the same neighbour remembered:

He was much less formal and much less concerned about the proper dress and time-keeping except for official occasions (when the Queen was notoriously unpunctual) than was the Queen. To the young, he was much less formidable than was she. I remember coming in late and rather dirty from duck-flighting with him and meeting the Queen coming down the stairs to dinner. She remarked that she supposed we just had time to change to which he responded, 'For Goodness' sake – we're on holiday. We'll go and wash!'

If the Queen thought the King was getting too informal in the presence of the young she would say 'Bertie!' in 'a little soft voice' and the high spirits would quickly subside. The King liked the young:

My principal and perhaps overriding memory is his extreme tolerance and kindness to the younger generation. I am sure as a teenager I and my friends were dogmatic and self-opinionated and I well remember solving most of the world's problems. He always seemed interested, always joined in, often kindly injecting some reality into what must often have been frightful rubbish! I vaguely recollect that he was a good deal less tolerant with the older generation . . . [but] overall he was one of the kindest, gentlest and most courteous people I have ever known. . . .[4]

As his health worsened the King became increasingly subject to fits of temper, known in the family as his 'gnashes', when his jaw muscles would work, his blue eyes would assume an alarming glare and a stream of invective, much of it consisting of expletives, would emerge. 'He would rant, noisily,' a courtier said. These fits of temper were unpredictable, uncontrollable and completely out of character with the King's natural courtesy and kindness. Servants and ladies-in-waiting, people whom the King would normally die rather than insult, could be in the firing-line; the 'gnashes' would be set off by something trivial, usually an arrangement going awry, and the shouting would normally be directed not at somebody but about something. The fits of temper were partly hereditary; even Princess Mary was, according to her son, subject to a certain 'Hanoverian spleen'. They were partly due, too, to the King's highly strung temperament, an outlet for the increasing strain of his public life. Some members of his Household, Peter Townsend in particular, learned to 'gentle him along like a high-mettled horse', avoiding these explosions, but once they began only the Queen or Princess Margaret could stop them until they had run their brief but fiery course. 'Once she [the Queen] held his pulse, and with a wistful smile, began to count – tick, tick, tick – which made him laugh, and the storm subsided.'[5] The King inherited the family habit of 'chaff' as a form of humorous communication to which both Edward VII and George V had been given. Defined by the *Oxford Dictionary* as 'banter, ridicule; badinage' dating from 1827, it was not always pleasant for the recipient since, although meant in a friendly spirit, it entailed harping on some weakness or foolish act on the part of the person at whom it was directed. In the King's case it was often used as a cover-up for his shyness.

On occasion the King's irritability seemed intimidating to strangers, such as young officers and their partners who fell foul of their sovereign at Windsor balls, when the King could react as any father might on finding his house cluttered with unknown people. One officer, finding himself the escort of the Prime Minister's daughter, Felicity Attlee, who, as a staunch left-winger was unhappy at such functions, and endeavouring to amuse her, took her on a tour of the Prince Consort's Suite which was open with all the lights on. Suddenly the King came in, evidently on his way to the bathroom at the end. 'What are you doing here?' His Majesty snapped. "You've no right to be here."' Discomfited, the couple retired, the Prime Minister's daughter in tears – 'he'll tell my father....'[6] On another occasion, the young man's partner was powdering her nose in the corridor when the King suddenly appeared, infuriated, and told her roundly, 'You do that kind of thing in the cloakroom. Now will you please get your coat and leave.'[7] Normally, according to Osbert Sitwell who had known him for many years, he was always 'a most kind and considerate host; his manner and manners with his guests were perfect, and he liked them to enjoy themselves'. Often, Sitwell suspected, the King would have preferred to be alone with his family, but he concealed his feelings. Sitwell recalled an occasion when he was staying at Balmoral with a large house-party which included the artist, Rex Whistler. The King had appeared to be in excellent humour, although he had been out stalking deer all day without success, walking twenty-five miles without seeing one, followed by a ghillies' ball in the evening so that it was after one o'clock when they went to bed. Half an hour later Whistler, occupying a connecting room next door to Sitwell, rushed in: 'Osbert, there's someone in the room beyond me! It's the King! I recognise his voice and he's talking to himself!' 'Well, what did he say?' 'He said: "I've never been so *tired* in my life – it's all these bloody guests!"' But the next morning at breakfast, the King was as charming to his guests as ever....'[8] To those young men, his daughters' friends whom he knew personally and his Lascelles nephews, the King appeared as exceptionally kind and courteous, going out of his way to make them feel at home. One young man, on his first royal shoot at Balmoral in 1945, missed everything on his first drive; the King came over to him from the next butt and, handing him some birds, said, 'I think these are yours....'[9]

The King, unlike most of his family, was considerate of his staff. In December 1949 Edward Ford, after a brief honeymoon with his wife, Virginia, went to Sandringham as resident Private Secretary, where he collapsed with jaundice.

The King invited his wife to Sandringham to help him convalesce and wrote him a sympathetic note in his own hand, showing an appreciation of his condition and, equally, of his work:

My dear Edward,

I hope you are not feeling too wretched being in bed & that your wife has cheered you up. She tells me that you are going to your father-in-law's house in the country, where you will soon recover.

Do please get completely well before returning to work.

Before you leave here tomorrow, you know I never really thanked you for your letter which I much appreciated.

I am glad that you like the work here, which is interesting & diverse at all times, & for my part I would like to tell you that during the last year you have acquired a real grasp of the way of the workings of this job while working with me. I have much to thank you for.

Yours very sincerely,

George R.[10]

Shooting and the countryside were the King's passion and relaxation. Out 'on the hill' at Balmoral or the Sandringham marshes, he could escape the constant stream of despatch boxes and official visitors which were a feature of his daily life in London. Even at Balmoral or Sandringham, however, he would have to work in the evening, but outdoors he was free, practising his favourite expertise in surroundings which he loved and with companions whom he chose. He had not inherited the family passion for racing, in which he was only mildly interested, although he was quite successful as an owner with Lime Kiln before the war, Sun Chariot in the Oaks at Newmarket in June 1942, Rising Light at the first post-war races at Ascot in August 1945 and Hypericum, named after a homoeopathic remedy, winner of the Thousand Guineas at Newmarket in 1946. Dutifully, because it was part of his inheritance, the King carried on the family racing traditions, keeping the Sandringham stud horses at Newmarket with Cecil Boyd-Rochfort and another string, leased from the National Stud, at Fred Darling's Beckhampton stables. He and the Queen encouraged their elder daughter's already manifest fascination with the sport. Racing remained a part of the royal ambience and Royal Ascot one of the highlights of the social season, but the King preferred his shooting where he was not 'on view' and it was not a Society event.

The King took his shooting very seriously; he had travelled a long way since the days of his father and especially his grandfather of heavy 'bags' and even heavier luncheons. The men he invited to shoot with him were people who were as knowledgeable and keen as he was, his brother, Prince Henry, his brothers-in-law, David and Michael Bowes-Lyon, friends like Lord Eldon, his Norfolk neighbours the Earl of Leicester and Harry Cator, and his Sandringham agent, Sir William Fellowes. Of the younger generation, his daughters' friends, only Lord Porchester, already an expert shot, was a regular and there was no family favouritism: his future son-in-law, Prince Philip, then only at the beginning of his shooting career, did not enjoy his lowly position on the outside of the line, as far away as possible from the experts in the centre next to the King. The King was prepared to spend four hours in a frozen kale field on a cold January morning waiting for wild pigeon, or to get up before dawn to lie in wait by a weed-fringed pond covered with a thin skin of ice for a flight of wild duck. King George v was one of the finest shots in the country; King George vi was a quick, alert shot with a faultless technique, but beyond that he was extremely knowledgeable in the ways of game, birds and animals. He planned the shoots with his keeper and he always picked up his birds himself with his dog while his keeper went further afield for the 'runners' to ensure that no bird was left wounded and half-dead. He would go out by himself or with two or three friends, as well as on the big, perfectly organized shoots, always with his favourite yellow Labradors as gun dogs, wearing his own tweed which he had designed himself. When it came to duck-shooting, he did not go in for 'blowing-up' the duck by having them driven on to the guns as his father used to— duck having been bred for shooting at Sandringham in George v's day. He belonged, thanks to the Bowes-Lyon family who introduced him to it and to Michael Bowes-Lyon's brother-in-law, Harry Cator, who owned the famous Ranworth Broad in Norfolk, to what his biographer called the 'elite' of wild-fowling (as opposed to mere mowing down of duck), 'the world of long waders and thick clothing; of punts, poles and oars; of torches and dogs hunting in the darkness; of ripples gently lapping the bows and the whispering of the wind in the rushes'.[11] Every evening during the shooting season, the King would carefully and neatly fill in his game book, the record of the day's sport not just in numbers but with technical comments on the weather and the game, his own score in woodcock always entered in red ink. His first game book entry was dated 23 December 1907; the last, dated 24 January 1952, was only a few days before his death. He was shooting with friends, keepers, staff and estate workers on an informal day in cold bright sunshine on the day before he died.

The King's other passion, a truly Windsor obession, was for things sartorial—clothes, medals, orders and decorations. Fascination with such trappings seems to have been a characteristic of the males of the family; Edward vii, George v and Edward viii were all fanatical on the subject, Queen Victoria, although neither chic nor clothes-obsessed, had laid the ground rules on this as she had on so many others connected with the science and practice of being royal. She wrote to her son, the future Edward vii, aged ten:

Dress is a trifling matter which might not be raised to too much importance in our own eyes. But it gives also the one outward sign from which people in general can and often do judge upon the *inward* state of mind and feeling of a person; for this they all see, while the other they cannot see. On that account it is of some importance particularly in persons of high rank.

This maxim was quoted by her great-grandson, the Duke of Windsor, in his *A Family Album,* a slim volume over half of whose pages (eighty-four out of

144) was devoted to clothes and tailors.[12] Clothes were a favourite topic of conversation with George V, usually in the form of a diatribe against those who dressed differently from himself, to whom he was wont to refer as 'cads', providing the battleground for continuing disagreements with his son and heir. One of George VI's younger courtiers explained this preoccupation with matters which other people might well regard as trivial as being as much a part of the royal mentality as the classic story of the princess and the pea under the mattress.

It is a different type of mind from ours ... the King, for instance, minds criticism for things that do not matter and simply ignores it when it applies to things that do. For instance he minds any suggestion of incorrect dress or deportment but does not care at all if it is suggested that he looks bored or cross or has no intellectual tastes.[13]

George VI, although not a style-setter like his elder brother, none the less gave his clothes a good deal of thought. He dressed conventionally in beautifully cut clothes and, with his slim, well-proportioned figure, wore them elegantly. He would spend hours with his tailors, Benson & Clegg, choosing cloth and fitting suits and uniforms, trying on his suits again and again until they were just right. He was interested in the symbolic significance of dress and appurtenances, particularly when it concerned uniforms. In November 1932 he addressed a four-page, handwritten letter to Lord Londonderry, then Secretary of State for Air, advocating the wearing of swords by RAF officers on ceremonial occasions, as the other two Services did. A sword, he told Londonderry, 'is the mark of an officer'.[14] Thirteen years later, while travelling to South Africa on HMS *Vanguard*, concerned at the suggested abolition of the Sam Browne belt and sword for Army officers, he expressed himself in much the same terms. The democratization of the Army, he thought, could be carried too far, with 'unhealthy results': '... the sudden abolition of what has been for many years regarded as the 2 outward and visible symbols of an officer's rank might have results which would be unexpectedly far-reaching, and not altogether healthy, both from the Army's point of view and from that of the general public. ...'[15] The Sam Browne belt and sword stayed. Only days before his death in 1952 he spent hours considering a new design for the wearing of the Garter on narrow evening trousers, 'overalls' (as opposed to the traditional knee breeches), and writing a six-page, handwritten letter to Halifax, Chancellor of the Order of the Garter, on the subject:

After much careful thought and trying out various ideas, I have devised a pair of trousers strapped at the bottom as is usual, but fuller round the seat and in front, and they are quite comfortable to sit down in. Sitting down in overalls is always uncomfortable as we know, but in this case part of the bottom strap is elastic and stretches. The old-fashioned elastic-sided plain fronted boots 'Jemimas' is the only form of footwear which looks neat and tidy ... I feel it will look very chic, as so few people are entitled to wear the Garter. ... My only one [comment] is the expense of having to buy the overall and boots ... the old proverb '*il faut souffrir pour être beau*' is more true nowadays.[16]

The King, having always had a particular interest in the Garter, had succeeded in 1946 on his own initiative in wresting control of nominations to it from the hands of the politicians, so that it had become once again what it originally had been, in the gift of the King. The King had perspicaciously seized the opportunity offered by a Labour Prime Minister to suggest this: 'I spoke to Attlee about the future K.G's [Knight of the Garter],' he wrote in his diary for 8 May 1946. 'His people are against accepting honours & most recipients would have to be of the other party. I want it non-political & in my gift. . . .' Attlee agreed – which no Conservative Prime Minister would have been likely to do – and so the Garter, together with the two other major Orders of Chivalry, the Thistle and the St Patrick, passed into the King's gift on the same basis as the Order of Merit, giving the King the right to confer the honour in consultation with, but not on advice from, his ministers. On 17 December 1946 he held the first investiture since before the Second World War, having taken the utmost pains over the wording of the ritual to stress what he saw as its historical significance in his address to the Knights:

Our Order, besides being one of Chivalry, is above all a Christian one. During the actual Investiture you will find that the Ancient Admonitions will be said as the separate emblems of the Order are presented, signifying their Christian purport. These Admonitions have been revived after many years of disuse. . . .

Among the seven new Knights on that occasion were only two political names, Lord Addison, leader of the House of Lords, as a gesture to Attlee, and the King's friend, Viscount Cranborne, the Opposition leader in the Lords, who as the heir to the Marquess of Salisbury and a man of outstandingly independent thought could hardly be considered a politician in the ordinary sense of the word. The majority could have been called 'knights' in the ancient, military sense of the term, or, as Churchill liked to put it to the King, 'paladins', Alan Brooke, Alexander, Mountbatten, Portal and Montgomery.

He adored medals and was an avid collector of them. In February 1944 he actually went so far as to have Eisenhower informed that he would 'be pleased to wear the American Service ribbon for the North Africa Campaign' so that the request could be passed on to General Marshall. When, almost two years later, he had still not received the actual medal, he caused Lascelles to write again to Eisenhower: 'His Majesty, who always wears the ribbon, has asked me to let you know that he hopes you will not forget to send him the actual Medal when it is struck.' The design was not ready until July 1947, when Eisenhower duly forwarded the King 'one of the first medals struck'.[17] He took a great personal interest in the design of the campaign medals awarded in his name; on one occasion the Duke of Windsor found him intently studying lengths of coloured silk. 'What does this remind you of?' the King asked his brother, indicating a strip of beige-coloured silk. 'Sand,' the Duke replied. 'That's just it,' the King said, pleased. 'It matches the sand out of the back of Montgomery's car. . . .' He had the ancestral eagle eye for correct dress and an encyclopaedic knowledge of his subject, even the most esoteric regimental rules such as the tradition in the Household Cavalry Regiment, known as the 'Blues', of wearing dark brown, not black, shoes with their blue dress uniforms, 'patrols'. Immediately after the war the officers of the sovereign's ceremonial escort were hastily issued with miniature sets of medals, properly embossed with the King's head on the obverse, but blank on the reverse. At Buckingham Palace that evening Lord Porchester was approached by the King. 'You're improperly dressed,' His Majesty said sternly. Porchester, panicking, began to explain about brown shoes and regimental custom. The King cut him short, 'It's nothing to do with your shoes, it's your medals,' he said, turning one round with his finger. 'Ha, ha,' he said and walked on.[18] In January 1944 it had been Montgomery's turn to fall foul of the King's sartorial punctiliousness, for his refusal to wear a general's peaked cap instead of his habitual black beret. The King told Alan Brooke to draw the General's attention to dress regulations, but received instead from the unrepentant Montgomery a lecture on 'the value of high morale throughout the Army and how it could be achieved'. Montgomery told the King that his black Royal Armoured Corps beret was 'one of his methods of building up a high morale', that all the soldiers recognised him by it, claiming that his beret was 'worth at least an Army Corps and that, while the War lasted, it was vital that he should continue to wear it'.[19] The King, in the run-up to OVERLORD, took the General's point and did not pursue the matter.

Investitures, in fact, were almost the only public ceremonies which the King seems to have viewed with equanimity and even enjoyed. On such occasions he was at his best, saying a charming, apposite word to each officer as he pinned the medal to his chest. In the long, wide, red-carpeted gallery between the Bow Room and the Grand Entrance giving on to the inner courtyard at Buckingham Palace, the King would, during the war years, hold investitures, week after week, standing for two hours at a time on a raised dais with a ramp on either side, up which 300 recipients of honours for civil and military gallantry would approach him to receive their medals or, in some cases, the tap on each shoulder with a sword signifying a knighthood. An equerry stood close beside ready to proffer the sword or a velvet cushion with the medals reposing upon it. The King's technique was so faultless that he could lay his hand on the medal each time without looking. 'If ever he failed, it was your fault.' He was very much at ease and at times could be heard humming the tune being played by the string orchestra. If he did not like the music, he might turn to the equerry and say, rather too loudly, 'For God's sake tell them not to make such a ghastly noise.' On such occasions in the latter years of his reign, he would wear make-up, upon whose advice it has proved impossible to discover. Courtiers strenuously deny that he did use 'sun tan and rouge', as was frequently reported, but the testimony of reliable witnesses, such as the French Ambassador, René Massigli, confirms it.[20]

Perhaps one of the King's principal weaknesses as a monarch was that, like his mother, he had no small talk. If he was interested, as he was in all subjects connected with war or things which he knew about, which could be as disparate as factory assembly lines or the breeding habits of game birds, he could be almost as talkative as his father. With foreign envoys whom he did not know making formal calls to present their credentials, he could be sticky. Sir Alexander Cadogan, whose task it was to present newly accredited envoys to the King, did not enjoy the experience. A typical diary entry recording such an occasion would read, 'Had three or four minutes' talk with HM before [presenting three South American ambassadors]. Very pleasant & easy. But he was sticky with the Ministers — couldn't bring himself to say a word to them & dismissed them almost at once. . . .' Cadogan later learned to prime the diplomats and, indeed, the King, 'Had to go to Palace to introduce new Venezuelan. It went fairly well; I told the V. beforehand that he must talk, and I told the King he must help the V. out with his English. So they both talked at once!'[21] Things went a great deal more easily with an African envoy who, upon receiving from the King a signed photograph of himself in a silver frame, insisted on dancing and shaking in the royal presence, which the King greatly enjoyed.

British Ambassadors, however, officially accredited as His Majesty's Representatives to foreign Heads of State, and regarded as such in a very real sense by the King, received very different treatment. Since they were usually urbane, upper-class figures with whom the King and Queen felt at home, they would be asked to lunch *en famille* at Buckingham Palace with the Queen and often one or both of the Princesses. The King would use these occasions for a private talk beforehand during which he could inform himself about the area in question, not hesitating to give his own opinions and sometimes criticisms of the Foreign Office. Talking to Sir Miles Lampson, British Ambassador in Cairo, about plans for the partition of Palestine in October 1937, for instance, he gave it as general opinion that 'Old Balfour was a silly old man; and had given (or promised to others) something already belonging to someone else!'[22] As Head of State he regarded it as his prerogative to be informed on foreign relations and, as in the case of Lindsay and the Windsor visit to the United States and in his correspondence with Halifax, to put his opinions directly to his representative.

Lord Crawford was shocked at the contrast between the treatment of diplomats, even those destined for minor posts, and the leaders of the artistic and scientific world, going so far as to call it a 'boycott of science and art by the King except in a very restricted semi-official degree' and to ask the Lord Chamberlain, Clarendon, to look into it. 'A minister sent to a small republic in South America is received in audience,' he wrote, 'but the President of the Royal Society, the Director of the British Museum, the chairman of the University Grants Commission, and so on — why never is their name or status whispered in Buckingham Palace? A whole section of British greatness and enterprise is taboo.'[23] Having thought he would be thanked for his suggestion which he had limited to a mere dozen audiences for such figures a year, he was amazed to receive a long, considered reply from the Lord Chamberlain saying that 'the King has no time for such a thing'. Anti-intellectualism and lack of interest in the arts had become a tradition at Court since the days of George v, who disliked clever men, describing them in his erratic orthography as 'eyebrows'. Helen Hardinge, descendant of the intellectual Cecils, having been crushed by Queen Mary when she attempted to argue the poetic qualities of certain books of the Bible, wrote that the Court of George v was a *'mauvais milieu'* as far as literary and artistic interests were concerned. His sons, with the exception of the Duke of Kent, carried on the family tradition; the King was quite simply uninterested and, beyond attending major exhibitions and the annual show at the Royal Academy in the line of duty, at which he would appear noticeably bored, regarded active patronage of the arts as outside his province. When it came to art, he followed his mother's precepts. Queen Mary, although more cultivated than her husband, had found family history absorbing to the exclusion of any other and a bad bust of a distant relative more worthy of regard than, say, a bust of Voltaire by Roubilliac. Nor did she have taste in paintings beyond portraits of the family. George vi, as trustee of one of the world's great art collections, took his mother's view that family connection was all. 'How many portraits are there at Buckingham Palace of Princess Caroline of Anspach?' he would ask a fledgling adviser on the royal collections as a test question. 'I am afraid I do not know, Sir.' 'But you *ought* to know.' Among the King's favourite pictures were, unsurprisingly, Gainsborough's group of the three eldest daughters of George iii, which the King hung in the Audience Room at Buckingham Palace, and the set of Gainsborough portraits of George iii's entire family, which the King arranged according to the artist's original scheme for them.

Generally, therefore, the art experts employed by the Crown did not find the King, as they did the Queen, sympathetic. Kenneth Clark, appointed in 1934 to be the Surveyor of the King's Pictures to George v, had found the new monarch 'as difficult to talk to as his mother', indeed, his initial impression of the royal couple had been that the Queen was 'not much better than the kind of person one met at a country house, and the King somewhat worse'. He quickly changed his opinion as far as the Queen was concerned, discovering that she had 'sense and good taste' in art. In fact, like many of the men subjected to the Queen's charm, he was extremely attracted by her. According to Clark's biographer, 'he might have been a little in love with her' and, 'When he talked about their romantic friendship in retrospect, he said that they saw as much of each other as they dared, adding that the King became unreasonably jealous and twice made scenes, once at Windsor Castle and again at Buckingham Palace.' The King probably thought his Surveyor's reaction to the Queen's normally mildly flirtatious manner excessive. He was very much in love with his wife and also sensitive to signs of *lèse-majesté*. At the end of a long and friendly reply to a letter from Walter Monckton, whom he addressed as 'My dear Walter', was a light reminder not to overstep the mark: 'I gave the Queen your "love and duty",' he wrote, 'at which she was both surprised and pleased. I wonder if you did not mean "loyal duty"!! Anyhow it made us laugh....'[24]

Encouraged by the Queen, however, he did not take his father's extreme line towards modern art (George v, on a visit with Clark to the National Gallery in 1934, had described Turner as a 'madman' and displayed a disconcerting desire to attack Cezanne's paintings with his cane). George vi and the Queen had agreed at the outset of their reign that they wanted to keep the monarchy in touch with as many aspects of modern life as possible and, as she told Clark, they were determined to start a collection of modern paintings. With Clark's advice she bought a Wilson Steer of Lulworth Castle, landscapes by Duncan Grant and works by younger British artists. He encouraged her to have her portrait painted by Augustus John, an idea suggested to the Queen by the artist's patron, Mrs Cazalet-Keir, and persuaded her to commission artists – including John Piper, whose brief was to do watercolours of Windsor Castle. The King's characteristic comment on seeing the finished works featuring grey wash and lowering clouds was how bad the weather must have been when Piper was painting them. The King had an extremely practical mind; on one occasion after a Toscanini concert, he asked the conductor, Sir Adrian Boult, 'When one player turns over the music for his partner and himself, does the other one play twice as loud?' Boult, taken aback, afterwards said it was the first time anyone had asked him that particular question before. The King preferred the solution of practical and mechanical problems and, according to his bbc sound engineer and broadcasting adviser, Robert Wood, he was 'very well versed mechanically and electrically', and during the war had a room at Windsor equipped for him where he could precision-finish various gun mechanisms by hand, the first monarch to do so.[25]

In fact, at Windsor during the War the King had, inadvertently, an artist-in-residence, Gerald Kelly, later President of the Royal Academy, an old Etonian Irishman of charm and talent, and brother-in-law of the satanist, Aleister Crowley. Kelly had been commissioned in 1938 by the King on Clark's recommendation to paint the huge State portraits of himself and the Queen, nine feet high and almost six feet wide, to hang in the private apartments at Windsor; however the portraits were still unfinished on the outbreak of war and were taken to Windsor Castle for safety. The artist followed them, staying with his friend, Sir Henry Marten, Princess Elizabeth's tutor and Vice-Provost of Eton, and then requesting permission for accommodation at the castle to 'apply the finishing touches'. Given a bedroom and the Grand Reception Room to work in, taking his meals with the royal Household and, in the improvised wartime arrangements, often with the King, the Queen and the two Princesses as well, Kelly dragged out 'the finishing touches' until the end of the war. It was rumoured that Kelly, like Ulysses' wife, got up at night to undo the work he had done during the day. The King, who had very much disliked having to pose in his theatrical Coronation costume comprising a full-skirted coat of violet satin with gold braid, white satin breeches and silk stockings, but had none the less frequently fulfilled his obligations to the artist, made 'mild and semi-humorous protests at the length of his guest's stay', but Kelly remained, finally completing the portraits in time to be exhibited at the Royal Academy in May

1945, for which, two months later, he received a knighthood from His Majesty.

Early in March 1942 Kelly, who by then had been two years in residence at Windsor, discussed the Court with Barrington-Ward, Dawson's successor as editor of *The Times*. He was 'eloquently critical of the old governing class' and complained particularly that 'the King is not told what he should be'.[26] In April, Lord Woolton, Minister of Food, after dining with the Queen's friend, Mrs Greville, at her suite in the Dorchester, reported his conversation with her on the same subject: 'She was telling me that the Queen had been to see her, and had told her that she was a little worried about the King's immediate entourage. She said that they wanted a little leaven to the Guards Officer mixture who are the King's private secretaries. . . .'[27] On 3 June Victor Cazalet confided to his diary a conversation he had recently had with Mrs Greville, identifying the subject of the complaints, the King's Principal Private Secretary, Alec Hardinge. 'Everyone is against A.H.,' he wrote. 'He prevents K & Q doing all sorts of things – says No to everyone. Apparently K & Q don't like him very much but it's hard to get rid of him. . . .'[28] These were the preliminary insider indications of a major upheaval unprecedented in recent Court history, the virtual dismisssal or 'resignation on grounds of ill-health' of the King's Private Secretary.

The King and Queen felt very strongly that it was important for the monarchy to keep in touch; they wanted to modernize the Court within its traditional framework and to make the overladen baroque structure bequeathed by George v and Queen Mary less rigidly formal. 'There is to be no more high-hat business,' the King had said after his North American tour. Robert Wood, who saw the King and Queen frequently during the war years, recorded how 'they liked to know what was going on', how 'the King and Queen were always anxious to know how the man in the street was getting on, how people managed. . . .' Increasingly they saw Hardinge, whose function as Private Secretary was to be the principal channel of communication between the King and the outside world and his interpreter of events, as obstructive and out of touch. One of the principal proponents of this complaint against Hardinge was the influential figure of David Bowes-Lyon, who as press officer for the Minister of Economic Warfare in the early part of the war was in charge of briefing foreign journalists and found that Hardinge kept people away from the King whom he should see, 'including American newspapermen'. As early as November 1941, Harvey, who was very pro-Hardinge as an anti-Munichois and supporter of Eden, reported that Bowes-Lyon was 'still intriguing' against him.[29]

Beyond that, there had been a behind-the-scenes personality conflict between the King and his Private Secretary. Hardinge had many excellent qualities, a first-class brain, integrity and discretion being principally among them, but he lacked two essentials for a courtier, tact and a phlegmatic temperament, both of which were a particular asset when dealing with a man as highly strung as George vi. Hardinge was himself highly strung, his physical health was not good after being wounded in the First World War and, after both stressful royal events, the abdication and his own 'resignation', he suffered breakdowns. He was a loyal and dedicated royal servant, but not an easy one. Even George V, who took criticism with a better grace than either of his elder sons, had his problems with Hardinge. 'Oh,' he would say to a courtier friend of his, 'That nephew of yours, my goodness me, I'm having trouble with him again!' Hardinge would say straight out if he thought his sovereign was wrong and would not hesitate to say something unpalatable. Edward VIII had not liked criticism of his actions, George VI and the Queen also did not take it well. There had been a major policy disagreement between them over Munich when the King, and even more strongly the Queen and David Bowes-Lyon, had been supporters of Chamberlain. Hardinge made no secret of his anti-feelings, speaking to Harvey at dinner of 'the shame of the appeasement period'; 'he is violent on the subject,' Harvey commented.[30]

There had been, from the first, friction between the King and his Secretary over ways of doing business. Hardinge, trained by Lord Stamfordham, had been accustomed to mark State papers for both George V and Edward VIII; George VI insisted on reading the whole thing himself. Hardinge resented this, as he resented the King's keeping things to himself. Under the Stamfordham system George V had, after seeing a minister, dictated a memorandum of the meeting to his Secretary; George VI would merely make a few remarks as to what had been said, keeping his own counsel. There was a fundamental divergence of style on the royal way of life. The King and Queen were determined to lead, as far as possible, the informal, aristocratic family existence they had enjoyed before their accession, which included their relations with their friends. They, therefore, insisted on writing their personal letters themselves and, as both were so busy, unanswered letters would pile up to Hardinge's frustration. An instance of the King's personal consideration was the case of Hardinge's son, who on his marriage in 1943 wrote to the King from Londonderry, where he was stationed, asking if he could borrow a small house on the Balmoral estate for his honeymoon. In the midst of the pressures of his wartime official life, the King wrote back, in his own hand and addressing the envelope himself, offering not just a cottage, but Birkhall, the house used by the royal family. The result, however, of this exercise in royal good manners was that some of the King's letters which he was determined to write himself, such as those which he often sent to Halifax in Washington, were sometimes months late. The King and Queen also liked to make impromptu visits to friends when on official tours, something which offended Hardinge's ordered mind, while the Queen's chronic unpunctuality and carelessness about hours when she was enjoying herself was agonizing to someone of the Secretary's temperament.

Hardinge's excessive punctiliousness, refusal to delegate and insistence on being the sole channel through which the King could be reached made him generally unpopular with the Palace secretariat. The last straw for his subordinate Secretaries came when he left for North Africa with the King taking the keys of the royal despatch boxes with him so that his colleagues were unable to open them to deal with business while he was away. On that trip Macmillan, as has been seen, blamed Hardinge for his lack of vision in planning the King's programme because 'he just doesn't seem to live in the modern world at all. He would have been out of date in the 1900s, and King Edward would have sacked him as outmoded then.' The fact that Hardinge's 'resignation', on 6 July 1943, took place within days of the King's return from North Africa, seems to indicate that it was immediately connected with either one or both of his failings connected with the tour. The official reason was 'ill-health', but the real reason was probably that the King, having long wanted to get rid of him took this as an opportunity to do so.

Hardinge's departure was immediately seen for what it was, an enforced one, in official circles where there was much speculation, much of it centring on the Queen's role in the affair. '. . . there has been friction for some time (beginning from Munich and Neville Chamberlain) largely caused by the Queen who was determined to get him out,' Harvey wrote of the episode, which he regarded strictly from a personal point of view as a 'grave loss' to his patron, Eden. 'The King', he added unflatteringly, was 'fundamentally a weak character and certainly rather a stupid one. The Queen is a strong one out of a reactionary stable.'[31]

Whatever role the Queen may or may not have played in the Hardinge affair, the King's feelings towards his former Private Secretary, as he revealed them to Cadogan a few weeks later, were not friendly. The King, who had always reacted strongly to any suggestion that he was 'run' by the courtiers or the politicians, had clearly seen Hardinge as overbearing and obstructive. 'He was sorry for A. Hardinge, but burst out with complaints,' Cadogan wrote in an unpublished section of his diary. 'A.H. had always strong & unhelpful views what was the use of suggesting anything to anyone who, one knew, would always say "No".'[32] The parting had clearly been a bitter and painful one; an intimate friend of the King's spoke of Hardinge's 'hysteria on dismissal'.[33] As far as the King was concerned, Hardinge became a non-person after his traumatic departure; he became angry if anyone tried to plead his case, his loyalty, his devotion to the family. Hardinge was rarely asked to the Palace after his dismissal and would ask his successor why, to the latter's embarrassment. 'The King can't stand the sight of him and won't have him in the house,' it was reported. Years later, after the King's death, there was a rapprochement when Queen Elizabeth visited Hardinge when he was dying of cancer in 1960.

The older courtiers, such as Hardinge and Lascelles, accustomed to the male-dominated Court of George v, where Stamfordham and even the King's valet, Howlett, had more influence over the sovereign than the beloved but repressed Queen, resented the partnership between George vi and his wife as something from which they were excluded. As one royal biographer put it, Lascelles, Hardinge's successor as Principal Private Secretary, 'found her a rival and sometimes obstructive influence in all that touched the Sovereign'. In cases such as the dismissal of Hardinge, they, therefore, tended to exaggerate that influence.

The Queen was a strong personality, with often concealed but deeply held views. She was also a highly visible figure, whose social abilities made public and private functions run smoothly. She had now established her public image as firmly as Queen Mary had, adopting her own distinctive style of dress which had a great deal to do with her preference for furs, ostrich feathers and hyacinth blue and very little to do with fashion. She was now entering middle age and had become distinctly plump, which in no way seemed to lessen her attraction. American reporters noticed that she skilfully avoided appearing with a double chin by holding her head well up and out and called her dress sense more like that of 'a retired actress than a queen', but all of them had to admit she radiated star quality. *Time*'s London correspondent, Alfred Wright, tracking the royal family at the height of the social season in June 1946, reported on the opening of an exhibition of American art at the Tate Gallery by the King and Queen:

Instinctively my attention was first attracted by the Queen. She was not beautiful and she was not wearing a spectacular get-up. It is just that she is the real star of the team.

She has a superb complexion; everyone notices it right away. She moves with the unselfconscious ease of a person who knows she is alone in a room and won't be disturbed. When someone is talking to her, she concentrates completely on what he is saying, despite any & all distractions. During all the time I watched her the Queen maintained a remarkable expression on her face – as if this was an experience she had been awaiting months, and it had turned out better than she hoped. . . .

This, the showbusiness side of royalty, was the Queen's public role; in private she saw it was her duty to be supportive and protective of the King, but she did not initiate policy or interfere in the political side of the King's affairs, nor did she make any attempt to create her own clique of courtiers. The King's servants remained very much the King's.

The King found Hardinge's successor, Tommy Lascelles, far easier to get on with, although if he and the Queen were seeking a change from the Guards officer mentality Lascelles would hardly have been the obvious choice. If he had not actually served in the Guards nor been at Eton or Harrow, he was deeply imbued with the traditional background of his class and had bitterly resented having been educated at Marlborough, which, as a school, he had regarded as beneath a person of his social connections as a grandson of the 4th Earl of Harewood and a cousin of the 6th Earl, Princess Mary's husband. He belonged to the intellectual generation immediately preceding the First World War at Oxford, where, again to his disappointment, he had attended not Christ Church but Trinity, and was, like Lord Esher at the Courts of Edward vii and George v, a highly cultivated man with an intense love of literature and a writer *manqué*, qualities which contrasted oddly with serving a master whose favourite reading was a treatise on the Resurrection. He was not, as most people were, seduced by the Queen's charm and would have penetrated any intellectual pretensions which she might have had. Mark Bonham-Carter, a friend of Princess Margaret, called him a 'stuffed shirt' and Peter Townsend, whose aspirations to the Princess's hand Lascelles was to greet with the famous remark, 'You must be mad or bad or both,' found him 'an Edwardian figure'. Lascelles confined his comments on his employers and his personal opinions to his diaries and his intimate friends, as outlets for confidences which were surprisingly and refreshingly indiscreet. Lascelles was a professional courtier, a man who had subordinated his intelligence to his *métier* or at least made it appear that he had. A colleague said of him:

Lascelles disliked most of the flummeries of the Court and his real interests were in literature, of which he had a very considerable knowledge, and public affairs, but he was very much an interpreter of the King's wishes and an excellent rapporteur to him about the political scene. . . .[34]

For the King, life was made a great deal easier; there were no more arguments, no more obstruction. 'He could say anything to Lascelles. . . .' Lascelles did not answer back.

The royal desire to dilute the Court's prevailing Guards officer mentality did not—with one notable exception which was to have momentous consequences for the family—go far beyond getting rid of Hardinge. The Master of the Household, Joey Legh, known to his intimates as 'Babe', had a typical Guards officer's languid manner, moving and speaking slowly and deliberately, so much so that ex-King Alfonso of Spain once asked Lascelles, 'when did Leg [*sic*] have his last stroke?' Macmillan, meeting him on the King's staff in North Africa, remarked, 'Joey Legh, although looking quite half-witted, is not so,' and the sleepy manner concealed considerable energy, efficiency and a prodigious memory for detail and for faces, a kind heart and cool judgement. He had a fund of stories of his experiences with both royal brothers, such as the occasion when as equerry to the then Prince of Wales touring Australia and dressed in the Windsor uniform of dark blue tailcoat with brass buttons, he had slipped outside after dinner to relieve himself only to be confronted as he tried to reenter the house by a furious Australian giant bellowing: 'How many more times must I say: WAITERS OUTSIDE!' Arriving at Boulogne on the King's visit to the BEF in December 1939, Legh, who had been 'silently and unobtrusively' seasick on the voyage over, was sent ashore at Boulogne to escort the French admiral and a posse of French generals aboard the destroyer to meet the King. The destroyer had two very similar-looking hatches within a few feet of each other and Legh led his party through the wrong one. Some of the French generals had considerable difficulty in squeezing through the hatch and negotiating the steep iron ladder with their spurs and swords. After a short time to the amazement of those on deck, Legh reappeared still leading the generals, all somewhat out of breath, and disappeared through the other hatch. 'What had happened', wrote an eyewitness, 'was that Joey, on opening what he thought was the door to the Ward Room where the King was waiting, discovered the Warrant Officers' lavatory. He was absolutely unperturbed and probably to this day the French Generals think that this is the normal ritual of going aboard a British Battleship!'[35] Legh amused the King, who liked him and trusted his judgement; he once said that of all his Household 'when it came down to really personal matters he trusted Joey's advice more than anybody else's'.[36] The King with his fierce quick temper was not always an easy man to handle, but Legh could do it. 'Joey could say things to the King nobody else could,' a colleague said of him. Once, out shooting, the King accidentally peppered one of the beaters; nobody dared say anything except Legh who had no hesitation in telling him quietly, 'Sir, you realize you've shot x. You'd better give him something.'[37]

The two younger members of the King's post-war Secretariat were both ex-Guards officers and old Etonians with Establishment backgrounds. Michael Adeane, after attending Cambridge and a spell as aide-de-camp to Lord Tweedsmuir in Canada, had become an Assistant Private Secretary in 1937 and left to do his wartime service in the Coldstream Guards, returning to the Palace in 1946. As the grandson of Lord Stamfordham, he had been literally born to the job. Edward Ford's father had been headmaster of Harrow and Dean of York, his mother a daughter of a Bishop of Winchester; he had a distinguished academic record as a scholar at Eton and New College, Oxford, an unsatisfactory stint as tutor to King Farouk of Egypt, and a brief practice as a barrister before wartime service with the Grenadier Guards. Adeane and Ford were of a different generation and outlook to Hardinge, Lascelles and Legh, but their backgrounds, particularly in Adeane's case, were very much in the Palace tradition. In March 1944 the first real outsider joined the Household ranks as equerry to the King, breaking the centuries-old mould of appointments drawn from the ranks of the aristocracy and from a narrow circle of interrelated families. He was thirty years old, a brave, much-decorated and exceptionally handsome Battle of Britain pilot. His name was Peter Townsend and his appointment, intended originally for a duration of three months, was to last ten years.

Townsend's appointment was at the King's initiative, an imaginative gesture designed to honour the Service which had saved the country but which was still not represented at Court, where the two senior Services had hitherto held exclusive sway. The King's original idea, as Chief of the Air Staff, Air Chief Marshal Sir Charles 'Peter' Portal, told Townsend, had been to change the personal basis upon which equerries had hitherto been chosen and to widen the net by appointing temporary equerries who would be picked not for their personal connections but for their fighting record. 'If you don't find the idea particularly revolting,' Portal continued, 'I propose to recommend you for the job of equerry to His Majesty. The appointment will be for three months.' 'We're made,' was the reaction of Townsend's pretty and socially ambitious wife, Rosemary, but, as Townsend himself wryly recorded, the appointment was to be the un-making of their marriage.

Townsend's background was the middle classes which were the backbone of the King's Empire. His father, educated at Haileybury and the Royal Military College, Sandhurst, had for years been a colonial administrator in Burma. Townsend had followed his father to Haileybury, where, as a fifteen-year-old schoolboy, he had watched nervously as a stammering Duke of York opened their dining hall. A real passion for flying had led him to Cranwell, followed by a commission in the RAF, and by 1940 he was a senior pilot, leading 'B' Flight of Hurricanes in No. 43 Squadron (known as Kate Meyrick's Own after the owner of the famous London watering-hole, the 43). He had played a leading part in the Battle of Britain, being responsible for many 'kills', had been shot down twice and, after twenty months of continual day and night operations, had been grounded with nervous exhaustion. He had made a lightning wartime marriage after a whirlwind romance with Rosemary Pawle, a brigadier's daughter, and already had one son.

The King and Townsend struck up an instant rapport, from the moment when, in Townsend's phrase, Legh ushered the Group-Captain, straight 'out of the cockpit into the Court', to be presented to the King in the green-carpeted Regency Room at Buckingham Palace. 'The King did not try, or even need, to put me at my ease,' Townsend wrote in an autobiography charged with emotional memories, '... the humanity of the man and his striking simplicity came across warmly, unmistakably ... sometimes he hesitated in his speech, and then I felt drawn towards him, to help keep up the flow of words. I knew myself the agonies of a stammerer.'[38] They had many qualities and characteristics in common, not least of which was a congenital shyness and a tendency to a stammer. A superior officer once described Townsend's shyness as 'a reluctance to attempt anything which might make him noticeable', a remark which could equally well have been applied to the King. Like the King's his was a tense and inhibited nature, which found expression in athletic prowess; he was a sensitive, expert pilot and later became a good horseman and a proficient stalker. Like the King, he was a religious man, with a deep appreciation of the beauties of Church of England ritual and a fondness for biblical allusions and quotations which could be made to have a double meaning. The suggestion that there was an element of the father–son relationship between the King and his equerry may have some foundation; certainly Townsend loved the King unreservedly and was able to 'manage' him in his nervous moments with the same understanding shown by the King's family.

The King's relationship with his family was central to his life; indeed, he would have regarded the warmth and closeness between 'us four' as an achievement on a par with his success in his public role. Their ease and happiness together was so noticeable that it was remarked upon by most visitors to the King's homes. Alan Brooke, whose own family life was equally important to him, noted in his diary after a shooting weekend at Appleton in January 1944 that 'the King and Queen and their two daughters provide one of the very best examples of English family life. A thoroughly close-knit and happy family all wrapped up in each other....'[39] It could hardly have been a greater contrast to the King's own early life with his parents and it is to the King's great credit that he did not, as many parents who have had an unhappy childhood so often do, repeat the pattern of his own upbringing. It seems that the King and Queen deliberately set out to create a family atmosphere which was closer to that of Glamis than to York Cottage.

One result of the King's determination that his children should not suffer, as he had, the feeling of discrimination and distinction between the heir and the second child, was that the two Princesses were treated in exactly the same way and as if there were not over four years' difference in age between them. The policy made for a happy family atmosphere, without strains, jealousies or sibling rivalries, but it had the side effect of making Princess Elizabeth young for her age (although this may have been also an inherited Windsor characteristic) and Princess Margaret precocious. On 26 April 1944 Princess Elizabeth had reached her majority with her eighteenth birthday and was of an age when she could accede to the throne, while her sister Princess Margaret, aged not yet fourteen, was still a schoolgirl. Yet they kept the same hours, were dressed the same and treated the same. The previous year Chips Channon, attending the Thanksgiving Service at St Paul's in May 1943, had noted that the seventeen-year-old Princess Elizabeth and the twelve-year-old Princess Margaret 'were dressed alike in blue which made them seem like little girls'.

'Poor darlings, they have never had any fun yet,' the King wrote in his diary for VE-Day, 8 May 1945, by which he meant that the war years had severely limited his daughters' social life. They had spent most of their time at Windsor with their nursery entourage consisting of the Queen's former nurse, Alla, their governess, Marion Crawford, and Princess Elizabeth's maid and later dresser, Bobo Macdonald. Although Princess Elizabeth, according to law, registered at the Windsor Labour Exchange after her sixteenth birthday in 1942, the King had still considered her too young to leave her governess, although, in view of the by now virtual certainty that she would succeed to the throne, she was rather better educated than she might otherwise have been, taking lessons in history and the constitution from the Vice-Provost of Eton, Sir Henry Marten. Otherwise the two Princesses were brought up as nice upper-class girls, not over-educated but with good habits and good manners towards guests, servants and animals. It was not until the spring of 1945, just a few months before the war ended, that the King yielded to his elder daughter's pleas to be allowed to 'join up'. As No. 230873, Second Subaltern Elizabeth Alexandra Mary Windsor, she was enrolled in the ATS (Auxiliary Territorial Service) at Camberley, and chauffeured over from Windsor every day to take part in a course of vehicle maintenance. She had scarcely completed her course when the war ended and with it her limited involvement in life outside the Palace circle.

Windsor Castle during the war presented a glum appearance, with chandeliers taken down and windows blacked out; the Princesses' lives there, however, although secluded, were not dull. The King and Queen took care to include their daughters as much as possible even when they had official guests. Princess Elizabeth would almost always be present when the King and Queen invited people to lunch or tea at Buckingham Palace, often Princess Margaret as well. Like most people in the war they had to make their own entertainment; at Windsor at Christmas in 1940 it had started with a simple nativity play; from then on they started a tradition of pantomimes produced by the two Princesses with scripts written by the headmaster of the royal school, *Cinderella*, *Aladdin* (which provided an opportunity for topical and uncomplimentary digs at the Japanese) and *Old Mother Red Riding Boots*. Hoary old jokes and costumes made out of old clothes and curtains were the order of the day and the King and Queen would invite friends to the performances. Princess Elizabeth decorated the hall with pantomime pictures hung in the great gilt frames from the Waterloo Chamber, whose paintings of figures of the Napoleonic Wars had been taken out for safety. When the war ended and the paintings were returned to their frames the King decided that the pictures of Aladdin, Mother Goose and Cinderella should remain in the frames underneath George III, George IV and the Duke of Wellington, as a secret joke and a memento of pantomime days. On one occasion he arranged a royal command performance of his favourite radio comedy programme, *ITMA*, at Windsor for Princess Elizabeth's birthday in 1942.[40]

The King adored his daughters. He took a particular pride in Princess Elizabeth, whose character and dignity evidently fitted her for the post she would now inevitably occupy. Even when she was only four or five years old he had liked to compare her with Queen Victoria, saying to Osbert Sitwell one night, 'From the first moment of talking, she showed so much character that it was impossible not to wonder whether history would not repeat itself.'[41] Years later, Lady Airlie, who drove up from Badminton with Queen Mary in March 1942 for Princess Elizabeth's confirmation, also saw the resemblance. 'The carriage of her head was unequalled, and there was about her that indescribable something which Queen Victoria had.' At the age of eighteen she already had a sense of what was properly due to Kings. Talking of her grandfather, King George V, she said, 'His manner was very abrupt; some people thought he was being rude.' When Townsend, to whom she was speaking, replied that he rather liked people like that, because you could always be rude back to them, she retorted, 'Yes, but you can't very well be rude to the King of England.'[42] She was, Lady Airlie wrote, her father's 'constant companion in shooting, walking, riding – in fact in everything. His affection for her was touching....' Princess Elizabeth was very like her father, with the same shyness, sense of duty and enjoyment of country life. Throughout her childhood and girlhood observers commented on her 'quiet simplicity', 'unselfishness', 'niceness'. Harold Nicolson, meeting her just before her eighteenth birthday, called her 'a clear, nice girl with a most lovely skin'. Like her father, however, she did not shine on social occasions.

Princess Margaret was entirely different. High-spirited and amusing she was spoiled and indulged as an *enfant terrible*, an image to which she continued to play up for the rest of her life. While Princess Elizabeth had inherited her shy, steady honourable character from her father, Princess Margaret had her mother's wit and ability to amuse and to mimic people. She also sang and played the piano with talent and spirit and would be the life and soul of the party. Queen Mary, who perhaps saw the younger Princess's failings better than her parents did, none the less found her irresistibly funny. Even the courtiers, who, as a whole, did not like Princess Margaret, admitted that she was from a child '*very amusing*', '*very* attractive'. Said one:

She was a wicked little girl, there were moments when I'd have given anything to have given her the hell of a slap. She really was *maddening* very often. The Queen was always much the nicest, no question about it, but Princess Margaret was very attractive, collected the men better than the Queen did. She played the piano, amused people for whole evenings, ran the whole thing really. They spoiled her. They adored her; the King used to look at her as if he couldn't believe anybody could be so much fun. But I think he fully realised that much as he admired Princess Margaret – he said something once that made it quite clear – that he realised that the Queen was the best of the two. . . .[43]

With a wife and two daughters whom he adored, the King had a perfect quartet, whose inevitable break-up he dreaded and, by the time Princess Elizabeth reached her eighteenth birthday, he was made formally aware of what he must already have suspected, that his daughter was in love with and wanted to marry her cousin, Prince Philip of Greece, whom she had first met at Dartmouth in July 1939. Prince Philip, born in Corfu in 1921, was now at twenty-three a lieutenant in the British Navy with a dashing war record. He was exceptionally handsome, tall, blond, blue-eyed and self-confident. He had, moreover, royal blood in his veins and was, through his father, Prince Andrew of Greece, the King's second cousin. Prince Andrew was the son of King George I of Greece and, therefore, the nephew of Queen Alexandra and the grandson of King Christian IX of Denmark. His mother was Princess Alice of Battenberg, a great-grand-daughter of Queen Victoria, and sister of Lord Louis Mountbatten. The Battenbergs, however, had genealogical flaws in their ascendance which rendered them imperfectly princely, a fact which Mountbatten strove to conceal. Their grandmother Julia Hauke, was a commoner of Dutch–German–Polish descent and was the morganatic wife of Prince Alexander of Hesse, who was himself illegitimate, although recognized by his putative father, the Grand Duke of Hesse.[44]

Prince Philip was, like all the Greek royal family except those who had managed to marry money, extremely poor, but that hardly mattered when Princess Elizabeth was the greatest heiress in Europe. His parents were separated, but not scandalously so. His father, whom Prince Philip greatly resembled in looks, had fought at the head of the Greek Army in Asia Minor, been condemned to death and almost executed but for British intervention, and had then lived the dilettante life of an exile, first in Paris and then in Monte Carlo, discreetly supported by his brother and other well-wishers; he had died there in 1944. His mother, who had become totally deaf and extremely religious, lived in Athens in conditions which Macmillan, who visited her there in October 1944, described as 'humble, not to say somewhat squalid', which he attributed to her English birth (she was born at Windsor Castle) and her 'unequivocal loyalties', which he contrasted with the more Germanophile tendencies of some of the other ladies connected with the Greek royal family. Unlike her dashing husband, Princess Andrew was, said Macmillan, 'rather blowsy, frumpish and very Hausfrau', not very intelligent and 'seemed nervous and clumsy'. She had stayed in Greece throughout the German occupation working for children's relief, and, although she made no complaint of poverty, when Macmillan had pressed her, she did admit to being short of food. Prince Philip himself, seven years younger than the youngest of his four sisters, had lived a peripatetic life, spending holidays with his royal relations, living in Paris until his parents separated in 1930, then as a virtual orphan in England with his maternal uncle George, Marquess of Milford Haven, and his wife, Nadejda, Countess Torby, until the death of Milford Haven in 1938, when he came under the wing of his other uncle, Lord Louis Mountbatten.

The King, however, did not view the prospect of his eldest daughter's marriage to Prince Philip with unqualified approval. The King and Queen had not, according to a courtier, been initially impressed. 'The family were at first horrified when they saw that Prince Philip was making up to Princess Elizabeth. They felt he was rough, ill mannered, uneducated and would probably not be faithful....'[45] As they had got to know him, they changed their opinion. Prince Philip with his naval background, his 'chaffing' sense of humour, honesty and independence of mind and love of the open air and sport, was very much the King's type of man. Having no real home in England, Prince Philip used to visit Windsor on leave from the Navy and when in March 1944, Prince Philip's first cousin, King George of Greece, bravely raised the subject of an engagement, the King's response was, although negative as far as marriage was concerned, personally favourable. 'We both think she is too young for that now, as she has never met any young men of her own age,' he wrote to Queen Mary. 'I like Philip. He is intelligent, has a good sense of humour & thinks about things in the right way.... We are going to tell George that P. had better not think any more about it for the present.' The King understandably felt that Princess Elizabeth, whose recent eighteenth birthday had presumably prompted the King of Greece to raise the question, had led a secluded life in wartime and needed time to look around and make up her mind before taking what was, for a future Queen, a hugely important step, of marriage to the first young man she had fallen in love with at the age of thirteen.

He liked the idea of his daughter returning to tradition in marrying a man of royal blood, something which must have seemed unlikely in view of the war, which had, as in 1918, cut off the supply of German princelings as eligible candidates. Prince Philip, as a naval officer fighting on the British side, and as a royal relation, 'thought about things in the right way'. The King had, however, a sense that Mountbatten and the Greek relations were applying too much pressure, trying to railroad the marriage through. Mountbatten had been the patron of the meeting at Dartmouth and, when Greece joined the war in 1940, had been considerably concerned that Philip's cousin, King George of Greece, might expect him, having newly passed out of Dartmouth, to join the Greek

Navy, which would not have helped either his nephew's naval career or his prospects of marrying Princess Elizabeth. King George, however, was to be Mountbatten's ally in pressing Prince Philip's claims; as early as January 1941 Chips Channon, on a visit to Athens, found the subject openly discussed among the Greek royal family. After a conversation with Prince Philip's aunt, Princess Nicholas, mother of Princess Marina, he met Prince Philip looking 'extraordinarily handsome' at a cocktail-party. 'He is to be our Prince Consort', Channon noted, 'and that is why he is serving in our Navy.' In 1944, the year of Princess Elizabeth's eighteenth birthday, Mountbatten and the Greeks made not one but two *démarches* towards advancing Prince Philip's cause. After King George of Greece had been rebuffed on the engagement front in March, Mountbatten returned to the charge in August with the idea that Prince Philip should change his Greek nationality for British citizenship as a first step and, after discussions with the King, flew to Cairo on 23 August to put the idea to his nephew, in Alexandria with his ship, and to the Greek King. Even before he arrived there, George VI sent a warning shot across his bows. 'I have been thinking the matter over since our talk', he wrote to Mountbatten on 10 August, 'and I have come to the conclusion that we are going too fast.' Mountbatten should confine his talks with George of Greece to the question of citizenship only. Mountbatten evidently took the hint to rein in family enthusiasm. 'Philip entirely understood that the proposal [British citizenship] was not connected with any question of marrying Lilibet,' he wrote to his mother on 28 August, '. . . though there is no doubt that he would very much like to one of these days.' Six months later, on 9 February 1945, he strongly advised his sister, Prince Philip's mother, not to raise the subject with the King and Queen; 'the best hopes are to let it happen—if it will—without parents interfering. The young people appear genuinely devoted and I think after the war it is very likely to occur.'[46]

Prince Philip himself pleaded humorously with his uncle to moderate his enthusiasm. 'Please, I beg of you, not too much advice in an affair of the heart', he wrote, 'or I shall be forced to do the wooing by proxy.' Mountbatten's pressure was counter-productive rather than otherwise; he was not as popular at the Palace as he liked to think, particularly with the Queen and Princess Elizabeth herself, who both thought that he was too pushy and tried to take advantage of his family connection with the King. It was a standing joke in Whitehall that he could never leave a meeting without murmuring that he was expected at the Palace; he did not hesitate to drop the King's name when he thought it might benefit him nor to enlist the King's help on subjects close to his heart, honours, titles, commands and his wife's trust funds. The King himself was fond of his cousin, liked swapping naval stories and jokes with him, and appreciated his undoubted qualities of leadership and drive and the skill with which he had handled the huge tasks which he had been given. He did not, however, take Mountbatten at his own estimation. Unburdening himself to the King about his great enemy, the French General de Lattre de Tassigny, in 1949,

Montgomery had summed up the General's shortcomings in the most pithy manner, describing his as 'the French equivalent of Dickie Mountbatten'. The monarch said nothing and did not look amused. Montgomery beat a hasty retreat to confess to Lascelles that he had 'dropped a tremendous brick'. Lascelles had reassured him by roaring with laughter, 'Don't you worry,' he said. 'The Monarch has no illusions whatever about dear cousin Dickie!'[47]

In the end the King dropped his objections in the face of the couple's obvious love for each other and, when the subject was broached at Balmoral in the late summer of 1946, he agreed on condition that they should wait until Princess Elizabeth was twenty-one and the family had completed their first – and last – overseas trip together to South Africa in the early months of 1947. In March while they were still abroad it was announced that Prince Philip had become a naturalized British subject, dropping the title of Prince. Since the Greek royal family had no family name apart from their former one, Schleswig-Holstein-Sonderburg-Glücksburg, which was both clumsy and too Teutonic sounding to be desirable at the time, and since it derived from the House of Oldenburg, it was tentatively suggested that this might be Anglicized to 'Oldcastle', but Prince Philip decided to take his uncle's name Mountbatten. From then on he was to be Philip Mountbatten RN. The King could hold out no longer; on 10 July 1947 the engagement was announced from Buckingham Palace:

It is with the greatest pleasure that the King and Queen announce the betrothal of their dearly beloved daughter The Princess Elizabeth to Lieutenant Philip Mountbatten, RN, son of the late Prince Andrew of Greece and Princess Andrew (Princess Alice of Battenberg), to which union the King has gladly given his consent.

But did he 'gladly' give his consent? Although knowing in his heart of hearts that his daughter's marriage was not only a love match but an eminently suitable one, he felt the coming separation from his daughter and the inevitable break-up of the family quartet more than most men. After the wedding he was to write Princess Elizabeth one of the most touching and revealing letters which any father could have written:

... I was so proud of you & thrilled at having you so close to me on our long walk in Westminster Abbey, but when I handed your hand to the Archbishop I felt that I had lost something very precious. You were so calm & composed during the Service & said your words with such conviction, that I knew everything was all right.

I am so glad you wrote & told Mummy that you think the long wait before your engagement & the long time before the wedding was for the best. I was rather afraid that you had thought I was being hard-hearted about it. I was so anxious for you to come to South Africa as you knew. Our family, us four, the 'Royal Family' must remain together with additions of course at suitable moments!! I have watched you grow up all these years with pride under the skilful direction of Mummy, who as you know is the most marvellous person in the World in my eyes, & I can, I know, always count on you, & now Philip, to help us in our work. Your leaving us has left a great blank in our lives but do remember that your old home is still yours & do come back to it as much & as

often as possible. I can see that you are sublimely happy with Philip which is right but don't forget us is the wish of
Your ever loving & devoted
PAPA

The wedding was to be at Westminister Abbey on 20 November in the depths of a grey, austerity, post-war winter. To the people of Great Britain and the Empire, however, it was, as Churchill put it, 'a flash of colour on the hard road we have to travel'. It was a true fairytale, the virginal princess and the handsome prince who had been through many trials imposed by his father-in-law, the King, to win her hand. Wedding presents showered in from all over the world including literally hundreds of pairs of nylon stockings, a valued gift in those days of clothes rationing, and an object which a disgusted Queen Mary identified as Gandhi's loin-cloth. It was simply a piece of cloth which the Mahatma, at Mountbatten's suggestion, had woven himself on his famous spinning-wheel, but Queen Mary, who was not favourably disposed to Gandhi in any case, would not be persuaded it was not his celebrated symbol. 'Such an indelicate gift.... What a horrible thing!' she exclaimed on seeing it on display with the other wedding presents at St James's Palace. Prince Philip bravely argued with her, 'I don't think it's horrible. Gandhi is a wonderful man; a very great man.' Queen Mary moved on in silence. The next day, when there was another royal tour of the presents, Princess Margaret darted ahead and hid the offending object behind some other presents.

Princess Elizabeth's wedding dress was magnificent, a *tour de force* by Norman Hartnell of ivory silk satin (derived, it was announced to a xenophobic nation, from Nationalist Chinese silkworms, thus avoiding the embarrassment of fascist enemy silkworms from Italy or Japan), with garlands of white York roses embroidered in raised pearls and ears of corn in crystal. Before the wedding the King made his daughter and her fiancé Lady and Knight of the Garter, created Philip a Royal Highness and bestowed upon him high-sounding titles:

I am giving the Garter to Lilibet next Tuesday, November 11th [he wrote to Queen Mary] so that she will be senior to Philip, to whom I am giving it on November 19th. I have arranged that he shall be created a Royal Highness & that the titles of his peerage will be: Baron Greenwich, Earl of Merioneth & Duke of Edinburgh.... It is a great deal to give a man all at once, but I know Philip understands his new responsibilities on his marriage to Lilibet.

Apart from this, the wedding celebrations were in keeping with the prevalent austerity. There was a wedding breakfast for 150 at Buckingham Palace, but Princess Alice, Countess of Athlone, noted that it was 'simpler than usual because the nation was still on rations'. The speeches, too, were short, the King and Queen remembering how bored they had been with the lengthy orations at their wedding nearly a quarter of a century before. The closest link with the past was provided by the bunches of white heather and sprigs of myrtle grown from the wedding bouquet of Queen Victoria which decorated the table. After the reception the newly married couple drove through cheering crowds in an open carriage, hot-water bottles and Princess Elizabeth's favourite corgi hidden under blankets, to take the train for Broadlands, Mountbatten's house in Hampshire, where they were to spend their honeymoon.

The wedding was attended by a sprinkling of royalty, a good many of whom had lost their thrones: the King and Queen of Denmark, the Kings of Norway, Romania and Iraq, the King and Queen of Yugoslavia, the Queen of the Hellenes, the Princess Regent and Prince Bernhard of the Netherlands, the Prince Regent of Belgium, the Crown Prince and Princess of Sweden, the Count and Countess of Barcelona, Queen Helen of Romania, Queen Ena of Spain, Prince Jean and Princess Elizabeth of Luxembourg, and the Duchess of Aosta. There were notable absentees and the gaps in the guest list reflected the problems of royalty in the post-war period. King Victor Emmanuel III, forced by the Allies to abdicate his throne because of his co-operation with the Italian fascists, was not present. Nor was his more innocent son and successor, Umberto, whose chaotic wedding as Prince of Piedmont King George had attended in 1930 and been deeply offended by lapses in protocol. Another royal absentee was King Leopold III of the Belgians, still an exile from his country and embroiled in bitter quarrels with socialist politicians; the Belgian royal family was represented by his brother, Prince Charles, now the Regent. Prince Paul of Yugoslavia and Princess Olga, still in exile in South Africa although comforted by the King and Queen's recent secret visit to them, were not there. The most notable family absentees, however, were the Duke of Windsor, who was not invited and supposed not to reveal the fact, and the Princess Royal, who allegedly stayed away in protest at her brother's omission, giving ill-health as the reason although she was seen to attend a public function two days later.[48]

The most delicate problem for the King concerned his, and indeed the bridegroom's, German relations. With the war a recent memory and in view of the socialist temper of the country, it was thought better not to remind the country of the royal family's German or fascist relations. The numerous descendants of Queen Victoria's 'royal mob' were not invited, including the bridegroom's three surviving sisters, all of whom had married German princes. Prince Philip's sister Cecilie, married to the Hereditary Grand Duke of Hesse, had been killed with her husband in a plane crash near Ostend in 1937, but Princess Margarita, wife of Gottfried of Hohenlohe-Langenburg, Princess Theodora, married to the Margrave of Baden, and Princess Sophie, widow of Prince Christopher of Hesse and now married to Prince George of Hanover, were all very much alive. This was a common problem for European royalty in the immediate post-war period; the former Princess Frederica of Hanover, now Queen of Greece since the death of George II in April 1947, had had four brothers fighting on the German side in the Second World War. The Hesse family, close relations of George VI, were in a particularly delicate position. Philipp of Hesse had been the go-between for Hitler with Mussolini, but his wife Mafalda died in Ravensbruck concentration camp (killed in an Allied bombing raid), where she had been interned by Hitler in revenge for her father, the King of Italy', turncoat to the Allies in 1943. Prince Christopher of Hesse, husband of Princess Sophie, Prince Philip's youngest sister, had died as a Luftwaffe pilot fighting in Italy; an enthusiastic Nazi sympathizer, he had frequently been heard declaring how much he would like to bomb Buckingham Palace. Princess Marina's sister, Elisabeth, was also not invited; her husband, Count Charles Theodore Toerring-Jettenbach, had also sympathized with the late regime. Most reprehensible from the British point of view was the Eton-educated Duke of Saxe-Coburg and Gotha, a grandson of Queen Victoria through his father, Leopold, Duke of Albany, and brother of Princess Alice, Countess of Athlone. As a declared Nazi his estates had been subsequently confiscated. A file in the Public Record Office reads 'Saxe-Coburg-Gotha: denazification Duke and guardianship grandson'. It is closed to public inspection as is an entire file relating to the interests of the royal family in the Saxe-Coburg properties in Austria and Germany. Both are files for the year 1947, the year of Princess Elizabeth's wedding.

The year 1947 was, in fact, that of the King's maximum preoccupation with the potentially embarrassing consequences of his family's relationship with Germany. It was a concern which had been growing since April 1945, when signals from US General Courtney Hodge's First Army in the Harz mountain region of Germany, an area designated for Russian occupation, alerted a team of Anglo-American experts to the existence of German official archives deposited in various locations and caches there. Four hundred and eighty-five tons of documents and sixty tons of books were then sent, as they were found, to a huge castle at Marburg for examination by the team headed by Colonel 'Tommy' Thomson, Assistant Librarian and senior translator of the Foreign Office, and Dr W.R. Perkins of the State Department. Subsequently, upon a tip-off from Karl Loesch, an assistant to Hitler's chief interpreter, Paul Schmidt, Thomson was led to a spot in the Thuringia Wald where Loesch and Schmidt had buried microfilms of Foreign Ministry files in a tin box wrapped in a torn mackintosh. Among thirty rolls of microfilm copies of files from the office of the State Secretary, Ernst von Weizsäcker, was an extensive collection entitled 'German-British Relations', which included a volume on the Duke and Duchess of Windsor, later dubbed the 'Marburg File'. A month later Thomson dug up in the same area a large wooden box containing Schmidt's personal papers. Among the records of Hitler's conversations with foreign statesmen one was noticeably absent; there was no transcript of the conversation between the Duke of Windsor and Hitler on the former's visit to Germany in October 1937. The contents of the Marburg File, however, which included an account of the Duke of Windsor's activities in Lisbon in July 1940, were considered sensitive enough to be abstracted from Marburg in complete secrecy on Eisenhower's orders and taken to his SHAEF Headquarters.[49] The King, however, was informed, exactly when is not known, but on 25 October 1945 Cadogan noted in his diary after an interview at Buckingham Palace: 'King fussed about the Duke of Windsor

File and Captured German Documents.' The King had, however, known about his brother's contacts with the Germans in Lisbon in 1940 for many years.

The evidence of the file and its potential for damaging the family upset him, all the more so since he had already ordered a highly secret, mopping-up operation in Germany which had been designed to save precisely such an archival embarrassment. Some time during the period when the Marburg File was discovered and not long after General Patton's Third Army had occupied the neighbouring village of Kronberg in the Taunus Mountains at the end of March 1945, the King's Librarian, Owen Morshead, accompanied by Anthony Blunt, who was then combining his intelligence duties with work in the Royal Library, drove up to the Freidrichshof, the castle built by Queen Victoria's eldest daughter, Princess Victoria, German Empress and Queen of Prussia, on a specific mission from the King. The King had provided Morshead with a letter requesting the Landgrave of Hesse, to whom the castle belonged, to allow his Librarian to remove sensitive papers to Windsor for safe keeping. The letter caused some embarrassment, first because the Hesse family had been evicted by the Americans to a house in the village of Kronberg and, second, because Philipp of Hesse, head of the family, had been arrested by the Americans for his Nazi activities. The family then produced a letter of authorization signed by the Prince's seventy-two-year-old mother, Princess Margarethe, and, armed with this, Morshead and Blunt succeeded in removing from the castle two crates of documents, the archive of the principal branch of the Hesse-Cassel family. Morshead had apparently been looking for, but had missed, the remaining volumes of correspondence between Queen Victoria and the Empress Frederick which were later discovered in Chicago in 1946 among property stolen from the castle and returned to the Windsor Archives.

While the King, perhaps prompted by Queen Mary's expert knowledge and concern for family heirlooms and objets d'art, may well have been originally concerned to save them from looting by the various armies during the disintegration of Germany, the contents of the Lisbon file and, it has been assumed, the modern section of the Hesse archive, made him aware that documentary evidence might be of more immediate concern. In June 1946 the British Foreign Office and the US State Department agreed jointly to publish documents from the captured archives of the German Foreign Ministry and Chancellery; John Wheeler-Bennett, who had already been involved in a consultative capacity on the German documents at Marburg, was appointed British editor-in-chief on the project. It was he who, having previously heard rumours of the existence of the Marburg File on the Duke of Windsor, discovered that it did, indeed, exist but had been taken from Marburg on Eisenhower's express orders and that the King already knew of it. 'Though I consider highly improbable that General Eisenhower acted on his own initiative,' Wheeler-Bennett later wrote, 'I never knew (nor do I to this day) whose initiative it was. The important consequence of the curious incident was that the Marburg File was speedily returned to our custody and that we duly included the bulk of its contents in the Series D, vol. X....'[50]

From the King's point of view, however, the first sifting of the documents seems to have been highly embarrassing and necessitated urgent action. In August 1947 Morshead and Blunt were sent to Haus Doorn, the late Kaiser's place of exile in the Netherlands, their mission apparently prompted by information from Wheeler-Bennett that he had found a reference in the Marburg File to the role played in the Windsor saga by the Kaiser, whose son Frederick William and his wife Cecilie were both used by Hitler as royal intermediaries. They located the Kaiser's Garter insignia and a Cosway portrait of the Duke of Clarence, which were later transferred to Windsor. No documentary material was found.[51] When, twenty years later, Blunt was investigated by Peter Wright in 1967, the Palace was to put any questioning about his missions to Germany out of bounds.

Early in March 1947 something so damaging had been revealed that it required Anglo–American co-operation at the highest level, an urgent request from the Foreign Secretary, Ernest Bevin, then in Moscow for the Foreign Ministers' Meeting which began on 10 March 1947, to his opposite number, the American Secretary of State, General George Marshall. Upon receiving Bevin's request, Marshall sent a top-secret 'Personal For Your Eyes Only' telegram to Dean Acheson in the State Department. Dated 'March 15, midnight', it read:

Bevin informs me that Department or White House has on file a microfilm copy of a paper concerning the Duke of Windsor. Bevin says only other copy was destroyed by Foreign Office, and asks that we destroy ours to avoid possibility of a leak to great embarrassment of Windsor's brother [George VI]. Please attend to this for me and reply for my eyes only.[52]

Declassified on 11 May 1988 as Document No. 841.001/3-1547 in the US National Archives, the State Department telegram bears a manuscript note 'no record in RM/R as of 2,28/58'. No record of the microfilm copy to which it referred with such urgency apparently now exists either in the National Archives or among the Roosevelt, Truman or Marshall Papers. Its precise contents cannot, therefore, now be known beyond the fact that it concerned the Duke of Windsor and that the King was extremely anxious to prevent a 'leak'. Nineteen forty-seven was, however, the year in which Wheeler-Bennett was engaged on his preliminary sifting of the Marburg File; his American contacts were exceptional and, having worked for PWE in New York during the war, his knowledge of American sources was extremely good. It is noticeable that in the memoir in which he deals with his editorship of the captured German documents and specifically with the Marburg File he does not follow the standard line of exonerating the Duke of Windsor. One might infer from his unusual silence on this point, upon which he was almost uniquely qualified to give an opinion, that what appeared in the captured German documents was not the whole story of the Duke of Windsor's relations with Germany. One might also infer from the Anglo–

American context of the telegram that it referred to an episode during the period in which the Duke of Windsor was Governor of the Bahamas from 1940 to 1945 and was under United States surveillance. Whatever it may have been, it was serious enough for the British Foreign Secretary, on behalf of the King, to ask his American counterpart to destroy the evidence.

The Marshall telegram is not the only instance of Anglo–American co-operation to suppress damaging evidence of the Duke of Windsor's pro-Nazi leanings arising directly from the captured German documents. Just over three months previously, on 2 November 1946, the British Ambassador in Washington, Lord Inverchapel (the Queen's old friend, Sir Archibald Clark-Kerr), wrote a letter of protest headed 'Top Secret and Personal' to Dean Acheson, in which he referred to a cutting from *Newsweek* of that week in which it was alleged that publication of the captured German documents was being held up in the State Department in deference to British wishes. The United States Government, the magazine said, had agreed some time ago 'to suppress documents dealing with the Duke of Windsor's pre-war ideas on European politics and the Third Reich'. Now, it charged, London wanted material on other subjects withheld and 'so far is having its way'. Inverchapel dismissed the first and last allegations as having 'as you know ... no foundation at all'. He was, however, protesting furiously at the sentence regarding the Duke of Windsor, not because, like the others, it was baseless, but because it was true and, therefore, indicated the leakage of a secret agreement:

You may remember the conversations which you had with Balfour last year on this subject, and the exchange of communications between him and your Department culminating in your personal letter to Balfour of 19th November 1945.

I am at a loss to know what explanation I can give to the Foreign Office with regard to this leakage in view of the special precautions which your Department agreed to undertake....[53]

The Duke of Windsor was clearly still an embarrassment to his brother and to the British Government. Without complete access to all the documentation it is impossible to evaluate the extent of the threat which he posed to the security of both. What there is in the public domain suggests that in his bitterness against his brother and his blinkered opinionatedness he contemplated dangerous paths, and that if he was an unconscious pawn in the German game he was not an unwilling one. The quarrel between George VI and his brother could have provided a theme for a Shakespearean tragedy had it not been conducted on such a petty level. Obstinacy and a certain paranoia characterized both sides. The central issue was the King's refusal to make the Duchess of Windsor a Royal Highness and the royal family's refusal to receive her; it was the primary cause of the Windsors' bitterness against the royal family and of the 'two camps' mentality which, alongside his personal opinions and his desire to regain a leading position, led the Duke into dealings with 'Peace Movements' which were Nazi fronts and, through intermediaries, with the Nazis themselves. An increasing obsession with money, partly inspired by Wallis's insistence on a quasi-royal style of life entailing an equivalent expenditure, was to place him, in the eyes of the US authorities, in the equivocal position of 'trading with the enemy'. It was also responsible for his insistence, for tax reasons, on an 'official' job which the post-war Labour Government was not prepared to give him.

On the central issue, there was never any chance that the King or the royal family would yield. The King saw the refusal of the people of Britain and the Empire to accept Wallis Simpson as a member of the royal family as the *raison d'être* of the Abdication, a decision which could not be reversed. Queen Mary had promised George V never to receive her, a pledge that she would not break; the Queen would never forgive her for what she had done. The Duke, equally obstinately, continued to press the question as a matter of honour. There was also the question, sadder because it was rooted in the psychology of the past, of the Duke's permanent return to England. The King, quite simply, could not bring himself to contemplate the prospect of his elder brother in permanent residence in England, upstaging him as he always had. It is hard to say that his instinctive fears were totally unjustified. The situation was perhaps best summed up by Herbert Morrison commenting in the Labour magazine *Forward* on the Duke of Windsor's German tour of 1937: 'The choice before ex-Kings is either to fade out of the public eye or to be a nuisance. It is a hard choice, perhaps, for one of his temperament, but the Duke will be wise to fade.' The King knew, far better than Morrison did, that his brother would never take this advice.

Even the outbreak of war in September 1939 had effected no cessation of hostilities between the King and his brother. As war became imminent, the Duke had offered his services to his country and the King had in return promised his own aeroplane to bring the Duke and Duchess back from the South of France to talk about a war job; arrangements were made via Monckton, who spent hours on the telephone to the Duke from Downing Street, for the Windsors' return on 2 September. At the last moment, however, the Duke, in an access of pique, began to make demands: he would not return unless he and his wife were personally invited to stay at Windsor by the King. 'The Duke of Windsor could have come back yesterday but for a sudden fit of temper,' the long-suffering Monckton told his daughter on 3 September. Unfortunately Monckton appears unwisely to have repeated the Duke's demands to the King, or, as Fruity Metcalfe put it, 'all the rot talked on the phone'. The King, furious, sent Monckton out to France with a message from Chamberlain that the Duke could return only if he accepted one of two jobs offered him, either Deputy Regional Commissioner to Sir Wyndham Portal in Wales, or liaison officer with the British Military Mission No. 1 to General Gamelin under General Howard-Vyse. Monckton was also to tell the Duke from the King that there would be no invitation to Windsor Castle and that the offer of the royal aeroplane was withdrawn. It was hardly an enviable mission; as the King remarked wryly to Monckton, he ought to write a book entitled 'Odd jobs I have done'. To undertake it Monckton deliberately chose a tiny RAF Leopard Moth, 'the sort of aeroplane in which the Duke and Duchess would be reluctant to make the return journey', as his biographer put it, as he feared they might otherwise have done so, leaving him to languish in France.

In the end the Duke of Windsor made his own arrangements with Churchill at the Admiralty, crossing the Channel on Mountbatten's new destroyer, the *Kelly*. Whatever had been said on the telephone, the atmosphere at the Palace towards the Duke on his first homecoming was by now icy. There was no royal representative to meet them at Portsmouth, nor indeed any message from the King. They were met by Randolph Churchill, whose spurs, the Duke noted, were upside down, bearing a welcoming note from his father. '... all will come right if we all work together to the end,' Churchill wrote meaningfully. The Palace had arranged no transport or even a place to stay, nor was it clear if and when the King intended to meet his brother. That he did so on 14 September was due to Monckton. 'Long and boring discussions took place', Monckton recalled, 'in order to bring about a meeting between the King and his brother which I finally achieved by excluding women, as I explained to Alec Hardinge that it would save trouble if it was a stag party....' Indeed, the strained atmosphere of this, the first meeting between the brothers since their emotional farewell at the Royal Lodge, showed how much their relations had deteriorated in the intervening three years. The King and his brother met for an hour, 'not a very pleasant interview' was how the King described it to Mountbatten, 'but quite friendly. I thought he had not changed one bit, but perhaps his behaviour was rather forced. He did not seem to think he had done anything wrong.'[54] The Duke told Monckton that the meeting had only, as the King described it, gone 'all right' because on Monckton's advice he had avoided anything controversial. It could in no way have been regarded as a reconciliation.

Moreover, in the interim the King seems to have changed his mind about offering his brother a military job at home and to have decided that he should take the liaison job in France. According to the diary of Hore-Belisha, then still Secretary of State for War, Chamberlain told him at a Cabinet meeting on the 15th that the Duke had agreed to this and that he had also expressed a desire to spend his remaining time in England before taking up his post in France with one of the home commands. The Duke, calling at the War Office at 4 p.m. that afternoon to discuss the appointment, repeated his desire to be attached to the different home commands 'so that he could be in contact with the soldiers again'. He added that he would like to take the Duchess with him. 'I began to see difficulties ...', Hore-Belisha recorded. The King was horrified; the principal reason that he had decided for the liaison job in France had been to get his brother out of the country and out of 'contact with the soldiers again'. The royal fears about the Duke of Windsor had recently been expressed by Mountbatten when he warned the officers of the *Kelly* not to be led away by the Windsor charm, as one of them recalled, 'He [Mountbatten] seemed to fear that the officers might be seduced into thinking that the wrong brother was King....'[55] The King and his family evidently feared that the Duke would not be able to resist encouraging demonstrations of affection by the troops which could produce a dangerous impression both at home and abroad and one which would be wholly at variance with the unity of a nation at war.

Summoned to Buckingham Palace the next morning, 16 September at 11 a.m., Hore-Belisha found the King 'in a distressed state':

He thought that if the Duchess went to the Commands, she might have a hostile reception, particularly in Scotland. He did not want the Duke to go to the Commands in England. He seemed very disturbed and walked up and down the room. He said the Duke had never had any discipline in his life.[56]

The King must, indeed, have been upset to reveal his feelings in this way to a minister whom he could in no way count as a personal friend; he was to be equally frank later that day when Hore-Belisha returned for further consultation bringing with him the CIGS, General Ironside. He no doubt saw his brother, far from being willing to take a back seat, yearning to be back in the limelight again, exercising his remarkable crowd-pulling qualities and establishing contact with the troops as he had in his days as the idolised Prince of Wales in the First World War. The King knew, too, that his brother still saw nothing wrong in the Abdication, that he had no conception of the widespread hostility to Wallis; he foresaw and dreaded the inevitable newspaper headlines, the raking up of old painful memories. Why, he wondered to himself, could his brother not leave him in peace to get on with his job? That afternoon he told Hore-Belisha and Ironside that he thought it best if the Duke left for Paris at once. 'All my ancestors succeeded to the throne after their predecessors had died,' he commented ruefully. 'Mine is not only alive, but very much so.'

The Duke of Windsor continued to trample on his brother's sensitivities. When he saw Hore-Belisha at 3 p.m. that afternoon, 16 September, he told him openly that he would like the colonelcy of the Welsh Guards back and said that he had ascertained that they wanted him. Hore-Belisha, not wishing to be drawn, replied that it was not his business and asked if he had discussed it with the King, thus effectively ending the subject. It was, at best, an insensitive suggestion and would have put the King in an impossible position if it had been raised openly. With the Duke's departure for France, orders went out to BEF Headquarters that he should, if possible, be kept from visiting the troops. 'There is, for the moment, an inhibition against his going round the troops,' Pownall wrote in his diary two days after the Duke had visited Gort's HQ on 6 October 1939; 'indeed I believe he was not supposed to come to GHQ but we can't help saying "Yes" if we are told he's coming'. An embarrassed Duke of Gloucester had tried to avoid meeting his brother by pleading a liaison meeting in Lille, but, Pownall wrote, 'I gather "David" informed "Harry" he would like to see him and the latter turned up.' On this occasion the Duke had behaved impeccably, 'very nice and agreeable and talked very intelligently', Pownall recorded. But, as the King had feared, while the Duke could contain himself with the Staff officers, he was unable to resist temptation when faced with massed ranks of the Guards. Pownall wrote on 18 October:

The Duke of Windsor is on us again today. Behaved charmingly here but badly up forward where he took the salute of all Guards which turned out. C-in-C [Gort] was there, a full General, and Master W. definitely should not have pushed in on that. He's here as a soldier, not as Royalty. C-in-C very annoyed about it and is getting it back to Proper Quarter. If Master W. thinks he can stage a comeback he's mighty wrong.[57]

The Duke of Gloucester, who was present on this occasion, was horrified and also reported it to the King. According to Gloucester's official biographer, 'the tour turned into something of a triumph for the Duke of Windsor and, therefore, as Prince Henry and the King obviously saw it, as something of a slight, if an unintentional one, to the King....' Charitably, the Duke's reactions could be interpreted as a trip into nostalgia; it was noted that on a visit to the Fourth and Fifth French Armies on the Vosges Sector of the Maginot Line he had chosen to wear the somewhat frayed overcoat, faded leggings and well-worn shoes which he had carefully preserved from the First World War a quarter of a century before. Nevertheless, in taking the salute, the Duke's behaviour had been militarily improper, if nothing else; he was banned from visiting the BEF for the immediate future.

The Duke was determined to defy the King and to appeal secretly to the man whom he regarded as his only friend in the Government, Winston Churchill. On 9 November, Oliver Harvey noted in his diary that his friend, Charles Peake, head of the Press Section at the Foreign Office, had news of an attempted undercover visit to London by the Duke:

Charles Peake tells me the Duke of Windsor has sent a message to Monckton from France to say he is flying over during the weekend in a private aeroplane and wants to see Winston but that the King is not to know! Monckton, after taking Charles's advice, has warned Winston who is saying that he has to visit the fleet over this weekend and is telling Hardinge about it. He is also telling Belisha and will ring up the Duke tonight to tell him he cannot come.[58]

The Duke was restless and dissatisfied with his job, as Lady Alexandra Metcalfe, who knew him well, had foreseen. 'I see endless trouble ahead with the job in France', she had predicted in September, 'as I don't think he will think it big enough & I doubt his getting on with the "Wombat" [his chief, Major-General Howard-Vyse, so-called because of his large ears and Australian service].' In the New Year of 1940 the Duchess expressed the feeling in the Windsor household, complaining that the Duke's job was 'too inactive, besides a lot of pressure from the Palace which makes it impossible to do well. Even the war can't stop the family hatred of us.'[59]

On 21 January 1940 the Duke made a further attempt to circumvent his brother, flying to London without advising the Palace he was doing so. In the course of this visit he revealed how far his frustration and bitterness against his brother had once again led him to contemplate the kind of action which the

King had always feared he might. In the second week of January Oliver Harvey, now Minister at the British Embassy in Paris, received a note from Charles Peake in London, which he marked 'Rec'd Jan 13 1940'. 'I have just heard that the D of Windsor arrives here on Monday. The Palace it seems have not been consulted & Walter Monckton is very worried.... Please burn this....'[60] While in London the Duke saw Churchill and Ironside and apparently persuaded them to lift the ban on his visiting the front since he subsequently was to do so on his return to France. He also, accompanied by Monckton, visited the Foreign Office to complain to Peake about the attitude towards himself of the new British Ambassador in Paris, Sir Eric Phipps's replacement, Sir Ronald Campbell. As Peake reported it, this interview provided a pathetic insight into the Duke's sensitivity to what he saw as Palace-inspired official slights. When the Duke complained that he and the Duchess had not yet been received at the Embassy, Peake soothed them by explaining that there had been a delay in transporting the new Ambassador's possessions from his previous post in Belgrade and that, under wartime conditions, only half the Embassy building was available for the Ambassador's private and social use. Peake reported:

HRH's brow then cleared. He smiled & said, 'Now I understand, why did nobody tell me this before.' He became quite different ... & showed all the signs of a man with a strong inferiority complex who has had his suspicions removed. There were constant references to 'The Duchess', & 'The Duchess thinks' and 'The Duchess says' & so on....

He also had a far more controversial interview with Beaverbrook, which, in the context of both his past and his future relations with Nazi Germany, shows how the idea of himself as the leader of an international 'Peace Movement', with, in his case, his setting himself up as a rival leader to his brother, had never left his mind. Peake reported the meeting from a first-hand source, Walter Monckton:

W.M. tells me that he was present at a frightful interview between the D of W & the Beaver two days ago. Both found themselves in agreement that the war ought to be ended at once by a peace offer to Germany. The Beaver suggested that the Duke should get out of uniform, come home, & after enlisting powerful City support, stump the country in which case he predicted that the Duke would have a tremendous success. W.M. contented himself with reminding the Duke that if he did this he would be liable to UK income tax. This made the little man blench & he declared with great determination that the whole thing was off.[61]

Peake later told Harold Nicolson that this conversation had taken place at Walter Monckton's house and, he said, the Duke had initiated the conversation: '... he spoke about the inevitable collapse of France and said that he would return to England and conduct a movement for peace with Germany. Beaverbrook was delighted. "Go ahead, Sir," he beamed, "and I shall back you."' Monckton, according to Peake, after Beaverbrook's departure, had to point out to the Duke of Windsor that 'he had been speaking high treason', something which he seems not to have taken into account. Perhaps the saddest part of the episode is the decisive effect which the thought of having to pay income tax had upon the Duke's plans: 'Walter ... pointed out ... that if he really came to live in this country he would have to pay income tax. The latter thought filled him with such appalling gloom that he gave up all idea of saving England by negotiating with Germany.'[62] Peake made two minutes of the conversation he had had with Monckton on 26 January and, by the next day, the information had reached the Prime Minister[63] and, no doubt, the King.

The King must have reflected on the similarities between the scenario put forward by the Duke and the plot of *The Apple Cart*, a possibility which he had envisaged, perhaps only half-seriously, when discussing the question of his brother's title in December 1936. He knew his brother far better than anyone else did and, now and in the future, he took his potential as a rival more seriously than as a traitor to his country. He regarded his brother as a threat to his position and, in view of repeated evidence of his brother's willingness to stage a come-back, however ill-thought out and woolly his plans to do so were, it is hard to say that he was entirely wrong. For reasons rooted in his own psyche he overestimated his brother's potential popularity in Britain; he may also have underestimated the threat which, as an embittered exile, the Duke represented. The Duke's nuisance-value was made more serious by the Nazis' desire to make use of him.

On the day of the Duke's interview with the King in London on 14 September 1939, Lord Crawford dined at The Club with Lord Howe, who was then working at the Admiralty. Howe reported that he had been horrified to see the Duke of Windsor, accompanied by Churchill emerging from the Secret Room – the basement apartment where the positions of the British and enemy fleets were plotted by the hour. Crawford commented:

He is too irresponsible a chatterbox to be entrusted with confidential information which will all be passed on to Wally at the dinner table. That is where the danger lies – namely that after nearly three years of complete obscurity, the temptation to show that he knows, that he is again at the centres of information will prove irresistible, and that he will blab and babble our state secrets without realising the danger.[64]

Within less than six months Crawford's fears appear to have been realized. The Duke was, of course, an obvious Nazi target; on 27 January 1940, Count Julius von Zech-Burkersroda, German Minister at The Hague, wrote to von Weizsäcker, State Secretary, of the Duke's openly expressed dissatisfaction during his recent visit to London and the 'personal relationships' which gave Zech the 'opportunity to establish certain lines leading to the Duke of Windsor. As of course you know,' he wrote, 'W. is a member of the British military mission with the French Army Command.'[65] In a further letter of 19 February 1940, Zech reported that the Duke of Windsor had leaked the highly secret subject of a recent meeting of the Allied War Council, which concerned their plans in the event of a German invasion of Belgium, revised in the light of the recent crash of an aeroplane in which the German plan for the invasion *Fall*

Gelb had been found.[66] The Duke continued to be regarded as a security risk in the later stages of the war. In Washington from 1942 staff on the Combined Chiefs of Staff Committee were warned that the Duke of Windsor was under no circumstances to be allowed to enter the basement room in which the strategic maps and plans were kept.[67]

After the fall of France in June 1940 the King was again presented with the problem of what to do with his brother. It was almost a carbon copy of September 1939; the Windsors arrived as refugees in Madrid on 23 June to find a cable from Churchill inviting them to return home as soon as possible, while the Foreign Office cabled the Ambassador, Sir Samuel Hoare, to invite 'Their Royal Highnesses' to proceed to Lisbon, a solecism for which they received, with the King's authorization, a rap over the knuckles from Hardinge. The Duke's reaction to Churchill's cable was to present his customary demands that his family receive and recognize his wife as a condition of his return to England, and that he himself be given some official post. Churchill replied on 25 June that they had better come to England as arranged, when 'everything can be considered', and, when this failed, sent the Duke, with the King's permission, a very strongly worded telegram: 'Your Royal Highness has taken active military rank and refusal to obey direct orders of competent military authority would create a serious situation. I hope it will not be necessary for such orders to be sent. I most strongly urge compliance with wishes of the Government.'[68]

The King – and Churchill – reacted very strongly to the Duke's demands. To them both it seemed incredible that he should haggle at such a moment when his country was facing invasion. The Palace was already considering alternatives to his return, for on 28 June, when Churchill submitted his telegram for the King's approval, Hardinge remarked that he did not see how the Duke as an ex-King could perform 'any useful service in this country' and suggested an appointment on Wavell's staff in Egypt. At some point between 28 June and 1 July the King seems to have come to a crisis decision that he could not face the prospect of his brother back in England. By the evening of 1 July a solution had been reached after a meeting between the King and Churchill at Buckingham Palace at 6.30 p.m. On his return to Downing Street, Churchill told Beaverbrook, in the presence of Jock Colville, that the Duke was to be offered an appointment as Governor and Commander-in-Chief of the Bahamas, claiming that the idea had been his: 'I think a very good suggestion of mine. Max, do you think he'll take it?' 'He'll find it a great relief,' Beaverbrook replied, at which Churchill commented, 'Not half as much as his brother will.' That the Duke would not now be returning to England seems to have been taken by Churchill as a foregone conclusion. On the following day, 2 July, the Grosvenor Estate which handled the property of Churchill's friend, the Duke of Westminster, wrote to Monckton that their proprietor's house, Saighton Grange, near Chester, which 'a short time ago a very important personage was thinking of taking ... for a short time', was not now available.[69]

It has been argued, from comments made by Lord Lloyd, the Colonial

Secretary, in whose department the appointment lay, that the idea of the Bahamas was not Churchill's but the King's. 'The Windsor appointment is the K[ing]'s idea to keep him at all costs out of England,' he told Sir Ronald Storrs. Windsor had accepted it 'on condition "that the family did not interfere" '.[70] An unpublished letter from the Duke of Kent to Prince Paul of Yugoslavia, however, throws new light on the affair, making it clear that Churchill was equally as strongly against the Duke of Windsor's return to England as was the King and that the general family view was, indeed, that the Duke 'would have caused trouble':

My brother has behaved disgracefully ... to accept to be Governor of a small place like that is fantastic! But they are both terrified of returning here & thank God they haven't. (I did my best to stop it as he would surely have caused trouble) & W.C. didn't want him back.[71]

The Queen, who would hardly have gone so far as to oppose the King's decision had he really been the principal proponent of the Bahamas appointment, did not entirely welcome it. On 6 July she made her strong views on the Duchess's unfitness to be the wife of a British Governor clear, although she realized the appointment was by now a *fait accompli*. A woman with three husbands living, would not, she thought, be acceptable to the people of the Islands and might set a precedent for a general lowering of standards. She suggested that the Windsors go to the Bahamas, but as visitors to gauge the local reaction. She also suggested, with some justification, that official American opinion would not approve and that the appointment might be dangerous.[72]

For the King and Churchill, however, the removal of the Duke of Windsor to the safe distance of the Bahamas was more important than the points raised by the Queen. The Bahamas appointment was a sentence of banishment and bitterly accepted as such by the Windsors, 'the St Helena of 1940' was how the Duchess referred to it. Churchill himself explicitly referred to it as such at dinner at Lambeth Palace a few weeks later. 'The Duke of Windsor's views on the war', he said, 'are such as to render his banishment a wise move.'[73] Even before the appointment had been formally offered to the Duke, Lloyd had drafted a telegram in strong terms which were omitted in the final version, justifying it to the Dominion Prime Ministers on the grounds that: 'The activities of the Duke of Windsor on the Continent in recent months have been causing HM and myself grave uneasiness as his inclinations are well known to be pro-Nazi and he may become a centre of intrigue.'[74]

The King's public reaction to such reports as this which were now circulating in well-informed London circles was to make light of them. On 10 July Cadogan, in conversation with the King after a luncheon-party at Venetia Montagu's house, with the King and Queen, Gort, Harold Nicolson, the Dowager Duchess of Devonshire and others, found him 'amused at C's [head of British intelligence] report of the quisling activities of my brother'.[75] The captured German Foreign Office documents already published have revealed at least some of the Duke of

Windsor's 'quisling activities' in Madrid and Lisbon, where, from the moment of his arrival on 23 June, the Germans in collaboration with the Spanish Government contemplated using him as a weapon either in the event of a successful invasion of England or, possibly, in peace negotiations, detaining him in Spain either with or without his co-operation.[76] Presumably in response to a request from the Duke in Madrid, the Germans agreed to keep watch on the Duke's Paris house,[77] although it was stressed, presumably for the Duke's protection, that no written statement to that effect was to be made. On 2 July the German Ambassador in Madrid, Eberhard von Stohrer, reported that the Duke had told the Spanish Minister that he would only return to England if his wife were recognized as a member of the royal family and if he were appointed to a military or civilian position of influence. The Duke was planning to go to Lisbon to 'confer with the Duke of Kent' (who was there for Portugal's quincentenary celebrations; the Duke did not go, at the request of Dr Salazar and to the relief of the British official party); as he realized that the fulfilment of his conditions was 'practically out of the question', he intended returning to Spain where the Spanish Government had offered him the Palace of the Caliph at Ronda as a residence. The Duke had made his views on the war quite plain: 'Windsor has expressed himself to the Foreign Minister and other acquaintances in strong terms against Churchill and against this war....'[78]

The contents of the documents if true show the Duke as contemplating something very like treason and would certainly have been enough to worry the King and Churchill, who later loyally dismissed them as attempts to blacken the Duke's reputation. On 11 July the German Minister in Lisbon, Baron Oswald von Hoyningen Huene, reported that the Duke of Windsor was trying to delay his departure for the Bahamas as long as possible 'in hope of a turn of events favourable to him'. 'He is convinced', Huene continued, 'that if he had remained on the throne war would have been avoided, and he characterizes himself as a firm supporter of peaceful arrangement with Germany. The Duke definitely believes that continued severe bombing would make England ready to sue for peace.' Ribbentrop now definitely contemplated getting the Duke back to Spain and keeping him there, by whatever means necessary, for future use:

... at a suitable occasion in Spain the Duke must be informed that Germany wants peace with the English people, that the Churchill clique stands in the way of it, and that it would be a good thing if the Duke would hold himself in readiness for further developments. Germany is determined to force England to peace by every means of power and upon this happening would be prepared to accommodate any desire expressed by the Duke, especially with a view to the assumption of the throne by the Duke and Duchess. If the Duke should have other plans, but be prepared to co-operate in the establishment of good relations between Germany and England, we would likewise be prepared to assure him and his wife of a subsistence which would permit him, either as a private citizen or in some other position, to lead a life suitable for a king.[79]

A further telegram of 23 July reported more indiscreet comments by the Duke and Duchess: 'Politically he was more and more distant from the King and the present English Government.... He was considering making a public statement and thereby disavowing present English policy and breaking with his brother.'[80] No evidence exists that the Duke was doing more than keeping his options open, and, indeed, from a further conversation the Windsors had two days later with an old Spanish friend of the Duke's, Miguel Primo de Rivera, Marqués de Estella, it appears that both the Duke and Duchess were astonished when the possibility of the Duke ascending the throne was put to them, replying that 'according to the English Constitution this would not be possible after the abdication'; but at the suggestion that the course of the war might bring about changes in the English Constitution, 'the Duchess especially became very pensive'.[81]

On 31 July, the eve of the Duke's final departure from Lisbon, Ribbentrop sent to Huene a message for transmission to the Duke by his Portuguese host, the banker, Ricardo Espirito Santo Silva. In essence it was the same as the message from Ribbentrop, which had been put to Huene in the cable of 12 July, but this time it was put directly to the Duke, when it apparently made 'the deepest impression upon him'. He replied, according to Huene's cable of 2 August, agreeing 'gladly' 'to the appeal made to him to co-operate at a suitable time in the establishment of peace', but that at the present time he must follow his Government's orders.

Disobedience would disclose his intentions prematurely, bring about a scandal and deprive him of his prestige in England. He was also convinced that the present moment was too early for him to come forward since there was as yet no inclination in England for an approach to Germany. However, as soon as this frame of mind changed, he would be ready to return immediately. To bring this about there were two possibilities. Either England would yet call upon him, which he considered to be entirely possible, or Germany would express the desire to negotiate with him. In both cases he was prepared for any personal sacrifice and would make himself available without the slightest personal ambition. He would remain in continuing communication with his previous host [Espirito Santo Silva], and had agreed with him on a code word, upon receiving which he would immediately come back over. He insisted that this would be possible at any time, since he had foreseen all eventualities and had already initiated the necessary arrangments....[82]

In a telegram of 15 August Huene reported that Espirito Santo Silva had just received a telegram from the Duke in Bermuda, asking him to send a communication as soon as action was advisable.[83] And there the documentary record ended.

The background to the Duke's threat made on 23 July to break publicly with his brother was so petty, indeed ludicrous, that it suggests the King may have been right not to take the Duke's 'quisling activities' altogether seriously. At this moment when the Battle of Britain had already begun, the Duke of Windsor chose to dig in his toes, sending angry telegrams to the authorities complaining of red tape and Palace persecution, refusing to travel to the Bahamas without going via New York and demanding that his soldier servants, Piper Alastair Fletcher and his chauffeur, be released from active service to accompany him to the Bahamas. The Duchess entered the fray with a cable to Lloyd complaining of 'obstacles' being put in her husband's way. The War Office, having refused a similar request from Lord Athlone, was not prepared, as Churchill cabled on 20 July, to accommodate the Duke of Windsor by releasing men of military age from the Army 'to act as servants to Your Royal Highness'. The King's first reaction, when consulted by Lloyd and Eden, was 'tell him to do what he is told'. Then, knowing his brother as he did, he had second thoughts, as Lloyd telephoned Churchill's office that same day:

He asked me to let you know as soon as possible that we should remain adamant on the subject of his [Windsor's] going to New York. On the point of servants he wanted you to appreciate that ... Lascelles and Sir Walter Monckton both agreed that HRH had to be treated as a petulant baby, and that there was a by no means remote possibility that he was prepared to face a break on this subject, and that he was unable to appreciate how ludicrous the affair would appear when made public....[84]

On 20 July, the day on which the King was discussing the Windsor problem in London, the US Minister in Lisbon, Herbert Claiborne Pell, sent a telegram to the Secretary of State, Cordell Hull, which underlined how right the King had been that Churchill should remain adamant on the question of his brother's not being allowed to go to Bermuda via New York. Pell had lunched that day with the Windsors at Espirito Santo Silva's house at Cascais and what he heard there caused him to send an urgent cable to his Government:

Duke and Duchess of Windsor are indiscreet and outspoken against British Government. Consider their presence in the United States might be disturbing and confusing. They say that they intend remaining in the United States whether Churchill likes it or not and desire apparently to make propaganda for peace....[85]

At this critical moment in his country's history, when Britain needed all the help she could get from America in her stand against Germany, the King was not prepared to contemplate the possibility of his brother's making 'propaganda for peace' in the United States. The price of removing the Duke of Windsor from the scope of German intrigue (Walter Monckton having been despatched to Lisbon on 28 July to persuade the Duke to leave on 1 August as planned, thus thwarting a German plot to kidnap him) was to bring him into proximity to America and thus cause the King, the British Government and especially Halifax, as Ambassador to Washington, endless preoccupation.

On 11 December 1940, the fourth anniversary of his accession, the King invited Halifax, then still Foreign Secretary but soon to become Ambassador to Washington, to luncheon à trois with himself and the Queen, and then for an hour's private conversation afterwards. The Windsors, 'certainly that problem is very intractable', Halifax noted in his diary, were very much a subject of conversation, arising out of their present visit to Miami for the Duchess's dental operation, and the articles which she had authorized, a series of intimate interviews with the Windsors by the American journalist Adela St Johns, which represented them as romantic figures very far from content with their paradise. The articles had been syndicated in US newspapers in the latter half of November, thus adding to the publicity the Windsors received when they arrived in Miami. The King and the British Government were extremely concerned at the effect the Duke of Windsor might have as a rallying-point for isolationist feeling in the United States. Churchill, indeed, had gone so far as to warn the Duke in courteous language to keep his mouth shut even before he left Lisbon:

Sir, may I venture upon a word of serious counsel. It will be necessary for the Governor of the Bahamas to express views about the war and the general situation which are not out of harmony with those of His Majesty's Government.... In particular, there will be danger of use being made of anything you say in the United States to do you injury, and to suggest divergence between you and the British Government....[86]

Indeed, from the fall of France until the attack on Pearl Harbor in December 1941, Anglo–American relations and the possibility of bringing the United States into the war were uppermost in the minds of the King and Churchill and fear of what the Duke might say was certainly the principal reason for the Government's anxiety to keep the Windsors out of the United States. Official opinion was not the problem; the Roosevelt Administration deeply disapproved of the Duke's pro-peace moves and of the right-wing, pro-Nazi businessmen whose company he kept. Public opinion, however, was a different matter; anything which could be perceived as official persecution of the Windsors by the British authorities could only result in anti-British feelings which were never far below the surface. The 'two camps' battlefields had now been extended to the United States.

The King made little effort to conciliate his brother, perhaps because the only thing that would have effected a reconciliation, the recognition of Wallis as a member of the royal family, was something which he was not prepared to offer. His main concern appears to have been to keep his brother as far away as possible and to leave the handling of him primarily to Churchill and, secondarily, although in the front line, to Halifax. He must have known that the Duke was incapable of distinguishing between public interest and private interests, that the Duke's resentment made him potentially dangerous and yet, between 1940 when he received no reply to a letter he had written to the Duke in July 1940 upon the appointment to the Bahamas, saying how glad he was that his brother realized he should not return to England, and 1943 he seems to have made no direct approach to him.

The Duke, for his part, saw the hand of the Palace behind every slight or obstacle, his indignation being particularly fired by finding, on file at Government House, Nassau, on his arrival, a telegram of instruction from Lord Lloyd laying down the rules of etiquette as far as the new Governor and his wife were concerned: 'You are no doubt aware that a lady when presented to HRH the Duke of Windsor should make a half-curtsey. The Duchess of Windsor is not entitled to this. The Duke should be addressed as "Your Royal Highness" and the Duchess as "Your Grace".' His anger was principally directed at the Queen; in a bitter letter which he wrote to Churchill in October 1940, but wisely did not send, he spoke of 'the mean and petty humiliations with which a now semi-Royal family [a dig at the Queen's commoner ancestry] with the co-operation of the Government has indulged itself over the years'.[87] Although the Duke, at an informal meeting with Roosevelt aboard the *Tuscaloosa* on 13 December 1940 (which Lothian and the Foreign Office had tried strenuously to prevent), was sensible enough to speak 'very charmingly' of his brother, underneath he was seething, an easy target once again for the pro-German peace faction. At the meeting with Roosevelt, Hopkins noted that 'the Duke's entourage was very bad'. Three years later, Assistant Secretary of State, Adolf Berle Jr, was to turn down a request from Halifax to exempt the Duchess of Windsor's letters from US censorship on precisely these grounds. Berle wrote:

Quite aside from the more shadowy activities of this family, it is to be recalled that both the Duke and Duchess of Windsor were in contact with Mr James Mooney, of General Motors, who attempted to act as mediator of a negotiated peace in the early winter of 1940; that they have maintained correspondence with Bedaux, now in prison in North Africa and under charges of trading with the enemy; that they have been in constant contact with Axel Wenner-Gren, presently on our Blacklist for suspicious activity....[88]

The Duke and Duchess cruised back from Miami with Wenner-Gren on his yacht, the *Southern Cross*, to spend Christmas among what was, according to American intelligence, his circle of men like Mooney, an anti-British Irish–American travelling with authorization from Göring to make peace with Hitler, and Alfred P. Sloan, chairman of General Motors, another Hitler sympathizer. During this period the Duke is alleged to have had several conversations on the subject of peace with Nazi Germany; on 6 February he gave an interview to an American journalist, Fulton Oursler, in which he appeared to advocate a nego-tiated peace and to advise America under no circumstances to enter the war. The timing could be regarded as significant. On 10 January 1941 the Lend-Lease Bill, Roosevelt's lifeline to Britain providing arms and supplies on credit, a particular target of isolationist hatred, was introduced into the House of Representatives, where it did not have an easy passage and was not passed until 8 February, two days after the Duke gave the Oursler interview, when it then faced the Senate.

When published in the influential American magazine *Liberty* and reproduced in Britain in the *Sunday Dispatch* of 16 March 1941, it earned the Duke a furious rebuke from Churchill. The Duke was then agitating for permission to make another visit to the United States; Churchill rounded on him in a furious exchange of telegrams, which should have warned the Duke of exactly what impression he was making. Firstly, he told him he should refrain from cruising on a yacht owned by Wenner-Gren who, according to reports I have received, [is] regarded as a pro-German financier, with strong leanings towards appeasement, and suspected of being in communication with the enemy. Your Royal Highness may not, perhaps, realise the intensity of feeling in the United States about people of this kind and the offence which is given to the Administration when any countenance is given them.

Among the Duke's other sins, of which British intelligence had knowledge at this time, was illegal currency dealing, again through pro-Nazi connections, but to this Churchill did not refer. He did, however, roundly castigate him for the *Liberty* interview, which he described as certainly to be interpreted as 'defeatist and pro-Nazi ... and approving of the isolationist aim to keep America out of the war',[89] and in a further telegram which hinted that the Duke, surrounded by fascist-minded millionaires, was out of touch, added a parting shot of barely suppressed anger and irritation:

That is not the policy of His Majesty's Government; nor is it the policy of the Government and vast majority of the people of the United States ... in this sad time of sacrifice and suffering it is not I think much to ask that deference be shown to the advice and wishes of His Majesty's Government and of Your Royal Highness's friends, among whom I have always tried to play my part.[90]

The Duke, in his reply, blamed the King and Queen, implicitly for his own behaviour, explicitly for their treatment of Wallis. He counterattacked with a recent article in *Life* magazine on the Queen in which Her Majesty was quoted as referring to the Duchess of Windsor as 'that woman' and, with a characteristic disregard of the larger issues, laid responsibility for his behaviour on his brother: 'Had my simple request conveyed to you by Sam Hoare [in Madrid, June–July 1940] been granted by my brother, I would have been proud to share these sad and critical times with my countrymen. ...'[91]

Against the shifting background of world war, the situation between the King and his brother remained static, the King refusing to budge, the Duke refusing to accept that he would not. Halifax, charged by the King with discovering whether the Duke's opinions had changed, reported after an interview in Washington in October 1941 that they had not. 'The Duke feels very keenly the difficulty about returning to England to resume the sort of life he might have expected,' Halifax wrote in what he described in a letter to Churchill of the same date as a 'bowdlerized account' of his conversation with the Duke of Windsor, 'but so long as these difficulties persist, he will not try to force the situation'. Halifax tried, no doubt on orders after a conversation with the King at Windsor the previous month, to explain to the Duke what the Abdication had meant to most people in Britain and that, although it was five years earlier, many people still felt that 'by abdicating from the duty he had inherited, he had let the show down ...' and that 'very large numbers of people disliked the marriage quite intensely because of her previous divorces'. He warned the King, however, 'I don't think anything I said would make any difference to his general thought.'[92] The King hoped that, with time, his brother would accept what he saw as the realities of the situation. 'The real fact of the matter which he does not realise', he wrote to Halifax, commenting on a long report the Ambassador had sent him of his conversation with the Duke of Windsor in Washington in October 1941, 'is that having occupied the throne of this country he can never live in this country as an ordinary citizen. We know this, so does Winston, but we can never tell my brother in so many words. He has got to realise it for himself. . . .'[93]

In the King's eyes the question of royal rank for the Duchess of Windsor had been irrevocably settled by the Abdication, and when, in November 1942, the Duke of Windsor submitted a request through Churchill to 'restore the Duchess's royal rank' in the New Year's Honours List, 'not only as an act of justice and courtesy to his sister-in-law, but also as a gesture of recognition of her two years' public service in the Bahamas', the King sent Churchill a memorandum which he intended to be seen as his last word on the subject. It was in essence the same as the letter which he had written to Baldwin in May 1937 during the discussions over the Letters Patent. The King wrote on 8 December 1942:

I feel I cannot alter a decision which I made with considerable reluctance at the time of his marriage. The reason for his abdication was that he wished to marry a lady who, having two husbands living, was not considered by the country to be a suitable Queen of England. When he abdicated, he renounced all the rights and privileges of succession for himself and his children – including the title 'Royal Highness' in respect of himself and his wife. There is therefore no question of his title being 'restored' to the Duchess – because she never had it.

I am sure that there are still large numbers of people in this country and in the Empire, to whom it would be most distasteful to have to do honour to the Duchess as a member of our family. . . . I know you will understand how disagreeable this is to me personally, but the good of my country and my family comes first. . . . I have consulted my family who share these views.[94]

And that, the King was intimating to Churchill, was that. The Duke was to make further attempts to get the decision reversed, notably in 1949, when Jowitt, then Labour Lord Chancellor and head of his profession, bluntly told the Duke that, whatever subtle arguments lawyers might produce on the legality or otherwise of the King's decision, to reverse it would require the issue of further Letters Patent by the King on advice of his ministers. In short, the ultimate decision was the King's.

The King, apparently, continued to hope that his brother would accept his ruling and in May 1943 he made, via Churchill, at least a gesture of reconciliation. The King was 'unhappy over this family estrangement', Churchill told the Duke of Windsor in Washington, and that he had never received any reply to his last letter of July 1940. The result was a bitter letter from the Duke to the King, charging him with 'studied insults' and 'persecuting me', a policy which he had suffered in silence. The family estrangement was, the Duke claimed, entirely the King's fault, and he himself felt frankly very bitter about it. 'The whole world knows we are not on speaking terms, which is not surprising in view of the impression you have given via the FO and in general that my wife and I are to have different treatment to other royal personages. . . .'[95]

For the King, and indeed for British officialdom, the question of the Duke of Windsor's future residence and employment after the Bahamas became more acute as the end of the European war approached. He was adamant that the ex-King could not return as a permanent resident to the United Kingdom, but he was not in principle against some form of official post for his brother. In July 1944 when Halifax and the King discussed the subject at Windsor, the King asked Halifax what he thought of a South American ambassadorship for the Duke. Halifax did not encourage the idea. 'We left it in agreement that he could not well return here, but that he might settle after the war in France ... or in the US where the interest that he excited would soon wear off.'[96] The trouble was, as Lascelles was to tell the Duke himself, that there was no place in the 'British imperial constitutional machinery' for 'an extra wheel – the wheel of an ex-King'. None of the principal government departments wanted to take the responsibility of the Duke of Windsor in a major post, as Halifax himself had discovered when, in conjunction with David Bowes-Lyon, he had tried in 1943 to persuade Oliver Stanley, then Colonial Secretary, to move the Duke of Windsor to a post further away from the United States.[97]

In October 1945 the King had two meetings in London with his brother, who had arrived there alone and was staying with Queen Mary. The meetings were amicable and the question of the Duke's future was discussed, the King making it clear that, as Churchill had already told the Duke the previous year, the Windsors' residence in England would not be welcome, and the Duke put forward the idea that he should live in America and work in the field of Anglo–American relations, a plan which he had apparently discussed during his visit with Churchill and with members of the new Labour Government, Attlee, Bevin and the Colonial Secretary, George Hall. In a friendly exchange of letters after the Duke's return to Paris, the King welcomed the idea, saying that he would write a letter of recommendation to President Truman. He did not, however, think there was any question of inventing an official post for the Duke. The King and his brother were soon again at loggerheads. What the Duke now wanted, a notion which apparently had been crystallized after a conversation with Churchill in Paris, was an official job in Anglo–American relations working 'within the ambit' of the British Embassy in Washington and officially accredited to it, as he explained to the King in a letter of 15 November. He needed this not only for prestige but for tax reasons, in order with diplomatic status to retain in the United States the tax privileges he had been granted in France. 'I hope', he concluded, with a strong hint of a *quid pro quo*, 'that you will make arrangements for me along these lines in the same spirit that I am willing to respect your feelings with regard to my living in Great Britain.'[98]

In fact, opposition to the Duke's ideas came not from the King, but, as the Duke admitted in a memorandum to Monckton of 8 December, from the Foreign Secretary and senior Foreign Office officials, who objected on the grounds that it would overshadow the British Ambassador in Washington and give the impression that there were two Ambassadors. The Duke saw his only hope as putting pressure on the King to have the appointment and accreditation effected as the King's personal wish ('your command in this personal instance would be obeyed,' he was to write), something the King could hardly be expected to have complied with. The most the King could do was to promise that Bevin would consult the diplomats concerned, including Halifax and his successor, Inverchapel. When Bevin consulted them by telegram early in March their reaction was against the appointment; among other experienced diplomats informally consulted by Lascelles, even Duff Cooper, the Duke's former supporter, now Ambassador in Paris, advised against it. Halifax's telegram to Bevin, forwarded to the King, was so particularly hostile that the King caused Lascelles to write instructing him to do nothing to obstruct the Duke's intention to live in the United States.

As early as 1943 Halifax had warned of the possibility that the Windsors were grooming themselves for 'future occupation of this embassy', which he thought could prove dangerous:

... familiarity with him and her is not unlikely to breed a certain kind of sympathy, and from that sympathy a transition to the thought of his having been unjustly treated and therefore of some resentment against those who unjustly treated them is not a large one. More than once [he continued] responsible Americans have spoken in this sense to me, even saying in some quarters American thought would almost regard the present King and Queen as place-holders for the in-justice-rightful occupant![99]

He was now advising that the Duke should be discouraged from living in the United States even as a private individual but, with the war over, the King was no longer worried by the 'two camps' possibilities as far as the United States was concerned. He was anxious to see the Duke of Windsor settled permanently and, so far as possible in the circumstances, contentedly. Lascelles had suggested to the Duke that he buy himself a house

somewhere in the southern states, and make it a centre of private hospitality ... where he could bring together worthwhile Americans, English and foreigners ... with this he could continue some line of his own (stock-raising, arboriculture, agricultural research, etc.) which would give him an interest, and which, with his considerable means, he could well afford to do on a useful, and even profitable scale....

Lascelles told Halifax:

The King feels strongly ... that USA is the only place in which he *can* live, and that he should be urged to make it his permanent home as soon as possible. He must not settle in the UK ... France today, and still less France tomorrow, is no place for him; and there are obvious difficulties in the way of his going to any corner of the British Empire. The King ... is strongly advising him to pack up and go to the USA as soon as possible; to make himself a permanent home there, and *in an unofficial capacity* to do what he can for the 'betterment of Anglo–American relations'.

The King, furthermore, hoped that if the Duke did settle there, it would be possible for the British Embassy to 'establish a friendly and unofficial relationship with the Duke whereby HRH's wish to make himself useful in the sphere of Anglo–American understanding may be encouraged, and, when necessary, controlled by private advice'.[100]

The Duke's plan foundered on Foreign Office opposition, but there was nothing to have prevented him playing a useful and interesting part on the lines he had envisaged as a private person, but for his extreme aversion to paying tax. The Duke loved the United States; his attraction towards America had changed his life. He had a long-standing aversion to things French and spoke the language badly but, for tax reasons, he was to spend most of the rest of his life there. He blamed his brother: '... you and your advisers have turned down the offer of my services,' he wrote stiffly. As the Duchess put it more straightforwardly to her aunt, giving her the news that the British Government was not prepared to do anything for them, there were 'taxes to be considered first of all and then the mounting costs everywhere'. Surrounded by the destitution and austerity of post-war Europe the Windsors were employing at their house in Boulevard Suchet twenty-eight people and two secretaries. As Wallis wrote, 'I imagine outside of embassies it is the only house run in this fashion in France and probably England today....' A decade later James Pope-Hennessy, visiting their country house outside Paris, Le Moulin des Tuileries, wrote: 'Every conceivable luxury and creature comfort is brought, called on, conscripted, to produce a perfection of sybaritic living. It is, of course ... consciously aimed. The Queen Mother at Clarence House is leading a lodging-house existence compared to this.'[101] The Duchess's clothes bills alone were estimated at £35,000 a year, excluding the huge sums paid by the Duke for his presents of jewellery to her. Money and status had been a continuing obsession with the Windsors since the Abdication, the root of the Duke's quarrels with his brother, of his tainted connections with Wenner-Gren and others. It was important to them both to show each other and the world that they had lost nothing by the Abdication.

In France the Windsors paid no taxes, enjoyed the privilege of buying liquor, tobacco and other goods duty free through the British Embassy and the military commissary. The Duke's fortune of £1 million or so in 1936 was now worth at least three times that amount, yet money, and perhaps a desire to live again in the public eye, must have prompted the Duke of Windsor to begin the very un-royal task of writing his memoirs in 1947. It began with a contract signed in February 1947 with Henry Luce, proprietor of Time-Life, to write four articles on his early life up to the First World War. Entitled 'The Education of a Prince' and ghosted by a Time-Life editor, Charles V. Murphy, who later fell out with the Windsors and went on to write a best-selling, if uncomplimentary, biography of the couple, the first series appeared in *Life* and the *Sunday Express* in December 1947. 'OK but he shouldn't have done them,' was Harold Nicolson's comment. The King said nothing publicly but he did not invite his brother to Princess Elizabeth's wedding.

That year, while the Duke was engaged on recalling his more distant, innocent past before the First World War, the King was engaged in minimizing the potential damage caused by the emergence of evidence of his brother's activities before and during the Second. In the autumn of 1949 the King learned definitely that rumours that had been circulating for the previous twelve months that the Duke was writing his memoirs were true, that he was writing them for world-wide publication and that they would include the Abdication. On 20 October 1949, Harold Nicolson, after talking to Lascelles, reported him as 'very distressed at the news of the Duke of Windsor's autobiography'. The King was appalled. The Abdication had been the first family betrayal; now, for money and in public print, his brother was resurrecting what had been for him the most traumatic experience of his life. In December 1949, uncomfortably close to the twelfth anniversary of what the King called 'the dreadful day', the Duke, having consulted Jowitt earlier that year as to the legal possibilities of reversing the King's decision on the Duchess's title, chose, with conspicuously bad timing, to raise the subject for the last time, making a personal appeal to his brother in an emotional interview. Having had Jowitt's opinion, the Duke now knew this was his only chance. In a letter written on 15 December the King turned him down, trying to convey to his brother what he had perhaps never been able to make him understand face to face. Reliving his own feelings during those weeks, he told him of his shock at learning that his brother intended to marry Mrs Simpson, the 'most ghastly void' which his abdication had left and which he himself had had to fill, the ordeal of the Coronation and what had followed. The one, single reason for all this horror, the King reminded his brother, was that the people of Britain and the Empire had concluded that Mrs Simpson was unfit to be their Queen and that he had accepted it. To reverse this decision, the King said, 'wouldn't make sense of the past'.

The Duke of Windsor did not reply to this letter for almost six months, by which time he had brought their mutual past again into the public domain. On 22 May 1950, *Life* began the second series of 'The Education of a Prince'. On 6 June the Duke of Windsor wrote his brother a cool note: 'Before leaving New York I arranged with Life magazine to send you the four issues in which my articles are being published. I hope you are receiving them.'[102] A year later, against a background of international social gossip as to the nature of the Duchess's relations with the questionable Jimmy Donahue, the full auto-biography, *A King's Story*, was published. The King was by then mortally ill: in September on the eve of his operation, perhaps with intimations of mortality, perhaps also sorry for his brother whose marriage seemed then to be fulfilling his family's expectations, he sent the Duke some grouse he had brought down from his last season at Balmoral.

The bitterness between the family and the Windsors had, however, by then gone too deep. The Duke, who had prepared a recording to coincide with the British launching of his book, was furious when the publishers cancelled it as a mark of respect when the King's serious illness was announced, his anger seeming principally to have been inspired by the fact that, on the afternoon his speech should have been delivered, the King's daughters were seen on a race-course. At some point in the three months before the King's death the Duke apparently wrote a letter to his mother of such bitterness concerning his brother and sister-in-law that even the Duchess, advising her husband from afar at the time of the King's funeral, realized it was unforgivable.[103] Their correspondence, as published, does not suggest that the Duke felt any grief at his brother's death, or that the Duke went to London for any reason other than to be seen publicly at his brother's funeral (at which he was described as appearing 'jaunty') and to obtain a continuance of his allowance under the new regime, the female representatives of which the Duke described as 'these ice-veined bitches'. 'Mama as hard as nails but failing,' the Duke noted. 'Cookie [the Queen Mother, to whom they also referred as Mrs Temple Senior] listened without comment [to his explanation of the 'offending letter'] & closed on the note that it was nice to be able to talk about Bertie to somebody who had known him so well.'[104] The widowed Queen's view was that if his elder brother had not abdicated, her husband would still be alive.

ᘓ 13 ᘓ

WALKING WITH DEATH

'During these last months the King walked with death, as if death were a companion, an acquaintance, whom he recognized and did not fear.... We all saw him approach his journey's end.'
Winston Churchill, broadcast, 7 February 1952

'As a result of the stress he was under the King used to stay up too late and smoked too many cigarettes – he literally died for England ...', Alec Hardinge, who had seen the King at close quarters during the darkest days of the war, told his son.[1] The years immediately following the war had been almost equally stressful as crisis piled upon crisis. The King had left for South Africa in January 1947 a deeply tired, anxious man. The tour, although a change from the daily grind at Buckingham Palace, was an exhausting one, taxing even the Queen's formidable constitution. The King lost a great deal of weight – seventeen pounds. By January the following year, 1948, he was already suffering from cramp in his legs, the early symptoms of Buerger's disease, arteriosclerosis as a result of smoking, which was restricting the flow of blood to his lower legs and feet. By August, he was, he noted, 'in discomfort most of the time'. His secretaries, going in to see him in his study after a day's shooting, would find him kicking his leg against the desk to restore the circulation. He did not, however, summon a doctor to examine him until a fortnight after he returned to London on 8 October.

Commander Sir Morton Smart, who had rejoiced in the title of Manipulative Surgeon to the King since 1937, was, according to the King's biographer, 'gravely alarmed' at the condition of the King's right foot and consulted the royal general medical adviser, Sir Maurice Cassidy. Their alarm, however, does not seem to have led to any urgent result, since it was another ten days before a further consultation was held, this time with the addition of Sir Thomas Dunhill, Serjeant-Surgeon to the King, another septuagenarian. All, Wheeler-Bennett writes, 'were agreed on the King's serious condition' and 'at once decided' to call in Professor James Learmonth, a considerably younger man, Regius Professor in Clinical Surgery, and the top expert in the country on vascular disease. Even then, Professor Learmonth, who was based in Edinburgh,

449

did not examine the King until almost two weeks later, on 12 November. Learmonth's diagnosis was, indeed, alarming – a condition of early arterio-sclerosis, with a danger of gangrene developing and even the possibility of the King's right leg requiring amputation. It was by now over three weeks since the King had first consulted Sir Morton Smart and, in the meantime, he had been carrying out severely taxing duties such as the Remembrance Day Service at the Cenotaph and a review of the Territorial Army in Hyde Park, both of which entailed a considerable amount of painful and potentially dangerous standing. Now, however, that the gravity of the situation was realized, the doctors took immediate action, ordering the cancellation of the King's con-templated tour of Australia and New Zealand. The King, determined to go, argued for a shorter programme, but the doctors forbade it. Reluctantly, two days after the birth of Prince Charles on 14 November 1948, the King agreed, the announcement of the cancellation and a bulletin giving the news of his health was issued on 23 November. (Princess Elizabeth had not been told of the seriousness of her father's condition until after the birth of her child.) The bulletin stated that the King was suffering from 'an obstruction to the circulation through the arteries of the legs' which had 'only recently become acute', the defective blood supply to the right foot being a cause for anxiety. There was no doubt, the doctors wrote, 'that the strain of the last twelve years has appreciably affected his resistance to fatigue'.

The King was confined to bed until mid-December, when he got up to find that the Queen had had new pictures hung in his Audience Chamber as a surprise for him when he left his bedroom. 'The poor King,' she told Ben Nicolson, who helped her hang them. Although the King was well enough to go to Sandringham for the New Year and even, on 18 January, to do a little shooting, the King could not lead a normal life. He bore his illness with great patience for a man with such a nervous temperament. Harold Nicolson, engaged to write the public life of King George v, was told by a member of the Court that he would not find King George vi difficult. 'Since he has become a recognised invalid he is as sweet and patient as can be,' he said. Rest and patience, however, were not curing him; on 3 March Learmonth told him that, if he wanted to live a normal life, he would have to have a right lumbar sympathectomy operation. The King's reaction was one of exasperation: 'So all our treatment has been a waste of time. . . .' It had not been, however; the King had been in danger of losing his right leg and, although Learmonth would have liked to have operated earlier, the King's general physical condition had been too weak to have withstood it. 'The first thing we've got to do', Learmonth told a member of the Court, 'is to get the King in shape to have an operation at all.' 'How are you going to do that?' 'With iron pills from Boots,' Learmonth retorted.[2]

Learmonth also said, 'Before we do this operation we've got to cut down on the smoking.' Nicotine addiction was a Windsor family curse, from Edward vii's generation down. Smoking had certainly played a major part in the deaths of the King's father and grandfather; King George v's respiratory difficulties before his death had necessitated oxygen tanks being kept in his bedroom. Even Queen Mary smoked; her present to her son 'Bertie' on his eighteenth birthday had been a cigarette case. George VI was only fifty-four, but his life was already endangered. The lumbar sympathectomy operation which Learmonth now proposed to carry out involved cutting a nerve at the base of the spine which functions as a thermostat contracting the blood vessels in the arteries on a hot day, opening them on a cold one, thus regulating the supply of blood. Without the operation of this nerve, the blood vessels would be permanently at maximum thus avoiding the claudification or blocking up of the arteries in the leg, but with the disadvantage that on a warm day the leg would feel extremely hot. The operation took place on 12 March 1949 in a specially fitted up operating theatre at Buckingham Palace. 'I am not in the least worried,' the King said as he went under the anaesthetic, but his family were. 'He is so ill, poor boy, so ill ....', Queen Mary told Harold Nicolson the day of the operation 'in such a sad voice'.

The operation was a success, seemingly giving the King a new lease of life. At the Ascot week ball at Windsor on 18 June he was seen to have his leg up on a foot rest, although he often danced none the less. Behind the scenes, however, the picture was not quite so encouraging. Learmonth had warned the King that the change in the tempo of his life must be permanent. The problem was apparently 'both psychological and physical', by which he meant that there was a constant danger of thrombosis which could be increased by the King's anxious temperament if he overstressed himself again. The King took the warnings seriously; at Balmoral he invented a kind of harness which would enable him to go out 'on the hill' without overworking his legs. It was attached to a pony which would pull him uphill and had a quick release clip as a precaution in case the pony bolted. He actively tried to 'worry less about matters political', as he wrote to Queen Mary from Balmoral in August, but Britain was on the verge of another economic crisis and for the King, as indeed for his Prime Minister, the spectre of the depression of 1931 seemed to loom. After a summer of strikes, including a damaging dock stoppage which hit exports, the British economy, heavily dependent on American aid, was in trouble again and in September the pound was devalued against the dollar from 4.03 to 2.80. Attlee informed the King that he proposed to call a general election. When the results came in on 23 February 1950, Attlee was still in power, but only just, with an overall majority of eight. With such a small majority and an aggressive Opposition scenting blood, there was now for the first time the possibility that the Government might be defeated, and a prolonged constitutional argument took place, mainly in newspaper columns, as to what course of action the King should take in such an eventuality, a controversy finally closed by Lascelles who took the unprecedented step of writing himself to the *The Times* on 2 May under the pseudonym 'Senex'.

The King was in noticeably good form that summer; at an Ascot week cocktail-party given by Princess Marina at Coppins on 15 June, he was described by Chips Channon as being 'in a rollicking mood – after several glasses of champagne' he touched Channon's cheek lightly with a finger and asked him how he managed to look so young for his age. Channon, although somewhat taken aback by the royal skittishness, was impressed by the King's obvious *joie de vivre*. 'Ascot this year was highly enjoyable', he wrote, 'and obviously the King, who now dotes on society and parties, adored it. He looks much younger than the Duke of Windsor.' Ten days later North Korean forces crossed the 38th Parallel and the Korean War began. Fears that the Americans might be contemplating the use of the atomic bomb sent Attlee on a flying visit to Truman in December. The Korean War weighed heavily on the King's horizon until mid-summer 1951. 'The incessant worries & crises through which we have to live have got me down properly,' he wrote to a friend.

The King was deeply interested in medicine both clinical and alternative. He took careful notes of his symptoms to facilitate his conversations with his doctors; he was also a firm believer in homoeopathy and had been for some thirty years. There had been previous links between the royal family and homoeopathy. Queen Alexandra's favourite doctor, Dr George Moore, was a homeeopath; Dr John Weir, whom the King made one of his official physicians on his accession in 1937, had been previously Physician-in-Ordinary to the Prince of Wales for almost ten years and was given the KCVO in 1932, and in 1944 became first President of the Brtish Faculty of Homoeopathy. The King had converted the Queen: 'I have now rather come round to a belief in homo-eopathy...,' she had written to a friend in 1944. Weir was also physician to Queen Mary, another fervent royal follower of homoeopathy, and to the Duchess of Gloucester. The King was one of his keenest patients: he even named one of his racehorses, Hypericum, after a homoeopathic remedy. Only three days before his death the King wrote Weir a touching letter from Sandringham in which he said that it was difficult for him to find words adequate to thank him for 'all the wonderful help' he had given him 'during a friendship, a deep friendship, which began over thirty years ago. I am a firm believer in your form of medicine', he added, 'and it suits me.'[3]

'The King walked with death', Churchill was to say of him, and, in a sense, he did. He knew that the possibility of a serious, even fatal, thrombosis was always there. He did not know, however, as his health worsened in the summer of 1951, that he had cancer of the lung. At the installation of the Duke of Gloucester as Great Master of the Order of the Bath in King Henry VII's chapel, Westminster Abbey, on 24 May, everyone remarked on how ill he looked. He had a temperature and, thinking that he had 'flu, retired to bed. The doctors subsequently diagnosed a small area of 'catarrhal inflammation' on the left lung, at which, or so the King wrote to Queen Mary, 'everyone is very relieved'.

At last the doctors have found the cause of the temperature. I have a condition on the left lung known as pneumonitis. It is not pneumonia though if left it might become it. I was X-rayed & the photographs showed a shadow. So I am having daily injections of penicillin for about a week. This condition has only been on the lung for a few days at the most so it should resolve itself with treatment.

The doctors think the cause of the cough was below the larynx & has now moved into the lung.... Everyone is very relieved at this revelation & the doctors are happier about me tonight than they have been for a week....

The doctors, it seems, were perhaps not quite so happy and relieved as the King thought. The King's illness was shrouded in secrecy at the time and it was only over ten years later that some of the facts of the case began to emerge. In an article in the St Mary's Hospital Gazette, Mr A. Dickson Wright, at that time a surgeon at the hospital, alleged that one of the doctors who attended the King that summer had made the correct diagnosis early on but that his warnings had been ignored by his colleagues, with the result that the doctor in question brooded over it for years and in April 1957 died of an overdose of barbiturates as a result. In a letter to the *People* Sir Geoffrey Marshall, one of the team of doctors and surgeons who attended the King at the time, denied that the doctor in question had ever issued any such warnings. Writing from 149 Harley Street, Marshall said that he had in front of him the doctor's reports dated 31 May, 6 June, 12 June and 10 July 1951. 'These', Marshall wrote, 'all describe an inflamed area in the left lung and in none of these reports was there any suggestion that a tumour was present, either cancerous or otherwise.' The fact that the doctor found it necessary to submit four separate reports on four separate occasions does, however, indicate that there was concern about the King's condition. Marshall, indeed, goes on to say that the clinicians – himself, Sir Horace Evans and Sir Daniel Davies – still suspected a growth in the lung and at their request the doctor took a series of chest films by a different technique known as tomography. These again failed to establish a diagnosis, so they invited a second doctor to co-operate with the first and take a second series of tomographs with a modified apparatus. 'These films for the first time showed the presence of a tumour at the root of the lung.'

Concerned or not, the royal doctors seem to have moved with the stately pace which had characterized their performance leading up to the operation to relieve the circulatory deficiency in the King's leg, a dilatorinesss which might have resulted in its amputation. Almost two months passed between the doctor's report on the first round of tests, dated 10 July 1951, and the King's tomograph tests in London on 8 September. Even then they were acting as a result of being summoned to a conference at Balmoral on 1 September. And yet the King had had what a courtier described as 'that awful cough' since Whitsun. The King took the overnight train down to London on 7 September, flying back on the evening of 8 September. A photographer for the *Sunday Pictorial* snapped him leaving the Wimpole Street clinic of his radiologist, Dr George Cordiner, after a visit of one and a half hours. The newspaper was slightly shamefaced about catching the monarch unawares: 'Why are we proud to print this picture?' the caption ran. 'Because it is news, because it is human, because it is symbolic. It is a happy and reassuring picture of a monarch about whom his people had been anxious for a long time.'[4] In fact, the results of that consultation were as bad as they could be, the tomograph showing at last the presence of a tumour on the King's left lung. The doctors recommended a bronchoscopy as soon as possible, to be carried out by Mr Clement Price Thomas, a leading chest surgeon, on 16 September. On 15 September the King, accompanied by Lord Porchester, who had been a shooting guest, and Sir Edward Ford, his Assistant Private Secretary, drove away from Balmoral for the last time. As they drove out of the gate, the King said, quoting a line from a comic song which the Queen and Princess Margaret used to sing at the piano. 'It may be that this is the end. Well it is. . . .'

The tomograph had been bad enough, but the result of the bronchoscopy was worse. The tumour was malignant. The King was not told, but the cautious language of the bulletin issued by the royal doctors on 18 September conveyed a grim message to those who knew how to interpret it. Churchill summoned Lord Moran, who, reading between the lines of previous bulletins, had warned him that it sounded as if there were a possibility of cancer of the lung. 'What do you make of it?' Churchill asked him as soon as he arrived. 'I don't like it at all,' Moran replied. 'The doctors would not have used a bronchoscope if they had not been worried about a possible cancer. But much more disturbing is their failure to say a single word of reassurance after the bronchoscopy. . . .' 'Why', Churchill asked, 'had the doctors used the words "structural changes"?' 'Because', Moran answered, 'they were anxious to avoid talking about cancer.' Two days later, Churchill learned the truth in a letter from Lascelles. 'The King has a growth in his lung. It means an operation – on Monday. The King did not know that Lascelles was writing to me. Poor fellow, he does not know what it means.'[5]

The King was told that his illness was caused by a blockage of one of the bronchial tubes which necessitated the removal of his left lung. He hated the idea of another operation: 'If it's going to help to get me well again I don't mind but the very idea of the surgeon's knife again is hell.' The operation took place at Buckingham Palace at 10 a.m. on Sunday 23 September, performed by Mr Clement Price Thomas over two hours. There were immediate complications; Price Thomas discovered that he might have to cut nerves in the larynx, which could mean that the King would never be able to speak above a whisper. The doctors decided to go ahead. For three hours as the royal family and Household waited anxiously for the King to recover consciousness, no news was given to the public. At 5 p.m. the doctor's first bulletin was posted on the railings outside the Palace. A crowd of 5,000 waiting on the steps of the Victoria Memorial opposite surged forward, breaking the police cordon. It took police three-quarters of an hour to form the anxious spectators into an orderly queue; two at a time they filed past to read the bulletin until late that night. It was not entirely encouraging: 'The King underwent an operation for lung resection this morning. Whilst anxiety must remain for some days, His Majesty's immediate post-operative condition is satisfactory.' There was always the danger that in his post-operative condition a thrombosis might occur as the bulletin indicated.

Privately in medical circles the long-term prognosis for the King's life was gloomy. On the evening of the King's operation, Wilson Harris, editor of the *Spectator*, telephoned Harold Nicolson to ask him to write an obituary of the King: 'It seems he had seen Lord Moran at the party given yesterday for Mr Cox of the London Library and that he had shaken his head gravely.' Moran's later opinion, according to Harris, was that 'even if the King recovers he can scarcely live more than a year'.[6]

On 24 September Harold Nicolson noted in his diary: 'The King pretty bad. Nobody can talk about anything else—and the Election is forgotten. What a strange thing is Monarchy!' The King had been worried about the uncertain political situation for some time; in the House of Commons the Conservative Opposition kept the Government's tiny majority under severe pressure. It was a situation to which only a general election—and a decisive one—could provide the solution. The King, unaware of how seriously ill he was, was still, as late as 1 September, contemplating making the tour of Australia and New Zealand which had been postponed due to his illness in the winter of 1948. On that day he had written to Attlee going over the points which they had previously discussed in the summer, pointing out that he could hardly embark on a long tour, which he had hoped to undertake in the following January, with the home political situation as it then was. Attlee replied on 5 September that he proposed dissolving Parliament in the first week of October. Despite the King's illness the election went ahead as planned, with polling taking place on 25 October. Within two weeks of his operation the King had been just well enough to fulfil the constitutional procedure necessary for the prorogation of Parliament. He had not been well enough to hold a Privy Council in the ordinary manner on 4 October, and the meeting approving the Order for the Prorogation had been presided over by the Queen and Princess Elizabeth as Councillors of State. The following day another Council was held in circumstances which were sadly reminiscent of King George v's last Council at Sandringham in January 1936. Five Councillors stood at the door to the King's bedroom while the Lord President read out the order of business. The King, speaking with difficulty, muttered the word 'Approved' and Lascelles held the necessary three documents at the bedside while the King signed his name. On 25 October the Conservative Party, led by the King's old friend and companion in arms, Winston Churchill, were returned with a majority of seventeen.

Churchill, however, was no longer physically the man he had been during their wartime partnership. He was seventy-six, rather deaf and had in 1949 suffered the first of his strokes. Power, however, had a rejuvenating effect; the pale, brooding old man with his leonine but almost bald head sunk into his shoulders could instantly become the rubicund, jovial figure of former days. His spirit remained indomitable and he still had the magical power to turn a phrase; but there was, as Moran said, a difference: then that indomitable spirit had been battling against a deadly threat to the world's freedom, now it was 'struggling only with the humiliations of old age and with economic problems that are quite beyond his ken'.[7] The King was twenty years younger but weak from a major operation, a man with only one lung and the threat of thrombosis hanging over him. None the less his eye for constitutional niceties was as sharp as ever. When Churchill submitted to him a first list of proposed ministerial appointments, he noticed that Anthony Eden's office of Secretary of State for Foreign Affairs was followed by another title, that of 'Deputy Prime Minister'. Although in Churchill's eyes this title was sanctified by his own invention of it as a distinction for Attlee as leader of the Labour Party in the coalition Government and had subsequently been in use for seven years, the King refused to sanction it as an official title. He saw this, rightly, as an infringement on his constitutional prerogative to choose a successor in the event of the death or resignation of a Prime Minister, a situation which was, in fact, to occur in his daughter's reign with the resignation on grounds of ill-health of Harold Macmillan. The title of Deputy Prime Minister implied a line of succession as, in the case of Eden, it was intended to.

The King conferred the Order of Merit on Attlee on 5 November; they had come to appreciate each other during the six years of Attlee's premiership. Attlee's final tribute to the King was to be less ringing than Churchill's, but in its plain language and honest assessment of the King's contribution to one of the most vital periods of British history, one which the King himself would have truly appreciated. Attlee told the House of Commons on 11 February 1952:

Few people realize how much time and care he gave to public affairs but visitors from overseas were often astonished at his close familiarity with all kinds of questions. With this close study went a good judgement and a sure instinct for what was really vital. During his reign there were developments in the Commonwealth, some of which entailed the abandonment of outward forms which a lesser man might have felt difficult to surrender, but he was essentially broad-minded and was ready to accept changes that seemed necessary.

The King made tremendous efforts both physical and pyschological to bring himself back to health. Not knowing that he had cancer, he made himself believe that the operation had cured him. He leaned, too, on his homoeopathic doctor, Dr Weir, for comfort and remedies. He seems to have brushed aside thoughts of thrombosis. His advisers, however, were already prepared for the worst. When, on 7 October, Princess Elizabeth and the Duke of Edinburgh finally took off on their tour of Canada and the United States, their original departure date having been put off because of the King's illness, the Princess's Private Secretary, Martin Charteris, travelled with all the papers necessary for the Queen's formal accession if her father died while they were abroad. Despite the King's illness, the tour was a tremendous success, photographs of a happy, smiling Princess, dressed in check shirt and flared, whirling skirt, square-dancing in Canada were flashed across the world. In Washington the couple stayed with the Trumans in the newly renovated White House. The Princess presented the President with gifts from the King for the White House: a rare pair of blue john (fluorite) and ormolu candelabra by Mathew Boulton and an early eighteenth-century, carved, gilt landscape mirror with a flower painting inset above, six foot eight inches high and four foot seven inches wide. (The King had written to President Truman asking if he would accept these presents 'for the White House to mark the occasion of its restoration', on 20 September, three days before his operation.) Truman was enchanted, writing to the King in a characteristically homely vein: 'We've just had a visit from a lovely young lady and her personable husband. They went to the hearts of all the citizens of the United States.... As one father to another', the President concluded, 'we can be very proud of our daughters. You have the better of me – because you have two!' The King was, indeed, proud of his daughter's success and to mark it he sent his private train to meet them at Liverpool where the ship docked and made them both Privy Counsellors.

The King was now a grandfather twice over, Princess Anne having been born on 15 August 1950. On 14 November he was well enough to attend Prince Charles's third birthday party and be photographed with him sitting beside him on a sofa. Before he left for Christmas at Sandringham on 21 December he pre-recorded his Christmas broadcast. He still hated broadcasting – the prospect of his 3 p.m. ordeal had cast a gloom over every Christmas Day. Once, when a younger member of the family was trying to catch his attention one Christmas morning, he suddenly burst out, 'I can't concentrate on anything because I've got that damned broadcast coming up this afternoon,' and he would be euphoric with joy afterwards if it had gone well. None the less he regarded it as an important part of his duty. He always wrote his own speech for the Christmas broadcast, with the help of the Queen. They worked together as a team; if they did not like the sound of a passage during rehearsal they would go away together and work on it, crossing things out, trying new phrases until they had exactly what they meant to get across.[8]

This was to be the only pre-recorded Christmas broadcast. The King, despite his distaste for it, had become a very good broadcaster; his broadcast for Christmas 1950 had come across very strongly with hardly any hesitation. He still wanted to try to do the 1951 broadcast live because he did not like the idea of recordings, feeling that he should make the effort to talk directly to his people. The Queen, however, knowing that the strain would prove too much for him in his post-operative state and on his voice in particular, ruled out the idea of a live broadcast. So the BBC engineer, Robert Wood, who had helped with all the King's broadcasts, brought his equipment to Buckingham Palace for a long, painful session lasting more than two hours, with the King only able to do a few words at a time, resting in between. By the time the King's ordeal was over, all three of them were anguished. 'It was very, very distressing for him, and the Queen, and for me,' Wood wrote, 'because I admired him so much and wished I could do more to help.' Remarkably, the King's voice came over strongly, with a supreme effort he managed to keep any sign of weakness out of it; it did, however, sound husky, hoarse, a wheezing as if he had a heavy cold audible between phrases. His grateful, optimistic words touched the hearts of his listeners:

... for not only by the grace of God and through the faithful skill of my doctors, surgeons and nurses have I come through my illness, but I have learned once again that it is in bad times that we value most highly the support and sympathy of our friends. From my peoples in these islands and in the British Commonwealth and Empire – as well as from many other countries – this support and sympathy has reached me and I thank you now from my heart....

At Sandringham that Christmas the King seemed in excellent form. He had started shooting again and taking an interest in the affairs of the estate. As ever, Anglo–American relations were in the forefront of his mind and he was anxious to do whatever he could personally to help. On 22 December, the day after his arrival from London, he wrote personally in his own hand to Truman, thanking him for his hospitality to Princess Elizabeth and stressing how much he welcomed the idea of Churchill's meetings with the President in Washington the following month:

Much has happened in the world since we met in Plymouth Sound in 1945. I am glad that you are going to renew your relations with Mr Churchill shortly. He is a wise man and understands the problems of this troubled world. I have always felt that our two countries cannot progress one without the other, & I feel that this meeting will unite us even more closely....[9]

On 7 January he wrote another personal, handwritten letter to Eisenhower, thanking him for his good wishes, and clearly wishing to enlist his goodwill on Churchill's behalf in the forthcoming meetings:

You, who have done so much to strengthen the friendship between our two countries, will, I am sure, agree with me as to the vital importance of the dicussions now going on in Washington, & will share my hope that they may achieve positive results. The chances of keeping the peace will obviously be deeply affected by their outcome....[10]

Other observers close to the King were not so confident about his health. Lascelles, who had lost his only and much beloved son John from an incurable disease the previous September, was perhaps over-conscious of the shadow of death and over-sensitive to the signs he saw, but he was worried enough to send Churchill, then still in the United States, a warning telegram on 20 January. The King, however, was making plans for a convalescent visit to South Africa, where the formerly hostile Nationalist leader, now the Prime Minister, Dr Malan, had offered Botha House, his official country residence, to the King and his entourage. Townsend had been sent out to reconnoitre and returned at the end of January to report to the King; plans were made for the King and Queen to leave for South Africa on 10 March. On 29 January the King went up to London for a consultation with his doctors, who, apparently, pronounced themselves 'very well satisfied' with their patient. The following evening the royal family, the King, the Queen, Princess Elizabeth and the Duke of Edinburgh, and Princess Margaret with Peter Townsend in attendance, went to a performance of *South Pacific* at Drury Lane. It was in the nature of a family celebration of the King's recovery and also a last get-together before the Princess and the Duke flew off the following morning to undertake the tour of Australia and New Zealand originally planned for the King. The following day, 31 January, the King, unusually, went to Heathrow to see his daughter off to Kenya, the first stage of her journey. He stood hatless in the cold wind, his eyes with the glaring look they took on in moments of emotion. Whatever brave front the King put on, he knew in his heart of hearts that he was living on the edge of life and that it was always possible that he would not see his beloved daughter again. Churchill, who was there at the airport, however, described him as 'gay and even jaunty, and drank a glass of champagne'. 'I think', he added, 'he knew he had not long to live.'

He returned on 1 February to Sandringham, the place which, like his father, he loved the best. On 5 February he was out shooting hares and rabbits. It was the tail-end of the season, a 'Keepers' Day', the kind of informal day which he liked. There were some twenty guns including estate tenants, local police, gamekeepers from neighbouring estates and friends. The day was perfect, the wide Norfolk sky an arch of pale blue. The King was on top gun form, his last shot caught a hare at full speed, killing it cleanly and expertly. He spent the evening happily, sending messages of congratulation to the gamekeepers, planning the next day's shooting, dining with the Queen and Princess Margaret, the Household and shooting friends, perhaps putting in pieces in the jigsaw which was always laid out on a table. He went to bed at 10.30, staying awake until midnight when a watchman in the garden saw him fiddling with a recently fixed latch at his bedroom window. Some time in the early hours of 6 February a blood clot stopped the King's heart. He died silently in his sleep.

The King's valet, James MacDonald, went into the King's bedroom carrying his early-morning cup of tea as he always did at 7.30 a.m. to find the King dead. Most of the royal staff were in London; Edward Ford was rung up at his Park Lane flat by Lascelles with the code-word they had already worked out for just such an emergency, 'Hyde Park Corner'. 'Hyde Park Corner last night,' Lascelles told Ford. 'Go and tell the Prime Minister and Queen Mary.' Ford went to Downing Street:

I found Mr Churchill in bed, papers scattered all over, a chewed cigar in his mouth and on the bedside table a green candle from which he was accustomed to relight it. I said 'I've got bad news, Prime Minister, the King died last night. I know nothing else.' He was shattered by it. There was a pause and then he said, 'Bad news? The worst', and then there was a flurry and flop and the papers going everywhere, and then 'Get me Anthony' and then 'Can we scramble [the telephone line]?' And we couldn't scramble and then in that curious way as if everybody was listening and as if they couldn't understand what he was saying, instead of saying 'The King is dead', he said 'Our Chief is dead'. He was preparing a speech on foreign affairs in the House and he just threw away the papers, saying 'How unimportant these matters are.'[11]

Jock Colville arrived to find Churchill 'sitting alone with tears in his eyes, looking straight in front of him and reading neither his official papers nor the newspapers. I had not realized how much the King meant to him.' Colville tried to cheer him up, saying how well he would get on with the new Queen, 'but all he could say was that he did not know her and that she was only a child'.[12] 'He is terribly upset, Sir,' Churchill's valet told Moran that evening, 'but nothing to [compared with how he was at] lunchtime. Then, when he was reading his speech he broke down.' A few weeks later, after Churchill suffered a minor arterial spasm which might have been the precursor of another stroke, Moran consulted Colville and Lord Salisbury about the possibility of persuading him to retire, or even, as Salisbury suggested, to continue as Prime Minister but in the House of Lords. Who, however, would succeed in persuading him? Moran, knowing Churchill's reverence for the monarchy, suggested the Queen. Lascelles was, therefore, consulted but disabused them of the idea: 'If she said her part, he would say charmingly: "It's very good of you, Ma'am, to think of it –" and then he would very politely brush it aside. The King might have done it ... but he is gone.'[13]

Ford continued his sad errand by going on to Marlborough House, where he found Colville's mother, Lady Cynthia, one of Queen Mary's ladies-in-waiting. 'Oh dear!' said an appalled Lady Cynthia. 'It's very difficult. Queen Mary's never forgiven me for telling her without any adornments that the Duke of Kent had been killed. Perhaps you'd better go up and say he's very ill.' 'I can't possibly say that,' Ford told her; 'within half an hour the world will know. I've got to tell her before.' Then she very kindly said that she would go up and prepare the Queen, came down and said simply, 'I've told her.' In fact, Queen Mary already seemed to know; as Lady Cynthia came through the door, she asked, 'Is it the King?' She was very controlled, Ford remembered. 'She was sitting there twiddling her fingers as many members of the royal family do.' 'What a shock!' she said. In the words of her biographer, 'From this, the last great emotional shock of her life, Queen Mary did not recover....' She aged rapidly and died only just over a year later on 24 March 1953, aged eighty-five.

The King's eldest daughter became Queen as she sat watching rhino at a waterhole from Treetops Hotel high up in a fig tree in the Aberdare Forest game reserve in Kenya. At dawn she, her husband and his equerry, Lieutenant-Commander Michael Parker, returned to the Sagana Royal Lodge, given them by the people of Kenya Colony as a wedding present. Martin Charteris visited her there that morning, 'she was looking wonderful in blue jeans, talking about the rhinoceros'. At the nearby Outspan Hotel, where he was to lunch en route for Treetops, he was called to the telephone. In the booth he found a local journalist, white-faced, who told him the news. He spoke to Michael Parker at Sagana. 'Mike, our employer's father is dead. I suggest you do not tell the lady at least until the news is confirmed.' Later Parker told the Duke of Edinburgh. 'He looked as if you'd dropped half the world on him' was how Parker described it. The Duke told his wife in private. When Charteris arrived at Sagana about fifteen minutes later, he found her 'very composed, absolute master of her fate, we thought'.[14] They left for Entebbe in a Dakota: 'I remember we were flying over this savannah country, you could see the fires burning in the bush and I was telling her what was going to happen when she got home.' At the age of only twenty-five, Princess Elizabeth had become, in the words of her accession proclamation, 'Queen Elizabeth the Second, by the Grace of God Queen of this Realm and of all Her other Realms and Territories, Head of the Commonwealth, Defender of the Faith'.

At Sandringham the atmosphere was one of stunned shock. For the Queen, now Queen Elizabeth The Queen Mother, and Princess Margaret, it was as if their world had suddenly come to an end. The King had been the centre of their universe; now he was suddenly gone and the world had shifted on its axis, its focal point to the new Queen. The widowed Queen had persuaded herself that all was well; to her the King had seemed to have taken on a new lease of life. As she wrote to a friend three months later:

It is very difficult to realise that the King has left us, he was so much better, & so full of plans & ideas for the future, and I really thought that he was going to have some years perhaps less anguished than the last fifteen. I think that those years after the war were terribly anxious & frustrating and it was all very hard & grinding work, and I longed for him to have some peace of mind. He was so young to die, and was becoming so wise in kingship. He was so kind too, and had a sort of natural nobility of thought & life, which sometimes made me ashamed of my narrower & more feminine point of view. Such sorrow is a very strange experience – it really changes one's whole life, whether for better or for worse I don't know yet....[15]

To General and Mrs Eisenhower she had written the previous month, using much the same words: 'One cannot imagine life without him,' she wrote sadly, 'but I suppose one must carry on as he would wish.'[16] 'She was absolutely heart-broken,' a friend said nearly forty years later; 'for a few months I thought she wasn't going to pull herself together.... I'm sure she thinks about him a great deal now, still misses him.'

In London, when the news was announced, people stopped their cars in the streets, got out and stood to attention as a mark of respect. Women wept openly. Internationally, Colville noted in his diary, 'the world showed a large and genuine measure of grief'. The reaction in America was perhaps the most surprising. President Truman wrote privately in his diary: 'He was a grand man. Worth a pair of his brother Ed.' At his weekly news conference, the Secretary of State, Dean Acheson, having read out his formal tribute, put it aside to say a few words of his own. 'The King's outstanding quality', he reflected, 'had been his selfless dedication to duty.' The House of Representatives passed a resolution of sympathy and, as a mark of respect, adjourned for the rest of the day. The Massachusetts Senate adopted a resolution which spoke of 'The beloved Monarch ... a King who was sincerely devoted to his subjects, who laboured to the point of exhaustion in showing to them, and to the world, the proper discharge of his royal duties.' In Los Angeles, which the King had never visited, the first newspaper editorial to break the news said: 'The late King may find his niche in history as "George the Good". Or perhaps Britons will remember him as "George the Steadfast". He was both. Great Britain's sorrow will find an echo all over the civilized world. He died well loved.'[17] On the morning of 6 February, Alexander Cadogan set down his professional opinion of the King, with whom he had so often worked over the past fifteen years: 'He was undoubtedly a model King, &, as I thought, a charming man.'[18]

One of the most perceptive summings-up of King George vi, his life, reign and what he had come to mean to his people, was sent by the French Ambassador in London, René Massigli, to his Foreign Minister, Maurice Schuman. The British people, he said, had felt a genuine grief at the passing of their sovereign, apart, perhaps, from a coterie in high Society who had looked down on him for his limited intellectual qualities and his mediocre artistic tastes, perhaps too because he lacked the royal panache of his grandfather Edward vii. But, the Ambassador continued, if the measure of a King lies in the manner in which his character and qualities correspond to the needs of a nation at a given moment in its history, then 'George vi was a great King, and perhaps a very great King'. 'Courage, work and austerity have been the watchwords of the country over the last fifteen years, and one could say that the King provided an example of them. . . . He had to learn everything at the age of 41 on ascending the throne. And he learned quickly and well.' Politicians and those who worked with him had high praise for his professionalism, his acute sense of duty and his constant desire to do the best for his subjects; Massigli particularly underlined the strict neutrality with which the King had behaved during the years of socialist government. He concluded:

By his simplicity, his goodwill, his courage, and his sense of duty, his respect for constitutional principles and the example of his private life, King George vi has amassed around the throne a capital of sympathy and loyalty upon which . . . he could call in case of crisis. Brought to the throne in a climate of dynastic and constitutional crisis, George vi has died leaving to his daughter a throne more stable than England has known throughout almost her entire history.[19]

During the weekend of 9 and 10 February, the King's body lay in the little family church at Sandringham, the coffin draped in the royal standard and guarded by his estate workers keeping vigil in groups of four; then, on the 11th, following the same route as his father's in January 1936 it was borne on the same gun-carriage from the church to Wolferton station, and by train to London. During the three days it lay in state in Westminster Hall 300,000 people filed past in tribute before the funeral on 16 February in St George's Chapel, Windsor. Among the wreaths was Churchill's final tribute to King George vi, a wreath of white flowers bearing a note with two words in the old Prime Minister's own hand, 'For Valour'.

SOURCE NOTES

All quotations from the letters and diaries of Queen Victoria, King Edward VII, King George V, Queen Mary, King Edward VIII (also as Prince of Wales and Duke of Windsor) and King George VI are from *King George VI* by Sir John Wheeler-Bennett (1958) unless otherwise indicated.

'Nicolson, Balliol' indicates unpublished passages from the manuscript diaries at Balliol College, Oxford, as distinct from the published versions edited by Nigel Nicolson (1966) and Stanley Olson (1980).

1: Heritage

1. James Pope-Hennessy, *Queen Mary* (1959), p. 316
2. *Ibid.*, p. 317
3. Virginia Cowles, *Edward VII and his Circle* (1956), pp. 158–9
4. *Ibid.*, p. 273
5. John Vincent (ed.), *The Crawford Papers* (1984), p. 39
6. Pope-Hennessy, *op. cit.*, p. 402
7. Elizabeth Longford, *Victoria R.I.* (1964), pp. 571, 574
8. Kenneth Rose, *King George V* (1983), p. 64
9. Nicolson, Balliol, 23 June 1949
10. Barrington-Ward Papers, Diary, 29 June 1942
11. See H. Montgomery Hyde, *The Cleveland Street Scandal* (1976)
12. Pope-Hennessy, *op. cit.*, p. 186
13. *Ibid.*, pp. 207–8
14. *Ibid.*, p. 242
15. *Ibid.*, p. 227
16. *Ibid.*, p. 272
17. *Ibid.*
18. John Gore, *King George V, a Personal Memoir* (1941), p. 20
19. HRH Duke of Windsor, *A King's Story* (1951), p. 6
20. Gore, *op. cit.*, p. 360n
21. *Ibid.*, p. 74
22. Nicolson, Balliol, 27 July 1949
23. Georgina Battiscombe, *Queen Alexandra* (1969), p. 143
24. Pope-Hennessy, *op. cit.*, p. 248
25. *Ibid.*, p. 105
26. *Ibid.*, p. 110
27. Mabell, Countess of Airlie, *Thatched with Gold* (1962), p. 102

2: A Cloistered World

1. Longford, *op. cit.*, p. 567
2. Pope-Hennessy, *op. cit.*, p. 392
3. Airlie, *op. cit.*, pp. 112–13

4. Windsor, *op. cit.*, p. 24
5. James Pope-Hennessy, *A Lonely Business* (1981), p. 215
6. Windsor, *op. cit.*, p. 27
7. Nicolson, Balliol, 7 September 1949
8. Earl of Harewood, *The Tongs and the Bones* (1981), p. 15
9. Pope-Hennessy, *Lonely Business*, p. 214
10. Windsor, *op. cit.*, p. 18
11. *Ibid.*, pp. 57–8
12. Airlie, *op. cit.*, p. 114
13. HRH Prince of Wales to Captain Bryan Godfrey-Faussett, 4 September 1916, Phillips Sale Catalogue, 12 February 1986, Lot 499
14. Windsor, *op. cit.*, p. 37
15. *Ibid.*, p. 39
16. *Ibid.*, p. 48
17. Christopher Hibbert, *Edward VII: A Portrait* (1976), p. 199
18. Viscount Esher, *Journals and Letters*, vol. II, *1903–10* (1934), p. 53

3: Ugly Duckling and Cock Pheasant

1. Imperial War Museum, Department of Sound Records, SR 10056/1/1
2. *The Lancet*, 18 February 1911, p. 460
3. Nicolson, Balliol, 20 September 1943
4. Windsor, *op. cit.*, pp. 69–70
5. Thomas Jones, *A Diary with Letters, 1931–1950* (1954), p. 302
6. Churchill Archives Centre, Diaries of Sir Bryan Godfrey-Faussett, BGGF 1/61, 21 April 1910
7. *Ibid.*, BGGF 1/66
8. Godfrey-Faussett to Ponsonby, 22 and 25 August 1911, Phillips sale, 12 August 1987, Lot 562
9. Harewood, *op. cit.*, p. 27
10. HRH Princess Alice, Countess of Athlone, *For my Grandchildren* (1966), p. 78
11. Sir Harold Nicolson, *King George V: His Life and Reign* (1952), p. 194
12. Private collection, HRH Prince Albert to Godfrey-Faussett, 21 July 1913
13. *Ibid.*, 22 July 1913
14. Imperial War Museum, Memoir by Captain E.M.C. Barraclough RN, MS 81/48/1
15. *Ibid.*, Memoir by Commander F.J. Chambers RN, MS 82/30/1
16. *Ibid.*, Papers of Commander F.J. Lambert RN, PP/MCR/318, 3 June 1914
17. *Ibid.*, Papers of Captain H. Hamilton RN, MS 75/41/1, n.d.
18. *Ibid.*, 13 June 1914
19. Pope-Hennessy, *op. cit.*, p. 482
20. Imperial War Museum, Hamilton Papers, MS 75/41/1, 19 July 1914
21. *Ibid.*, n.d., ?29 July 1914
22. Winston S. Churchill, *The World Crisis* (1931), p. 126
23. Imperial War Museum, Hamilton Papers, MS 75/41/1, n.d. (*c.* 26 August 1914)
24. *Ibid.*, 20 June 1915
25. Rose, *op. cit.*, p. 172
26. James Lees-Milne, *Harold Nicolson: A Biography*, vol. II: *1930–1968* (1981), p. 241
27. Rose, *op. cit.*, pp. 178–9
28. Sir Frederick Ponsonby, *Recollections of Three Reigns* (1951), p. 329
29. Private collection, Prince Albert to Godfrey-Faussett, 23–27 January 1916
30. *Ibid.*, 13 March 1916
31. *Ibid.*, 27 January 1916
32. Arthur J. Marder, *From the Dreadnought to Scapa Flow*, vol. III (1966), p. 205
33. *Ibid.*, p. 194
34. Private collection, Prince Albert to Mrs Godfrey-Faussett, 11 June 1916
35. Imperial War Museum, Special Miscellaneous A5, Prince of Wales to Godfrey-Faussett, 14 June 1916
36. Private collection, Prince Albert to Mrs Godfrey-Faussett, 9 July 1916
37. Interview with Captain A.V.S. Yates RN (retd), 15 August 1986
38. College Archives, Royal Air Force College Cranwell, Papers of Wing-Commander A.E.F. McCreary RAF (retd), unpublished memoir
39. Rose, *op. cit.*, p. 387
40. Private collection, Prince Albert to Godfrey-Faussett, 1 March 1918
41. *Ibid.*

42. Cranwell, typescript memoir: 'Some Recollections of Cranwell' by Wing-Commander S.E. Townson
43. Cranwell, unpublished memoir: 'Memories of Cranwell from end of year 1917 to May 1918' by Wilfred A. Goss
44. Cranwell, McCreary memoir
45. *Ibid.*

4: Love and Duty

1. Vincent, *op. cit.*, p. 398
2. Recollections by the Prince of Wales's chauffeur, Henry Jacobs, in *Empire News and Sunday Chronicle*, 20 January 1957
3. Robert R. Hyde, *Industry Was my Parish* (1968), p. 105
4. Grant Family Archive, courtesy of Sir Hector Laing
5. *Ibid.*
6. Interview with Sir David Llewellyn, 2 February 1987
7. James Warner Bellah, 'Passed with Flying Colors', *Reader's Digest*, pp. 11–12, condensed from *Air Facts* (1948)
8. Imperial War Museum, Department of Sound Records, SR 3190/3
9. Ministry of Defence, Air Historical Research Centre, Ref. AHB5/67A, Royalty and the Royal Air Force 1918–58
10. Cited in Philip Ziegler, *Mountbatten* (1985), p. 50
11. *The Freemason*, vol. LIX, 6 December 1919
12. Hannah Pakula, *The Last Romantic: A Biography of Queen Marie of Roumania* (1985), p. 267
13. PRO, FO 371/7679. C5413/266/92
14. *Ibid.*, C8097/266/92
15. *Ibid.*
16. *Ibid.*, C87541/266/92
17. Pope-Hennessy, *Queen Mary*, pp. 521–2
18. *Ibid.*
19. Airlie, *op. cit.*, p. 163
20. Interview with the Dowager Duchess of Rutland, 11 March 1987
21. Vincent, *op. cit.*, p. 406
22. James Stuart himself, writing in 1967 over forty years after the event, gave,

incorrectly, a different date and place for that first meeting, placing it a year later and in a different setting, at a Royal Air Force ball at the Ritz: *Within the Fringe* (1967), p. 57
23. Airlie, *op. cit.*, p. 166
24. Elizabeth Longford, *The Queen Mother* (1981), p. 16
25. The Monster appears to have been the eldest son of Patrick, Master of Glamis, and his wife Charlotte, officially declared dead at birth in 1821 but who, apparently, died a centenarian in 1921.
26. Dorothy Laird, *Queen Elizabeth the Queen Mother* (1966), p. 32
27. Private collection, HM the Queen to Osbert Sitwell, 18 December 1944
28. Penelope Mortimer states that Lady Elizabeth Bowes-Lyon was born somewhere in London, either at her grandparents' flat in Grosvenor Gardens or perhaps in an ambulance, and not at St Paul's, Walden Bury, as her father declared, probably for reasons of convenience, six weeks later when he returned to Hertfordshire from Scotland: *Queen Elizabeth* (1986), p. 16
29. Longford, *The Queen Mother*, p. 18
30. Bodleian Library, Department of Western Manuscripts, Violet Milner Papers, MS VM 28, Helen Cecil to Violet Milner, 15 September 1920
31. Airlie, *op. cit.*, pp. 166–7
32. Private information
33. Airlie, *op. cit.*, p. 167
34. Typescript in the possession of a member of the family and cited with some omissions in Robert Rhodes James (ed.), *Memoirs of a Conservative: J.C.C. Davidson's Memoirs and Papers, 1910–1937* (1969), pp. 109–10
35. Robert Rhodes James (ed.), *Chips: The Diaries of Sir Henry Channon* (1967), p. 397
36. Longford, *op. cit.*, p. 23
37. Cited in Rose, *op. cit.*, p. 311
38. Interview with the Dowager Duchess of Rutland, *op. cit.*
39. Private information
40. Airlie, *op. cit.*, p. 168

5: The Yorks

1. Osbert Sitwell, *Rat Week* (1984), p. 42
2. Brian Masters, *Great Hostesses* (1982), p. 88
3. *Ibid.*, pp. 99–100
4. Private collection, HM the Queen to Osbert Sitwell, 27 September 1942
5. Masters, *op. cit.*, p. 152
6. PRONI, Londonderry Papers, D. 3099/13/29, The Queen to Edith, 7th Marchioness of Londonderry, 3 March 1938
7. Sitwell, *op. cit.*, p. 38
8. Alan Clark, (ed.), *A Good Innings: The Private Papers of Viscount Lee of Fareham* (1974), p. 272
9. PRO WORK 19/771, Sir Frederick Ponsonby to Sir Lionel Earle, 10 November 1924
10. *Ibid.*, WORK 19/772, Sir Lionel Earle to Sir Warren Fisher, 11 November 1924
11. *Ibid.*, Sir Frederick Ponsonby to Sir Lionel Earle, 15 October 1926
12. Airlie, *op. cit.*, p. 179
13. Private information
14. *News Chronicle*, 13 April 1953
15. *Sunday Express*, 29 October 1967, extract from Reginald Pound, *Harley Street* (1967)
16. Cecil Edwards, *Lord Bruce of Melbourne* (1966), p. 135
17. Private information
18. Nicolson, Balliol, 20 September 1943
19. Nicolson, Balliol, 14 December 1936
20. MS Diary of Victor Cazalet MP, 6 March 1920
21. PRONI, Londonderry Papers, D. 3099/3/13/3, HRH Duke of York to 7th Marquess of Londonderry, 18 November 1920
22. Duff Hart-Davis (ed.), *In Royal Service: The Letters and Journals of Sir Alan Lascelles 1920–1936* vol. II (1989), p. 4
23. *Ibid.*, p. 50
24. *Ibid.*, p. 109
25. Rose, *op. cit.*, p. 362
26. Clark, *op. cit.*, pp. 289–90
27. HRH Duke of Windsor, *A Family Album* (1960), p. 130
28. Airlie, *op. cit.*, pp. 183–4
29. Cited in Robert Lacey, *Majesty* (1977), pp. 74–5
30. Sitwell, *op. cit.*, p. 44
31. Marion Crawford, *The Little Princesses* (1950), p. 19
32. *Ibid.*, p. 16
33. *Ibid.*, p. 28
34. Private information
35. Gloria Vanderbilt and Thelma, Lady Furness, *Double Exposure* (1959), p. 261
36. *Ibid.*, p. 281
37. *Ibid.*, p. 382

6: The Year of Three Kings

1. Michael Bloch (ed.), *Wallis & Edward, Letters 1931–1937* (1986), p. 70
2. Charles Higham, *Wallis: Secret Lives of the Duchess of Windsor* (1988), p. 1
3. Bloch, *op. cit.*, pp. 10–11
4. Duchess of Windsor, *The Heart Has its Reasons* (1956), p. 170
5. Dugdale Typescript Diary, 'Constitutional Crisis November to December 1936 by Nancy Dugdale', written from data supplied by Thomas Dugdale, 8 December 1936
6. Kenneth Young (ed.), *The Diaries of Sir Robert Bruce Lockhart*, vol. I: *1915–1938* (1973), p. 215
7. Airlie, *op. cit.*, p. 195
8. Columbia University Libraries, Bakhmeteff Archive, HRH Duke of Kent to Prince Paul Karageorgevic, 26 September [1934]
9. Bloch, *op. cit.*, Duchess of Windsor to Mrs Merriman, 30 December 1934, p. 105
10. *Ibid.*, p. 104
11. Lambeth Palace Library, MS 2862, Diary of Rev. Dr Alan Campbell Don, 10 May 1935
12. Archives du Ministère des Affaires Etrangères, Quai d'Orsay, Direction d'Europe 1930–1940 Grande Bretagne, Z 274.3. File no. 176. f. 34
13. *Ibid.*, f.44
14. Cazalet Diary, 2 June 1935
15. Cited by Francis Watson, 'The Death of

George V', in *History Today*, December 1986, p. 24

16. *Ibid.*

17. Cazalet Diary, notes on conversation with Walter Monckton on 1 December 1937

18. Nicolson, Balliol, 13 July 1937

19. Bloch, *op. cit.*, p. 179

20. Private information

21. Private collection, Duchess of York to Osbert Sitwell, 28 August 1935

22. Watson, *op. cit.*, pp. 24–5

23. Lambeth MS 2863, Don Diary, 20 September 1935

24. Watson, *op. cit.*, p. 27

25. *Ibid.*, p. 28

26. Sitwell, *op. cit.*, pp. 73–4

27. Nicolson, Balliol, 14 December 1936

28. Bloch, *op. cit.*, p. 145

29. Watson, *op. cit.*, p. 30

30. Vincent, *op. cit.*, p. 571

31. Brian Inglis, *Abdication*, (1966), p. 2

32. Cited in Francis Watson, *Dawson of Penn* (1950), p. 285

33. Rhodes James (ed.), *Chips*, p. 58

34. Masters, *op. cit.*, p. 140

35. Bloch, *op. cit.*, p. 154

36. Lambeth Palace, Papers of Cosmo Gordon Lang, Archbishop of Canterbury, Lambeth MS vol. 22, f. 390, Lord Wigram to Archbishop Lang, 27 January 1936

37. PRO, CAB 63/53, memorandum by Hankey

38. Bloch, *op. cit.*, p. 158

39. Stanley Olson (ed.), *Harold Nicolson: Diaries and Letters 1930–1964* (1980), p. 116

40. Rhodes James (ed.), *Chips*, pp. 45–6

41. Churchill Archives Centre, Papers of Major-General Sir Edward Spears, Sprs 2/1

42. Robert Rhodes James, *Victor Cazalet* (1976) p. 189

43. Rhodes James (ed.), *Chips*, p. 73

44. Helen Hardinge, *Loyal to Three Kings* (1967), p. 89

45. Nicolson, Balliol, 14 December 1936

46. Lambeth MS 2862, Don Diary, 15 November 1934

47. Lambeth MS 2864, Don Diary, 29 January 1936

48. Lambeth Palace, Lang Papers, vol. 22, f. 128, Archbishop Lang to Bishop Barnes, 11 November 1936

49. Rhodes James, *Cazalet*, p. 203

50. University of Birmingham Library, Papers of Neville Chamberlain, NC 18/1/947

51. Vincent, *op. cit.*, p. 568

52. Young (ed.), *op. cit.*, p. 342

53. Cited in Inglis, *op. cit.*, p. 113

54. *Ibid.*

55. *Documents on German Foreign Policy 1918–1945*, Series C, vol. IV (1962), Doc. No. 27

56. *Ibid.*, Doc. No. 531, Pt III

57. *Ibid.*, Series C, vol. V (1966), Doc. No. 77

58. Airlie, *op. cit.*, p. 198

59. Michael Thornton, *Royal Feud* (1985), p. 101

60. Hardinge, *op. cit.*, p. 91

61. At the age of twenty-one George IV, then Prince of Wales, fell in love with Maria Fitzherbert, a twice-widowed Roman Catholic six years his senior. Despite her reluctance, he persuaded her to marry him in secret on 15 December 1785 in defiance of the Act of Settlement of 1701, which forbade any member of the royal family to become a Roman Catholic or to marry one; and also of the Royal Marriages Act of 1772, by which the Prince of Wales required his father's consent to marry. The marriage remained a secret and ten years later the Prince married his first cousin, Princess Caroline of Brunswick, whom he subsequently sensationally tried to divorce. Mrs Fitzherbert behaved nobly, George IV less so, twice abandoning her for aristocratic married mistresses, but on his death-bed he left instructions that a picture of 'my beloved wife, my Maria Fitzherbert' be interred with him.

62. Martin Gilbert, *Winston S. Churchill* vol. V: *1922–1939* (1976), p. 811

63. House of Lords Record Office, Beaverbrook Library, BBK/G/23, Folder XIII

64. Windsor, Duchess, *op. cit.*, p. 225

65. Pembroke College, Cambridge, Papers of Sir Ronald Storrs, Box VI/2, 20 August 1935

66. Nicolson, Balliol, 9 June 1936

67. *Ibid.*, 13 July 1936

68. Pembroke, Storrs Diary, Box VI/4, 4 March 1941; private information

69. Thornton, *op. cit.*, p. 113

70. Hardinge, *op. cit.*, p. 113

71. Bodleian Library, Department of Western Manuscripts, Papers of Geoffrey Dawson, MS Dawson 79 ff. 1–9

72. News International plc Record Office, Papers of Geoffrey Dawson, Hardinge to Dawson, 27 October 1936

73. Bodleian Library, Papers of Sir Donald Somervell, Manuscript Journal 1934–7

74. Cazalet Diary, 20 November 1936. In the published text Rhodes James has mistranscribed 'Simpson had deceived her' as 'Simpson had divorced her'.

75. Sitwell, *op. cit.*, p. 55

76. Nigel Nicolson (ed.), *Sir Harold Nicolson: Diaries and Letters 1930–1939* (1966), p. 277

77. Rhodes James (ed.), *Chips*, pp. 74–5

78. Cited in H. Montgomery Hyde, 'The Windsors and the Londonderrys', in *Harpers & Queen*, July 1980

79. Rhodes James (ed.), *Chips*, pp. 77–8

80. Cited in Frances Donaldson, *Edward VIII* (1974), pp. 235–6

81. Windsor, *A King's Story*, p. 327

82. Donaldson, *op. cit.*, p. 248

83. HRH Princess Alice, Duchess of Gloucester, *Memoirs* (1983), pp. 113–14

84. Pope-Hennessy, *Queen Mary*, p. 575

85. *Sunday Express*, 10 June 1962

86. Windsor, *A King's Story*, p. 335

87. Rhodes James (ed.), *Chips*, p. 91

88. *Ibid.*, p. 206

89. H. Montgomery Hyde, *Baldwin* (1973), p. 474

90. Keith Middlemas and John Barnes, *Baldwin* (1969), p. 1001

91. Cited in *ibid.*, p. 993

92. Olson (ed.), *op. cit.*, p. 106

93. PRO, DO 127/21 108504

94. *Ibid.*

95. *Ibid.*

96. Dugdale Diary, 2 December 1936

97. Wheeler-Bennett, p. 285 *nb*, incorrectly states that the King put this suggestion of a broadcast to Baldwin on 4 December

98. Bloch, *op. cit.*, p. 215

99. Cazalet Diary, entry opposite page dated 1 December 1937

100. PRO, DO 127/23 108504

101. Cited in Neil Balfour and Sally Mackay, *Paul of Yugoslavia* (1980), pp. 135–6

102. Borthwick Institute of Historical Research, Papers of the Earl of Halifax, A7.8.6, 11 December 1940

103. Cited in Hyde, *op. cit.*, p. 406

104. Second Earl of Birkenhead, *Walter Monckton* (1969), p. 143

105. Bloch, *op. cit.*, pp. 220–1

106. House of Lords Record Office, Beaverbrook Papers BBK/G/23, Folder III

107. Cited in Birkenhead, *op. cit.*, p. 147

108. Dugdale Diary, 9 December 1936

109. *Ibid.*, 8 December 1936

110. Balfour, *op. cit.*, p. 137

111. Cited in Rhodes James, *Cazalet*, pp. 188–9

112. Dugdale Diary, 8 December 1936

113. Notes by Sir Edward Peacock, cited in Birkenhead, *op. cit.*, p. 149

114. *Ibid.*

115. Donaldson, *op. cit.*, p. 292

116. Cited in Watson, *op. cit.*, p. 30

117. Cited in Birkenhead, *op. cit.*, p. 151

118. See *Daily Telegraph*, 9 December 1979, for report on Lot 40 in Sotheby's sale

119. Halifax Papers, A7.8.6, 11 December 1940

120. Windsor, *A King's Story*, p. 410

121. PRO, DO 127/23 108504

122. Bodleian, Dawson Papers, MS Dawson 93, Papers of Cecilia Dawson including working papers of Evelyn Wrench, G.M. Young to Dawson, 16 June n.y.

123. Sitwell, *op. cit.*, p. 114

124. Birkenhead, *op. cit.*, p. 152

125. Charles Stuart (ed.), *The Reith Diaries* (1975), p. 193

7: Consecration

1. Walter Bagehot, *The English Constitution* (World's Classics edn, 1928), pp. 34–7
2. Wheeler-Bennett incorrectly states on p. 302 that this announcement was made on 2 January
3. India Office, L/PO/5/19 (iii), Linlithgow to Zetland, 14 December 1936
4. *Ibid.*, Zetland to Linlithgow, 18 January 1937
5. *Ibid.*, 31 January 1937
6. Lambeth MS, Lang Papers, vol. 21, f. 203
7. *Ibid.*, vol. 152, f. 1, Dawson of Penn to Lang, 15 March 1937
8. Lambeth MS 2865, Don Diary, 23 March 1937
9. Robert Wood, *A World in Your Ear...* (1979), pp. 102–3
10. Lambeth MS, Lang Papers, vol. 223, 'Notes on the Coronation of King George VI and Queen Elizabeth'
11. Nicolson Diaries, p. 301
12. Lambeth MS, Lang Papers, vol. 22, ff. 48 & 59, Sir Gerald Wollaston to Lang, 8 and 20 April 1937
13. Interview with the Lady Priscilla Aird, 12 June 1986
14. HRH Princess Alice, Countess of Athlone, *op. cit.*, p. 104
15. Lambeth MS 2865, Don Diary, 21 July 1937
16. Bloch, *op. cit.*, p. 238
17. Nicolson Diaries, pp. 297–8
18. Norman Hartnell, *Silver and Gold* (1955), p. 94
19. Meryle Secrest, *Kenneth Clark* (1984), p. 119
20. India Office, L/PO/5/19 (ii), Linlithgow to Zetland, 30 August 1937
21. *Ibid.*, Zetland to Linlithgow, 12 September 1937
22. *Ibid.*, Linlithgow to Zetland, 7 October 1937
23. *Ibid.*, extract from Cabinet Conclusions 38(37) of 20 October 1937; secret letter from 'H' to Sir Rupert Howorth, 22 October 1937
24. *Ibid.*, Zetland to Linlithgow, 15 November 1937
25. *Ibid.*, L/PO/5/19 (i), 'Most Secret' memo: 'Question of the Royal Visit to India in the Cold Weather of 1938–1939'
26. *Ibid.*, Hardinge to Zetland, 14 December 1937
27. *Ibid.*, Extract from Cabinet Conclusions 3(38) of 2 February 1938
28. *Ibid.*, Zetland to Linlithgow, 7 February 1938
29. *Ibid.*, Zetland to Neville Chamberlain, 9 February 1938
30. Lambeth MS 2864, Don Diary, 16 December 1936
31. Alfred Shaughnessy, *Both Ends of the Candle* (1978), p. 62
32. Birkenhead, *op. cit.*, pp. 163–4
33. Bakhmeteff Archive, Columbia University, Papers of Prince Paul of Yugoslavia, HM Queen Mary to HRH Prince Paul, 16 December 1936
34. Rhodes James, *Cazalet*, pp. 188–9
35. Lambeth MS, Lang Papers MS 2884, Lang to Parker, 29 December 1936
36. Rhodes James, *Cazalet*, pp. 188–9
37. Stuart, *op. cit.*, p. 194
38. Diana Cooper, *Light of Common Day* (1959), pp. 191–3
39. Sitwell, *op. cit.*, pp. 70–1

8: Two Camps

1. Jones, *op. cit.*, p. 302
2. John Barnes and David Nicholson (eds), *The Empire at Bay: The Leo Amery Diaries 1929–1945* (1988), p. 435: Lord Brownlow's account of the Abdication to Amery on 28 December 1936
3. Birkenhead, *op. cit.*, p. 165
4. Donaldson, *op. cit.*, p. 310
5. Bloch, *op. cit.*, p. 231
6. *Ibid.*, p. 233
7. *Ibid.*, pp. 245–6
8. Bodleian, Somervell Papers, Typescript: 'Politics by D.B.S....'
9. Bloch, *op. cit.*, p. 257

10. Bodleian, Somervell Papers, Manuscript Journal 1934–7
11. See Michael Bloch, *The Secret File of the Duke of Windsor* (1988), pp. 45–6, where the 'Belvedere Agreement' is printed, not, apparently, in its entirety
12. *Ibid.*, p. 50
13. Frances Stevenson, *Lloyd George: A Diary* (1971), pp. 326–7
14. Martin Gilbert, *Winston S. Churchill*, vol. v Companion Pt 3: *The Coming of War 1936–1939* (1982), p. 634
15. *Ibid.*, p. 635
16. Barnes and Nicholson, *op. cit.*, p. 439
17. Gilbert, *op. cit.*, p. 644
18. Chamberlain Papers, NC 18/1/1001, Chamberlain to Hilda, 10 April 1937
19. *Ibid.*, NC 2/23A, Diary, 12 April 1937
20. *Ibid.*, NC 18/1/1001, 10 April 1937
21. Gilbert, *op. cit.*, p. 659
22. *Proceedings of the Select Committee on the Civil List* (HMSO, 1937), p. 18
23. Private information
24. House of Lords, Beaverbrook Papers, BBK/G/23, Folder XIII
25. Bodleian, Monckton Papers, Dep. Monckton Trustees, MS1, f. 170, William Gibson to Monckton, 8 November 1937
26. Lambeth MS, Lang Papers, vol. 48, Ulick Alexander to Lang, 21 December 1936
27. Young (ed.), *op. cit.*, vol. II, p. 641
28. News International plc Record Office, Dawson Papers, Dawson to Willmott Lewis, 21 October 1937
29. Young (ed.), *op. cit.*, vol. II, p. 748
30. Bloch, *Wallis & Edward*, p. 257
31. *Ibid.*, p. 268
32. *Ibid.*, p. 279
33. Lambeth MS 2865, Don Diary, 5 April 1937
34. *Ibid.*
35. Bloch, *Wallis & Edward*, p. 285
36. British Library, Papers of Lord Harvey of Tasburgh, Diary, BL Add MS 56379, 21 April 1937
37. Gilbert, *op. cit.*, p. 674
38. Mills Memorial Library, McMaster University, H. Montgomery Hyde Papers, typescript of *Baldwin*, p. 448
39. Chamberlain Papers, NC 2/24A, 23 May 1937
40. Gilbert, *op. cit.*, p. 653
41. Chamberlain Papers, NC 2/24A, 30 May 1937
42. Cited in Bloch, *Secret File*, pp. 91–2: George VI to Duke of Windsor, 15 December 1949
43. Birkenhead, *op. cit.*, p. 166
44. Halifax Papers, Diaries, A7.8.5, 19 July 1940
45. Gilbert, *op. cit.*, p. 659
46. *Ibid.*, pp. 651–3, note of remarks to Wigram on 25 April 1937
47. Cited in Donaldson, *op. cit.*, p. 324
48. *Ibid.*, p. 326
49. Hugo Vickers, *Cecil Beaton* (1985), p. 199
50. News International plc Record Office, Dawson Papers, Dawson to Wigram, 17 June 1937; Wigram to Dawson, 20 June 1937
51. PRO, Avon Papers, FO 954/33/5, Hardinge to Vansittart, 1 May 1937
52. *Ibid.*, FO 954/33/6, Vansittart to Hardinge, 4 May 1937
53. *Ibid.*, FO 954/33/32, Vansittart to Hardinge, 31 August 1937
54. *Ibid.*, FO 954/33/36, Hardinge to Vansittart, 2 September 1937
55. *Ibid.*, FO 954/33/52
56. *Ibid.*, FO 954/33/59, Vansittart to Hardinge, 1 October 1937
57. *Ibid.*, FO 954/33/61
58. *Ibid.*, FO 954/33/69, Sir Eric Phipps to FO, 4 October 1937
59. Churchill Archives Centre, Phipps Papers, PHPP I/I/19, Phipps to Eden, 12 October 1937
60. PRO, FO 954/33/67–8, Vansittart to Hardinge, 4 October 1937
61. *Ibid.*, FO 954/33/71, Hardinge to Oliver Harvey, 6 October 1937
62. *Ibid.*, FO 954/33/47–8
63. Bedaux was captured by the Americans in North Africa in 1943 and indicted for treason and communicating with the enemy; he committed suicide in prison awaiting trial.

64. Cazalet Diary, 1 December 1937
65. Cited in J. Bryan III and Charles J.V. Murphy, *The Windsor Story* (1979), p. 359
66. PRO, FO 954/33/65–6, Vansittart to Hardinge, 4 October 1937
67. Vincent, *op. cit.*, p. 582
68. *Ibid.*, pp. 617–18
69. PRO, FO 954/33/94–6, Ogilvie-Forbes to Eden, 17 October 1937
70. *Ibid.*, FO 954/33/183, Lindsay to Hardinge, 29 November 1937
71. Michael Bloch, *The Duke of Windsor's War* (1982), p. 155
72. PRO, FO 954/33/125, Washington tel. 383, 5 November 1937
73. Cited in Vincent, *op. cit.*, p. 619
74. Churchill Archives Centre, Phipps Papers, PHPP I/I/19, Phipps to Eden, 28 December 1937
75. Bloch, *Secret File*, p. 62
76. Cazalet Diary, n.d. (1 December 1937)
77. *Ibid.*, 17 December 1937

9: Bulwark against Dictatorship

1. Churchill Archives Centre, Papers of Sir Hughe Knatchbull-Hugessen, KNAT 2/70, Hardinge to Knatchbull-Hugessen, 10 August 1937
2. Vincent, *op. cit.*, p. 617
3. Young (ed.), *op. cit.*, vol. II, 6 April 1947
4. *Sunday Express*, 17 June 1967
5. Olson (ed.), *op. cit.*, p. 348
6. Stevenson, *op. cit.*, pp. 376–7
7. Halifax Papers, A7.8.6, 7 November 1940
8. Chamberlain Papers, NC 18/1/940, Chamberlain to Hilda, 23 November 1935
9. *Ibid.*, NC 18/1/1003, same to same, 25 April 1937
10. *Ibid.*, NC 18/1/1006, same to same, 30 May 1937
11. *Ibid.*, NC 18/1/1009, same to same, 26 June 1937
12. *Ibid.*, NC 18/1/1014, same to same, 1 August 1937
13. *Ibid.*, NC 18/1/1019, Chamberlain to Ida, 7 September 1937

14. *Ibid.*, NC 7/3/21, Chamberlain to George VI, 2 September 1937
15. Martin Gilbert, *op. cit.*, vol. v, p. 626
16. Earl of Birkenhead, *Halifax* (1965), p. 372
17. Alan Bullock, *Hitler: A Study in Tyranny* (rev. edn, 1973), p. 368
18. Birkenhead, *Halifax*, p. 370
19. Cited in Bullock, *op. cit.*, p. 371
20. Orville H. Bullitt (ed.), *For the President ... Correspondence between Franklin D. Roosevelt and William C. Bullitt* (1973), p. 310
21. PRO, FO 371/21606 C174/17, Phipps to Cadogan, 10 January 1938
22. Richard Dubreuil, '*La visite des souverains britanniques*' in *La France et les français en 1939* (Paris, 1978), pp. 88–91
23. Chamberlain Papers, NC 7/4/8, HM Queen to Chamberlain, 2 July 1938
24. Quai d'Orsay, Archives du Ministère des Affaires Etrangères, Direction d'Europe, 1939–40, Grande Bretagne, File Z 274.3.sd.2, no. 1822, Bonnet to Cambon, 18 July 1938, and PRO, FO 371/21607 C5966/174/17
25. PRO, 371/21608, Campbell to Halifax, 29 July 1938
26. Dubreuil, *op. cit.*, p. 84
27. Interview with the Dowager Duchess of Rutland, *op. cit.*
28. Earl of Halifax, *Fullness of Days* (1957), p. 196
29. Cooper, *op. cit.*, p. 223
30. Quai d'Orsay, File Z 274.3.sd.2, no. 671, f. 100, Corbin to Bonnet, 23 July 1938
31. Bodleian, Violet Milner Papers, MS VM 49, 25 July 1938
32. Gilbert, *op. cit.*, vol. v, p. 972
33. *Ibid.*, p. 1001
34. Malcolm Muggeridge (ed.), *Galeazzo Ciano: Diaries* (1947), 7 January 1939, p. 7
35. *Ibid.*, 11 January 1939, pp. 9–10
36. Chamberlain Papers, NC 7/3/31, Chamberlain to George VI, 17 January 1939
37. *Ibid.*, NC 7/3/35, George VI to Chamberlain, 18 March 1939

38. J.W. Pickersgill, *The Mackenzie King Record*, vol. I: *1939–44* (Toronto, 1960), p. 255

39. Elliott Roosevelt and James Brough, *A Rendezvous with Destiny* (New York, 1977), p. 230

40. Franklin D. Roosevelt Library, PSF Great Britain Kings and Queens

41. *Ibid.*, 2 November 1938

42. Bodleian, Dawson Papers, MS Dawson 80, Wharton to Dawson, 18 January 1939, f. 129; Miéville to Dawson, 8 February 1939, f. 134

43. *Ibid.*, MS Dawson 80*

44. *Daily Express*, 9 May 1939

45. See 'The Queen's Uncle', *Sunday Express*, 5 March 1967

46. Birkenhead, *Monckton*, p. 169

47. House of Lords, Beaverbrook Papers, BBK G24, Folder xvi, Duke of Windsor to Beaverbrook, 13 March 1939

48. Roosevelt Library, PSF France, Bullitt

49. Queen's University Archives, John Buchan Papers, Tweedsmuir to Hardinge, 22 May 1939

50. *Ibid.*

51. Tweedsmuir to Stair Gillon in Wheeler-Bennett

52. *Ibid.*

53. Buchan Papers, Tweedsmuir to Baldwin, 19 June

54. News International plc Record Office, Dawson Papers, Stevenson to Dawson, 11 July 1939

55. *Daily Mirror*, 10 July 1939

56. Buchan Papers, Mackenzie King to Tweedsmuir, 30 May 1939

57. Buchan Papers, Tweedsmuir to Baldwin, 19 June 1939

58. Roosevelt Library, PSF Great Britain Kings & Queens, Bullitt to Roosevelt, 23 March 1939

59. Eleanor Roosevelt, *This I Remember* (New York, 1949), p. 153

60. *Ibid.*, pp. 154–5

61. *Ibid.*, p. 156

62. Joseph P. Lash, *Eleanor and Franklin* (1972), p. 582

63. Roosevelt, *op. cit.*, p. 156

64. PRO, FO 371/2279, 'Helen' to Stella, Lady Reading, 6 February 1939

65. *Ibid.*, FO 371/22800, extract from a letter to Sir L. Oliphant

66. Roosevelt, *op. cit.*, p. 153

67. PRO, FO 371/22800

68. Roosevelt Library, PSF, Mackenzie King to Roosevelt, 1 July 1939

69. Elliott Roosevelt and James P. Lash, *The Roosevelt Letters...*, vol. III (New York, 1952), p. 266

70. PRO, FO 371/22801, FO despatch 677, 20 June 1939

71. Nicolson Diaries, p. 403

72. *Daily Mirror*, 23 June 1939

10: The King at War

1. Chamberlain Papers, NC 18/1/1108, Chamberlain to Ida, 23 July 1939

2. *Ibid.*, NC 18/11/1112, Chamberlain to Hilda, 13 August 1939

3. Trefor Evans (ed.), *The Killearn Diaries* (1972), p. 107

4. Olson (ed.), *op. cit.*, p. 156–7

5. Gilbert, *op. cit.*, vol. v, p. 1109

6. Interview with Lieutenant-General Sir Ian Jacob, 26 July 1988

7. Philip Ziegler, *Mountbatten* (1985), p. 125

8. Liddell Hart Centre, Papers of Lt-Gen. Sir Henry Pownall, Diary, 18–20 November 1939

9. *Ibid.*, 22 November 1939

10. Chamberlain Papers, NC 2/24A, memo headed 'France 1939'

11. Pownall Diary, 8 December 1939

12. Rhodes James (ed.), *Chips*, p. 229

13. Pownall Diary, 11 January 1940

14. Chamberlain Papers, NC 18/1/1137, 7 January 1940

15. *Ibid.*, NC 7/3/42, Chamberlain to George vi, 8 January 1940

16. R.J. Minney (ed.), *The Private Papers of Hore-Belisha* (1960), p. 281

17. Chamberlain Papers, NC 7/3/45, George vi to Chamberlain, 25 March 1940

18. *Ibid.*, NC 7/4/10, Queen Elizabeth to Chamberlain, 17 May 1940

19. *Ibid.*, NC 7/3/47, George VI to Chamberlain, 5 August 1940
20. *Ibid.*, NC 2/24A, 14 October 1940
21. Nicolson, Balliol, 6 April 1955
22. John Colville, *The Fringes of Power...* (1985), p. 122
23. Martin Gilbert, *Winston S. Churchill* vol. VI: *1939–41, Finest Hour* (1983), p. 313
24. The King had invited Halifax to use the Palace gardens as a short cut between his home in Eaton Square and the Foreign Office.
25. Halifax Papers, A7.8.4, Diary, 11 May 1940
26. *Ibid.*, 5 June 1940
27. *Ibid.*, 18 June 1940
28. Colville, *op. cit.*, 7 August 1940, p. 211
29. Interview with Hon. Lady Lindsay of Dowhill, 28 July 1986
30. Colville, *op. cit.*, p. 733
31. *Ibid.*, p. 145
32. Gilbert, *op. cit.*, pp. 453–4
33. *Ibid.*, p. 454
34. Cited in Roger Keyes, *Outrageous Fortune: The Tragedy of King Leopold III of the Belgians 1901–1941* (1984), p. 310
35. Liddell Hart Centre, Alanbrooke Papers, Diaries 5/2, 23 May 1940
36. A.D. Divine, *Dunkirk* (1945), p. 240
37. Roosevelt Library, Hopkins Papers, Box 304, memorandum by Hopkins to Roosevelt, 30 January 1941
38. Ben Pimlott (ed.), *The Second World War Diary of Hugh Dalton 1940–45* (1986), 31 May 1940, p. 31
39. *Ibid.*, 11 June 1940, p. 38
40. Halifax Papers, A7.8.3, Diary, 20 March 1940
41. *Ibid.*, A7.8.4, Diary, 5 June 1940
42. Olson (ed.), *op. cit.*, p. 188
43. David Dilks (ed.), *The Diaries of Sir Alexander Cadogan, 1938–1945* (1971), p. 294
44. Keyes, *op. cit.*, p. 152
45. Dilks (ed.), *op. cit.*, p. 307
46. Bodleian, MS Eng. hist. c.498, David Euan Wallace Diary, 9 September 1940
47. Bodleian, Papers of Frederick Marquis, 1st Earl of Woolton, MS Woolton 2, Diary, 31 October 1940
48. Bodleian, Wallace Diary, 27 September 1940
49. Interview with the Dowager Viscountess Hambleden, 12 August 1986
50. Private information
51. Hartnell, *op. cit.*, pp. 101–2
52. Bodleian, MS Woolton 2, Diary, 11 October 1940
53. Queen Elizabeth to Osbert Sitwell, 1 February 1940
54. Bodleian, MS Woolton 2, 31 October 1940
55. *Ibid.*, 20 December 1940
56. Nicolson, Balliol, 10 July 1940
57. Bodleian, MS Woolton 2, 19 March 1942
58. *Time*, 2 July 1941
59. Roosevelt Library, PSF, Great Britain: King and Queen File, Box 69
60. *Ibid.*
61. 'The first time he came over here, Harry Hopkins told me that the President had finally become doubtful of Kennedy's reports and that one of the reasons Hopkins visited us was to see whether British morale was really as bad as Kennedy pretended...', J. Colville to Ismay, Ismay Papers, I/14/31/3c, Liddell Hart Centre
62. Roosevelt Library, Hopkins memorandum
63. Halifax Papers, A4.410.4.8/2, Halifax to George VI, 7 March 1941
64. *Ibid.*, A7.8.19, Secret Diary, 7 March 1942
65. John G. Winant, *A Letter from Grosvenor Square* (1947), p. 19
66. Halifax Papers, A2.278.26/4, George VI to Halifax, 14 April 1941
67. *Ibid.*, A4.410.1.8/3, Halifax to George VI, 16 May 1941
68. Roosevelt Library, PSF, GB Folder, Box 82
69. Rhodes James, *Cazalet*, p. 261
70. 'Mr President,' Wilkie replied, 'I had as many drinks as Churchill all the time I was with him, and no one has ever called me a drunk.' Halifax Papers,

A7.8.19, Secret Diary, 17 February 1941

71. Cazalet Diary, 3 June 1942
72. *Ibid.*, 19 August 1942
73. Interview with Sir Edward Ford, 22 July 1986
74. Halifax Papers, A2.278.26/5, George VI to Halifax, 1 March 1942
75. Bodleian, MS Woolton 2, 29 March 1942
76. Roosevelt Library, PSF, GB Folder, Box 96
77. Halifax Papers, A7.8.10, 9 May 1942
78. *Ibid.*, 15 May 1942
79. Liddell Hart Centre, Alanbrooke Diaries, 5/5, 15 April 1942
80. Cited in Martin Gilbert, *Winston S. Churchill*, vol. VII: *1941–1945, Road to Victory* (1986), p. 159
81. *Ibid.*, p. 160
82. PRO, PREM 3/76A/8 f. 2, 17 August 1942
83. Gloucester, *op. cit.*, p. 128
84. 'The Duke of Windsor has gone for three days to the Saar front and Gloucester is now "said to be ill" but that does not debar him from carrying on a continual conversation with frequent pulls at the bottle and outbursts of gruesome noises said to represent a laugh.' Earl of Munster to Monckton, 21 February 1940, Bodleian, Monckton Papers, Dep. Monckton Trustees, MS2
85. Liddell Hart Centre, Alanbrooke Diaries, 5/4, 18 March 1941
86. Private information
87. Liddell Hart Centre, Alanbrooke Diaries, 5/5, 28 August 1942
88. Wheeler-Bennett, *op. cit.*, p. 550
89. Roosevelt, *op. cit.*, p. 209
90. Captain Harry C. Butcher, *My Three Years with Eisenhower, the Personal Diary...1942–1945* (1946), 12 July 1942
91. Mark Clark, *Calculated Risk* (1951), p. 94
92. Gilbert, *op. cit.*, vol. VII, p. 249
93. *Ibid.*, p. 251
94. John Harvey (ed.), *The War Diaries of Oliver Harvey* (1978), p. 218
95. Gilbert, *op. cit.*, vol. VII, p. 358
96. Kay Summersby, *Eisenhower Was my Boss* (1949), p. 68

97. Harold Macmillan, *War Diaries: Politics and War in the Mediterranean, January 1943–May 1945* (1984), p. 120
98. Alistair Horne, *Macmillan, vol. 1: 1894–1956* (1988), p. 188
99. Clark, *op. cit.*, pp. 169–70
100. Macmillan, *op. cit.*, p. 123
101. N.A. Rose (ed.), *Baffy: The Diaries of Blanche Dugdale, 1936–47* (1973), p. 207
102. Nigel Hamilton, vol. II: *Monty, Master of the Battlefield, 1942–44* (1983), p. 293
103. Imperial War Museum, Montgomery Papers, Diary Notes, BLM 37/1
104. Macmillan, *op. cit.*, p. 130
105. David Eisenhower, *Eisenhower at War, 1943–45* (1986), p. 234
106. Liddell Hart Centre, Ismay Papers IV/Las/4, Lascelles to Ismay, 20 June 1944
107. Alexander of Tunis, 1st Earl, *Memoirs* (1962), pp. 129–30
108. Imperial War Museum, Leese Papers, Box 4, letter from Leese to his wife, 31 July 1944
109. Macmillan, *op. cit.*, p. 495
110. *Ibid.*, p. 497
111. Imperial War Museum, BLM 92/4, George VI to Montgomery, 24 August 1944
112. Nigel Hamilton, vol. III: *Monty the Field Marshal 1944–76* (1986), pp. 115–16
113. Imperial War Museum, BLM 92/8, Legh to Montgomery, 18 October 1944
114. Cited Hamilton, *op. cit.*, vol. III, p. 116
115. Imperial War Museum, BLM 92/9, Lascelles to Montgomery, 28 October 1944
116. Dwight D. Eisenhower, *At Ease, Stories I Tell my Friends* (1967), p. 279
117. Dwight D. Eisenhower Library, ERL Personal File #3, Lee to Lascelles, 14 November 1944
118. Hamilton, *op. cit.*, vol. III, p. 623n
119. Barnes and Nicholson, *op. cit.*, p. 1033
120. Hamilton, *op. cit.*, vol. III, p. 532

11: A New World

1. Nicolson, Balliol, 8 and 14 May 1945
2. British Library, Add. MS 56389, Harvey Diary, 12 June 1941

3. Halifax Papers, 4.410.4.16, Halifax to Cadogan, 13 September 1941
4. Harvey, *op. cit.*, p. 111
5. Liddell Hart Centre, Alanbrooke Diaries 5/5, 19 December 1941
6. Churchill Archives Centre, Cadogan Papers, ACAD 1/13, Diary, 19 March 1944
7. Gilbert, *op. cit.*, vol. VII, p. 1241
8. Sir John Wheeler-Bennett, *Friends, Enemies and Sovereigns* (1976), p. 163
9. PRO, FO 954/34/7–8, Churchill to Tito, 8 January 1944
10. Balfour and Mackay, *op. cit.*, p. 251
11. *Ibid.*, p. 284
12. PRO, FO 371/59538, Henderson to Lascelles, 23 July 1946
13. *Ibid.*, FO 954/33/25
14. *Ibid.*, FO 954/34/217
15. Halifax Papers, A7.8.15, Diary, 3 July 1944
16. *Ibid.*, A7.8.16, Diary, 17 April 1945
17. Birkenhead, *Halifax*, pp. 249–50
18. PRO, FO 954/2/285, Churchill to Stalin, 15 June 1945
19. Imperial War Museum, BLM 92/14, Lascelles to Montgomery, 21 June 1945
20. PRO, FO 954/2/299, Churchill to Stalin, 1 July 1945
21. Lord Moran, *Winston Churchill, The struggle for Survival 1940–1965* (1966), p. 274
22. *Ibid.*, pp. 311–12
23. Martin Gilbert, *Winston S. Churchill*, vol. VIII: *1945–1965*, 'Never Despair' (1988), pp. 114–15
24. Moran, *op. cit.*, pp. 282 and 285
25. Olson (ed.), *op. cit.*, 8 August 1945, p. 293
26. Moran, *op. cit.*, p. 312
27. Roosevelt Library, Hopkins Papers, Box 304, unpublished passage from Hopkins memorandum to Roosevelt, 30 January 1941
28. Herbert Morrison, *An Autobiography* (1960), pp. 247–8
29. Cited in Kenneth Harris, *Attlee* (1982), p. 352
30. Michael Foot, *Aneurin Bevan*, vol. 2 (1973), p. 349 *n2*

31. Cited in Wheeler-Bennett, *King George VI*, p. 650
32. Halifax Papers, A7.8.17, Diary, 1 August 1945
33. Morrison, *op. cit.*, p. 248
34. Pimlott (ed.), *op. cit.*, 4 March and 2 December 1942, p. 388, pp. 528–9
35. Ben Pimlott, *Hugh Dalton* (1985), p. 408
36. Philip M. Williams (ed.), *Diary of Hugh Gaitskell, 1945–1956* (1983), pp. 249–50
37. 7th Earl of Longford, *Born to Believe* (1953), p. 159
38. Williams, *op. cit.*, May 1951, pp. 250–51
39. *Ibid.*, p. 244
40. *Ibid.*, pp. 250–1
41. *Ibid.*, p. 78
42. Hamilton, *op. cit.*, vol. III, p. 679
43. Bodleian, Woolton MS 3, Diary, 24 October 1942
44. Peter Townsend, *The Last Emperor* (1975), p. 146
45. PRO, FO 371/65575, Baring to Addison
46. Bodleian, Violet Milner Papers, VM 48, Major G.R. Richards to Lady Milner, 23 April 1947
47. Peter Townsend, *Time and Chance* (1978), pp. 177–8
48. Cited in Mortimer, *op. cit.*, p. 213
49. Cited by Inverchapel in despatch to Bevin of 24 June 1947, PRO, FO 371/61001
50. Liddell Hart Centre, Ismay Papers, IV/Las/9a-b, Lascelles to Ismay, 27 December 1947
51. C.L. Sulzberger, *A Long Row of Candles: Memoirs and Diaries 1934–1954* (1969), p. 338
52. Ziegler, *op. cit.*, p. 407
53. *Ibid.*, p. 406
54. *Ibid.*, p. 409
55. *Ibid.*, p. 413
56. *Ibid.*, p. 415
57. Nicolson, Balliol, 15 August 1947
58. *Ibid.*, 27 October 1948

12: The House of Windsor

1. Nicolson, Balliol, 4 May 1946
2. Private information

3. Interview with John Blythe, 16 February 1989

4. Private information

5. Townsend, *Time and Chance*, p. 144

6. Private information

7. Private information

8. Sitwell, *op. cit.*, p. 46

9. Interview with Lord Bonham-Carter, 17 January 1989

10. Courtesy of Sir Edward Ford, King George VI to Ford, 15 January 1950

11. Aubrey Buxton, *The King in his Country* (1955), p. 50

12. Windsor, *A Family Album*, pp 11–12

13. Nicolson, Balliol, 9 May 1951

14. Durham Record Office, Londonderry Papers, D/Lo/c 237(i), 16 November 1932

15. Imperial War Museum, Leese Papers, Lascelles to Leese, February 1947

16. Halifax Papers, A2.278.26.7, George VI to Halifax, 4 February 1952

17. Dwight D. Eisenhower Library, Pre-Presidential Papers, Lascelles to Eisenhower, 13 March 1946, Eisenhower to Lascelles, 25 July 1947

18. Interview with the Earl of Carnarvon, 25 January 1989

19. Imperial War Museum, BLM 74, Notes on Planning the Campaign in NW Europe Jan–Jun 1944

20. See Nicolson, Balliol, 14 March 1950, and Quai d'Orsay, Direction d'Europe, No. 287, report by René Massigli to Maurice Schumann, 19 February 1952

21. Churchill Archives Centre, ACAD 1/6, 24 March 1937 and 15 March 1939

22. Evans (ed.), *op. cit.*, 22 October 1937, pp. 84–5

23. Vincent, *op. cit.*, p. 601

24. Bodleian, Dep. Monckton Trustees, MS 9 f. 52, George VI to Monckton, 1 March 1942

25. Wood, *op. cit.*, p. 158

26. News International plc Record Office, Barrington-Ward Diaries, 9 March 1942

27. Bodleian, MS Woolton 2, 21 April 1942

28. Cazalet Diary, 3 June 1942

29. BL Add. MS 5638A, 10 November 1941

30. BL Add. MS 56387, 20 June 1947

31. Harvey (ed.), *War Diaries*, p. 275

32. Churchill Archives Centre, ACAD 1/2, 3 August 1943

33. Pembroke College, Storrs Diary, 1 November 1944

34. Interview with Sir Edward Ford

35. Noble Frankland, *Prince Henry, Duke of Gloucester* (1980), p. 146

36. Interview with Group-Captain Peter Townsend, 20 March 1986

37. Interview with Sir Edward Ford

38. Townsend, *Time and Chance*, pp. 120–1

39. Liddell Hart Centre, Alanbrooke Diaries 5/8, 13 January 1944

40. Wood, *op. cit.*, pp. 148–50

41. Sitwell, *op. cit.*, p. 44

42. Townsend, *Time and Chance*, p. 145

43. Private information

44. See Antony Lambton, *The Mountbattens* (1989)

45. Nicolson, Balliol, 12 June 1955

46. Ziegler, *op. cit.*, p. 308

47. Hamilton, *op. cit.*, vol. III, p. 750

48. Pembroke College, Storrs Papers, Box VI/8, 18 January 1948, where he writes of 'Princess Mary's absence from the wedding in anger at the Duke of Windsor not having been invited, & markedly attending a public function later'.

49. Ann and John Tusa, *The Nuremberg Trial* (1983), pp. 97–8

50. Wheeler-Bennett, *Friends, Enemies and Sovereigns*, p. 82

51. John Costello *Mask of Treachery* (1988), p. 460

52. US National Archives, Diplomatic Branch, 841.001/3-1547, Marshall to Acheson, 15 March 1947

53. PRO, FO 371/55526, Inverchapel to Acheson, 2 November 1946

54. Cited in Patrick Howarth, *King George VI* (1988), p. 104

55. Ziegler, *op. cit.*, p. 125

56. Minney (ed.), *op. cit.*, p. 238

57. Liddell Hart Centre, Pownall Diaries, 6 and 18 October 1939

58. Harvey (ed.), *Diplomatic Diaries*, p. 328

59. Bloch, *Secret File*, p. 151

60. BL Add. MS 56402

61. *Ibid.*, Peake to Harvey, 26 January 1940
62. Nicolson, Balliol, 1 October 1940
63. Chamberlain Papers, NC 18/1/1140, Chamberlain to Ida, 27 January 1940: 'I have heard on unimpeachable authority that while the Duke of Windsor was here this week Beaverbrook tried to induce him to head a peace campaign in this country promising him the full support of his papers.'
64. Vincent, *op. cit.*, p. 604
65. *Documents on German Foreign Policy*, Series D, vol. VIII (1954), no. 580
66. *Ibid.*, no. 621
67. Private information
68. Gilbert, *op. cit.*, vol. VI, p. 698
69. Bodleian, Dep. Monckton Trustees, MS 3, 2 July 1940
70. Pembroke College, Storrs Diary, Box VI/3, 14 July 1940
71. Bakhmeteff Archive, Duke of Kent to Prince Paul Karageorgevitch, 17 July 1940
72. Private information
73. Lambeth MS 2868, Don Diary, 1 August 1940
74. Cited in Gilbert, *op. cit.*, vol. VI, p. 707. Churchill vetoed Lloyd's wording which was not, therefore, sent.
75. Churchill Archives Centre, ACAD 1/9, 10 July 1940
76. *Documents on German Foreign Policy*, Series D, vol. X (1957), no. 2
77. *Ibid.*, no. 66
78. *Ibid.*, no. 86
79. *Ibid.*, no. 152
80. *Ibid.*, no. 211
81. *Ibid.*, no. 224
82. *Ibid.*, no. 276
83. *Ibid.*, p. 398
84. Cited in Gilbert, *op. cit.*, vol. VI, p. 703
85. US National Archives, Diplomatic Branch, 841.0011.102 1/2, 4 p.m. 20 July, Herbert Claiborne Pell to Secretary of State
86. Gilbert, *op. cit.*, vol. VI, p. 707
87. Bloch, *Secret File*, p. 175
88. US National Archives, 811.711/4039, memo by A.A. Berle Jr in response to request forwarded by Halifax
89. Gilbert, *op. cit.*, vol. VI, p. 984n, Churchill to Duke of Windsor, 17 March 1941
90. Bloch, *Secret File*, pp. 187–8, Churchill to Duke of Windsor, 20 March 1941
91. *Ibid.*, p. 186
92. Halifax Papers, A4.410.4.8, Halifax to George VI, 19 October 1941
93. *Ibid.*, A2.278.26.5, George VI to Halifax, 1 March 1942
94. Cited in Howarth, *op. cit.*, p. 143
95. Bloch, *Secret File*, pp. 202–3
96. Halifax Papers, A7.8.15, Diary, 3 July 1944
97. see *ibid.*, A4.410.4.18(1): 'I am sorry to seem unhelpful but, much as I should like to help, I cannot do it at the expense of what I believe might well be a political catastrophe in a major Colony,' Stanley to Halifax, 1 December 1943
98. Bloch, *Secret File*, p. 220
99. Halifax Papers, A4.410.4.18(1), Halifax to Oliver Stanley, 22 November 1943
100. *Ibid.*, A4.410.4.10, Lascelles to Halifax, 10 March 1946
101. Pope-Hennessy, *A Lonely Business*, p. 211
102. Bloch, *Secret File*, pp. 92–3
103. See *ibid.*, pp. 261 and 263, where Duchess of Windsor describes it as 'the offending letter', advising the Duke to do his best to explain it away to 'the widow': '. . . but I am afraid Mrs Temple Sr [the Queen Mother] will never give in – all due to that letter which your mother should have kept to herself.' (14 and 17 February 1952)
104. *Ibid.*, p. 265

13: Walking with Death

1. Interview with Lord Hardinge of Penshurst, 22 March 1988
2. Interview with Sir Edward Ford
3. Cited in Constance Babington-Smith, *Champion of Homoeopathy: The Life of Margery Blackie* (1986), p. 130
4. *Sunday Pictorial*, 9 September 1951
5. Moran, *op. cit.*, pp. 340–2

6. Nicolson, Balliol, 23 September and 2 October 1951
7. Moran, *op. cit.*, p. 351
8. Wood, *op. cit.*, p. 115
9. Harry S. Truman Library, PSF, George VI to Truman, 22 December 1951
10. Eisenhower Library, King George VI to Eisenhower, 7 January 1952
11. Interview with Sir Edward Ford
12. Colville, *op. cit.*, p. 640
13. Moran, *op. cit.*, p. 378
14. Interview with Lord Charteris of Amisfield, 29 July 1986
15. Private collection, Queen Elizabeth The Queen Mother to Osbert Sitwell, 3 May 1952
16. Eisenhower Library, Queen Elizabeth The Queen Mother to General and Mrs Eisenhower, 11 March 1952
17. Facts collected by Leonard Miall for 'American Commentary, "The Impact of the King's Death in the United States"', 11 February 1952
18. Churchill Archives Centre, ACAD 1/23, 6 February 1952
19. Quai d'Orsay, Direction d'Europe, No. 287, Massigli to Schumann, 19 February 1952

COPYRIGHT PERMISSIONS

I am grateful to the following for their kind permission to quote from copyright material: Crown copyright records in the Public Record Office are quoted by permission of the Controller of Her Majesty's Stationery Office; Times Newspapers Ltd, for the Dawson Papers, and Mark Barrington-Ward for the Barrington-Ward Diaries in the News International Record Office; University of Birmingham for the Chamberlain Papers; Bodleian Library for the Papers of Lord Somervell, Violet, Lady Milner, Lord Woolton and Geoffrey Dawson, the Earl of Woolton for the Woolton Diaries, Mrs Laura Morland and Mrs Davina Howell for the Euan Wallace Diaries, the Master and Fellows of Balliol College, Oxford, for the Monckton Papers – all deposited in the Bodleian; manuscripts from the College Archives, Royal Air Force College Cranwell, are quoted by kind permission of the Air Officer Commanding and Commandant; The Lady Mairi Bury for the Londonderry Papers at PRONI; The Durham County Archivist and the Marquess of Londonderry for the Londonderry Papers at Durham County Record Office; The Hon. Sir Edward Cazalet for the Diaries of Victor Cazalet MP; The Clerk of the Record, House of Lords and the Trustees of the Beaverbrook Foundation for the Beaverbrook Papers in the House of Lords Record Office; The Master, Fellows and Scholars of Churchill College in the University of Cambridge for the Papers of Sir Eric Phipps, and for the Knatchbull-Hugessen Papers and the Godfrey-Faussett Diaries, the late Sir Alexander Cadogan and Cassell & Co. for permission to quote from the published edition and unpublished passages from the Cadogan Diaries, the Hon. Julian Hardinge for permission to quote from a letter by Sir Alexander Hardinge – all in the Churchill Archive Centre; The Lord Crathorne for the Dugdale Diary; Lady Peake for permission to quote from letters by Sir Charles Peake and the Hon. John Harvey for passages both published and unpublished from the Diaries of Lord Harvey of Tasburgh in the Harvey of Tasburgh Papers in the British Library; The Trustees of the Imperial War Museum for the Montgomery Papers and other collections in their Department of Documents and Department of Sound Records, the Executors of Captain E.M.C. Barraclough for permission to quote from a memoir by Captain Barraclough, M.L.F. Chambers for a memoir by Commander Chambers, Miss Eloise Lambert for permission to quote from a letter by Commander F.S. Lambert, Mrs M. Hamilton, for the letters of Captain H. Hamilton, Mrs Frances Denby for the papers of Lieutenant-General Sir Oliver Leese – all deposited in the Imperial War Museum; The kind permission of the Master and Fellows of Pembroke College for the Diaries of Sir Ronald Storrs; The Trustees of the Liddell Hart Centre for Military Archives, King's College, University of London, for the Ismay and Pownall Papers; Mrs David Smyly for the Ismay Papers; Nigel Nicolson, the Master and Fellows of Balliol College, Oxford, and Collins Publishers for the Harold Nicolson Diaries, published and unpublished; Martin Gilbert and Heinemann Publishers for permission to quote from *Winston S. Churchill*, vols v–vii; The Earl of Halifax for the Halifax Papers on deposit at the Borthwick Institute of Historical Research, University of York.

BIBLIOGRAPHY

Manuscript Sources

UNITED KINGDOM:

PRO Kew
  Dominion Office Files
  Foreign Office General Correspondence,
FO 371
  War Office Files
  Works Office Files

  Prime Minister's Papers (Churchill) Prem. 4
  Prime Minister's Papers (Attlee) Prem. 8

  Private Collections:
  Avon Papers, FO 954
  Bevin Papers, FO 800
  Halifax Papers, FO 800

PRONI, Belfast
  Cabinet Papers CAB 9R
  Londonderry Papers

Balliol College, Oxford
  Harold Nicolson Diaries

Birmingham University Library
  Chamberlain Papers

Bodleian Library Oxford
  Crookshank Papers
  Dawson Papers (including the papers of
Sir Evelyn Wrench)

Gwynne Papers
Iverchapel Papers
Monckton Papers
Sankey Papers
Simon Papers
Somervell Papers
Euan Wallace Diary
Violet Milner Papers
Woolton Papers

Borthwick Institute of Historical Research, University of York
  Halifax Papers

British Library
  Harvey of Tasburgh Papers

Churchill Archives Centre, Churchill College, Cambridge
  Cadogan Papers
  Godfrey-Faussett Diaries
  P. J. Grigg Papers
  Hankey Papers
  Knatchbull-Hugessen Papers
  Phipps Papers
  Spears Papers
  Swinton Papers
  Thurso Papers
  Vansittart Papers

Durham County Record Office
Londonderry Papers

Freemason's Hall, Great Queen Street
Archives and Records

House of Lords, Beaverbrook Library
Beaverbrook Papers
J.C.C. Davidson Papers

Imperial War Museum
Department of Documents:
Barraclough Papers
Chambers Papers
Hamilton Papers
Lambert Papers
Leese Papers
Montgomery Papers
Robinson Papers
Swinley Papers

Department of Sound Records:
Coryton Interview
Denham Interview

India Office Records
Private Office Papers (L/PO)

Industrial Society
Archives of the Industrial Welfare Society

Lambeth Palace Library
A.C. Don Diaries
Lang Papers

Liddell Hart Centre, King's College, London
Alanbrooke Diaries
Ismay Papers
Pownall Diaries

News International plc Record Office
Dawson Papers
Barrington-Ward Papers

Pembroke College, Cambridge
Storrs Papers

Royal Air Force College, Cranwell
Goss Papers
McCreary Papers
Parker Papers
Townson Papers

CANADA:

Queen's University Archives, Kingston
John Buchan Papers

Mills Memorial Library, McMaster University, Hamilton
H. Montgomery Hyde Papers

FRANCE:

Archives du Ministère des Affaires Etrangères, Palais du Quai d'Orsay, Paris
Section Europe: Direction des affaires politiques et commerciales. Z 274.3. Questions dynastiques et Cours.

UNITED STATES:

Bakhmeteff Archive, Columbia University
Jacob B. Hoptner Papers
Herbert H. Lehman Papers
Prince Paul of Yugoslavia Papers

Dwight D. Eisenhower Library
Pre-Presidential Papers: George VI folder, Lascelles folder

Franklin D. Roosevelt Library
Correspondence and papers of Mrs Franklin D. Roosevelt concerning the British royal family (ER correspondence)
Materials among the papers of Franklin D. Roosevelt concerning the relationship of Franklin D. Roosevelt to the British royal family
Harry L. Hopkins Papers
President's Secretary's File (PSF) Great Britain: King and Queen File
President's Personal File (PPF) 5565-King George VI

Harry S. Truman Library
President's Secretary's File: correspondence with George VI, President Truman's diaries, log of the President's trip to the Berlin Conference

PRIVATE COLLECTIONS IN THE UNITED
KINGDOM:

Diaries of Victor Cazalet MP
'Constitutional Crisis November to
December 1936', diary written by Nancy

Dugdale from data supplied by Thomas
Dugdale diary
Papers of Sir Alexander Grant
Osbert Sitwell Papers
Royal correspondence in the possession of
various owners

Published Sources

ACHESON, Dean, *Present at the Creation: My Years in the State Department* (1969)
AIRLIE, Mabell Countess of, *Thatched with Gold* (1962)
ALEXANDER of Tunis, First Earl, *Memoirs* (1962)
ALEXANDRA, Queen of Yugoslavia, *For Love of a King* (1956)
ALEXANDRA, Queen of Yugoslavia, *Prince Philip, a Family Portrait* (1960)
ALICE, HRH Princess, Countess of Athlone, *For my Grandchildren* (1966)
AMERY, L.S., *My Political Life*, 3 vols (1953–5)
ASQUITH, Lady Cynthia, *The Family Life of Her Majesty Queen Elizabeth* (1937)
ASQUITH, Lady Cynthia, *Haply I May Remember* (1950)
ASQUITH, Lady Cynthia, *Diaries 1915–1918* (1968)
ASTOR, Michael, *Tribal Feeling* (1963)
ATTLEE, C.R., *As It Happened* (1954)
AVON, Earl of, *Eden Memoirs*, vol. 1 (1962)
BABINGTON-SMITH, Constance, *Champion of Homoeopathy: The Life of Margery Blackie* (1986)
BAGEHOT, Walter, *The English Constitution* (World classics edn 1928)
BALDWIN, A.W., *My Father, the True Story* (1955)
BALFOUR, Neil, and MACKAY, Sally, *Paul of Yugoslavia* (1980)
BALFOUR, Sir John, *Not Too Correct an Aureole: The Recollections of a Diplomat* (1983)
BARNES, John, and NICHOLSON, David (eds), *The Empire at Bay: The Leo Amery Diaries 1929–1945* (1988)
BATTISCOMBE, Georgina, *Queen Alexandra* (1969)
BEAVERBROOK, Lord, *The Abdication of King Edward VIII* (1966)

BIRKENHEAD, Second Earl of, *Halifax* (1965)
BIRKENHEAD, Second Earl of, *Walter Monckton* (1969)
BLOCH, Michael, *The Duke of Windsor's War* (1982)
BLOCH, Michael (ed.), *Wallis & Edward, Letters 1931–1937* (1986)
BLOCH, Michael, *The Secret File of the Duke of Windsor* (1988)
BOCCA, Geoffrey, *She Might Have Been Queen* (1955)
BOND, Brian, *France and Belgium, 1939–1940* (1975)
BOOTHROYD, Basil, *Philip* (1971)
BRYAN III, J., and MURPHY, Charles J.V., *The Windsor Story* (1979)
BULLITT, Orville H. (ed.), *For the President ... Correspondence between Franklin D. Roosevelt and William C. Bullitt* (1973)
BULLOCK, Alan, *Ernest Bevin* (1960)
BULLOCK, Alan, *Hitler: A Study in Tyranny* (rev. edn, 1973)
BULLOCK, Alan, *Ernest Bevin, Foreign Secretary* (1985)
Burke's Royal Families of the World, vol. 1: *Europe & Latin America* (1977)
BUTCHER, Captain Harry C., *My Three Years wih Eisenhower, the Personal Diary ... 1942–1945* (1946)
BUXTON, Aubrey, *The King in his Country* (1955)
CARTLAND, Barbara, *We Danced all Night* (1970)
CAZALET-KEIR, Thelma, *From the Wings* (1967)
CHARMLEY, John, *Duff Cooper* (1986)
CHARMLEY, John, *Lord Lloyd and the Decline of the British Empire* (1987)
CHRISTOPHER, HRH Prince of Greece, *Memoirs* (1938)

CHURCHILL, Randolph S., *Lord Derby: King of Lancashire* (1959)

CHURCHILL, Sir Winston S., *The World Crisis* (1931)

CHURCHILL, Sir Winston S., *The Second World War*, 6 vols (1948–54)

CLARK, General Mark, *Calculated Risk* (1951)

CLARK, Alan (ed.), *A Good Innings: The Private Papers of Viscount Lee of Fareham* (1974)

COATS, Peter, *The Gardens of Buckingham Palace* (1978)

COLVILLE, Lady Cynthia, *Crowded Life* (1963)

COLVILLE, Sir John, *The Fringes of Power: Downing Street Diaries 1939–1955* (1985)

COOPER, Diana, *The Light of Common Day* (1959)

COOPER, Duff, *Old Men Forget* (1953)

COOPER, A. (ed.), *A Durable Fire: The Letters of Duff and Diana Cooper, 1939–50* (1983)

COSTELLO, John, *Mask of Treachery* (1988)

COWLES, Virginia, *Edward VII & His Circle* (1956)

CRAWFORD, Marion, *The Little Princesses* (1950)

CUNNINGHAM, Admiral of the Fleet Lord, *A Sailor's Odyssey* (1951)

CURZON OF KEDLESTON, Marchioness, *Reminiscences* (1955)

DALTON, Hugh, *The Fateful Years, 1931–45* (1947)

DAY, James Wentworth, *The Queen Mother's Family Story* (1967)

DEMPSTER, Nigel, *Princess Margaret* (1981)

DILKS, David (ed.), *The Diaries of Sir Alexander Cadogan, 1938–1945* (1971)

DIXON, Piers, *Double Diploma: The Life of Sir Pierson Dixon* (1968)

Documents on German Foreign Policy 1918–1945, series C, vols IV & VI; series D, vols VIII & X (1962–83–54–57)

DONALDSON, Frances, *Edward VIII* (1974)

DONALDSON, Frances, *King George VI and Queen Elizabeth* (1977)

DUBREUIL, Richard, 'La visite des souverains britanniques' in *La France et les français en 1939* (Paris, 1978)

DUFF, David, *Elizabeth of Glamis* (1973)

ECCLES, David and Sybil, *By Safe Hand, Letters 1939–42* (1983)

EDWARDS, Cecil, *Lord Bruce of Melbourne* (1966)

EISENHOWER, David, *Eisenhower at War, 1943–45* (1986)

EISENHOWER, Dwight D., *At Ease, Stories I Tell my Friends* (1967)

ESHER, Viscount, *Journals and Letters*, vol. II: *1903–10* (1934)

EVANS, Trefor (ed.), *The Killearn Diaries* (1972)

FEILING, Keith, *The Life of Neville Chamberlain* (1946)

FLANNER, Janet, *London was Yesterday, 1934–39* (1975)

FOOT, Michael, *Aneurin Bevan*, 2 vols (1965–73)

FRANKLAND, Noble, *Prince Henry, Duke of Gloucester* (1980)

GAULLE, General Charles de, *The Call to Honour* (1955)

GILBERT, Martin, *Winston S. Churchill*, vol. V: *1922–1939* (1976)

GILBERT, Martin, *Winston S. Churchill*, vol. V Companion Pt 3: *The Coming of War 1936–1939* (1982)

GILBERT, Martin, *Winston S. Churchill*, vol. VI: *1939–1941, Finest Hour* (1983)

GILBERT, Martin, *Winston S. Churchill*, vol. VII: *1941–1945, Road to Victory* (1986)

GILBERT, Martin, *Winston S. Churchill*, vol. VIII: *1945–1965, 'Never Despair'* (1988)

GLOUCESTER, HRH Princess Alice, Duchess of, *Memoirs* (1983)

GOODWIN, Doris K., *The Fitzgeralds and the Kennedys* (1987)

GORE. John, *King George V, a Personal Memoir* (1941)

GRAVES, Robert, and HODGE, Alan, *The Long Weekend: A Social History of Great Britain, 1918–39* (1950)

GRIGG, Sir James, *Prejudice and Judgment* (1948)

HALIFAX, Earl of, *Fulness of Days* (1957)

HAMILTON, Nigel, vol. I: *Monty, The Making of a General, 1887–1942* (1981); vol. II: *Monty, Master of the Battlefield, 1942–44* (1983); vol. III: *Monty the Field Marshal, 1944–76* (1986)

HANCOCK, Sir William K. *Smuts*, vol. II: *The Fields of Force 1919–1950* (1968)

HARDINGE, Helen, *Loyal to Three Kings* (1967)

HAREWOOD, Earl of, *The Tongs and the Bones* (1981)

HARRIS, Kenneth, *Attlee* (1982)

HART-DAVIS, Duff (ed.), *In Royal Service: The Letters and Journals of Sir Alan Lascelles 1920–1936*, vol. II (1989)

HARTNELL, Norman, *Silver and Gold* (1955)

HARVEY, J. (ed.), *The Diplomatic Diaries of Oliver Harvey 1937–40* (1970)

HARVEY, J. (ed.), *The War Diaries of Oliver Harvey* (1978)

HENDERSON, George F., 'The 1939 Royal Visit to Kingston', in *Historic Kingston*, vol. 29 (1981)

HESSE, Fritz, *Hitler and the English* (1954)

HIBBERT, Christopher, *Edward VII: A Portrait* (1976)

HIGHAM, Charles, *Wallis: Secret Lives of the Duchess of Windsor* (1988)

HORNE, Alistair, *Macmillan, vol. 1: 1894–1956* (1988)

HOWARTH, Patrick, *King George VI* (1988)

HUDSON, Derek, *For Love of Painting: The Life of Sir Gerald Kelly* (1975)

HUGHES, E.A., *The Royal Naval College, Dartmouth* (1950)

HYDE, H. Montgomery, *Baldwin* (1973)

HYDE, H. Montgomery, *The Cleveland Street Scandal* (1976)

HYDE, Robert R., *The Camp Book* (1930)

HYDE, Robert R., *Industry Was my Parish* (1968)

ICKES, Harold L., *Secret Diary*, vol. II: *1936–1939* (1955)

INGLIS, Brian, *Abdication* (1966)

ISMAY, Lord, *Memoirs* (1960)

JONES, Thomas, *A Diary with Letters, 1931–1950* (1954)

JUDD, Denis, *King George VI* (1982)

KEYES, Roger, *Echec au Roi: Léopold III 1940–1951* (Paris, 1986)

KEYES, Roger, *Outrageous Fortune: The Tragedy of King Leopold III of the Belgians 1901–1941* (1984)

KNIGHT, Stephen, *The Brotherhood* (1983)

LACEY, Robert, *Majesty* (1977)

LAIRD, Dorothy, *Queen Elizabeth The Queen Mother* (1966)

LAMBTON, Antony, *The Mountbattens* (1989)

LASH, Joseph P., *Eleanor and Franklin* (1972)

LEAHY, Admiral William D., *I Was There* (1950)

LEEPER, Sir Reginald, *When Greek Meets Greek* (1950)

LEES-MILNE, James, *Harold Nicolson: A Biography*, vol. II: *1930–1968* (1981)

LEES-MILNE, James, *The Enigmatic Edwardian: The Life of Reginald 2nd Viscount Esher* (1986)

LOCKHART, J.G., *Cosmo Gordon Lang* (1949)

LONGFORD, Elizabeth, *Victoria R.I.* (1964)

LONGFORD, Elizabeth, *The Queen Mother* (1981)

LONGFORD, Earl of, *Born To Believe* (1953)

LOWNDES, Susan (ed.), *Marie Belloc Lowndes: Diaries and Letters 1911–1947* (1971)

LYTTELTON, Oliver, *The Memoirs of Lord Chandos* (1962)

MACMILLAN, Harold, *War Diaries: Politics and War in the Mediterranean January 1943–May 1945* (1984)

MAILER, Chloe, and MUSGRAVE, Peter, *The History of the Industrial Society 1918–1986* (1986)

MARDER, Arthur J., *From the Dreadnought to Scapa Flow: The Royal Navy in the Fisher Era, 1904–19*, vol. III: *Jutland & After, May–December 1916* (1966)

MARIE LOUISE, HRH Princess, *My Memories of Six Reigns* (1956)

MASTERS, Brian, *Great Hostesses* (1982)

Memoirs of Cordell Hull (New York, 1955)

MIDDLEMAS, Keith, and BARNES, John, *Baldwin* (1969)

MIDDLEMAS, Keith, *The Life and Times of George VI* (1974)

MINNEY, R.J. (ed.), *The Private Papers of Hore-Belisha* (1960)

MORAN, Lord, *Winston Churchill, The Struggle for Survival 1940–1965* (1966)

MORRISON, Herbert, *An Autobiography* (1960)

MORTIMER, Penelope, *Queen Elizabeth: A Life of the Queen Mother* (1986)

MOSLEY, Diana, *The Duchess of Windsor* (1980)

MUGGERIDGE, Malcolm (ed.), *Galeazzo Ciano: Diaries 1939–43* (1947)

NICOLSON, Sir Harold, *King George V: His Life and Reign* (1952)

NICOLSON, Nigel (ed.), *Sir Harold Nicolson: Diaries and Letters 1930–1939* (1966)

OLSON, Stanley (ed.), *Sir Harold Nicolson: Diaries and Letters 1930–1964* (1980)

PAKULA, Hannah, *The Last Romantic: A Biography of Queen Marie of Roumania* (1985)

PICKERSGILL, J.W., *The Mackenzie King Record*, vol. I: *1939–44* (Toronto, 1960)

PIMLOTT, Ben, *Hugh Dalton* (1985)

PIMLOTT, Ben (ed.), *The Second World War Diary of Hugh Dalton 1940–45* (1986)

PONSONBY, Sir Frederick, *Recollections of Three Reigns* (1951)

POPE-HENNESSY, James, *A Lonely Business* (1981)

POPE-HENNESSY, James, *Queen Mary* (1959)

REID, Michaela, *Ask Sir James* (1987)

REITH, Lord, *Into the Wind* (1949)

REYNOLDS, David, *FDR's Foreign Policy and the British Royal Visit to the USA, 1939*, offprint from *The Historian*, vol. XLV, no. 4 (1983)

RHODES JAMES, Robert (ed.), *Chips: The Diaries of Sir Henry Channon* (1967)

RHODES JAMES, Robert, *Memoirs of a Conservative: J.C.C. Davidson's Memoirs and Papers, 1910–1937* (1969)

RHODES JAMES, Robert, *Victor Cazalet* (1976)

RHODES JAMES, Robert, *Anthony Eden* (1986)

RIBBENTROP, Joachim von, *The Ribbentrop Memoirs*, tr. O. Watson (1954)

ROOSEVELT, Eleanor, *An Autobiography* (1962)

ROOSEVELT, Eleanor, *This I Remember* (New York, 1949)

ROOSEVELT, Elliott, and BROUGH, James, *A Rendezvous with Destiny* (New York, 1977)

ROOSEVELT, Elliott, and LASH, James P., *The Roosevelt Letters...*, vol. III (New York, 1952)

ROOSEVELT, James, and SHALETT, Sidney, *Affectionately, F.D.R.: A Story of a Courageous Man* (New York, 1960)

ROSE, Kenneth, *King George V* (1983)

ROSE, Kenneth, *Kings, Queens & Courtiers* (1985)

ROSE, N.A. (ed.), *Baffy: The Diaries of Blanche Dugdale, 1936–47* (1973)

SECREST, Meryle, *Kenneth Clark* (1984)

SENCOURT, R., *Reign of Edward VIII* (1962)

SHAUGHNESSY, Alfred, *Both Ends of the Candle* (1978)

SHAW, G.B., *The Apple Cart* (1930)

SHERWOOD, Robert E., *The White House Papers of Harry L. Hopkins*, 2 vols (1949)

SITWELL, Osbert, *Queen Mary and Others* (1974)

SITWELL, Osbert, *Rat Week* (1986)

SOAMES, Mary, *Clementine Churchill* (1979)

SPEARS, Sir Edward, *Assignment to Catastrophe*, 2 vols (1954)

STEVENSON, Frances, *Lloyd George: A Diary* (1971)

STUART, Charles (ed.), *The Reith Diaries* (1975)

STUART, James (Viscount Stuart of Findhorn), *Within the Fringe, An Autobiography* (1967)

SULZBERGER, C.L., *A Long Row of Candles: Memoirs and Diaries 1934–1954* (1969)

SUMMERSBY, Kay, *Eisenhower Was my Boss* (1949)

TAYLOR, A.J.P., *English History 1914–1945* (1970)

TEMPLEWOOD, Viscount, *Nine Troubled Years* (1954)

THORNTON, Michael, *Royal Feud* (1985)

THE TIMES, *The History of The Times*, vol. IV (1952)

TISDALL, E.E.P., *Royal Destiny, the Royal Hellenic Cousins* (1955)

TOWNSEND, Peter, *The Last Emperor* (1975)

TOWNSEND, Peter, *Time and Chance* (1978)

TRUMAN, Harry S., *Year of Decisions* (New York, 1955)

VANDERBILT, Gloria, and FURNESS, Thelma, Lady, *Double Exposure* (1959)

VANSITTART, Lord, *The Mist Procession* (1958)

VICKERS, Hugo, *Cecil Beaton* (1985)

VICTORIA, Queen of England, *The Letters of Queen Victoria*, Third Series, 1886–1901, vols I–III (1930–2)

VINCENT, John (ed.), *The Crawford Papers* (1984)

WARWICK, Christopher, *Princess Margaret* (1983)

WARWICK, Christopher, *George and Marina* (1988)

WATSON, Francis, *Dawson of Penn* (1951)

WESTMINSTER, Loelia Duchess of, *Grace and Favour* (1961)

WHEELER-BENNETT, Sir John W., *King George VI: His Life and Reign* (1958)

WHEELER-BENNETT, Sir John W., *Friends, Enemies and Sovereign* (1976)

WILLIAMS, Philip M. (ed.), *Diary of Hugh Gaitskell, 1945–1956* (1983)

WINANT, John G., *A Letter from Grosvenor Square* (1947)

WINDSOR, Duchess of, *The Heart Has its Reasons* (1956)

WINDSOR, HRH Duke of, *A King's Story* (1951)

WINDSOR, HRH Duke of, *A Family Album* (1960)

WINTERTON, Earl, *Orders of the Day* (1953)

WOOD, Robert, *A World in Your Ear...* (1979)

WRENCH, Sir Evelyn, *Geoffrey Dawson and our Times* (1955)

YOUNG, Kenneth (ed.), *The Diaries of Sir Robert Bruce-Lockhart, 1915–65*, 2 vols (1973–80)

ZIEGLER, Philip, *Mountbatten* (1985)

INDEX

NOTE: Titles and ranks are generally the highest mentioned in the text. Where appropriate, cross-references are given. The following abbreviations are used: KG = King George VI; QE = Queen Elizabeth (wife of George VI); QM = Queen Mary; DW = Duke of Windsor (earlier Prince of Wales, then King Edward VIII)

THE HOUSE OF WINDSOR

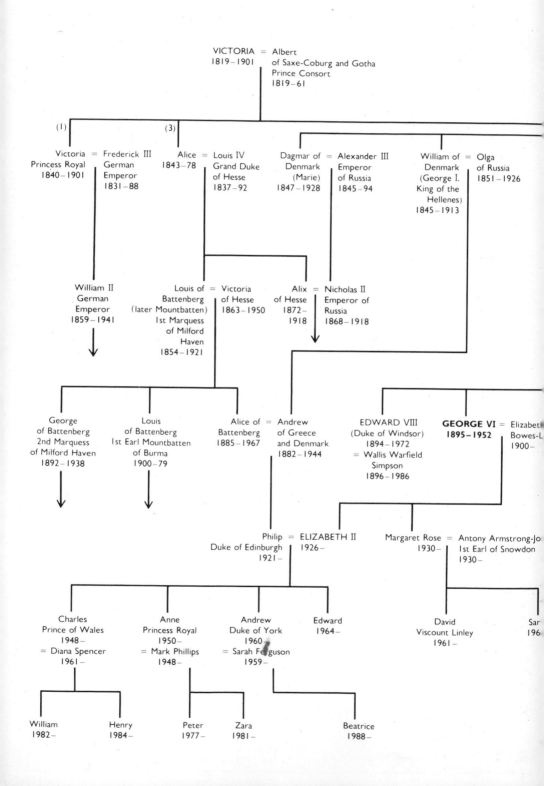

VICTORIA = Albert
1819–1901 of Saxe-Coburg and Gotha
Prince Consort
1819–61

(1)
Victoria = Frederick III
Princess Royal German
1840–1901 Emperor
1831–88

(3)
Alice = Louis IV
1843–78 Grand Duke
of Hesse
1837–92

Dagmar of = Alexander III
Denmark Emperor
(Marie) of Russia
1847–1928 1845–94

William of = Olga
Denmark of Russia
(George I. 1851–1926
King of the
Hellenes)
1845–1913

William II
German
Emperor
1859–1941

Louis of = Victoria
Battenberg of Hesse
(later Mountbatten) 1863–1950
1st Marquess
of Milford
Haven
1854–1921

Alix = Nicholas II
of Hesse Emperor of
1872– Russia
1918 1868–1918

George
of Battenberg
2nd Marquess
of Milford Haven
1892–1938

Louis
of Battenberg
1st Earl Mountbatten
of Burma
1900–79

Alice of = Andrew
Battenberg of Greece
1885–1967 and Denmark
1882–1944

EDWARD VIII
(Duke of Windsor)
1894–1972
= Wallis Warfield
Simpson
1896–1986

GEORGE VI = Elizabeth
1895–1952 Bowes-L
1900–

Philip = ELIZABETH II
Duke of Edinburgh 1926–
1921–

Margaret Rose = Antony Armstrong-Jo
1930– 1st Earl of Snowdon
1930–

Charles
Prince of Wales
1948–
= Diana Spencer
1961–

Anne
Princess Royal
1950–
= Mark Phillips
1948–

Andrew
Duke of York
1960–
= Sarah Ferguson
1959–

Edward
1964–

David
Viscount Linley
1961–

Sar
196

William
1982–

Henry
1984–

Peter
1977–

Zara
1981–

Beatrice
1988–